Innovations in
Insurance, Risk- and
Asset Management

Innovations in Insurance, Risk- and Asset Management

Conference at the Technical University of Munich,
5 – 7 April 2017

Editors

Kathrin Glau
Queen Mary University of London, UK

Daniël Linders
University of Illinois at Urbana-Champaign, USA

Aleksey Min
Technical University of Munich, Germany

Matthias Scherer
Technical University of Munich, Germany

Lorenz Schneider
Technical University of Munich, Germany & EMLYON Business School, France

Rudi Zagst
Technical University of Munich, Germany

World Scientific

NEW JERSEY · LONDON · SINGAPORE · BEIJING · SHANGHAI · HONG KONG · TAIPEI · CHENNAI · TOKYO

Published by

World Scientific Publishing Co. Pte. Ltd.

5 Toh Tuck Link, Singapore 596224

USA office: 27 Warren Street, Suite 401-402, Hackensack, NJ 07601

UK office: 57 Shelton Street, Covent Garden, London WC2H 9HE

Library of Congress Cataloging-in-Publication Data

Names: Innovations in Insurance, Risk- and Asset Management (Conference)
(2017 : Technical University of Munich), sponsoring body. | Glau, Kathrin, editor.
Title: Innovations in insurance, risk- and asset management / [edited by]
Kathrin Glau [and five others].
Description: New Jersey : World Scientific, [2018] | Contributions selected from
participants at the The conference "Innovations in Insurance, Risk- and Asset Management"
held on the campus of Technical University of Munich in Garching-Hochbrück (Munich)
from April 5th until April 7th, 2017. | Includes bibliographical references.
Identifiers: LCCN 2018026883 | ISBN 9789813272552 (alk. paper)
Subjects: LCSH: Insurance--Congresses. | Risk (Insurance)--Congresses. |
Risk management--Congresses. | Finance--Congresses.
Classification: LCC HG8017 .I475 2017 | DDC 368--dc23
LC record available at https://lccn.loc.gov/2018026883

British Library Cataloguing-in-Publication Data
A catalogue record for this book is available from the British Library.

For any available supplementary material, please visit
https://www.worldscientific.com/worldscibooks/10.1142/11051#t=suppl

Desk Editors: Herbert Moses/Shreya Gopi

Typeset by Stallion Press
Email: enquiries@stallionpress.com

Foreword

The conference "Innovations in Insurance, Risk- and Asset Management" was held on the campus of Technical University of Munich in Garching-Hochbrück (Munich) from April 5th until April 7th, 2017. Thanks to the great efforts of the organizers, the scientific committee, the keynote speakers, contributors, and all other participants, the conference was a huge success, bringing together academics and practitioners. More than 200 participants had many fruitful discussions and exchanges during three days of talks.

The conference and this book are part of an initiative that was founded in 2012 as a cooperation between the Chair of Mathematical Finance at the Technical University of Munich and KPMG AG Wirtschaftsprüfungsgesellschaft. This cooperation was based on three pillars: first, strengthening a scientifically challenging education of students that at the same time addresses real world topics, second, supporting research with particular focus on young researchers, and third, bringing together academic researchers with practitioners from the financial industry in order to develop trendsetting and viable improvements in the effective management of financial risks.

The topic of financial risk management is a subject of great importance for banks, insurance companies, and asset managers alike. It has been of even greater attention ever since the financial crisis of 2008 and still is today in the light of difficult market circumstances such as low interest rates, regulatory requirements, and ongoing technological evolvements. The conference brought together risk management practitioners from insurance, banking and asset management and academics conducting research in these fields to present and discuss state-of-the-art research in financial mathematics as well as current trends and innovations. Overall, the topics presented during the conference covered a large spectrum, ranging from developments in financial theory, new applications to actuarial and capital models to practical trends and challenges in risk management.

We would like to thank everyone who contributed to make this event a great success. In particular, we express our gratitude to the scientific committee, namely Kathrin Glau, Daniël Linders, Aleksey Min, Matthias Scherer, Lorenz Schneider, and Rudi Zagst, the organization team led by Bettina Haas, the key note speakers, the invited professional experts, all speakers of invited and contributed talks, and all participants that attended the conference.

Finally, we would like to thank Rudi Zagst and Matthias Scherer for many great years of cooperation and for making this third large conference of the KPMG Center of Excellence in Risk Management possible.

We are convinced that this book will help you to gain insights about state-of-the-art research in the areas of risk management and mathematical finance.

Franz Lorenz, Dr. Matthias Mayer and Dr. Daniel Sommer,
KPMG AG Wirtschaftsprüfungsgesellschaft

Preface

The third international conference organized by the *KPMG Center of Excellence in Risk Management* took place in April 5–7, 2017 in Garching–Hochbrück and attracted more than 200 participants from academia and the financial industry. The conference was titled *Innovations in Insurance, Risk- and Asset Management*, reflecting the dynamic growth of these industry segments in the wider Munich area on the one hand, and the scientific interests of our research group, i.e. the Chair of Mathematical Finance at Technical University of Munich (TUM) and its many collaborators, on the other hand. In charge of the scientific organization of the event, and responsible for editing the proceedings volume, were Kathrin Glau, Daniël Linders, Aleksey Min, Matthias Scherer, Lorenz Schneider, and Rudi Zagst. Responsible for the splendid local organization was a team, led by Bettina Haas, consisting of Maria Dech Pons, Susanne Deuke, Andrea Grant, and Annette Wenninger.

We were very proud to host as keynote speakers Hansjörg Albrecher (HEC Lausanne), Daniel Bauer (Georgia State University), Damiano Brigo (Imperial College London), Damir Filipović (Ecole Polytechnique Fédérale de Lausanne and Swiss Finance Institute), Ralf Korn (TU Kaiserslautern), Steven Kou (National University of Singapore), Stéphane Loisel (Ecole ISFA — Université Lyon), Alfred Müller (Universität Siegen), Johanna Nešlehová (McGill University, Montréal), Giovanni Puccetti (University of Milano), Bruno Remillard (HEC Montréal), David Saunders (University of Waterloo), and Josef Teichmann (ETH Zürich). These renowned researchers were complemented by our invited industry experts Christian Bluhm (CRO, UBS), Iain Clark (Efficient Frontier Consulting Ltd), Bernhard Kaufmann (CRO, Munich Re), and Frank Schiller (Head Actuarial & Pricing, Munich Re). Invited talks were provided by Nicole Bäuerle (Karlsruher Institut für Technologie), Carole Bernard (Grenoble Ecole de Management), Philippe Bertrand (Aix-Marseille Université), Francesca Biagini (LMU München), Sam Cohen (University of Oxford), Claudia Czado (TUM), Ernst Eberlein (Universität Freiburg), Walter Farkas (University of Zurich and ETH Zürich), Massimo Fornasier

(TUM), Peter Hieber (Universität Ulm), Monique Jeanblanc (Université d'Evry), Martin Keller-Ressel (TU Dresden), Jan-Frederik Mai (TUM), Thilo Meyer-Brandis (LMU München), Peter Ott (KPMG), Luis Seco (University of Toronto), Stefan Weber (Leibniz Universität Hannover), and Ralf Werner (Universität Augsburg). Moreover, as many as 26 contributed talks were offered. After the conference, we kindly asked all speakers to submit a manuscript to this proceedings volume. All submissions undergone a peer-review process to guarantee good academic standards. We thank all reviewers for their time and expertise.

Besides the academic program, our guests enjoyed a traditional Bavarian dinner at the castle Schleißheim and a visit to the Flugwerft Schleißheim, where a guided tour to the aviation history on the historic airfield was offered.

The Chair of Mathematical Finance at Technical University Munich would like to express its deepest thankfulness to KPMG AG Wirtschaftsprüfungsgesellschaft for five years of continuing support via the *KPMG Center of Excellence in Risk Management*, which enabled us to significantly improve the quality of our research and education and, last but not least, host conferences like the one we are documenting with this proceedings volume. In particular, we would like to thank Franz Lorenz, Matthias Mayer, and Daniel Sommer for their huge personal commitment to our joint project.

Best regards,
Matthias Scherer and Rudi Zagst
March 2018, Munich

About the Editors

Kathrin Glau was a Junior Professor at the Technical University of Munich and is a Lecturer in Financial Mathematics at the Queen Mary University of London since 2017. Her research focuses on modeling and computing asset prices. Her approach merges recent advances from numerical analysis and stochastic modeling to develop complexity reduction methods for finance.

Daniël Linders is an Assistant Professor in the Department of Mathematics at the University of Illinois. He obtained his PhD in 2013 under the supervision of Professor Jan Dhaene (KU Leuven). He was a Visiting Lecturer at the University of Antwerp (Belgium), Université Libre de Bruxelles (Belgium), University of Waterloo (Canada), and ISM Adonaï (Benin). His research interests are in the field of multi-asset derivative pricing, pension financing, and pricing of combined financial–actuarial claims.

Aleksey Min obtained his PhD at the University of Göttingen and is currently a Research Associate at the Technical University of Munich. His research focuses on copulas, Markov chain Monte Carlo methods, generalized linear models, factor models, and limit theorems.

Matthias Scherer is a Professor of Mathematical Finance at the Technical University of Munich. His research interests comprise various topics in financial mathematics, actuarial science, probability theory, and the history of mathematics. He is an active member of the executive boards of the DGVFM and the KPMG Center of Excellence in Risk Management. He is co-author of the book *Simulating Copulas: Stochastic Models, Sampling Algorithms, and Applications.*

Lorenz Schneider is an Associate Professor in Finance at EMLYON Business School, Lyon, France, and was KPMG Visiting Professor at the chair of Mathematical Finance at TU Munich. His research interests include multifactor models of commodity futures curves with stochastic volatility, asset distributions obtained via maximum entropy techniques, share pricing in emerging network markets, and fair value of executive compensation.

Rudi Zagst is a Professor of Mathematical Finance at the Technical University of Munich and member of the executive board of the KPMG Center of Excellence in Risk Management. He has held various teaching positions at the Universities of Augsburg, St. Gallen, Toronto, Ulm, and Singapore. He has also held different positions in the industry as Head of Product Development in the Institutional Investment Management of HypoVereinsbank AG, Head of Consulting at Allfonds International Asset Management GmbH, and as Managing Director of RiskLab GmbH — Private Research Institute for Financial Studies. He serves as a professional trainer for a number of leading institutions. His research interests are in financial engineering, risk- and asset management.

Contents

4. Examples of Wrong-Way Risk in CVA Induced by Devaluations on Default 95

Damiano Brigo and Nicola Pede

8.   Pathwise Construction of Affine Processes   185

Nicoletta Gabrielli and Josef Teichmann

Part II. Innovations in Insurance and Asset Management   215

9.   Fixed-Income Returns from Hedge Funds with Negative Fee Structures: Valuation and Risk Analysis   217

Mohammad Shakourifar, Ranjan Bhaduri,
Ben Djerroud, Fei Meng, David Saunders
and Luis Seco

12. Option Pricing and Hedging for Discrete Time Autoregressive Hidden Markov Model   313

Massimo Caccia and Bruno Rémillard

13. Interest Rate Swap Valuation in the Chinese Market   349

Wei Cui, Min Dai, Steven Kou, Yaquan Zhang, Chengxi Zhang and Xianhao Zhu

14. On Consistency of the Omega Ratio with Stochastic Dominance Rules   367

Bernhard Klar and Alfred Müller

Part I
Innovations in Risk Management

Chapter 1

Behavioral Value Adjustments for Mortgage Valuation

M. Bissiri* and R. Cogo

Cassa Depositi e Prestiti S.p.A.
Rome, Italy
*matteo.bissiri1@gmail.com

Behavioral risk affects the pricing of assets and liabilities with embedded prepayment/extension options whenever the option holder does not act purely on the strength of financial convenience but follows an uncertain and sub-optimal exercise strategy, if seen from the viewpoint of the option seller. Such behavior is particularly relevant for mortgage valuation, since mortgage prepayments are clearly influenced by exogenous and individual factors besides financial reasons. In this paper we apply the general framework, proposed by Bissiri and Cogo, for modeling behavioral risk to the particular case of the valuation of a fixed-rate mortgage portfolio. We also extend the formulas by considering a pool of heterogeneous mortgagors, leading to the introduction of specific behavioral risk adjustments (βVA) in the pricing formulas.

Keywords: behavioral risk, prepayment, mortgage, MBS, RMBS, XVA, embedded option, OAS.

1. Introduction

Many financial instruments are characterized by the presence of embedded options, which allow one of the counterparts to terminate the contract before maturity or modify contractual conditions, according to clauses specified at the inception. We do not refer here to the so-called automatic options, such as a cap or floor on an interest rate, but rather to options that require a decision to be taken by the option holder, such as prepayment or switch options.

On the asset side, the most typical example are mortgage loans, whose valuation is the focus of this paper. In many countries mortgagors are allowed to cancel a debt at any time by paying back the outstanding notional without any penalty (see, e.g., Davidson and Levin [1]). Prepayments also influence the pricing of mortgage backed securities (MBS), callable bonds, retail loans, loan commitments, etc. Liabilities can also embed explicit or implicit options, like in the case of puttable bonds or non-maturity deposits, which can be withdrawn by the investor at any time (see, e.g., Castagna and Fede [2] for a review of these instruments). Insurance policies may also incorporate complex prepayment features.

Due to the presence of behavioral risk, the valuation of instruments with embedded options can be an extremely challenging task. This occurs whenever the option holder does not act purely on the strength of financial convenience but follows a sub-optimal and uncertain exercise strategy, if seen from the perspective of the option seller. Various reasons can be invoked to explain this behavior, such as a different valuation and/or modeling of the underlying contract, no financial interest in early exercise, regulatory constraints, the presence of large transaction costs, the impact of exogenous factors or, as in the case of retail customers, the lack of information or sophistication. According to a more rigorous and quantitative definition, provided by Bissiri and Cogo [3], behavioral risk can be identified with the additional source of uncertainty in the time and amount of future cash flows that an option seller faces, due to the unpredictable exercise strategy followed by the option holder.

In this paper we reconsider the impact of prepayment features ion the valuation of a mortgage portfolio from the lender's viewpoint. For this purpose, we apply the general pricing approach for contracts affected by behavioral risk, which was recently developed by Bissiri and Cogo [4]. In particular, we examine the pricing of a basket of fixed-rate mortgages, issued at different times and with different contractual rates. We also extend pricing formulas to the case of a heterogeneous pool of mortgagors, with different creditworthiness and prepayment behavior. The aim is to develop a coherent and flexible enough framework, that can be tailored and calibrated to specific instruments depending on available data.

Clearly, mortgage valuation depends also on credit risk (i.e. the borrower is unable to repay the loan), although mitigated by the underlying asset acting as collateral (e.g. the house property). For instance, the recent sub-prime crisis in the US market was caused by large-scale mortgagor defaults. However, a detailed modeling of default risk is out of scope of the present paper.

Nonetheless, the approach used to model mortgage prepayments takes advantage of a full parallel with credit risk modeling and combines the features of option-based and intensity models reported in literature. A particular emphasis is placed on the calibration of the risk premium. Since exercise decisions taken by irrational option holders are influenced at the same time by financial, exogenous and individual reasons, behavioral risk clearly has a hybrid nature. However, whilst it is possible to implement a replicating strategy to hedge (or significantly reduce) portfolio sensitivity to financial risk factors, exogenous or idiosyncratic risk can only be diversified in a large portfolio. Therefore, a mixed approach seems the most appropriate choice for pricing purposes. A market risk premium for all financial risk factors is inferred from the quotes of liquid traded instruments, which could be used to set up a replicating strategy. In contrast, a traditional risk charge is calculated in order to compensate for unexpected losses arising from other sources of risk, leading to the definition of behavioral value adjustment (βVA).

The paper is divided into three sections: (i) Firstly, the literature about mortgage valuation is summarized briefly; (ii) Secondly, the general pricing framework proposed by Bissiri and Cogo [4] and its underlying hypotheses are described in more detail; (iii) Finally, a pricing formula for a basket of fixed-rate mortgages is derived.

2. Literature review

The valuation of baskets of mortgages has been studied since early 1980s and several pricing approaches have been proposed.

Econometric models assume that prepayment rates are dependent variables, and functions of a set of explanatory variables. Although they potentially allow a detailed description of a debtor's behavior by means of a large set of regressors, econometric models are less practical for pricing purposes, since risk-neutral dynamics have to be specified for all risk factors.

Option-based models were introduced along with the development of the no-arbitrage pricing theory for derivatives. In order to account for deviations from rationality, exercise constraints or transaction costs are introduced as in the models of Dunn and McConnell [5], Stanton [6], Longstaff [7], Kalotay *et al.* [8], Davidson and Levin [9]. Conditionally to a specific market scenario, the strategy followed by the option holder is still deterministic but sub-optimal, if seen by the option seller. Although option-based models permit valuations that are theoretically consistent with prepayment scenarios, their use seems to be a more natural choice only if prepayments are almost rational from a financial standpoint.

Intensity-based models have been proposed as a valid alternative by several authors, such as Schwartz and Torous [10], Deng *et al.* [11], Kau *et al.* [12], Kwok *et al.* [13], Consalvi and Scotto di Freca [14] and Chernov *et al.* [15]. They exploit the similar methodology widely applied in credit risk modeling. Like default probabilities, prepayment probabilities are stochastic variables, depending on a set of risk drivers. Intensity models naturally incorporate exogenous sources of risk, accounting for the residual variability in prepayment rates not determined by financial reasons. Our understanding is that intensity-based models are particularly suitable for those situations where early prepayments mainly depend on exogenous factors rather than on financial variables.

Finally, hybrid models have recently been proposed by combining the features of different approaches, such as in the works of Goncharov [16], Castagna and Fede [2], Kolbe and Zagst [17], [18]. For instance, Kolbe and Zagst [17] have generalized the traditional proportional hazard approach by developing and calibrating an extended hybrid model. Mortgage prepayment rates are explained in terms of a combination of market and non-financial drivers, like, e.g., gross-domestic-product (GDP).

All models reported in literature have to be calibrated with historical data. It is important to stress that mortgage prepayments are a very complex phenomenon. Despite the model family and regardless of its complexity, there are always some latent risk factors not captured by the model, as demonstrated by the fit residuals, which result after the calibration process. A similar issue is found when comparing theoretical model prices to the market quotes of liquid RMBS. Typically, an option-adjusted-spread has to be applied to discount factors in order to obtain a perfect match (see, e.g., Davidson and Levin [1] or Gabaix *et al.* [19]). Such residual dispersion cannot be neglected, since it may contribute significantly to the variability in the future cash flows of a mortgage portfolio. In this paper we model it as an exogenous error process, leading to a prudential correction in the pricing formula. In our opinion, such an approach is particularly suitable for calibrating the risk premium in the absence of liquid market benchmarks.

3. A general framework for modeling behavioral risk

In this section we summarize the general framework recently proposed by Bissiri and Cogo [4] for the pricing of financial products with embedded options in the presence of behavioral risk. The approach is intended to be general and adaptable to model the behavior of different categories of investors and to price different types of financial instruments.

It takes advantage of the similarities with credit risk modeling. For a review of interest and credit models see e.g. the books of Brigo and Mercurio [20] or Schönbucher [21].

3.1. *Defining behavioral risk*

Although there is no unanimous consensus about a single definition, behavioral risk, as well as all sources of risk, can always be identified as the additional source of uncertainty in the future cash flows of a contract that it generates. More precisely, it can be identified with the additional source of uncertainty in the time and amount of future cash flows that an option seller faces, due to the unpredictable exercise strategy followed by the option holder, see Bissiri and Cogo [3], [4].

In a world where all investors are fully rational from a financial standpoint and agree on a no-arbitrage model for market factors, the optimal exercise strategy for the prepayment option is uniquely determined.

In the particular case of a mortgage with no prepayment penalties, the optimal exercise time, which maximizes the return for the option holder, occurs whenever the redemption value (i.e. the outstanding balance of the loan) falls below the so-called continuation value (i.e. the present value of all future installments).[1] Conditional to a specific market scenario of mortgage rates, cash flows are completely deterministic.

In contrast, only a probability for option exercise can be estimated under the presence of behavioral risk. More importantly, cash flows are uncertain and cannot be predicted purely on the strength of financial convenience. Historical aggregate prepayment rates relative to baskets of mortgages imply that some debtors prepay when this is not convenient and some others do not prepay even if this is convenient. Typically, a S-shaped dependence from the rate shift[2] is observed (see, e.g., Peristiani [22]).

Thus, empirical evidence demonstrates that prepayments must be influenced by exogenous and/or individual reasons besides financial factors. Such behavior results in an additional variability in the future cash flows, even subject to a particular market scenario. More precisely, behavioral risk can be associated with the conditional variance which arises whenever the option holder does not follow an optimal exercise strategy as seen from the option seller's perspective.

---

[1]In practice, such condition is met as soon as mortgage rates prevailing in the market decrease so that it is possible to refinance the debt at lower cost.

[2]The rate shift can be defined as the difference between the mortgage contractual rate and the new rate prevailing in the market at a point in time.

3.2. *A general framework in parallel with credit risk*

Exercise probabilities, $Q_i(t)$, like default probabilities, are modeled as stochastic variables, depending on both market $X(t)$ and exogenous factors $Z(t)$.

$$\ln[Q_i(t)] = R_i(t, X(t), Z(t); \theta(t)) \tag{1}$$

where R_i is a generic response function of the i-th mortgagor and $\theta(t)$ is a set of model parameters.

Potentially, the responsiveness to changing market conditions of two different debtors may vary significantly. It is well known that heterogeneity plays a crucial role in determining the aggregate prepayment rate of a basket of mortgages and can be responsible, at least to some extent, for the so-called burnout effect, namely, the tendency of prepayment rates to decline over the lifetime of a contract.

Financial factors, X, include all market variables that impact on contractual payments and are required for the valuation of the full rational cost of the option. For instance, in the case of mortgages, interest rates and credit spreads (or default probabilities) should be taken into account.

In principle, a large set of economic or individual observables can be selected in order to explain exercise rates besides financial factors, such as gross-domestic-product, unemployment rate, personal income, age, etc. By adopting a reduced-form approach, we introduce generic exogenous drivers, Z, orthogonal to the financial ones and characterized by a systemic component (i.e. common to all investors) and a purely idiosyncratic one.

Conditional independence is also assumed. Subject to the realization of a scenario of all risk factors $\{X, Z\}$, prepayment decisions are taken independently by each single mortgagor. In addition, if a debtor holds several positions, the exercise decisions of options embedded in different contracts are independent from each other, subject to the same risk scenario.[3]

Mathematically,

$$\mathbb{V}\left[\mathbb{I}(\tau_p^i > t_k), \mathbb{I}(\tau_q^j > t_h) \middle| X, Z\right] = 0 \qquad \text{for } i \neq j \text{ or } p \neq q \tag{2}$$

---

[3]For example, let us consider a borrower holding two distinct mortgages A e B with contractual fixed rates of 1% and 5%, respectively, when prevailing market rates are around 3%. The exercise probability of two loans will satisfy the inequality $Q_A << Q_B$, if computed through a reasonable specification of (1). However, subject to that particular scenario, exercise decisions are taken independently. It is worth noting that in typical residential mortgage portfolios most mortgagors hold a single contract.

A further hypothesis consists in assuming that exogenous factors follow a mean-reverting process, so that their effect tends to vanish over a long period of time. Without loss of generality, we can reformulate the problem by taking advantage of conditional probabilities and set

$$R_i\left(t, X(t), Z(t); \theta(t)\right) = \phi_t\left(X(t); \theta(t)\right) + \eta_t\left(Z(t) \mid X(t); \theta(t)\right) \qquad (3)$$

The function η_t can be interpreted as a sort of error process which quantifies the variability in option exercise frequencies around the historical average, ϕ_t, conditionally to a particular scenario of market factors.

Since we expect that such deviations tend to cancel out over a long observation period, we impose that η_t follows a mean-reverting process with an asymptotic distribution with zero mean and finite variance.

$$\begin{cases} \mathbb{E}_Z^P\left[\eta_\infty \mid X\right] = 0 \\ \mathbb{V}_Z^P\left[\eta_\infty \mid X\right] \approx s_\infty^2(X) \end{cases} \qquad (4)$$

where variance s_∞^2 is the empirical conditional variance.[4] Refer to the paper by Bissiri and Cogo [4] for more details.

3.3. *Behavioral risk adjustments*

A mixed-approach has been proposed by Bissiri and Cogo [4] for computing behavioral risk premium in the absence of a market benchmark.

On the one hand, risk-neutral dynamics (Q) are calibrated for all relevant market factors affecting contractual cash flows and, to some extent, option exercise decisions. A market risk premium is implied from the prices of actively-traded and liquid hedging instruments.

On the other hand, exogenous or individual risk factors cannot easily be hedged but rather diversified away in a large portfolio. In this case, the traditional risk-adjusted pricing, followed, for example, by insurance companies, seems more appropriate. Firstly, the return of an instrument or portfolio is simulated under the physical measure (P). Secondly, the expectation of future discounted cash flows is computed. Thirdly, a prudential risk charge is applied. Typically, this is equal to the remuneration on the risky capital which has to be set apart as a compensation for unexpected losses. Capital absorption is computed by means of a coherent risk measure and the premium is proportional to a hurdle rate for shareholders.

---

[4]A similar issue characterizes credit modeling, where we distinguish between default probabilities estimated at a particular time ("point-in-time" perspective) from their historical averages ("through-the-cycle" perspective). A data-set spanning over a long interval of time is needed to perform a robust calibration.

In practice, we proceed as follows: (*i*) we select a specific market scenario X; (*ii*) we apply the risk charge approach to the conditional cash flow distribution; (*iii*) finally, we average across all possible market scenarios. Summing up, the price of a generic contract $V(t)$ with embedded options can be expressed by the following general formula

$$V(t) = V_E(t) - V_U(t) \tag{5}$$

$$V_E(t) = \mathbb{E}_X^Q \left[\mathbb{E}_{Z,\tau}^P \left[\Psi | X \right] \right] \tag{6}$$

$$V_U(t) = k \cdot \mathbb{E}_X^Q \left[\Phi_{Z,\tau}^P \left[\Psi; q | X \right] \right] \tag{7}$$

where Φ is a coherent risk measure, q is a target quantile and k is the unitary cost of capital.

The first term, $V_E(t)$, corresponds to the expectation of discounted cash flows, Ψ, under a risk-neutral probability measure, where behavioral risk is costless ($k = 0$) or completely diversified ($\Phi^P = 0$).

The second term, $V_U(t)$, is the premium required by a risk averse investor to bear behavioral risk. It can also be interpreted as the potential extra-cost necessary to compensate for unavoidable hedging errors of a replicating strategy based on instruments, whose price is affected by market risk factors only.

In line with XVA methodology, it is possible to introduce the concept of behavioral value adjustment βVA. For a review of the most widespread value adjustments refer, e.g., to Brigo *et al.* [23].

From the option seller's viewpoint, the price of a contract with embedded options can be written in the general form

$$V(t) = \mathbb{E}_{X,Z,\tau}^Q \left[\Psi \right] = V_H(t) - \mathrm{OVA}(t) + \beta\mathrm{VA}(t) \tag{8}$$

where

- $V_H(t)$ is the price of the host instrument, i.e. the contract without any prepayment option;
- $\mathrm{OVA}(t)$ is the option value adjustment corresponding to the full rational cost of the option;
- $\beta\mathrm{VA}(t)$ is the behavioral value adjustment quantifying the potential benefit for the option seller that the option holder does not take advantage of.

Behavioral risk adjustments $\beta\mathrm{VA}$ can be split as follows:

$$\beta\mathrm{VA}(t) = \beta\mathrm{VA}_E(t) - \beta\mathrm{VA}_U(t) \tag{9}$$

$$\beta\mathrm{VA}_E(t) = \mathbb{E}_X^Q \left[\mathbb{E}_{Z,\tau}^P \left[\Psi \,|\, X \right] \right] - V_H(t) + \mathrm{OVA}(t) \tag{10}$$

$$\beta\mathrm{VA}_U(t) = k \cdot \mathbb{E}_X^Q \left[\Phi_{Z,\tau}^P \left[\Psi; q \,|\, X \right] \right] \tag{11}$$

The two components, $\beta\mathrm{VA}_E(t)$ and $\beta\mathrm{VA}_U(t)$, quantify the expected gain and the potential unexpected losses due to the uncertain sub-optimal exercise strategy followed by the option holder, respectively.

Finally, an appropriate and coherent risk measure, Φ^P, in (7) has to be chosen. Typically, one can select expected shortfall (ES) relative to the present value of future cash flows through the entire life of the contract. Unfortunately, this may require time-consuming Monte Carlo simulations of all risk factors.

In order to improve analytical tractability and speed up calculations, if the distribution is not excessively skewed, we can adopt an analytical risk measure, linked to the conditional standard deviation.

$$\Phi^P \left(\Psi | X \right) = \chi_q \cdot \sqrt{\mathbb{V}_{Z,\tau}^P \left[\Psi \,|\, X \right]} \tag{12}$$

where χ_q is a scaling factor which depends on the shape of the distribution and a quantile q. As a result, formula (5) can be rewritten as

$$V(t) = \mathbb{E}_X^Q \left[\mathbb{E}_{Z,\tau}^P \left[\Psi \right] - k \cdot \chi_q \cdot \sqrt{\mathbb{V}_{Z,\tau}^P \left[\Psi \right]} \,\Big|\, X \right] \tag{13}$$

3.4. *A general formula for portfolio valuation*

The discounted payoff of a single mortgage can be expressed by the following formula[5]

$$\Psi = \sum_{k=1}^{T} D_k \cdot C_k \cdot \mathbb{I}(\tau > t_k) + \sum_{k=1}^{T} D_k \cdot E_k \cdot \mathbb{I}(\tau = t_k) \tag{14}$$

where τ is the exercise time and, for each date k,

- D_k is the aleatory discount factor
- C_k is the contractual cash flow if the option is not exercised
- E_k is the prepayment amount

---

[5]For the sake of simplicity and consistent with standard numerical pricing algorithms, we assume that early exercise can occur at a discrete set of dates, like in Bermudan-style prepayment options.

In the case of level payment mortgages without prepayment penalties, C_k is constant and equal to the installment amount, while E_k coincides with the outstanding balance of the loan. As a consequence, D and τ are the only aleatory variables. The former depends on market factors only, while the latter is also affected by exogenous factors.

The payoff can be rewritten in terms of survival indicator functions with simple passages:

$$\Psi = \sum_{k=0}^{T} D_k \cdot M_k \cdot \mathbb{I}(\tau > t_k) \tag{15}$$

where

$$\begin{cases} M_0 = E_1 \cdot D_1 & \text{with } D_0 = 1, \ \mathbb{I}(\tau > t_0) = 1 \\ M_T = C_T - E_T \\ M_k = C_k - E_k + E_{k+1} \cdot D_{k+1}/D_k & \text{for } 0 < k < T \end{cases} \tag{16}$$

We consider now a portfolio of mortgages, issued continually at different times and with different contractual conditions. Let us define:

- N, the total number of mortgage debtors
- M, the number of mortgage contract types (i.e. same issue time, maturity, coupon rate and frequency, etc.)
- N^p, the number of contracts of type p
- N^{ip}, the number of contracts of type p closed with the i-th debtor ($\sum_{i=1}^{N} N^{ip} = N^p$).

The discounted payoff of the portfolio can be written as

$$\Psi = \sum_{i=1}^{N} \sum_{p=1}^{M} N^{ip} \cdot \left(\sum_{k=0}^{T} D_k \cdot M_k^p \cdot \mathbb{I}(\tau^{ip} > t_k) \right) \tag{17}$$

By applying (13) and the law of total variance

$$\mathbb{V}\left[\Psi(x,y)\right] = \mathbb{V}_x\left[\mathbb{E}_y\left[\Psi \,|\, x\right]\right] + \mathbb{E}_x\left[\mathbb{V}_y\left[\Psi \,|\, x\right]\right] \tag{18}$$

we can derive a general pricing formula for the portfolio

$$V(0) = \mathbb{E}_X^Q\left[\Pi_0(X) - k \cdot \chi_q \cdot \sqrt{\Pi_1(X) + \Pi_2(X)}\right] \tag{19}$$

with

$$\Pi_0(X) = \mathbb{E}_Z^P \left[\mathbb{E}_\tau^P \left[\sum_{i=1}^{N} \sum_{p=1}^{M} \sum_{k=0}^{T} \Psi_k^{ip} \middle| X, Z \right] \middle| X \right] \tag{20}$$

$$\Pi_1(X) = \mathbb{E}_Z^P \left[\mathbb{V}_\tau^P \left[\sum_{i=1}^{N} \sum_{p=1}^{M} \sum_{k=0}^{T} \Psi_k^{ip} \middle| X, Z \right] \middle| X \right] \tag{21}$$

$$\Pi_2(X) = \mathbb{V}_Z^P \left[\mathbb{E}_\tau^P \left[\sum_{i=1}^{N} \sum_{p=1}^{M} \sum_{k=0}^{T} \Psi_k^{ip} \middle| X, Z \right] \middle| X \right] \tag{22}$$

where we have defined

$$\Psi_k^{ip} = N^{ip} \cdot D_k \cdot M_k^p \cdot \mathbb{I}(\tau^{ip} > t_k) \tag{23}$$

The first term, $\Pi_0(X)$, is the revised expectation of discounted cash flows, conditionally to a particular market scenario and including the impact of exogenous factors. It quantifies the expected benefit for the option seller due to the sub-optimal exercise strategy followed by the option holder.

The second term, $\Pi_1(X)$, can be interpreted as a sort of granularity adjustment. It reflects the variability of future cash flows, since the option exercise time τ is not uniquely determined by the market scenario but it can occur potentially at any time. However, in the limit of a granular portfolio[6] it tends to vanish and can be disregarded.

The third term, $\Pi_2(X)$, quantifies the additional uncertainty induced by exogenous factors, which alter exercise probabilities for the same market scenario. It becomes negligible in a large portfolio only if exogenous factors are purely idiosyncratic (no system component).

By applying condition (2), we obtain:

$$\Pi_0(X) = \sum_{i=1}^{N} \sum_{p=1}^{M} \sum_{k=0}^{T} L_k^{ip} \cdot \Gamma_{k,i,p}^0 \tag{24}$$

$$\Pi_1(X) = \sum_{i=1}^{N} \sum_{p=1}^{M} \sum_{k,h=0}^{T} L_k^{ip} L_h^{ip} \cdot \Gamma_{i,kh,p}^1 \tag{25}$$

$$\Pi_2(X) = \sum_{i,j=1}^{N} \sum_{p,q=1}^{M} \sum_{k,h=0}^{T} L_k^{ip} L_h^{jq} \cdot \Gamma_{ij,kh,pq}^2 \tag{26}$$

---

[6]A granular portfolio is characterized by a large number of positions with different counterparts and almost equal sizes.

where we have defined

$$L_k^{ip} = N^{ip} \cdot D_k \cdot M_k^p \tag{27}$$

$$\Gamma_{i,k,p}^0 = \mathbb{E}_Z^P \left[S_k^{ip} \middle| X \right] \tag{28}$$

$$\Gamma_{i,kh,p}^1 = \mathbb{E}_Z^P \left[S_{\max(k,h)}^{ip} \middle| X \right] - \mathbb{E}_Z^P \left[S_k^{ip} S_h^{ip} \middle| X \right] \tag{29}$$

$$\Gamma_{ij,kh,pq}^2 = \mathbb{V}_Z^P \left[S_k^{ip}, S_h^{jq} \middle| X \right] \tag{30}$$

and S_k^{ip} are survival probabilities, conditionally to a risk scenario $\{X, Z\}$. For each borrower, contract and possible exercise date

$$S_k^{ip}(X, Z) \begin{cases} = \mathbb{E}\left[\mathbb{I}\left(\tau^{ip} > t_k \right) \middle| X, Z \right] & \forall k > 0 \\ = 1 \ \text{if} \ k = 0 \end{cases} \tag{31}$$

It is worth noting that the price depends only on the specification of the dynamics of both market and exogenous factors, as well as their functional dependence with survival probabilities $S_k^{ip}(X, Z)$.

4. Mortgage portfolio valuation with BIX model

In this section, we apply the general pricing framework described above to the valuation of a portfolio of mortgages, issued at different times and with different contractual rates, by Bissiri and Cogo [4], by extending pricing formulas to the case of a heterogeneous pool of mortgagors.

From the previous section we recognize that a particular model choice consists in: (*i*) characterizing mortgagor creditworthiness and behavioral attitude to early prepayment; (*ii*) selecting all market and exogenous factors $\{X(t), Z(t)\}$; (*iii*) specifying their dynamics; (*iv*) assuming a marginal probability response function, R, as defined in (1).

4.1. *Heterogeneity and granularity*

Firstly, heterogeneity in the pool is taken into account by dividing mortgagors into C distinct clusters, with homogeneous degree of creditworthiness and prepayment attitude.[7]

We denote with N^c the number of mortgagors in cluster c and similarly with N^{cp} the number of contracts of type p owned by borrowers belonging

---

[7]We implicitly assume that the issuer has a good knowledge of the characteristics of all counterparts.

to cluster c. Clearly,

$$\sum_{i=1}^{N} \mathbb{I}(i \in c) = N^c \qquad \sum_{c=1}^{C} N^c = N \tag{32}$$

$$\sum_{i=1}^{N} \mathbb{I}(i \in c) \cdot N^{ip} = N^{cp} \qquad \sum_{c=1}^{C} N^{cp} = N^p \tag{33}$$

4.2. *Market factors*

Mortgage valuation is affected by interest and credit risk, besides behavioral risk. A sound and realistic model should capture the joint evolution of market interest rates and credits spread for all debtors. Several approaches can be chosen with increasing complexity.[8]

In this paper, for the sake of simplicity, we select a standard two-factor Gaussian model, belonging to the so-called family of intensity-based models, whose risk neutral dynamics is described by the stochastic processes

$$\begin{cases} dX_1(t) = -\alpha_1 \cdot dX_1(t) \cdot dt + \sigma_1 \cdot dW_1(t) \\ dX_2(t) = -\alpha_2 \cdot dX_2(t) \cdot dt + \sigma_2 \cdot dW_2(t) \end{cases} \tag{34}$$

$$\mathbb{E}^Q \left[dW_1(t) \cdot dW_2(t) \right] = \rho_X \cdot dt \tag{35}$$

The first risk factor models essentially interest rates, while the second one accounts for default intensities for all mortgagors in the portfolio. Conditional to a specific risk factor scenario, defaults occur independently. A correlation between factors, ρ_X, is also introduced. See e.g. Brigo and Mercurio [20] or Schönbucher [21] for more details.

Due to the affine properties of the Gaussian models, interest rates and credit spreads, $Y(t)$, can be computed analytically

$$Y(t) = a + b \cdot X_1(t) + c \cdot X_2(t) \tag{36}$$

In particular, discount factors for cash flows of mortgages held by any debtor i belonging to cluster c are stochastic variables, expressed by

$$D_k^i = D_k^c = \exp \left\{ -\psi_k^c - \int_0^{t_k} X_1(u)du - \int_0^{t_k} X_2(u)du \right\} \quad \forall i \in c \tag{37}$$

where ψ_k^c are deterministic shifts that account for the initial term structure of interest rates and credit spread for each cluster of borrowers.

---

[8]Credit spreads depend both on default probabilities and recovery rates. A full detailed model of mortgagor creditworthiness as well as the impact of collateral on recovery rates is beyond the scope of the present paper.

4.3. *Exogenous factors*

We adopt a micro-structural (reduced-form) approach, by assigning a single (synthetic) exogenous factor to each single debtor in the portfolio. In order to capture additional correlation besides financial convenience, we assume that each factor can be split into a systemic component, ξ_k^0, and a purely idiosyncratic one, ξ_k^i.

$$Z_k^i = Z^i(t_k) = \rho_Z \cdot \xi_k^0 + \sqrt{1 - \rho_Z^2} \cdot \xi_k^i \qquad (38)$$

where ρ_Z is the weight of the systemic component, $\rho_Z \in [0,1]$.[9]

In order to mimic fluctuations of observed prepayment rates around their historical mean, we also model the dynamics of each exogenous factor by means of an auto-regressive process, AR(1), with common parameters (α, β), so that

$$\xi_k^i = \alpha \cdot \xi_{k-1}^i + \beta \cdot \varepsilon_k^i \qquad (39)$$

$$\mathbb{E}_Z^P\left[\varepsilon_k^i\right] = 0; \qquad \mathbb{E}_Z^P\left[\varepsilon_k^i \varepsilon_h^j\right] = \delta_{kh}\delta_{ij} \quad \forall\, i, j \geq 1, \ k, h > 0 \qquad (40)$$

We also assume that $\varepsilon_0^i = 0 \ \forall\, i > 0$, while ε_0^0 is a model parameter.

It is easy to compute that

$$\xi_k^i = \lambda_{k,0} \cdot \varepsilon_0^i + \sum_{h=1}^{k} \lambda_{k,h} \cdot \varepsilon_h^i \qquad (41)$$

$$\lambda_{k,0} = \alpha^k; \qquad \lambda_{k,h} = \alpha^{k-h} \cdot \beta \qquad (42)$$

The exogenous process has to satisfy conditions (4) on the asymptotic distribution. When applied to the logarithm of $Q(t)$, model parameters are subject to the following constraints:

$$\mathbb{E}_Z^P\left[\xi_\infty \,|\, X\right] = 0 \ \Rightarrow \ |\alpha| < 1 \qquad (43)$$

$$\mathbb{V}_Z^P\left[\xi_\infty \,|\, X\right] = 1 \ \Rightarrow \ \beta = \sqrt{1 - \alpha^2} \qquad (44)$$

4.4. *Marginal exercise probabilities*

Finally, we need to specify the dependence of marginal exercise probabilities on market and exogenous factors. In principle, a different response function Q_k^{ip} can be calibrated for each mortgage with respect to contract type, loan age and mortgagor cluster. However, a large historical data-set

---

[9] A similar approach can be found in the Vasicek model, which is at the foundation for Basel standardized approach to credit risk measurement.

would be needed to achieve a robust calibration. In practice, a simplified parametrization is more appropriate in most situations.

In the BIX model [4], Q_k^{ip} at time t_k for i-th owner of contract of type p has the general form

$$\ln\left[1 - Q_k^{ip}\right] = A_k^{ip}(X) + B_k^{ip}(X) \cdot Z_k^i \tag{45}$$

where A and B are generic functions. By taking cluster homogeneity into account, the following conditions hold

$$A^{ip} = A^{cp}, B^{ip} = B^{cp} \quad \forall i \in c \tag{46}$$

All response functions (45) have to be calibrated with historical prepayment data. For this purpose, it is convenient to select some representative market observables, $Y(t)$, such as interest rates and credit spreads. Thanks to the analytical properties of Gaussian models, their exact expression as a function of X can easily be derived, so that

$$Y(t) = \{Y_1(t, X(t)), Y_2(t, X(t)), ...\} \tag{47}$$
$$A_k^{ip}(X) \to A_k^{ip}[Y(X)] \quad B_k^{ip}(X) \to B_k^{ip}[Y(X)] \tag{48}$$

In order to capture the S-shaped dependence of prepayment rates on the market scenario X, A can be selected among the family of logit-like functions, with a set of shape parameters for calibration. In contrast, B can be assumed, to a first approximation, constant and independent on X.

4.5. *Hints for calibration*

In this paragraph we provide some hints for model calibration. Further details can be found in Bissiri and Cogo [4].

Undoubtedly, it is worth pointing out that a crucial role is played by the extent of the available data-set with time-series of historical prepayments. In practice, we follow a three-step procedure:

- We assume that risk neutral Q-dynamics for all market factors can be calibrated with the prices of quoted instruments. Such an assumption is quite reasonable when interest rate risk is concerned, but rather questionable for credit risk, since hedging instruments are not often liquid or traded.[10] Nonetheless, because this paper

---

[10]Indeed, interest rate dynamics can be calibrated with the quotes of several liquid instruments such as deposits, swaps, swaptions, etc. In contrast, only a few single-name CDS are actively traded so that risk-neutral default probabilities cannot easily be

focuses on behavioral risk, we assume that a term structure of interest rates and credit spreads is available for all borrowers and used to calibrate ψ_k^c in formula (37) for each cluster.

- Formula (45), as a particular case of (3), has a financial interpretation. Function A represents the long-term mean of prepayment rates subject to market scenario X, whilst function B accounts for the amplitude of deviations induced by (unitary) exogenous factors. If aggregate prepayment rates of mortgage baskets are observed for a long enough period of time, the impact of exogenous factors tends to cancel out on average. Thus A and be B can be estimated by fitting historical prepayments as a function of market regressors. Basically, A corresponds to the best fit line, while B accounts for the residual variance. Typically, A can be chosen among the family of logit or sigmoid functions of the rate shift in order to reproduce quite accurately the average S-shaped observed in historical data, see, e.g., prepayment rates reported in Davidson and Levin [1] or Peristiani [22]. The size of residuals is given by function B.

- Fit residuals can be explained in terms of latent exogenous risk factors, besides financial reasons. The time-evolution of Z_t can be deduced by inverting formula (45). Model parameters in (39) can be calibrated by means of a maximum-likelihood-estimation algorithm (see, e.g., Hamilton [24]). A similar approach can be found in Kolbe and Zagst [17].

4.6. *Survival exercise probabilities*

It is also useful to derive an analytical expression for survival probabilities. For each mortgagor belonging to cluster c and holding a contract of type p we can write

$$S_k^{ip}(X, Z) = \prod_{h=1}^{k} \left[1 - Q_h^{ip}(X, Z) \right] = e^{W_k^{ip}(X, Z)} \tag{49}$$

where, according to (45) and (46),

$$W_k^{ip}(X, Z) = \sum_{h=1}^{k} A_h^{cp}(X) + \sum_{h=1}^{k} B_h^{cp}(X) \cdot Z_h^i \tag{50}$$

---

inferred from the market. This is even more obvious when dealing with retail mortgagors. However, it is worth noting that in several cases, like residential mortgages, credit risk is remarkably mitigated by the presence of a collateral, i.e. the house property.

With simple passages

$$W_k^{ip}(X, Z) = \sum_{h=1}^{k} A_h^{cp}(X) + \sum_{h=1}^{k} B_h^{cp}(X) \cdot Z_h^i$$

$$= \sum_{h=1}^{k} A_h^{cp}(X) + \sum_{h=1}^{k} B_h^{cp}(X) \cdot \rho \cdot \left(\lambda_{h,0} \cdot \varepsilon_0^0 + \sum_{l=1}^{h} \lambda_{h,l} \cdot \varepsilon_l^0 \right)$$

$$+ \sum_{h=1}^{k} B_h^{cp}(X) \cdot \sqrt{1 - \rho^2} \cdot \left(\sum_{l=1}^{h} \lambda_{h,l} \cdot \varepsilon_l^i \right) \tag{51}$$

Summing up, we obtain

$$W_k^{ip}(X, Z) = \sum_{h=1}^{k} F_h^{cp}(X) + \sum_{h=1}^{k} G_{h,k}^{cp}(X) \cdot \left(\rho \cdot \varepsilon_h^0 + \sqrt{1 - \rho^2} \cdot \varepsilon_h^i \right) \tag{52}$$

where

$$F_h^{cp}(X) = A_h^{cp}(X) + B_h^{cp}(X) \cdot \rho \cdot \lambda_{h,0} \cdot \varepsilon_0^0 \tag{53}$$

$$G_{h,k}^{cp}(X) = \sum_{l=h}^{k} B_l^{cp}(X) \cdot \lambda_{l,h} \tag{54}$$

For each $i \in c$ and conditionally to a market scenario, W_k^{ip} are normal variables with mean and variance

$$\mu_k^{ip}(X) = \mu_k^{cp}(X) = \mathbb{E}_Z^P \left[W_k^{ip} \middle| X \right] = \sum_{h=1}^{k} F_h^{cp}(X) \tag{55}$$

$$\sigma_k^{ip\,2}(X) = \sigma_k^{cp\,2}(X) = \mathbb{V}_Z^P \left[W_k^{ip} \middle| X \right] = \sum_{h=1}^{k} G_{h,k}^{cp\,2}(X) \tag{56}$$

4.7. *Portfolio pricing*

The price, $V(0)$, can be computed by using formulas derived in Section 3.4. We need to compute the three quantities in (24), (25) and (26):

$$\Pi_0(X) = \sum_{i=1}^{N} \sum_{p=1}^{M} \sum_{k=0}^{T} L_k^{ip} \cdot \mathbb{E}_Z^P \left[S_k^{ip} \middle| X \right] \tag{57}$$

$$\Pi_1(X) = \sum_{i=1}^{N} \sum_{p=1}^{M} \sum_{k,h=0}^{T} L_k^{ip} L_h^{ip} \cdot \mathbb{E}_Z^P \left[S_{\max(k,h)}^{ip} - S_k^{ip} S_h^{ip} \middle| X \right] \tag{58}$$

$$\Pi_2(X) = \sum_{i,j=1}^{N} \sum_{p,q=1}^{M} \sum_{k,h=0}^{T} L_k^{ip} L_h^{jq} \cdot \mathbb{V}_Z^P \left[S_k^{ip}, S_h^{jq} \middle| X \right] \tag{59}$$

where

$$L_k^{ip} = L_k^{ip}(X) = N^{ip} \cdot D_k^i \cdot M_k^p \qquad (60)$$

Given the sub-portfolio of mortgages of type p held by borrowers in cluster c, let us define $L_k^{cp}(X)$ as the aggregate discounted cash flows exchanged at time t_k

$$L_k^{cp} = L_k^{cp}(X) = \sum_{i \in c} N^{ip} \cdot D_k^c \cdot M_k^p = N^{cp} \cdot D_k^c \cdot M_k^p \qquad (61)$$

and H^{cp} as the Herfindahl-Hirschman Index (HHI)[11]

$$H^{cp} = \sum_{i \in c} \left(\frac{N^{ip}}{N^{cp}} \right)^2 \qquad (62)$$

4.7.1. *Expression for* $\Pi_0(X)$

By using (55) and (56), the conditional expectation $\Pi_0(X)$ can be computed as

$$
\begin{aligned}
\Pi_0(X) &= \sum_{p=1}^{M} \sum_{c=1}^{C} \sum_{i \in c} \sum_{k=0}^{T} L_k^{ip} \cdot \mathbb{E}_Z^P \left[e^{W_k^{ip}} \Big| X \right] \\
&= \sum_{p=1}^{M} \sum_{c=1}^{C} \left[L_0^{cp} + \sum_{k=1}^{T} L_k^{cp} \cdot e^{\mu_k^{cp} + \frac{1}{2}(\sigma_k^{cp})^2} \right]
\end{aligned}
\qquad (63)
$$

4.7.2. *Expression for* $\Pi_1(X)$

The second term $\Pi_1(X)$ is also linear with respect to the number of contracts and investors.

$$
\begin{aligned}
\Pi_1(X) &= \sum_{p=1}^{M} \sum_{i=1}^{N} \sum_{k,h=0}^{T} L_k^{ip} L_h^{ip} \cdot \mathbb{E}_Z^P \left[e^{W_{\max(k,h)}^{ip}} - e^{W_k^{ip} + W_h^{ip}} \Big| X \right] \\
&= \sum_{p=1}^{M} \sum_{c=1}^{C} H^{cp} \cdot \sum_{k=0}^{T} L_k^{cp} \cdot I_k^{cp} \cdot e^{\mu_k^{cp} + \frac{1}{2}(\sigma_k^{cp})^2}
\end{aligned}
\qquad (64)
$$

---

[11]HHI is a widespread indicator of the granularity of a portfolio, see e.g. Gordy [25].

where I_k^{cp} is approximated by[12]

$$I_k^{cp} = I_k^{cp}(X) \approx L_k^{cp} \cdot \left(1 - e^{\mu_k^{cp} + \frac{3}{2}(\sigma_k^{cp})^2}\right)$$

$$+2 \cdot \sum_{h=0}^{k-1} L_h^{cp} \cdot \left(1 - e^{\mu_h^{cp} + \frac{1}{2}(\sigma_h^{cp})^2 + \sigma_k^{cp}\sigma_h^{cp}}\right) \qquad (65)$$

It is worth noting that H^{cp} is usually vanishingly small in the granularity limit and, in turn, $\Pi_1(X)$ can be disregarded in large and equal-sized portfolios.

4.7.3. *Expression for $\Pi_2(X)$*

Finally, the computation for $\Pi_2(X)$ is less straightforward and more time-consuming, due to the double loop on the number of contracts. Since it arises from conditional survival probability covariances, it becomes negligible only in the unrealistic case that exogenous risk is fully idiosyncratic.

Therefore, a different approach has to be followed with some suitable but accurate enough approximations.

- Firstly, we observe that $\Pi_2(X)$ is the variance of a sum of log-normal variables. Although an analytical expression for the resulting distribution is not available, we can apply one of the several approximations that have been derived in order to calculate analytically the first moments.[13]
- Secondly, the formula can be further simplified by assuming that the number of mortgagors with more than one position is relatively small if compared to the entire portfolio.

In this paper we adopt Gentle's approximation [26] by replacing the arithmetic weighted average with the geometric one,[14] so that we can

---

[12]It can be shown that the following condition holds for $v_{hk} = \mathbb{V}[W_k + W_h|X]$. If $h < k$, $L_1 < v_{hk} < L_2$ where $L_1 = \sigma_k^2 + 3\sigma_h^2$ and $L_2 = 3\sigma_k^2 + \sigma_h^2$. As a proxy, we take the geometric mean so that $v_{hk} \approx \sigma_k^2 + \sigma_h^2 + 2\sigma_k\sigma_h$. The impact of approximation has negligible impact especially if $\mu << \sigma^2$ or σ is almost constant as a function of time.

[13]For instance, this is the typical mathematical problem that one encounters in the pricing of equity Asian options in a Black-Scholes framework.

[14]Although several alternative and even more refined approximations have been developed, Gentle's approach is accurate enough as reported in the extensive literature about the pricing of Asian options.

rewrite the expression for $\Pi_2(X)$ in the following way

$$\Pi_2(X) = \mathbb{V}_Z^P \left[\sum_{p=1}^{M} \sum_{i=1}^{N} \sum_{k=1}^{T} L_k^{ip}(X) \cdot S_k^{ip}(X,Z) \middle| X \right] \tag{66}$$

$$\approx \mathbb{V}_Z^P \left[\prod_{p=1}^{M} \prod_{i=1}^{N} \prod_{k=1}^{T} e^{L_k^{ip}(X) \cdot W_k^{ip}(X,Z)} \middle| X \right] = \mathbb{V}_Z^P \left[e^{\Omega(X,Z)} \middle| X \right]$$

where $\Omega(X,Z)$ is a normal random variable, with mean $M_\Omega(X)$ and variance $\Sigma_\Omega^2(X)$, respectively (see the Appendix (Section 6) for their analytical expressions). Thus, $\Pi_2(X)$ can be approximated with

$$\Pi_2(X) \approx e^{2 \cdot M_\Omega(X) + \Sigma_\Omega^2(X)} \cdot \left(e^{\Sigma_\Omega^2(X)} - 1 \right) \tag{67}$$

4.8. *Simulation*

Portfolio evaluation can be performed by means of Montecarlo simulations as in the full rational case. The only difference lies in the fact that, subject to a market scenario, cash flows are uniquely determined only if the option holder follows an optimal exercise strategy. In contrast, under the presence of behavioral risk, we need to compute the first two moments of the conditional distribution for each simulated path of market factors. However, we can rely on analytical formulas (63), (64), (67). Since all formulas essentially depend on linear sums over the number of contracts and the number of dates, the additional computational burden is usually limited.

5. Conclusion

In conclusion, we have described a coherent and flexible framework for accounting the impact of behavioral risk on the valuation of a basket of mortgages. The approach consists in a prepayment model based on financial observables, which is needed to reproduce sub-optimal early prepayments in line with other models reported in the literature. At the same time, it introduces a pricing correction which accounts for the residuals that are observed when fitting historical data, as a consequence of the effect of exogenous factors. Due to their non-financial nature of these sources of risk, an additional adjustment is added to the pricing formula by adopting the traditional risk charge approach. We believe that our methodology is a valid and more transparent alternative to the practice of applying an option-adjusted-spread (OAS) to the discount factors in order to account for risk factors not capture by the financial prepayment model.

6. Appendix

In this paragraph we derive an expression for the random variable $\Omega(X, Z)$, defined in (66), and we provide an analytical formula for its two conditional moments, $M_\Omega(X)$ and $\Sigma^2_\Omega(X)$.

$$\Omega(X, Z) = \sum_{p=1}^{M} \sum_{k=1}^{T} \sum_{i=1}^{N} L_k^{ip}(X) \cdot W_k^{ip}(X, Z) \tag{68}$$

$$= \sum_{k=1}^{T} \sum_{p=1}^{M} \sum_{c=1}^{C} \left[J_k^{cp}(X) + K_k^{cp}(X) \cdot \left(\rho_Z \cdot \varepsilon_k^0 + \sqrt{1 - \rho_Z^2} \cdot \sum_{i \in c} \left(\frac{N^{ip}}{N^{cp}} \right) \varepsilon_k^i \right) \right]$$

where

$$J_k^{cp}(X) = L_k^{cp}(X) \cdot \sum_{h=1}^{k} F_h^{cp}(X) \tag{69}$$

$$K_k^{cp}(X) = \sum_{h=k}^{T} L_h^{cp}(X) \cdot G_{k,h}^{cp}(X) \tag{70}$$

We can easily compute the conditional mean and variance of $\Omega(X, Z)$ as

$$M_\Omega(X) = \mathbb{E}_Z^P \left[\Omega \middle| X \right] = \sum_{k=1}^{T} \sum_{p=1}^{M} \sum_{c=1}^{C} J_k^{cp}(X) \tag{71}$$

$$\Sigma^2_\Omega(X) = \mathbb{V}_Z^P \left[\Omega \middle| X \right] = \sum_{k=1}^{T} \left[\rho_Z^2 \cdot U_k^1(X) + \left(1 - \rho_Z^2 \right) \cdot U_k^2(X) \right] \tag{72}$$

where

$$U_k^1(X) = \left(\sum_{p=1}^{M} \sum_{c=1}^{C} K_k^{cp}(X) \right)^2 \tag{73}$$

$$U_k^2(X) = \sum_{c=1}^{C} \sum_{i \in c} \left(\sum_{p=1}^{M} \frac{N^{ip}}{N^{cp}} \cdot K_k^{cp}(X) \right)^2 \tag{74}$$

The expression can be further simplified in the quite realistic case where most mortgagors own a single contract, but contracts of a given type p are owned by various mortgagors.

$$U_k^2 = \sum_{p=1}^{M} \sum_{c=1}^{C} H^{cp} K_k^{cp\,2} \tag{75}$$

$$\Sigma_\Omega^2 = \sum_{k=1}^{T} \left[\rho_Z^2 \left(\sum_{p=1}^{M} K_k^p \right)^2 + (1 - \rho_Z^2) \sum_{p=1}^{M} \sum_{c=1}^{C} H^{cp} K_k^{cp\,2} \right] \tag{76}$$

References

1. A. Davidson and A. Levin, *Mortgage Valuation Models: Embedded Options, Risk, and Uncertainty* (Oxford University Press, 2014).
2. A. Castagna and F. Fede, *Measuring and Managing Liquidity Risk* (Wiley Finance, 2013).
3. M. Bissiri and R. Cogo, Modeling behavioral risk, *Available at SSRN:* `https://ssrn.com/abstract=2523349` (2014).
4. M. Bissiri and R. Cogo, Behavioral Value Adjustments, *Available at SSRN:* `https://ssrn.com/abstract=2941815` (2017).
5. K. Dunn and J. McConnell, Valuation of GNMA mortgage-backed securities, *Journal of Finance* **36**, 3 (1981), pp. 599–616.
6. R. Stanton, Rational Prepayment and the valuation of mortgage-backed securities, *The Review of Financial Studies* **8**, 3 (1995), pp. 677–708.
7. F. Longstaff, Borrower credit and the valuation of mortgage-backed securities, *Real Estate Economics* **33**, 4 (2005), pp. 619–661.
8. A. Kalotay, D. Yang and F. Fabozzi, An option-theoretic prepayment model for mortgages and mortgage-backed securities, *International Journal of Theoretical and Applied Finance* **7**, 8 (2004), pp. 949–978.
9. A. Davidson and A. Levin, Prepayment risk and option-adjusted valuation of MBS, *The Journal of Portfolio Management* **31**, 4 (2005), pp. 73–85.
10. E. S. Schwartz and W. N. Torous, Prepayment and the value of mortgage-backed securities, *The Journal of Finance* **44**, 2 (1989), pp. 375–392.
11. Y. Deng, J. M. Quigley and R. Van Order, Mortgage terminations, heterogeneity, and the exercise of mortgage options, *Econometrica* **68**, 2 (2000), pp. 275–307.
12. J. Kau, D. Keenan and A. Smurov, Reduced form mortgage pricing as an alternative to option-pricing models, *The Journal of Real Estate Finance and Economics* **33**, 3 (2006), pp. 183–196.
13. Y. K. Kwok, M. Dai and H. You, Intensity-based framework and penalty formulation of optimal stopping problems, *Journal of Economic Dynamics and Control* **31**, 12 (2007), pp. 3860–3880.

14. M. Consalvi and G. Scotto di Freca, Measuring prepayment risk: an application to Unicredit Family Financing, *Unicredit and Universities, Working paper series* **5**, (2010).

15. M. Chernov, B. Dunn and F. Longstaff, Macroeconomic-Driven Prepayment Risk and the Valuation of Mortgage-Backed Securities, *National Bureau of Economic Research*, Working paper 220968 (2016).

16. Y. Goncharov, An intensity-based approach to the valuation of mortgage contracts and computation of the endogenous mortgage rate, *International Journal of Theoretical and Applied Finance* **9**, 6 (2006), pp. 889–914.

17. A. Kolbe and R. Zagst, A hybrid-form model for the prepayment-risk-neutral valuation of mortgage-backed securities, *International Journal of Theoretical and Applied Finance* **11**, 6 (2008), pp. 635–656.

18. A. Kolbe and R. Zagst, Valuation of mortgage-backed securities and mortgage derivatives: A closed-form approximation, *Applied Mathematical Finance* **16**, 5 (2009), pp. 401–427.

19. X. Gabaix, A. Krishnamurthy and O. Vigneron, Limits of arbitrage: Theory and evidence from mortgage-backed-securities market, *Journal of Finance* **62**, 2 (2007), pp. 557–595.

20. D. Brigo and F. Mercurio, *Interest Rate Models: Theory and Practice with Smile, Inflation and Credit*, 2nd edn. (Springer-Verlag, Berlin Heidelberg, 2006).

21. P. J. Schönbucher, *Credit Derivatives Pricing Models* (Wiley Finance, 2003).

22. S. Peristiani, Modeling the instability of mortgage-backed prepayments, *The Journal of Fixed Income* **13**, 3 (2003), pp. 33–41.

23. D. Brigo, M. Morini and A. Pallavicini, *Counterparty Credit Risk, Collateral and Funding: With Pricing Cases for all Asset Classes* (Wiley Finance, 2013).

24. J. D. Hamilton, *Time Series Analysis* (Princeton University Press, 1994).

25. M. B. Gordy and E. Lütkebohmert, Granularity adjustment for Basel II, *Deutsche Bundesbank Series* **2**, 1 (2007).

26. D. Gentle, Basket weaving, *Risk* **6** (1993), pp. 51–52.

Chapter 2

Wrong-Way Risk Adjusted Exposure: Analytical Approximations for Options in Default Intensity Models

Damiano Brigo

Department of Mathematics, Imperial College London,
London SW7 2AZ, UK
damiano.brigo@imperial.ac.uk

Thomas Hvolby

Department of Mathematical Sciences, Aalborg Universitet,
Fredrik Bajers Vej 7G, DK-9220 Aalborg Øst, Denmark
thomas@math.aau.dk

Frédéric Vrins

Louvain Finance Center & CORE, Université catholique de Louvain,
Voir du Roman Pays 34, B-1348 Louvain-la-Neuve, Belgium
frederic.vrins@uclouvain.be

We examine credit value adjustment (CVA) estimation under wrong-way risk (WWR) by computing the expected positive exposure (EPE) under an equivalent measure as suggested in [1], adjusting the drift of the underlying for default risk. We apply this technique to European put and call options and derive the analytic formulas for EPE under WWR obtained with various approximations of the drift adjustment. We give the results of numerical experiments based on 4 parameter sets, and supply figures of the CVA based on both of the suggested proxys, comparing with CVA based on a 2D-Monte Carlo scheme and Gaussian Copula resampling. We also show the CVA obtained by the formulas from Basel III. We observe that the Basel III formula does not account for the credit-market correlation, while the Gaussian Copula resampling method estimates a too large impact of this correlation. The two proxies account for the credit-market correlation, and give results that are mostly similar to the 2D-Monte Carlo results.

Keywords: counterparty risk, CVA, wrong-way risk, change of measure, drift adjustment, wrong way measure, put and call options.

1. Introduction

In this paper we aim at computing the credit valuation adjustment (CVA) expressions of European calls and puts under the Black-Scholes-Merton-Cox model, that is when the underlying stock follows GBM dynamics and the default is governed by a totally inaccessible stopping time corresponding to the first jump time of a Cox process. Specifically, we assume that the default intensity follows a CIR-process.

Let us consider a portfolio with maturity T and whose discounted price process is $\tilde{V}$. The CVA associated to such a portfolio traded with a counterparty whose recovery rate is R and default time is τ with survival (risk-neutral) probability curve $G(t) := \mathbb{Q}(\tau > t)$ is given by

$$\text{CVA} = -(1 - R) \int_0^T \mathbb{E}^{\mathbb{Q}} \left[\tilde{V_s}^+ \middle| \tau = s \right] dG(s) , \tag{1}$$

where $x^+ := \max(x, 0)$. It has been shown in [1] that when the default time is modeled as the first jump's time of a Cox process, the "$\tau = s$" condition in the expectation in Eq. (1) — associated to market-credit dependency that is, to wrong-way risk — can be absorbed in the drift of the portfolio price process:

$$\text{CVA} = -(1 - R) \int_0^T \mathbb{E}^{\mathbb{Q}^{\mathcal{C}_s}} \left[\tilde{V_s}^+ \right] dG(s) .$$

Here, $\mathcal{C}_t$ is a rolling numéraire corresponding to the default leg of a CDS offering protection in a small interval around t, and is not to be confused with the call option price at t, noted C_t. We refer the reader to [1] for more details about this technique.

We define the expected positive exposure (EPE) without taking wrong-way risk into account as the expectation in Eq. (1) without the condition. Thus the no-WWR EPE is simply the function $\text{EPE}^{\perp}(s) := \mathbb{E}^{\mathbb{Q}} \left[\tilde{V_s}^+ \right]$ for $s \in [0, T]$. The EPE under wrong-way risk (referred to as the WWR EPE) is defined as

$$\text{EPE}(s) = \mathbb{E}^{\mathbb{Q}} \left[\tilde{V_s}^+ \middle| \tau = s \right] = \mathbb{E}^{\mathbb{Q}^{\mathcal{C}_s}} \left[\tilde{V_s}^+ \right] .$$

From Girsanov theorem, a $\mathbb{Q}$-Brownian motion on $[0, s]$ will become, under $\mathbb{Q}^{\mathcal{C}_s}$, a Brownian motion plus a drift. In particular, we note $\theta_{\cdot}^s$ the drift associated to the $\mathbb{Q}$-Brownian motion driving the exposure. Its analytical expression is derived explicitly in [1]. We now show that when this (stochastic) drift is approximated by a deterministic function $\theta(\cdot, s)$, the quantity $\mathbb{E}^{\mathbb{Q}^{\mathcal{C}_s}} \left[\tilde{V_s}^+ \right]$ is available in closed form for calls and puts, leading to an analytical approximation for the CVA under wrong-way risk, and compare the effect on CVA of two approximations of this drift to the Monte Carlo setup.

2. Call and put risk-neutral dynamics

We assume GBM dynamics for the stock under the risk-neutral measure $\mathbb{Q}$, with constant risk-free rate r and volatility $\sigma > 0$. Hence, denote by W a $\mathbb{Q}$-Brownian motion,

$$dS_t = rS_t dt + \sigma S_t dW_t \ ,$$

whose solution is

$$S_t = S_0 e^{(r-\frac{\sigma^2}{2})t+\sigma W_t} \ .$$

Let us note C the price process of a European call option on the stock S with maturity T and strike K. Hence, using the Theta-Delta-Gamma relationship,

$$dC_t = \Theta_t dt + \Delta_t dS_t + \frac{1}{2}\Gamma_t d\langle S\rangle_t = rC_t dt + \sigma S_t \Delta_t dW_t \ ,$$

and it is well-known that

$$C_t = S_t \Phi(d(T-t)) - Ke^{-r(T-t)}\Phi\left(d(T-t) - \sigma\sqrt{T-t}\right) \ ,$$
$$\Delta_t = \Phi(d(T-t)) \ ,$$
$$d(s) := \frac{1}{\sigma\sqrt{s}}\left(\ln\frac{S_t}{K} + \left(r + \frac{\sigma^2}{2}\right)s\right) \ .$$

Let us note the time-t discounted value of any process $X = (X_t)_{t\geq 0}$ as $\tilde{X}_t := X_t e^{-rt}$. The discounted call price process $\tilde{C}$ can be written in terms of the discounted stock price process $\tilde{S}$:

$$\tilde{C}_t = \tilde{S}_t \Phi\left(d(t,T)\right) - Ke^{-rT}\Phi\left(d(t,T) - \sigma\sqrt{T-t}\right) \ ,$$
$$d(t,T) = \frac{1}{\sigma\sqrt{T-t}}\left(\ln\frac{\tilde{S}_t}{K} + rT + \frac{\sigma^2}{2}(T-t)\right) \ ,$$

where we have used that $\ln S_t = \ln \tilde{S}_t + rt$. Using $W_t \overset{(\mathbb{Q})}{\sim} \sqrt{t}Z$ where $Z \overset{(\mathbb{Q})}{\sim} \mathcal{N}(0,1)$, one obtains

$$\tilde{S}_t = S_0 e^{-\frac{\sigma^2}{2}t+\sigma W_t} \sim S_0 e^{-\frac{\sigma^2}{2}t+\sigma\sqrt{t}Z} \ ,$$
$$\Delta_t = \Phi\left(\frac{1}{\sigma\sqrt{T-t}}\left(\ln\frac{S_0}{K} + \left(r + \frac{\sigma^2}{2}\right)T - \sigma^2 t\right) + \frac{W_t}{\sqrt{T-t}}\right)$$
$$\sim \Phi\Big(\underbrace{\frac{1}{\sigma\sqrt{T-t}}\left(\ln\frac{S_0}{K} + \left(r + \frac{\sigma^2}{2}\right)T - \sigma^2 t\right)}_{:=\alpha(t)} + \underbrace{\frac{\sqrt{t}}{\sqrt{T-t}}Z}_{:=\beta(t)}\Big) \ ,$$

so that

$$\tilde{C}_t = S_0 e^{-\frac{\sigma^2}{2}t + \sigma W_t} \Phi\left(\alpha(t) + W_t/\sqrt{T-t}\right)$$
$$-Ke^{-rT}\Phi\left(\alpha(t) - \sigma\sqrt{T-t} + W_t/\sqrt{T-t}\right)$$
$$\sim S_0 e^{-\frac{\sigma^2}{2}t + \sigma\sqrt{t}Z}\Phi\left(\alpha(t) + \beta(t)Z\right)$$
$$-Ke^{-rT}\Phi\left(\alpha(t) - \sigma\sqrt{T-t} + \beta(t)Z\right).$$

A similar development yields the dynamics and the marginal distributions of the corresponding put

$$\tilde{P}_t = Ke^{-rT}\Phi\left(\sigma\sqrt{T-t} - \alpha(t) - W_t/\sqrt{T-t}\right)$$
$$-S_0 e^{-\frac{\sigma^2}{2}t + \sigma W_t}\Phi\left(-\alpha(t) - W_t/\sqrt{T-t}\right)$$
$$\sim Ke^{-rT}\Phi\left(\sigma\sqrt{T-t} - \alpha(t) - \beta(t)Z\right)$$
$$-S_0 e^{-\frac{\sigma^2}{2}t + \sigma\sqrt{t}Z}\Phi\left(-\alpha(t) - \beta(t)Z\right).$$

3. Expected positive exposures under no WWR

As $\tilde{C} \geq 0$ and $\tilde{P} \geq 0$, the expected (discounted) exposure corresponds to the expected *positive* (discounted) exposure. Hence,

$$\mathbb{E}^{\mathbb{Q}}\left[\tilde{C}_t\right] = S_0 e^{-\frac{\sigma^2}{2}t}\mathbb{E}^{\mathbb{Q}}\left[e^{\sigma\sqrt{t}Z}\Phi\left(\alpha(t) + \beta(t)Z\right)\right]$$
$$-Ke^{-rT}\mathbb{E}^{\mathbb{Q}}\left[\Phi\left(\alpha(t) - \sigma\sqrt{T-t} + \beta(t)Z\right)\right]$$
$$= S_0\Phi\left(\frac{\alpha(t) + \beta(t)\sigma\sqrt{t}}{\sqrt{1+\beta^2(t)}}\right) - Ke^{-rT}\Phi\left(\frac{\alpha(t) - \sigma\sqrt{T-t}}{\sqrt{1+\beta^2(t)}}\right),$$

$$\mathbb{E}^{\mathbb{Q}}\left[\tilde{P}_t\right] = Ke^{-rT}\mathbb{E}^{\mathbb{Q}}\left[\Phi\left(\sigma\sqrt{T-t} - \alpha(t) - \beta(t)Z\right)\right]$$
$$-S_0 e^{-\frac{\sigma^2}{2}t}\mathbb{E}^{\mathbb{Q}}\left[e^{-\sigma\sqrt{t}Z}\Phi\left(-\alpha(t) - \beta(t)Z\right)\right]$$
$$= Ke^{-rT}\Phi\left(\frac{\sigma\sqrt{T-t} - \alpha(t)}{\sqrt{1+\beta^2(t)}}\right) - S_0\Phi\left(\frac{-\alpha(t) - \beta(t)\sigma\sqrt{t}}{\sqrt{1+\beta^2(t)}}\right),$$

where we have used

$$\mathbb{E}^{\mathbb{Q}}\left[e^{\eta Z}\Phi\left(\mu + \sigma Z\right)\right] = e^{\frac{\eta^2}{2}}\Phi\left(\frac{\mu + \sigma\eta}{\sqrt{1+\sigma^2}}\right).$$

It can be checked that $\mathbb{E}^{\mathbb{Q}}\left[\tilde{C}_t\right] = C_0$ and $\mathbb{E}^{\mathbb{Q}}\left[\tilde{P}_t\right] = P_0$ for all $t \in [0,T]$ as expected from the martingale property of discounted price processes under

Q. Nevertheless, because of the drift-adjustment, those expressions will become time-dependent as soon as WWR will enter the picture.

4. Expected positive exposures under WWR

Under no WWR (risk-neutral measure $\mathbb{Q}$), $\tilde{C}$ is a martingale,

$$d\tilde{C}_t = \sigma \tilde{S}_t \Delta_t dW_t ,$$

whose solution is given by the standard Black-Scholes-Merton equation in Sec. 3. As discussed above, Girsanov theorem yields

$$dW_t = dW_t^s + \theta_t^s dt ,$$

where W^s is a $\mathbb{Q}^{\mathcal{C}_s}$-Brownian motion on $[0, s]$. We assume that under $\mathbb{Q}$, the default intensity λ is governed by a CIR process with volatility η, i.e.

$$d\lambda_t = \kappa(\theta - \lambda_t)dt + \eta\sqrt{\lambda_t}dW_t^\lambda ,$$

where W_t^λ is a $\mathbb{Q}$-Brownian motion whose correlation with W is ρ. A non-zero value for ρ introduces a dependency between S and λ that controls wrong-way risk. The drift adjustment is given by [1]

$$\theta_t^s = \theta_t^s(\lambda_t) = \rho\eta\sqrt{\lambda_t}\left(\frac{A^\lambda(t,s)B_s^\lambda(t,s)}{A^\lambda(t,s)B_s^\lambda(t,s)\lambda_t - A_s^\lambda(t,s)} - B^\lambda(t,s)\right) , \quad (2)$$

where A^λ, B^λ are known zero-coupon bond functions in affine models [2]:

$$\mathbb{E}^{\mathbb{Q}}\left[e^{-\int_t^s \lambda_u du}\,\Big|\,\mathcal{F}_t\right] = A^\lambda(t,s)e^{-B^\lambda(t,s)\lambda_t}.$$

The subscripts refer to the variable with respect to which we compute the derivatives of A^λ and B^λ.

Let us now look at the dynamics of the call for $t \in [0, s]$ under $\mathbb{Q}^{\mathcal{C}_s}$. First, observe that we can write $\tilde{C}$ as a deterministic function of the variables (t, W_t) (instead of the usual (t, S_t) couple):

$$\tilde{C}_t = v(t, W_t) ,$$

with

$$v(s, x) := S_0 e^{-\frac{\sigma^2}{2}s + \sigma x}\Phi\left(\alpha(s) + x/\sqrt{T - s}\right)$$
$$-Ke^{-rT}\Phi\left(\alpha(s) + x/\sqrt{T - s} - \sigma\sqrt{T - s}\right) .$$

Applying Ito's lemma,

$$d\tilde{C}_t = \left(v_t(t, W_t) + \frac{1}{2}v_{xx}(t, W_t)\right) dt + v_x(t, W_t)dW_t ,$$

and we have, for all (s, x) where $s \in [0, T]$ and $x \in \mathbb{R}$ the following relationships for the partial derivatives of v:

$$v_t(s, x) + \frac{1}{2}v_{xx}(s, x) = 0 \tag{3}$$

$$v_x(s, x) = \sigma S_0 e^{-\frac{\sigma^2}{2}s + \sigma x} \Phi\left(\alpha(s) + x/\sqrt{T - s}\right) . \tag{4}$$

Now let us look at the dynamics of the call as a function of the $\mathbb{Q}^{\mathcal{C}_s}$-Brownian motion W^s on $t \in [0, s]$:

$$\tilde{C}_t := v\left(t, W_t^s + \int_0^t \theta_u^s du\right) .$$

Using Ito's lemma and the relationships between v_t, v_x and v_{xx} in Eqs. (3) and (4), we have

$$d\tilde{C}_t = \left(v_t\left(t, W_t^s + \int_0^t \theta_u^s du\right) + \frac{1}{2}v_{xx}\left(t, W_t^s + \int_0^t \theta_u^s du\right)\right) dt$$

$$+ v_x\left(t, W_t^s + \int_0^t \theta_u^s du\right)(dW_t^s + \theta_t^s dt)$$

$$= v_x\left(t, W_t^s + \int_0^t \theta_u^s du\right)\theta_t^s dt + v_x\left(t, W_t^s + \int_0^t \theta_u^s du\right) dW_t^s .$$

Defining now

$$\hat{S}_t := \tilde{S}_t e^{\sigma \int_0^t \theta_u^s du} ,$$

$$\hat{\Delta}_t := \Phi\left(\hat{d}(t, T)\right) ,$$

$$\hat{d}(t, T) := \frac{1}{\sigma\sqrt{T - t}}\left(\ln\frac{\hat{S}_t}{K} + rT + \frac{\sigma^2}{2}(T - t)\right) ,$$

one gets

$$d\tilde{C}_t = \sigma\tilde{S}_t e^{\sigma \int_0^t \theta_u^s du}\hat{\Delta}_t\theta_t^s dt + \sigma\tilde{S}_t e^{\sigma \int_0^t \theta_u^s du}\hat{\Delta}_t dW_t^s$$

$$= \sigma\hat{S}_t\hat{\Delta}_t\theta_t^s dt + \sigma\hat{S}_t\hat{\Delta}_t dW_t^s . \tag{5}$$

Clearly, $\tilde{C}$ is a $\mathbb{Q}$-martingale. This is no longer true under the new measure: it features a drift. Moreover, the martingale part is impacted by the drift as well as $\hat{S}$ features θ.

Let us consider the deterministic approximation $\theta_t^s \approx \theta(t, s)$ where λ_t is replaced by a deterministic proxy $\lambda(t)$. By replacing λ_t with $\lambda(t)$ in Eq. (2), we have

$$\theta(t, s) := \rho\eta\sqrt{\lambda(t)}\left(\frac{A^\lambda(t, s)B_s^\lambda(t, s)}{A^\lambda(t, s)B_s^\lambda(t, s)\lambda(t) - A_s^\lambda(t, s)} - B^\lambda(t, s)\right) . \tag{6}$$

Then, the WWR EPE expression $\text{EPE}(s) = \mathbb{E}^{\mathbb{Q}^{\mathcal{C}_s}}\left[\tilde{C}_s\right]$ is known analytically. To compute $\text{EPE}(t)$, the WWR EPE at time t, we need to evaluate the expectation of $\tilde{C}_t$ under $\mathbb{Q}^{\mathcal{C}_t}$. We thus set $s = t$ and define

$$\Theta(t) \; := \; \int_0^t \theta(u, t)du \, ,$$

$$\hat{\alpha}(t) \; := \; \alpha(t) + \frac{\Theta(t)}{\sqrt{T-t}} \, ,$$

$$Z^t \overset{(\mathbb{Q}^{\mathcal{C}_t})}{\sim} \mathcal{N}(0, 1) \, .$$

This yields (up to the approximation of the stochastic drift by its deterministic expression)

$$\begin{aligned}
\tilde{C}_t &= v\left(t, W_t^t + \Theta(t)\right) \\
&= S_0 e^{-\frac{\sigma^2}{2}t + \sigma\Theta(t) + \sigma W_t^t} \Phi\left(\hat{\alpha}(t) + W_t^t/\sqrt{T-t}\right) \\
&\quad - Ke^{-rT}\Phi\left(\hat{\alpha}(t) - \sigma\sqrt{T-t} + W_t^t/\sqrt{T-t}\right) \\
&\sim S_0 e^{-\frac{\sigma^2}{2}t + \sigma\Theta(t) + \sigma\sqrt{t}Z^t} \Phi\left(\hat{\alpha}(t) + \beta(t)Z^t\right) \\
&\quad - Ke^{-rT}\Phi\left(\hat{\alpha}(t) - \sigma\sqrt{T-t} + \beta(t)Z^t\right) \, ,
\end{aligned}$$

showing that the WWR EPE takes a similar form as the No-WWR EPE:

$$\mathbb{E}^{\mathbb{Q}^{\mathcal{C}_t}}\left[\tilde{C}_t\right] \approx S_0 e^{\sigma\Theta(t)} \Phi\left(\frac{\hat{\alpha}(t) + \beta(t)\sigma\sqrt{t}}{\sqrt{1 + \beta^2(t)}}\right) - Ke^{-rT}\Phi\left(\frac{\hat{\alpha}(t) - \sigma\sqrt{T-t}}{\sqrt{1 + \beta^2(t)}}\right) \, ,$$

where the approximation results from the fact that we have replaced the random variable $\int_0^t \theta_u^t du$ by the deterministic quantity $\int_0^t \theta(u, t)du$. As regards to the WWR EPE of the put, one easily gets

$$\mathbb{E}^{\mathbb{Q}^{\mathcal{C}_t}}\left[\tilde{P}_t\right] \approx Ke^{-rT}\Phi\left(\frac{\sigma\sqrt{T-t} - \hat{\alpha}(t)}{\sqrt{1 + \beta^2(t)}}\right) - S_0 e^{\sigma\Theta(t)}\Phi\left(\frac{-\hat{\alpha}(t) - \beta(t)\sigma\sqrt{t}}{\sqrt{1 + \beta^2(t)}}\right) \, .$$

5. Proxys of θ_t^s

Here we use two different proxys for θ_t^s. As presented in [1], we consider a proxy where the $\mathbb{Q}$-expectation of λ_t is used in the formula for the drift adjustment (6). However, here we also present an alternative proxy, by using an approximation of the $\mathbb{Q}^{\mathcal{C}_T}$-expectation of λ_t and compare the impact on CVA in Sec. 7.

5.1. Q-*expectation*

Here we use $\theta(t,s) = \theta_t^s(\bar{\lambda}_t)$, where $\bar{\lambda}_t := \mathbb{E}^{\mathbb{Q}}[\lambda_t]$. One strength for this proxy is that we have an analytic formula for $\bar{\lambda}_t$ and the proxy $\theta(t,s)$ is straight-forward to obtain. The disadvantage is that we are 'operating' under other measures than $\mathbb{Q}$. Specifically when estimating the WWR EPE at time t, we have changed measure to $\mathbb{Q}^{C_t}$. This changes the dynamics of λ, but it is ignored in this approach.

5.2. *Approximation of* $\mathbb{Q}^{C_T}$-*expectation*

In order to improve the deterministic approximation of θ_t^s, we aim to obtain an approximation for the $\mathbb{Q}^{C_T}$-expectation of λ_t. Remark that we use the measure for the maturity of the contract for all $t \in [0, T]$. A possible weakness of this proxy is that for calculating WWR EPE at time t we should use the $\mathbb{Q}^{C_t}$-dynamics not the (terminal) $\mathbb{Q}^{C_T}$-dynamics. However, using the terminal measure is a more convenient choice, since it is just necessary to obtain one 'term structure' of λ_t, $t \in [0, T]$, whereas using the $\mathbb{Q}^{C_t}$-dynamics for the WWR EPE at time t will have the effect that it is necessary to compute separate values for λ_u, $u \in [0, t]$, corresponding to each $t \in [0, T]$. This may be computationally heavy, and thus we assume the simpler version with the benefit that only one term structure has to be computed while the effect of the drift-adjustment in λ from the change of measure may be accounted for. A closed-form expectation of λ_t under $\mathbb{Q}^{C_T}$ can however not be readily found, but in the following we present an approximation of this expectation.

One further remark is that the $\mathbb{Q}^{C_T}$-dynamics of λ is completely independent of the correlation between the underlying stock and λ, but is solely determined by the parameters of the $\mathbb{Q}$-dynamics of λ as well as the maturity of the contract. This allows for computed λ's to be used for calculating CVA on several contracts with the same counterparty, since the dynamics of the contract and its correlation with the default intensity does not enter any of the expressions.

Firstly, consider the $\mathbb{Q}^{C_T}$-dynamics of λ_t for $t \in [0, T]$:

$$d\lambda_t = \kappa(\theta - \lambda_t)dt + \eta\sqrt{\lambda_t}\left(dW_t^T + \eta\sqrt{\lambda_t}\tilde{\theta}_t^T(\lambda_t)dt\right), \qquad (7)$$

$$\tilde{\theta}_t^T(x) := \frac{a(t,T)}{a(t,T)x - b(t,T)} - c(t,T),$$

where

$$a(t,T) := A^\lambda(t,s)B_s^\lambda(t,s) \ , \quad b(t,T) := A_s^\lambda(t,s) \quad \text{and} \quad c(t,T) := B^\lambda(t,s) \ .$$

Hence, integrating both sides of the above SDE in Eq. (7),

$$\lambda_t = \lambda_0 + \kappa\theta t - \kappa \int_0^t \lambda_s ds + \eta^2 \int_0^t \lambda_s \tilde{\theta}_s^T(\lambda_s) ds + \eta \int_0^t \sqrt{\lambda_s} dW_s^T$$

and using Tonelli's theorem,

$$\mathbb{E}^{\mathbb{Q}^{C_T}}[\lambda_t] = \lambda_0 + \kappa\theta t - \kappa \int_0^t \mathbb{E}^{\mathbb{Q}^{C_T}}[\lambda_s] ds + \eta^2 \int_0^t \mathbb{E}^{\mathbb{Q}^{C_T}}\left[\lambda_s \tilde{\theta}_s^T(\lambda_s)\right] ds , \quad (8)$$

where the Ito integral has zero expectation, and thus has vanished. We want to simplify the term that includes

$$\lambda_s \tilde{\theta}_s^T(\lambda_s) = \frac{a(t,T)\lambda_s}{a(t,T)\lambda_s - b(t,T)} - c(t,T)\lambda_s ,$$

and therefore we use a first-order Taylor-expansion of the function $a(t,T)x/(a(t,T)x - b(t,T))$ around some point $x(t) > 0$. We use a positive function since $\mathbb{Q}^{C_T}$ is an equivalent measure to $\mathbb{Q}$ and thus the expectation of λ_t is always positive. Expanding the function around zero also turns out to be an undesirable choice that leads to unstable estimates of the expectation close to maturity, as $a(t,T)/b(t,T)$ diverges for $t \to T$. We choose to make the expansion around the $\mathbb{Q}$-expectation of λ_t, since this is indeed a positive function, and the $\mathbb{Q}$-expectation may give some reasonable input to the $\mathbb{Q}^{C_T}$-expectation. The Taylor expansion looks as follows

$$\frac{a(t,T)x}{a(t,T)x - b(t,T)} = \frac{a(t,T)x(t)}{a(t,T)x(t) - b(t,T)}$$

$$- \frac{a(t,T)b(t,T)}{(a(t,T)x(t) - b(t,T))^2}(x - x(t)) + o(x)$$

$$= \left(\frac{a(t,T)x(t)}{a(t,T)x(t) - b(t,T)}\right)^2 - \frac{a(t,T)b(t,T)}{(a(t,T)x(t) - b(t,T))^2}x$$

$$+ o(x) .$$

Setting $g(t) := \mathbb{E}^{\mathbb{Q}^{C_T}}[\lambda_t]$ we have

$$g(t) \approx \lambda_0 + \kappa\theta t - \kappa \int_0^t g(s)ds$$

$$- \eta^2 \int_0^t \left(\frac{a(s,T)b(s,T)}{(a(s,T)x(s) - b(s,T))^2} + c(s,T)\right) g(s)ds$$

$$+ \eta^2 \int_0^t \left(\frac{a(s,T)x(s)}{a(s,T)x(s) - b(s,T)}\right)^2 ds .$$

Differentiating both sides we obtain a first-order linear inhomogeneous ODE

$$g'(t) \approx \kappa\theta + \eta^2 \left(\frac{a(t,T)x(t)}{a(t,T)x(t) - b(t,T)} \right)^2 - h(t,T)g(t) \, ,$$

where

$$h(t,T) := \kappa + \eta^2 \left(\frac{a(t,T)b(t,T)}{(a(t,T)x(t) - b(t,T))^2} + c(t,T) \right) \, .$$

Disregarding the drift approximation the solution to this SDE is

$$g(t) = e^{-H(t,T)} \left(g(0) + \int_0^t \left(\kappa\theta + \eta^2 G(s,T) \right) e^{H(s,T)} ds \right) \, ,$$

where in this context, $g(0) = \lambda_0$, and

$$H(s,T) := \int_0^s h(u,T)du \, ,$$

$$G(s,T) := \left(\frac{a(s,T)x(s)}{a(s,T)x(s) - b(s,T)} \right)^2 \, .$$

6. Potential future exposures (PFE)

We would like to compare the risk-neutral CVA (CVA computed with market-implied default probabilities and WWR EPE) with actuarial CVA, computed with PFE (e.g. 99% quantile of exposures) and historical default probabilities.

From above, the time-t call price takes the form $C_t = f(t, W_t)$ where

$$f(t,x) = S_0 e^{(r-\frac{\sigma^2}{2})t + \sigma x} \Phi \left(\alpha(t) + x/\sqrt{T-t} \right)$$
$$- Ke^{-r(T-t)} \Phi \left(\alpha(t) - \sigma\sqrt{T-t} + x/\sqrt{T-t} \right)$$

is a continuous increasing function. Under the risk-neutral measure, the k-PFE is defined as the profile of the exposure's quantile at level k: Functions f being continuous and strictly increasing wrt x, this means that

$$q(t) = f \left(t, \Phi^{-1}(k)\sqrt{t} \right) \, .$$

A similar expression holds for WWR PFE : one just needs to account for the measure change. This can be achieved by inserting the drift adjustment, replacing $f(t,x)$ by $f(t, x + \Theta(t))$ so that $q(t) = f \left(t, \Phi^{-1}(k)\sqrt{t} + \Theta(t) \right)$.

The move from "risk-neutral" to "historical" PFEs can be handled in a similar way. Clearly, C_t is a deterministic function of S_t, so that the historical distribution of C_t is obtained by using μ (instead of r) as rate of return of S on the period $[0, t)$. Because S_t is a deterministic function of W_t and $W_t = \tilde{W}_t + \frac{\mu - r}{\sigma} t$ where $\tilde{W}$ is a Brownian motion under the physical measure, the "historical quantile" is obtained by evaluating the "risk-neutral" function f at a shifted point compared to the Normal quantile: $q(t) = f\left(t, \Phi^{-1}(k)\sqrt{t} + \frac{\mu - r}{\sigma} t\right)$, and similarly for the WWR case.

Notice that in the previous sections — when dealing with CVA based on EPE — we assume that the specified CIR-process is the true risk-neutral dynamics of the default intensities. Thus we do not consider fitting the survival probability curve to any exogenously given CDS quotes and to obtain the CVA from Eq. (1) we apply $G(t) = P^{\mathrm{CIR}}(0, t)$ where P^{CIR} is the CIR-bond price.

This approach needs adjustment to obtain the actuarial CVA part. Here we assign a rating and a flat equivalent spread (or hazard rate) γ to each pair of maturity and parameter set. We apply a historical survival probability curve based on the rating: $G(t) = \exp\{-\gamma t\}$. To ensure that we can recover the historical probability curve when applying the intensities process we use the CIR++ model, see e.g. [2], and apply deterministic shifts $\phi(t)$ such that the shifted intensity process $y_t = \lambda_t + \phi(t)$ is inline with the flat hazard rate γ. The survival probabilities implied by the shifted intensity process are found by

$$P^y(t, s) := \mathbb{E}^{\mathbb{Q}}\left[e^{-\int_t^s y_u du}\right] = e^{-\int_t^s \phi(u) du} P^{\mathrm{CIR}}(t, s) \ , \quad s \geq t.$$

In the approximation of the actuarial CVA based on the drift adjustments, the shifted intensities y_t replace λ_t in Eq. (2). Further we choose $\phi(0) = 0$ such that $y_0 = \lambda_0$ and replace $A(t, s)$ by $A^*(t, s) = \exp\{-\int_t^s \phi(u) du\} A(t, s)$, while $B(t, s)$ remains.

7. Numerical experiments

We use the four parameter sets for the CIR-process of λ used in [1]. Thus in the forthcoming we will regard parameters in Table 1 as set 1–4. Further we use $S_0 = K = 15$, $r = 1\%$, $\mu = 3\%$ and $\sigma = 30\%$, and call options with a time to maturity of 1 year and 5 years, respectively. For simplicity we assume that there is no recovery upon default, i.e. $R = 0$ in Eq. (1). The corresponding CVA figures are given in Figs. 1 and 2, and are compared with a 2D Monte Carlo scheme as well as the Gaussian Copula resampling approach (for more details about this approach, see e.g. [3], [4] or [5]).

Table 1.   Parameter sets for the dynamics of λ in the numerical experiments.

	λ_0 (bps)	κ	θ (bps)	η	Rating used for actuarial CVA
Set 1	300	02%	1610	8%	B
Set 2	350	35%	450	15%	B
Set 3	100	80%	200	20%	B
Set 4	300	50%	500	50%	B

We also consider the actuarial CVA; CVA calculated from the 99% PFE, which is described in Sec. 6, and on historical rather than risk-neutral default probabilities. We use the default rates from [6], and we consider all parameter sets to have rating B, which ensures that all shifts are positive and thus the shifted default intensity is ensured to be non-negative. Specifically the flat hazard rates used for B rating are 458.8 bps for 1 year contracts and 507.6 bps for 5 year contracts. The actuarial CVA is shown in Figs. 3 and 4.

In the following, we use the terms $\mathbb{Q}^{\mathcal{C}_T}$-proxy and $\mathbb{Q}$-proxy for the proxys of θ_t^s using the λ expectation under $\mathbb{Q}^{\mathcal{C}_T}$ and $\mathbb{Q}$, respectively.

Consider the CVA on 1 year contracts in Fig. 1. We observe a pattern that for negative correlations, we tend to estimate a higher CVA compared to the 2D Monte Carlo scheme. Generally this overestimation of CVA is stronger for the $\mathbb{Q}^{\mathcal{C}_T}$-proxy than for the $\mathbb{Q}$-proxy. The exception is parameter set 4, where the $\mathbb{Q}$-proxy which estimates a slightly lower CVA. For positive correlations — when we experience WWR on the call — we observe a very good fit of the $\mathbb{Q}^{\mathcal{C}_T}$-proxy and the Monte Carlo CVAs parameter set 1–3, while the $\mathbb{Q}$-proxy also tends to overestimate the CVA on this end.

Comparing the results for the two proxys, we observe that the $\mathbb{Q}$-proxy tends to suggest a larger WWR-effect, giving a larger compensation than the $\mathbb{Q}^{\mathcal{C}_T}$-proxy for positive correlations, while it suggests a lower compensation in the case of negative correlations. Thus the $\mathbb{Q}$-proxy suggests a higher impact of the "market-credit correlation".

Consider now the CVA on the 5 year contract in Fig. 2. Firstly, we observe that even for one million sample paths and a time step of 0.01, the Monte Carlo simulations of the CVA does include some bias, since the zero-correlation case does not completely correspond with the analytic formula. This is especially pronounced for parameter set 4. Here we experience a weakness of the 2D Monte Carlo approach; it is computationally heavy, but

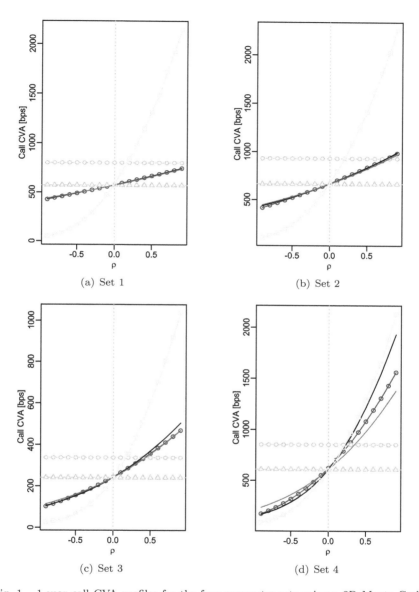

Fig. 1. 1 year call CVA profiles for the four parameter sets using a 2D Monte Carlo scheme (line with circles) with 10^6 paths and a time step of 0.01, compared with the analytic approximation using the $\mathbb{Q}$-expectation (black) and $\mathbb{Q}^{C_T}$-approximation (grey). CVA based on the Gaussian Copula resampling approach (line with squares) and the analytic CVA with zero-correlation (vertical dashed grey line) are included. The Basel no-WWR CVA is indicated by the line with triangles and the WWR CVA using $\alpha = 1.4$ is indicated by grey dots.

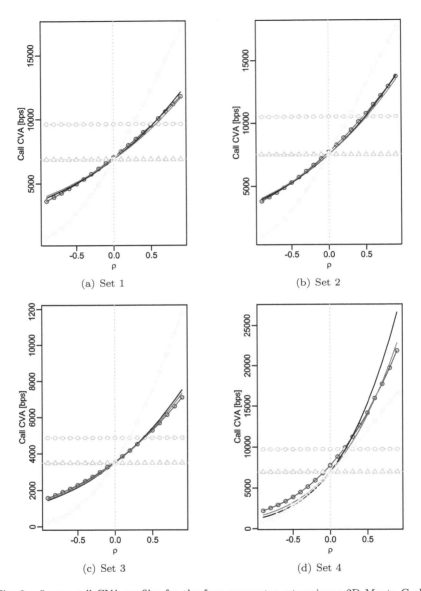

(a) Set 1

(b) Set 2

(c) Set 3

(d) Set 4

Fig. 2.   5 year call CVA profiles for the four parameter sets using a 2D Monte Carlo scheme (line with circles) with 10^6 paths and a time step of 0.01, compared with the analytic approximation using the $\mathbb{Q}$-expectation (black) and $\mathbb{Q}^{\mathcal{C}_T}$-approximation (grey). CVA based on the Gaussian Copula resampling approach (line with squares) and the analytic CVA with zero-correlation (dashed grey line) are included. The Basel no-WWR CVA is indicated by line with triangles and the WWR CVA using $\alpha = 1.4$ is indicated by grey dots.

moreover includes a bias with a very small time-step and large number of paths. Comparing the CVA of the two proxys, we observe similar behavior as in the 1 year case.

For both 1 and 5 year CVA — and for all parameter sets — we observe that the resampling approach is highly sensitive to the market-credit correlation. This allows to model very strong WWR impact. The problem however is that it is unclear how the value of the dependence parameter (the correlation between τ and the exposure V_{t_i} at any given point in time t_i) has to be chosen.

Further, we provide the CVA under Basel, based on [7], [8]. In this context (T being the contract maturity, where we consider 1 and 5 years), the No-WWR figure is given by

$$\mathrm{CVA}^{\mathrm{basel}} = (1 - G(T)) \frac{\mathrm{EPE}^{\perp}(0) + \mathrm{EPE}^{\perp}(T)}{2} \,,$$

where $\mathrm{EPE}^{\perp}(t)$ is the (No-WWR) EPE at time t, which is constant and equal to $\tilde{C}_0$ for the call and $\tilde{P}_0$ for the put. The WWR CVA is given by

$$\mathrm{CVA}_{\alpha}^{\mathrm{basel}} = (1 - G(T)) \alpha \mathrm{EPE}^{\perp}(T/2) \,, \tag{9}$$

where $\alpha \mathrm{EPE}^{\perp}(T/2)$ is called the "exposure at default" (EAD) and the scaling coefficient α is typically set to 1.4. The corresponding levels are indicated on Figs. 1 and 2.

The Basel III parameter α cannot be considered as a way to represent market-credit correlation, but in fact capture the "market-credit covariance". This is a crucial point, that complicates drastically the choice of a reasonable value for α. In order for the Basel type formula to be a decent approach to account for WWR, α has to be chosen not only with regards to dependence between portfolio and credit, but also according to both market and credit volatilities. This observation suggests that it is a bit naive to hope that a kind of "universal constant" would be able to account for this effect. The approximation proposed in [1] is therefore, from this perspective, a significant improvement to Basel type formulae. Table 2 show the values of α that make the CVA in the Basel type formulae agree with the ones obtained from Monte Carlo simulation for 1 year contracts. Across parameter sets the value changes quite significantly. Obviously $\alpha \approx 1$ for zero-correlation, and the values are larger (smaller) for positive (negative) correlations. Thus the Basel approach cannot capture right-way risk, which is experienced when the correlation is negative, while the performance of the method is highly dependent both on the correlation and the parameter set used.

Table 2.   The values of α for which Eq. (9) agrees with the
2D-MC results for 1 year call options.

ρ	-0.9	-0.6	-0.3	0	0.3	0.6	0.9
Set 1	0.75	0.83	0.92	1.01	1.10	1.20	1.30
Set 2	0.63	0.74	0.87	1.01	1.16	1.31	1.48
Set 3	0.42	0.58	0.78	1.01	1.28	1.59	1.95
Set 4	0.29	0.45	0.70	1.03	1.44	1.95	2.57

The interpretation of the actuarial CVA in Figs. 3 and 4 are similar to the interpretation of the risk-neutral CVA results. We generally observe a larger impact of the correlation on the CVA when using the $\mathbb{Q}$-proxy than what suggested by the $\mathbb{Q}^{\mathcal{C}_T}$-proxy.

8. Conclusion

From the change-of-measure approach suggested in [1], we have examined the CVA on put and call options under WWR. In the Basel III framework, WWR is treated by a multiplier. But it should not be based on "market-credit correlation", but rather on "market-credit covariance". We find that the Basel III approach is a naive way of estimating the CVA that does not recognize right-way risk and cannot capture the wrong-way risk in a desirable way. However, using the set-up in this paper, one can obtain CVA on put and call options, and capture the effect of the market-credit correlation by analytic formulas. Specifically, we present the formulas for two proxys of the drift-adjustment process, using each proxy, the CVA can be obtained analytically. Further the actuarial CVA based on PFE also has an analytic expression, based on the formulas in the paper.

In the numerical experiments, we examine the estimated CVA — both the risk-neutral and actuarial CVA — from the formulas supplied in the paper, compared with joint (exposure-credit) Monte Carlo simulations, Gaussian Copula resampling and Basel III figures. We observe that the Gaussian Copula resampling approach is very sensitive to the correlation, leading to too high CVA estimates when experiencing WWR. We do not find 2D Monte Carlo to be a desirable method, since it is computationally heavy, and in some cases includes a bias, even for a small time-step and large number of sample paths.

On the other hand, we get very encouraging results from the CVA based on the two proxys, both when calculating the risk-neutral CVA and the actuarial CVA. The simple $\mathbb{Q}$-proxy is performing quite reasonably and

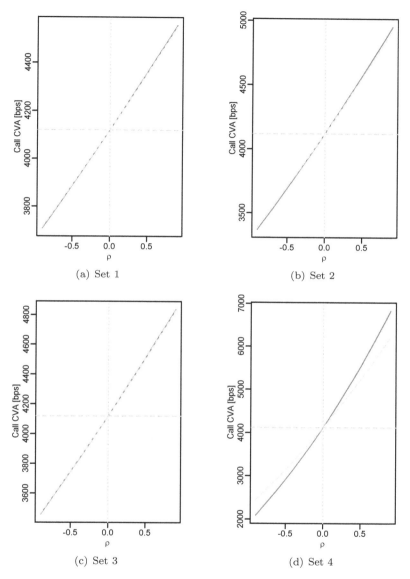

Fig. 3. 1 year actuarial call CVA profiles for the four parameter sets using the analytic approximation with the $\mathbb{Q}$-expectation (solid line) and $\mathbb{Q}^{\mathcal{C}_T}$-approximation (dashed line). The dashed grey line shows the analytic CVA with zero-correlation is included.

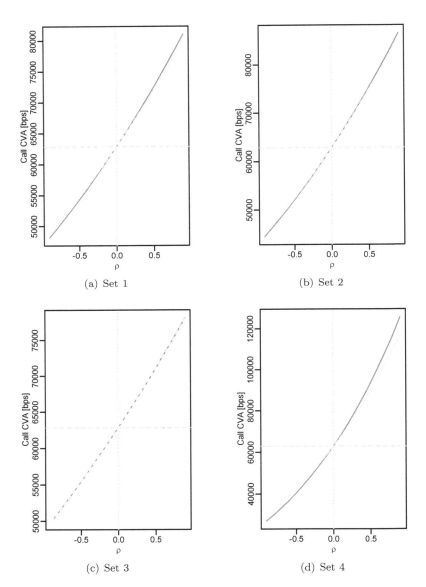

Fig. 4.   5 year actuarial call CVA profiles for the four parameter sets using the analytic approximation with the $\mathbb{Q}$-expectation (solid line) and $\mathbb{Q}^{\mathcal{C}_T}$-approximation (dashed line). The dashed grey line shows the analytic CVA with zero-correlation is included.

captures the general behavior of the CVA. This proxy is very easy to implement and fast to compute since all formulas are analytic (up to the deterministic approximation of the drift adjustment). Using the $\mathbb{Q}^{\mathcal{C}_T}$-proxy requires an additional approximation (to compute the corresponding expectation of λ_t), but gives a slightly more realistic (considering the MC-results to be the true CVA) CVA when experiencing WWR.

References

[1] D. Brigo and F. Vrins, Disentangling Wrong-Way Risk: Pricing CVA via change of measures and drift adjustment (2017), preprint available at `https://arxiv.org/abs/1611.02877`.

[2] D. Brigo and F. Mercurio, *Interest Rate Models — Theory and Practice* (Springer, 2006).

[3] A. Sokol, Modeling and hedging Wrong Way Risk in CVA with exposure sampling, in *RiskMinds USA*, (Risk, 2011).

[4] D. Rosen and D. Saunders, Cva the Wrong Way, *Journal of Risk Management in Financial Institutions* **5**, 252 (2012).

[5] F. Vrins, Wrong-way risk CVA models with analytical EPE profiles under gaussian exposure dynamics, *International Journal of Theoretical and Applied Finance* **20** (2017).

[6] *Corporate One-to-Five-Year Rating Transition Rates*, tech. rep., Moody's (2008).

[7] *Basel III: A global regulatory framework for more resilient banks and banking systems*, tech. rep., Basel Committee on Banking Supervision (2010), `http://www.bis.org/publ/bcbs189.pdf`.

[8] *Basel III framework (Annex 4)*, tech. rep., Basel Committee on Banking Supervision. `https://www.bis.org/publ/bcbs128d.pdf`.

Chapter 3

Consistent Iterated Simulation of Multivariate Defaults: Markov Indicators, Lack of Memory, Extreme-Value Copulas, and the Marshall–Olkin Distribution

Damiano Brigo

Department of Mathematics, Imperial College London,
London, SW7 2AZ, UK
damiano.brigo@imperial.ac.uk

Jan-Frederik Mai
Xaia Investment,
Sonnenstr. 19, 80331 München, Germany
jan-frederik.mai@xaia.com

Matthias Scherer
Technische Universität München, Lehrstuhl für Finanzmathematik
Parkring 11, 85748 Garching, Germany
scherer@tum.de

Henrik Sloot
Technische Universität München, Lehrstuhl für Finanzmathematik
Parkring 11, 85748 Garching, Germany
henrik.sloot@tum.de

A current market-practice to incorporate multivariate defaults in global risk-factor simulations is the iteration of (multiplicative) i.i.d. survival indicator increments along a given time-grid, where the indicator distribution is based on a copula ansatz. The underlying assumption is that the behavior of the resulting iterated default distribution is similar to the one-shot distribution. It is shown that in most cases this assumption is not fulfilled and furthermore numerical analysis is presented that shows sizable differences in probabilities assigned to both "survival-of-all" and "mixed default/survival" events. Moreover, the classes of distributions for which probabilities from the "terminal one-shot" and "terminal iterated" distribution coincide are derived for problems considering "survival-of-all" events as well as "mixed default/survival" events. For the former problem, distributions must fulfill a lack-of-memory type property, which is, e.g., fulfilled by min-stable multivariate exponential distributions. These correspond in a copula-framework to exponential margins coupled via extreme-value copulas. For the latter problem, while looping default inspired multivariate Freund distributions and more generally multivariate phase-type

---

distributions could be a solution, under practically relevant and reasonable additional assumptions on portfolio rebalancing and nested distributions, the unique solution is the Marshall–Olkin class.

Keywords: stepwise default simulation, default dependence, extreme-value copulas, Marshall–Olkin distribution, nested margining, Freund distribution, looping default models, multivariate phase-type distribution.

1. Introduction

The increasingly global nature of financial products and risks calls for adequately complex stochastic models and simulation procedures. These are required for valuation purposes as well as for risk analysis and often involve thousands of risk factors that can be different in nature. Investment banks and financial service companies are devoting a sizable effort to design software and hardware architectures that support such global simulations effectively, see, e.g. [1]. The path-dependent nature of many risks and the necessity to analyze risks at different time horizons lead to an iterated simulation of all risk factors across time steps. The consistent statistical representation of default-times of multiple entities and their inter-dependence-structure is the main motivation for this paper. For the simulation of default-times, up to a final horizon, two possible approaches are considered:

(i) Simulate the default-times, at the beginning, once and for all in each given scenario. The resulting values are stored and the other risk factors are simulated iteratively up to the final time horizon.

(ii) Alternatively, one simulates in each given scenario for every time-period a "default/no default" indicator of all non-defaulted entities conditional on the default history — i.e. the survival of non-defaulted entities up to the beginning of this period and the default-times of already defaulted entities.

We anticipate that we will be concerned with the consistency of the two approaches above under a number of additional specifications. The basic question is:

When is an iterated default simulation, often done by sampling a given type of multivariate distribution, equivalent to a one-shot simulation under essentially the same distribution?

Although this appears to be a simple question, it is in fact rather nuanced. For this question to fully make sense we need to be a little more precise on our definitions and on our problem specification, and it is indeed one of the main purposes of this paper to fully clarify this question, its implications, and some possible answers. It is worth putting this pre-question in the open now, and we would like to mention that the first named author has witnessed cases in the industry where the two procedures were assumed to be equivalent when they were not, and this both in the valuation/hedging space and in the risk measurement space. While the author is not allowed to provide details on such cases for confidentiality issues, we will see some numerical examples clarifying this discrepancy in the course of the paper.

Going back to our introduction, the dependence between default-times and other risk factors has to be introduced on the whole risk factor evolution in approach (i) and on the period steps in approach (ii), respectively. In this formulation both approaches are mathematically equivalent — however, this equivalence is based on conditional probabilities, which can be arbitrarily complex.[1] Consider, for example, the case of wrong way risk for credit valuation adjustments for credit default swap (CDS) trades under collateralization in [2], where the first approach is used: even with just three default times involved, the CDS and the two trading parties, the formulas become very involved and cumbersome. Thus, generally, one either has a model for the default-times in approach (i) with complex conditional probabilities, or one has a model for the indicator increment process in approach (ii) with unknown "terminal iterated" dependence. The mathematical underpinning — if any — for company-wide, global simulation of defaults is often, or can be translated into, a copula-based ansatz. Such a model originates from the statistical literature and renders approach (i) more natural from the company-default perspective. However, when dealing with large portfolios, the literature on financial risk management mostly prefers models relying on a repeated evolution of risk factors on common time grids. Approach (ii) is more consistent with this way of thinking and therefore more desirable both from a theoretical and practical point of view, for the following reasons:

- **Software consistency with "Brownian-driven" asset classes**: Consider a bank that runs a global simulation on a large portfolio, including complex products and defaults, in order to obtain a risk measure.

---

[1]Contrary to the univariate case, where sampling from conditional probability distributions can be handled using the distributional transform, even if we can calculate the probabilities, conditional multivariate probability distributions can be very difficult to sample from.

One example would be computing the value-at-risk or the expected short-fall of CVA, a task that is numerically very intensive, see, e.g. [3]. In this context, there is need to evolve risk factors according to controlled time steps that are common to all factors, to have all required variables at each step of the simulation. While this is relatively natural for asset models that are driven by Brownian-type processes and even extensions with jumps, it becomes harder when trying to include defaults of under-lying entities or counterparties. The reason for this is that default-times, typically represented through intensity models, should be simulated just once, being static random variables as opposed to stochastic processes. Once simulated, there would be nothing left to iterate. However, the consistency of the global simulation and the desire to have all variables simulated at every step is prompting the design of iterated survival or default flags across the time steps that are already used in the simulation of more traditional assets.

- **Basel III requirement for risk horizons:** A further motivation for iterating the global simulation across standard time steps is coming from the Basel III framework when trying to address liquidity risk. The Bank of International Settlements (BIS) suggests the following solution, see [4].
  "The Committee has agreed that the differentiation of market liquidity across the trading book will be based on the concept of liquidity hori-zons. It proposes that banks' trading book exposures be assigned to a small number of liquidity horizon categories: [10 days, 1 month, 3 months, 6 months, 1 year]. The shortest liquidity horizon (most liquid exposures) is in line with the current 10-day VaR treatment in the trading book. The longest liquidity horizon (least liquid exposures) matches the banking book horizon at one year. The Committee believes that such a frame-work will deliver a more graduated treatment of risks across the balance sheet. Among other benefits, this should also serve to reduce arbitrage opportunities between the banking and trading books."
  It is clear then that a bank will need to simulate the risk factors of the portfolio across a grid including the standardized holding periods above. In this sense it will be practical to simulate all variables, including de-faults and survivals, in common time steps. Software architecture and the possibility to effectively decompose the simulation across steps, prompt to the possibility to iterate the default simulation rather than trying to simulate random default-times just once.
- **General need for dependence modeling in the context of the cur-rent counterparty credit risk debate:** As an example, the current

debate on valuation adjustments (as the partly overlapping credit CVA, debit DVA, and funding FVA adjustments, see, e.g., [3]), is forcing financial institutions to run global simulations over very large portfolios. By nature, CVA is an option on a very large portfolio containing the most disparate risk factors. A key quantity in valuing this option is the dependence between the default of a counterparty and the value of the underlying portfolio that is traded with that counterparty. When such dependence is adverse for the agent making the calculation we have wrong way risk (WWR), a risk that is at the center of the agenda of the Bank of International Settlements in reforming current regulation. Modeling the dynamics of dependence is not only essential for the current emergencies of the industry, such as CVA/DVA/FVA and risk measures on these quantities, but it is also necessary for the management of pure credit products, such as, e.g., Collateralized Debt or Loan Obligations (CDO, CLO).

Before shifting the focus solely to default-times, it is important to consider not only the distribution of default-times but also the dependence on other risk factors:

(a) In reality, default risk is correlated with other risk-factors. These can be risk-factors belonging to other asset classes, e.g. equity, or even macro-economic risk factors. These dependencies, however, are usually not considered in model building for the following reasons: It might be easy to reject the independence-assumption between a default-time and some other risk-factor with qualitative arguments or statistical tests, but the determination of a good model for this dependence (or directly for the joint distribution) is usually far from trivial. Even if one can formulate a satisfying model for other risk-factors and default-times — or the survival-indicator increments — the additional complexity can lead to computational problems (as explained in the following). Furthermore, the design of such a global model, including dependence between risk-factor classes, would require different departments of the financial institution to work together. For most institutions this is infeasible as business is often separated into different sections, of which each models their relevant risk factors to their own appropriate level of complexity.

(b) The computation of transition probabilities, or sampling from these transition-distributions, for the risk-factor evolution will be very difficult and non-trivial in most cases. In particular, if there are no closed-form expressions, one usually has to rely on numerical-integration techniques — if available — which becomes time-consuming and is difficult to implement.

(c) Dependency information requires additional storage — especially if the dependency is conditional on the full histories of risk-factors, which is even challenging in low, but especially in high dimensions.

Focussing on the (discrete) survival-indicator process, there are more problems which have to be considered:

(d) Assume that there are d entities and N simulation steps up to the final time-horizon. In the worst case of full default-evolution-dependence this leads to $\sum_{k=0}^{N-1}(k+2)^d$ transition-probabilities. In the case of simple time-dependence, we have $N \cdot 3^d$ transition-probabilities. In the case of complete time-homogeneity, one "only" has 3^d transition-probabilities. For a large number of entities d or/and a large number of simulation steps N the issue of over-parameterization becomes apparent.

(e) Let T be the final time-horizon. Then the number of time-steps, and subsequently the number of parameters, depends on the step-size Δ, i.e. $N = T/\Delta$. This can lead to problems if different step-sizes have to be simulated (e.g. days, weeks, months, ...) as all probabilities should be consistent.

An additional problem is that the definition of all transition-probabilities have to be re-assessed in case the composition of the defaultable portfolio changes.

In summary, approach (i) appears more natural from the perspective of default modeling itself, however, in a global risk factor model, approach (ii) might be more desirable and is mostly used in the financial industry. Summing up, this involves the following questions:

(1) What are convenient conditions on the multivariate distribution of the default-times such that approach (i) and approach (ii) are consistent in the sense that if one knows the distribution of default-times for approach (i), one has a manageable "default/no default" indicator process for approach (ii) yielding the same results, and vice versa.

(2) What can go wrong, if one uses some indicator evolution which is not consistent in the sense of (1) — e.g. based on a Gaussian coupling of exponential random variables?

The consistency in question (1) can be weakened if the problem only concerns "survival-of-all" events instead of "mixed default/survival" events. The class of consistent distributions in the sense of question (1) might be very large — as the requirement of understanding the distribution as a model in approach (i) and approach (ii) can be fulfilled for many distributions with enough time at hand. However, most of these distributions are not feasible in practice, as we do not only need a model which is fully understood, but also feasible for simulation in terms of memory usage and sampling strategy. Therefore, a convenient *assumption*, which resolves — or at least diminishes — problems (a)–(e) from above, is a (continuous-time) time-homogeneous Markovian survival-indicator process. This is equivalent to conditional probabilities being determined by the current set of defaulted entities, but not on their specific default-times. The idea of using Markovian survival-indicator processes (even possibly time-inhomogeneous and only Markovian conditional on a set of intensity processes) is not new and has been discussed in [5] and [6]. These papers focus on the issue of pricing portfolio-credit derivatives. In the following we give a short overview on the "survival-of-all" and "mixed default/survival" problems.

1.1. *Problem one: "Survival-of-all" events*

In this special case the underlying problem only concerns the default/survival-of-all entities up to certain points in time. An example for such a problem is the valuation of a first-to-default swap on a basket of entities. Subsequently, one can demand a weaker version of consistency and feasibility — namely that the "survival-of-all" event and the corresponding indicator process are consistent and feasible. The class of consistent and feasible distributions for this problem was first studied in [7] and is related to a multivariate generalization of the univariate lack-of-memory property. In particular, a subclass fulfilling this property are min-stable multivariate exponential distributions. These are multivariate distributions with exponential margins and an extreme-value copula. Fundamental examples of this subclass, such as the Marshall–Olkin and the Gumbel–Hougaard distribution, are presented in this paper.

1.2. *Problem two: "Mixed default/survival" events*

Problems which depend on "mixed default/survival" events — and thus do not fall in the same category as problem one — require the original strict version of consistency. This leads (under previously outlined feasibility conditions) to time-homogeneous Markovian survival-indicators. This general class is already known under the name *multivariate phase-type distributions*. This article analyzes further desirable theoretical and practical conditions on the resulting simulation process and as a result focuses on the subclasses of Marshall–Olkin distributions as well as a multivariate extension of the bivariate Freund distribution. In particular, the practically important requirement of having the Markov property also for sub-vectors of indicators leads to a new characterization of the Marshall–Olkin law that has been first discussed in [8] and is recalled here in the context of the present paper. Our general aim is to increase awareness of the fact that the stepwise simulation of default indicators (approach (ii) above) is a hard task in general, and in particular that the practical implementation is not feasible without huge efforts (both theoretical and computational), and that sizable errors and undesired effects may occur by iterating under the wrong conditions.

1.3. *Structure of the paper*

In Sec. 2 the survival-indicator process is introduced. It is shown that Markovianity of this process can be identified on a distributional level with a lack-of-memory type property. Subsequently, multiple lack-of-memory properties are presented and associated with certain classes of multivariate probability distributions. In particular, the min-stable multivariate exponential property (MSMVE) is introduced and is related to its characterization via extreme-value copulas and exponential margins.

Section 3 addresses the "survival-of-all" problem. Therefore, the concepts of self-chaining distributions and copulas, which were introduced in [7], are revisited and advanced. In particular, it is shown that the MSMVE characterization in terms of extreme-value copulas with exponential margins solves the problem. Then it is outlined that the widely used Gaussian-coupled exponential distributions do not fulfill that property. Moreover, choosing such a distribution for the step-innovations leads asymptotically to independence of the default-times, completely destroying dependence in the limit if the step size in time tends to zero.

In Sec. 4 the "mixed default/survival" problem is discussed, for looping default models, Freund distributions, and multivariate phase-type distributions. A special focus lies on the Marshall–Olkin class, leveraging its new characterization in terms of Markov property of vectors and subvectors of indicators, as in [8], and different simulation strategies as well as a convenient construction through Lévy-frailty models.

The final section concludes the article.

2. Default-time distributions and survival-indicator processes

Assume that $(\Omega, \mathcal{F}, \mathbb{P})$ is a probability space on which all random objects of this section are defined. Throughout this article, let $\boldsymbol{\tau} = (\tau_1, \ldots, \tau_d)'$ be a (non-negative) random vector of default-times[2] for d entities with joint- and marginal survival function(s) $\bar{F}$ and $\bar{F}_i, i \in [d] := \{1, \ldots, d\}$, respectively[3] and $\boldsymbol{Z} = \boldsymbol{Z}(t)$ be the corresponding survival indicator process which is defined by

$$Z_i(t) := 1_{\{\tau_i > t\}}, \ i \in [d], t \geq 0.$$

In light of the introduction — and particularly as our questions of interest rely on iterating the survival-indicator process over periods with fixed length Δ — it may seem more appropriate (and also simpler) to work with the discretized version of $\boldsymbol{Z}$, hereby denoted by $\boldsymbol{Z}^{(\Delta)}$ and defined by

$$Z_i^{(\Delta)}(j) := Z_i(j\Delta), \ j \in \{0, \ldots, N\}, \ i \in [d].$$

As outlined in the introduction, there are various arguments why it is convenient to assume that the underlying continuous-time process $\boldsymbol{Z}$ is also time-homogeneous Markovian. In the following another technical and a model building argument for this assumption are presented:

(a) *Technical argument:* The period-length, $\Delta > 0$, is usually an externally given quantity — e.g. set by the regulator as liquidity horizon or it is implicitly given from the existing IT-infrastructure. Hence, a model which can only be used consistently and feasible for very specific Δ is not desirable, as any (externally driven) change in Δ might destroy the models usability.

(b) *Model building argument:* From a model building perspective it is reasonable to assume that $\boldsymbol{Z}^{(\Delta)}$ has a representation with an underlying continuous-time process $\boldsymbol{Z}$. A deviation from the Markovian assumption above implies that the process $\boldsymbol{Z}$ either violates the time-homogeneity or the Markovian assumption entirely. However, if one

---

[2]For consistency, these "event"-times are referred to as default-times throughout this article, however, other notions such as fatality-, inter-arrival-, or inter-failure-times are equally applicable.

[3]For $\boldsymbol{\tau}$ and $\boldsymbol{s}, t \geq 0$, the multivariate survival function is defined by $\bar{F}(\boldsymbol{s}) := \mathbb{P}(\boldsymbol{\tau} > \boldsymbol{s})$ and the ith marginal survival function by $\bar{F}_i(t) := \mathbb{P}(\tau_i > t)$.

assumes that the time-homogeneous Markovian property of $\boldsymbol{Z}^{(\Delta)}$ is a tolerable deviation from reality — one should avoid choosing a model which violates those very properties on the continuous-time scale.

In summary, one can conclude that assuming an implied continuous-time, time-homogeneous Markovian survival-indicator process $\boldsymbol{Z}$ is a reasonable assumption, if one wants a feasible and consistent approach. In particular, this assumption is desirable from a technical aspect and also from a model building view if the underlying entities do note make the time-homogeneity assumption in itself unusable. Therefore, it is assumed throughout this article that, as a feasibility condition, $\boldsymbol{Z}$ is a continuous-time, time-homogeneous Markovian survival-indicator process.

2.1. *Markovian survival indicator-processes*

Let $\mathcal{I} = \{0,1\}^d$ and define the auxiliary function h to establish a bijection between the power set of $[d]$, denoted by $\mathcal{P}([d])$, and $\mathcal{I}$ by

$$h : \mathcal{P}([d]) \to \mathcal{I}, I \mapsto (1_{\{1 \in I\}}, \ldots, 1_{\{d \in I\}})'.$$

A *survival-indicator process* is a stochastic process $\boldsymbol{Z} = \boldsymbol{Z}(t)$ on $\mathcal{I}$ fulfilling for all $s, t \geq 0$ and $J \subsetneq I \subseteq [d]$

$$\mathbb{P}(\boldsymbol{Z}(t+s) = h(I) \mid \boldsymbol{Z}(t) = h(J)) = 0.$$

This process is *Markovian* if for all $I, J \subseteq [d]$, $A \in \sigma(\boldsymbol{Z}(v) : v \leq t)$, and $s, t \geq 0$

$$\mathbb{P}(\boldsymbol{Z}(t+s) = h(I) \mid \boldsymbol{Z}(t) = h(J), A)$$
$$= \mathbb{P}(\boldsymbol{Z}(s+t) = h(I) \mid \boldsymbol{Z}(t) = h(J)).$$

It is furthermore called *time-homogeneous* if additionally for all $s, t, v \geq 0$

$$\mathbb{P}(\boldsymbol{Z}(t+s+v) = h(I) \mid \boldsymbol{Z}(t+v) = h(J))$$
$$= \mathbb{P}(\boldsymbol{Z}(t+s) = h(I) \mid \boldsymbol{Z}(t) = h(J)).$$

A time-homogeneous Markovian process satisfies

$$\mathbb{P}(\boldsymbol{Z}(t+s) = h(I) \mid \boldsymbol{Z}(t) = h(J)) = (\vec{e}_{\tilde{h}(J)})' \exp\{Qs\}\vec{e}_{\tilde{h}(I)},$$

where $\tilde{h} : \mathcal{P}([d]) \to \{0,1\}^{2^d}$ is an arbitrary bijection between the power set of $[d]$ and the set $\{1, \ldots, 2^d\}$, which fulfills $\tilde{h}(I) < \tilde{h}(J) \Leftrightarrow |I| > |J|$ for all $I, J \subseteq [d]$,[4] $\vec{e}_k, k \in [2^d]$, is the canonical basis of $\mathbb{R}^{2^d}$, and $Q \in \mathbb{R}^{2^d \times 2^d}$ is an

---

[4]This property guarantees, that the resulting intensity matrix Q is an upper-triagonal matrix.

intensity matrix.[5] As it is assumed that $\tilde{h}$ is chosen such that for two sets with different cardinality, the one with more elements has the lower index, the matrix Q is upper trigonal with non-negative off-diagonal values and rows summing up to zero, i.e.

$$Q = \begin{pmatrix} q_{1,1} & & \star \\ & \ddots & \\ 0 & & q_{d,d} \end{pmatrix}.$$

Remark 2.1 (Intensities of a Markovian Process). *Let $Q \in \mathbb{R}^{n \times n}$ be a (not necessarily upper trigonal) intensity matrix for n states S — w.l.o.g. assume $S = [n]$. Then, one can construct a continuous-time, time-homogeneous Markovian process Z as follows (see [9]):*

(i) *Let X_0 be the (possibly random) initial state, i.e. define $Z(0) := X_0$.*
(ii) *For $k \in \mathbb{N}_0$ define the kth jump time of Z by T_k (for $k = 0$ let $T_0 := 0$). Furthermore, assume that $Z(T_k) = i \in S$.*

   (a) *Let $E_{k+1} \sim \text{Exp}(-q_{ii})$ be an exponential random variable with rate $-q_{ii}$ which is, conditional on $Z(T_k)$, independent of $\sigma(\{E_l, T_l, l \leq k\})$.*
   (b) *Define $T_{k+1} := T_k + E_{k+1}$ and define $Z(t) = i \; \forall t \in (T_k, T_{k+1})$.*
   (c) *Let X_{k+1} be a discrete random variable on $S \backslash \{i\}$ with probabilities proportional to the ith row, i.e. $\mathbb{P}(X_{k+1} = j) = -q_{ij}/q_{ii}$. Moreover, assume that X_{k+1} is independent of $\sigma(\{E_l, T_l, l \leq k\})$ as well as independent of T_{k+1}.*
   (d) *Let $Z(T_{k+1}) = X_{k+1}$.*

(iii) *Repeat (ii) either infinitely often or until an absorbing state is reached, i.e. a state i with $q_{ii} = 0$. Note that for practical application the algorithm stops if $T_{k+1} > T$ for some terminal time-horizon $T > 0$.*

It is useful to know that a time-homogeneous Markovian survival-indicator process is uniquely defined if for every non-zero transition, i.e. $h(J) \to h(I), I \subseteq J$, the transition probability for an arbitrary positive transition-time is known. This will be shown in the sequel. Let τ be a default-vector with corresponding time-homogeneous Markovian survival-process Z and intensity-matrix Q. Furthermore, let $1 \leq K \leq d$,

---

[5]For a thorough introduction to continuous-time Markovian processes and a reference for this result, see [9], Ch. 8 and 9.

$I = \{i_1, \ldots, i_K\} \subseteq [d]$, $t_I \geq 0$, $\pi \in \mathcal{S}_d$ be a permutation[6] with $\pi([K]) = I$ and $t_{\pi(1)} \geq \ldots \geq t_{\pi(K)}$, and define $A_{\pi,K}$ as the finite set

$$A_{\pi,K} := \{(I_1, \ldots, I_K) : \pi([k]) \subseteq I_k, I_k \subseteq I_{k+1} \ \forall k = 1, \ldots, K\},$$

where $t_{\pi(K+1)} = 0$ and $I_{K+1} = [d]$. Then

$$\mathbb{P}(\boldsymbol{\tau}_I > \boldsymbol{t}_I) = \sum_{(I_1,\ldots,I_K)\in A_{\pi,K}} \prod_{k=1}^{K} (\vec{e}_{\bar{h}(I_{k+1})})' \exp\left\{(t_{\pi(k)} - t_{\pi(k+1)})Q\right\} \vec{e}_{\bar{h}(I_k)}.$$

The assumption that the survival-indicator process is time-homogeneous Markovian has an important implication: Let $\boldsymbol{s} = (s_1, \ldots, s_d)' \geq 0$ be a deterministic vector of non-negative times and let $\pi \in \mathcal{S}_d$ be a permutation such that $s_{\pi(1)} \geq \ldots \geq s_{\pi(d)}$. Then for $t \geq 0$, $\boldsymbol{v} = \boldsymbol{s} + t$, and $v_{\pi(d+1)} = 0$ as well as $I_{d+1} = [d]$

$$\mathbb{P}(\boldsymbol{\tau} > \boldsymbol{s} + t) = \sum_{(I_1,\ldots,I_K)\in A_{\pi,d}} \prod_{k=1}^{d} (\vec{e}_{\bar{h}(I_{k+1})})' \exp\left\{(v_{\pi(k)} - v_{\pi(k+1)})Q\right\} \vec{e}_{\bar{h}(I_k)}$$

$$= (\vec{e}_{\bar{h}([d])})' \exp\{tQ\}\vec{e}_{\bar{h}([d])}$$

$$\times \sum_{(I_1,\ldots,I_K)\in A_{\pi,d}} \prod_{k=1}^{d} (\vec{e}_{\bar{h}(I_{k+1})})' \exp\left\{(s_{\pi(k)} - s_{\pi(k+1)})Q\right\} \vec{e}_{\bar{h}(I_k)}$$

$$= \mathbb{P}(\boldsymbol{\tau} > \boldsymbol{s})\mathbb{P}(\boldsymbol{\tau} > t).$$

This is equivalent to

$$\mathbb{P}(\boldsymbol{\tau} > \boldsymbol{s} + t \mid \boldsymbol{\tau} > t) = \mathbb{P}(\boldsymbol{\tau} > \boldsymbol{s}). \tag{1}$$

Analogously, one can derive for some $\emptyset \neq I \subseteq J \subseteq [d]$, and $t, v \geq 0$, that

$$\mathbb{P}(\boldsymbol{\tau}_I > \boldsymbol{s}_I + t + v \mid \boldsymbol{\tau}_J > t + v, \tau_{[d]\backslash J} \leq t + v)$$
$$= \mathbb{P}(\boldsymbol{\tau}_I > \boldsymbol{s}_I + t \mid \boldsymbol{\tau}_J > t, \tau_{[d]\backslash J} \leq t).$$

2.2. Lack-of-memory properties

It is not a coincidence that Eq. (1) collapses in the univariate case to the well-known *univariate lack-of-memory property* — also known as Cauchy's

---

[6]A permutation on $[d]$ is a bijection from $[d]$ to $[d]$; the set of all permutations on $[d]$ is denoted by $\mathcal{S}_d$.

functional equation — as in that case the time-homogeneity of the survival-indicator process implies exactly that *the probability of a survival-time bigger than $s+t$ conditional on a survival-time bigger than s is stationary with respect to t*, i.e.

$$\mathbb{P}(\tau > s + t \mid \tau > t) = \mathbb{P}(\tau > s). \tag{2}$$

It is a well-known fact that the class of non-negative distributions fulfilling Eq. (2) and having at least one continuity point[7] are exponential distributions — see, e.g., [10], p. 190. This property implies a very convenient simulation scheme if one is interested in the exponentially distributed survival-time of some entity:

$$1_{\{\tau > j\Delta\}} \overset{d}{=} \prod_{k=1}^{j} 1_{\{\tau^{(k)} > \Delta\}},$$

where $\tau^{(k)} \sim \tau$ are i.i.d. copies of τ and $\overset{d}{=}$ denotes equality in distribution.

The univariate lack-of-memory property, Eq. (2), can be extended to a multivariate property in multiple ways. In the following, a few of these are presented. Therefore, let $\boldsymbol{\tau}$ be a vector of non-negative random default-times and assume that the following conditions hold for all $\emptyset \neq I \subseteq [d]$ and $s_I, t_I, c_I, s, t \geq 0$.

- *Multivariate independent exponential lack-of-memory (MIELOM):*

$$\mathbb{P}(\boldsymbol{\tau}_I > \boldsymbol{s}_I + \boldsymbol{t}_I \mid \boldsymbol{\tau}_I > \boldsymbol{t}_I) = \mathbb{P}(\boldsymbol{\tau}_I > \boldsymbol{s}_I). \tag{3}$$

- *Multivariate Marshall–Olkin lack-of-memory (MMOLOM):*

$$\mathbb{P}(\boldsymbol{\tau}_I > \boldsymbol{s}_I + t \mid \boldsymbol{\tau}_I > t) = \mathbb{P}(\boldsymbol{\tau}_I > \boldsymbol{s}_I). \tag{4}$$

- *Min-stable multivariate exponential lack-of-memory (MSMVE):*

$$\mathbb{P}(\boldsymbol{\tau}_I > \boldsymbol{c}_I(s + t) \mid \boldsymbol{\tau}_I > \boldsymbol{c}_I t) = \mathbb{P}(\boldsymbol{\tau}_I > \boldsymbol{c}_I s). \tag{5}$$

- *Exponential-minima lack-of-memory (EM):*

$$\mathbb{P}(\boldsymbol{\tau}_I > s + t \mid \boldsymbol{\tau}_I > t) = \mathbb{P}(\boldsymbol{\tau}_I > s). \tag{6}$$

---

[7]This condition can be weakened in this context.

It was shown in [11] that (MIELOM) is equivalent to $\boldsymbol{\tau}$ having independent exponential components and (MMOLOM) is equivalent to $\boldsymbol{\tau}$ having a *Marshall–Olkin distribution*, i.e. there exist $\lambda_I \geq 0$, $\emptyset \neq I \subseteq [d]$, with $\sum_{I : i \in I} \lambda_I > 0$ for all $i \in [d]$, such that for all $\boldsymbol{t} \geq 0$

$$\mathbb{P}(\boldsymbol{\tau} > \boldsymbol{t}) = \exp\left\{ - \sum_{I : \emptyset \neq I \subseteq [d]} \lambda_I \max_{i \in I} t_i \right\}. \tag{7}$$

Furthermore, the authors provided the following stochastic model: Let $E^I, \emptyset \neq I \subseteq [d]$, be exponential random variables with rates $\lambda_I, \emptyset \neq I \subseteq [d]$, as above. Then the random vector $\boldsymbol{\tau}$ has the survival function in Eq. (7), where $\boldsymbol{\tau}$ is defined by

$$\tau_i := \min\{E^I : i \in I\}, \ i \in [d]. \tag{8}$$

Marshall–Olkin distributions and continuous-time, time-homogeneous Markovian survival-indicator processes are deeply connected. In [8] it was shown that $\boldsymbol{\tau}$ has a Marshall–Olkin distribution if and only if for every non-empty subset I the marginal survival-indicator process $\boldsymbol{Z}_I(t) := (1_{\{\tau_i > t\}}, i \in I)'$ is time-homogeneous Markovian. The following theorem shows that every continuous-time, time-homogeneous Markovian survival-indicator process can be constructed using a finite sequence of Marshall–Olkin distributed random vectors.

Theorem 2.1. *Let Q be an intensity matrix of a time-homogeneous Markovian survival-indicator process. Consider the process $\boldsymbol{Z}$, which is constructed as follows:*

(i) *Define $\boldsymbol{Z}(0) = h([d]) = (1, \ldots, 1)'$ (All entities are alive at time 0).*

(ii) *Assume that $\boldsymbol{Z}$ jumped $k \in \mathbb{N}_0$ times and define the time of the kth jump by T_k (for $k = 0$ let $T_0 := 0$). Furthermore, assume that $h^{-1}(\boldsymbol{Z}(T_k)) = I \subseteq [d]$.*

    (a) *For $\emptyset \neq J \subseteq I$, let $E_{k+1}^J \sim \text{Exp}(q_{h(I),h(I \setminus J)})$ be independent exponential random variables with rates $q_{h(I),h(I \setminus J)}$, which are, conditional on $\boldsymbol{Z}(T_k)$, also independent of all previously used random variables.*

    (b) *Define*
    $T_{k+1} := T_k + \min_{\emptyset \neq J \subseteq I} E_{k+1}^J$ and $D_{k+1} := \text{argmin}_{\emptyset \neq J \subseteq I} E_{k+1}^J$. Furthermore, define $\boldsymbol{Z}(t) := h(I) \ \forall t \in (T_k, T_{k+1})$ and $\boldsymbol{Z}(T_{k+1}) := h(I \setminus D_{k+1})$.

The resulting process $\boldsymbol{Z}$ is time-homogeneous Markovian with intensity matrix Q. Note how the minimum operation in (b) is related to the Marshall–Olkin fatal shock model.

Proof. The statement follows directly from Thm. A.1. □

It is a well-known fact, see e.g. [12], p. 174, that the class of MSMVE distributions is characterized by having exponential margins and a survival copula of *extreme-value kind*, i.e. a copula $\hat{C}$ that satisfies

$$\hat{C}(\boldsymbol{u}^t) = \hat{C}(\boldsymbol{u})^t, \ \forall \boldsymbol{u} \in [0,1]^d, t \geq 0. \tag{9}$$

Furthermore, it holds that (see, e.g., [13])

$$\mathrm{MIELOM} \subsetneq \mathrm{MMOLOM} \subsetneq \mathrm{MSMVE} \subsetneq \mathrm{EM}.$$

For the purpose of this article, we also define weaker versions of these properties, where the respective property only has to be fulfilled for $I = [d]$, and these are then referred to as weak versions of the respective properties, e.g., *weak exponential minima property (WEM)*.

3. Problem one: Iterating "survival-of-all"

This section addresses problem one, for which only "survival-of-all" events are relevant. Let the vector of default-times be denoted by $\boldsymbol{\tau} = (\tau_1, \ldots, \tau_d)'$. A "survival-of-all" event (similarly for a "first-to-default" event) has the form

$$\left\{ \min_{i \in [d]} \tau_i > s \right\}, \ \text{for some } s > 0.$$

In practical applications, one has the options of either directly modeling the joint minimum of all default-times, or modeling the vector of all default-times and considering its minimum. Note that these approaches are sometimes called top-down- and bottom-up approach, respectively, not to be confused with the related but different top-down and bottom-up approaches for collateralized debt or loan obligations, see for example [14]. The top-down approach has the appealing advantage that everything becomes simpler and more advanced models, e.g. with stochastic intensity, become feasible. On the contrary, the bottom-up approach has the advantage that the default-times themselves are more "natural," compared to their joint minimum, as a model. This means in particular that in bottom-up models:

- There is usually good knowledge on the single default-times τ_i through historic data or CDS-quotes.
- On the contrary, there is comparably little understanding of the "first-to-default"-time that, barring heroic assumptions on pool homogeneity, granularity, and dependence, is usually accessed through brute force simulation methods.
- The dependence of other risk factors, e.g. equity, to the default-times is usually less complex than their dependence to the "first-to-default" time.
- A dependence-structure between default-times can be found, e.g., by mixtures of expert-judgment and model calibration to portfolio credit derivative data (e.g. CDO's), even though at the moment these markets are much less liquid than before the 2007-2008 crisis.

For the rest of this section the second option of modeling the default-times vector, namely the bottom up option, is considered.

The assumption of a continuous-time, time-homogeneous Markovian survival-indicator process has been motivated with the need to understand the increment- as well as the "terminal iterated"-distribution and to limit the data which has to be stored for simulation. For this very problem we can weaken these requirements by simply asking that the survival-indicator process has a time-homogeneous probability to stay in the "no default"-state. In other words, for this particular problem, the distribution of default-times is feasible if it fulfills the *weak exponential minima (WEM)* property:

$$\mathbb{P}(\boldsymbol{\tau} > s + t \mid \boldsymbol{\tau} > t) = \mathbb{P}(\boldsymbol{\tau} > s). \tag{10}$$

Another formulation of this class, fulfilling Eq. (10), is the following:

"terminal one-shot survival probability up to $t_1 + \ldots + t_N$"
$$= \mathbb{P}(\boldsymbol{\tau} > t_1 + \ldots + t_N) = \mathbb{P}(\boldsymbol{\tau}^{(1)} > t_1) \cdot \ldots \cdot \mathbb{P}(\boldsymbol{\tau}^{(N)} > t_N)$$
$$= \text{"terminal iterated survival probability with steps } t_1, \ldots, t_N,"$$

where $\boldsymbol{\tau}^{(k)}, k \in [d]$, are i.i.d. copies of $\boldsymbol{\tau}$. The class of distributions fulfilling the WEM-property is potentially large, as the following examples show, and to the best knowledge of the authors it is not characterized in any other way.

Example 3.1. Let $\boldsymbol{\tau}$ have a bivariate survival function corresponding to an independence survival-copula and the marginal survival functions $\bar{F}_1(t) = (t+1)\exp\{-t\}$ and $\bar{F}_2(t) = (1+t)^{-1}$, respectively. The functions $\bar{F}_i, i \in [2]$, are both proper survival functions as they are decreasing, continuous, and tend to zero and one for $t \to 0$ and $t \to \infty$, respectively. Then the joint minimum, $\min_{i \in [2]} \tau_i$, is exponential, and in particular $\boldsymbol{\tau}$ fulfills the WEM-property, but neither τ_1 nor τ_2 are exponential,

$$\mathbb{P}\left(\min_{i \in [2]} \tau_i > t\right) = (t+1)\exp\{-t\} \cdot (1+t)^{-1} = \exp\{-t\}.$$

Example 3.2. Let $\boldsymbol{\eta}$ be a $(d-1)$-dimensional non-negative random vector, E an exponential random variable with rate $\lambda > 0$, and Π a random variable on the set of permutations on $[d]$. Define $\tilde{\boldsymbol{\tau}} := (E, E + \boldsymbol{\eta}')'$ and $\boldsymbol{\tau}$ by

$$\boldsymbol{\tau} := (\tilde{\tau}_{\Pi(1)}, \ldots, \tilde{\tau}_{\Pi(d)})'.$$

Then $\boldsymbol{\tau}$ has the WEM-property, as by construction $\min_{i \in [d]} \tau_i = E$.

The rest of this section has two purposes:

- The assumption of a time-homogeneous Markovian first-default survival indicator has strong links to multivariate lack-of-memory properties. It is shown that, in particular, all MSMVE distributions fulfill this property. As a well-known representative of this class, the Gumbel–Hougaard copula and the corresponding Gumbel–Hougaard exponential distribution[8] are introduced as an example.
- Showing that the popular approach of (independent in time) Gaussian-coupled exponential increments does not fulfill the WEM-property. Furthermore, it is shown that this approach kills dependence asymptotically for $N \to \infty$ — meaning the "terminal iterated" dependence is approximately that of independent-coupled exponential random variables.

3.1. *Lack-of-memory properties revisited*

Let Δ be the period step-size, T the final horizon, and N the number of periods up to T, i.e. $T = N\Delta$.

In [7], in the context of the problem of "survival-of-all", the authors tried to bridge the gap between the question

---

[8]The Gumbel–Hougaard distribution is the multivariate extension defined later in Eq. (12). This was originally introduced in [15] for the bivariate case. It is not to be confused with the two other bivariate exponential distributions introduced in that very paper that are also named after Emil J. Gumbel. One of those, with the survival function $\exp\{-\lambda_1 t_1 - \lambda_2 t_2 - \theta t_1 t_2\}$, is characterized by a lack-of-memory property called *bivariate remaining life constancy*, see, e.g., [16], [17], which has the interpretation that, conditional on the survival of the respective other component up to an arbitrary time, both variables are exponential, cf. [18].

> *Which distributions have equal "terminal one-shot" and "terminal*
> *iterated" survival probabilities for common step-size Δ?*

and properties of survival copulas corresponding to multivariate exponential distributions. This leads to the definition of so called *self-chaining* copulas — or *self-chaining distributions*.

In the following, this approach will be (broadly) outlined, advanced and generalized, exploring the full lack-of-memory implications and characterization for the extreme-value copula with exponential margin solution obtained initially in [7]. We will confirm also the special solutions found in [7], namely the Gumbel–Hougaard copula and the Marshall–Olkin copula, further specifying the properties of these solutions, although we will not address the bivariate Pickands functions solution here. For further details on Pickands functions see, for example, [19] or [20].

Definition 3.1. The distribution of τ has the *weak common Δ-period exponential minima* (WCPEM(Δ))-property if for every two natural numbers $j, k \in \mathbb{N}$

$$\mathbb{P}(\tau > (j+k)\Delta \mid \tau > j\Delta) = \mathbb{P}(\tau > k\Delta).$$

It has the *common Δ-period exponential minima (CPEM (Δ))*-property if for all non-empty $I \subseteq [d]$ the vector τ_I has the (WCPEM(Δ))-property.

It can be easily shown that this property can be rewritten as follows:

Definition 3.2. A random vector τ is Δ-*periodic self-chaining* if for all $j \in \mathbb{N}$

$$\mathbb{P}(\tau > j\Delta) = \mathbb{P}(\tau > \Delta)^j.$$

For a Δ-periodic self-chaining distribution, the corresponding survival-copula $\hat{C}$ is called $\mathbb{N}$-*self-chaining in the point* $(\bar{F}_1(\Delta), \dots, \bar{F}_d(\Delta))'$.

From Def. 3.1 it is visible that a distribution fulfilling the (W)CPEM(Δ)-property for all $\Delta > 0$ fulfills the (W)EM-property and vice versa. Therefore, in light of Def. 3.2, the following definition follows.

Definition 3.3. A random vector τ is *self-chaining* if for all $t > 0$

$$\mathbb{P}(\tau > t) = \mathbb{P}(\tau > 1)^t.$$

For a self-chaining distribution, the corresponding survival-copula $\hat{C}$ is called $\mathbb{R}$-*self-chaining* (or *self-chaining*) in the point $(\bar{F}_1(1), \dots, \bar{F}_d(1))'$.

Let $\boldsymbol{\tau}$ have exponential margins and define $\boldsymbol{u} := (\bar{F}_1(1), \ldots, \bar{F}_d(1))'$. Then $\boldsymbol{\tau}$ is self-chaining if and only if the survival-copula $\hat{C}$ fulfills (for the specific $\boldsymbol{u}$)

$$\hat{C}(\boldsymbol{u}^t) = \hat{C}(\boldsymbol{u})^t, \ \forall t > 0. \tag{11}$$

Equation (11) is well-known from extreme-value theory, as the class of copulas fulfilling Eq. (11) for all $\boldsymbol{u} \in [0,1]^d$, cf. Eq. (9), is that of *extreme-value copulas (EVCs)* and furthermore, that the class of min-stable multivariate exponential distributions, cf. Eq. (5), is characterized by a coupling of EVC's and exponential margins, see [12], p. 174.

A self-chaining survival-copula in the point $\boldsymbol{u} \in [0,1]^d$ can only be coupled with exponential margins with rates $\lambda_i = -\ln u_i, i \in [d]$, to a self-chaining distribution, while an extreme-value copula can be coupled with any exponential margin to a self-chaining distribution. In general, it should be noted that almost all lack-of-memory properties get lost if the underlying survival-copula is re-coupled with different marginal distributions — even if one stays in the exponential class.

An example for a (survival-)copula which is self-chaining in arbitrary points $\boldsymbol{u} \in [0,1]^d$ is the *Gumbel–Hougaard copula*, see [15],[16],[21],[22], which is implicitly defined by the following multivariate exponential distribution ($\boldsymbol{\lambda} > 0, \theta \geq 1$)

$$\mathbb{P}(\boldsymbol{\tau} > \boldsymbol{s}) = \exp\left\{-\left(\sum_{i=1}^{d}(\lambda_i s_i)^\theta\right)^{\frac{1}{\theta}}\right\}, \ \boldsymbol{s} \geq 0. \tag{12}$$

In [22], it was proven that the class of Gumbel–Hougaard copulas are the only copulas which are both extreme-value- and Archimedean copulas, see also [7] for an alternative proof.

An example for a distribution with exponential minima, which is not min-stable multivariate exponential, with a recipe from [13] for the bivariate case.

(1) Let $E_I^{(k)}$ be independent exponential random variables with rates $\lambda_I^{(k)}, k \in [2], \emptyset \neq I \subseteq [2]$.
(2) Let $\tilde{\boldsymbol{\tau}}^{(k)} = (\tilde{\tau}_1^{(k)}, \tilde{\tau}_2^{(k)})', k \in [2]$, be defined by

$$\tilde{\tau}_i^{(k)} := \min\{E_{\{i\}}^{(k)}, E_{[2]}^{(k)}\}, \ i, k \in [2],$$

i.e. both $\tilde{\boldsymbol{\tau}}^{(1)}$ and $\tilde{\boldsymbol{\tau}}^{(2)}$ are Marshall–Olkin distributed.

(3) Let $\boldsymbol{\tau}$ for $p \in (0,1)$ and $a_i^{(k)}, i, k \in [2]$, be defined by

$$\tau_i = X a_i^{(1)} \tilde{\tau}_i^{(1)} + (1 - X) a_i^{(2)} \tilde{\tau}_i^{(2)}, \ i \in [2],$$

where X is a Bernoulli variable with "success probability" p.

Choose $\lambda_{\{1\}}^{(1)} = 1/2$, $\lambda_{\{2\}}^{(1)} = 1$, $\lambda_{[2]}^{(1)} = 2$, $\lambda_{\{1\}}^{(2)} = 2/3$, $\lambda_{\{2\}}^{(2)} = 1/2$, $\lambda_{[2]}^{(2)} = 1$ as well as $a_1^{(1)} = 1/2$, $a_2^{(1)} = 1$, $a_1^{(2)} = 1/3$, and $a_2^{(2)} = 1/2$; then the attained distribution has EM but is not MSMVE. The attained distribution is a mixture of MO-coupled, i.e. having a copula from a Marshall–Olkin survival copula, exponential random variables. The key for the EM-property to hold is to make sure that the mixed MO-coupled exponential distributions have equal diagonal-functions for all margins. This concept can be extended to arbitrary dimensions for the creation of distributions with EM.

In more basic terms, this discussion highlights a tension between the full Marshall–Olkin law and the Marshall–Olkin copula with possibly different exponential margins. The initial results in [7] include the solution given by the Marshall–Olkin copula with possibly re-scaled exponential margins, leading to a multivariate distribution that is different from a fully consistent Marshall–Olkin law. In more intuitive terms, we can say that re-scaling the margins with new exponentials breaks the natural consistency between margins and dependence that is a key property of the Marshall–Olkin law. In general, arbitrarily decoupling the margins and the dependence structure may result in paradoxical results when analyzing wrong way risk in CDS trades, see, for example, the low dimensional examples in [23], [3], [2], and [24].

For the construction of high-dimensional models it might be convenient to know that there is another recent approach for the generation of (extendible) EM-distributed random vectors via first hitting times of matrix-mixtures of subordinators which are weakly infinitely divisible with respect to time over random exponential barriers, see [25], [26].

3.2. *Change in dependence when iterating non-self chaining copulas*

In the following, a standard approach which is widely used in the financial industry is critically analyzed: The discretely iterated Gaussian-coupled exponential margins survival-indicator process. Let, as before, $T > 0$, $N \in \mathbb{N}$, and $\Delta := T/N$ and define for $j \in \mathbb{N}$

$$\boldsymbol{Z}^{(\Delta)}(j+1) \mid \{\boldsymbol{Z}^{(\Delta)}(j) = 1\} := 1_{\{\varsigma_{j+1} > \Delta\}},$$

for independent and identically distributed $\boldsymbol{\zeta}_{j+1} \sim C_\Phi(\rho) \oplus (\bar{F}_1, \ldots, \bar{F}_d)$, where $C_\Phi(\rho)$ is the Gaussian copula with equi-correlation $\rho > 0$ and $\bar{F}_i, i \in [d]$, are exponential survival functions.

Assume first that $\boldsymbol{\zeta}_j, j \in [N]$, are constructed with an arbitrary copula coupled with exponential margins; then the "terminal iterated" probability for the "survival-of-all" event is

$$\mathbb{P}\left(\boldsymbol{Z}^{(T/N)}(N) = \mathbf{1}\right) = \left(\mathbb{P}\left(\zeta > \frac{T}{N}\right)\right)^N. \tag{13}$$

From multivariate extreme-value theory it is known that for $N \to \infty$ the expression in Eq. (13) either converges to a min-stable multivariate exponential distribution[9] or does not converge at all, see [12].

Definition 3.4. Let $\hat{C}$ be an extreme-value copula. Every copula $\hat{C}_F$ with

$$\lim_{n \to \infty} \hat{C}_F(\boldsymbol{u}^{1/n})^n = \hat{C}(\boldsymbol{u}), \ \forall \boldsymbol{u} \in [0,1]^d,$$

is said to be in the *domain of attraction* of $\hat{C}$.

Theorem 3.1. *Let $d = 2$, then the* Clayton copula, Frank copula, *and the* Gaussian copula *for $\rho < 1$ are in the domain of attraction of the independence copula.*

Proof. See [12],[27]–[29]. $\square$

This implies in particular for $d = 2$ and large N that the distribution of $\boldsymbol{\tau}$ is approximately that of independent exponential random variables. Hence, and this is a word of warning, for large N the Gaussian-coupling kills the correlation of the "terminal iterated" law.

Remark 3.1. The asymptotic "terminal iterated" dependence can be inferred if the survival-copula of the iterated law lies in the domain of attraction of some extreme-value copula, e.g. in Thm. 3.1, it was shown that the bivariate non-comonotonic Gaussian-, Clayton-, and Frank copulas are in the domain of attraction of the independence copula, see [12], p. 141 and also [29] for an early account on asymptotic independence of the Gaussian copula. The bivariate exchangeable t-copula lies in the domain of attraction of the *t-EV copula*, which is for finite degrees of freedom not the independence copula and depends on the degrees of freedom as well as the correlation parameter, see [30]. Furthermore, if $\hat{C}_F$ lies in the domain of

---

[9]A vector of independent exponentially distributed random variables is also MSMVE.

attraction of $\hat{C}$, then their upper-tail-dependence coefficient coincides — in particular, if a copula $\hat{C}_F$ incorporates asymptotic independence and lies in the domain of attraction of an extreme-value copula $\hat{C}$, then $\hat{C}$ is the independence copula, see e.g. [30], pp. 587–588. Moreover, if $\hat{C}_F$ is a d-dimensional copula which lies in the domain of attraction of $\hat{C}$ and incorporates pairwise asymptotic independence, then $\hat{C}$ is the independence copula, see, e.g., [30], p. 591. This implies in particular that also the d-dimensional exchangeable Gaussian-copula with $\rho < 1$ lies in the domain of attraction of the independence copula.

In the following example, this effect is analyzed numerically for bivariate Gaussian-coupled exponential distributions with rates $\lambda_{IG} = 1\%$ and $\lambda_{SG} = 4.5\%$, corresponding to an investment grade (IG) or speculative grade (SG) entity. The "terminal one-shot" and "terminal iterated" probability for the "survival-of-all" event is denoted by

$$p_T := \mathbb{P}(\zeta > T) \text{ or } p_\Delta^N := \mathbb{P}(\zeta > \Delta)^N = \mathbb{P}(\tau > T).$$

In Tables 1 and 2, the result of this analysis for two different settings with different final time-horizons as well as different numbers of iterations can be observed. The results illustrate the statement from Thm. 3.1, i.e. that Gaussian-coupled exponential distributions with $\rho < 1$ do not have the WEM-property. Moreover, the relative error is sizable and becomes larger for higher marginal rates and higher correlation, which is especially undesirable.

Table 1. Comparison of "terminal one-shot" and "terminal iterated" survival probabilities for $T = 5y$ and $N = 1000$.

λ_1	λ_2	ρ	p_T	p_Δ^N	% Diff.
0.010	0.010	0.25	0.9084	0.9049	0.38%
0.010	0.010	0.50	0.9142	0.9057	0.95%
0.010	0.010	0.75	0.9238	0.9103	1.48%
0.010	0.045	0.25	0.7679	0.7598	1.07%
0.010	0.045	0.50	0.7785	0.7614	2.24%
0.010	0.045	0.75	0.7908	0.7698	2.73%
0.045	0.045	0.25	0.6592	0.6382	3.29%
0.045	0.045	0.50	0.6851	0.6421	6.7%
0.045	0.045	0.75	0.7187	0.6605	8.81%

In Fig. 1, the relative error is visualized for four additional survival-copulas, i.e. the t-, Clayton-, Frank-, and Gumbel-copula, and multiple

Table 2. Comparison of "terminal one-shot" and "terminal iterated" survival probabilities for $T = 30y$ and $N = 1000$.

λ_1	λ_2	ρ	p_T	p_Δ^N	% Diff.
0.010	0.010	0.25	0.5765	0.5496	4.91%
0.010	0.010	0.50	0.6084	0.5545	9.71%
0.010	0.010	0.75	0.6483	0.5766	12.43%
0.010	0.045	0.25	0.2169	0.1929	12.47%
0.010	0.045	0.50	0.2389	0.1974	21.01%
0.010	0.045	0.75	0.2553	0.2142	19.2%
0.045	0.045	0.25	0.0949	0.0682	39.17%
0.045	0.045	0.50	0.1268	0.0728	74.09%
0.045	0.045	0.75	0.1667	0.0899	85.38%

Kendall's τ, denoted by τ_K, where the underlying copula parameters are calibrated such that a certain τ_K is achieved. One can see that the error is strongly dependent on the chosen rank correlation. Furthermore, the Gaussian coupling seems to have the largest errors for $\tau_K \leq 75\%$, while the error for the t-coupling is rather small in comparison. An explanation for the latter observation could be that the bivariate t-copula converges for a low degree of freedoms comparably fast, see [27], and the t-EV copula still incorporates information on ν and τ_K.

In conclusion, these calculations show that a coupling with the Gaussian-, Frank-, or Clayton copula can lead to sizable differences in the terminal probabilities. This is not a surprising result, as it was already shown theoretically that the terminal probabilities can only match if the iterated distribution has the WEM-property (e.g. an MSMVE-distribution) and that the iteration of Gaussian-copulas leads asymptotically to independence; however, this analysis underscores the severity of the mismatch.

4. Problem two: "Mixed default/survival" events

So far, the problem of finding conditions under which the "survival-of-all" simulation can be iterated (feasible) in a way that makes it consistent to a single step simulation was addressed. However, while the "survival-of-all" may be of interest in situations where one wishes to exclude even a single default, or for the valuation of a first-to-default CDS, it is more interesting to look at the general problem of iterating in presence of "mixed-default/survival"-states. This problem, "problem two," is the topic of the present section and conditions for the feasible and consistent simulation of "mixed-default/survival"-indicators up to a terminal time are analyzed.

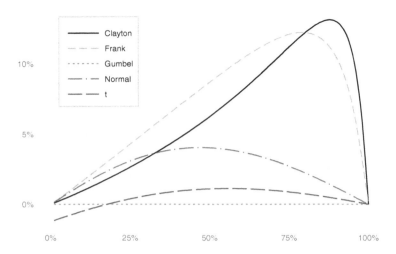

Fig. 1.   Relative deviation of p_T and p_Δ^N in % vs. Kendalls's τ for $T = 5y$, $\lambda_i = 4.5\%$, $i = 1, 2$, $N = 10$, and 3 degrees of freedom for the t-distribution, see [28].

Finally, examples such as the Marshall–Olkin distribution and a multivariate extension of the Freund distribution are presented.

4.1. *The looping default model and the Freund distribution*

One of the most intuitive models for contagion effects in portfolio-credit risk is the so-called "looping default"-model, the terminology being introduced in one of the first works on counterparty credit risk pricing, see [31]. In the bivariate case, the model can easily be explained: Let C_1 and C_2 be two companies with respective default intensities for $t \geq 0$

$$\tilde{\lambda}_1(t) = \lambda_1 + 1_{\{\tau_2 \leq t\}}(\eta_1 - \lambda_1),$$
$$\tilde{\lambda}_2(t) = \lambda_2 + 1_{\{\tau_1 \leq t\}}(\eta_2 - \lambda_2),$$

where $\lambda_1, \lambda_2, \eta_1, \eta_2 > 0$.   Loosely speaking, this means that the default/survival-probabilities of company C_1 depend on the default/survival of company C_2 and vice versa.   This explains the notion of a "looping-default" model, as the influence of companies on each-others default/survival-probabilities can be depicted as a loop. This model formulation can easily be generalized to non-linear or stochastic hazard functions. Constructing a well-defined probability space, however, supporting such a multivariate distribution is non-trivial. Therefore, it was initially assumed that the set of companies can be divided into two classes $\mathcal{A}$ and $\mathcal{B}$, such that the default of a company from set $\mathcal{A}$ can influence the default of a company from $\mathcal{B}$, but not vice versa. As a consequence the model can be formulated recursively in the spirit of a classical intensity-based model, see [31]. The problem of constructing the distribution in the general model (with hazard-rate functions which are deterministic functions of time and default history) on a well-defined probability space has been investigated in subsequent articles and finally was resolved in [32], where the "looping-default" model is defined using the so-called "total hazard construction," which originates from the statistical literature, see [33] and [34]. The total hazard construction defines a d-dimensional random vector $\boldsymbol{\tau}$ of default-times as a function of d independent unit exponential random variables $E_1, \ldots, E_d$, such that the corresponding default intensities satisfy certain relations that are specified a priori. This construction algorithm is, however, rather complicated to implement in practice, and in particular has no natural coherence with stepwise simulation — rendering it inconvenient for our purpose. As a first example of the total hazard construction, [32] reconsiders the "looping default" of [31] in a two-dimensional setup. In [6] and [5], it was shown that the "looping default" model falls into the class of default models whose survival indicator process is a Markov chain, which provides an alternative stochastic construction being naturally consistent with stepwise simulation. Interestingly, in the bivariate case the probability law of $\boldsymbol{\tau} = (\tau_1, \tau_2)'$ is well-known in the statistical literature as well.

Remark 4.1 (Looping default model/Freund distribution). *The bivariate distribution which is derived in [32] coincides precisely with the so-called bivariate Freund distribution, which is an "old friend" from reliability theory, see [35]. In other words, the looping default has incidentally been known for many years in the statistical literature by the name "Freund distribution." The fact that both distributions coincide can be observed by comparing the bivariate densities derived in [32] and [35], respectively. The details are provided below.*

In the sequel, a new construction for the Freund distribution based on continuous-time, time-homogeneous Markovian processes is presented. This construction provides an alternative access to this probability law, which is in particular based on a stepwise-simulation ansatz. Moreover, it can be easily generalized to dimensions $d > 2$ and to extensions with simultaneous defaults.

Consider two companies' default-times $\tau = (\tau_1, \tau_2)'$. We construct the associated survival indicator process $\mathbf{Z}(t) := (1_{\{\tau_1 > t\}}, 1_{\{\tau_2 > t\}})'$ as a continuous-time, time-homogeneous Markov chain. This process is fully described by its intensity matrix Q. Let the four states $(1,1), (0,1), (1,0)$, and $(0,0)$ be indexed by the numbers $1, 2, 3$, and 4 and define the intensity matrix $Q \in \mathbb{R}^{4 \times 4}$ by

$$
Q = \begin{pmatrix}
-(\lambda_1 + \lambda_2) & \lambda_1 & \lambda_2 & 0 \\
0 & -\eta_2 & 0 & \eta_2 \\
0 & 0 & -\eta_1 & \eta_1 \\
0 & 0 & 0 & 0
\end{pmatrix},
$$

where the "initial intensities" $\lambda_i > 0, i \in [2]$, and the "intensities conditional on second-party default" $\eta_i > 0, i \in [2]$, are positive real numbers. It is easy to verify that in case the condition $\eta_i \neq \lambda_1 + \lambda_2, i \in [2]$, is fulfilled the matrix Q is diagonalizable,[10] i.e. we can find a matrix M such that

$$
M^{-1}QM = \text{diag}(-(\lambda_1 + \lambda_2), -\eta_2, -\eta_1, 0),
$$

where the transformation-matrix M has the eigenvectors of Q as column vectors, i.e.

$$
M = \begin{pmatrix}
1 & \frac{\lambda_1}{\lambda_1 + \lambda_2 - \eta_2} & \frac{\lambda_2}{\lambda_1 + \lambda_2 - \eta_1} & 1 \\
0 & 1 & 0 & 1 \\
0 & 0 & 1 & 1 \\
0 & 0 & 0 & 1
\end{pmatrix}.
$$

This intensity matrix Q can be interpreted as follows (cf. Thm. 2.1): Being in a certain state corresponds to a certain row of the matrix — e.g. the process starts in state $(1,1)$ corresponding to row 1. For each other state $(0,1), (1,0)$, and $(0,0)$ there are independent latent exponential random variables with rates $Q_{(1,1),(0,1)}, Q_{(1,1),(1,0)}$, and $Q_{(1,1),(0,0)}$. The process $\mathbf{Z}$ reacts only on the smallest of these random variables and moves to the corresponding target state. A rate of zero corresponds to the corresponding random variable being "degenerate," i.e. almost surely equal to infinity. Therefore, the chain cannot go directly from no default $(1,1)$ to joint default $(0,0)$. Finally, as Q has vanishing row sums, the ith diagonal entry corresponds to the negative rate of the minimum of all latent exponential random variables for transition out of i. The same logic applies to the other rows of Q. In particular, after the default of one company, the hazard rate

---

[10]The case $\eta_i = \lambda_1 + \lambda_2$ for some $i \in [2]$ is still a valid model. However, as the matrix Q is not diagonalizable, the analytical calculation of probabilities becomes more involved.

of the remaining company changes from λ_i to η_i, and the bottom row of Q is zero because the state of two defaults is an absorbing state. Using diagonalization, one can show that for $t > 0$ the entries of the transition matrix

$$P[t] := e^{tQ} = M^{-1} \exp\{tMQM^{-1}\}M$$

are given by

$$P_{(1,1),(1,1)}[t] = e^{-(\lambda_1+\lambda_2)\,t},$$

$$P_{(1,1),(0,1)}[t] = \frac{\lambda_1}{\lambda_1 + \lambda_2 - \eta_2}\left(e^{-\eta_2\,t} - e^{-(\lambda_1+\lambda_2)\,t}\right),$$

$$P_{(1,1),(1,0)}[t] = \frac{\lambda_2}{\lambda_1 + \lambda_2 - \eta_1}\left(e^{-\eta_1\,t} - e^{-(\lambda_1+\lambda_2)\,t}\right),$$

$$P_{(1,1),(0,0)}[t] = -\frac{\lambda_1}{\lambda_1 + \lambda_2 - \eta_2}\,e^{-\eta_2\,t} - \frac{\lambda_2}{\lambda_1 + \lambda_2 - \eta_1}\,e^{-\eta_1\,t}$$
$$+ 1 + \left(\frac{\lambda_1}{\lambda_1 + \lambda_2 - \eta_2} + \frac{\lambda_2}{\lambda_1 + \lambda_2 - \eta_1} - 1\right)e^{-(\lambda_1+\lambda_2)\,t},$$

$$P_{(0,1),(0,1)}[t] = e^{-\eta_2\,t}, \quad P_{(0,1),(0,0)}(t) = 1 - e^{-\eta_2\,t},$$

$$P_{(1,0),(1,0)}[t] = e^{-\eta_1\,t}, \quad P_{(1,0),(0,0)}(t) = 1 - e^{-\eta_1\,t},$$

and all other entries of P being zero. In particular, we calculate

$$\mathbb{P}(\tau_1 > t_1, \tau_2 > t_2)$$

$$= \begin{cases} P_{(1,1),(1,1)}(t_1)\left(P_{(1,1),(1,1)}(t_2 - t_1) + P_{(1,1),(0,1)}(t_2 - t_1)\right), & t_2 \geq t_1 \\ P_{(1,1),(1,1)}(t_2)\left(P_{(1,1),(1,1)}(t_1 - t_2) + P_{(1,1),(1,0)}(t_1 - t_2)\right), & t_1 > t_2 \end{cases}$$

$$= \begin{cases} \frac{\lambda_2 - \eta_2}{\lambda_1 + \lambda_2 - \eta_2}\,e^{-(\lambda_1+\lambda_2)\,t_2} + \frac{\lambda_1}{\lambda_1 + \lambda_2 - \eta_2}\,e^{-\eta_2\,t_2 - (\lambda_1+\lambda_2-\eta_2)\,t_1}, & t_2 \geq t_1 \\ \frac{\lambda_1 - \eta_1}{\lambda_1 + \lambda_2 - \eta_1}\,e^{-(\lambda_1+\lambda_2)\,t_1} + \frac{\lambda_2}{\lambda_1 + \lambda_2 - \eta_1}\,e^{-\eta_1\,t_1 - (\lambda_1+\lambda_2-\eta_1)\,t_2}, & t_1 > t_2. \end{cases}$$

The latter distribution is precisely the Freund distribution, which can be seen by comparing it to Eq. (47.26) in [16], p. 356. Note additionally, that the so-called $\mathrm{ACBVE}(\tilde{\eta}_1, \tilde{\eta}_2, \tilde{\eta}_{12})$-distribution, defined in [36], arises as the three-parametric subfamily of the Freund distribution, obtained from the parameters

$$\lambda_1 = \tilde{\eta}_1 + \frac{\tilde{\eta}_{12}\tilde{\eta}_1}{\tilde{\eta}_1 + \tilde{\eta}_2}, \quad \lambda_2 = \tilde{\eta}_2 + \frac{\tilde{\eta}_{12}\tilde{\eta}_2}{\tilde{\eta}_1 + \tilde{\eta}_2}, \quad \eta_1 = \tilde{\eta}_1 + \tilde{\eta}_{12}, \quad \eta_2 = \tilde{\eta}_2 + \tilde{\eta}_{12}.$$

Multivariate extensions of the described Markov chain construction, leading to the Freund distribution, are now clearly straightforward. One can simply define the intensity matrix Q as follows: For each set $I \subseteq [d]$ one has to define exponential rates η_J for all subsets $J \subseteq I$ with $|J| = |I| - 1$, i.e. corresponding to exactly one additional default scenario, and write them in the respective entry $Q_{h(I),h(J)}$. All other off-diagonal entries of Q are set to zero, and then the diagonal elements are computed as the negative of the sum over all previously defined row entries. Similarly, one can generalize the model to allow for multiple defaults and also assign positive exponential rates to subsets $J \subseteq I$ with $|J| = |I| - k$, $k \geq 1$.

For stepwise simulation along the Δ-grid, one only requires the matrix $P[\Delta] = \exp\{\Delta\, Q\}$, which can be computed easily if Q is diagonalizable or otherwise numerically (e.g. `expm` in MATLAB or `Matrix::expm` in R).

Remark 4.2. The class of distributions attained in continuous-time, time-homogeneous Markovian survival-indicator processes coincides with the class of *multivariate phase-type distributions* which were introduced in [37], see also [38]. Multivariate phase-type distributed random vectors τ are defined implicitly through a continuous-time, time-homogeneous Markovian process Z and absorbing sets $A_i, i \in [d]$, such that $\bigcap_{i \in d} A_i$ is absorbing and

$$\tau_i := \inf\{t > 0 : Z(t) \in A_i\}, \ i \in [d].$$

In particular, it follows that all resulting marginal distributions of τ are univariate phase-type distributions.

4.2. *Marshall–Olkin distributions*

Throughout this section, we denote by Z_I the I-margin of the survival-indicator process Z which only consists of the components indexed by $I \subseteq [d]$. This section starts with summarizing the findings and results of [8], in which it is emphasized that for practical applications even the assumption of a continuous-time, time-homogeneous Markovian survival-indicator process has serious drawbacks if the corresponding default-times vector τ does not have a Marshall–Olkin distribution. The findings are:

(a) In general, even if Z is time-homogeneous Markovian the survival-indicator Z_I, corresponding to a subportfolio $\emptyset \neq I \subsetneq [d]$, might not fulfill this property. As a result, even if a certain study involves only the default-times τ_I one has to simulate the full survival-indicator process Z. This is undesirable for two reasons: Firstly, simulations only considering subportfolios cannot be performed more efficiently than via the full portfolio simulation. Second, every restructuring of the credit portfolio requires a careful adjustment and possibly a reevaluation of the whole default model (see (b) for a detailed account).

(b) If the underlying credit portfolio is subject to restructuring, the Markovian survival-indicator model is, in general, problematic. This is best explained in the case where an additional entity $d + 1$ is added to the credit portfolio. Then, each state L splits into two separate states L and $\tilde{L} := L \cup \{d+1\}$, and following this logic each "transition-rate" in the intensity matrix has the interpretation

$$P_{h(I), h(J)}[\Delta] = \mathbb{P}\left(Z((k+1)\Delta) \in h(\{J, \tilde{J}\}) \mid Z(k\Delta) \in h(\{I, \tilde{I}\})\right),$$

with an extended version of h. Hence, to be consistent with the model before restructuring, generally all transition probabilities have to be carefully translated into a new model. Therefore, models which have a "dimension-less" specification are very popular in the industry — an example for such a model, which particularly does not correspond to a Markovian survival-indicator, is the Gaussian one-factor model.

(c) A general drawback of *all* Markovian survival-indicator models is that one-dimensional marginals are heavily dependent on the specification of Q. Moreover, given an intensity-matrix Q, the construction of finite state space Markovian processes, cf. Rmk. 2.1 or Thm. 2.1, gives a particular interpretation of the joint behavior, which is lost after applying arbitrary marginal transformation. Finally, if there exists a positive rate $q_{h(I), h(J)}$ for two sets with $|J| \leq |I| - 2$, the default-time distribution has a singular component, i.e. joint defaults are possible. As a result, marginal transformation is even more difficult and can introduce undesired effects if performed without care, see e.g. [39], Sec. 5.

A Markovian characterization of the Marshall–Olkin law

The problem described in (a) can easily be resolved by requiring that also all marginal survival-indicator processes $\boldsymbol{Z}_I$ have to be time-homogeneous Markovian. The main result of [8] is the following theorem.

Theorem 4.1. (*Markovian characterization of MO*). *The $|I|$-dimensional survival indicator processes $\boldsymbol{Z}_I$ are time-homogeneous Markovian for all subsets $\emptyset \neq I \subseteq [d]$ if and only if $\boldsymbol{\tau} = (\tau_1, \dots, \tau_d)'$ has a Marshall–Olkin distribution.*

Simulation and Application

There are multiple stochastic models that produce Marshall–Olkin distributed random vectors, which can be used for model specification and simulation. We will consider three models. The seminal interpretation is an exogenous shock model representation with $2^d - 1$ independent exponential shock arrival-times, one for each subset of components, cf. Eq. (8), see also [11]. An alternative model, in the following denoted as the *Arnold model*, was introduced in [40] and is based on compound sums of exponential random variables. The model can be summarized as follows: Let $\{E_i\}_{i\in\mathbb{N}}$ be an i.i.d. family of exponential random variables with a rate $c = \sum_{\emptyset \neq I \subseteq [d]} \lambda_I$ and $\{X_i\}_{i\in\mathbb{N}}$ a discrete Markov-chain on $\{I : \emptyset \neq I \subseteq [d]\}$, which has a probability of λ_I/c for a transition from an arbitrary state each into I. Then, the random vector $\boldsymbol{\tau}$ is defined by

$$\tau_i := \inf\{t > 0 : i \in X_{N(t)}\},$$

where $N(t) := \sum_{i=1}^{\infty} 1_{\{E_1 + \ldots + E_i \leq t\}}$. The latter is closely linked to the classical model for the underlying Markovian survival-indicator as introduced in the previous sections, which is the third model.

Remark 4.3 (Comparison of MO-models). *All three models require a full model specification, i.e. $2^d - 1$ parameters, one for every non-empty set of components. The original model has the advantage of being very simple and easy to implement, however, for large dimensions d one has to sample $2^d - 1$ exponential shocks — therefore the simulation of n independent samples has a runtime of the order $\mathcal{O}(n2^d)$, see [41]. The Arnold-model is a little more difficult to implement efficiently, see [41], Alg. 3.3 and Alg. 3.4 for details, however the sampling of n independent samples has an expected runtime of the order $\mathcal{O}(2^d + nd^3)$. The classical Markov simulation is very similar to the Arnold model, with two important differences, which make this approach either more or less desirable. The Arnold model has the property that the distributions of waiting times to the next "event" as well as the random set-variable of "killed" components corresponding to that event are i.i.d. However, if all set-components have already defaulted nothing happens. In the classical Markovian setup the exponential-rates of the waiting times as well as the (random) new state depend on the current state. As a result the initial setup and storage for transition probabilities of the Arnold model is less costly. The price to pay is that not every "event" corresponds to an action. In summary, which of these models is most appropriate depends on the dimension d, the number of simulations n, and the computational capabilities.*

A possible way to reduce the number of model parameters as well as the computational effort for simulation (with all models) is to assume that all, but a few selected shock-rates equal zero: In [42] the shock model is defined using only idiosyncratic shocks, a global shock, and a few additional shocks which are chosen on some classification, e.g. industry segment, country, etc., see also [43] for a similar approach.

Considering default modeling, the dynamic properties of the aggregated default counting process and the related loss process have been studied in [44] and [45] under pool homogeneity assumptions and time-inhomogeneous *cluster default-intensities*[11] in dimensions up to $d = 125$. These authors build on the framework of [43], one of the few frameworks allowing for an explicit joint bottom-up and top-down approach, where a Marshall–Olkin bottom up setting corresponds to a generalized Poisson process top-down setup. The GPL model in [44] is one of the first pre-crisis arbitrage-free aggregate loss model to be consistently calibrated to the whole panel of different CDO tranches and maturities for the iTraxx (or CDX) portfolio, including a discussion on tranchelets. For a summary of related models and a calibration study ranging from 2005 to 2009 iTraxx tranches data see [14]. For an example of the calibration of a (time-inhomogeneous) Markovian model to market data, see [46] and [47].

Marshall–Olkin one-factor models

While survival-indicator processes defined on a latent Marshall–Olkin distribution solve the problem described in (a), it is still a model with a large number of parameters, which is in general inefficient to sample. Furthermore, the problem described in (b) is not resolved, as a Marshall–Olkin distributed vector τ attained with the classical shock model representation as a model tied to a specific dimension d, and certain objects indexed by $\{1, \ldots, d\}$. Assume, that a $d + 1$ dimensional Marshall–Olkin distribution $\tilde{\tau}$ exists with $\tilde{\tau}_{[d]} \overset{d}{=} \tau$. Then, for $i \in [d]$, it holds that (cf. Eq. (8))

$$\tilde{\tau}_i = \min\{\tilde{E}^I : i \in I\}$$
$$= \min\{\min\{\tilde{E}^I, \tilde{E}^{I \cup \{d+1\}}\} : i \in I \subseteq [d]\},$$

where $\tilde{E}^I, \emptyset \neq I \subseteq [d + 1]$, are the independent exponential random shocks from the shock model representation of $\tilde{\tau}$. In particular, it follows for the rates of τ that

$$\lambda_I = \tilde{\lambda}_I + \tilde{\lambda}_{I \cup \{d+1\}}, \quad \emptyset \neq I \subseteq [d],$$

---

[11]In this model, all defaults are triggered by independent, time-inhomogeneous Poisson processes for subsets (clusters) of entities.

which shows that there are infinitely many possibilities to embed a Marshall–Olkin distribution into a higher dimensional Marshall–Olkin distribution. Summarizing, one can conclude that, in general, for large d the Marshall–Olkin distribution has too many parameters and has no direct intuition for the extension into higher dimensions.

The simplest way to circumvent this issue is to assume that there exists an exchangeable sequence $\tilde{\tau}_i$, $i \in \mathbb{N}$, such that for every finite $\emptyset \neq I \subseteq \mathbb{N}$ the random vector $\tilde{\boldsymbol{\tau}}_I := (\tilde{\tau}_i)_{i \in I}$ has a Marshall–Olkin distribution. Random vectors $\boldsymbol{\tau}$ which have such a construction are said to have an *extendible Marshall–Olkin distribution*. A thorough treatment of these distributions can be found in [20], which also shows that an extendible Marshall–Olkin distribution can be characterized and constructed by a Lévy-subordinator Λ.

Theorem 4.2 (Lévy-frailty construction). *Let $\{\tau_i\}_{i \in \mathbb{N}}$ be an exchangeable sequence on some probability space, such that each finite margin has a Marshall–Olkin distribution. Denote by $\mathcal{H} = \bigcap_{n \geq 1} \sigma(\tau_n, \tau_{n+1}, \ldots)$ the tail-σ-field of $\{\tau_i\}_{i \in \mathbb{N}}$.*

(a) *The stochastic process $\Lambda(t) := -\log \mathbb{P}(\tau_1 > t \mid \mathcal{H}), t \geq 0$, is a (possibly killed) Lévy subordinator.*

(b) *There exists a sequence of i.i.d. unit exponential random variables $\{E_i\}_{i \in \mathbb{N}}$, independent of Λ, such that almost surely*

$$\tau_i = \inf\{t > 0 : \Lambda(t) > E_i\}, \ i \in \mathbb{N}.$$

(c) *Denote by $x \mapsto \psi(x)$ the associated Bernstein function,[12] i.e. $\exp\{-t\psi(x)\} = \mathbb{E}[\exp\{-x\Lambda(t)\}]$, then*

$$\mathbb{P}(\boldsymbol{\tau} > \boldsymbol{t}) = \prod_{i=1}^{d} e^{-t_{\pi(i)}(\psi(i) - \psi(i-1))}$$

for each $d \geq 1$ and $\boldsymbol{\tau} = (\tau_1, \ldots, \tau_d)'$, $\boldsymbol{t} \in \mathbb{R}_+^d$ and a permutation π on $[d]$ with $t_{\pi(1)} \geq \ldots \geq t_{\pi(d)}$.

Proof. By De Finetti's Theorem, conditional on $\mathcal{H}$ the sequence $\{\tau_i\}_{i \in \mathbb{N}}$ is i.i.d., with distribution function $1 - \exp\{-\Lambda(t)\}$ for $\Lambda(t) := -\log \mathbb{P}(\tau_1 > t \mid \mathcal{H})$, see [50]. The claim on the variables $\{E_i\}_{i \in \mathbb{N}}$ can be established

---

[12]A Bernstein function ψ is characterized by a Lévy-triplet (a, b, ν) for $a, b \geq 0$ and a Lévy-measure ν on $(0, \infty)$ fulfilling the integrability condition $\int_{(0,\infty)} 1 \wedge v \nu(dv) < \infty$, where $\psi(x) = a 1_{(0,\infty)}(x) + bx + \int_{(0,\infty)} (1 - e^{-xv}) \nu(dv), x \geq 0$, see [48], [49].

with a modified distribution function, see [51], Prop. 2.1. Furthermore, the law of $\{\Lambda(t)\}_{t \geq 0}$ is almost surely uniquely determined by $\mathcal{H}$, and by [41], Chapter 3.3, it is a (possibly killed) Lévy subordinator with the claimed properties. □

The alternative stochastic model of extendible Marshall–Olkin distributions via the so-called Lévy-frailty construction in Thm. 4.2 has the advantage of being a *De Finetti model* for extendible sequences, which renders the approach independent of the dimension d. This solves not only the problem described in (b), but also provides an alternative simulation strategy, see [8] for a detailed account. The alternative simulation strategy has the advantage that its runtime scales linearly with increasing dimension, which makes it particularly interesting for large d. The approach comes with the drawback that a simulation bias is introduced as we can only sample the random walk corresponding to some embedding of Λ on a discrete time-grid. This bias, however, can be controlled through the step size of the discrete time-grid.

In the following we present five examples of Lévy-subordinators which can be used to define parametric one-factor Marshall–Olkin distributions.

Example 4.1 (Linear drift). *Let $\Lambda(t) = bt, t \geq 0$ for some $b > 0$, then τ corresponds to d independent exponentially distributed random variables with common rate b. A simple extension can be attained assuming a "global shock" $E \sim \text{Exp}(a)$, $a > 0$, which "kills" all entities. This corresponds to a (killed) Lévy-subordinator $\Lambda(t) = bt + \infty \cdot 1_{\{E \leq t\}}, t \geq 0$ with the convention $0 \cdot \infty = 0$. The corresponding Bernstein-function is $\psi(x) = a1_{(0,\infty)}(x) + bx$.*

This model is, e.g., implicitly used in [52]. A "global shock" can analogously be introduced in every Lévy-frailty model by assuming that Λ is "killed" — that is, sent to the absorbing state ∞ — at a rate $a > 0$, i.e. there exists an independent exponential random variable E with rate a and we assume that $\Lambda(t) = \infty$ for $t > E$. The corresponding new Bernstein-function can be attained by adding the term $a1_{(0,\infty)}(x)$ to the old one.

Example 4.2 (Compound Poisson subordinator). *Let $\Lambda(t) = bt + \sum_{k=1}^{N(t)} J_k$ for independent N and $\{J_k\}_{k \in \mathbb{N}}$, where the former is a classical Poisson-process with rate $\lambda > 0$ and the latter an i.i.d. family of random variables on $(0, \infty)$. The corresponding Bernstein-function is $\psi(x) = bx + \lambda(1 - \mathcal{L}(x; J_1))$, where $\mathcal{L}(x; J_1)$ is the Laplace-transformation corresponding to J_1.*

For a compound Poisson subordinator, defined as above, the number of jumps in the time-intervals $(0, t_1], (t_1, t_2], \ldots$ are independent and $\mathrm{Poi}(\lambda(t_k - t_{k-1}))$ distributed on $\mathbb{N}_0$, respectively, and the jth jump-size is J_j.

Example 4.3 (Gamma subordinator). *Let Λ have a Bernstein function of the form $\psi(x) = \alpha \ln(1 + x/\beta)$ for $\alpha, \beta > 0$. The corresponding increments $\Lambda(s) - \Lambda(t)$ are Gamma-distributed and can easily be sampled, see e.g. [41], Alg. 6.5 and Alg. 6.6, pp. 242–243.*

Example 4.4 (Inverse-Gaussian subordinator). *Let Λ have a Bernstein function of the form $\psi(x) = \beta(\sqrt{2x + \eta^2} - \eta)$ for $\beta, \eta > 0$. The corresponding increments $\Lambda(s) - \Lambda(t)$ are Inverse-Gaussian distributed and can easily be sampled, see e.g. [41], Alg. 6.10, p. 245.*

Example 4.5 (Stable subordinator). *Let Λ have a Bernstein function of the form $\psi(x) = x^\alpha$ for some $1 \geq \alpha > 0$. Then the increments $\Lambda(s) - \Lambda(t)$ belong to the class of stable distributions and can be sampled, see e.g. [41], Alg. 6.11, p. 246.*

Marshall–Olkin multi-factor models

The Lévy-frailty model has the serious drawback of being a one-factor model. This implies not only homogeneity with respect to marginal distributions, but also an exchangeable dependence structure. However, we can exploit that independent Lévy subordinators form a cone and we can consider the extended Lévy-frailty model, where $\boldsymbol{\tau}$ is defined by

$$\tau_i := \inf\{t > 0 : \Lambda_i(t) > E_i\}, \ i \in [d], \tag{14}$$

where $\Lambda_i, i \in [d]$, are Lévy subordinators from the cone spanned from independent Lévy subordinators $\Upsilon_1, \ldots, \Upsilon_n$ and $E_1, \ldots, E_d$ are i.i.d. unit exponentials, which are independent thereof. In the following, a result of [26] regarding this model is presented. Assume that $\boldsymbol{\Upsilon}$ is an n-dimensional vector of independent Lévy subordinators corresponding to Bernstein functions $\hat{\psi}_1, \ldots, \hat{\psi}_n$ and $\Theta = (\boldsymbol{\theta}_1, \ldots, \boldsymbol{\theta}_d) \in \mathbb{R}_+^{n \times d}$ is a matrix with non-negative entries. Define the process $\boldsymbol{\Lambda}$ by $\Lambda_i := \boldsymbol{\theta}_i' \boldsymbol{\Upsilon}, i \in [d]$.

Theorem 4.3. *Let $\boldsymbol{t} \geq 0$ and $\pi \in \mathcal{S}_d$ be a permutation with $t_{\pi(1)} \geq \ldots \geq t_{\pi(d)}$ and let $\boldsymbol{\tau}$ be defined as in Eq. (14). Then*

$$\mathbb{P}(\boldsymbol{\tau} > \boldsymbol{t}) = \exp\left\{ -\sum_{i=1}^{d} t_{\pi(i)} \sum_{k=1}^{n} \hat{\psi}_k\left(\sum_{j=1}^{i} \Theta_{k,\pi(j)}\right) - \hat{\psi}_k\left(\sum_{j=1}^{i-1} \Theta_{k,\pi(j)}\right)\right\}.$$

Furthermore, $\boldsymbol{\tau}$ has a Marshall–Olkin distribution.

Proof. See [26]. □

A slightly simplified extension with $n = 1$ has the interpretation of allowing inhomogeneous trigger rates in the original Lévy-frailty model, cf. [53]. Furthermore, a useful alternative representation of the vector in Thm. 4.3 can be attained as follows, cf. [41], Sec. 3.3.4: Let $\boldsymbol{\tau}^{(k)}$ be independent random vectors corresponding to Lévy-frailty models with inhomogeneous trigger rates $\boldsymbol{\theta}_k$ and trigger processes $\hat{\psi}_k$ for $k = 1, \ldots, n$. Then $\boldsymbol{\tau}$ has the survival function in Thm. 4.3, where $\boldsymbol{\tau}$ is defined by

$$\tau_i := \min\{\tau_i^{(k)} : k \in [n]\}, \ i \in [d].$$

Remark 4.4 (Constructing the full Marshall–Olkin class). The multi-factor Lévy-frailty construction is general enough to comprise the full family of Marshall–Olkin distributions. To this end, we use $m = 2^d - 1$ independent killed subordinators $\Upsilon^{(I)}(t) := \infty \mathbf{1}_{\{E_I \leq t\}}$ and $\Lambda^{(k)}(t) := \sum_{I:k \in I} \hat{\Lambda}^{(I)}(t)$, which is basically just a complicated way of writing the original Marshall–Olkin shock model, cf. Eq. (8). This construction is not unique in the class of Lévy-frailty models and provides an alternative proof of [54], Thm. 4.2.

Closely related, a hierarchical and h-extendible Marshall–Olkin law is constructed in [55] and [56]. The idea is to group the components according to some (economic) criterion (e.g., geographic region, industry segment, etc.). In the simplest case one has only one classification criterion, say for illustration purposes the industry segment, and each component is affected by a global and an industry specific factor. With respect to the factor model described in Thm. 4.3, assume that the components can be separated into J industry segments. Let $\Upsilon_1, \ldots, \Upsilon_J$ be independent Lévy subordinators, each corresponding to a specific segment. Furthermore, let Υ_0 be another independent Lévy subordinator corresponding to a global factor affecting all components. For component $i \in [d]$ which is in segment k, an individual trigger-processes Λ_i is defined using the weights $\boldsymbol{\theta}_i$ which are for $\alpha, \beta_k > 0$ defined by

$$\boldsymbol{\theta}_i = (\alpha, \underbrace{0, \ldots, 0}_{k-1 \text{ times}}, \beta_k, \underbrace{0, \ldots, 0}_{(J-k) \text{ times}})' \in \mathbb{R}_+^{J+1}$$

and by

$$\Lambda_i = \boldsymbol{\theta}_i' \boldsymbol{\Upsilon} = \sum_{k=0}^{n} \Theta_{k,i} \Upsilon_k.$$

This model is said to be h-extendible with two levels of hierarchy — meaning that there exists a σ-algebra $\mathcal{G}_0$ such that, conditional on this $\mathcal{G}_0$, the vector of default-times separates into independent groups and there exist group specific σ-algebras $\mathcal{G}_k$ such that the marginal group vectors of default-times are conditionally i.i.d., see [56]. For more levels of hierarchy, say one wants an additional regional classification, the model can be extended easily.

This model specification solves the problems (a), (b), and partially also (c), which were described at the beginning of this section:

(a) As shown in the previous paragraph, Marshall–Olkin distributions have the unique property that all marginal survival indicators are time-homogeneous Markovian. Therefore, simulation-studies on subportfolios can be performed efficiently using lower dimensional Markovian processes.

(b) The hierarchical construction gives an intuitive way to deal with portfolio restructuring. In case of a downsize, we can simply use the reduced model as each of the factors should be chosen in a way that they are (mostly) independent of the portfolio. If an additional component has to be modeled, one only has to specify factor-loadings corresponding to the "risk" regarding to each factor.

(c) Even though this model setup is not a copula ansatz, the factor approach offers a schematic picture of the inner- and outer-group dependence between components. In particular, it follows that the dependence, measured with the upper-tail dependence coefficient, between two components of the same group is higher than that of two components of different groups, see [55] for a similar result with temporal-, instead of spatial scaling of the underlying subordinators. However, the complete dependence structure, in form of the underlying copula, as well as the marginal distributions, are influenced by the specific weights. If only marginal distributions should be altered, this is possible by using a component specific factor. However, the choice of the marginal is restricted to the class of exponential distributions (as otherwise the Markov property is lost) and the minimal marginal rate is determined by the remaining weights.

In default modeling, the historical data is rarely substantial enough to perform goodness-of-fit tests for the chosen copula. Therefore, a good qualitative understanding of the schematic dependence is crucial. A slight modification of this model, which then partially solves (c), can be specified, if the loadings are assumed to be constant, e.g. $\alpha_i = \beta_i = 1$, and the group-components of the resulting vector are scaled with group specific scalar values to attain a group specific exponential-rate.

In Fig. 2, most of the distributional classes discussed in this paper are summarized in a schematic picture.

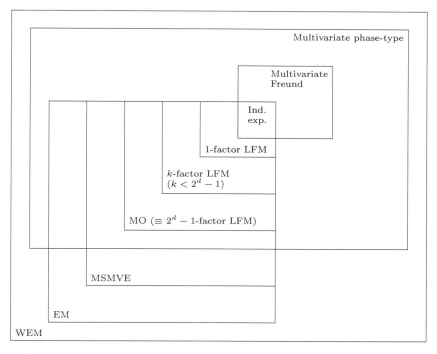

Fig. 2.   Venn-diagram of (selected) multivariate exponential, Phase-type distributions, and distributions fulfilling the WEM-property. See Chap. 2.2 as well as [41], [37], [35], [13] for details.

4.3. Case study: Iteration bias for selected multivariate distributions

In Thm. 3.1 it was highlighted that iterating bivariate (non-comonotonic) Gaussian-, Clayton-, or Frank-coupled exponential margins "kills" dependence asymptotically. In the first numerical case study, cf. Sec. 3.2, it was demonstrated that probabilities for "survival-of-all" events can divert significantly if "terminal one-shot" are compared to "terminal iterated" laws. Only distributions fulfilling the weak exponential minima property have the property that "survival-of-all" events have the same probability under the "terminal one-shot" and "terminal iterated" law.

In Thm. 4.1 it was shown that the "terminal one-shot" and the "terminal iterated" law are equal if and only if it is a Marshall–Olkin distribution. The purpose of this section is to underscore this statement with a second numerical case study.

The model

Before numerical results are presented, it is specified mathematically what was referred to loosely as the "terminal one-shot" and "terminal iterated" law. It is assumed that the multivariate probability and survival distribution of "mixed default/survival" events are replaced by corresponding events using discretely iterated survival indicators, i.e. instead of

$$\mathbb{P}\left(\left(\bigcap_{i \in I}\{\tau_i > k_i \Delta\}\right) \cap \left(\bigcap_{i \notin I}\{\tau_i \le k_i \Delta\}\right)\right)$$

we consider the probabilities

$$\mathbb{P}\left(\left(\bigcap_{i \in I}\{\tilde{Z}_i^{(\Delta)}(k_i) = 1\}\right) \cap \left(\bigcap_{i \notin I}\{\tilde{Z}_i^{(\Delta)}(k_i) = 0\}\right)\right),$$

where $\tilde{\boldsymbol{Z}}^{(\Delta)}$ is a (discrete-time) Markov-chain with i.i.d. multiplicative increments that are fully determined by

$$\tilde{\boldsymbol{Z}}^{(\Delta)}(1) \stackrel{d}{=} (1_{\{\tau_1 > \Delta\}}, \dots, 1_{\{\tau_d > \Delta\}})'.$$

This approach corresponds to the widespread industry-practice of defining a default distribution and iterating (multiplicative) i.i.d. increments of the corresponding survival-indicator for the step-size Δ through a discrete time grid up to the final horizon $T = N\Delta$.

The case study

It is assumed that $\Delta = 1$, $k_1 = 10$, and $k_2 \in \{5, 10\}$ for the event $\{\tau_1 > k_1 \Delta, \tau_2 > k_2 \Delta\}$ and the following distributions with common marginal rate $\lambda > 0$ are considered:

- *Marshall–Olkin:* A bivariate exchangeable Marshall–Olkin distribution with copula-parameter $\alpha_{MO} \in [0, 1]$, in the exchangeable Cuadras-Augé parameterization.
- *Gumbel:* A bivariate Gumbel distribution with parameter $\theta_{Gu} \in [1, \infty]$.
- *Clayton:* An exchangeable Clayton-coupled exponential distribution with parameter $\theta_{Cl} \geq -1$.
- *Frank:* An exchangeable Frank-coupled exponential distribution with parameter $\theta_{Fr} \in \mathbb{R}$.
- *Gaussian:* An exchangeable Gaussian-coupled exponential distribution with parameter $\rho_{Ga} \in [-1, 1]$.
- *t:* An exchangeable t-coupled exponential distribution for $\nu = 3$ degrees of freedom, parameter $\rho_t \in [-1, 1]$.

The marginal rates are assumed to be $\lambda_{SG} = 4.5\%$ (speculative grade) and the copula parameters are calibrated such that Kendall's τ equals 50%, see [30], pp. 260–261 for an overview on the Gumbel, Clayton, and Frank copula. Additionally, the following distributions are considered:

- *Freund:* An exchangeable Freund distribution with rates $\lambda_1 = \lambda_2 = \lambda_{SG}$ and $\eta_1 = \eta_2 = 3\lambda_{SG}$. The corresponding marginal distributions are not exponential and the resulting Kendall's τ is not set up to equal 50%.
- *Independent:* Two independent exponential random variables with common marginal rate $\lambda_{SG} > 0$. The independence copula is contained in all previously mentioned copulas families and is included as a reference point in this analysis.

In Tables 3 and 4 the results for both events can be observed. As expected, apart from Marshall–Olkin, Gumbel, Freund, and the independence copula, all copulas yield sizable differences for the "survival-of-all" event. For the "mixed default/survival" event only the Marshall–Olkin distribution and the independence copula yield equal "terminal one-shot" and "terminal iterated" probabilities. The effect is particularly strong for the Clayton- and Frank copula, where the "terminal iterated" probabilities are almost at the level of the independence copula.

Table 3.   Comparison of "terminal one-shot" and "terminal iterated" survival probabilities for $k_1 = 10$, $k_2 = 10$, and $\Delta = 1y$ (survival-of-all case).

Copula	Exact law	Iterated law	%Diff
Marshall–Olkin	0.5488	0.5488	0%
Gumbel	0.5292	0.5292	0%
Clayton	0.5051	0.4220	19.71%
Frank	0.5299	0.4388	20.77%
Gaussian	0.5205	0.4788	8.72%
t	0.5219	0.5053	3.28%
Independent	0.4066	0.4066	0%
Freund	0.4066	0.4066	0%

Table 4.   Comparison "terminal one-shot" and "terminal iterated" survival probabilities for $k_1 = 10$, $k_2 = 5$, and $\Delta = 1y$ (mixed default-survival case).

Copula	Exact law	Iterated law	%Diff
Marshall–Olkin	0.5916	0.5916	0%
Gumbel	0.6046	0.5809	4.09%
Clayton	0.5747	0.5187	10.79%
Frank	0.5965	0.5289	12.77%
Gaussian	0.5956	0.5525	7.8%
t	0.5956	0.5676	4.93%
Independent	0.5092	0.5092	0%
Freund	0.4885	0.5042	−3.13%

5. Conclusions

The problem of simulating the survival-indicator process on a discrete time-grid along with the remaining risk-factors has been investigated. It has been argued that, especially for high dimensions, good candidates for consistent and feasible joint simulations are continuous-time, time-homogeneous Markovian survival-indicators processes. In particular, the market practice of modeling the survival-indicator process as a discrete-time Markov chain with i.i.d. multiplicative increments, corresponding to a step distribution which is based on a copula-based ansatz, has been analyzed, criticized, and rectified. It has been shown theoretically and demonstrated with numerical examples that if we are concerned only with the "survival-of-all" event, then in order for "terminal one-shot" and "terminal iterated" probabilities to coincide, the multivariate default times distribution must fulfill the weak exponential minima property. In particular, this property is fulfilled for exponential margins with a survival copula of extreme-value kind. If we are concerned with more general "mixed default/survival" events, this consistency is only achieved by Marshall–Olkin distributions. A special emphasis is on warning practitioners who are iterating Gaussian-coupled exponential distributions, which fulfill neither the weak exponential minima property nor do they belong to the class of Marshall–Olkin distributions. Indeed, since these distributions lie in the domain of attraction of the independence copula, iterating them completely "kills" dependence asymptotically, when the number of iterations increases.

Appendix A. Alternative construction of Markovian processes

An alternative construction of continuous-time, time-homogeneous Markovian processes on finite state spaces is presented. The construction is a variation of the classical construction, where (state specifically) jumps are constructed with exponential waiting times and independent new (random) states, cf. Rmk. 2.1.

Theorem A.1. *Let Q be an intensity matrix of a continuous-time, time-homogeneous Markovian process on a finite state space S (which is w.l.o.g. assumed to be $\{1, \ldots, |S|\}$). Consider a process Z which is constructed as follows:*

(i) Let X_0 be the (possibly random) initial state, i.e. define $Z(0) := X_0$.

(ii) Assume that Z jumped $k \in \mathbb{N}_0$ times and define the time of the kth jump by T_k (for $k = 0$ we define $T_0 := 0$). Furthermore, assume that $Z(T_k) = i \in S$.

> *(a) For $j \in S \backslash \{i\}$ let $E_{k+1}^j \sim \mathrm{Exp}(q_{ij})$ be independent exponential random variables and define $E_{k+1}^i := \infty$. Assume additionally that $\boldsymbol{E}_{k+1}$, conditional on $Z(T_k)$, is independent of $\{\boldsymbol{E}_l : l \leq k\}$, $\boldsymbol{E}_{k+1} := (E_{k+1}^1, \ldots, E_{k+1}^d)'$.*
>
> *(b) Define $T_{k+1} := T_k + \min_{j \in S} E_{k+1}^j$ and $Z(t) := i \; \forall t \in (T_k, T_{k+1})$.*
>
> *(c) Define $Z(T_{k+1}) := \mathrm{argmin}_{j \in S} E_{k+1}^j$.*

(iii) Repeat (ii) either infinitely often or until an absorbing state is reached.

Then the process Z is time-homogeneous Markovian with intensity-matrix Q.

Proof. For $k \geq 0$ and $i \in S$ define $\mathbb{P}_k(\cdot) = \mathbb{P}(\cdot \mid Z(T_k) = i)$. It suffices to show that for every $k \geq 0$ and $i \in S$ the following three conditions hold, as this implies the classical construction:

(I) $\mathbb{P}_k(\min_{j \in S} E_{k+1}^j > t) = \exp\{q_{ii}t\} \ \forall t > 0$.

(II) $\mathbb{P}_k(\operatorname{argmin}_{j \in S \setminus \{i\}} E_{k+1}^j = j^\star) = -q_{ij^\star}/q_{ii} \ \forall j^\star \in S \setminus \{i\}$.

(III) The random variables $\min_{j \in S} E_{k+1}^j$ and $\operatorname{argmin}_{j \in S \setminus \{i\}} E_{k+1}^j$ are independent conditional on $\{Z(T_k) = i\}$.

Condition (I) holds as the minimum of independent exponential random variables is again exponential with the rate corresponding the sum of all rates. In this particular case this implies, conditional on $\{Z(T_k) = i\}$, $\min_{j \in S} E_{k+1}^j$ is exponential with rate

$$\sum_{j \in S \setminus \{i\}} q_{ij} \overset{(\star)}{=} -q_{ii},$$

where $(\star)$ follows because Q is an intensity matrix.

The following calculation shows that condition (II) hold:

$$\mathbb{P}_k \left(\operatorname*{argmin}_{j \in S \setminus \{i\}} E_{k+1}^j = j^\star \right) = \mathbb{P}_k \left(E_{k+1}^{j^\star} < \min_{j \in S \setminus \{i, j^\star\}} E_{k+1}^j \right)$$

$$\overset{(\star)}{=} \mathbb{E}_k \left[\exp \left\{ -E_{k+1}^{j^\star} \sum_{j \in S \setminus \{i, j^\star\}} q_{ij} \right\} \right]$$

$$\overset{(\dagger)}{=} \frac{q_{ij^\star}}{q_{ij^\star} + \sum_{j \in S \setminus \{i, j^\star\}} q_{ij}} \overset{(\ddagger)}{=} -\frac{q_{ij^\star}}{q_{ii}},$$

where $(\star)$ follows using the tower property conditioning on $E_{k+1}^{j^\star}$, $(\dagger)$ follows with the Laplace-transform of the exponential distribution, and $(\ddagger)$ follows using that Q has vanishing row sums.

Finally, the following calculate proves that condition (III) holds:

$$\mathbb{P}_k \left(\min_{j \in S \setminus \{i\}} E_{k+1}^j > t, \operatorname*{argmin}_{j \in S \setminus \{i\}} E_{k+1}^j = j^\star \right)$$

$$\overset{(\star)}{=} \mathbb{E}_k \left[1_{\{E_{k+1}^{j^\star} > t\}} \exp \left\{ -E_{k+1}^{j^\star} \sum_{j \in S \setminus \{i, j^\star\}} q_{ij} \right\} \right]$$

$$\overset{(\dagger)}{=} -\frac{q_{ij^\star}}{q_{ii}} \exp\{q_{ii}t\},$$

where $(\star)$ follows using the tower property conditioning on $E_{k+1}^{j^\star}$ and $(\dagger)$ follows using that for an exponential random variable E with rate $\eta > 0$

one has for $t, x > 0$

$$\mathbb{E}\left[1_{\{E > t\}} \exp\{-xE\}\right] = \int_t^\infty \eta \exp\{-(x + \eta)v\}dv$$
$$= \frac{\eta}{\eta + x} \exp\{-(x + \eta)t\}.$$

$\square$

Acknowledgments

We thank the anonymous referees and the handling editor for useful remarks. Valuable help by Annette Wenninger to organize the references is appreciated.

References

1. C. Albanese, T. Bellaj, G. Gimonet and G. Pietronero, Coherent global market simulations and securitization measures for counterparty credit risk, *Quantitative Finance* **11**, 1–20 (2011).
2. D. Brigo, A. Capponi and A. Pallavicini, Arbitrage-free bilateral counterparty risk valuation under collateralization and application to credit default swaps, *Mathematical Finance* **24**, 125–146 (2014).
3. D. Brigo, A. Pallavicini and M. Morini, *Counterparty Credit Risk, Collateral and Funding: With Pricing Cases for all Asset Classes* (Wiley, 2013).
4. Bank of International Settlement, Fundamental review of the trading book, consulting document, annex 4 (May 2012), Available at BIS.org.
5. T. R. Bielecki, S. Crépey and A. Herbertsson, Markov chain models of portfolio credit risk, in *The Oxford Handbook of Credit Derivatives*, eds. A. Lipton and A. Rennie (Oxford University Press, 2011) pp. 327–382.
6. A. Herbertsson and H. Rootzen, Pricing kth-to-default swaps under default contagion: the matrix-analytic approach, *Journal of Computational Finance* **12**, 49–78 (2008).
7. D. Brigo and K. Chourdakis, Consistent single-and multi-step sampling of multivariate arrival times: a characterization of self-chaining copulas, Available at SSRN: https://ssrn.com/abstract=2047474 or http://dx.doi.org/10.2139/ssrn.2047474 (April, 2012).
8. D. Brigo, J.-F. Mai and M. Scherer, Markov multi-variate survival indicators for default simulation as a new characterization of the Marshall–Olkin law, *Statistics & Probability Letters* **114**, 60–66 (2016).

9. P. Brémaud, *Markov chains*, Texts in applied mathematics, Vol. 31 (Springer, 1999).

10. P. Billingsley, *Probability and measure*, Wiley Series in Probability and Statistics, 3 edn. (Wiley, 1995).

11. A. W. Marshall and I. Olkin, A multivariate exponential distribution, *Journal of the American Statistical Association* **62**, 30–44 (March 1967).

12. H. Joe, *Multivariate Models and Multivariate Dependence Concepts* (CRC Press, 1997).

13. J. D. Esary and A. W. Marshall, Multivariate distributions with exponential minimums, *The Annals of Statistics* **2**, 84–96 (1974).

14. D. Brigo, A. Pallavicini and R. Torresetti, *Credit Models and the Crisis: A Journey into CDOs, Copulas, Correlations and Dynamic Models* (Wiley, 2010).

15. E. J. Gumbel, Bivariate exponential distributions, *Journal of the American Statistical Association* **55**, 698–707 (December 1960).

16. S. Kotz, N. Balakrishnan and N. L. Johnson, *Continuous multivariate distributions, models and applications (volume 1)* (John Wiley & Sons, 2000).

17. N. Ebrahimi and H. Zahedi, Testing for bivariate gumbel against bivariate new better than used in expectation, *Communications in Statistics - Theory and Methods* **18**, 1357–1371 (1989).

18. K. M. Nair and N. U. Nair, On characterizing the bivariate exponential and geometric distributions, *Annals of the institute of Statistical Mathematics* **40**, 267–271 (1988).

19. G. Gudendorf and J. Segers, Extreme-value copulas, in *Copula Theory and Its Applications*, eds. P. Jaworski, F. Durante, W. K. Härdle and T. Rychlik, Lecture Notes in Statistics, Vol. 198 (Springer, Berlin, Heidelberg, 2010) pp. 127–145.

20. J.-F. Mai, Extendibility of Marshall–Olkin distributions via Lévy subordinators and an application to portfolio credit risk, dissertation, Technische Universität München 2010. Available at http://mediatum.ub.tum.de?id=969547.

21. J.-C. Lu and G. K. Bhattacharyya, Inference procedures for a bivariate exponential model of Gumbel based on life test of component and system, *Journal of Statistical Planning and Inference* **27**, 383–396 (March 1991).

22. C. Genest and L.-P. Rivest, A characterization of Gumbel's family of extreme value distributions, *Statistics & Probability Letters* **8**, 207 (1989).

23. D. Brigo and K. Chourdakis, Counterparty risk for credit default swaps: impact of spread volatility and default correlation, *International Journal of Theoretical and Applied Finance* **12**, 1007–1026 (2009).

24. M. Morini, *Understanding and Managing Model Risk: A Practical Guide for Quants, Traders and Validators* (John Wiley & Sons, 2011).

25. J.-F. Mai and M. Scherer, Characterization of extendible distributions with exponential minima via processes that are infinitely divisible with respect to time, *Extremes* **17**, 77–95 (2014).

26. J.-F. Mai, Multivariate exponential distributions with latent factor structure and related topics, habilitation, Technische Universität München 2014.

27. D. K. Dey and J. Yan (eds.), *Extreme value modeling and risk analysis: methods and applications* (Chapman and Hall/CRC, 2015).

28. C. Fang, *Terminal vs. iterated statistics of multivariate default times*, UROP project report, Imperial College of London (2016), Supervised by Brigo, D.

29. M. Sibuya, Bivariate extreme statistics, *Annals of the Institute of Statistical Mathematics* **11**, 195–210 (1960).

30. P. Embrechts, R. Frey and A. McNeil, *Quantitative risk management*, Princeton Series in Finance, Vol. 5, revised edn. (Princeton University Press, 2015).

31. R. A. Jarrow and F. Yu, Counterparty risk and the pricing of defaultable securities, *The Journal of Finance* **56**, 1765–1799 (2001).

32. F. Yu, Correlated defaults in intensity-based models, *Mathematical Finance* **17**, 155–173 (2007).

33. I. Norros, A compensator representation of multivariate life length distributions, with applications, *Scandinavian Journal of Statistics* **13**, 99–112 (1986).

34. M. Shaked and G. J. Shanthikumar, The multivariate hazard construction, *Stochastic Processes and Their Applications* **24**, 241–258 (1987).

35. J. E. Freund, A bivariate extension of the exponential distribution, *Journal of the American Statistical Association* **56**, 971–977 (December 1961).

36. H. W. Block and A. P. Basu, A continuous, bivariate exponential extension, *Journal of the American Statistical Association* **69**, 1031–1037 (1974).

37. D. Assaf, N. A. Langberg, T. H. Savits and M. Shaked, Multivariate phase-type distributions, *Operations Research* **32**, 688–702 (1984).

38. J. Cai and H. Li, Conditional tail expectations for multivariate phase-type distributions, *Journal of Applied Probability* **42**, 810–825 (September 2005).

39. J.-F. Mai and M. Scherer, What makes dependence modeling challenging? Pitfalls and ways to circumvent them, *Statistics & Risk Modeling* **11**, 287–306 (2013).

40. B. C. Arnold, A characterization of the exponential distribution by multivariate geometric compounding, *Sankhyā: The Indian Journal of Statistics, Series A* **37**, 164–173 (1975).

41. J.-F. Mai and M. Scherer, *Simulating copulas: stochastic models, sampling algorithms and applications*, Series in Quantitative Finance, Vol. 6, 2 edn. (World Scientific, 2017).

42. K. Giesecke, A simple exponential model for dependent defaults, *The Journal of Fixed Income* **13**, 74–83 (2003).

43. F. Lindskog and A. J. McNeil, Common Poisson shock models: applications to insurance and credit risk modelling, *Astin Bulletin* **33**, 209–238 (2003).

44. D. Brigo, A. Pallavicini and R. Torresetti, Calibration of CDO tranches with the dynamical Generalized-Poisson Loss model, *Risk Magazine* (June 2007).

45. D. Brigo, A. Pallavicini and R. Torresetti, Cluster-based extension of the generalized Poisson loss dynamics and consistency with single names, *International Journal of Theoretical and Applied Finance* **10**, 607–632 (2007), Also in: Liption, A., Rennie, A. (Eds.), Credit Correlation – Life after Copulas, World Scientific, 2007.

46. T. R. Bielecki, A. Cousin, S. Crépey and A. Herbertsson, A bottom-up dynamic model of portfolio credit risk; part i: Markov copula perspective, Available at SSRN: https://ssrn.com/abstract=1844574 or http://dx.doi.org/10.2139/ssrn.1844574 (March, 2013).

47. T. R. Bielecki, A. Cousin, S. Crépey and A. Herbertsson, A bottom-up dynamic model of portfolio credit risk: part ii: common-shock interpretation, calibration and hedging issues, Available at SSRN: https://ssrn.com/abstract=2245130 or http://dx.doi.org/10.2139/ssrn.2245130 (March, 2013).

48. R. L. Schilling, R. Song and Z. Vondracek, *Bernstein functions*, De Gruyter Studies in Mathematics, Vol. 37 (De Gruyter, Berlin, 2010).

49. C. Berg, J. P. R. Christensen and P. Ressel, *Harmonic analysis on semigroups*, Graduate Texts in Mathematics, Vol. 100 (Springer New York, 1984).

50. D. J. Aldous, Exchangeability and related topics, in *École d'Été de Probabilités de Saint-Flour XIII — 1983*, ed. P. L. Hennequin (Springer Berlin Heidelberg, Berlin, Heidelberg, 1985) pp. 1–198.

51. L. Rüschendorf, On the distributional transform, Sklar's theorem, and the empirical copula process, *Journal of Statistical Planning and Inference* **139**, 3921–3927 (2009), Special Issue: The 8th Tartu Conference on Multivariate Statistics & The 6th Conference on Multivariate Distributions with Fixed Marginals.

52. X. Burtschell, J. Gregory and J.-P. Laurent, A comparative analysis of CDO pricing models under the factor copula framework, in *The Definitive Guide to CDOs*, ed. G. Meissner (Risk Books, 2009) pp. 389–427.

53. J. Engel, M. Scherer and L. Spiegelberg, One-factor lévy-frailty copulas with inhomogeneous trigger rates, in *Soft Methods for Data Science*, eds. M. B. Ferraro, P. Giordani, B. Vantaggi, M. Gagolewski, M. Ángeles Gil, P. Grzegorzewski and O. Hryniewicz (Springer International Publishing, 2017) pp. 205–212.

54. Y. Sun, R. Mendoza-Arriaga and V. Linetsky, Marshall–Olkin distributions, subordinators, efficient simulation, and applications to credit risk, Available at SSRN: https://ssrn.com/abstract=1702087 or http://dx.doi.org/10.2139/ssrn.1702087 (December, 2016).

55. J.-F. Mai and M. Scherer, Reparameterizing Marshall–Olkin copulas with applications to sampling, *Journal of Statistical Computation and Simulation* **81**, 59–78 (2011).

56. J.-F. Mai and M. Scherer, H-extendible copulas, *Journal of Multivariate Analysis* **110**, 151–160 (2012).

Chapter 4

Examples of Wrong-Way Risk in CVA Induced by Devaluations on Default

Damiano Brigo

Dept. of Mathematics – Mathematical Finance Group & Stochastic Analysis Group –
Imperial College,
London, SW7 2AZ, U.K.
damiano.brigo@imperial.ac.uk
www.imperial.ac.uk

Nicola Pede

Dept. of Mathematics – Mathematical Finance Group & Stochastic Analysis Group –
Imperial College,
London, SW7 2AZ, U.K.
n.pede13@imperial.ac.uk
www.imperial.ac.uk

When calculating *Credit Valuation Adjustment* (CVA), the interaction between the portfolio's exposure and the counterparty's credit worthiness is referred to as *Wrong-Way Risk* (WWR). Making the assumption that the Brownian motions driving both the market (exposure) and the (counterparty) credit risk-factors dynamics are correlated represents the simplest way of modeling the dependence structure between these two components. For many practical applications, however, such an approach may fail to account for the right amount of WWR, thus resulting in misestimates of the portfolio's CVA. We present a modeling framework where a further — and indeed stronger — source of market/credit dependence is introduced through devaluation jumps on the market risk–factors' dynamics. Such jumps happen upon the counterparty's default and are a particularly realistic feature to include in case of sovereign or systemically important counterparties. Moreover, we show that, in the special case where the focus is on FX/credit WWR, devaluation jumps provide an effective way of incorporating market information coming from quanto Credit Default Swap (CDS) basis spreads and we derive the corresponding CVA pricing equations as a system of coupled PDEs.

Keywords: credit default swaps, liquidity spread, liquidity premium, credit liquidity correlation, liquidity pricing, intensity models, reduced form models, capital asset pricing model, credit crisis, liquidity crisis.

MSC Codes: 60H10, 60J60, 91B70.

1. Introduction

Credit Valuation Adjustment (CVA) is a risk adjustment to the fair value of a portfolio of derivative contracts that reflects the credit risk of the common counterparty with which such contracts have been agreed. It accounts for the potential losses incurred due to the default of the counterparty before the contracts' expiries, and, as such, it heavily depends on the correct modeling of the credit risk factors, the market risk factors, and of the interaction between them. One of the main challenges in calculating CVA is indeed constituted by the lack of liquid market data to be used to infer risk-neutral credit/market joint distributions.

The calibration and approximation techniques showed in this paper can be used, for example, to connect currency devaluation with multi-currency Credit Default Swap (CDS) par-spreads (see [1] for more details) and that, in turn, allows to calculate CVA more accurately. The resulting FX/credit cross modeling improvement is crucial where the interaction between the counterparty credit and the FX is strong, i.e. with emerging market credits and systemically relevant counterparties where the right/wrong wayness is more relevant.

Throughout this work, we will often refer to the interaction between market and credit risk factors as *Wrong-Way Risk* (WWR).

1.1. *Overview of the modeling framework*

In this work, we will be using *unilateral*, as opposed to bilateral, CVA to illustrate the impact of WWR modeling. 'Unilateral' in this context means that we will be assuming only the counterparty to be a defaultable entity, while we neglect our own default risk. This assumption effectively amounts to considering ourselves as a default–free entity. On the one hand, the assumptions made in a bilateral framework are more realistic (both counterparties are subject to default risk), but, on the other hand, they introduce additional complexity in the form of the default time/default time interaction that, we think, might obfuscate the main points with respect to WWR modeling that this article wants to illustrate. We will use a probability space $(\Omega, \mathcal{F}, \mathbb{Q}, (\mathcal{F}_t, t \geq 0))$ satisfying the usual hypotheses. In particular $(\mathcal{F}_t, t \geq 0)$ is a filtration under which the dynamics of the risk factors are adapted and under which the default time of the reference entity is a stopping–time.

In the setting just described, CVA can be represented through the following formula:

$$\text{CVA}_t = \mathbb{E}_t \left[\left(\phi(\tau, X_\tau^{(0)}, \ldots, X_\tau^{(N)}) \right)^+ \frac{B_t}{B_\tau} \mathbb{1}_{\{\tau \leq T\}} \right] \tag{1}$$

where

- $\mathbb{E}_t [\cdot] = \mathbb{E} [\cdot | \mathcal{F}_t]$ is the expected value calculated with respect to the filtration $\mathcal{F}_t$;
- $(t, x_0, \ldots, x_N) \mapsto \phi(t, x_0, \ldots, x_N)$ is the value of the portfolio at time t and for a realization $x_0, \ldots, x_N$ of the market risk–factors;
- τ is the counterparty's default time;
- $(B_t, t \geq 0)$ is the numeraire associated to the pricing measure.

For the same reason, and given that the main examples shown throughout this work focus on equity/credit WWR and FX/credit WWR, we will neglect the randomness in interest rates and just assume deterministic interest rate term–structures. We will generically refer to the FX and equity related risk–factors as the *market risk–factors*.

The plan of the work is the following: in Section 2 we will present a PDE approach based on reduced-form framework for credit risk modeling. We will show how to handle the case where the market risk–factor is a jump-diffusion process and how to link the jump times to the default time of the counterparty. In Section 4 we will show how this approach is able to provide a more effective way to model WWR.

For the equity case, in Section 3 we will present an alternative credit modeling framework called AT1P and we will show how it naturally links equity and credit risk factors. In Section 4 we will compare this approach to the jump-diffusion approach in reduced-form framework.

We refer to [2] and [3] for a general overview on CVA modeling with applications to multiple asset classes. In [2], both unilateral and bilateral CVA calculation frameworks are described. Techniques for calculations of extreme CVA values, in the context of bilateral CVA modeling, have been recently shown in [4].

2. A PDE approach for both FX-driven and equity-driven WWR

In this section we present a modeling approach to handle the case where the counterparty's hazard rate is stochastic and where one additional market risk-factor is modeled as a jump-diffusion process whose only jump occurs upon the counterparty's default.

This approach can be effectively applied to both the case where the market risk-factor is an FX rate and to the case where the market risk-factor is an equity asset or index. Test cases with respect to both the examples are presented in Section 4.

2.1. *FX*

Let us consider the existence of multiple risk-neutral pricing measures, each of them linked to a specific currency. In this context, we will denote by $(B(t), t \geq 0)$ the money market account denominated in the (arbitrarily chosen) domestic currency, while we will denote by $(\hat{B}(t), t \geq 0)$ the money market account denominated in another foreign currency. Both of them are assumed deterministic. Furthermore, we will denote by Z_t the spot FX rate expressing the cost of one unit of foreign currency in the domestic currency and we will be using $(D_t, t \geq 0)$ for the default process:

$$D_t = \mathbb{1}_{\{\tau \leq t\}}, \quad t \geq 0. \tag{2}$$

Let us consider the following specification for the dynamics of $(Z_t, t \geq 0)$ and of the counterparty's hazard rate, $(\lambda_t, t \geq 0)$:

$$\mathrm{d}Y_t = a(b - Y_t)\,\mathrm{d}t + \sigma^Y\,\mathrm{d}W_t^Y, \ t \geq 0, \tag{3}$$

$$Y_0 = y, \tag{4}$$

$$\mathrm{d}Z_t = \mu^Z Z_t\,\mathrm{d}t + \sigma^Z Z_t\,\mathrm{d}W_t^Z + \gamma^Z Z_{t-}\,\mathrm{d}D_t, \ t \geq 0, \tag{5}$$

$$Z_0 = z, \tag{6}$$

$$\mathrm{d}\langle W^Y, W^Z \rangle_t = \rho\,\mathrm{d}t, \ t \geq 0, \tag{7}$$

$$\lambda_t = e^{Y_t}, \ t \geq 0. \tag{8}$$

An application of the generalized Itô formula (see [5]) allows us to write the $\mathbb{Q}$–dynamics of $(\mathrm{CVA}_t, t \geq 0)$. Using $f(t, Z_t, Y_t, D_t) = \mathrm{CVA}_t$:

$$
\begin{aligned}
\mathrm{d}f = {} & \partial_t f\,\mathrm{d}t + \partial_z f\left(\mu^Z z\,\mathrm{d}t + \sigma^Z z\,\mathrm{d}W_t^Z + \gamma^Z z\,\mathrm{d}D_t\right) \\
& + \partial_y f\left(a(b - Y_t)\,\mathrm{d}t + \sigma^Y\,\mathrm{d}W_t^Y\right) + \frac{1}{2}\left(\sigma^Z z\right)^2 \partial_{zz} f\,\mathrm{d}[Z, Z]_t \\
& + \frac{1}{2}\left(\sigma^Y\right)^2 \partial_{yy} f\,\mathrm{d}[Y, Y]_t + \rho\sigma^Z\sigma^Y z\partial_{zy} f\,\mathrm{d}[Z, Y]_t \\
& \hspace{5cm} + \Delta f\Delta D_t - \partial_z f\Delta Z_t \quad (9)
\end{aligned}
$$

where, with some abuse of notation, we have defined the jump-to-default term as

$$\Delta f := f(t, Z_{t-} + \Delta Z_t, Y_t, D_{t-} + \Delta D_t) - f(t, Z_{t-}, Y_t, D_{t-}). \tag{10}$$

Definition of Δf. Δf depends on the jumps of $(Z_t, t \geq 0)$ and $(D_t, t \geq 0)$. The two jump components, however, are driven by a common jump driver $((D_t, t \geq 0)$ itself, see Eq. (5)), and the jumps in the FX rate dynamics are given by

$$\Delta Z_t = \gamma^Z Z_{t-} \Delta D_t. \tag{11}$$

It must be noted that $(D_t, t \geq 0)$ starts at 0 and jumps to 1 at a single time, τ, upon default. This means, in particular, that $D_{t-} + \Delta D_t$ takes a value different from zero only upon default, and that, for all the times previous to that, the following equation holds:

$$D_t = 0, \quad t < \tau. \tag{12}$$

The first term in Eq. (10) can then be rewritten as

$$f(t, Z_{t-} + \Delta Z_t, Y_t, D_{t-} + \Delta D_t) = f(t, Z_{t-} + \Delta Z_t, Y_t, \Delta D_t) \tag{13}$$

and, considering also Eq. (11), the equation for Δf can be written as

$$\Delta f = f(t, (1 + \gamma^Z) Z_{t-}, Y_t, 1) - f(t, Z_{t-}, Y_t, 0). \tag{14}$$

Compensated martingale for $(D_t, t \geq 0)$. A compensator for $(D_t, t \geq 0)$ in the measure $\mathbb{Q}$ is defined as the process $(A_t, t \geq 0)$ such that $D_t - A_t$ is a $\mathbb{Q}$–martingale with respect to $(\mathcal{F}_t, t \geq 0)$. The compensator for $(D_t, t \geq 0)$ is given by (see Lemma 7.4.1.3 in [5])

$$\mathrm{d}A_t = \mathbb{1}_{\{\tau > t\}} \lambda_t \, \mathrm{d}t. \tag{15}$$

We define the resulting martingale as $(M_t, t \geq 0)$, where

$$M_t = D_t - A_t. \tag{16}$$

Consequently, the compensator of the term $\Delta f \Delta D_t$ in Eq. (9) can be written as

$$(1 - D_t) e^{Y_t} \Delta f \, \mathrm{d}t, \tag{17}$$

which, conditional on $\mathcal{F}_t$, $D_t = d$, $Z_{t-} = z$, and $Y_t = y$, is equal to

$$(1 - d) e^y \left(f(t, z(1 + \gamma^Z), y, 1) - f(t, z, y, 0) \right) \mathrm{d}t. \tag{18}$$

2.1.1. *No–arbitrage drift for the market risk–factor (FX)*

Any specification of the FX rate dynamics is subject to arbitrage constraints. One way to formulate them is by requiring that the Radon–Nikodym derivative defined by

$$L_t = \frac{Z_t \hat{B}_t}{Z_0 B_t}, \quad L_0 = 1. \tag{19}$$

is a martingale. The drift specification that satisfies such condition is provided by

$$\mu^Z = r(t) - \hat{r}(t) - \lambda_t \gamma^Z \mathbb{1}_{\{\tau > t\}} = r(t) - \hat{r}(t) - \lambda_t \gamma^Z (1 - D_t), \tag{20}$$

where $r(t)$ and $\hat{r}(t)$ are the — assumed deterministic — domestic and foreign short rates, respectively.

FX symmetry. Each FX rate links two risk-neutral pricing measures and, in deciding how to set its no-arbitrage drift, we arbitrarily started from one of them. We could as well have started from the other risk-neutral pricing measure. An argument equivalent to the one discussed in the previous paragraph would lead, in this case, to set a drift condition for the process $(X_t, t \geq 0)$ defined as $X_t = \frac{1}{Z_t}$. When the FX rate is specified as a geometric Brownian motion, it does not matter if we start from one measure or from the other one, as the two approaches lead to consistent results.

Despite the introduction of the jump in the FX rate dynamics, the consistency between $(X_t, t \geq 0)$ and $(Z_t, t \geq 0)$ is maintained. This is stated in the next proposition.

Prop 2.1 (FX symmetry and devaluation jumps). *Let us consider an FX rate process whose dynamics in the domestic risk-neutral measure $\mathbb{Q}$ is specified by Eq. (5) and whose drift is given by Eq. (20). Then the dynamics of the process $(X_t, t \geq 0)$ where $X_t = 1/z_t$ in the foreign risk–neutral measure $\hat{\mathbb{Q}}$ is given by*

$$dX_t = (\hat{r} - r)X_t \, dt - \sigma^Z X_t \, d\hat{W}_t^Z + X_{t-}\gamma^X \, d\hat{M}_t, \tag{21}$$

$$X_0 = \frac{1}{z},$$

where the devaluation rate for $(X_t, t \geq 0)$ is given by

$$\gamma^X = -\frac{\gamma^Z}{1 + \gamma^Z} \tag{22}$$

and where $(\hat{M}_t, t \geq 0)$ is the martingale defined in Eq. (16) expressed in $\hat{\mathbb{Q}}$. In particular, (21) is such that the Radon–Nikodym derivative $(\hat{L}_t, t \geq 0)$ defined by

$$\hat{L}_t = \frac{B_t}{\hat{B}_t} \frac{X_t}{X_0}, \quad \hat{L}_0 = 1. \tag{23}$$

is a $\hat{\mathbb{Q}}$-martingale.

A proof of this proposition is presented in [1].

It is now possible to write a Feynman–Kac PDE to compute the value of $\text{CVA}_t(T)$. Indeed, $(CVA_t, t \geq 0)$ is a $\mathbb{Q}$–price and, as such, it must locally grow at the rate r. Therefore, its drift must satisfy the following equation:

$$\partial_t f + \left(r - \hat{r} - \lambda_t \gamma^Z (1 - d) \right) z \partial_z f + a(b - Y_t) \partial_y f$$
$$+ \frac{1}{2} \left(\sigma^Z z \right)^2 \partial_{zz} f + \frac{1}{2} \left(\sigma^Y \right)^2 \partial_{yy} f + \rho \sigma^Z \sigma^Y z \partial_{zy} f$$
$$+ e^y (1 - d) \Delta f = rf \, dt,$$

where the explicit dependence of f on the state variables (x, y, t, d) has been omitted for clarity of reading. It is worth noting that, if it wasn't for the last term, this would be the typical PDE for default-free payoffs. Incidentally, this jump-to-default term is also the only term of the equation where the two default-specific components $f(t, (1 + \gamma^Z)z, y, 1)$ and $f(t, z, y, 0)$ appear together. In fact, by conditioning first on $d = 1$ and then on $d = 0$ we can decouple the two functions

$$u(t, z, y) := f(t, (1 + \gamma^Z)z, y, 1) \tag{24}$$
$$v(t, z, y) := f(t, z, y, 0) \tag{25}$$

and calculate them by solving iteratively two separate — lower dimension — PDE problems. We first solve for u, as for $d = 1$ the last term does not appear in the equation, and, once u has been calculated, we use it to solve for v.

Remark 2.1 (Interpretation of u and v). *The functions u and v account for the post-default and pre-default values respectively of a derivative with payoff $\phi(x, y, d)$. The price of this derivative can be written as*

$$V_t = \mathbb{1}_{\{\tau > t-\}} \mathbb{E}_t \left[\phi(X_T, Y_T, D_T) | X_t = x, Y_t = y, D_t = d \right], \tag{26}$$

where, due to the strong Markov property of the processes $(X_t, t \geq 0)$, $(Y_t, t \geq 0)$, and $(D_t, t \geq 0)$, the expected value on the right-hand side *can be written as*

$$f(t, x, y, d) = \mathbb{E}_t \left[\phi(X_T, Y_T, D_T) | X_t = x, Y_t = y, D_t = d \right]. \qquad (27)$$

This can be decomposed as $f(t, x, y, d) = \mathbb{1}_{\{d=1\}} u(t, x, y) + \mathbb{1}_{\{d=0\}} v(t, x, y)$
where

$$v(t, x, y) := \mathbb{E}_t \left[\phi(X_T, Y_T, D_T) | X_t = x, Y_t = y, D_t = 0 \right], \qquad (28)$$

$$u(t, x, y) := \mathbb{E}_t \left[\phi(X_T, Y_T, D_T) | X_t = x, Y_t = y, D_t = 1 \right], \qquad (29)$$

in fact

$$\begin{aligned}
f(t, x, y, d) &= \mathbb{E}_t \left[\phi(X_T, Y_T, D_T) | X_t = x, Y_t = y, D_t = d \right] \\
&= \mathbb{1}_{\{\tau > t\}} \mathbb{E}_t \left[\phi(X_T, Y_T, D_T) | X_t = x, Y_t = y, D_t = 0 \right] \\
&\quad + \mathbb{1}_{\{\tau \le t\}} \mathbb{E}_t \left[\phi(X_T, Y_T, D_T) | X_t = x, Y_t = y, D_t = 1 \right] \\
&= \mathbb{1}_{\{\tau > t\}} v(t, x, y) + \mathbb{1}_{\{\tau \le t\}} u(t, x, y) \qquad (30)
\end{aligned}$$

as both $\mathbb{1}_{\{\tau > t\}}$ *and* $\mathbb{1}_{\{\tau \le t\}}$ *are measurable in the* $\mathcal{F}_t$ *filtration. The derivative price can then be written as*

$$V_t = \mathbb{1}_{\{\tau > t\}} v(t, X_t, Y_t) + \Delta D_t u(t, X_t, Y_t), \qquad (31)$$

where we defined

$$\Delta D_t := \mathbb{1}_{\{\tau > t\}} - \mathbb{1}_{\{\tau > t-\}}. \qquad (32)$$

2.1.2. *Final conditions — CVA payoff*

The final conditions for functions u and v depend on the portfolio for which the CVA is going to be calculated. For the sake of explanation, let us consider a stylized portfolio where we expect to receive a single — deterministic and constant in time — cash-flow payment from our counterparty at maturity $T > 0$. The payment will be settled in a different currency from the one used to determine the risk-neutral pricing measure. Furthermore, we consider null interest rates. Under these assumptions, the CVA is given by:

$$\text{CVA}_0 = \mathbb{E}_0 \left[Z_\tau \mathbb{1}_{\{\tau \le T\}} \right]. \qquad (33)$$

The final conditions for the two functions can be written as:

$$u(T, z, y) = f(T, (1 + \gamma^Z)z, y, 1) = (1 + \gamma^Z)z, \qquad (34)$$

$$v(T, z, y) = f(T, z, y, 0) = 0. \qquad (35)$$

Remark 2.2 (Terminal condition for u). *In order to get a better understanding of the conditions set above, it might be useful to write the terminal condition for u in terms of conditioned expected values:*

$$u(T, z, y) = f(T, (1 + \gamma^Z)z, y, 1)$$

$$= \mathbb{E}\left[Z_\tau \mathbb{1}_{\{\tau \leq T\}} \middle| \mathcal{F}_T, \tau \leq T \right] = Z_\tau. \quad (36)$$

It is also worth recalling that $u(t, z, y)$ is only needed in solving v in the term representing the jump-on-default component Δf, that is, the change in value given to a default happening at t (see Remark 2.1).

The PDE problem that must be solved to obtain u is then given by

$$\partial_t u = -(r - \hat{r})z\partial_z u - a(b - y)\partial_y u - \frac{1}{2}\left(\sigma^Z x\right)^2 \partial_{zz} u$$

$$- \frac{1}{2}\left(\sigma^Y\right)^2 \partial_{yy} u - \rho\sigma^Z\sigma^Y z\partial_{zy} u, \quad (37a)$$

$$u(T, z, y) = (1 + \gamma^Z)z. \quad (37b)$$

Once the solution to this problem has been calculated, it can be used to solve the PDE for v, which is then given by

$$\partial_t v = -(r - \hat{r})z\partial_z v - a(b - y)\partial_y v - \frac{1}{2}\left(\sigma^Z z\right)^2 \partial_{zz} v$$

$$- \frac{1}{2}\left(\sigma^Y\right)^2 \partial_{yy} v - \rho\sigma^Z\sigma^Y z\partial_{zy} v$$

$$+ e^y \left(v - u - \gamma^Z z\partial_z v\right), \quad (38a)$$

$$v(T, z, y) = 0. \quad (38b)$$

Remark 2.3. From the PDE system (38) above it is clear why it makes sense to define $u(t, z, y) := f(t, (1 + \gamma^Z)z, y, 1)$ rather than $u(t, z, y) := f(t, z, y, 1)$ as we need the term in Δf.

2.2. *Equity*

We can use the same modeling approach presented in Section 2.1 to calculate the CVA of an equity portfolio. Similarly to the previous case, we consider an exponential Ornstein–Uhlenbeck process for the stochastic hazard rate and a geometric Brownian motion with a deterministic relative jump occurring upon the counterparty's default for the other relevant risk-factor — in this case, equity, rather than FX.

We specify the model as:

$$dS_t = \mu^S S_t \, dt + \sigma^S S_t \, dW_t^S + \gamma^S S_{t-} \, dD_t, \tag{39}$$

$$S_0 = s_0, \tag{40}$$

$$dY_t = a(b - Y_t) \, dt + \sigma^Y \, dW_t^Y, \tag{41}$$

$$Y_0 = y_0, \tag{42}$$

$$d \langle W^S, W^Y \rangle_t = \rho \, dt, \tag{43}$$

where the stochastic intensity of default $(\lambda_t, t \geq 0)$ is given — as in the FX/credit case — by

$$\lambda_t = e_t^Y. \tag{44}$$

2.2.1. No-arbitrage drift for the market risk-factor (equity)

The no-arbitrage condition on $(S_t, t \geq 0)$'s drift is given by requiring that its discounted price is a martingale. In formulas:

$$\mathbb{E}_t \left[\frac{S_T}{B_T} \right] = \frac{S_t}{B_t}. \tag{45}$$

Under the assumption of deterministic interest rates, that translates into

$$\mu^S = r(t) - \gamma^S (1 - D_t) \lambda_t. \tag{46}$$

2.2.2. Final conditions — CVA payoff

In this case, the prototype portfolio we are interested in studying is made of a single put option and it can be written as

$$V_t = (1 - R)\mathbb{E}_t \left[(K - S_\tau)^+ \mathbb{1}_{\{\tau \leq T\}} \right]. \tag{47}$$

This is a classic example of a position carrying a high level of WWR, and therefore highly sensitive to correlation assumptions. In order to get some intuition about the correlation effect in this type of trade, it might be useful to consider the limit case where the equity option's underlying is the counterparty's stock. In case of, for example, financial problems of the reference entity, these will be reflected in their balance account, and, arguably, in their stock price (that will decrease) and in their credit quality (that will decrease). Both these changes will affect the CVA of the position in the same direction (it will increase) and, moreover, they can reinforce each other. Therefore, taking in account their joint effect can have a dramatic effect on our calculations.

Given the strong Markov property of all the processes involved, the CVA can be assumed to be a function of their values at valuation time:

$$f(t, s, y, d) := (1 - R)\mathbb{E}_t \left[(K - S_\tau)^+ \mathbb{1}_{\{\tau \le T\}} \right]. \tag{48}$$

The PDE system that must be solved to calculate the value above can be deduced using the same techniques showed in Section 2.1 in the FX/credit case. Let us then define the conditioned on default and on survival values of f

$$u(t, s, y) := f(t, s(1 + \gamma^S), y, 1), \tag{49}$$
$$v(t, s, y) := f(t, s, y, 0), \tag{50}$$

so that the final conditions on the newly defined functions are given by

$$u(T, s, y) := f(T, s, y, 1) = (1 - R)(K - s), \tag{51}$$
$$v(T, s, y) := f(T, s, y, 0) = 0. \tag{52}$$

The same equations can therefore be used, with two important differences to take into account:

i) the no-arbitrage drift of the market risk-factor (equity in this case, rather than FX) is given by Eq. (46) rather than Eq. (20)
ii) the terminal conditions are given by Equations (51) and (52).

The resulting PDE system is then given by:

$$\partial_t u = -rs\partial_s u - a(b - y)\partial_y u - \frac{1}{2}\left(\sigma^S x\right)^2 \partial_{ss} u$$
$$- \frac{1}{2}\left(\sigma^Y\right)^2 \partial_{yy} u - \rho\sigma^S \sigma^Y s\partial_{sy} u \tag{53a}$$
$$u(T, s, y) = (1 - R)(K - s). \tag{53b}$$

Once the solution to this problem has been calculated, it can be used to solve the PDE for v, which is then given by

$$\partial_t v = -(r)s\partial_s v - a(b - y)\partial_y v - \frac{1}{2}\left(\sigma^S s\right)^2 \partial_{ss} v$$
$$- \frac{1}{2}\left(\sigma^Y\right)^2 \partial_{yy} v - \rho\sigma^S \sigma^Y s\partial_{sy} v$$
$$+ e^y \left(v - u - \gamma^S s\partial_s v\right) \tag{54a}$$
$$v(T, s, y) = 0. \tag{54b}$$

3. A structural approach for equity/credit WWR

In contrast to the reduced-form approach presented in Section 2.2, the model that we show in this section is based on a *structural* approach to credit modeling. Structural models seem a particularly good candidate to model WWR in equity as they naturally link credit risk and stock prices through their knowledge of balance account quantities. Furthermore, in the equity case, differently from the FX rate case, we don't have the constraint provided by the existence of quanto CDS basis. On the one hand, this means that we have more freedom on modeling the underlying process dynamics. For the sake of illustration, we will be using a simple *Geometric Brownian Motion* (GBM) to do that. On the other hand, by doing that we lose one "correlation" parameter (the devaluation-on-default parameter γ), thus delegating the whole WWR effect to the instantaneous correlation between the equity process and the credit process. The effects on WWR of this modeling choice are compared with reduced-form based models both in a purely diffusive case and in a jump-diffusion setting in Section 4 showing that, from a WWR perspective, a structural approach lies in between the other two modeling approaches.

3.1. *AT1P*

We will be using a model based on *Analytically Tractable First-Passage* (AT1P) to model the dependence between equity and credit in this section. AT1P was first presented in [6] where the authors extended the original Merton and Black Cox setting in two important ways:

i) by considering a deterministic non-flat barrier (see Eq. (57) below);
ii) by allowing for a time–dependent volatility for the firm value process (see Eq. (56) below).

$$\tau = \inf\{t \geq 0 : V_t \leq H(t)\}, \quad \inf \varnothing := +\infty. \tag{55}$$

This approach has been used by [7] for pricing Lehman equity swaps taking into account counterparty risk. In that work, the use of a random default barrier associated with misreporting and risk of fraud was also considered. Here we use the first version of the model, having deterministic non-flat barriers.

The reason for imposing a particular shape for the barrier and for considering different maturities for the outstanding debt of the firm is to make the calibration and pricing processes as feasible and practical as possible, as, under these assumptions, the survival probabilities of the firm can be recovered using closed form formulas. Indeed, the main achievement of the AT1P generalization relies in the possibility of calibrating the model to the whole CDS term structure of the firm, as illustrated for Parmalat and Lehman in [6], [7].

In addition to those works, we refer to [8] for the deduction of results on the pricing formulas for one-touch barriers in AT1P and to [9] for an application of AT1P to *Contingent Conversion* (CoCo) bond pricing, where a technique to calibrate AT1P to the spot stock price, the entity Tier-1 Capital Ratio, and the CDS spreads is introduced.

We present here a formulation of the model in the simplified setting where — in addition to the debt barrier being deterministic — the dividends and the risk free short rate are constant. The firm-value process is specified by the following SDE:

$$dV_t = (r - q)V_t \, dt + \sigma(t)V_t \, dW_t^V, \quad V_0 = v, \tag{56}$$

while a time-dependent barrier is parameterized as

$$\hat{H}(t) = He^{(r-q)t - B\int_0^t \sigma^2(s) \, ds}, \quad \hat{H}(0) = H_0. \tag{57}$$

Next, we look separately at how this model can be used to model both the credit risk and the equity component when calculating CVA for an equity trade.

3.1.1. *Credit risk*

Survival probabilities are given in closed-form expression as

$$\mathbb{Q}(\tau > T) = \Phi(d_1) - \left(\frac{H}{V_0}\right)^{2B-1} \Phi(d_2), \tag{58}$$

where τ is defined in (55) and where

$$d_1 := \frac{\log \frac{V_0}{H} + \frac{2B-1}{2}\int_0^T \sigma(s)^2 \, ds}{\left(\int_0^T \sigma(s)^2 \, ds\right)^{1/2}},$$

$$d_2 := d_1 - \frac{2\log \frac{V_0}{H}}{\left(\int_0^T \sigma(s)^2 \, ds\right)^{1/2}}.$$

Closed-form formulas for survival probabilities are sufficient for CDS calibration in a single-currency framework and when credit is assumed to be independent of interest rates.

3.1.2. *Equity price*

In AT1P an entity can default at any time and not only at its debt maturity. If we assume that the debt still has a clear single final maturity T and that early default is given by safety covenants, it is not unreasonable to model equity as an option on the firm value with maturity T that is killed if the default barrier is reached before T (see also [2], Chapter 8). We calculate the stock price E_t (in this framework) as a down-and-out European call option, that is

$$E_t = B(t)\mathbb{E}_t\left[\frac{\left(V_T - \hat{H}(T)\right)^+ \mathbb{1}_{\{\tau > T\}}}{B(T)}\right] = f(t, V_t). \tag{59}$$

This equation can be used both to calculate the stock price both inside a simulation of an equity-dependent payoff and in the calibration procedure.

A closed form solution for the price of the option is given for example in [8], see also the Equity chapter in [2]. The formula is as follows:

$$\begin{aligned}
f = \frac{B(t)}{B(T)}\Bigg(&V_t e^{\int_t^T (v(s) + \frac{\sigma(s)^2}{2})\,\mathrm{d}s}\left(1 - \Phi(d_3)\right) \\
&- \hat{H}(T)\left(1 - \Phi(d_4)\right) \\
&- \hat{H}(t)\left(\frac{\hat{H}(t)}{V_t}\right)^{2B} e^{\int_t^T (v(s) + \frac{\sigma(s)^2}{2})\,\mathrm{d}s}\left(1 - \Phi(d_5)\right) \\
&+ \hat{H}(T)\left(\frac{\hat{H}(t)}{V_t}\right)^{2B-1}\left(1 - \Phi(d_6)\right)\Bigg),
\end{aligned}$$

$$\tag{60}$$

where

$$v(t) = r - q - \frac{\sigma(t)^2}{2},$$

$$d_3 = \frac{\left(\log\frac{\hat{H}(T)}{H}\right)^+ - \log\frac{V_t}{H} - \int_t^T (v(s) + \sigma(s)^2)\,\mathrm{d}s}{\left(\int_t^T \sigma(s)^2\,\mathrm{d}s\right)^{1/2}},$$

$$d_4 = \frac{\left(\log\frac{\hat{H}(T)}{H}\right)^+ - \log\frac{V_t}{H} - \int_t^T (v(s))\,\mathrm{d}s}{\left(\int_t^T \sigma(s)^2\,\mathrm{d}s\right)^{1/2}},$$

$$d_5 = \frac{\left(\log \frac{\hat{H}(T)}{H}\right)^+ - \log \frac{\hat{H}(t)^2}{HV_t} - \int_t^T (v(s) + \sigma(s)^2) \, ds}{\left(\int_t^T \sigma(s)^2 \, ds\right)^{1/2}},$$

$$d_6 = \frac{\left(\log \frac{\hat{H}(T)}{H}\right)^+ - \log \frac{\hat{H}(t)^2}{HV_t} - \int_t^T (v(s)) \, ds}{\left(\int_t^T \sigma(s)^2 \, ds\right)^{1/2}}.$$

3.2. *Introducing WWR*

We introduce WWR in AT1P by allowing the option's underlying process, $(S_t, t \geq 0)$, to be correlated to the firm's stock price process. Similarly to the case analysed in Section 2.2 — but with the crucial difference that in this case we don't assume a jump-to-default component — the dynamics of the option's underlying process is specified as a geometric Brownian motion:

$$dS_t = rS_t \, dt + \sigma^S S_t \, dW_t^S, \quad S_t = S_0. \tag{61}$$

The instantaneous correlation between processes $(S_t, t \geq 0)$ and $(V_t, t \geq 0)$ is in principle difficult to estimate, because it mixes together information of fundamentally different nature: a stock price S, that is observable and traded, and a firm-value V, that is not traded, and that is only observable at most quarterly or at any planned balance account public disclosure. The link provided by firm-value and stock price in AT1P Eq. (60), however, proves useful in this respect, because it allows, as a first approximation, to use the empirical correlation between the firm's stock price and the underlying equity process as a firm-value/underlying equity's correlation estimate. In formulas, we will be assuming that:

$$d \langle W^S, W^V \rangle = d \langle W^S, W^E \rangle. \tag{62}$$

4. Results

In this section, we show results produced by all the models described in the previous sections and we compare the different "WWR power" that each model is able to provide. From an asset class perspective, we will present tests on FX/credit interaction and on equity/credit interaction. From a modeling perspective, we will test impact on WWR of instantaneous correlation in both reduced–form model and in structural model (the latter only in equity case). We will also test the devaluation jump impact on WWR.

We will use acronyms to refer to models. We will use *exponential Ornstein–Uhlenbeck* (expOU) for the reduced-form models, and we will denote by a (+J) the addition of jumps to default on the market risk factor. We will use AT1P for the structural model. A test/asset class summary is presented in Table 1.

Table 1.   Summary of the models tested in Section 4.

Test case	Reduced-form model		Structural model
	expOU	expOU+J	AT1P
FX	✓	✓	
Equity	✓	✓	✓

4.1. *Models calibrations*

For the tests presented in this section we considered a dummy set of market data. Specifically, we used

- a flat term-structure or CDS par-spreads (200 bps);
- a flat term-structure of zero rates (100 bps);
- we fixed the lognormal volatility of both equity and FX rate to 20%;
- in the reduced-form approach, we fixed the the normal volatility of the OU process driving the stochastic hazard rate to 50% and its speed of mean reversion speed to 0.001.

For the AT1P calibration, we refer to [7], [6] for further discussions and examples around calibration. We also refer to [9] for a more recent example and for a detailed description on how to use balance account information to fix the barrier level H_0 (see Eq. (57)).

For the expOU model calibration, we refer in particular to [1] where calibration is discussed extensively and where 3 year daily calibration outputs relying on quanto CDS spreads are presented.

4.2. *Equity WWR: Correlation impact*

In Figure 1 we present the correlation impact on CVA calculation of a portfolio consisting of a single trade: an ATM put option with expiry 1 year.

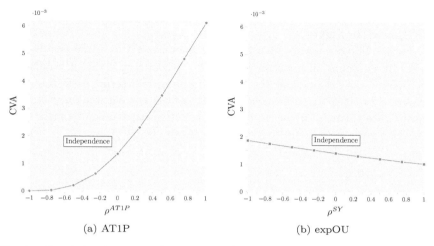

Fig. 1.   Correlation impact in the structural AT1P approach versus the reduced-form expOU approach. The CVA values obtained in case of credit-market independence (highlighted in both plots) are the same.

The agreement between the expOU and AT1P graphs on the zero correlation case provides a good safety check on the two model implementations.

It is worth highlighting that we used a common x-axis for the two charts, as indeed both the CVA calculated using expOU and using AT1P depend on a correlation parameter. The correlation parameter, however, has a very different interpretation in the two cases. As discussed in Section 3.2, in AT1P a possible proxy for it is provided by the equity/equity correlation between the counterparty and the option's underlying. In expOU, instead, the correlation to be used is the one between the counterparty's credit and the option's underlying. Unsurprisingly, the two parameters have opposite impact on CVA. Given the fact that the stochastic factor driving the asset value in AT1P is more directly linked to the counterparty's default time (through Eq. (55)) than the stochastic hazard rate in expOU, AT1P's correlation parameter has a stronger impact than expOU's correlation on WWR.

4.3. *Equity WWR: Devaluation impact*

The impact of the devaluation factor γ^S on the CVA of a portfolio constituted of a single 1-year expiry at-the-money equity put option is showed in Figure 2. The maximum CVA values that could be produced through correlation both in this reduced–form framework (for negative equity/credit correlation) and in AT1P (for positive equity/equity correlation) have been highlighted in Figure 2.

Figure 2 illustrates an unsurprising behavior of CVA — and that applies to credit modeling in general: the more a parameter is directly linked to the default time definition, the higher its impact in terms of WWR. This phenomenon is akin to tranche pricing, where correlation on stochastic hazard rate turns up being a much less effective mechanism to price CDO tranche than a copula approach (see, for example, [10]).

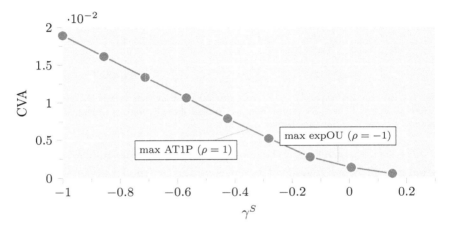

Fig. 2. Devaluation jump impact in reduced-form (BK) approach.

4.4. *FX WWR: FX Vega*

In this section, we show a less intuitive, yet of high practical importance, effect that correlation has on CVA pricing. For this example, we considered a portfolio constituted of a single cash payment that is settled in a currency different from the one in which the numeraire is denominated (like in Eq. (33)). We used a reduced-form approach to calculate the CVA with no devaluation jumps on the FX rate. The correlation impact on FX vega is plotted on Figure 3, showing that, when FX and credit are independent, the CVA has no FX Vega. This is not the case when instead we introduce correlation between FX and credit. The practical impact of having or not having correlation/dependence is in this case quite relevant as it would drastically change the hedging strategy to be used to hedge the CVA risk.

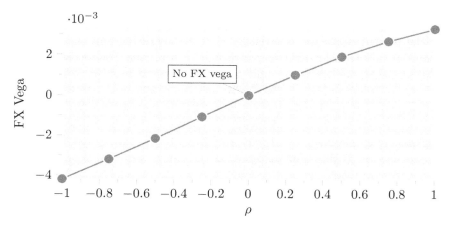

Fig. 3.   Correlation impact on FX vega in a reduced–form model (BK).

We can explain the results above in formulas: when **FX** and credit are independent — and considering zero interest rates for simplicity — the CVA from Eq. (33) can be written as:

$$\text{CVA}_0 = \mathbb{E}_0\left[X_\tau \mathbb{1}_{\{\tau \leq T\}}\right] = \int_0^T \mathbb{E}_0\left[X_s\right] \mathbb{Q}(s \leq \tau < s + \mathrm{d}s)$$

$$= X_0 \mathbb{Q}(\tau \leq T) \quad (63)$$

showing in fact no dependence on $(X_t, t \geq 0)$ dynamics. It is worth nothing that the same would happen also for more complicated derivatives as far as their only dependence on the FX rate is given by a mismatch in the pricing/payment currencies. Let us consider a derivative paying off an amount $\phi(Y_T)$ at T if the counterparty has not defaulted before T, where $(Y_t, t \geq 0)$ is a non-FX market risk factor. CVA can be written in this case as:

$$\text{CVA}_0 = \mathbb{E}_0\left[\phi(Y_T)X_\tau \mathbb{1}_{\{\tau \leq T\}}\right]$$

$$= \int_0^T \mathbb{E}_0\left[\phi(Y_s)X_s\right] \mathbb{Q}(s \leq \tau < s + \mathrm{d}s)$$

$$= X_0 \int_0^T \hat{\mathbb{E}}_0\left[\phi(Y_s)\right] \mathbb{Q}(s \leq \tau < s + \mathrm{d}s) \quad (64)$$

where we denoted as $\hat{\mathbb{E}}_0\left[\cdot\right]$ the expected value calculated in the payment currency pricing measure. The formula shows, again, no dependence on $(X_t, t \geq 0)$ dynamics.

5. Conclusions

In the present work, we investigated different modeling approaches to account for the credit/market dependence in CVA pricing. We focused on two distinct cases, one where the only market risk-factor was the FX rate and one where the only market risk-factor was the equity asset. In both cases, we showed how to calculate CVA in a PDE framework using a reduced-form approach for credit modeling and we investigated the impact that the inclusion of a default-driven devaluation jump to the market risk-factor dynamics has on WWR. Furthermore, in the equity case, we showed how a structural approach can also be effectively used to model the WWR.

Consistently with our intuition, the more directly a given modeling approach links the credit risk component to the market risk component, the higher is the variation in WWR that can be achieved by adopting it. In particular, delegating the whole credit/market dependence to instantaneous correlation provides the smallest range of WWR variation, while the inclusion of a jump-to-default effect on the market risk factor provides the largest one, with the structural approach — in the equity case — lying somewhere in between these two extreme cases.

In future works, we plan to include testing with more realistic portfolios, where impacts coming from variations on moneyness can be studied and, possibly, we will introduce a modeling approach that could consistently account for the observed skew in the market risk factor.

References

1. D. Brigo, N. Pede and A. Petrelli, Multi-Currency Credit Default Swaps: Quanto Effects and FX Devaluation Jumps https://papers.ssrn.com/sol3/papers.cfm?abstract_id=2703605, (2015).
2. D. Brigo, M. Morini and A. Pallavicini, *Counterparty Credit Risk, Collateral and Funding: With Pricing Cases for all Asset Classes* (Wiley, 2013).
3. G. Cesari and L. Gordon, *Modelling, Pricing, and Hedging Counterparty Credit Exposure* (Springer, 2006).
4. M. Scherer and T. Schulz, Extremal dependence for bilateral credit valuation adjustments, *International Journal of Theoretical and Applied Finance* **19**, 7 (2016).
5. M. Jeanblanc, M. Yor and M. Chesney, *Mathematical Methods for Financial Markets* (Springer, 2009).

6. D. Brigo and M. Tarenghi, Credit Defaulty Swap Calibration and Equity Swap Valuation under Counterparty Risk with a Tractable Structural Model, in *Proceedings of the FEA 2004 Conference at MIT*, 2004.

7. D. Brigo, M. Morini and M. Tarenghi, Credit Calibration with Structural Models and Equity Return Swap valuation under Counterparty Risk, in *Credit Risk Frontiers: Sub- prime crisis, Pricing and Hedging, CVA, MBS, Ratings and Liquidity*, ed. Bielecki, T., Brigo, D., and Patras, F. (Wiley, 2010) pp. 457–484.

8. F. Rapisarda, Barriers Option on Underlyings with Time–Dependent Parameters: a Perturbation Approach `https://papers.ssrn.com/sol3/papers.cfm?abstract_id=682184`, (2003), Technical report, available at SSRN.com.

9. D. Brigo, J. Garcia and N. Pede, CoCo Bond Pricing with Credit and Equity Calibrated First-Passage Firm Value Models, *International Journal of Theoretical and Applied Finance* **18**, 3 (2015) pp. 1550015–1550030.

10. D. Brigo and F. Mercurio, *Interest Rate Models — Theory and Practice: With Smile, Inflation and Credit*, second edn. (Springer, 2006).

Chapter 5

Implied Distributions from Risk-Reversals and Brexit/Trump Predictions

Iain J. Clark

Efficient Frontier Consulting Ltd.,
Level39 Technology Accelerator,
One Canada Square, London E14 5AB, U.K.
iain.clark@efficientfrontierconsulting.com
www.efficientfrontierconsulting.com

Saeed Amen

Cuemacro Ltd.,
Level39 Technology Accelerator,
One Canada Square, London E14 5AB, U.K.
saeed@cuemacro.com
www.cuemacro.com

In the 12 months from the middle of June 2016 to the middle of June 2017, a number of events occurred in a relatively short period of time, all of which either had, or had the potential to have, a considerably volatile impact upon financial markets.

The events referred to here are the Brexit referendum (23 June 2016), the US election (8 November 2016), the 2017 French elections (23 April and 7 May 2017) and the surprise 2017 UK parliamentary election (8 June 2017).

All of these events — the Brexit referendum and the Trump election in particular — were notable both for their impact upon financial markets after the event and the degree to which the markets failed to anticipate these events. A natural question to ask is whether these could have been predicted, given information freely available in the financial markets beforehand. In this paper, we focus on market expectations for price action around Brexit and the Trump election, based on information available in the traded foreign exchange options market.

Keywords: Brexit, Trump, foreign exchange options, implied distributions, forecasting, event risk.

1. Introduction

The year 2016 was notable for two major events in financial markets and world politics: Brexit and Trump. By these, we mean the UK referendum held on 23 June 2016 as to whether the UK should remain in the European

Union [EU] or leave it, and the US election on 8 November 2016 in which Donald Trump, once a relative outsider for the office of the President, won the election as Republican Party presidential nominee against the Democratic candidate Hillary Clinton.

These events share certain factors: they were both originally viewed as very unlikely from the viewpoint of mainstream political and economic commentary, but in the period of time before the UK referendum and the US election, both campaigns (for Brexit and for Trump) managed to marshal enough popular sentiment to achieve the result they sought.

After these two surprise results, commentators naturally turned their attention to two questions. Firstly, potentially using information available in financial markets or betting markets, could these results have been better predicted? Secondly, could similar techniques be used to assess the probability of similar unlikely but potentially very market-sensitive events occurring in 2017?

One natural possibility to analyse in the second quarter of 2017, as a potential consequence of the continuation of Brexit/Trump populism spreading to the Eurozone, was the possibility of the election of Marine Le Pen in the French elections held in two rounds on 23 April and 7 May 2017, which was won convincingly by Emmanuel Macron in the second round. A second and unexpected opportunity for modeling political event risk arose on 18 April 2017, when Theresa May (UK Prime Minister since 13 July 2016, following the Brexit referendum) announced that a UK general election would be held on 8 June 2017. It was generally felt beforehand that her position was unassailable, however the result was a net loss of thirteen seats for the Conservative Party, which was then no longer able to govern with an outright majority and needed to form a minority government supported by the Conservative-DUP agreement.

Our contribution to this volume seeks to empirically investigate the implied probability distributions around these event dates. We have already considered the case of Brexit [1] and we shall review our analysis herein, and then extend the analysis to Trump and the 2017 elections mentioned above.

2. Literature Review

We know from Breeden and Litzenberger [2] that if we know the price of European options on a tradable asset at all strikes, for a specific time to expiry T, then we can infer the future risk-neutral probability distribution for that asset at the future time T. This is described with reference to foreign exchange [FX] markets in Malz [3]. An application of this principle is made by the same author [4] in connection with the specific example of the British pound/Deutsche Mark exchange rate in the European Exchange Rate Mechanism. More recently, in other works [5]–[8], the case of EURCHF is considered, which between 6 September 2011 to 15 January 2015 had an effective floor maintained at 1.20 Swiss francs per Euro due to Swiss National Bank policy and intervention in currency markets.

As well as our own work [1], Dupire [9] and Hanke *et al.* [10] use similar methods to model potential FX moves around the dates of the Brexit referendum and the 2016 US election (specifically considering the FX example of the Mexican peso quoted against the US dollar). Dupire [9] also discusses the 2017 French elections, with respect to equity markets, which have a traded market in volatility through the VIX [11].

It is therefore clear that there is a historical body of work that analyses the short-dated volatility skew in FX markets in order to construct implied distributions for currency exchange rates at various time horizons of interest, aligned with real world events subject to political event risk on those dates. This is the scope of this work.

3. Method

Historical spot and implied volatility quotes have been obtained from Bloomberg (`www.bloomberg.com`) for various currency pairs (EURUSD, GBPUSD, USDMXN) together with historical timeseries of bookmaker quotes from the Oddschecker web site (`www.oddschecker.com`) for bets on the event that the UK votes to leave the EU.

Spot market quotes are merely the price in units of domestic currency of one unit of foreign currency. Volatility quotes, however, are more complex. At-the-money straddles and 25-delta and 10-delta strangles and risk reversals with expiries corresponding to the overnight maturity, 1, 2 and 3 weeks, and at 1, 2, 3, 6 and 12 months.

For each expiry T_j, we have five market quotes from the volatility surface: σ_{ATM}, $\sigma_{25-d-SS}$, $\sigma_{10-d-SS}$, $\sigma_{25-d-RR}$ and $\sigma_{10-d-RR}$, where σ_{x-d-SS} denotes the x-delta smile strangle and σ_{x-d-RR} denotes the x-delta risk reversal, both expressed in units of volatility; see [12]. Consequently, we have five implied volatilities σ_{10-d-P}, σ_{25-d-P}, σ_{ATM}, σ_{25-d-C}

and σ_{10-d-C} satisfying

$$\sigma_{x-d-SS} = \frac{1}{2}[\sigma_{x-d-C} + \sigma_{x-d-P}] - \sigma_{ATM}, \tag{1a}$$

$$\sigma_{x-d-RR} = \sigma_{x-d-C} - \sigma_{x-d-P}, \tag{1b}$$

where $x \in \{25, 10\}$ and with the strikes K_{10-d-P}, K_{25-d-P}, K_{ATM}, K_{25-d-C} and K_{10-d-C} chosen such that

$$\sigma_{\text{imp}}(K_i) = \sigma_i, \tag{2a}$$

$$\Delta(-1, K_{x-d-P}, T, \sigma_{x-d-P}) = -x/100, \tag{2b}$$

$$\Delta(+1, K_{x-d-C}, T, \sigma_{x-d-C}) = x/100, \tag{2c}$$

$$\Delta(+1, K_{ATM}, T, \sigma_{ATM}) + \Delta(-1, K_{ATM}, T, \sigma_{ATM}) = 0, \tag{2d}$$

with $\omega = -1$ for a put and $\omega = +1$ for a call in

$$\Delta(\omega, K, T, \sigma) = \begin{cases} \omega N(\omega d_1), & \text{for GBPUSD}, \\ \omega \frac{K}{F_{0,T}} N(\omega d_2), & \text{for EURGBP}. \end{cases} \tag{3}$$

As we have five implied volatilities available for each maturity we have sufficiently many data points to interpolate between, or to calibrate a mixture model to the market.

Premium adjusted deltas are used for EURGBP and USDMXN but not for GBPUSD or EURUSD in (3), following usual FX market conventions [12]. In all cases we solve numerically for K_i to obtain a strike based representation for the volatility surface which we then extend to a full volatility surface $\sigma_{\text{imp}}(K, T)$ using flat forward volatility interpolation in the temporal dimension, and polynomial in delta interpolation in the moneyness dimension, to account for smile. For flat forward volatility interpolation in time, for interpolating volatility at time t in between two prespecified tenors t_1 and t_2, we use

$$\sigma(t) = \sqrt{\frac{t_2(t - t_1)}{t(t_2 - t_1)}\sigma^2(t_2) + \frac{t_1(t_2 - t)}{t(t_2 - t_1)}\sigma^2(t_1)}. \tag{4}$$

For polynomial in delta interpolation we use an expression of the form

$$\sigma_X(K) = \exp(f(\ln(F_{0,T}/K))) \tag{5a}$$

with

$$f(x) = \sum_{i=0}^{4} c_i[\delta(x)]^i \tag{5b}$$

where $F_{0,T}$ is the T-forward, $\sigma_0 = \exp(c_0)$ and

$$\delta(x) = N(x/(\sigma_0\sqrt{T})). \tag{5c}$$

Note that we first interpolate in time, for each of the five points on the smile, and then we interpolate in strike, thereby obtaining a volatility surface $\sigma(K,T)$, which immediately gives call prices for all strikes K and tenors T

$$C(K,T) = S_0 e^{-r^f T} N(d_1) - K e^{-r^d T} N(d_2) \tag{6a}$$

using

$$d_{1,2} = \frac{\ln\left(\frac{F_{0,T}}{K}\right) \pm \frac{1}{2}[\sigma(K,T)]^2 T}{\sigma(K,T)\sqrt{T}}. \tag{6b}$$

Once we have this, we can employ Breeden-Litzenberger [2] to obtain the implied distribution for the terminal FX spot rate S_T in the (domestic) risk-neutral measure

$$f_{S_T}^d(K) = e^{r^d T} \frac{\partial^2 C(K,T)}{\partial K^2}. \tag{7}$$

Note that the risk-free rate r^d is determined separately for each maturity given the underlying yield curve, rather than being presumed constant.

As well as the empirical approach based around the Breeden-Litzenberger analysis above, we construct a mixture model, as described in [1] and references therein, which has a specific probability P_E of a **risk event** (such as a vote for Brexit, Trump, Le Pen or a vote against a Theresa May majority government) on the referendum/election date which we expect the market could well be sensitive to, and thereby associated with an event risk potentially likely to cause a jump in FX rates. We let T^* denote the time to that referendum/election date and use P_{NE} to denote the probability of no such risk event happening (clearly $P_E + P_{NE} = 1$).

In the case of a vote for a risk event (such as one of the above), we model this with a post-event exchange rate S_{T^*} by integrating the stochastic process $dS_t = \mu_E S_t dt + \sigma_E S_t dW_t$ from 0 to T^*, with drift and volatility terms μ_E and σ_E. If, however, the risk event does not come to pass, we model the distribution for S_{T^*} using Black-Scholes $dS_t = \mu_{NE} S_t dt + \sigma_{NE} S_t dW_t$ with a compensated drift μ_{NE} and a "no risk event" volatility σ_{NE} (both σ_E and σ_{NE} are annualized volatilities).

By risk-neutrality, we require

$$F_{0,T^*} = \mathbb{E}^d[S_{T^*}] = (1 - P_E)S_0 \exp(\mu_{NE}T^*) + P_E S_0 \exp(\mu_E T^*), \tag{8}$$

so the "no risk event" scenario has a terminal distribution for S_{T^*} equal to that of a Black-Scholes model with compensated risk-neutral drift term

$$\mu_{NE} = \frac{1}{T^*} \ln \left(\frac{F_{0,T^*} - P_E S_0 \exp(\mu_L T^*)}{S_0(1 - P_E)} \right). \tag{9}$$

We write the terminal distribution of the FX rate under the mixture model

$$S_{T^*} = \begin{cases} S_0 \exp\left((\mu_{NE} - \frac{1}{2}\sigma_{NE}^2)T^* + \sigma_{NE}W_{T^*}\right), & \text{with probability } 1 - P_E, \\ S_0 \exp\left((\mu_E - \frac{1}{2}\sigma_E^2)T^* + \sigma_E W_{T^*}\right), & \text{with probability } P_E. \end{cases} \tag{10}$$

Valuation of any European option with strike K is simply obtained by taking a weighted sum of the two Black-Scholes prices corresponding to integration of the payout function over the two density kernels.

Integrating the expression in the second case of (10) yields

$$S_{T^*,E} = S_E \exp\left(\left(\sigma_E \xi \sqrt{T^*} - \frac{1}{2}\sigma_E^2 T^* \right) \right), \tag{11}$$

where $S_E = S_0 \exp(\mu_E T^*)$ denotes the point estimate for the FX rate under the "risk event" scenario and $\xi \sim N(0,1)$, i.e. ξ is normally distributed.

We use market volatility surfaces as described earlier to estimate risk event probabilities P_E based on the observed skew. Since we have five implied volatilities at each time slice, we conduct a least squares calibration of the parameter set $\{P_E, S_E, \sigma_E, \sigma_{NE}\}$ using Levenberg-Marquardt optimization.

4. Results

4.1. *2016 Brexit referendum*

As already presented elsewhere in the literature [1], Figures 1 and 2 show implied densities for GBPUSD and EURGBP respectively from 1 May 2015 to 23 June 2016 for options expiring the day after the Brexit referendum date, and also the implied density as seen on Friday 24 June 2016 for the FX rate one business day later. These results suggest probability mass for GBPUSD between 1.10 and 1.30, and for EURGBP between 0.825 and 0.95 at the referendum date.

Nothing in the above provides directional support for making the claim that a "leave" vote in the Brexit referendum need be associated with the lower mode for the GBPUSD distribution, of course. In order to make a case for this, we have collected information from betting markets from the Oddschecker web site (www.oddschecker.com), an odds comparison web site where prices for digital bets on certain political events are published (and tradable). The raw data, expressed as betting odds, is transformed into an implied probability for "leave".

By considering the historical behavior of moves in FX spot relative to absolute changes in the betting market implied odds of a "leave" vote, displayed in Figure 3, we see that a 1% increase in the probability of a "leave" vote is correlated with a 0.16% decrease in GBPUSD. This we contend suggests that the probability mass for GBPUSD between 1.10 and 1.30 (and for EURGBP between 0.825 and 0.95) can be associated with the regime in which the actual Brexit vote is for "leave" on the referendum date.

In Tables 1 and 2 we see the parameters for the calibrated mixture model for each analysis date, where we show the implied probability P_E of a "leave" vote and the point estimate S_E for the FX spot price in the event of a Brexit "leave" vote, together with the expected GBP percentage appreciation $S_E/S_0 - 1$ (negative numbers, indicating devaluation in the event of a Brexit "leave" vote) and a 95% confidence interval for the realized post-referendum FX spot rate for GBPUSD in the event of a "leave vote", together with "remain" and "leave" volatilities σ_{NE} and σ_E respectively (corresponding to no risk event and risk event respectively).

In Figure 4 we show the "leave" point estimate S_E and the "remain" point estimate S_{NE} together with the GBPUSD FX spot rate S_0 on each trading day, from 24 February to 22 June 2016, and in Figure 5 we show the mixture model implied "leave" probability P_E together with the two volatilities σ_E and σ_{NE}, also from 24 February to 22 June 2016.

We can see in these two figures that the implied "leave" probability varied between 15.3% and 45.3% during the period of analysis, with an average level of 30.6%, with a considerable amount of uncertainty from late April 2016 onwards (reflecting the market confusion during the approach to the referendum). From 25 June 2016 onwards, i.e. a month before the referendum date, we see a clear upward trend in both "leave" and "remain" volatilities σ_E and σ_{NE}, and an increasing separation between the point estimates S_E and S_{NE} for the "leave" and "remain" states. While there is some parameter uncertainty, perhaps not surprisingly given the uncertainty in the market, the average value of the estimate S_L over the two weeks (ten business days) before the referendum was 1.3727, very consistent indeed with the actual FX spot level decline from 1.4877 to 1.3622 which was realized after the announcement of the "leave" vote.

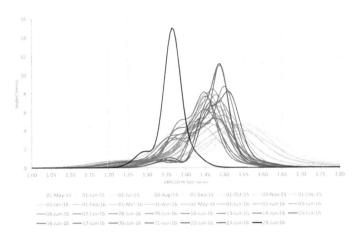

Fig. 1.   GBPUSD implied densities for the Brexit referendum date from 1 May 2015 to 23 June 2016, sampled monthly from 1 May 2015 to 1 June 2016, then sampled daily, and for the next business day on 24 June 2016 (Source: [1]).

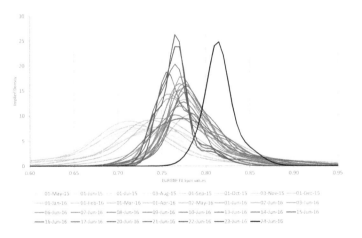

Fig. 2.   EURGBP implied densities for the Brexit referendum date from 1 May 2015 to 23 June 2016, sampled monthly from 1 May 2015 to 1 June 2016, then sampled daily, and for the next business day on 24 June 2016 (Source: [1]).

Table 1. Calibrated mixture model parameters for GBPUSD from 24 February to 26 April 2016 (Source: [1]).

Date	S_0	P_E	S_E	$S_E/S_0 - 1$	95% CI for $S_{T^*,E}$		σ_{NE}	σ_E
24 Feb 2016	1.3927	30.8%	1.3250	−4.9%	1.0316	1.6184	8.8%	18.6%
25 Feb 2016	1.3962	31.5%	1.3319	−4.6%	1.0390	1.6247	8.4%	18.6%
26 Feb 2016	1.3871	32.0%	1.3252	−4.5%	1.0383	1.6120	8.3%	18.4%
29 Feb 2016	1.3917	32.6%	1.3340	−4.1%	1.0553	1.6128	8.2%	18.1%
01 Mar 2016	1.3952	32.5%	1.3378	−4.1%	1.0656	1.6100	8.1%	17.7%
02 Mar 2016	1.4078	32.4%	1.3541	−3.8%	1.0824	1.6258	7.9%	17.6%
03 Mar 2016	1.4178	33.4%	1.3666	−3.6%	1.0982	1.6349	7.9%	17.3%
04 Mar 2016	1.4229	33.0%	1.3711	−3.6%	1.1072	1.6351	7.7%	17.0%
07 Mar 2016	1.4265	33.5%	1.3773	−3.4%	1.1209	1.6337	7.7%	16.7%
08 Mar 2016	1.4215	33.3%	1.3737	−3.4%	1.1211	1.6262	7.6%	16.6%
09 Mar 2016	1.4217	33.5%	1.3753	−3.3%	1.1255	1.6252	7.5%	16.5%
10 Mar 2016	1.4281	33.7%	1.3830	−3.2%	1.1322	1.6339	7.6%	16.6%
11 Mar 2016	1.4382	32.7%	1.3936	−3.1%	1.1534	1.6337	7.1%	15.8%
14 Mar 2016	1.4302	33.5%	1.3885	−2.9%	1.1602	1.6167	7.0%	15.4%
15 Mar 2016	1.4151	33.5%	1.3701	−3.2%	1.1405	1.5998	7.3%	15.7%
16 Mar 2016	1.4259	34.1%	1.3800	−3.2%	1.1483	1.6117	7.4%	15.8%
17 Mar 2016	1.4482	33.9%	1.4011	−3.3%	1.1691	1.6331	7.5%	15.7%
18 Mar 2016	1.4476	34.5%	1.4015	−3.2%	1.1702	1.6328	7.6%	15.7%
21 Mar 2016	1.4369	34.7%	1.3902	−3.3%	1.1690	1.6113	7.7%	15.4%
22 Mar 2016	1.4208	35.6%	1.3751	−3.2%	1.1413	1.6089	8.2%	16.5%
23 Mar 2016	1.4117	27.9%	1.3189	−6.6%	1.0065	1.6314	9.5%	22.3%
24 Mar 2016	1.4153	27.4%	1.3159	−7.0%	1.0107	1.6210	9.5%	21.9%
25 Mar 2016	1.4132	27.7%	1.3156	−6.9%	1.0099	1.6212	9.6%	22.0%
28 Mar 2016	1.4254	30.6%	1.3471	−5.5%	1.0402	1.6540	9.6%	22.3%
29 Mar 2016	1.4384	27.2%	1.3403	−6.8%	1.0542	1.6264	9.4%	20.7%
30 Mar 2016	1.4378	26.6%	1.3394	−6.8%	1.0519	1.6269	9.4%	21.0%
31 Mar 2016	1.4360	27.9%	1.3453	−6.3%	1.0555	1.6350	9.5%	21.3%
01 Apr 2016	1.4227	27.8%	1.3326	−6.3%	1.0490	1.6161	9.5%	21.1%
04 Apr 2016	1.4264	27.6%	1.3383	−6.2%	1.0718	1.6048	9.2%	20.2%
05 Apr 2016	1.4161	28.5%	1.3349	−5.7%	1.0632	1.6067	9.5%	20.8%
06 Apr 2016	1.4123	27.8%	1.3246	−6.2%	1.0629	1.5864	9.8%	20.3%
07 Apr 2016	1.4056	28.8%	1.3222	−5.9%	1.0596	1.5849	9.9%	20.6%
08 Apr 2016	1.4128	30.4%	1.3377	−5.3%	1.0779	1.5975	9.6%	20.4%
11 Apr 2016	1.4239	30.2%	1.3520	−5.1%	1.1070	1.5970	9.4%	19.4%
12 Apr 2016	1.4275	31.3%	1.3611	−4.7%	1.1158	1.6064	9.4%	19.5%
13 Apr 2016	1.4204	31.1%	1.3552	−4.6%	1.1200	1.5904	9.4%	19.0%
14 Apr 2016	1.4155	32.4%	1.3566	−4.2%	1.1203	1.5929	9.5%	19.2%
15 Apr 2016	1.4202	30.6%	1.3590	−4.3%	1.1322	1.5858	9.4%	18.5%
18 Apr 2016	1.4278	33.0%	1.3801	−3.3%	1.1684	1.5918	9.0%	17.6%
19 Apr 2016	1.4398	37.5%	1.4026	−2.6%	1.2009	1.6043	8.4%	16.7%
20 Apr 2016	1.4332	37.7%	1.3991	−2.4%	1.2071	1.5911	8.1%	16.1%
21 Apr 2016	1.4323	37.8%	1.3993	−2.3%	1.2120	1.5866	8.1%	15.9%
22 Apr 2016	1.4403	39.5%	1.4118	−2.0%	1.2282	1.5955	7.9%	15.6%
25 Apr 2016	1.4482	42.8%	1.4305	−1.2%	1.2643	1.5968	7.6%	14.4%
26 Apr 2016	1.4582	22.6%	1.3546	−7.1%	1.1698	1.5394	9.3%	16.0%

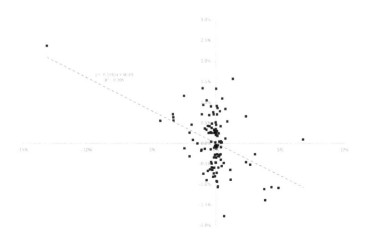

Fig. 3.   Percentage change in GBPUSD FX spot rates [y-axis] vs. the change in the leave probability from betting markets [x-axis] (12 January to 23 June 2016).

4.2. *2016 US election – Trump*

Figure 6 shows implied distributions for USDMXN (the Mexican peso equivalent of one US dollar) based on FX options expiring on Wednesday 9 November 2016, i.e. the day after the 2016 US election. We see a notable skew in the distribution, suggesting the possibility of a devaluation in the Mexican peso in accordance with a move in USDMXN to above 20, in the event of a Trump victory — a move in FX which indeed came to pass after the election result became known.

Calibrating the mixture model to the observed FX volatility surfaces for USDMXN, we obtain the results shown in Table 3, which similarly suggest a "risk event" move upwards in USDMXN of around 5% from prevailing FX spot levels below 19.5 up towards the region of 20, which indeed happened after the Trump victory. We also see a mixture model implied probability of a Trump victory between 23.7% and 55.0% during the period shown in Table 3, with an average level of 38.6% — while these parameters seem unstable, it is worth remembering that many different factors were influencing the markets at this time, so we would not expect too much stability.

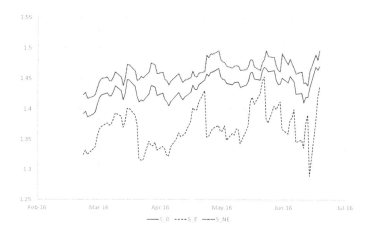

Fig. 4. Mixture model implied point estimates for S_E and S_{NE} (corresponding to "leave" and "remain" states of the world resp.) together with FX spot S_0 (24 February to 22 June 2016).

4.3. *2017 French elections*

In Figures 7 and 8 we apply the same technique to obtain implied distributions for EURUSD for the day after the first round and second round respectively. We see downside risk for the Euro, though not as extreme an FX risk as for the Brexit and Trump events of 2016, with potential decline in the Euro to around 1.05, which we would expect to be associated with a victory for Marine Le Pen. However, this sequence of events did not happen thanks to Emmanuel Macron's success in the election. We note for the first round of the French election, that the probability of very large downside moves in EURUSD is higher, compared with the second round, presumably reflecting the greater uncertainty at the first round stage.

We attempted to calibrate the mixture model to FX EURUSD volatilities but found that the calibration scheme experienced numerical problems when detecting any bimodality, perhaps not surprisingly given the relatively small levels of FX skew compared with the earlier levels seen for Brexit and Trump scenarios. This manifests as degeneracy in the parameter set (due to $S_E \approx S_{NE}$) and parameter instability. It would be interesting to conduct an analysis of the skew dependency of the mixture model, with

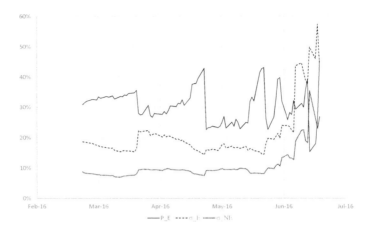

Fig. 5. Mixture model implied "leave" probability P_E together with σ_E and σ_{NE} for Brexit under "leave" and "remain" states of the world (24 February to 22 June 2016).

a view to improving the small skew behavior. This is an area we hope to revisit.

4.4. *2017 UK general election*

A final and unexpected opportunity to investigate empirically implied FX distributions in relation to contemporary political events arose on 18 April 2017, and we can therefore present implied distributions for the GBPUSD currency pair for Friday 9 June 2017, the day on which the election results would be known. We see in Figure 9 some probability mass in the range 1.25 to 1.275, which we would have expected to be realized if Theresa May had unexpectedly lost the election or proceeded to a hung parliament, and in contrast a decisive Conservative Party victory would be likely to be slightly stronger for the British pound. The result in June 2017, with Theresa May's Conservative government losing the majority in the House of Commons after a net loss of 13 seats, was accompanied by a sudden fall in GBPUSD from levels around 1.29 to a levels around 1.275, very much in line with our expectations based on implied distributions.

Table 2. Calibrated mixture model parameters for GBPUSD from 27 April to 22 June 2016 (Source: [1]).

Date	S_0	P_E	S_E	$S_E/S_0 - 1$	95% CI for $S_{T^*,E}$		σ_{NE}	σ_E
27 Apr 2016	1.4543	23.2%	1.3549	−6.8%	1.1727	1.5371	9.2%	16.0%
28 Apr 2016	1.4609	23.3%	1.3620	−6.8%	1.1818	1.5423	9.2%	15.9%
29 Apr 2016	1.4612	23.7%	1.3684	−6.3%	1.1856	1.5512	9.2%	16.2%
02 May 2016	1.4673	23.2%	1.3737	−6.4%	1.2001	1.5472	9.4%	15.8%
03 May 2016	1.4535	23.7%	1.3639	−6.2%	1.1845	1.5432	9.6%	16.6%
04 May 2016	1.4496	25.0%	1.3650	−5.8%	1.1768	1.5533	9.8%	17.6%
05 May 2016	1.4485	26.9%	1.3732	−5.2%	1.1839	1.5625	9.5%	17.9%
06 May 2016	1.4427	23.1%	1.3495	−6.5%	1.1766	1.5223	9.5%	16.6%
09 May 2016	1.4407	25.0%	1.3604	−5.6%	1.1875	1.5332	9.5%	17.2%
10 May 2016	1.4442	23.7%	1.3580	−6.0%	1.1915	1.5245	9.7%	16.7%
11 May 2016	1.4448	26.0%	1.3682	−5.3%	1.2027	1.5337	9.4%	16.7%
12 May 2016	1.4451	25.0%	1.3677	−5.4%	1.2038	1.5316	9.5%	16.8%
13 May 2016	1.4365	22.8%	1.3439	−6.4%	1.1860	1.5018	10.0%	16.4%
16 May 2016	1.4402	24.9%	1.3649	−5.2%	1.2061	1.5236	9.8%	17.1%
17 May 2016	1.4463	24.7%	1.3737	−5.0%	1.2286	1.5188	9.2%	15.8%
18 May 2016	1.4599	31.8%	1.4141	−3.1%	1.2637	1.5645	8.3%	16.4%
19 May 2016	1.4611	33.2%	1.4203	−2.8%	1.2744	1.5662	8.3%	16.1%
20 May 2016	1.4502	32.0%	1.4089	−2.8%	1.2700	1.5479	8.3%	15.7%
23 May 2016	1.4484	41.5%	1.4266	−1.5%	1.2974	1.5557	8.3%	15.2%
24 May 2016	1.4636	42.7%	1.4464	−1.2%	1.3241	1.5686	8.2%	14.5%
25 May 2016	1.4697	43.0%	1.4536	−1.1%	1.3325	1.5747	8.2%	14.5%
26 May 2016	1.4670	26.2%	1.3841	−5.6%	1.2358	1.5324	9.2%	18.1%
27 May 2016	1.4623	22.6%	1.3784	−5.7%	1.2207	1.5362	10.0%	19.7%
30 May 2016	1.4640	26.7%	1.4060	−4.0%	1.2592	1.5528	9.8%	19.4%
31 May 2016	1.4483	32.3%	1.4006	−3.3%	1.2511	1.5500	10.8%	20.3%
01 Jun 2016	1.4416	39.2%	1.4067	−2.4%	1.2538	1.5596	11.3%	21.3%
02 Jun 2016	1.4423	39.7%	1.4130	−2.0%	1.2740	1.5520	10.6%	19.8%
03 Jun 2016	1.4518	31.9%	1.3676	−5.8%	1.2025	1.5328	13.4%	23.9%
06 Jun 2016	1.4442	25.8%	1.3600	−5.8%	1.2081	1.5118	14.4%	23.8%
07 Jun 2016	1.4545	28.1%	1.3825	−4.9%	1.2359	1.5292	13.3%	23.5%
08 Jun 2016	1.4504	27.5%	1.3865	−4.4%	1.2511	1.5218	13.2%	22.4%
09 Jun 2016	1.4458	32.1%	1.4002	−3.2%	1.2742	1.5263	12.7%	21.6%
10 Jun 2016	1.4257	29.2%	1.3461	−5.6%	1.1033	1.5889	18.8%	43.6%
13 Jun 2016	1.4270	31.2%	1.3497	−5.4%	1.1287	1.5708	22.4%	44.5%
14 Jun 2016	1.4114	29.9%	1.3369	−5.3%	1.1417	1.5321	22.4%	41.6%
15 Jun 2016	1.4204	35.7%	1.3769	−3.1%	1.2023	1.5515	18.8%	38.9%
16 Jun 2016	1.4203	39.1%	1.3914	−2.0%	1.2319	1.5510	18.3%	37.5%
17 Jun 2016	1.4358	15.3%	1.2900	−10.2%	1.0893	1.4906	35.3%	49.7%
20 Jun 2016	1.4698	18.0%	1.3779	−6.3%	1.2308	1.5249	26.1%	46.0%
21 Jun 2016	1.4652	26.1%	1.4198	−3.1%	1.2588	1.5809	22.9%	57.3%
22 Jun 2016	1.4707	45.3%	1.4378	−2.2%	1.3323	1.5434	26.7%	44.2%

5. Conclusions

In this contribution we have surveyed the literature employing option pricing theory to analyse information embedded in the volatility surfaces

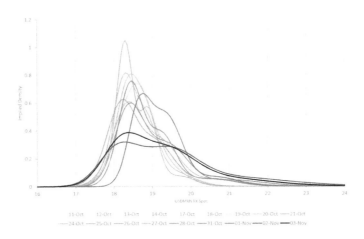

Fig. 6.   USDMXN implied densities for the day after the 2016 US election date (11 October to 3 November 2016).

pertaining to political event risk over the decade so far (2010–2017). We have cited several works that model the Swiss National Bank's defense level for the Swiss franc and the floor on EURCHF thereby imposed. We mention our own analysis of Brexit, with reference to GBPUSD and EURGBP, and we obtain implied distributions for USDMXN at the date of the US election, thereby describing the potential collapse in the Mexican peso to levels of 20 or more to the US dollar (a scenario which came to pass). Finally, we construct implied distributions for the 2017 French presidential and UK general elections, finding currency rate distributions which we attempt to ascribe to potential outcomes in the election. In the case of the French elections, no particular event risk analogous to Brexit came to pass, whereas the surprise factor of the Conservative Party's poor result in the June 2017 UK general election is consistent with our expectations based on implied distributions.

It would be of interest to extend and strengthen this analysis by utilizing more quantitative methods such as the mixture model approach [1] and including additional predictive information such as betting market odds and polls data [10], which would allow us to strengthen the analysis, both in terms of describing market regimes and apportioning them to potential

Table 3. Calibrated mixture model parameters for USDMXN from 3 October to 3 November 2016.

Date	S_0	P_E	S_E	$S_E/S_0 - 1$	95% CI for $S_{T^*,E}$		σ_{NE}	σ_E
03 Oct 2016	19.3007	52.0%	19.9551	2.7%	17.2743	22.6360	12.2%	19.9%
04 Oct 2016	19.3255	46.9%	19.8175	2.7%	17.4099	22.2251	12.8%	19.6%
05 Oct 2016	19.2087	53.6%	19.8480	2.2%	17.5032	22.1928	11.4%	18.1%
06 Oct 2016	19.2361	41.9%	19.6346	4.8%	17.5119	21.7574	13.2%	20.5%
07 Oct 2016	19.2980	41.6%	20.1660	5.0%	17.7925	22.5396	13.5%	21.0%
10 Oct 2016	18.9274	49.4%	20.2575	4.3%	17.8513	22.6637	12.5%	20.9%
11 Oct 2016	18.9143	45.7%	19.7422	4.4%	17.5051	21.9792	14.4%	21.7%
12 Oct 2016	18.9151	35.4%	19.7560	5.4%	17.4737	22.0382	14.3%	19.5%
13 Oct 2016	18.9267	39.6%	19.9271	4.5%	17.9097	21.9445	12.9%	18.7%
14 Oct 2016	18.9914	40.0%	19.7775	4.0%	17.8697	21.6853	11.6%	17.4%
17 Oct 2016	18.8745	41.4%	19.7597	3.2%	18.0105	21.5090	10.8%	15.4%
18 Oct 2016	18.6130	31.0%	19.4787	3.9%	18.0344	20.9230	11.0%	13.3%
19 Oct 2016	18.5225	42.6%	19.3428	2.6%	18.1400	20.5457	10.2%	13.3%
20 Oct 2016	18.6182	55.0%	19.0058	1.3%	17.8360	20.1756	9.9%	14.1%
21 Oct 2016	18.6182	55.0%	18.8651	1.3%	17.6488	20.0814	9.8%	13.9%
24 Oct 2016	18.5507	25.3%	18.8645	3.7%	17.6939	20.0350	10.0%	14.4%
25 Oct 2016	18.5507	23.7%	19.2417	3.6%	18.1321	20.3512	9.7%	13.1%
26 Oct 2016	18.6858	26.1%	19.2106	5.4%	18.2321	20.1892	13.7%	25.8%
27 Oct 2016	18.8390	26.1%	19.7031	5.4%	17.8192	21.5870	14.5%	26.2%
28 Oct 2016	18.9923	28.1%	19.8471	5.5%	17.9833	21.7110	14.6%	30.5%
31 Oct 2016	18.8611	26.8%	20.0413	4.5%	17.9416	22.1410	13.8%	27.2%
01 Nov 2016	19.1948	25.7%	19.7114	4.3%	18.0891	21.3336	14.8%	26.1%
02 Nov 2016	19.3732	38.1%	20.0187	6.0%	18.5177	21.5198	29.2%	52.5%
03 Nov 2016	19.1728	36.2%	20.5365	5.5%	17.6777	23.3953	27.8%	48.1%

political outcomes; for now, we present this empirical study as a topical and timely contribution to the conference "Innovations in Insurance, Risk-and Asset Management".

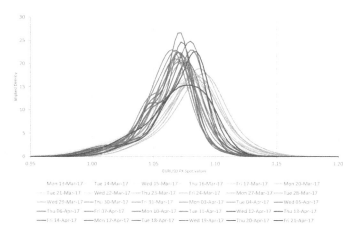

Fig. 7.   EURUSD implied densities from 13 March to 21 April 2017 for the day (Monday 24 April 2017) after the first round French presidential election.

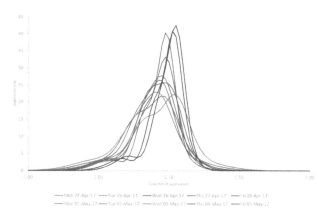

Fig. 8.   EURUSD implied densities from 24 April to 5 May 2017 for the day (Monday 8 May 2017) after the second round French presidential election.

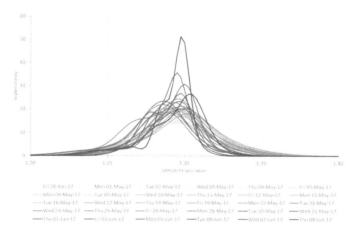

Fig. 9. GBPUSD implied densities from 28 April to 8 June 2017 for the day (Friday 9 June 2017) after the 2017 UK general election.

References

1. I. J. Clark and S. Amen, Implied distributions from GBPUSD risk-reversals and implication for Brexit scenarios, *Risks* **5**(3), 35–52 (2017).
2. D. T. Breeden and R. H. Litzenberger, Prices of state-contingent claims implicit in option prices, *The Journal of Business* **51**, 621–651 (1978).
3. A. M. Malz, Estimating the probability distribution of the future exchange rate from option prices, *Journal of Derivatives* **5**, 18–36 (1997).
4. A. M. Malz, Using option prices to estimate realignment probabilities in the European Monetary System: The case of sterling-mark, *Journal of International Money and Finance* **15**(5), 717–748 (1996).
5. M. Hanke, R. Poulsen, and A. Weissensteiner, Where would the EUR/CHF exchange rate be without the SNB's minimum exchange rate policy?, *Journal of Futures Markets* **35**, 1103–1116 (2015).
6. C.-H. Hui, C.-F. Lo, and T. P.-W. Fong, Swiss franc's one-sided target zone during 2011–2015, *International Review of Economics and Finance* **44**, 54–67 (2016).

7. M. Hertrich and H. Zimmermann, On the credibility of the Euro/Swiss Franc Floor: A financial market perspective, *Journal of Money, Credit and Banking* **49**, 567–578 (2017).
8. U. J. Jermann, Financial Markets' Views about the Euro-Swiss Franc Floor, *Journal of Money, Credit and Banking* **49**, 553–565 (2017).
9. B. Dupire, Special techniques for special events, Paper presented at Global Derivatives, Barcelona, Spain, 10 May (2017).
10. M. Hanke, R. Poulsen, and A. Weissensteiner, Event-related exchange rate forecasts combining betting quotes and risk-neutral densities from option prices, *Journal of Financial and Quantitative Analysis* (forthcoming).
11. J. Dhaene, J. Dony, M.B. Forys, D. Linders and W. Schoutens, FIX: The Fear Index – Measuring market fear, **in** M. Cummins, F. Murphy and J.J.H. Miller (Eds.), *Topics in Numerical Methods for Finance* (Springer, Heidelberg, 2012).
12. I. J. Clark, *Foreign Exchange Option Pricing: A Practitioner's Guide* (Wiley, Chichester, 2011).

Chapter 6

Data and Uncertainty in Extreme Risks: A Nonlinear Expectations Approach

Samuel N. Cohen

Mathematical Institute, University of Oxford
Oxford, UK
* samuel.cohen@maths.ox.ac.uk
http://people.maths.ox.ac.uk/cohens/

Estimation of tail quantities, such as expected shortfall or Value at Risk, is a difficult problem. We show how the theory of nonlinear expectations, in particular the Data-robust expectation introduced in [1], can assist in the quantification of statistical uncertainty for these problems. However, when we are in a heavy-tailed context (in particular when our data are described by a Pareto distribution, as is common in much of extreme value theory), the theory of [1] is insufficient, and requires an additional regularization step which we introduce. By asking whether this regularization is possible, we obtain a qualitative requirement for reliable estimation of tail quantities and risk measures, in a Pareto setting.

Keywords: nonlinear expectation, extreme value theory, risk measure, uncertainty quantification.

1. Introduction

Statistics is, in part, the art of combining data and probabilistic models to predict the unknown. This necessarily results in uncertainty, not only as described by the estimated probabilistic model,[1] but also in the correctness of the model itself. In many situations, it is important to describe this uncertainty, and to incorporate it in our decision making.

One area where these issues are particularly prominent is when considering extreme outcomes. By their very nature, this involves looking at unlikely events, often beyond the range of available data. Justifying this extrapolation from observations is a key purpose of 'extreme value theory'. In particular, the Fisher–Tippett–Gnedenko and Pickands–Balkema–de Haan theorems tell us that, assuming they exist, the possible distributions of

---

[1]Since the work of Knight [2], uncertainty that is described by a probabilistic model is sometimes called 'risk', while lack of knowledge of the model is called 'uncertainty'.

renormalized extremes are in a small class, allowing asymptotic approximation methods to be used. Nevertheless, one must still estimate parameters of these distributions, and intuition suggests that there remains a significant level of uncertainty when working with these models.

The question of how to incorporate uncertainty in decision making has a long history. Bayesian approaches to statistics do this by placing a distribution over the unknown quantities, conditioning on observations, and then integrating over the possible unknowns. This effectively forces all uncertainty to be treated 'linearly', and one cannot describe an agent's aversion to uncertainty separately to their aversion to risk (i.e. to the randomness which is included within the model). Conversely, classical methods in statistics allow for uncertainty in parameters (for example, through the use of confidence sets), but these are frequently used with relatively limited axiomatic decision-theoretic support.

One approach, building from an axiomatic approach to valuations of outcomes, is 'nonlinear expectations'. These are mathematical generalizations of the classical expected value, allowing for risk and uncertainty to be represented in a rigorous and precise manner. Nonlinear expectations can be seen as generalizations of worst-case valuation, considered in a statistical context by Wald [3], but with an increased focus on making valuations of *multiple* random outcomes, rather than on minimizing a particular fixed risk. In finance, nonlinear expectations have played a particular role in the theory of convex risk measures, see for example Föllmer and Schied [4]. In a recent paper [1], a method of connecting these nonlinear expectations with statistical estimation was introduced.

In this paper, we shall look at some of the implications that this way of thinking has on extreme value theory. In particular, we will consider how quantifying our uncertainty leads to skepticism in extreme extrapolation, and how different approaches to measuring the riskiness of a decision require different quantities of data.

This paper proceeds as follows. Following an initial summary of the theory of nonlinear expectations and their connection with estimation, we will consider how to combine these expectations with measures of risk, corresponding in some cases to extrapolation into the tail. We will then look at methods of regularizing these nonlinear expectations, which are often needed when considering unbounded outcomes. Finally, we will apply this theory to a classic estimation problem with heavy tails, and draw conclusions for the estimation of a variety of measures of risk.

Remark 1.1. In their well known textbook on extreme value theory in finance and insurance, Embrechts, Klüppelberg and Mikosch [5] consider the challenges of extrapolation. In particular, they discuss their preference for looking at only moderately high quantiles of distributions, rather than estimating deeper into the tail. They state,

> The reason why we are *very reluctant* to produce plots for high quantiles like 0.9999 or more, is that we feel that such estimates are to be treated *with extreme care.* [...] The statistical reliability of these estimates becomes, as we have seen, very difficult to judge in general. Though we can work out approximate confidence intervals for these estimators, such constructions strongly rely on mathematical assumptions which are unverifiable in practice.
>
> — Embrechts, Klüppelberg and Mikosch, [5], p. 364
>
> (emphasis in original)

In this paper, we give a partial attempt at a formal analysis supporting this reticence. We shall see that the theory of nonlinear expectations gives certain bounds (which depend on the amount of data at hand) beyond which the uncertainties from estimation dominate the computation of high quantiles (and similar quantities), hence statistical inference is problematic.

2. DR-expectations

Consider the following problem. Suppose we have a family $\{X\} \cup \{X_i\}_{i \in \mathbb{N}}$ of real-valued random variables on the canonical space $(\Omega, \mathcal{F}) = (\mathbb{R}^{\mathbb{N}}, \mathcal{B}(\mathbb{R}^{\mathbb{N}}))$, where $\mathcal{B}(\mathbb{R}^{\mathbb{N}})$ denotes the Borel cylinder σ-algebra. We observe $\mathbf{x}_N = \{X_n\}_{n=1}^N$, and seek to draw conclusions about the likely values of $\phi(X)$, where ϕ is some (known, Borel measurable) real function. Our aim, therefore, is to estimate the distribution of X, accounting for the uncertainty in our estimation.

Beginning classically, we first propose a family $\mathcal{Q}$ of measures, assumed equivalent on $\sigma(\mathbf{x}_N)$ for each $N < \infty$, corresponding to possible joint distributions of $\{X\} \cup \{X_n\}_{n \in \mathbb{N}}$. For each of these distributions, we obtain the log-likelihood

$$\ell(\mathbf{x}_N; Q) = \log\left(\frac{dQ|_{\sigma(\mathbf{x}_N)}}{dQ_{\text{ref}}|_{\sigma(\mathbf{x}_N)}}\right)(\mathbf{x}_N)$$

(relative to some reference measure Q_{ref} on Ω). We can then define the divergence, or negative log-likelihood ratio,

$$\alpha_{\mathcal{Q}|\mathbf{x}_N}(Q) = -\ell(\mathbf{x}_N; Q) + \sup_{Q \in \mathcal{Q}} \ell(\mathbf{x}_N; Q).$$

If we knew the 'true' measure Q, a natural estimate for $\phi(X)$ given our observations $\mathbf{x}_N$ would be the conditional expectation $E_Q[\phi(X)|\mathbf{x}_N]$. Formally, as this is only defined for almost every observation $\mathbf{x}_N$, and we have a possibly uncountable family of measures $\mathcal{Q}$, this may cause technical difficulties. As we are working with countably generated Borel spaces,[2] simultaneously for every $Q \in \mathcal{Q}$, we can define the regular conditional Q-probability distribution of X given $\mathbf{x}_N$, that is, a probability kernel $\mathbf{Q}$: $\mathbb{R}^N \times \mathcal{B}(\mathbb{R}) \to [0, 1]$ such that

$$\mathbf{Q}(\mathbf{x}_N(\omega), A) = Q(X \in A | \mathbf{x}_N)(\omega),$$

and so obtain a 'regular' conditional expectation

$$E_Q[\phi(X)|\mathbf{x}_N] := \int_{\mathbb{R}} \phi(x) \mathbf{Q}(\mathbf{x}_N, dx).$$

We use this regular conditional expectation in what follows.

Remark 2.1. We shall focus our attention on the simpler case where $\{X\} \cup \{X_n\}_{n \in \mathbb{N}}$ are iid under each $Q \in \mathcal{Q}$. In this case, each measure in $\mathcal{Q}$ can be described by the density f_Q of X under Q, and we obtain the simplifications $\ell(\mathbf{x}_N; Q) = \sum_{i=1}^{N} \log f_Q(X_i)$ and $E[\phi(X)|\mathbf{x}_N] = E[\phi(X)]$.

The key idea of [1] is to define the following operator.

Definition 2.1. For fixed constants $k > 0$, $\gamma \in [1, \infty]$, define the nonlinear expectation

$$\mathcal{E}^{k,\gamma}_{\mathcal{Q}|\mathbf{x}_N}(\phi(X)) = \sup_{Q \in \mathcal{Q}} \left\{ E[\phi(X)|\mathbf{x}_N] - \left(\frac{1}{k}\alpha_{\mathcal{Q}|\mathbf{x}_N}(Q)\right)^{\gamma} \right\},$$

where we write $|x|^{\infty} = 0$ for $|x| \leq 1$, and ∞ otherwise. We call this the DR-expectation (with parameters k, γ). 'DR' is a deliberately ambiguous acronym, and refers to either 'divergence robust' or 'data-driven robust'.

We can see that $\mathcal{E}^{k,\gamma}_{\mathcal{Q}|\mathbf{x}_N}$ is built from considering the expected values under a range of models $\mathcal{Q}$, penalized by how well each model fits the observed data $\mathbf{x}_N$. This allows the DR-expectation to encode the uncertainty inherent in statistical estimation.

---

[2]See, for example, Cohen and Elliott [6], Section 2.6 or Shiryaev [7], Section II.7 for further details on the mathematics of this construction.

This nonlinear expectation has many elegant properties. From the perspective of the theory of nonlinear expectations, it is monotone, convex, constant equivariant and assigns all constants their values. One can obtain a risk measure, in the sense of Föllmer and Schied [4], Frittelli and Rosazza-Gianin [8] and Artzner, Delbaen, Eber and Heath [9], by specifying $\rho(\phi(X)) = \mathcal{E}^{k,\gamma}_{\mathcal{Q}|\mathbf{x}_N}(-\phi(X))$, or by treating $\phi(X)$ as 'losses'. The nonlinear expectation is coherent (in particular, it is positively homogeneous) if $\gamma = \infty$.

At the same time, unlike most risk measures in the literature, the DR-expectation is directly built from the observed data to represent statistical uncertainty. In order to perform classical statistical estimation, an agent needs to specify a class of models $\mathcal{Q}$ to be considered (and in a Bayesian analysis, a prior distribution over models); the only remaining inputs to the problem are the observations $\mathbf{x}_N$. In the DR-expectation framework, one additionally needs the uncertainty aversion parameter k and the curvature parameter γ. Rather than separating statistical inference from the valuation of outcomes, the DR-expectation combines the two, as the likelihood is part of the definition of the expectation. Observations $\mathbf{x}_N$ do not simply affect our expectation through conditioning (as in a Bayesian analysis), they also determine which models $Q \in \mathcal{Q}$ are 'good', in the sense of fitting our past observations well.

Remark 2.2. A key advantage of this approach is that we define the DR-expectation for every function ϕ. This allows the comparison of different ϕ to be consistently carried out, and the impact of statistical uncertainty on different ϕ may vary. While we have assumed above that X is real-valued, there is no issue if X is taken to be $\mathbb{R}^d$-valued (or more generally, Borel measurable and valued in some separable Banach space), which allows a great deal of flexibility in modeling.

In the setting where $\{X\} \cup \{X_n\}_{n \in \mathbb{N}}$ are iid, and under some regularity assumptions on $\mathcal{Q}$ detailed in [1], one can show that the DR-expectation is a consistent estimator of the expected value of $\phi(X)$, that is,

$$\mathcal{E}^{k,\gamma}_{\mathcal{Q}|\mathbf{x}_N}(\phi(X)) \to_P E_P[\phi(X)] \quad \text{as } N \to \infty, \text{ for every } P \in \mathcal{Q},$$

for any value of $k > 0$ and $\gamma \in [1, \infty]$. It is also clear that the case $\gamma = \infty$ is closely related to the Neyman–Pearson lemma from hypothesis testing, as it considers models where the negative log-likelihood-ratio $\alpha_{\mathcal{Q}|\mathbf{x}_N}(Q)$ is sufficiently small.

In order to give precise asymptotic statements, the following definition will prove useful. Here P^* is the outer measure associated with P, to deal with any potential lack of measurability.

Definition 2.2. Consider sequences $f = \{f_n\}_{n\in\mathbb{N}}$ and $g = \{g_n\}_{n\in\mathbb{N}}$ of functions $\Omega \to \mathbb{R}$.

(i) We write $f = O_P(g)$ whenever f_n/g_n is stochastically bounded, that is, $P^*(|f_n/g_n| > M) \to 0$ as $M \to \infty$ for each n,

(ii) We write $f = o_P(g)$ whenever $\lim_{n\to\infty} P^*(|f_n/g_n| > \epsilon) = 0$ for all $\epsilon > 0$.

Note that this depends on the choice of measure P.

Remark 2.3. In [1], a range of large-sample asymptotic results were obtained, for iid observations and X, under varying assumptions on the family $\mathcal{Q}$. Suppose that $\mathcal{Q}$ is a subset of a 'nice' exponential family parametrized by $\theta \in \Theta$ (in particular, Assumption 3.1, as detailed below, holds) and the maximum likelihood estimator based on a sample of size N, denoted $\hat{\theta}_N$, is well defined. For bounded ϕ, the following large sample approximations were obtained:

$$\mathcal{E}^{k,1}_{\mathcal{Q}|\mathbf{x}_N}(\phi(X)) = E_{\hat{\theta}_N}[\phi(X)] + \frac{k}{2N}V(\phi, \hat{\theta}_N) + O_P(N^{-3/2}),$$

$$\mathcal{E}^{k,\infty}_{\mathcal{Q}|\mathbf{x}_N}(\phi(X)) = E_{\hat{\theta}_N}[\phi(X)] + \sqrt{\frac{2k}{N}V(\phi, \hat{\theta}_N)} + O_P(N^{-3/4}),$$

for every $P \in \mathcal{Q}$, where $V(\phi, \hat{\theta}_N)$ is the 'local variance' at the MLE, defined by

$$V(\phi, \hat{\theta}) := \left(\frac{\partial E_\theta[\phi(X)]}{\partial \theta}\Big|_{\hat{\theta}}\right)^\top (\mathfrak{I}_{\hat{\theta}}^{-1})\left(\frac{\partial E_\theta[\phi(X)]}{\partial \theta}\Big|_{\hat{\theta}}\right),$$

for $\mathfrak{I}_{\hat{\theta}_N}$ the observed information matrix (the Hessian of the negative log-likelihood) at $\hat{\theta}_N$.

Remark 2.4. The results in [1] focus on the case where $\{X\}\cup\{X_n\}_{n\in\mathbb{N}}$ are iid under every model in $\mathcal{Q}$. This is clearly restrictive from a modeling perspective. However, it is clear from the definition that the DR-expectation depends on the set $\mathcal{Q}$ only through the conditional expectation and the log-likelihood, evaluated at the observed data $\mathbf{x}_N$. Therefore, provided our models are 'close' to an iid setting, in the sense that our expectations and likelihoods are similar to those from an iid model (possibly after some transformation of the space), the asymptotic behavior of the DR-expectation should not be significantly affected.

Remark 2.5. The DR-expectation is particularly designed to highlight statistical uncertainty, rather than an individual's risk aversion. In particular, the above results (particularly when combined with the classic analysis of White [10]) show that as the sample size $N \to \infty$, in the iid case,

$$\mathcal{E}^{k,\gamma}_{\mathcal{Q}|\mathbf{x}_N}(\phi(X)) \approx -\mathcal{E}^{k,\gamma}_{\mathcal{Q}|\mathbf{x}_N}(-\phi(X)) \approx E_P[\phi(X)],$$

where P is the measure in $\mathcal{Q}$ which is closest to the empirical distribution of the data. In this way, an individual's preferences can be seen not to play any role in the DR-expectation when samples are large (that is, when statistical uncertainty is low).

2.1. *Data-robust risk measures*

To focus attention on extreme events, or to include an individual's risk aversion, we may wish to extend our focus from the DR-expectation. Classically, when we ignore statistical uncertainty (so the DR-expectation would be replaced by the expectation with respect to the known distribution), a standard approach would be to take X to denote losses and ϕ to be a utility function. In our setting, following this approach would lead to a version of expected utility theory where the expectation is replaced with the DR-expectation.

Further interesting cases can be obtained by directly combining the DR-expectation with a risk assessment depending directly on the law of the random outcome. As we shall see, many common risk assessments are of this type, for example the value at risk and expected shortfall, as well as classical statistics such as the expectation and variance. Writing $\mathcal{M}_1$ for the space of probability measures on $\mathbb{R}$, we consider a map $\mathcal{R} : \mathcal{M}_1 \to \mathbb{R}$ which represents the 'riskiness' of a gamble with specified distribution. We can then combine the risk aversion of $\mathcal{R}$ (which treats the law of X as fixed) with the uncertainty aversion of the DR-expectation (which considers our uncertainty in this law). We formalize this construction in the following definition.

Definition 2.3. Write $\mathcal{M}_1$ for the space of probability measures on $\mathbb{R}$ and $\mathcal{L}_Q(\xi|\mathbf{x})$ for the (regular conditional) law of a random variable ξ under the measure Q (given observations $\mathbf{x}$). Let $\mathcal{R} : \mathcal{M}_1 \to \mathbb{R}$ be a map with $\mathcal{R}(\mathcal{L}_Q(\xi|\mathbf{x}))$ representing the risk of our position ξ assuming $Q \in \mathcal{Q}$ is a 'true' model. We combine $\mathcal{E}^{k,\gamma}_{\mathcal{Q}|\mathbf{x}}$ and $\mathcal{R}$ through the definition

$$(\mathcal{E}^{k,\gamma}_{\mathcal{Q}|\mathbf{x}} \circ \mathcal{R})(\xi) := \sup_{Q \in \mathcal{Q}} \left\{ \mathcal{R}(\mathcal{L}_Q(\xi|\mathbf{x})) - \left(\frac{1}{k}\alpha_{\mathcal{Q}|\mathbf{x}}(Q)\right)^\gamma \right\}$$

Remark 2.6. For the sake of simplicity, we will identify this construction by adding a prefix 'DR-'. For example, combining the DR-expectation and the expected shortfall, as in the example below, we obtain the 'DR-expected shortfall', similarly the 'DR-Value at Risk'.

Example 2.1. Consider the risk assessment given by the (upper) expected shortfall at level ϵ (also called the conditional value at risk, tail value at risk or average value at risk, by various authors). For a model P such that ξ has a continuous distribution, this can be written

$$\mathcal{R}(\mathcal{L}_P(\xi)) = E_P[\xi | \xi \geq F_P^{-1}(1 - \epsilon)] = \mathrm{ES}_\epsilon(\xi)$$

where F_P is the cdf of X under the measure P. This is a coherent risk measure (or nonlinear expectation), and can also be written (see Föllmer and Schied [4] or further discussion in McNeil, Frey and Embrechts [11])

$$\mathrm{ES}_\epsilon(\xi) = \sup_{P' \sim P} \left\{ E_{P'}[\xi] - \tilde{\alpha}(P'; P) \right\}$$

where

$$\tilde{\alpha}(P'; P) = \begin{cases} 0 & \text{if } \|dP'/dP\|_\infty < \epsilon^{-1}, \\ \infty & \text{otherwise.} \end{cases}$$

In the special case where $\mathcal{R}$ corresponds to a convex expectation (based on a reference measure), this construction can simplify in a natural way.

Proposition 2.1. *Suppose that, for each measure $P \in \mathcal{Q}$, our risk assessment $\mathcal{R}$ has representation*

$$\mathcal{R}(\mathcal{L}_P(\xi|\mathbf{x})) = \sup_{P' \in \tilde{\mathcal{Q}}} \{E_{P'}[\xi|\mathbf{x}] - \tilde{\alpha}(P'; P)\},$$

where $\tilde{\mathcal{Q}}$ is a collection of probability measures on Ω with $\mathcal{Q} \subseteq \tilde{\mathcal{Q}}$ and $\tilde{\alpha} : \tilde{\mathcal{Q}} \times \tilde{\mathcal{Q}} \to \mathbb{R}$ is an arbitrary penalty function. The composition of $\mathcal{E}_{\mathcal{Q}|\mathbf{x}}^{k,\gamma}$ and $\mathcal{R}$ is a nonlinear expectation, and has representation

$$(\mathcal{E}_{\mathcal{Q}|\mathbf{x}}^{k,\gamma} \circ \mathcal{R})(\xi) = \sup_{P' \in \tilde{\mathcal{Q}}} \left\{ E_{P'}[\xi|\mathbf{x}] - \alpha^*(P') \right\}$$

where α^* is the inf-sum (cf. the inf-convolution in Barrieu and El Karoui [12])

$$\alpha^*(P') = \inf_{Q \in \mathcal{Q}} \left\{ \left(\frac{1}{k} \alpha_{\mathcal{Q}|\mathbf{x}}(Q) \right)^\gamma + \tilde{\alpha}(P'; Q) \right\}.$$

Proof. To obtain the representation, simply expand

$$(\mathcal{E}^{k,\gamma}_{\mathcal{Q}|\mathbf{x}} \circ \mathcal{R})(\xi) = \sup_{Q \in \mathcal{Q}} \left\{ \mathcal{R}(\mathcal{L}_Q(\xi|\mathbf{x})) - \left(\frac{1}{k}\alpha_{\mathcal{Q}|\mathbf{x}}(Q)\right)^\gamma \right\}$$

$$= \sup_{Q \in \mathcal{Q}, P' \in \tilde{\mathcal{Q}}} \left\{ E_{P'}[\xi|\mathbf{x}] - \left(\frac{1}{k}\alpha_{\mathcal{Q}|\mathbf{x}}(Q)\right)^\gamma - \tilde{\alpha}(P';Q) \right\}$$

$$= \sup_{P' \in \tilde{\mathcal{Q}}} \left\{ E_{P'}[\xi|\mathbf{x}] - \alpha^*(P') \right\}$$

This defines a nonlinear expectation by duality, as in Föllmer and Schied [4]. □

3. Regularization from data

The above approach, based on simply penalizing with the divergence, often fails to give bounded values when considering unbounded random variables. In some sense, this is because of the difficulty in using data to determine the probabilities of extreme outcomes. To motivate our discussion, we consider the following simple example.

Example 3.1. Consider the case where $\xi = \phi(X) = \beta X$, and $\{X\} \cup \{X_n\}_{n \in \mathbb{N}}$ are iid $N(\mu, \sigma^2)$ distributed random variables, with $\mu \in \mathbb{R}$ and $\sigma^2 > 0$ unknown. Writing $\bar{X} = N^{-1} \sum_{i=1}^N X_i$ and $\hat{\sigma}^2 = N^{-1} \sum_i (X_i - \bar{X})^2$ for the MLE estimates of μ and σ^2, it is straightforward to calculate (see [1] for details)

$$\mathcal{E}^{k,1}_{\mathcal{Q}|\mathbf{x}_N}(\beta X) = \sup_{\mu, \sigma^2} \left\{ \beta\mu - \frac{N}{2k}\left(\log(\sigma^2/\hat{\sigma}^2) + \frac{\frac{1}{N}\sum_{n=1}^N (X_n - \mu)^2}{\sigma^2} - 1 \right) \right\}$$

$$= \sup_{\mu, \sigma^2} \left\{ \beta\mu - \frac{N}{2k\sigma^2}(\bar{X} - \mu)^2 - \frac{N}{2k}\left(\log(\sigma^2/\hat{\sigma}^2) + \frac{\hat{\sigma}^2}{\sigma^2} - 1 \right) \right\}$$

$$= \beta\bar{X} + \sup_{\sigma^2} \left\{ \frac{\beta^2 k}{2N}\sigma^2 - \frac{N}{2k}\left(\log(\sigma^2/\hat{\sigma}^2) - 1 + \frac{\hat{\sigma}^2}{\sigma^2} \right) \right\}. \tag{1}$$

This is problematic, as for any finite N, the growth of σ^2 will dominate the term in braces as $\sigma^2 \to \infty$, which implies $\mathcal{E}^{k,1}_{\mathcal{Q}|\mathbf{x}_N}(\beta X) = \infty$.

However, the function to be optimized is increasing near zero, and we can find a local minimum value of the derivative at $\sigma^2 = 2\hat{\sigma}^2$, where

$$\frac{\partial}{\partial \sigma^2}\left(\frac{\beta^2 k}{2N}\sigma^2 - \frac{N}{2k}\left(\log(\sigma^2/\hat{\sigma}^2) - 1 + \frac{\hat{\sigma}^2}{\sigma^2} \right) \right)\bigg|_{\sigma^2 = 2\hat{\sigma}^2} = \frac{\beta^2 k}{2N} - \frac{N}{2k}\frac{1}{4\hat{\sigma}^2}.$$

Provided this quantity is negative, that is, $\hat{\sigma}^2 > (\beta k/2N)^2$, we know that the derivative has changed sign at least once on the interval $\sigma^2 \in (0, 2\hat{\sigma}^2)$, so we can be sure that the function will have a local maximum, and (we shall see that) this occurs near $\sigma^2 \approx \hat{\sigma}^2$.

This example leads us to consider further ways of restricting our attention, to ensure that it is a *local* maximum which is chosen in the DR-expectation, as this corresponds to a value close to the MLE, and avoids the explosion of the expectation caused by considering the implausible model $\sigma^2 \to \infty$.

The following are some natural approaches to preventing this explosion:

- We could place a prior probability on σ^2, with density f, which collapses sufficiently quickly when $\sigma^2 \to \infty$, and then incorporate this prior into the penalty. This would result in a penalty given by the negative log-posterior density,

$$\alpha_{\mathcal{Q}|\mathbf{x}_N}(Q) = -\ell(\mathbf{x}_N; Q) - \log f(\sigma_Q^2) + \text{normalization term}$$

  where the normalizing term is constant with respect to Q, and ensures $\inf_{Q \in \mathcal{Q}} \alpha_{\mathcal{Q}|\mathbf{x}_N}(Q) = 0$. In order to ensure $\mathcal{E}_{\mathcal{Q}|\mathbf{x}_N}^{k,1}(\beta X) < \infty$ for large N, we require $f(\sigma^2)e^{a\sigma^2} \to 0$ as $\sigma^2 \to \infty$, for some $a > 0$, which is not the case for the classical (inverse Gamma) conjugate prior. This also seems a rather *ad hoc* fix, and raises the concern that the conclusions drawn, no matter how much data is available, depends principally on the choice of prior distribution $f(\sigma^2)$.
- We could *a priori* truncate σ^2 away from ∞ (i.e. set a maximum value $\bar{\sigma}^2$ which will be considered). This is equivalent to a uniform prior $f(\cdot) \propto I_{[0, \bar{\sigma}^2]}$ for σ^2, and will result in the local maximum being chosen whenever N is sufficiently large. However this has the drawback that it requires us to posit a maximum value of σ^2 independently of the data, and again our conclusions will depend on the choice of this upper bound, for all finite values of N.
- We could restrict to the case $\gamma = \infty$, and thus only consider a likelihood interval of values for σ^2. This has the implication that our DR-expectation is then positively homogeneous, and we 'flatten out' the interaction between the choice of model and the variable being considered. (In particular, the penalty term only takes the values 0 and ∞ — models are either excluded or are considered as reasonable as the best-fitting model, with no middle ground.)

The final of these options has the particular, advantage that the conclusions are purely based on the data, rather than our prior assumptions. At the same time, the flattening of our expectation may be undesirable, as it makes it difficult to see how different models will be chosen when evaluating different random variables. For this reason, we propose an alternative regularization technique, combining the $\gamma < \infty$ and $\gamma = \infty$ cases. To achieve this, we define the following transformation of the divergence.

Definition 3.1. The δ-truncation of the divergence, based on a sample of size N, is given by

$$\alpha^{(\delta)}_{\mathcal{Q}|\mathbf{x}_N}(Q) = \begin{cases} \alpha_{\mathcal{Q}|\mathbf{x}_N}(Q) & \text{if } \alpha_{\mathcal{Q}|\mathbf{x}_N}(Q) \le N^\delta, \\ \infty & \text{otherwise.} \end{cases}$$

The corresponding DR-risk-assessment is defined by

$$(\mathcal{E}^{k,\gamma,\delta}_{\mathcal{Q}|\mathbf{x}_N} \circ \mathcal{R})(\xi) = \sup_{Q \in \mathcal{Q}} \left\{ \mathcal{R}(\mathcal{L}_Q(\xi)|\mathbf{x}_N) - \left(\frac{1}{k} \alpha^{(\delta)}_{\mathcal{Q}|\mathbf{x}_N}(Q) \right)^\gamma \right\}. \qquad (2)$$

Remark 3.1. For bounded random variables ξ, taking $\mathcal{R}(\mathcal{L}_Q(\xi|\mathbf{x})) = E_Q[\xi|\mathbf{x}_N]$, the optimization step in calculating the DR-expectation implies that only those measures in $\{Q : \alpha_{\mathcal{Q}|\mathbf{x}_N}(Q) < \|\xi\|_\infty\}$ need be considered. Therefore, provided $N^\delta > \|\xi\|_\infty$, we have $\mathcal{E}^{k,\gamma,\delta}_{\mathcal{Q}|\mathbf{x}_N}(\xi) = \mathcal{E}^{k,\gamma}_{\mathcal{Q}|\mathbf{x}_N}(\xi)$.

Remark 3.2. Suppose $\mathcal{Q}$ is sufficiently regular and N sufficiently large that Wilks' theorem holds.[3] Then the set of measures $\{Q : \alpha_{\mathcal{Q}|\mathbf{x}_N}(Q) < N^\delta\}$ corresponds to a confidence set with confidence level $F^{-1}_{\chi^2_d}(2N^\delta)$, for d the dimension of (a parametrization of) $\mathcal{Q}$, where $F^{-1}_{\chi^2_d}$ is the inverse cdf of the χ^2_d distribution. In this case, we observe that the δ truncation corresponds to considering only those measures in a confidence set around the MLE (and then penalizing further using their divergences based on the data). However, the confidence level of this set will grow quickly with N (when $d = 1$, already for $N^\delta \approx 2$ we are considering a 95% confidence set).

We now consider the behavior of a sequence $\{\mathcal{R}_N\}_{N \in \mathbb{N}}$ of risk assessments, which may vary with our sample size N.

Definition 3.2. We say that $(\mathcal{E}^{k,\gamma,\delta}_{\mathcal{Q}|\mathbf{x}_N} \circ \mathcal{R}_N)(\xi)$ is regular whenever the supremum in its definition is finite and attained at a point where $\alpha_{\mathcal{Q}|\mathbf{x}_N}(Q) < N^\delta$.

---

[3]This classical theorem states that $\alpha_{\mathcal{Q}|\mathbf{x}_N}(P)$ has an asymptotic χ^2_d distribution under P, where d is the dimension of a parameter space representing $\mathcal{Q}$. Conditions under which this holds (which can be interpreted as requirements on the family $\mathcal{Q}$) can be found in Lehmann and Casella [13].

This definition gives us a criterion, which can be evaluated for a particular set of observations, to determine whether the estimation of our truncated DR-risk assessment is reliable. If our DR-risk assessment is not regular, then our estimate is based on parameters on the boundary of the admissible region $\{Q : \alpha_{Q|\mathbf{x}_N}(Q) < N^\delta\}$. This suggests our estimate depends critically on the choice of truncation parameter δ. On the other hand, when our DR-risk assessment is regular, we know that we have chosen a local maximum within the admissible region, which suggests that the variation in the truncation parameter δ has no marginal impact on our estimates.

The fact that Definition 3.2 depends on the particular observations $\mathbf{x}_N$ is important, as it provides us with a qualitative criterion to assess reliability of estimates which can be calculated from our observations. At the same time, it is interesting to know whether there exists a choice of truncation parameter δ which will typically result in a regular DR-risk assessment.

Definition 3.3. We say $(\mathcal{E}^{k,\gamma}_{Q|\mathbf{x}_N} \circ \mathcal{R}_N)(\xi)$ is ($\mathcal{Q}$-)regularizable if, for some $\delta > 0$, for all $P \in \mathcal{Q}$, with P-probability tending to 1, as $N \to \infty$, we have that $(\mathcal{E}^{k,\gamma,\delta}_{Q|\mathbf{x}_N} \circ \mathcal{R}_N)(\xi)$ is regular.

Remark 3.3. Typically, the divergence will grow like $O(N)$ outside of any neighborhood of the MLE. Therefore, regularizing with $\delta < 1$ is sufficient to guarantee that only points in a neighborhood of the MLE are considered in the optimization. The question is then whether, for risk assessments $\mathcal{R}_N$, we can choose δ sufficiently large that the local maximum is strictly in the interior of the restricted neighborhood. If this can be done, then the problem is regularizable. This leads to a delicate interplay between the class of risk assessments, the sample size, and the estimation problem itself.

Example 3.2. In the normal example above, $\mathcal{E}^{k,1,\delta}_{Q|\mathbf{x}_N}(\beta X)$ is regular whenever $\beta = o(N^{(\delta+1)/2})$ and $\delta < 1$ (for large N, with P-probability approaching 1 for every $P \in \mathcal{Q}$). Consequently, $\mathcal{E}^{k,1}_{Q|\mathbf{x}_N}(\beta X)$ is regularizable for any fixed β. This is suggested by the following sketch argument (and will be rigorously proven later).

As $\delta < 1$, we are restricting to a neighborhood of the MLE, so we can be confident that we will select a local extremum. We need only to verify that this occurs at a point with penalty $\alpha_{Q|\mathbf{x}_N}(\mu_*, \sigma^2_*) < N^\delta$. For large N, we approximate $\alpha_{Q|\mathbf{x}_N}$ by a quadratic in (μ, σ^2). This gives us the approximate optimization problem

$$\mathcal{E}^{k,1,\delta}_{Q|\mathbf{x}_N}(\beta X) \approx \sup_{\mu,\sigma^2} \left\{ \beta\mu - \left\{ \frac{N}{2k\sigma^2}(\bar{X} - \mu)^2 + \left(\frac{N}{4k}\right)\left(\frac{\sigma^2}{\hat{\sigma}^2} - 1\right)^2 \right\} \right\}.$$

The extremum of this approximation is attained by

$$\mu_* = \bar{X} + \frac{k}{N}\beta\sigma^2, \qquad \sigma_*^2 = \hat{\sigma}^2\left(1 + \frac{\beta^2 k^2}{N^2}\hat{\sigma}^2\right).$$

We now substitute back into the quadratic approximation, to obtain

$$\alpha_{\mathcal{Q}|\mathbf{x}_N}(\mu_*, \sigma_*^2) \approx \frac{k\beta^2}{2N}\hat{\sigma}^2\left(1 + \frac{\beta^2 k^2}{N^2}\hat{\sigma}^2\right) + \left(\frac{N}{4k}\right)\left(\frac{\beta^2 k^2}{N^2}\hat{\sigma}^2\right)^2$$

$$= O_P(N^{-1}\beta^2 + N^{-3}\beta^4).$$

Provided $\beta = o(N^{(\delta+1)/2})$, this guarantees $\alpha_{\mathcal{Q}|\mathbf{x}_N}(\mu_*, \sigma_*^2) = o_P(N^\delta)$, so our DR-expectation is regular.

For fixed β (or more generally $\beta = o(N^{1-\eta})$ for some $\eta > 0$), we can find a δ satisfying these conditions. Therefore, with P-probability approaching one for every $P \in \mathcal{Q}$, as $N \to \infty$, the DR-expectation is regular. Therefore, the DR-expectation is regularizable.

To make the argument above rigorous and more generally applicable, we proceed under the following assumption on our observations.

Assumption 3.1. *Assume that*

(i) *The family $\mathcal{Q}$ is parametrized by an open set $\Theta \subseteq \mathbb{R}^d$.*

(ii) *Under each $Q \in \mathcal{Q}$, the observations $\{X\} \cup \{X_n\}_{n \in \mathbb{N}}$ are iid with density of the form*

$$f(x; Q) = h(x)\exp\left\{\langle \theta, T(x)\rangle - A(\theta)\right\}.$$

(in other words, $\mathcal{Q}$ is an exponential family with its natural parametrization), where T and A are fixed functions (called respectively the sufficient statistic and the log-partition function).

(iii) *The variable of interest is $\xi = \phi(X)$, for some Borel function ϕ.*

(iv) *The Hessian $\mathfrak{I}_\theta = \partial^2 A(\theta)$ (commonly known as the information matrix) is strictly positive definite at every point of Θ.*

(v) *The Q-MLE exists and is consistent, with probability tending to 1 as $N \to \infty$ (that is, for every $P \in \mathcal{Q}$, a maximizer $\hat{Q}_N$ of the likelihood in $\mathcal{Q}$ exists with P-probability approaching 1 and $\hat{\theta}_N = \theta_{\hat{Q}_N} \to_P \theta_P$).*

The above assumption leads to the following estimate, which gives us a good understanding of the asymptotic behavior of $\alpha_{\mathcal{Q}|\mathbf{x}_N}$. For simplicity of notation, we shall write $\alpha_{\mathcal{Q}|\mathbf{x}_N}(\theta)$ for $\alpha_{\mathcal{Q}|\mathbf{x}_N}(Q_\theta)$, where Q_θ is the measure parametrized by $\theta \in \Theta$.

Lemma 3.1. *Suppose Assumption 3.1 holds. Then for every $P \in \mathcal{Q}$, there exists a constant $C > 0$ depending on P but independent of N, such that we have the uniform bound*

$$P\left(\alpha_{\mathcal{Q}|\mathbf{x}_N}(\theta) \geq \frac{N}{C}\|\theta - \hat{\theta}_N\|(1 \wedge \|\theta - \hat{\theta}_N\|) \text{ for all } \theta\right) \to 1.$$

Proof. This follows from the proof of Lemma 3 in [1]. □

The following abstract approximation result will be useful.

Theorem 3.1. *Consider the maximization of the general function*

$$f_N(\psi) := g_N(\psi) - \frac{1}{k}\alpha_{\mathcal{Q}|\mathbf{x}_N}(\hat{\theta} + \psi)$$

Suppose that $\alpha_{\mathcal{Q}|\mathbf{x}_N}$ arises from a setting where the result of Lemma 3.1 can be applied and, for some $\epsilon \in]0, 1/2]$, for every $P \in \mathcal{Q}$, for every N the function g_N is C^3 and satisfies, for B a ball of constant radius around $\psi = 0$,

(i) $g_N(0) = 0$,
(ii) $\|g_N'(\psi)\| = o_P(N^{1-\epsilon})$ uniformly on B,
(iii) $\|g_N''(0)\| = o_P(N)$,
(iv) $\|g_N'''(\psi)\| = O_P(N)$ uniformly on B.

Then defining

$$\delta = 1 - 2\epsilon$$

there exists a point ψ_N^* such that, for each $P \in \mathcal{Q}$, with P-probability approaching 1 as $N \to \infty$, we know that ψ_N^* maximizes the value of f_N on the set $\{\psi : \alpha_{\mathcal{Q}|\mathbf{x}_N}(\hat{\theta} + \psi) \leq N^\delta\}$ and, furthermore, $\alpha_{\mathcal{Q}|\mathbf{x}_N}(\hat{\theta} + \psi_N^*) = o_P(N^\delta)$.

Proof. See Appendix. □

Example 3.3. In the normal setting considered in Example 3.2, we are seeking to maximize

$$\beta\mu - \frac{1}{k}\alpha_{\mathcal{Q}|\mathbf{x}}(\mu, \sigma^2) = \beta\bar{X} + \left\{\beta\psi_\mu - \frac{1}{k}\alpha_{\mathcal{Q}|\mathbf{x}}(\psi)\right\}$$

where $\psi = (\psi_\mu, \psi_{\sigma^2}) = (\mu - \bar{X}, \sigma^2 - \hat{\sigma}^2)$. Provided $\beta = o(N^{1-\eta})$ for some $\eta > 0$, we can take $g(\psi) = \beta\psi_\mu$, which satisfies the conditions of Theorem 3.1. By application of the theorem, it follows that the DR-expectation is regularizable in this case, giving a rigorous proof of the condition obtained by quadratic approximation in Example 3.2.

In the above example, we have considered the case $\gamma = 1$. We can also obtain a sufficient condition for the case $\gamma > 1$ using an extension of this method, assuming that $\epsilon = 1/2$.

Lemma 3.2. *Suppose that, in the case $\gamma = 1$, our truncated optimization problem* (2) *has a maximizer Q_1^* where $\alpha_{\mathcal{Q}|\mathbf{x}_N}(Q_1^*) < 1$, when taking a truncation parameter $\delta \geq 0$. Then the truncated problem in the case $\gamma \geq 1$ certainly has a maximizer Q_γ^* with $\alpha_{\mathcal{Q}|\mathbf{x}_N}(Q_\gamma^*) < 1$, using the same truncation parameter.*

Proof. This is immediate from the fact that $|x|^\gamma < |x|$ for $|x| < 1$ and $|x|^\gamma > |x|$ for $|x| > 1$. □

Example 3.4. In the normal setting, we see that if $\beta = o(N^{1/2})$ then Theorem 3.1 yields the regularization parameter $\delta = 1 - 2\epsilon = 0$. In other words, we truncate to a set $\alpha_{\mathcal{Q}|\mathbf{x}_N} < o_P(1)$. By Lemma 3.2, this implies that the same regularization will be sufficient for all choices of $\gamma < \infty$.

This argument suggests that $\beta = o(N^{1/2})$ is a fundamental requirement for reliable statistical estimation of $E[\beta X]$ from N observations, under the assumption that X and our observations are iid normal with unknown mean and variance. Comparing with the case $\gamma = \infty$, where the DR-expectation is the upper bound of a confidence interval, we would need $\beta = o(N^{1/2})$ to ensure that

$$\left| \mathcal{E}_{\mathcal{Q}|\mathbf{x}_N}^{k,\infty}(\beta X) - E_{\hat{Q}}[\beta X] \right| \approx \sqrt{2k}\,\frac{|\beta|}{\sqrt{N}}\hat{\sigma} \to 0,$$

where $\hat{Q}$ is the MLE.

Remark 3.4. The example above shows that there is a close asymptotic relationship between regularity and the convergence of confidence intervals. However, the concept of regularity has the advantage that it can be applied for a given sample (of fixed size), rather than only being meaningful in an asymptotic sense. In particular, for a given sample, we can evaluate (for fixed $\delta \geq 0$) whether our truncated DR-expectation is regular, which allows us to qualitatively assess the statistical reliability of our estimates *based on the data at hand, and for the variables of interest.* In particular, if the function to be maximized when calculating $(\mathcal{E}_{\mathcal{Q}|\mathbf{x}_N}^{k,\gamma} \circ \mathcal{R})(\xi)$ does not have a local maximum near the MLE, then we know that the DR-risk assessment is not regular for any δ. This is unlike a confidence interval, which will generally not give a qualitative assessment of reliability for any fixed sample.

If we find that our problem is not regular, then we know that the observed data are insufficient to guide our calculation of DR-expectations — our choice of regularization has an overriding impact on our conclusions.

4. Heavy tails

The example given in the previous section shows us that, in a Gaussian setting, provided β is not too large relative to N (in particular $\beta = o(N^{1-\eta})$ for some $\eta > 0$), the DR-expectation $\mathcal{E}_{\mathcal{Q}|\mathbf{x}_N}^{k,1}(\beta X)$ is regularizable. This suggests asymptotic bounds on the size of random variables we are willing to consider, if we wish to account for our statistical uncertainty. In what follows, we shall seek to show that a similar relationship exists in a heavy tailed setting, when we calculate expected shortfall and related quantities.

We shall focus our attention on the following special case.

Assumption 4.1. *The family of measures $\mathcal{Q}$ describes models under which our observations $\{X\} \cup \{X_n\}_{n\in\mathbb{N}}$ are iid from a Pareto distribution (with known minimal value 1), that is, for a model parametrized by θ, we have the density*

$$f(x; \theta) = \theta x^{-(1+\theta)}; x > 1.$$

The possible values of θ will be assumed to satisfy one of two cases:

(i) $\mathcal{Q}$ corresponds to all $\theta > 0$ (which implies a valid probability distribution for X, but no integrability),

(ii) $\mathcal{Q}$ corresponds to all $\theta > 1$ (which implies X is integrable).

We should note that this is an exponential family of distributions, so the above approximation results (in particular Lemma 3.1) can be applied. Clearly Assumption 4.1(ii) is stronger than Assumption 4.1(i).

It is an easy exercise to show the following:

Proposition 4.1. *In the setting of Assumption 4.1, the MLE is given by*

$$\hat{\theta} = \frac{N}{\sum_i \log(x_i)}$$

and the divergence by

$$\alpha_{\mathcal{Q}|\mathbf{x}_N}(\theta) = N\left(-\log\left(\frac{\theta}{\hat{\theta}}\right) - 1 + \frac{\theta}{\hat{\theta}}\right).$$

Remark 4.1. This is a significantly simplified version of a standard extreme value estimation problem. In particular, consider a model for excesses over a threshold u. By the Pickands–Balkema–de Haan theorem (see for example Embrechts, Klüppelberg and Mikosch [5]), we know that for large u, the probability distribution in such a setting is typically approximated by the generalized Pareto distribution

$$P(X - u \le y | X > u) \approx \begin{cases} 1 - \left(1 + \frac{ky}{\sigma}\right)^{-1/k} & \text{if } k \ne 0, \\ 1 - e^{-y/\sigma} & \text{if } k = 0. \end{cases}$$

If we assume that this is the correct distribution family (so we are in the limiting regime), the scale variable σ is known (for simplicity) and $k > 0$ (so our distribution is unbounded and not exponential), then estimating k is equivalent to estimating θ in the above (classical) Pareto setting (after reparametrization).

Of course, in practice, the estimation of σ and the choice of cut-off value u are significant issues in their own right. What we shall see is that, even without these additional concerns, the estimation error associated with k (equivalently θ) is sufficient to restrict which risk assessments can be reliably estimated.

In what follows, we shall give relationships, for a variety of common risk assessment methods, between the growth of a parameter β (which will describe the 'extremity' of our risk assessment) and the sample size N, such that the DR-risk assessment is regularizable. This gives a method of assessing the reliability of our statistical estimates. We should point out that, if this were to be used in the context of fitting the excesses over a threshold, our sample size N would refer exclusively to the number of excesses we observe, and any probabilities would be conditional on being over the threshold point.

4.1. *Expected shortfall*

The first example we shall consider is the DR-expected shortfall, as defined in Example 2.1. As expected shortfall is a convex expectation, we know that the DR-expected shortfall is also a convex expectation. Given the expected shortfall is only defined for integrable random variables, we shall work under Assumption 4.1(ii).

Lemma 4.1. *Without truncation, under Assumption 4.1(ii), the DR-expected shortfall is infinite for all N, and all probability levels β, that is*

$$(\mathcal{E}_{\mathcal{Q}|\mathbf{x}_N}^{k,\gamma} \circ \mathrm{ES}_\beta)(X) = \infty$$

for every set of observations $\mathbf{x}_N$ and all choices of $k, \gamma < \infty$.

Proof. Under Assumption 4.1, for a given $\theta > 1$, we can calculate the Expected shortfall with tail probability β,

$$\mathrm{ES}_\beta = E[X | X > F_\theta^{-1}(1 - \beta)] = \frac{\theta}{\theta - 1} \beta^{-1/\theta}.$$

As $\theta \downarrow 1$, we observe that $\mathrm{ES}_\beta \to \infty$, but $\alpha_{\mathcal{Q}|\mathbf{x}_N}(\theta) \not\to \infty$. Therefore, for every $\gamma < \infty$, it is easy to see that $(\mathcal{E}_{\mathcal{Q}|\mathbf{x}_N}^{k,\gamma} \circ \mathrm{ES}_\beta)(X) = \infty$. $\square$

Remark 4.2. In the case $\gamma = \infty$, by monotonicity we will have

$$(\mathcal{E}_{\mathcal{Q}|\mathbf{x}_N}^{k,\gamma} \circ \mathrm{ES}_\beta)(X) = \frac{\theta^*}{\theta^* - 1} \beta^{-1/\theta^*},$$

where θ^* is the smallest value[4] such that $\alpha_{\mathcal{Q}|\mathbf{x}_N}(\theta) \le k$. This condition is the same for all N – in particular, using only a single observation, we give a finite estimate of the expected shortfall at any level $\beta \approx 0$ (i.e. arbitrarily far into the tail), which is intuitively unreasonable. This is the 'confidence interval' bound discussed in Embrechts, Klüppelberg and Mikosch [5].

This problem can be treated through regularization techniques, giving qualitatively different conclusions.

Theorem 4.1. *Under Assumption 4.1(ii), in the case $\gamma = 1$, the DR-expected shortfall with tail probability β is regularizable whenever $\beta^{-1} = o(N^{1-\eta})$, for some $\eta > 0$.*

Proof. As the MLE is consistent, we know that for large N, $\hat{\theta} > 1$ with P-probability approaching 1, for every $P \in \mathcal{Q}$. In what follows, we assume this is the case.

The quantity to be (locally) maximized when calculating (2) is

$$\frac{\theta}{\theta - 1} \beta^{-1/\theta} - \frac{N}{k} \Big(\log(\hat{\theta}/\theta) - 1 + \theta/\hat{\theta} \Big).$$

To apply Theorem 3.1, as we are interested in small values of β, we calculate the derivatives

$$\frac{d}{d\theta} \Big(\frac{\theta}{\theta - 1} \beta^{-1/\theta} \Big) = \beta^{-1/\theta} \Big(\frac{\log \beta}{\theta(\theta - 1)} - \frac{1}{(\theta - 1)^2} \Big),$$

$$\frac{d^2}{d\theta^2} \Big(\frac{\theta}{\theta - 1} \beta^{-1/\theta} \Big) = \beta^{-1/\theta} \Big(\frac{2}{(\theta - 1)^3} - \frac{2 \log \beta}{\theta(\theta - 1)^2} + \frac{(\log \beta)^2}{\theta^3(\theta - 1)} \Big),$$

$$\frac{d^3}{d\theta^3} \Big(\frac{\theta}{\theta - 1} \beta^{-1/\theta} \Big) = O(\beta^{-1/\theta}(\log \beta)^3) \quad \text{uniformly near } \theta > 1.$$

---

[4]This assumes $\theta^* > 1$, otherwise our risk assessment takes the value ∞.

For N large, uniformly in a neighborhood of $\hat{\theta} > 1$, taking

$$g_N(\psi) = \frac{\hat{\theta} + \psi}{\hat{\theta} + \psi - 1} \beta^{-1/(\hat{\theta}+\psi)} - \frac{\hat{\theta}}{\hat{\theta} - 1} \beta^{-1/\hat{\theta}}$$

the requirements of Theorem 3.1 are guaranteed by the simple condition

$$\frac{1}{\beta} = o_P(N^{\hat{\theta}-\eta}) \qquad \text{for some } \eta > 0, \text{ for all } P \in \mathcal{Q}.$$

As $\hat{\theta} > 1$ with P-probability approaching 1 for $P \in \mathcal{Q}$ (by consistency of the MLE), we obtain the deterministic bound desired. $\qquad\square$

Remark 4.3. This result places a qualitative bound on the extremity of the expected shortfall that can be reliably estimated, when we measure uncertainty through the DR-expected shortfall with $\gamma = 1$. Given N observations, for Pareto distributed models assuming only integrability, we cannot generally claim to estimate expected shortfalls for probabilities below c/N, where c is some constant. In particular, estimating extreme tails from small numbers of observations is shown to be unreliable.

Corollary 4.1. *Under Assumption 4.1(ii), in the case $\gamma < \infty$, the DR-expected shortfall with tail probability β is regularizable whenever $\beta^{-1} = o_P(N^{1/2-\eta})$, in particular when $\beta^{-1} = o(N^{1/2-\eta})$, for some $\eta > 0$.*

Proof. By assumption, we know that $\beta^{-1} = o_P(N^{\hat{\theta}/2-\eta})$, we can apply Theorem 3.1 with $\epsilon = 1/2$. This gives us a regularization parameter $\delta = 0$, and from Lemma 3.2 we observe regularity for all $\gamma < \infty$. $\qquad\square$

Remark 4.4. In practice, this is still a very optimistic requirement for reliable estimation, as we have assumed that our simple Pareto model is correct (and no further parameters need to be estimated). In this sense, these results give 'best-case' bounds on how far into the tail we can look before losing reliability of expected shortfall estimation using a Pareto model.

4.2. *Value at risk*

The Value at Risk (with tail probability β) is not a convex risk measure, so it is not generally true that $\mathcal{E}^{k,\gamma}_{\mathcal{Q}|\mathbf{x}_N} \circ \mathrm{VaR}_\beta$ is a convex expectation. Nevertheless, we can calculate

$$\mathrm{VaR}_\beta(X) = F_\theta^{-1}(1 - \beta) = \beta^{-1/\theta}.$$

Given this is well defined (and finite) for every distribution, we shall proceed under Assumption 4.1(i).

Lemma 4.2. *Without truncation, under Assumption 4.1(i), the DR-value at risk is infinite for all N, and all probability levels $\beta < 1$, that is*

$$(\mathcal{E}^{k,\gamma}_{\mathcal{Q}|\mathbf{x}_N} \circ \mathrm{VaR}_\beta)(X) = \infty$$

for every set of observations $\mathbf{x}_N$ and all choices of $k, \gamma < \infty$.

Proof. As in the Expected Shortfall case, we observe that $\beta^{-1/\theta} \to \infty$ as $\theta \downarrow 0$, but $\alpha_{\mathcal{Q}|\mathbf{x}_N}(\theta) \not\to \infty$ as $\theta \to 0$. The result follows. $\qquad\square$

Remark 4.5. If we assumed Assumption 4.1(ii), then for $\beta \to 0$ and finite N, we would obtain $(\mathcal{E}^{k,\gamma}_{\mathcal{Q}|\mathbf{x}_N} \circ \mathrm{VaR}_\beta)(X) \approx 1/\beta$, independently of the observed values. Clearly this is not reliable statistically, as it is the assumption of integrability, rather than the observations, which is leading to finiteness of the estimate.

Theorem 4.2. *Under Assumption 4.1(i), for all $\gamma < \infty$, the DR-Value at Risk with tail probability β is regularizable whenever $\beta^{-1} = O(1)$ (as $N \to \infty$), for some $\eta > 0$.*

Proof. As in the Expected Shortfall case, we see that

$$\frac{d^n}{d\theta^n}\left(\beta^{-1/\theta}\right) = O(\beta^{-1/\theta}((\log \beta)^n + 1)).$$

Applying Theorem 3.1 leads to the proposed condition for regularizability (in the case $\gamma = 1$)

$$\frac{1}{\beta} = o_P(N^{\hat{\theta}-\eta}) \qquad \text{for some } \eta > 0, \text{ for all } P \in \mathcal{Q}.$$

Again, using Lemma 3.2, for regularizability of the $\gamma > 1$ case, we obtain the condition $\beta^{-1} = o_P(N^{\hat{\theta}/2-\eta})$ for some $\eta > 0$. Consistency of the MLE (and the assumption $\theta > 0$ for all P), shows that this is guaranteed when $\beta^{-1} = O(1)$ as $N \to \infty$. $\qquad\square$

Remark 4.6. The requirement $\beta^{-1} = O(1)$ is quite restrictive, but comes from the fact we are assuming nothing beyond Assumption 4.1(i), i.e. that our distribution is well defined. Strengthening Assumption 4.1(i) to restrict to $\theta > \tilde{\theta}$ for some $\tilde{\theta} > 0$, we have regularizability whenever $\beta^{-1} = o(N^{\tilde{\theta}/2-\eta})$ for some $\eta > 0$.

4.3. *Probability of loss*

The probability of a loss exceeding a level β is given by (under Assumption 4.1(i)

$$\mathrm{PL}_\beta(X) = P(X > \beta) = 1 - F_\theta(\beta) = \beta^{-\theta}.$$

This is not a convex expectation, however we can equivalently express it as $P(X > \beta) = E[I_{X>\beta}]$, and then consider the regularity of

$$(\mathcal{E}^{k,\gamma}_{\mathcal{Q}|\mathbf{x}_N} \circ \mathrm{PL}_\beta)(X) = \mathcal{E}^{k,\gamma}_{\mathcal{Q}|\mathbf{x}_N}(I_{X>\beta}).$$

Theorem 4.3. *The DR-probability of a loss is regular, for all N, γ and β.*

Proof. As $I_{X>\beta}$ is bounded, this is well behaved without regularization, no matter what the choice of β. $\qquad\square$

Remark 4.7. The asymptotic behavior of the DR-probability of loss (and other bounded random variables) is described by [1], Section 3.2.

4.4. *Integrated tail and Cramér–Lundberg failure probability*

From an insurance perspective, it is sometimes of interest to look at the integrated tail, which under Assumption 4.1(ii) is given by

$$\mathrm{IT}_\beta(X) := E[(X - \beta)^+] = \int_\beta^\infty (1 - F_\theta(x))dx = \int_\beta^\infty x^{-\theta}dx = \frac{\beta^{1-\theta}}{\theta - 1}.$$

Remark 4.8. For $\beta \geq 1$, this a convex map, but not translation invariant, so the DR-integrated tail, $(\mathcal{E}^{k,\gamma}_{\mathcal{Q}|\mathbf{x}_N} \circ \mathrm{IT}_\beta)(\cdot)$, is not generally a convex expectation.

As in the previous cases, without truncation, the DR-integrated tail poses some problems.

Lemma 4.3. *Without truncation, under Assumption 4.1(ii), the DR-integrated tail is infinite for all N, and all $\beta \geq 1$, that is*

$$(\mathcal{E}^{k,\gamma}_{\mathcal{Q}|\mathbf{x}_N} \circ \mathrm{IT}_\beta)(X) = \infty$$

for every set of observations $\mathbf{x}$ and all choices of $k, \gamma < \infty$.

Proof. By direct calculation, considering $\theta \downarrow 1$,

$$(\mathcal{E}^{k,\gamma}_{\mathcal{Q}|\mathbf{x}_N} \circ \mathrm{IT}_\beta)(X) = \sup_\theta \left\{ \frac{\beta^{1-\theta}}{\theta - 1} - \frac{N}{k}\left(\log(\hat{\theta}/\theta) - 1 + \theta/\hat{\theta} \right) \right\} = \infty.$$

$\qquad\square$

The surprising result is that, while we need to truncate to avoid infinite values, the DR-integrated tail is always regularizable.

Theorem 4.4. *Under Assumption 4.1(ii), for all $\gamma < \infty$, the DR-integrated tail is regularizable for all choices of $\beta \geq 1$ (with any desired dependence on N).*

Proof. For all $P \in \mathcal{Q}$, as in the earlier settings, we calculate

$$\frac{d^n}{d\theta^n}\left(\frac{\beta^{1-\theta}}{\theta-1}\right) = O\big(\beta^{1-\theta}((\log\beta)^n + 1)\big).$$

However, for $\beta \geq 1$, $\theta > 1$, the right hand side is $o(1)$ with respect to β, in particular (by consistency of the MLE) it is $o_P(1)$ for every $P \in \mathcal{Q}$. Therefore, the integrated tail is regularizable with no restriction on the value of β, for every value of $\gamma < \infty$. $\qquad\square$

A closely related quantity is the related failure probability under a Cramér–Lundberg model, given by (under Assumption 4.1(ii))

$$\mathrm{CL}_\beta(X) = \frac{\mathrm{IT}_\beta}{E[X]} = \frac{\beta^{1-\theta}}{\theta}.$$

Theorem 4.5. *For all choices of $\beta \geq 1$, under Assumption 4.1(ii), the DR-Cramér–Lundberg failure probability is regularizable.*

Proof. We calculate

$$(\mathcal{E}^{k,\gamma}_{\mathcal{Q}|\mathbf{x}_N} \circ \mathrm{CL}_\beta)(X) = \sup_\theta\left\{\frac{\beta^{1-\theta}}{\theta} - \frac{N}{k}\Big(\log(\hat{\theta}/\theta) - 1 + \theta/\hat{\theta}\Big)\right\}.$$

For $\beta \geq 1$, we know $\frac{\beta^{1-\theta}}{\theta}$ is (uniformly) bounded for all $\theta > 1$. Therefore, from the consistency of the MLE and Theorem 3.1, $(\mathcal{E}^{k,\gamma}_{\mathcal{Q}|\mathbf{x}_N} \circ \mathrm{CL}_\beta)(X)$ is regularizable. $\qquad\square$

4.5. *Distortion risk*

As a final example, we consider a distortion based nonlinear expectation. This is given by taking a convex increasing bijective map $\lambda : [0,1] \to [0,1]$, then calculating the expectation with the transformed cdf $F_\lambda(x) = \lambda(F(x))$. As λ is convex, it is differentiable almost everywhere, and we can calculate the transformed density under Assumption 4.1,

$$f_\lambda(x) = \lambda'(F(x))f(x) = \lambda'(1 - x^{-\theta})\theta x^{-(1+\theta)}.$$

so the distortion risk is given by

$$D_\lambda(X) = \int_1^\infty \lambda'(1 - x^{-\theta})\theta x^{-\theta}dx. \tag{3}$$

Lemma 4.4. *The distortion risk is finite whenever there exists $\zeta > 1/\theta$ such that*

$$\lambda'(y) = O((1 - y)^{-1+\zeta}) \qquad as\ y \to 1.$$

Proof. In order for D_λ to be finite, as $\theta > 0$, for large x we require $\lambda'(1 - x^{-\theta})$ not to be too large, else we lose integrability in (3). As we know $x^{-(1+\zeta)}$ is integrable on $[1, \infty[$, the result follows by dominated convergence. $\square$

As λ is increasing and convex, for any $y < 1$, we know that $\{\lambda'(x)\}_{x<y}$ is bounded, so it is the behavior of λ' near 1 which is of interest. For this reason, we will focus our attention on the following example.

Definition 4.1. We say λ is the 'minmaxvar' transform (with parameter $\beta \in (0, 1]$) if $\lambda(x) = \lambda_\beta(x) := 1 - (1 - x)^\beta$.

This case is interesting from our perspective, as it describes the critical growth of λ near the boundary $x = 1$. Other classic examples, for example the Wang transform $\lambda(x) = \Phi(\Phi^{-1}(x) - \beta)$, where Φ is the normal cdf, are also of interest in some settings, but do not have this critical growth. This is closely related to the 'minmaxvar' risk measure considered by Cherny and Madan [14].

Lemma 4.5. *Without truncation, under Assumption 4.1(ii), the DR-minmaxvar risk is infinite for all N, and all $\beta \in (0, 1)$, that is*

$$(\mathcal{E}_{\mathcal{Q}|\mathbf{x}_N}^{k,\gamma} \circ D_{\lambda_\beta})(X) = \infty$$

for every set of observations $\mathbf{x}_N$ and all choices of $k, \gamma < \infty$.

Proof. We know $\lambda_\beta'(x) = \beta(1 - x)^{\beta-1}$, so

$$D_{\lambda_\beta} = \int_1^\infty \lambda_\beta'(1 - x^{-\theta})\theta x^{-\theta}dx = \int_1^\infty \beta(x^{-\theta})^{\beta-1}\theta x^{-\theta}dx = \frac{\beta\theta}{\beta\theta - 1}$$

provided $\beta > 1/\theta$, and is otherwise infinite. As $\alpha_{\mathcal{Q}|\mathbf{x}}(1/\beta) < \infty$ for all $\beta \in (0, 1)$, our DR-minmaxvar risk will be infinite. $\square$

Theorem 4.6. *Under Assumption 4.1(ii), the DR-minmaxvar risk is not regularizable for any $\beta < 1$. However, under the stronger assumption that we restrict our models to those where $\theta > \tilde{\theta}$ for some $\tilde{\theta} > 1$, then the DR-minmaxvar risk is regularizable whenever*

$$\beta \geq \frac{1}{\tilde{\theta}} + \frac{1}{|O(N^\eta)|}.$$

where $\eta = 1/4$ in the case $\gamma = 1$, and $\eta < 1/4$ in the case $\gamma < \infty$.

Proof. For any fixed $\beta < 1$, Assumption 4.1(ii), is insufficient to guarantee that the MLE $\hat{\theta} > 1/\beta$ (as $\hat{\theta}$ may be arbitrarily close to 1). As this is the condition for finiteness of D_{λ_β} and the MLE satisfies $\alpha_{\mathcal{Q}|\mathbf{x}_N}(\hat{\theta}) \equiv 0$, the non-regularizability follows.

Under our stronger assumption, to determine conditions on β such that the DR-minmaxvar risk is regularizable, we proceed as before. We can calculate

$$(\mathcal{E}^{k,1}_{\mathcal{Q}|\mathbf{x}_N} \circ D_{\lambda_\beta})(X) = \sup_\theta \left\{ \frac{\beta\theta}{\beta\theta - 1} - \left(\frac{N}{k} \left(\log(\hat{\theta}/\theta) - 1 + \theta/\hat{\theta} \right) \right)^\gamma \right\}.$$

We have the derivatives

$$\frac{d}{d\theta} \left(\frac{\beta\theta}{\beta\theta - 1} \right) = \frac{-\beta}{(\beta\theta - 1)^2},$$

$$\frac{d^2}{d\theta^2} \left(\frac{\beta\theta}{\beta\theta - 1} \right) = \frac{2\beta^2}{(\beta\theta - 1)^3},$$

$$\frac{d^3}{d\theta^3} \left(\frac{\beta\theta}{\beta\theta - 1} \right) = \frac{-6\beta^3}{(\beta\theta - 1)^4}.$$

With $g_N(\psi) = \frac{\beta(\hat{\theta}+\psi)}{\beta(\hat{\theta}+\psi)-1} - \frac{\beta\hat{\theta}}{\beta\hat{\theta}-1}$, Theorem 3.1 is satisfied by assuming $(\hat{\theta}\beta - 1)^{-4} = O_P(N)$, or equivalently,

$$\beta \geq \frac{1}{\hat{\theta}} + \frac{1}{|O_P(N^{1/4})|}.$$

Using the consistency of the MLE we know $\hat{\theta} > \tilde{\theta}$, and the result follows. If we make the further assumption that $\beta = \tilde{\theta}^{-1} + 1/|O(N^\eta)|$ for $\eta < 1/4$, we can take $\epsilon = 1/2$ in Theorem 3.1, to obtain regularizability for all $\gamma < \infty$. $\qquad \square$

Remark 4.9. Many further cases can also be considered, using this general approach. It would be interesting also to apply DR-regularization in a more general estimation problem, where we do not assume simply that we have a Pareto distribution, but must use a generalized extreme value or generalized Pareto model, with the associated estimation difficulties.

Appendix

To prove our key approximation result (Theorem 3.1) we begin with the following lemma.

Lemma A.1. *Consider a C^3 function $f : \mathbb{R}^N \to \mathbb{R}$, with negative definite Hessian at zero H. Suppose we wish to find a local maximum in a small ball B_δ of radius δ around 0. Let $c_\delta = \sup_{x \in B_\delta} \|f'''(x)\|$. If a local maximum exists in the interior of the ball, then it has position*

$$x^* = -H^{-1}f'(0) + c_\delta \|H^{-1}\|O(\delta^2).$$

Proof. By Taylor's theorem, we can write the expansion

$$f(x) = f(0) + x^\top f'(0) + \frac{1}{2}x^\top H x + R(x)$$

where R is some remainder term with $|R(x)| \leq (c_\delta/6)\|x\|^3$ and derivative $\|R'(x)\| \leq (c_\delta/2)\|x\|^2 = c_\delta O(\delta^2)$ on our ball. To find a local extremum x^*, we differentiate to obtain the vector equation

$$0 = f'(0) + Hx^* + R'(x^*)$$

which rearranges to give the approximation (which is true for every interior local extremum)

$$x^* = -H^{-1}f'(0) - H^{-1}R'(x^*).$$

For an extremum within the ball, we have the desired approximation

$$x^* = -H^{-1}f'(0) + c_\delta \|H^{-1}\|O(\delta^2).$$

$\square$

We now combine Lemma A.1 and Lemma 3.1 to give a proof of Theorem 3.1, which we repeat here for the ease of the reader.

Theorem A.1. *Consider the maximization of the general function*

$$f_N(\psi) := g_N(\psi) - \frac{1}{k}\alpha_{\mathcal{Q}|\mathbf{x}_N}(\hat{\theta} + \psi)$$

Suppose that $\alpha_{\mathcal{Q}|\mathbf{x}_N}$ arises from a setting where the result of Lemma 3.1 can be applied and, for some $\epsilon \in]0, 1/2]$, for every $P \in \mathcal{Q}$, for every N the function g_N is C^3 and satisfies, for B a ball of constant radius around $\psi = 0$,

(i) $g_N(0) = 0$,
(ii) $\|g'_N(\psi)\| = o_P(N^{1-\epsilon})$ uniformly on B,

(iii) $\|g_N''(0)\| = o_P(N)$,
(iv) $\|g_N'''(\psi)\| = O_P(N)$ *uniformly on B.*

Then there exists a point ψ_N^* such that, for each $P \in \mathcal{Q}$, with P-probability approaching 1 as $N \to \infty$, we know that ψ_N^* maximizes the value of f_N on the set $\{\psi : \alpha_{\mathcal{Q}|\mathbf{x}_N}(\hat{\theta} + \psi) \le N^{1-2\epsilon}\}$ and, furthermore, $\alpha_{\mathcal{Q}|\mathbf{x}_N}(\hat{\theta} + \psi_N^*) = o_P(N^{1-2\epsilon})$.

Proof. By Lemma 3.1, for all N sufficiently large, with arbitrarily high P-probability, for ψ in a neighborhood of zero of fixed radius, there exists a constant $C > 0$ (depending on P) such that

$$\alpha_{\mathcal{Q}|\mathbf{x}_N}(\hat{\theta} + \psi) > \frac{N}{C}\|\psi\|^2$$

and outside this neighborhood $\alpha_{\mathcal{Q}|\mathbf{x}_N}(\hat{\theta} + \psi) \ge O(N)$. In all that follows, we restrict our attention to this constant radius ball.

Omitting subscript N for simplicity, from our assumptions on g we know

$$g(\psi) = o_P(N^{1-\epsilon})\|\psi\|.$$

Consequently, except possibly on a ball of radius $O_P(N^{-\epsilon})$ around zero, we know that

$$\alpha_{\mathcal{Q}|\mathbf{x}_N}(\hat{\theta} + \psi) > \frac{N}{C}\|\psi\|^2 > o_P(N^{1-\epsilon})\|\psi\| = |g(\psi)|.$$

It follows that, for all ψ outside a ball of radius $O_P(N^{-\epsilon})$, we know that $f(\psi) < 0$. As $f(0) = 0$, there must exist a local maximum within the ball of radius $O_P(N^{-\epsilon})$.

We know that,

$$f'(0) = g'(0) = o_P(N^{1-\epsilon})$$
$$\|f''(0)^{-1}\| \le \|(g''(0) - N/C)^{-1}\| = O_P(N^{-1})$$
$$f'''(\psi) = g'''(\psi) + \alpha_{\mathcal{Q}|\mathbf{x}_N}'''(\hat{\theta} + \psi) = O_P(N).$$

Applying Lemma A.1, we know that any local maximum of f within a ball of radius $o_P(N^{-\epsilon/2})$ will be at a point satisfying

$$\psi^* = -f''(0)^{-1}f'(0) + O_P(N)\|f''(0)^{-1}\|o_P(N^{-\epsilon}) = o_P(N^{-\epsilon}).$$

Therefore, *all* local maxima within the ball of radius $o_P(N^{-\epsilon/2})$ will be within the ball of radius $o_P(N^{-\epsilon})$.

Taking a Taylor approximation of the C^3 function $\alpha_{\mathcal{Q}|\mathbf{x}_N}$ we see that, within the ball of radius $o_P(N^{-\epsilon})$,

$$\alpha_{\mathcal{Q}|\mathbf{x}_N}(\hat{\theta} + \psi) = N\psi^\top(\mathfrak{I}_{\hat{\theta}} + O_P(\|\psi\|))\psi = \|\mathfrak{I}_{\hat{\theta}}\|o_P(N^{1-2\epsilon}) + o_P(N^{1-3\epsilon})$$
$$= o_P(N^{1-2\epsilon}).$$

Conversely, outside the ball of radius $o_P(N^{-\epsilon/2})$, we know that $\alpha_{\mathcal{Q}|\mathbf{x}_N}(\hat{\theta} + \psi) > N^{1-\epsilon}/C$ for some $C > 0$. Therefore, we can be certain that a point $\psi^* = o_P(N^{-\epsilon})$ will be the maximizer within the region $\{\psi : \alpha_{\mathcal{Q}|\mathbf{x}_N}(\hat{\theta} + \psi) < N^{1-2\epsilon}\}$, as desired. $\qquad\square$

Acknowledgments

Research supported by the Oxford–Man Institute for Quantitative Finance and the Oxford–Nie Financial Big Data Laboratory.

References

1. S. Cohen, Data-driven nonlinear expectations for statistical uncertainty in decisions, *Electronic Journal of Statistics* **11**, 1858–1889 (2017).
2. F. Knight, *Risk, Uncertainty and Profit* (Houghton Mifflin, 1921).
3. A. Wald, Statistical decision functions which minimize the maximum risk, *Annals of Mathematics* **46**, 265–280 (1945).
4. H. Föllmer and A. Schied, *Stochastic Finance: An introduction in discrete time* (de Gruyter, 2002).
5. P. Embrechts, C. Klüppelberg and T. Mikosch, *Modelling Extremal events for Insurance and Finance* (Springer, 1997).
6. S. N. Cohen and R. J. Elliott, *Stochastic Calculus and Applications*, second Edn. (Birkhäuser, 2015).
7. A. N. Shiryaev, *Probability*, 2nd Edn. (Springer, 2000).
8. M. Frittelli and E. Rosazza Gianin, Putting order in risk measures, *Journal of Banking & Finance* **26**(7), 1473–1486 (2002).
9. P. Artzner, F. Delbaen, J.-M. Eber and D. Heath, Coherent measures of risk, *Mathematical Finance* **9**(3), 203–228 (1999).
10. H. White, Maximum likelihood estimation of misspecified models, *Econometrica* **50**(1), 1–25 (1982).
11. A. J. McNeil, R. Frey and P. Embrechts, *Quantitative Risk Management* (Princeton, 2005).
12. P. Barrieu and N. El Karoui, Inf-convolution of risk measures and optimal risk transfer, *Finance and Stochastics* **9**(2), 269–298 (2005).

13. E. Lehmann and G. Casella, *Theory of Point Estimation* (Springer, 1998).
14. A. Cherny and D. Madan, New measures for performance evaluation, *The Review of Financial Studies* **22**(7), 2571–2606 (2009).

Chapter 7

Intrinsic Risk Measures

Walter Farkas

University of Zurich, Department of Banking and Finance,
Plattenstrasse 14, 8032 Zürich, Switzerland
walter.farkas@bf.uzh.ch

Department of Mathematics, ETH Zurich
Swiss Finance Institute, Switzerland

Alexander Smirnow

University of Zurich, Department of Banking and Finance,
Andreasstrasse 15, 8050 Zürich, Switzerland
alexander.smirnow@bf.uzh.ch

Monetary risk measures classify a financial position by the minimal amount of external capital that must be added to the position to make it acceptable.

We propose a new concept: intrinsic risk measures. The definition via external capital is avoided and only internal resources appear. An intrinsic risk measure is defined by the smallest percentage of the currently held financial position which has to be sold and reinvested in an eligible asset such that the resulting position becomes acceptable.

We show that this approach requires less nominal investment in the eligible asset to reach acceptability. It provides a more direct path from unacceptable positions towards the acceptance set and implements desired properties such as monotonicity and quasi-convexity solely through the structure of the acceptance set. We derive a representation on cones and a dual representation on convex acceptance sets and we detail the connections of intrinsic risk measures to their monetary counterparts.

Keywords: intrinsic risk measures, monetary risk measures, acceptance sets, coherence, conicity, quasi-convexity, value-at-risk.

1. Introduction

Risk measures associated with acceptance criteria as introduced by P. Artzner, F. Delbaen, J. Eber, and D. Heath [1] are maps $\rho_{\mathcal{A},r}$ from a function space $\mathcal{X} \subseteq \mathbb{R}^{\Omega}$ to $\mathbb{R}$ of the form

$$\rho_{\mathcal{A},r}(X_T) = \inf \left\{ m \in \mathbb{R} \mid X_T + mr\mathbf{1}_{\Omega} \in \mathcal{A} \right\}. \tag{1}$$

These maps are means to measure the 'risk' of a financial position $X_T \in \mathcal{X}$ with respect to certain acceptability criteria and a risk-free investment. The latter are specified as a subset $\mathcal{A} \subset \mathcal{X}$, the *acceptance set*, and the risk-free return rate $r > 0$, respectively. Geometrically,[1] the risk of an unacceptable position $X_T \in \mathcal{X} \setminus \mathcal{A}$ in Equation (1) is defined as a scalar 'distance' to the acceptance set in direction $r\mathbf{1}_\Omega$. Such risk measures are known as *cash-additive* risk measures. Evidently, the acceptance set forms the primary object, whereas the risk-free asset contributes only a constant factor. More recent research has revisited the original idea using eligible assets with random return rates $r : \Omega \to \mathbb{R}_{>0}$, as for example P. Artzner, F. Delbaen, and P. Koch-Medina [2] and D. Konstantinides and C. Kountzakis [3]. W. Farkas, P. Koch-Medina, and C. Munari [4], [5] focus on general eligible assets $r : \Omega \to \mathbb{R}_{\geq 0}$, revealing significant shortcomings of the simplified constant approach. They point out that an appropriate interplay between eligible assets and acceptance sets is crucial for a consistent and successful risk measurement. They incorporate eligible assets as traded assets $S = (S_0, S_T)$ with initial unitary price $S_0 \in \mathbb{R}_{>0}$ and random payoff $S_T : \Omega \to \mathbb{R}_{\geq 0}$, and replace $r\mathbf{1}_\Omega$ in Equation (1) by the random return S_T/S_0. This alteration yields the extended definition

$$\rho_{\mathcal{A},S}(X_T) = \inf \left\{ m \in \mathbb{R} \mid X_T + \tfrac{m}{S_0} S_T \in \mathcal{A} \right\}. \tag{2}$$

Beside the geometric interpretation of $\tfrac{m}{S_0} S_T$ as a 'vector' it is economically interpreted as the payoff of $\tfrac{m}{S_0}$ units of asset S.

The more general definition in (2) can be consistently reduced to (1) if S_T is bounded away from zero, this means if $S_T \geq \varepsilon$, for some $\varepsilon > 0$.[2] This constitutes the basis for the simplified approach with constant return. However, payoffs of relevant financial instruments such as defaultable bonds and options do not satisfy this condition, and thus, the generalization to *S-additive* risk measures in (2) is justified.

Referring to eligible assets, P. Artzner, F. Delbaen, J. Eber, and D. Heath suggest in [1], Section 2.1, p. 205 that

> '*The current cost of getting enough of this or these [commonly accepted] instrument(s) is a good candidate for a measure of risk of the initially unacceptable position.*'

---

[1] See Figure 1(a) for a visual example.
[2] See [4], Section 1, p. 146ff. for a detailed discussion.

Both cash-additive and S-additive risk measures are conceptually in line with this suggestion, and we broadly refer to them as *monetary risk measures*.[3] This is a suitable name as these risk measures are defined as actual money which can be used to buy the eligible asset. Hence, they can be interpreted as more than just measurement tools. Referring to cash-additivity (or Axiom T), P. Artzner, F. Delbaen, J. Eber, and D. Heath claim in [1], Remark 2.7, p. 209 that

> '*By insisting on references to cash and to time, [...] our approach goes much further than the interpretation [...] that "the main function of a risk measure is to properly rank risks."*'

The application of this approach requires to raise the monetary amount $\rho_{A,S}(X_T)$ and carry it in the eligible asset S. However, the possible acquisition of additional capital is not completely accounted for by monetary risk measures. This raises the questions as to what effect this has on the risk measure and to which extent this method is applicable in reality.

Another approach is to restructure the portfolio and directly raise capital from the current position to invest it in the eligible asset, as was already mentioned in [1], Section 2.1, p. 205:

> '*For an unacceptable risk [...] one remedy may be to alter the position.*'

The aim of this article is to reflect about this thought and develop it towards a new class of risk measures, which we will call *intrinsic risk measures*. For great adaptability, we develop our approach based on acceptance sets $A \subset X$ as primary objects and the extended framework of general eligible assets $S = (S_0, S_T) \in \mathbb{R}_{>0} \times A$.

In the 'future wealth' approach described in [1], p. 205, it is not possible to change the current financial position, representing the principle of 'bygones are bygones'. The authors argue that the knowledge of the initial value of the position is not needed. So the risk measure is only used to determine the size of the buffer with respect to the eligible asset which sufficiently absorbs losses of this fixed position. However, we believe that a reconstruction of the financial position is possible and beneficial, since losses are not absorbed but essentially reduced as the eligible asset becomes part of the position. The intention to sell part of the current position requires the knowledge

---

[3] A definition is given in Section 2.2.

of the initial value. So while monetary risk measures are defined on $\mathcal{X}$, intrinsic risk measures take the initial value $X_0 \in \mathbb{R}_{>0}$ into account and are defined on $\mathbb{R}_{>0} \times \mathcal{X}$. For financial positions $X = (X_0, X_T)$ the intrinsic risk measure is given by

$$R_{\mathcal{A},S}(X) = \inf \left\{ \lambda \in [0,1] \,\middle|\, (1-\lambda)X_T + \lambda \tfrac{X_0}{S_0} S_T \in \mathcal{A} \right\}. \tag{3}$$

In words, we search for the smallest $\lambda \in [0,1]$ such that selling the fraction λ of our initial position and investing the monetary amount λX_0 in the eligible asset S yields an acceptable position. Using the convex combination $(1-\lambda)X_T + \lambda \frac{X_0}{S_0} S_T$, $\lambda \in [0,1]$, instead of $X_T + \frac{m}{S_0} S_T$, $m \in \mathbb{R}$, changes the form of risk measures and suggests a new way to shift unacceptable positions towards the acceptance set.[4] Furthermore, standard properties such as monotonicity and, in contrast to monetary risk measures, also quasi-convexity are imposed solely through the structure of the underlying acceptance set.

The subsequent work has grown from the master's thesis of A. Smirnow [6]. We will introduce acceptance sets and traditional risk measures, give economic motivation, and review important properties in Section 2 to build a foundation for comparison. In Section 3, we define the new class of intrinsic risk measures and we derive basic properties. We derive an alternative representation on cones and show that intrinsic risk measures require less investment in the eligible asset to yield acceptable positions. Finally, we study a dual representation of intrinsic risk measures on convex acceptance sets.

2. Terminology and preliminaries

In this section, we establish the foundations on which we can build our framework. Common terminology such as acceptance sets and traditional risk measures are introduced and discussed.

Throughout this chapter we work on an atomless probability space $(\Omega, \mathcal{F}, \mathbb{P})$. For the sake of exposition we consider financial positions on the space of essentially bounded random variables $\mathcal{X} = L^\infty(\Omega, \mathcal{F}, \mathbb{P})$ endowed with the $\mathbb{P}$-almost sure order and the $\mathbb{P}$-essential supremum norm. The majority of our results can be stated on arbitrary ordered real topological vector spaces.

---

[4]See Figure 1(b).

2.1. *Acceptance sets*

In the financial world, it is a central task to hold positions that satisfy certain acceptability criteria, may they represent own preferences or be of regulatory nature. These criteria can be brought into a mathematical framework via what is known as acceptance sets.

Definition 2.1. A subset $\mathcal{A} \subset \mathcal{X}$ is called an *acceptance set* if it satisfies

1. *Non-triviality*: $\mathcal{A} \neq \emptyset$ and $\mathcal{A} \subsetneq \mathcal{X}$, and
2. *Monotonicity*: $X_T \in \mathcal{A}$, $Y_T \in \mathcal{X}$, and $Y_T \geq X_T$ imply $Y_T \in \mathcal{A}$.

An element $X_T \in \mathcal{A}$ is called $\mathcal{A}$-*acceptable*, or just *acceptable* if the reference to $\mathcal{A}$ is clear. Similarly, we say $X_T \notin \mathcal{A}$ is ($\mathcal{A}$-)*unacceptable*.

Non-triviality is mathematically important and also representative of real world requirements, as generally not every situation is acceptable and any event requires near-term reactions. Monotonicity implements the idea that any financial position dominating an acceptable position must be acceptable. These two axioms constitute the basis for acceptance sets and reflect the 'minimal' human rationale.

Depending on the context, it is often necessary to impose further structure and we recall three relevant properties.

Definition 2.2. An acceptance set $\mathcal{A} \subset \mathcal{X}$ is called

- a *cone* or *conic* if $X_T \in \mathcal{A}$ implies for all $\lambda > 0 : \lambda X_T \in \mathcal{A}$,
- *convex* if $X_T, Y_T \in \mathcal{A}$ implies for all $\lambda \in [0,1] : \lambda X_T + (1 - \lambda)Y_T \in \mathcal{A}$,
- *closed* if $\mathcal{A} = \bar{\mathcal{A}}$.

The cone property allows for arbitrary scaling of financial positions invariant of their acceptability status. Convexity represents the principle of diversification: given two acceptable positions, any convex combination of these will be acceptable. In Section 2.2, we will see how these two properties translate to monetary risk measures. Finally, closedness is of mathematical importance when considering limits of sequences of acceptable positions. Apart from this, it is economically motivated as it prohibits arbitrarily small perturbations to make unacceptable positions acceptable.

The next lemma summarizes some useful properties of acceptance sets, which will be used in subsequent sections.

Lemma 2.1. *Let $\mathcal{A} \subset \mathcal{X}$ be an acceptance set. Then*

1. $\mathcal{A}$ *contains sufficiently large constants but no sufficiently small constants.*
2. $S_T \in \text{int}(\mathcal{A})$ *if and only if there exists an* $\varepsilon > 0$ *such that* $S_T - \varepsilon \mathbf{1}_\Omega \in \mathcal{A}$.
3. *The interior* $\text{int}(\mathcal{A})$ *and the closure* $\bar{\mathcal{A}}$ *are both acceptance sets, and* $\text{int}(\mathcal{A}) = \text{int}(\bar{\mathcal{A}})$.
4. *If* $\mathcal{A}$ *is a cone, then* $\text{int}(\mathcal{A})$ *and* $\bar{\mathcal{A}}$ *are cones, and* $0 \notin \text{int}(\mathcal{A})$ *and* $0 \in \bar{\mathcal{A}}$.

Proof. 1. Since $\mathcal{A}$ is a nonempty, proper subset of $\mathcal{X}$, the first assertion follows from monotonicity of $\mathcal{A}$.

2. The second assertion also follows directly from monotonicity of $\mathcal{A}$.

3. The proof of the third assertion goes along the lines of the proof of Lemma 2.3 in [5], p. 60 and is omitted here.

4. Given $S_T \in \text{int}(\mathcal{A})$, Assertion 2 together with the cone property imply $\lambda(S_T - \varepsilon \mathbf{1}_\Omega) \in \mathcal{A}$, for some $\varepsilon > 0$ and all $\lambda > 0$. The other direction of Assertion 2 implies $\lambda S_T \in \text{int}(\mathcal{A})$. Given $S_T \in \bar{\mathcal{A}}$, take a sequence $\{S_T^n\}_{n \in \mathbb{N}} \subset \mathcal{A}$ with limit S_T. Then conicity implies $\{\lambda S_T^n\}_{n \in \mathbb{N}} \subset \mathcal{A}$, for any $\lambda > 0$, and we conclude that λS_T belongs to $\bar{\mathcal{A}}$. The last two claims follow by similar arguments. □

We conclude this section with the well-known example of the *Value-at-Risk acceptance set.*

Example 2.1 (Value-at-Risk acceptance). *For any probability level* $\alpha \in \left(0, \frac{1}{2}\right)$ *the set*

$$\mathcal{A}_\alpha = \{X_T \in \mathcal{X} \mid \mathbb{P}[X_T < 0] \leq \alpha\}$$

defines a closed, conic acceptance set which, in general, is not convex.

Indeed, a few calculations show that $\mathcal{A}_\alpha$ *is a conic acceptance set. For closedness in* $L^\infty(\mathbb{P})$ *consider a sequence* $\{X_T^n\}_{n \in \mathbb{N}} \subset \mathcal{A}_\alpha$ *converging to some* X_T. *For any* $\delta > 0$ *and any* $n \in \mathbb{N}$ *the following inequality holds,*

$$\mathbb{P}[X_T < -\delta] = \mathbb{P}[X_T < -\delta, X_T^n < -\tfrac{\delta}{2}] + \mathbb{P}[X_T < -\delta, X_T^n \geq -\tfrac{\delta}{2}]$$
$$\leq \alpha + \mathbb{P}[|X_T^n - X_T| > \tfrac{\delta}{2}].$$

Since norm convergence implies convergence in probability, letting $n \to \infty$ *we get* $\mathbb{P}[X_T < -\delta] \leq \alpha$. *It follows* $\mathbb{P}[X_T < 0] = \lim_{\delta \to 0} \mathbb{P}[X_T < -\delta] \leq \alpha$. *To show that* $\mathcal{A}_\alpha$ *is not convex, we use its conicity to reduce the problem to finding* $X_T, Y_T \in \mathcal{A}_\alpha$ *such that* $X_T + Y_T \notin \mathcal{A}_\alpha$. *For two disjoint subsets* $A, B \in \mathcal{F}$ *with* $\mathbb{P}[A] = \mathbb{P}[B] = \alpha$ *the choices* $X_T = -\mathbf{1}_A$ *and* $Y_T = -\mathbf{1}_B$ *yield the desired inequality.*

2.2. *Traditional risk measures*

Traditional risk measures, commonly known as just risk measures, are instruments to measure risk in the financial world. Acceptance sets determine the meaning of 'good' and 'bad', acceptable or not. Traditional risk measures refine this differentiation and allow us to rank financial positions with respect to their distance to the acceptance set. To clearly distinguish between these risk measures and intrinsic risk measures, we define the broad class of traditional risk measures following [1], Definition 2.1, p. 207.

Definition 2.3. A *traditional risk measure* is a map from $\mathcal{X}$ to $\mathbb{R}$.

In Section 3, we will see that intrinsic risk measures are defined on $\mathbb{R}_{>0} \times \mathcal{X}$. In what follows we recall some well-known traditional risk measures. For the remainder of this section, let X_T, Y_T, Z_T and $\mathbf{r} = r\mathbf{1}_\Omega$ be elements of $\mathcal{X}$, and let ρ denote a traditional risk measure.

2.2.1. *Coherent risk measures*

Coherent risk measures form the historical foundation of modern risk measure theory. P. Artzner, F. Delbaen, J. Eber, and D. Heath define them in [1], Definition 2.4, p. 210 by the following set of axioms. A traditional risk measure is called *coherent* if it satisfies

- *Decreasing Monotonicity*: $X_T \geq Y_T$ implies $\rho(X_T) \leq \rho(Y_T)$,
- *Cash-additivity*: for $m \in \mathbb{R}$ we have $\rho(X_T + m\mathbf{r}) = \rho(X_T) - m$,
- *Positive Homogeneity*: for $\lambda \geq 0$ we have $\rho(\lambda X_T) = \lambda \rho(X_T)$, and
- *Subadditivity*: $\rho(X_T + Y_T) \leq \rho(X_T) + \rho(Y_T)$.

Monotonicity allows us to rank financial positions according to their risk. It is cash-additivity that constitutes the basis for the interpretation of a risk measure as an additionally required amount of capital. Adding this capital to the financial position, its risk becomes 0, since by cash-additivity, $\rho(X_T + \rho(X_T)\mathbf{r}) = 0$. These assumptions seem natural in the context of capital requirements and they are truly characterized by the term *monetary risk measures*, as coined by H. Föllmer and A. Schied in [7], Definition 4.1, p. 153.

2.2.2. *Convex risk measures*

Positive homogeneity, however, may not be satisfied, as risk can behave in non-linear ways. A possible variation is the following property around which H. Föllmer and A. Schied [7] base their discussion of risk measures.

- *Convexity*: for all $\lambda \in [0,1]$ we have

$$\rho(\lambda X_T + (1 - \lambda)Y_T) \leq \lambda\rho(X_T) + (1 - \lambda)\rho(Y_T).$$

A short calculation reveals that under positive homogeneity, subadditivity and convexity are equivalent. H. Föllmer and A. Schied decide in [7], Definition 4.4, p. 154 to drop the homogeneity axiom and replace subadditivity by convexity, and call the result a *convex measure of risk* — a convex monetary risk measure.

The axioms we have seen so far form a canonical connection to our acceptance sets.

Proposition 2.1. *Any monetary risk measure* $\rho : \mathcal{X} \to \mathbb{R}$ *defines via*

$$\mathcal{A}_\rho = \{X_T \in \mathcal{X} \,|\, \rho(X_T) \leq 0\} \qquad (4)$$

an acceptance set. Moreover, if ρ *is positive homogeneous, then* $\mathcal{A}_\rho$ *is a cone, and if* ρ *is convex, then* $\mathcal{A}_\rho$ *is convex.*

On the other hand, each acceptance set $\mathcal{A}$ *defines a monetary risk measure*

$$\rho_\mathcal{A}(X_T) = \inf\{m \in \mathbb{R} \,|\, X_T + m\mathbf{r} \in \mathcal{A}\}. \qquad (5)$$

Similarly, if $\mathcal{A}$ *is a cone, then* $\rho_\mathcal{A}$ *is positive homogeneous, and if* $\mathcal{A}$ *is convex, then* $\rho_\mathcal{A}$ *is convex.*
In particular, this means $\rho_{\mathcal{A}_\rho} = \rho$ *and* $\mathcal{A} \subseteq \mathcal{A}_{\rho_\mathcal{A}}$, *with equality* $\mathcal{A} = \mathcal{A}_{\rho_\mathcal{A}}$ *if the acceptance set is closed.*

Proof. The proof goes along the lines of the proofs of Proposition 4.6 and Proposition 4.7 in [7], p. 155f. for bounded measurable functions on $(\Omega, \mathcal{F})$, and is omitted here. □

Proposition 2.1 allows us to define acceptance sets via known risk measures and vice versa. Example 2.2 illustrates how properties can be inferred. A more general version of Proposition 2.1 is stated in Proposition 2.2.

Example 2.2 (Value at Risk acceptance). *For a given probability level* $\alpha \in \left(0, \frac{1}{2}\right)$ *we define the risk measure* Value-at-Risk (VaR$_\alpha$) *for all random variables on* $(\Omega, \mathcal{F})$ *by*

$$\mathrm{VaR}_\alpha(X_T) = \inf\{m \in \mathbb{R} \,|\, \mathbb{P}[X_T + m < 0] \leq \alpha\},$$

the negative of the α-quantile of X_T. Corresponding to Proposition 2.1, the VaR$_\alpha$-acceptance set is given by

$$\mathcal{A}_{\text{VaR}_\alpha} = \{X_T \in \mathcal{X} \mid \text{VaR}_\alpha(X_T) \leq 0\}.$$

Recalling the closed, conic set $\mathcal{A}_\alpha = \{X_T \in \mathcal{X} \mid \mathbb{P}[X_T < 0] \leq \alpha\}$ from Example 2.1, we find that it defines the Value-at-Risk via Equation (5). So with Proposition 2.1 we conclude that $\mathcal{A}_\alpha = \mathcal{A}_{\text{VaR}_\alpha}$ and that VaR_α is a positive homogeneous monetary risk measure which, in general, is not convex, and thus, not coherent.

Convexity also allows for an alternative treatment of risk measures. The rich literature on convex functional analysis finds convenient application in the theory of risk measures. And risk measures are enriched with a dual representation and more possibilities of interpretation.

We recall two important results for completeness and for the comparison to the intrinsic dual representation in Section 3.4. The first one is given in [7], Theorem 4.31, p. 172.

Theorem 2.1. *Let $\mathcal{M}_\sigma(\mathbb{P}) = \mathcal{M}_\sigma(\Omega, \mathcal{F}, \mathbb{P})$ be the set of all σ-additive probability measures on $\mathcal{F}$ which are absolutely continuous with respect to $\mathbb{P}$. Let $\mathcal{A} \subset \mathcal{X}$ be a convex, $\sigma(L^\infty, L^1)$-closed (weak*-closed) acceptance set. Let $\rho_\mathcal{A}$ be defined as in Equation (5) with $\mathbf{r} = \mathbf{1}_\Omega$. The risk measure has the representation*

$$\rho_\mathcal{A}(X_T) = \sup_{\mathbb{Q} \in \mathcal{M}_\sigma(\mathbb{P})} \{\mathbb{E}_\mathbb{Q}[-X_T] - \alpha_{\min}(\mathbb{Q}, \mathcal{A})\}, \tag{6}$$

with the minimal penalty function $\alpha_{\min}$ defined for all $\mathbb{Q} \in \mathcal{M}_\sigma(\mathbb{P})$ by

$$\alpha_{\min}(\mathbb{Q}, \mathcal{A}) = \sup_{X_T \in \mathcal{A}} \mathbb{E}_\mathbb{Q}[-X_T]. \tag{7}$$

Theorem 2.1 can now be directly applied to coherent risk measures, which of course are convex and positive homogeneous. But one can additionally show that with positive homogeneity we can restrict the supremum to a subset $\mathcal{M} \subset \mathcal{M}_\sigma(\mathbb{P})$ on which $\alpha_{\min}(\,\cdot\,, \mathcal{A}) = 0$. For further details see [7], Corollary 4.18 and Corollary 4.34, p. 165 and p. 175.

Corollary 2.1. *Let $\mathcal{A}$ be a conic, convex, $\sigma(L^\infty, L^1)$-closed acceptance set. Define the subset $\mathcal{M} = \{\mathbb{Q} \in \mathcal{M}_\sigma(\mathbb{P}) \mid \alpha_{\min}(\mathbb{Q}, \mathcal{A}) = 0\}$. Then the coherent risk measure $\rho_\mathcal{A} : \mathcal{X} \to \mathbb{R}$ can be written as*

$$\rho_\mathcal{A}(X_T) = \sup_{\mathbb{Q} \in \mathcal{M}} \mathbb{E}_\mathbb{Q}[-X_T].$$

2.2.3. *Cash-subadditivity and quasi-convexity of risk measures*

N. El Karoui and C. Ravanelli [8] point out that in presence of *stochastic interest rates* a financial position must be discounted before a cash-additive risk measure is applied. Consequently, the axiom of cash-additivity relies on the assumption that the discounting process does not carry additional risk. To relax this restriction they suggest the property of *cash-subadditivity*, where the equality in the cash-additivity condition is changed to the inequality '$\geq$'. However, S. Cerreia-Vioglio, F. Maccheroni, M. Marinacci and L. Montrucchio [9] explain that under cash-subadditivity, convexity is not a rigorous representative of the diversification principle, which translates into the following requirement for risk measures.

- *Diversification Principle*: if $\rho(X_T), \rho(Y_T) \leq \rho(Z_T)$ is satisfied, then

$$\text{for all } \lambda \in [0,1] : \rho(\lambda X_T + (1 - \lambda)Y_T) \leq \rho(Z_T).$$

Substituting $\rho(Z_T)$ by $\max\{\rho(X_T), \rho(Y_T)\}$ yields the equivalent and recently importance gaining property of

- *Quasi-convexity*: for all $\lambda \in [0,1]$ we have

$$\rho(\lambda X_T + (1 - \lambda)Y_T) \leq \max\{\rho(X_T), \rho(Y_T)\}.$$

Interestingly, quasi-convexity is equivalent to convexity under cash-additivity. Indeed, for any two positions with $\rho(X_T) \leq \rho(Y_T)$ we find an $m \in \mathbb{R}_{\geq 0}$ such that $\rho(X_T - m\mathbf{r}) = \rho(Y_T)$ so that for any $\lambda \in [0,1]$ we get

$$\rho(\lambda X_T + (1 - \lambda)Y_T) + \lambda m \leq \max\{\rho(X_T - m\mathbf{r}), \rho(Y_T)\}$$
$$= \lambda\rho(X_T) + (1 - \lambda)\rho(Y_T) + \lambda m.$$

This equivalence does not hold under cash-subadditivity as shown in [6], Example 2.10, p. 12, resulting in the necessity to explicitly implement the diversification principle and thus, in the introduction of cash-subadditive, quasi-convex risk measures.

2.2.4. *General monetary risk measures*

Stochastic interest rates can also be directly addressed through risk measures of the form

$$\rho_{\mathcal{A},S}(X_T) = \inf \left\{ m \in \mathbb{R} \,\middle|\, X_T + \tfrac{m}{S_0} S_T \in \mathcal{A} \right\}, \tag{8}$$

as introduced in [4] and [5]. This approach avoids implicit discounting, since the stochastic eligible asset is now part of the risk measure. C. Munari provides a broad discussion of the discounting argument, revealing fundamental issues with discounting in the context of acceptance sets in [10], Section 1.3, p. 26.

Equation (8) defines a generalized monetary risk measure which satisfies the following property for its defining eligible asset $S = (S_0, S_T)$,

- *S-additivity*: for $m \in \mathbb{R}$ we have $\rho_{\mathcal{A},S}(X_T + mS_T) = \rho_{\mathcal{A},S}(X_T) - mS_0$.

This general setup also yields the equivalence of quasi-convexity and convexity, and it exhibits a similar correspondence between acceptance sets and risk measures. The following result extends Proposition 2.1 to stochastic eligible assets.

Proposition 2.2. *Proposition 2.1 holds true if we replace $L^\infty(\Omega, \mathcal{F}, \mathbb{P})$ by any real ordered topological vector space, cash-additivity by S-additivity, and Equation (5) by Equation (8), for any eligible asset $S = (S_0, S_T) \in \mathbb{R}_{>0} \times \mathcal{A}$.*

Proof. See the proofs of propositions 3.2.3, 3.2.4, 3.2.5, and 3.2.8 in [10], p. 87f. The second claim in Proposition 2.1 follows from two short calculations. $\qquad\square$

3. Intrinsic risk measures

The risk measures in the previous section all yield the same procedure to make an unacceptable position X_T acceptable — raise the required 'minimal' capital $\rho_{\mathcal{A},S}(X_T)$ and get the acceptable position $X_T^\rho :=$ $X_T + \frac{\rho_{\mathcal{A},S}(X_T)}{S_0} S_T$. A procedure to acquire the required capital-level and the risk of failing to obtain it are not addressed by these risk measures. But what if we do not use external capital?

3.1. *Fundamental concepts*

In this section, we explore a different procedure to obtain acceptable positions. We suggest to sell part of the risky position and invest the acquired capital in the acceptable eligible asset. Hereby, the distance to the acceptance set is directly reduced and therefore also the risk.

In order to sell our original position we require the knowledge of the initial value $X_0 \in \mathbb{R}_{>0}$. Following the definition of general eligible assets $S = (S_0, S_T) \in \mathbb{R}_{>0} \times \mathcal{A}$ in Section 2.2.4, we consider financial positions $X =$

(X_0, X_T) on the product space $\mathbb{R}_{>0} \times \mathcal{X}$. The main object in this approach is the net worth of the convex combination of the risky position and a multiple of the eligible asset

$$X_T^{\lambda,S} := (1 - \lambda)X_T + \lambda\frac{X_0}{S_0}S_T \in \mathcal{X}, \ \lambda \in [0,1].$$

The notation $X_T^{\lambda,S}$ is convenient and we extend it to the whole position $X \in \mathbb{R}_{>0} \times \mathcal{X}$ as

$$X^{\lambda,S} := (X_0, X_T^{\lambda,S}) \in \mathbb{R}_{>0} \times \mathcal{X}.$$

Hence, $X^{\lambda,S}$ describes a position with initial value X_0 which is split in $(1 - \lambda)X_0$ and λX_0 and is then invested to get $(1 - \lambda)X_T$ and $\lambda\frac{X_0}{S_0}S_T$, respectively. We aim to find the smallest λ such that $X_T^{\lambda,S}$ is acceptable, this defines the intrinsic risk measure.

Definition 3.1 (Intrinsic Risk Measure). *For an acceptance set $\mathcal{A} \subset \mathcal{X}$ and an eligible asset $S \in \mathbb{R}_{>0} \times \mathcal{A}$ the intrinsic risk measure is a map $R_{\mathcal{A},S} : \mathbb{R}_{>0} \times \mathcal{X} \to [0,1]$ defined by*

$$R_{\mathcal{A},S}(X) = \inf \left\{ \lambda \in [0,1] \,|\, X_T^{\lambda,S} \in \mathcal{A} \right\}. \tag{9}$$

For well-definedness two short considerations yield that the acceptance set must either be a cone or that 0 must be contained in it.[5] In both cases, $\lambda\frac{X_0}{S_0}S_T$ is acceptable for $\lambda \in (0,1]$, or $\lambda \in [0,1]$ if $\mathcal{A}$ is closed. This means selling all of the original position leaves us always with an acceptable net worth $\frac{X_0}{S_0}S_T$.

A brief comparison of the intrinsic approach and the traditional monetary approach is provided below. Consider the conceptual Figure 1 and imagine that $\mathcal{A}$ is an arbitrary closed acceptance set.

While the monetary approach, illustrated in Figure 1(a), yields the position $X_T^{\rho} := X_T + \frac{\rho_{\mathcal{A},S}(X_T)}{S_0}S_T$, the intrinsic approach, illustrated in Figure 1(b), gives us

$$X_T^{R_{\mathcal{A},S}(X),S} := (1 - R_{\mathcal{A},S}(X))X_T + R_{\mathcal{A},S}(X)\frac{X_0}{S_0}S_T,$$

which we abbreviate with $X_T^{R,S}$ if the reference to $\mathcal{A}, S$, and X is clear.

---

[5]The assumption $0 \in \mathcal{A}$ is widely used in the financial literature, as for example the equivalent Axiom 2.1 in [1], p. 206 or, if $\mathcal{A}$ is closed, the *normalization property* $\rho(0) = 0$ in [7], above Remark 4.2, p. 154.

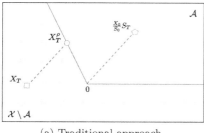

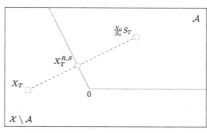

(a) Traditional approach   (b) Intrinsic approach

Figure 1. The payoff of the eligible asset (○) is used to make the unacceptable position (□) acceptable (◯).

1. We notice that, since $\mathcal{A}$ is closed, both risk measures are strictly positive if and only if $X_T \notin \mathcal{A}$. In this case, and if $S_T \in \mathrm{int}(\mathcal{A})$, both altered positions X_T^ρ and $X_T^{R,S}$ lie on the boundary of the acceptance set. Moreover, if $\mathcal{A}$ is either a cone or convex with $0 \in \mathcal{A}$, then the set $\{X_T^{\lambda,S} \mid \lambda \in [R_{\mathcal{A},S}(X), 1]\}$ belongs to $\mathcal{A}$. A similar result holds true for monetary risk measures.

2. If we assume a conic acceptance set as in Figure 1, we intuit that $X_T^{R,S}$ must be a multiple of X_T^ρ. And indeed, in Corollary 3.3 we will derive the relation

$$X_T^{R_{\mathcal{A},S}(X),S} = (1 - R_{\mathcal{A},S}(X))X_T^\rho. \tag{10}$$

3. By Definition 3.1, it is apparent that intrinsic risk measures cannot attain infinite values as opposed to traditional risk measures. W. Farkas, P. Koch-Medina, and C. Munari have shown in [5], Theorem 3.3 and Corollary 3.4, p. 62 that on closed, conic acceptance sets

$$\rho_{\mathcal{A},S} \text{ is finite if and only if } S_T \in \mathrm{int}(\mathcal{A}).$$

For a graphical illustration imagine that in Figure 1, $S_T \in \partial\mathcal{A}$. Then in Figure 1(a), a possible X_T^ρ would move along a line 'parallel' to the boundary, thus it would never reach $\mathcal{A}$. Consequently, $\rho_{\mathcal{A},S}(X_T) = +\infty$ and X_T^ρ is actually not defined.

In contrast, one can show[6] that on closed, conic acceptance sets

$$R_{\mathcal{A},S} < 1 \text{ on } \mathbb{R}_{>0} \times \mathcal{X} \setminus \mathcal{A} \text{ if and only if } S_T \in \mathrm{int}(\mathcal{A}).$$

---

[6]For a direct proof one can use Lemma 2.1 and the fact that $X_T^{R,S} \in \mathcal{A}$. For a proof via monetary risk measures consider Theorem 3.1 and Corollary 3.1 below.

Hence, if $S_T \in \partial \mathcal{A}$ in Figure 1(b), then $X_T^{R,S}$ and $\frac{X_0}{S_0} S_T$ coincide on the boundary with $R_{\mathcal{A},S}(X) = 1$.

Having established a basic intuition for this approach, we will now take a deeper look at some of its properties. For this we introduce the notions of monotonicity and convexity on $\mathbb{R}_{>0} \times \mathcal{X}$.

1. The monotonicity of $\mathcal{A}$ should be reflected by the corresponding intrinsic risk measure. So we need to extend the ordering on $\mathcal{X}$ to $\mathbb{R}_{>0} \times \mathcal{X}$. Two possible orderings are *element-wise* and *return-wise* defined respectively by

$$X \geqslant_{\mathrm{el}} Y \text{ if } X_0 \geq Y_0 \text{ and } X_T \geq Y_T, \text{ and}$$

$$X \geqslant_{\mathrm{re}} Y \text{ if } \frac{X_T}{X_0} \geq \frac{Y_T}{Y_0}.$$

2. On $\mathbb{R}_{>0} \times \mathcal{X}$, we think of convex combinations element-wise as

$$\alpha X + (1-\alpha)Y := (\alpha X_0 + (1-\alpha)Y_0, \, \alpha X_T + (1-\alpha)Y_T) \in \mathbb{R}_{>0} \times \mathcal{X}.$$

We can now show monotonicity and quasi-convexity of intrinsic risk measures with respect to these rules.

Proposition 3.1 (Monotonicity, Quasi-convexity). *Let $\mathcal{A}$ be an acceptance set containing 0, let $S \in \mathbb{R}_{>0} \times \mathcal{A}$ be an eligible asset and let $X, Y \in \mathbb{R}_{>0} \times \mathcal{X}$.*

1. The orders $X \geqslant_{el} Y$ and, on conic acceptance sets, $X \geqslant_{re} Y$, imply $R_{\mathcal{A},S}(X) \leq R_{\mathcal{A},S}(Y)$.

2. Let $\mathcal{A}$ be additionally convex. Then $R_{\mathcal{A},S}$ is quasi-convex, that means for all $\alpha \in [0,1]$, and any $X, Y \in \mathbb{R}_{>0} \times \mathcal{X}$

$$R_{\mathcal{A},S}(\alpha X + (1-\alpha)Y) \leq \max\{R_{\mathcal{A},S}(X), R_{\mathcal{A},S}(Y)\}.$$

Proof. 1. If $X \geqslant_{\mathrm{el}} Y$, then $X_T^{\lambda,S} \geq Y_T^{\lambda,S}$ and thus, by monotonicity of the acceptance set, $R_{\mathcal{A},S}(X) \leq R_{\mathcal{A},S}(Y)$. Similarly, $X \geqslant_{\mathrm{re}} Y$ implies $X_T^{\lambda,S} \geq \frac{X_0}{Y_0} Y_T^{\lambda,S}$. By conicity we have $\frac{X_0}{Y_0} Y_T^{R(Y),S} \in \mathcal{A}$ and again by monotonicity we get $X_T^{\lambda,S} \in \mathcal{A}$.

2. Assume without loss of generality $R_{\mathcal{A},S}(X) \leq R_{\mathcal{A},S}(Y)$. As mentioned above, since $\mathcal{A}$ is convex, $\{X_T^{\lambda,S} \mid \lambda \in [R_{\mathcal{A},S}(X), 1]\} \subset \mathcal{A}$. Hence, if $\lambda \in [R_{\mathcal{A},S}(Y), 1]$, then the convex combinations $Y_T^{\lambda,S}, X_T^{\lambda,S}$ lie in $\mathcal{A}$ and also their convex combinations $\alpha X_T^{\lambda,S} + (1-\alpha)Y_T^{\lambda,S} \in \mathcal{A}$, for all $\alpha \in [0,1]$. But

these convex combinations commutate so that

$$R_{\mathcal{A},S}(\alpha X + (1-\alpha)Y) = \inf\left\{\lambda \in [0,1] \mid \alpha X_T^{\lambda,S} + (1-\alpha)Y_T^{\lambda,S} \in \mathcal{A}\right\}$$
$$\leq R_{\mathcal{A},S}(Y) = \max\left\{R_{\mathcal{A},S}(X), R_{\mathcal{A},S}(Y)\right\},$$

showing quasi-convexity of the intrinsic risk measure. $\qquad\square$

So while monotonicity of $\mathcal{A}$ is passed on to underlying intrinsic risk measures, convexity of the acceptance set implies quasi-convexity and not convexity of the measures as we have seen in Proposition 2.1 for monetary risk measures. A counter-example to convexity can be constructed with the transition property for unacceptable X and $\alpha \in [0, R_{\mathcal{A},S}(X)]$,

$$R_{\mathcal{A},S}(X^{\alpha,S}) = \frac{R_{\mathcal{A},S}(X) - \alpha}{1-\alpha},$$

which can be derived using the bijection $[0,1] \to [\alpha,1]$ with $\lambda \mapsto (1-\lambda)\alpha + \lambda$, and the fact that $(1-\beta)X + \beta X^{\alpha,S} = X^{\alpha\beta,S}$. With help of Example 2.1 it can be shown that convexity of $\mathcal{A}$ is necessary for quasi-convexity of the intrinsic risk measure. Finally, a similar argument yields quasi-convexity with respect to eligible assets $S^1, S^2 \in \mathbb{R}_{>0} \times \mathcal{A}$ with same initial price $S_0^1 = S_0^2$,

$$R_{\mathcal{A},\alpha S^1 + (1-\alpha)S^2}(X) \leq \max\{R_{\mathcal{A},S^1}(X), R_{\mathcal{A},S^2}(X)\}.$$

3.2. *Representation on conic acceptance sets*

In this section, we will use cash- or S-additivity of monetary risk measures to derive an alternative representation of intrinsic risk measures on cones. This representation allows us to apply important results from monetary to intrinsic risk measures.

Theorem 3.1 (Representation on cones). *Let $\rho_{\mathcal{A},S} : \mathcal{X} \to \mathbb{R}$ be a monetary risk measure defined by a closed, conic acceptance set $\mathcal{A}$ and an eligible asset $S \in \mathbb{R}_{>0} \times \mathcal{A}$. Then the intrinsic risk measure with respect to $\mathcal{A}$ and S can be written as*

$$R_{\mathcal{A},S}(X) = \frac{(\rho_{\mathcal{A},S}(X_T))^+}{X_0 + \rho_{\mathcal{A},S}(X_T)}. \tag{11}$$

Proof. Since $\mathcal{A}$ is closed, we can use Proposition 2.2 to write

$$R_{\mathcal{A},S}(X) = \inf\{\lambda \in [0,1] \mid X_T^{\lambda,S} \in \mathcal{A}\} = \inf\{\lambda \in [0,1] \mid \rho_{\mathcal{A},S}(X_T^{\lambda,S}) \leq 0\}.$$

But $\rho_{\mathcal{A},S}$ is S-additive and positive homogeneous, so that we have

$$R_{\mathcal{A},S}(X) = \inf\left\{\lambda \in [0,1] \mid \rho_{\mathcal{A},S}(X_T) \leq \lambda(X_0 + \rho_{\mathcal{A},S}(X_T))\right\}.$$

If $\rho_{\mathcal{A},S}(X_T) > 0$, then we can solve for λ to get the form in Equation (11). If $\rho_{\mathcal{A},S}(X_T) \leq 0$, then $X_T \in \mathcal{A}$ and therefore $R_{\mathcal{A},S}(X) = 0$. We abbreviate these two cases with $(\rho_{\mathcal{A},S}(X_T))^+$ in the numerator. $\qquad\square$

Example 3.1. For continuous X_T and constant eligible assets $S_T = rS_0\mathbf{1}_\Omega > 0$ we can directly derive the representation in Equation (11) on the conic Value-at-Risk acceptance set $\mathcal{A}_\alpha = \{X_T \in \mathcal{X} \mid \mathbb{P}[X_T < 0] \leq \alpha\}$ from Example 2.2. Let F_X be the continuous cumulative distribution function of X_T with inverse F_X^{-1}. For $X_T \notin \mathcal{A}_\alpha$, this means $F_X^{-1}(\alpha) < 0$, we get

$$
\begin{aligned}
R_{\mathcal{A}_\alpha,S}(X) &= \inf\left\{\lambda \in (0,1) \mid \mathbb{P}[X_T^{\lambda,S} < 0] \leq \alpha\right\} \\
&= \inf\left\{\lambda \in (0,1) \mid F_X(-(1-\lambda)^{-1}\lambda rX_0) \leq \alpha\right\} \\
&= \frac{F_X^{-1}(\alpha)}{F_X^{-1}(\alpha) - rX_0} = \frac{\mathrm{VaR}_\alpha(X_T)}{rX_0 + \mathrm{VaR}_\alpha(X_T)},
\end{aligned}
$$

an expression similar to Equation (11). Of course, while we use the constant eligible asset $S_T = rS_0\mathbf{1}_\Omega$, the Value-at-Risk is of the form $\rho_{\mathcal{A}_\alpha}(X) = \inf\{m \in \mathbb{R} \mid X_T + m\mathbf{1}_\Omega \in \mathcal{A}_\alpha\}$ with $r = 1$.

In our opinion, Theorem 3.1 is a very convenient result that allows us to draw connections to traditional risk measures. This is true for all conic acceptance sets, including the commonly used Value-at-Risk and Expected Shortfall acceptance sets. In particular, some important results from traditional risk measures can be directly applied to intrinsic risk measures.

Corollary 3.1. *Let $\mathcal{A}$ be a closed, conic acceptance set.*

1. *$R_{\mathcal{A},S} < 1$ on $\mathbb{R}_{>0} \times \mathcal{X} \setminus \mathcal{A}$ if and only if $S_T \in \mathrm{int}(\mathcal{A})$.*
2. *If $S_T \in \mathrm{int}(\mathcal{X}_+)$, then $R_{\mathcal{A},S}$ is continuous on $\mathbb{R}_{>0} \times \mathcal{X}$.*
3. *If $\mathcal{A}$ is additionally convex, then $S_T \in \mathrm{int}(\mathcal{A})$ implies continuity of $R_{\mathcal{A},S}$.*
4. *$R_{\mathcal{A},S}$ is scale-invariant, meaning $R_{\mathcal{A},S}(\alpha X) = R_{\mathcal{A},S}(X)$, for $\alpha > 0$.*

Proof. 1. With the representation in Theorem 3.1 and the finiteness result in [5], Theorem 3.3, p. 62 the assertion follows directly.
2. By [4], Proposition 3.1, p. 154, if $S_T \in \mathrm{int}(\mathcal{X}_+)$, then $\rho_{\mathcal{A},S}$ is continuous. The map $f : (x_0, x) \mapsto \frac{x^+}{x_0 + x}$ is jointly continuous on $\mathbb{R}_{>0} \times \mathbb{R}$. Therefore, as the composition of two continuous maps the intrinsic risk measures is continuous on $\mathbb{R}_{>0} \times \mathcal{X}$.

3. In this case, [4], Theorem 3.16, p. 159 gives us continuity of $\rho_{\mathcal{A},S}$. The assertion follows as in the second part.

4. If $X_T \in \mathcal{A}$, then so is αX_T and thus, $R_{\mathcal{A},S}(\alpha X) = R_{\mathcal{A},S}(X) = 0$. If $X_T \notin \mathcal{A}$, then $\rho_{\mathcal{A},S}(X_T) > 0$ and the assertion follows from positive homogeneity of $\rho_{\mathcal{A},S}$ and Theorem 3.1. $\qquad\square$

Another version of Theorem 3.1 is the representation of monetary risk measures on $\mathcal{X} \setminus \mathcal{A}$ in terms of intrinsic risk measures.

Corollary 3.2. *Let $\mathcal{A}$ be a closed, conic acceptance set, $S \in \mathbb{R}_{>0} \times \text{int}(\mathcal{A})$ and $X = (X_0, X_T) \in \mathbb{R}_{>0} \times \mathcal{X} \setminus \mathcal{A}$. Then*

$$\rho_{\mathcal{A},S}(X_T) = \frac{X_0 R_{\mathcal{A},S}(X)}{1 - R_{\mathcal{A},S}(X)}. \tag{12}$$

Proof. We have $\rho_{\mathcal{A},S}(X_T) > 0$ on $\mathcal{X} \setminus \mathcal{A}$ and by Corollary 3.1, $S_T \in \text{int}(\mathcal{A})$ implies $R_{\mathcal{A},S} < 1$ on $\mathbb{R}_{>0} \times \mathcal{X} \setminus \mathcal{A}$. Setting $X = (X_0, X_T)$, for any $X_0 > 0$, and rearranging Equation (11) yields the assertion. $\qquad\square$

With this representation we confirm our claim that $X_T^\rho = X_T + \frac{\rho_{\mathcal{A},S}(X_T)}{S_0} S_T$ is a multiple of $X_T^{R,S}$.

Corollary 3.3. *In the setting of Corollary 3.2, we have*

$$X_T^{R_{\mathcal{A},S}(X),S} = (1 - R_{\mathcal{A},S}(X)) X_T^\rho. \tag{13}$$

Proof. Dividing $X_T^{R,S}$ by $1 - R_{\mathcal{A},S}(X)$ and using Equation (12) yields the desired relation. $\qquad\square$

The representation in (11) does not hold for convex, non-conic acceptance sets. However, it does give us an upper bound.

Proposition 3.2. *Let $\mathcal{A}$ be a closed, convex acceptance set containing 0, which is not a cone. Then the following inequality holds,*

$$R_{\mathcal{A},S}(X) \le \frac{(\rho_{\mathcal{A},S}(X_T))^+}{X_0 + \rho_{\mathcal{A},S}(X_T)}. \tag{14}$$

Proof. Using Proposition 2.2, we establish with S-additivity, and then convexity and the fact that $\rho_{\mathcal{A},S}(0) \le 0$ the inequality

$$\rho_{\mathcal{A},S}(X_T^{\lambda,S}) = \rho_{\mathcal{A},S}((1-\lambda)X_T) - \lambda X_0 \le (1-\lambda)\rho_{\mathcal{A},S}(X_T) - \lambda X_0.$$

With this we arrive at the inclusion

$$\{\lambda \in [0,1] \,|\, (1-\lambda)\rho_{\mathcal{A},S}(X_T) - \lambda X_0 \le 0\} \subseteq \{\lambda \in [0,1] \,|\, \rho_{\mathcal{A},S}(X_T^{\lambda,S}) \le 0\},$$

which implies (14). $\qquad\square$

3.3. *Efficiency of the intrinsic approach*

In the previous section, we have derived all necessary results to compare the intrinsic and the traditional approach on a monetary basis. We find that on conic or convex acceptance sets the intrinsic approach requires less investment in eligible assets. But on cones it yields positions with the same performance.

Corollary 3.4. *Let $\mathcal{A}$ be a closed acceptance set, either conic or convex. For an unacceptable position $X = (X_0, X_T)$ and an eligible asset S we have*

$$X_0 R_{\mathcal{A},S}(X) \leq \rho_{\mathcal{A},S}(X_T).$$

Proof. With Theorem 3.1 for conic acceptance sets, and Proposition 3.2 for the convex case we establish $X_0 R_{\mathcal{A},S}(X) \leq X_0 \frac{\rho_{\mathcal{A},S}(X_T)}{X_0 + \rho_{\mathcal{A},S}(X_T)}$. For unacceptable X_T the inequality $X_0 \frac{\rho_{\mathcal{A},S}(X_T)}{X_0 + \rho_{\mathcal{A},S}(X_T)} \leq \rho_{\mathcal{A},S}(X_T)$ holds true, proving the assertion. $\qquad\square$

So while the magnitude of the initial value X_0 controls the required monetary amount, Corollary 3.4 shows that the amount $X_0 R_{\mathcal{A},S}(X)$ is always less than $\rho_{\mathcal{A},S}(X_T)$. This means using the intrinsic approach, less capital is transitioned to the eligible asset.

But since less money is invested in the eligible asset, one could think that the intrinsic approach yields worse acceptable positions compared to the traditional approach. However, comparing the resulting positions in terms of returns, for example with the (revised) Sharpe ratio, shows otherwise. Given a financial position $X = (X_0, X_T)$, a monetary risk measure yields the acceptable position $X_T^\rho = X_T + \frac{\rho_{\mathcal{A},S}(X_T)}{S_0} S_T$. This means that at inception, the initial value must be $X_0^\rho := X_0 + \rho_{\mathcal{A},S}(X_T)$. On the other hand, an intrinsic risk measure does not change the initial value X_0 to get the acceptable position $X_T^{R,S}$. Interestingly, the returns of these positions are equal on cones.

Corollary 3.5. *Let $\mathcal{A}$ be a closed, conic acceptance set, X an unacceptable position, and S an eligible asset. The returns of the positions $(X_0, X_T^{R(X),S})$ and (X_0^ρ, X_T^ρ) are equal.*

Proof. Dividing both sides of Equation (13) by X_0 and using Equation (11) yield the assertion. $\qquad\square$

3.4. *Dual representations on convex acceptance sets*

Referring to duality results of convex and coherent risk measures stated in Section 2.2.2, we derive a dual representation of intrinsic risk measures. The derivation is based on a representation of convex acceptance sets by $\mathcal{M}_\sigma(\mathbb{P})$, the set of σ-additive, absolutely continuous probability measures $\mathbb{Q} \ll \mathbb{P}$, similar to that of S. Drapeau and M. Kupper in [11], Lemma 2, p. 52.

Lemma 3.1. *Let $\mathcal{A}$ be a $\sigma(L^\infty, L^1)$-closed, convex acceptance set. Then $X_T \in \mathcal{A}$ if and only if for all probability measures $\mathbb{Q} \in \mathcal{M}_\sigma(\mathbb{P})$*

$$\inf_{Y_T \in \mathcal{A}} \mathbb{E}_\mathbb{Q}[Y_T] \leq \mathbb{E}_\mathbb{Q}[X_T].$$

Proof. The 'only if' implication is evidently true. We outline the proof of the 'if' direction. Using a version of the Hahn-Banach Separation Theorem, see for example N. Dunford and J. T. Schwartz [12], Theorem V.2.10, p. 417, one shows that for any $X_T \in \mathcal{X} \setminus \mathcal{A}$ there is a linear functional ℓ in the topological dual space $\mathcal{X}^*$ such that $\inf_{y \in \mathcal{A}} \ell(y) > \ell(x)$. The structure of $\mathcal{A}$ implies that ℓ is positive on the positive cone $\{X_T \in \mathcal{X} \mid X_T \geq 0\}$. Under the weak*-topology $\sigma(L^\infty, L^1)$, using the Radon-Nikodým Theorem, as for example stated in [12], Theorem III.10.2, p. 176, these linear functionals can be identified with expectations with respect to σ-additive, absolutely continuous probability measures $\mathbb{Q} \ll \mathbb{P}$ in $\mathcal{M}_\sigma(\mathbb{P})$. $\square$

Using this result we can now derive a dual representation for intrinsic risk measures.

Theorem 3.2 (Dual representation). *Let $\mathcal{A}$ be a $\sigma(L^\infty, L^1)$-closed, convex acceptance set containing 0 and let S be an eligible asset. For $\mathbb{Q} \in \mathcal{M}_\sigma(\mathbb{P})$ define the penalty function[7] $\alpha(\mathbb{Q}, \mathcal{A}) = \inf_{X_T \in \mathcal{A}} \mathbb{E}_\mathbb{Q}[X_T]$. The intrinsic risk measure can be written as*

$$R_{\mathcal{A},S}(X) = \sup_{\mathbb{Q} \in \mathcal{M}_\sigma(\mathbb{P})} \frac{(\alpha(\mathbb{Q}, \mathcal{A}) - \mathbb{E}_\mathbb{Q}[X_T])^+}{\frac{X_0}{S_0} \mathbb{E}_\mathbb{Q}[S_T] - \mathbb{E}_\mathbb{Q}[X_T]}. \tag{15}$$

Proof. By Lemma 3.1, we have the equivalence $X_T^{\lambda,S} \in \mathcal{A}$ if and only if for all $\mathbb{Q} \in \mathcal{M}_\sigma(\mathbb{P})$: $\mathbb{E}_\mathbb{Q}[X_T^{\lambda,S}] \geq \alpha(\mathbb{Q}, \mathcal{A})$, or rewritten,

$$\lambda \mathbb{E}_\mathbb{Q}\left[\tfrac{X_0}{S_0} S_T - X_T\right] \geq \alpha(\mathbb{Q}, \mathcal{A}) - \mathbb{E}_\mathbb{Q}[X_T].$$

For $X_T \in \mathcal{A}$, Lemma 3.1 directly implies that the infimum over λ is equal to 0, for all $\mathbb{Q} \in \mathcal{M}_\sigma(\mathbb{P})$. For $X_T \notin \mathcal{A}$, Lemma 3.1 gives the inequality

---

[7]The negative of the minimal penalty function $\alpha_{\min}$ in Equation (7).

$\mathbb{E}_{\mathbb{Q}}[\frac{X_0}{S_0}S_T] - \mathbb{E}_{\mathbb{Q}}[X_T] \geq \alpha(\mathbb{Q}, \mathcal{A}) - \mathbb{E}_{\mathbb{Q}}[X_T] > 0$ so that we can solve for λ and get

$$R_{\mathcal{A},S}(X) = \inf \left\{ \lambda \in [0,1] \, \middle| \, \forall \mathbb{Q} \in \mathcal{M}_\sigma(\mathbb{P}) : \lambda \geq \frac{\alpha(\mathbb{Q}, \mathcal{A}) - \mathbb{E}_{\mathbb{Q}}[X_T]}{\frac{X_0}{S_0}\mathbb{E}_{\mathbb{Q}}[S_T] - \mathbb{E}_{\mathbb{Q}}[X_T]} \right\}$$

$$= \sup_{\mathbb{Q} \in \mathcal{M}_\sigma(\mathbb{P})} \frac{\alpha(\mathbb{Q}, \mathcal{A}) - \mathbb{E}_{\mathbb{Q}}[X_T]}{\frac{X_0}{S_0}\mathbb{E}_{\mathbb{Q}}[S_T] - \mathbb{E}_{\mathbb{Q}}[X_T]}.$$

From here the representation in (15) follows. □

It is interesting to find the same terms in the numerator in Equation (15) and the expression in Equation (6). But here, the numerator is normalized by an expected distance between financial position and eligible asset before the supremum over $\mathcal{M}_\sigma(\mathbb{P})$ is taken.

In case of a conic acceptance set and a constant eligible asset, we can link Theorem 3.2 via the dual representation of coherent risk measures in Corollary 2.1 to Theorem 3.1.

Corollary 3.6. *Let $\mathcal{A}$ be a $\sigma(L^\infty, L^1)$-closed, convex cone and $S_T = S_0\mathbf{1}_\Omega$. Then we recover the representation in Equation (11).*

Proof. A short calculation confirms that on cones, $\alpha(\mathbb{Q}, \mathcal{A}) = \lambda\alpha(\mathbb{Q}, \mathcal{A})$ is satisfied for all $\lambda > 0$, and thus, $\alpha(\mathbb{Q}, \mathcal{A}) \in \{0, \pm\infty\}$. Using Theorem 3.2, but taking the supremum over $\mathcal{M} = \{\mathbb{Q} \in \mathcal{M}_\sigma(\mathbb{P}) \,|\, \alpha(\mathbb{Q}, \mathcal{A}) = 0\}$, yields

$$R_{\mathcal{A},S}(X) = \sup_{\mathbb{Q} \in \mathcal{M}} \frac{(\mathbb{E}_{\mathbb{Q}}[-X_T])^+}{X_0 + \mathbb{E}_{\mathbb{Q}}[-X_T]}.$$

But for any constant $c > 0$ the map $x \mapsto \frac{x}{c+x}$ is increasing on $\mathbb{R}_{\geq 0}$ and therefore, we can split the supremum and then use the dual representation of coherent risk measures from Corollary 2.1 to get

$$R_{\mathcal{A},S}(X) = \frac{\sup_{\mathbb{Q} \in \mathcal{M}}(\mathbb{E}_{\mathbb{Q}}[-X_T])^+}{X_0 + \sup_{\mathbb{Q} \in \mathcal{M}} \mathbb{E}_{\mathbb{Q}}[-X_T]} = \frac{(\rho_{\mathcal{A},S}(X_T))^+}{X_0 + \rho_{\mathcal{A},S}(X_T)},$$

the representation of intrinsic risk measures on cones from Theorem 3.1. □

4. Conclusion

In this article, we have extended the methodology of risk measurement with a new type of risk measure: the intrinsic risk measure. We argued that since traditional risk measures are defined via hypothetical external capital, it is natural to consider risk measures that only allow the usage of internal capital contained in the financial position.

We discussed basic properties of intrinsic risk measures and provided some examples. We derived an alternative representation on conic acceptance sets, such as the ones associated with Value-at-Risk and Expected Shortfall. With this we showed that the intrinsic approach requires less investment in the eligible asset, and at the same time yields acceptable positions with the same performance. As the representation on cones does not hold on convex acceptance sets, we established a dual representation in terms of σ-additive probability measures.

Finally, we mention two ideas for further studies. First of all, the extension to general ordered topological vector spaces is necessary to provide greater adaptivity. The setting with multiple financial positions and multiple eligible assets should be studied in the context of portfolio rearrangement and how the intrinsic risk measure could help the process of optimization.

Bibliography

1. P. Artzner, F. Delbaen, J.-M. Eber and D. Heath, Coherent measures of risk, *Mathematical Finance* **9**(3), 203–228 (1999).
2. P. Artzner, F. Delbaen and P. Koch-Medina, Risk measures and efficient use of capital, *Astin Bulletin* **39**, 101–116 (2009).
3. D. G. Konstantinides and C. E. Kountzakis, Risk measures in ordered normed linear spaces with non-empty cone-interior, *Insurance: Mathematics and Economics* **48**, 111–122 (2011).
4. W. Farkas, P. Koch-Medina and C. Munari, Beyond cash-additive risk measures: when changing the numéraire fails, *Finance and Stochastics* **18**, 145–173 (2014).
5. W. Farkas, P. Koch-Medina and C. Munari, Capital requirements with defaultable securities, *Insurance: Mathematics and Economics* **55**, 58–67 (2014).
6. A. Smirnow, Risk measures: recent developments and new ideas, Master's thesis, Universität Zürich, ETH Zürich (2016).
7. H. Föllmer and A. Schied, *Stochastic Finance. An Introduction in Discrete Time* (Walter de Gruyter, Berlin, Boston, 2004).
8. N. El Karoui and C. Ravanelli, Cash subadditive risk measures and interest rate ambiguity, *Mathematical Finance* **19**(4), 561–590 (2009).
9. S. Cerreia-Vioglio, F. Maccheroni, M. Marinacci and L. Montrucchio, Risk measures: Rationality and diversification, *Mathematical Finance* **21**, 743–774 (2011).

10. C. Munari, Measuring risk beyond the cash-additive paradigm, PhD thesis, Diss. ETH no. 22541, ETH Zürich (2015).
11. S. Drapeau and M. Kupper, Risk preferences and their robust representation, *Mathematics of Operations Research* **38**(1), 28–62 (2013).
12. N. Dunford and J. T. Schwartz, *Linear Operators. Part I: General Theory* (Interscience Publishers Inc., New York, 1958).

Chapter 8

Pathwise Construction of Affine Processes

Nicoletta Gabrielli*

Bank Julius Bär, Switzerland
nicoletta.gabrielli@juliusbaer.com

Josef Teichmann*

ETH Zürich, Switzerland
josef.teichmann@math.ethz.ch

Based on the theory of multivariate time changes for Markov processes, we show how to identify affine processes as solutions of certain time change equations. The result is a strong version of a theorem presented by J. Kallsen in [1] which provides a representation in law of an affine process as a time–change transformation of a family of independent Lévy processes. This also leads to a new perspective on strong approximations for affine processes.

Keywords: affine processes, Lamperti transform, time–change.
MSC[2010]: 60G99, 91B70

1. Introduction

During the last decades, many alternatives to the Black-Scholes model have been proposed in the literature to overcome its deficiencies. Possible extensions include jumps, stochastic volatility and/or other high dimensional models. Among the most popular ones, we recall the exponential Lévy models, which generalize the Black-Scholes model by introducing jumps. They allow to generate implied volatility smiles and skews similar to the ones observed in the markets. However, in some occasions, independence of increments is too big a restriction. Stochastic volatility models give a way to overcome this problem: when we model the variance parameter in the Black–Scholes model by a CIR model, we get the Heston model, see [2]. The Heston model can be extended by adding jumps in the return component, as in the Bates model (see [3]), and also in the stochastic variance

---

*Both authors are grateful to the reviewer and the editors of this volume for numerous important suggestions to improve this article. Both authors acknowledge support by ETH foundation and SNF project 144130.

component, as in the Barndorff–Nielsen and Shephard model (see [4]). The class of affine processes includes all the above mentioned examples.

Affine processes are a class of time homogeneous Markov processes $X = (X(t))_{t \geq 0}$ taking values in a state space $D \subset \mathbb{R}^d$ characterized by the fact that, for all $(t, x) \in \mathbb{R}_{\geq 0} \times D$, their characteristic function has the following exponential affine form

$$\mathbb{E}^x \left[e^{\langle u, X(t) \rangle} \right] = e^{\varphi(t, u) + \langle x, \psi(t, u) \rangle}, \qquad u \in i\mathbb{R}^d,$$

where φ and ψ are two functions taking values in $\mathbb{C}$ and $\mathbb{C}^d$, respectively. The theory of affine processes is dominated by weak characterizations, since affine processes are characterized by a property of their marginal distributions. The functions φ and ψ in the specification of the affine property, solve a system of ODEs, also known in the literature with the name of *generalized Riccati equations*. These equations arise from the regularity property of affine processes. More precisely, in [5] it has been proved that, even on a general state space, stochastically continuous processes having the aforementioned affine property admit a version with càdlàg trajectories. The path regularity implies that the process is a semimartingale with differentiable characteristics up to its lifetime. From this characterization it is possible to conclude differentiability with respect to time of the Fourier–Laplace transform. This property, also called regularity property, is crucial to relate the marginal laws of affine processes with a solution of a system generalized Riccati equations.

This paper is devoted to a pathwise construction of affine processes, when the state space is specified by $\mathbb{R}_{\geq 0}^m \times \mathbb{R}^n$. The representation proposed in this paper is a multivariate generalization of the Lamperti transformation of Lévy processes in $\mathbb{R}$ with no negative jump. When $D = \mathbb{R}_{\geq 0}$, it has been proved that there exists a one-to-one correspondence between affine processes taking values in D and Lévy processes, see [6]. More precisely, let $Z^{(1)} = (Z^{(1)}(t))_{t \geq 0}$ be a Lévy process starting from 0 taking values in $\mathbb{R}$, whose Lévy measure has support $\mathbb{R}_{\geq 0}$ and let $Z^{(0)}$ be an independent subordinator. In [6], Theorem 2 shows that there exists a solution of the following time–change equation

$$X(t) = x + Z^{(0)}(t) + Z^{(1)} \left(\int_0^t X(s) ds \right)$$

for all $(t, x) \in \mathbb{R}_{\geq 0} \times \mathbb{R}_{\geq 0}$. Moreover, it is proved that the solution is a time homogeneous Markov process, taking values in $\mathbb{R}_{\geq 0}$ starting from x, characterized by the property that the logarithm of the characteristic function of the transition semigroup is given by an affine function of the initial state x. Hence, by definition, it is an affine process taking values in $\mathbb{R}_{\geq 0}$.

In this paper we aim to obtain the analogous result in the multivariate case. In [1] it has been proved that — in distribution — affine processes can be represented by means of $d+1$ independent Lévy processes taking values in $\mathbb{R}^d$. Under some assumptions on the Lévy triplets, the time change equation

$$X(t) = x + Z^{(0)}(t) + \sum_{i=1}^{d} Z^{(i)} \left(\int_0^t X_i(s) ds \right), \qquad t \geq 0, \qquad (1)$$

admits a *weak solution*. Existence of a solution for (1) (also in distribution) holds only under some conditions on the Lévy triplet.

In [1] the following problem is left unsolved: is X a strong solution of the time change equation (1)? In this paper we address this problem using an approximation of the underlying Lévy processes. Recently, an alternative time change construction of affine processes has been presented in [7]. The exposition is organized as follows. In Chapter 2 we provide an overview of some basic results for affine processes. Chapter 3 contains the core of the proof of existence of a strong solution of (1). We show how to path-wisely construct affine processes on the positive orthant solving a family of deterministic ODEs. Then, using the results from Chapter 3, we will see how to construct a solution X of (1) which lives on the same probability space where the Lévy processes are defined. In Chapter 4 we show that, starting from a family of Lévy processes $\{Z^{(k)}\}_{k=0,1,\dots,d}$ specified by some restrictions on their Lévy triplets, the solution time–change equation (1) is a time homogeneous Markov process having the affine property. Observe that, this new existence proof of affine processes gives, as straightforward consequence, the càdlàg property for affine processes.

2. Preliminaries

2.1. *Notation*

Henceforth D denotes the subset $\mathbb{R}_{\geq 0}^m \times \mathbb{R}^n$ of $\mathbb{R}^d$. The canonical basis of $\mathbb{R}^d$ is denoted by $\{e_i\}_{i=1,\dots,d}$. Given $\Delta \notin D$ define $D_\Delta = D \cup \{\Delta\}$. The set $\mathcal{B}(D)$ is the space of measurable function on D, while $B(D)$ is the space of measurable bounded function on D.

In order to simplify the notation, we introduce the sets of indices I and J defined as

$$I = \{1, \dots, m\} \qquad \text{and} \qquad J = \{m+1, \dots, d\}.$$

Moreover, given a set $H \subseteq \{1, \ldots, d\}$, the map π_H is the projection of $\mathbb{R}^d$ on the lower dimensional subspace with indices in H.

Comment. In particular

$$\pi_I : \mathbb{R}_{\geq 0}^m \times \mathbb{R}^n \to \mathbb{R}_{\geq 0}^m$$

$$x \mapsto \pi_I x := (x_i)_{i \in I}$$

and

$$\pi_J : \mathbb{R}_{\geq 0}^m \times \mathbb{R}^n \to \mathbb{R}^n$$

$$x \mapsto \pi_J x := (x_j)_{j \in J} .$$

Due to the geometry of the state space, the function

$$f_u(x) := e^{\langle x, u \rangle} , \qquad x \in D \tag{2}$$

is bounded if and only if u is an element in

$$\mathcal{U} := \mathbb{C}_{\leq 0}^m \times i\mathbb{R}^n , \tag{3}$$

where $\mathbb{C}_{\leq 0}^m = \{w \in \mathbb{C}^m \text{ such that } \mathcal{Re}(w) \in \mathbb{R}_{\leq 0}^m\}$. The notation $\langle \cdot, \cdot \rangle$ with input variables in $\mathbb{R}^d$ denotes the usual scalar product. The same notation is used also when the scalar product is considered in the space $\mathbb{R}^d + i\mathbb{R}^d$. In this case we mean the extension of $\langle \cdot, \cdot \rangle$ in $\mathbb{R}^d + i\mathbb{R}^d$ without conjugation. Unless differently specified, the notation $\mathbb{E}^x[\cdot]$ indicates that the expectation is taken under the probability measure $\mathbb{P}^x$.

Fix $N \in \mathbb{N}$ and let $s \in \mathbb{R}_{\geq 0}^N$. Whenever we are going to consider s as a time parameter, we emphasize its multidimensionality by writing $\underline{s}$. When $\underline{s} = (s_1, \ldots, s_N)$ is a multivariate time parameter and X is a stochastic process in $\mathbb{R}^N$, we use the notation

$$\underline{X}(\underline{s}) := (X_1(s_1), \ldots, X_N(s_N)) \in \mathbb{R}^N .$$

2.2. *Affine processes*

In line with the literature, we introduce the affine processes as a class of time homogeneous Markov processes characterized by two additional properties. The first one being stochastic continuity, the second one a condition which characterizes the Fourier–Laplace transform of the one time marginal distributions. This introduction of affine processes is taken from [8], [5] and [9].

Definition 2.1. Let

$$(\Omega, (X(t))_{t\geq 0}, (\mathcal{F}(t))_{t\geq 0}, (p(t))_{t\geq 0}, (\mathbb{P}^x)_{x\in D})$$

be a time homogeneous Markov process. In particular we assume that

- Ω is a probability space,
- $(X(t))_{t\geq 0}$ is a stochastic process taking values in D_Δ,
- $\mathcal{F}(t) = \sigma(\{X(s) , s \leq t\})$ is the filtration generated by canonical coordinates,
- $(p(t))_{t\geq 0}$ is a semigroup of transition functions on $(D_\Delta, \mathcal{B}(D_\Delta))$,
- $(\mathbb{P}^x)_{x\in D_\Delta}$ is a probability measures on $(\Omega, \mathcal{F})$, with $\mathcal{F} = \bigvee_{t\geq 0} \mathcal{F}(t)$,

satisfying

$$\mathbb{E}^x\Big[f(X(t+s))\big|\mathcal{F}(t)\Big] = \mathbb{E}^{X(t)}\Big[f(X(s))\Big], \quad \mathbb{P}^x\text{-a.s. for all } f \in B(D_\Delta). \quad (4)$$

The process X is said to be an *affine process* if it satisfies the following properties:

- for every $t \geq 0$ and $x \in D$, $\lim_{s\to t} p(s)(x, \cdot) = p(t)(x, \cdot)$ weakly,
- there exist functions $\varphi : \mathbb{R}_{\geq 0} \times \mathcal{U} \to \mathbb{C}$ and $\psi : \mathbb{R}_{\geq 0} \times \mathcal{U} \to \mathbb{C}^d$ such that

$$\mathbb{E}^x\Big[e^{\langle u, X(t)\rangle}\Big] = \int_D e^{\langle u,\xi\rangle} p(t)(x, d\xi) = e^{\varphi(t,u)+\langle x,\psi(t,u)\rangle}, \quad (5)$$

  for all $x \in D$ and $(t, u) \in \mathbb{R}_{\geq 0} \times \mathcal{U}$.

Regularity is a key feature for an affine process. It gives differentiability of the Fourier–Laplace transform with respect to time.

Definition 2.2. An affine process X is called *regular* if, for every $u \in \mathcal{U}$, the derivatives

$$F(u) := \partial_t\varphi(t, u)\Big|_{t=0}, \qquad R(u) := \partial_t\psi(t, u)\Big|_{t=0}, \qquad (6)$$

exist for all $u \in \mathcal{U}$ and are continuous in

$$\mathcal{U}_m = \Big\{u \in \mathbb{C}^d \mid \sup_{x\in D} \mathcal{R}e(\langle u, x\rangle) \leq m\Big\},$$

for all $m \geq 1$.

Regularity has been proved in [5]. The proof is based on the fact that affine processes always admit a version which has càdlàg paths. From this path regularity it is possible to conclude differentiability of the Fourier–Laplace transform. We summarize here the main results.

Theorem 2.1 (Theorem 6.4 in [5]). *Every affine process is regular. On the set* $\mathbb{R}_{\geq 0} \times \mathcal{U}$, *the functions* φ *and* ψ *satisfy the following system of generalized Riccati equations:*

$$\partial_t \varphi(t, u) = F(\psi(t, u)), \quad \varphi(0, u) = 0,$$
$$\partial_t \psi(t, u) = R(\psi(t, u)), \quad \psi(0, u) = u, \tag{7}$$

with

$$F(u) = \langle b, u \rangle + \frac{1}{2} \langle u, au \rangle - c$$
$$+ \int_{D \setminus \{0\}} \left(e^{\langle u, \xi \rangle} - 1 - \langle \pi_J u, \pi_J h(\xi) \rangle \right) m(d\xi), \tag{8}$$

$$R_k(u) = \langle \beta_k, u \rangle + \frac{1}{2} \langle u, \alpha_k u \rangle - \gamma_k$$
$$+ \int_{D \setminus \{0\}} \left(e^{\langle u, \xi \rangle} - 1 - \langle \pi_{J \cup \{k\}} u, \pi_{J \cup \{k\}} h(\xi) \rangle \right) M_k(d\xi), \tag{9}$$

for $k = 1, \ldots, d$ *where here we take as truncation function* $h(x) = x \mathbb{1}_{\{|x| \leq 1\}}$. *The set of parameters*

$$(b, \beta, a, \alpha, c, \gamma, m, M) \tag{10}$$

is specified by

- $b, \beta_i \in \mathbb{R}^d$ *for* $i = 1, \ldots, d$,
- $a, \alpha_i \in S_+^d$ *for* $i = 1, \ldots, d$, *where* S_+^d *denotes the cones of positive semidefinite* $d \times d$ *matrices,*
- $c, \gamma_i \in \mathbb{R}_{\geq 0}$ *for* $i = 1, \ldots, d$,
- m, M_i *for* $i = 1, \ldots, d$ *are Lévy measures.*

This set of parameters is called *admissible* if the previous conditions are satisfied. The set of admissible parameters fully characterizes an affine process in D.

Remark 2.1. If, additionally, the semigroup of transition functions $(p(t))_{t \geq 0}$ is homogeneous in the space variable, meaning that, for all $x \in D$ and $B \in \mathcal{B}(D)$

$$p(t)(x, B) = p(t)(0, B - x),$$

then necessarily $R = 0$ and it holds

$$\mathbb{E}^x \left[e^{\langle u, X(t) \rangle} \right] = \int e^{\langle u, \xi \rangle} p(t)(x, d\xi) = e^{t F(u) + \langle x, u \rangle},$$

for all $(t, x) \in \mathbb{R}_{\geq 0} \times D$ and $u \in \mathcal{U}$. Hence X is a (possibly killed) Lévy process with Lévy exponent F starting from x.

2.3. *Towards the multivariate Lamperti transform*

When $D = \mathbb{R}_{\geq 0}$, it has been proved that there exists a one-to-one correspondence between affine processes taking values in D and Lévy processes, see [6].

Comment. More precisely, let $Z^{(1)} = (Z^{(1)}(t))_{t \geq 0}$ be a Lévy process starting from 0 taking values in $\mathbb{R}$ whose Lévy measure has support $\mathbb{R}_{\geq 0}$. This implies that there exists a function $R : i\mathbb{R} \to \mathbb{C}$ such that

$$\mathbb{E}^0 \left[e^{u Z^{(1)}(s)} \right] = e^{s R(u)},$$

for all $(s, u) \in \mathbb{R}_{\geq 0} \times i\mathbb{R}$. Due to the restrictions on the jump measure, the function R takes the form

$$R(u) = \beta u + \frac{1}{2} \alpha^2 u^2 - \gamma + \int_{\mathbb{R}_{\geq 0}} \left(e^{u\xi} - 1 - u\xi \mathbb{1}_{\{|\xi| \leq 1\}} \right) M(d\xi),$$

where $u \in i\mathbb{R}$, $\alpha, \beta \in \mathbb{R}$ and M is a measure on $\mathbb{R}_{\geq 0}$ which satisfies

$$\int (1 \wedge |\xi|^2) M(d\xi) < \infty.$$

Moreover, let $Z^{(0)}$ be an independent subordinator with

$$\mathbb{E}^0 \left[e^{u Z^{(0)}(s)} \right] = e^{s F(u)},$$

for all $(s, u) \in \mathbb{R}_{\geq 0} \times i\mathbb{R}$. Since $Z^{(0)}$ is a subordinator, there exists a constant $b \in \mathbb{R}_{\geq 0}$ and a measure m in $\mathbb{R}_{\geq 0}$ satisfying

$$\int (1 \wedge |\xi|) m(d\xi) < \infty,$$

such that, for all $u \in i\mathbb{R}$,

$$F(u) = bu + \int_{\mathbb{R}_{\geq 0}} \left(e^{u\xi} - 1 \right) m(d\xi).$$

Theorem 2 in [6] shows that there exists a solution of the following time–change equation

$$X(t) = x + Z^{(0)}(t) + Z^{(1)} \left(\int_0^t X(s) ds \right)$$

for all $(t, x) \in \mathbb{R}_{\geq 0} \times \mathbb{R}_{\geq 0}$.

The theorem therein shows that the solution of the one-dimensional time change equation is a time homogeneous Markov process, taking values in $\mathbb{R}_{\geq 0}$ starting from x, such that the logarithm of the characteristic function of the transition semigroup is given by an affine function of the initial state x. Hence, by definition, it is an affine process taking values in $\mathbb{R}_{\geq 0}$.

Here we are interested in the multivariate generalization of this result, whose weak version is already known in the literature:

Theorem 2.2 (Theorem 3.4 in [1]). *Let X be an affine process with admissible parameter satisfying*

$$\int_{\{|\xi|\geq 1\}} |\xi_k| M_i(d\xi) < \infty \quad and \quad c = 0, \gamma_i = 0, \quad for \quad 1 \leq i, k \leq m.$$

On a possibly enlarged probability space, there exist $d+1$ independent Lévy processes $Z^{(k)}$ such that

$$X(t) \overset{d}{=} x + Z^{(0)}(t) + \sum_{k=1}^{d} Z^{(k)} \left(\int_0^t X_k(s) ds \right) \qquad t \geq 0. \tag{11}$$

This result has to be understood in distributional sense, because, without any additional assumptions, it is not clear how to conclude that the process X is adapted with respect to the (properly time–changed) filtration generated by the Lévy processes.

In this paper we provide a strong solution of (11) defined on the probability space $(\Omega, \mathcal{G}, \mathbb{P})$ which carries $Z^{(0)}, \ldots, Z^{(d)}$.

Remark 2.2. Note that Theorem 2.2 makes use of the theory of martingale problems related to the generator of affine processes to derive a time change representation in law. In this paper, the proof is based on a pathwise approximation and solution, respectively, of the time change equation. Hence, measurability of the solution with respect to the filtration generated by the Lévy process is obtained by construction.

2.4. *Affine processes of Heston type*

Comment. In this section, we are going to specify a particular subclass of affine processes, which we will call *affine processes of Heston type*. They are characterized by more restrictive admissible parameters but, at the same time, they constitute a canonical family, in the sense that every affine process can be obtained as a pathwise transformation of a canonical one. Instead of stating directly the conditions, we work through an example, where we point the main motivations and reasonings for the forthcoming Assumptions 2.1–2.3.

Let X be an affine process taking values in D and denote by $(b, \beta, a, \alpha, c, \gamma, m, M)$ its set of admissible parameters. The next condition implies that the function φ in the definition of affine property is identically zero.

Assumption 2.1. *The condition* $\mathbf{A}^\infty$ *is satisfied if* $(b, a, c, m) = (0, 0, 0, 0)$.

The next assumption implies that the process is homogeneous in the last n variables.

Assumption 2.2. *The condition* $\mathbf{A}^H$ *is satisfied if, for all* $i, j \in J$ *it holds* $(\beta_i)_j = 0$.

Finally, to ensure that a solution of the system exists for all $t \geq 0$, we introduce this last set of conditions.

Assumption 2.3. *The condition* $\mathring{\mathbf{A}}$ *is satisfied if, for all* $i \in I$ *it holds* $c = 0$, $\gamma_i = 0$ *and*

$$\int \left(|\pi_I \xi| \wedge |\pi_I \xi|^2 \right) M_i(d\xi), \quad \text{for all} \quad i \in I \,.$$

Definition 2.3. We call an affine process with admissible parameters $(b, \beta, a, \alpha, c, \gamma, m, M)$ satisfying $\mathbf{A}^\infty$, $\mathbf{A}^H$ and $\mathring{\mathbf{A}}$ an *affine process of Heston type*.

Among the previous assumptions, only Assumption 2.3 is a real restriction on the structure on the admissible parameters. As observed also in [1] (also compare with [8], Lemma 9.2) Assumption 2.3 guarantees that the solution process does not explode in finite time and hence the time–change process is always well defined. Up to an enlargement of the state space and a pathwise transformation, there is no loss of generality in assuming that both Assumption 2.1 and Assumption 2.2 hold.

In the following proposition we present all steps which allow us to reduce a general affine process into an affine process of Heston type.

3. Existence of the solution of the time–change equation

3.1. *The setting*

Let $Z^{(1)}, \dots, Z^{(d)}$ be d independent càdlàg $\mathbb{R}^d$-valued Lévy processes, each of them with Lévy triplet (β_k, α_k, M_k), $k = 1, \dots, d$, defined on the same probability space.

Now we consider the process $Z = (Z^{(1)}, \ldots, Z^{(d)}) \in \mathbb{R}^{d^2}$ on the product space $(\Omega, \mathcal{G}, P)$.

We fix $x \in D$ and consider the functions

$$f_k(y) := x_k + \sum_{i=1}^{d} y_k^{(i)} \text{ for } k = 1, \ldots, d, \ y \in \mathbb{R}^{d^2}. \tag{12}$$

In the next section it will be essential to construct the solution of a system of time–change equations of type

$$Y_i^{(k)}(t) := Z_i^{(k)}\left(\int_0^t f_k(Y(s))ds\right), \quad k, i = 1, \ldots, d, \text{ and }, t \geq 0, \tag{13}$$

with $Y = (Y_1^{(1)}, \ldots, Y_d^{(1)}, \ldots, Y_1^{(d)}, \ldots, Y_d^{(d)})$.

Introduce

$$\tau_k(t) := \int_0^t f_k(Y(s))ds, \text{ for } k = 1 \ldots, d \text{ and } t \geq 0, \tag{14}$$

and define

$$\underline{\tau}(t) := (\tau_1(t), \ldots, \tau_d(t)). \tag{15}$$

Existence of a solution of (13) is equivalent to the existence of a solution of the following system of ODEs

$$\begin{cases} \dot{\tau}_k(t) = f_k\left(\underline{Z}(\underline{\tau}(t))\right), & \text{for all } k = 1, \ldots, d, t \geq 0, \\ \tau_k(0) = 0, \end{cases} \tag{16}$$

where

$$\underline{Z}(\underline{\tau}(t)) := \left(Z^{(1)}(\tau_1(t)), \ldots, Z^{(k)}(\tau_k(t)), \ldots, Z^{(d)}(\tau_d(t))\right).$$

3.2. The core of the proof

We start studying the time–change representation of affine processes in $\mathbb{R}^m_{\geq 0}$. Under the assumption that $n = 0$, (11) reads

$$X(t) \stackrel{d}{=} x + \sum_{i=1}^{m} Z^{(i)}\left(\int_0^t X_i(s)ds\right) \qquad t \geq 0, \tag{17}$$

where $Z^{(1)}, \ldots, Z^{(m)}$ are m independent Lévy processes on $\mathbb{R}^m$, each of them with Lévy triplets (β_i, α_i, M_i), $i = 1 \ldots, m$, satisfying

$$(\alpha_i)_{kl} = 0 \text{ for all } k, l \in I \text{ such that } (k, l) \neq (i, i),$$
$$(\beta_i)_k \geq 0 \text{ for all } i \in I \text{ and } k \in I \setminus \{i\}.$$

Suppose that we can show existence of the solution of the following problem

$$\begin{cases} \dot{\tau}_k(t) = x_k + \mathcal{Z}_k(\underline{\tau}(t)), & k = 1, \ldots, m\,, t \geq 0\,, \\ \tau_k(0) = 0\,, \end{cases} \tag{18}$$

where

$$\mathcal{Z} : \underline{s} \mapsto \sum_{i=1}^{m} Z^{(i)}(s_i)\,. \tag{19}$$

Then, we can construct X as

$$X_t = x + \sum_{i=1}^{m} Z^{(i)}(\tau_i)\,, t \geq 0\,.$$

Observe that (18) in vector notation reads

$$\begin{cases} \underline{\dot{\tau}}(t) = x + \mathcal{Z}(\underline{\tau}(t))\,, t \geq 0\,, \\ \underline{\tau}(0) = 0\,. \end{cases} \tag{20}$$

3.2.1. *Approximation of the vector field*

In order to construct a solution for (20), we seek for a decomposition of type

$$\mathcal{Z} = \widetilde{\mathcal{Z}} + \widetilde{\widetilde{\mathcal{Z}}}$$

such that the system

$$\begin{cases} \underline{\dot{\tau}}(t) = (x + \widetilde{\mathcal{Z}})(\underline{\tau}(t))\,, t \geq 0 \\ \underline{\tau}(0) = 0\,, \end{cases} \tag{21}$$

reduces to a decoupled system of m one dimensional problems and $\widetilde{\widetilde{\mathcal{Z}}} := \mathcal{Z} - \widetilde{\mathcal{Z}}$.

The Lévy–Itô decomposition, together with the canonical form of the admissible parameters, gives

$$Z^{(i)}(t) = \beta_i t + \sigma_i B^{(i)}(t) + \int_0^t \int \xi \mathbb{1}_{\{|\xi|>1\}} \mathcal{J}^{(i)}(d\xi, ds)$$

$$+ \int_0^t \int \xi \mathbb{1}_{\{|\xi|\leq 1\}} (\mathcal{J}^{(i)}(d\xi, ds) - M_i(d\xi)ds)$$

where $\sigma_i = \sqrt{(\alpha_i)_{ii}}$, $B^{(i)}$ is a process in $\mathbb{R}^m$ which evolves only along the i-th coordinate as Brownian motion and $\mathcal{J}^{(i)}$ is the jump measure of the process $Z^{(i)}$.

Now, from the assumption on the set of admissible parameter,

$$\pi_{I\setminus\{i\}}\beta_i \in \mathbb{R}^{m-1}_{\geq 0} \quad \text{and} \quad \pi_i\beta_i \in \mathbb{R}.$$

Decompose

$$Z^{(i)} =: \widetilde{Z}^{(i)} + \overset{\approx}{Z}{}^{(i)}$$

where $\widetilde{Z}^{(i)}$ and $\overset{\approx}{Z}{}^{(i)}$ are two stochastic processes on $\mathbb{R}^m$ defined by

$$
\begin{aligned}
\widetilde{Z}^{(i)}_k(t) &:= 0, \quad \text{for } k \neq i, \\
\widetilde{Z}^{(i)}_i(t) &:= \sigma_i B^{(i)}_i(t) + \pi_i\beta_i t + \int_0^t \int \xi_i \mathbb{1}_{|\xi|>1} \mathcal{J}^{(i)}(d\xi, ds), \\
&\quad + \int_0^t \int \xi_i \mathbb{1}_{|\xi|\leq 1}(\mathcal{J}^{(i)}(d\xi, ds) - M_i(d\xi)ds), \\
\overset{\approx}{Z}{}^{(i)}(t) &:= \overset{\approx}{\beta}_i t + \int_0^t \int (\xi - \xi_i e_i) \mathbb{1}_{\{|\xi|>1\}} \mathcal{J}^{(i)}(d\xi, ds), \\
&\quad + \int_0^t \int (\xi - \xi_i e_i) \mathbb{1}_{\{|\xi|\leq 1\}}(\mathcal{J}^{(i)}(d\xi, ds) - M_i(d\xi)ds),
\end{aligned}
$$

where

$$\overset{\approx}{\beta}_i = \beta_i - e_i\pi_i\beta_i.$$

Remark 3.1. It is worth noticing that the proposed decomposition stems from the Lévy–Itô decomposition but there is a different separation among the infinite variation jump component and the finite variation part. Indeed, due to the restriction on the admissible parameters, for every $i = 1, \ldots, m$ the Lévy measure M_i generates jumps of finite variation on all directions but the i-th. We decompose each Lévy process $Z^{(i)}$ as a spectrally positive Lévy process evolving along the i-th direction (we call it $\widetilde{Z}^{(i)}_i$) and a correlated Lévy process of finite variation (the one we call $\overset{\approx}{Z}{}^i$).

The following lemma, which is an obvious consequence of the restrictions on the admissible parameters, collects some path properties of the processes $\widetilde{Z}^{(i)}$ and $\overset{\approx}{Z}{}^{(i)}$. We would like to remark that both càdlàg property and this special structure of the paths are essential ingredients of our proof.

Lemma 3.1. *For all $i = 1, \ldots, m$ it holds*

(1) $\widetilde{Z}^{(i)}$ is a Lévy process with no negative jumps,

(2) $\overset{\approx}{Z}{}^{(i)}$ is a process with increasing paths.

Introduce, for all $\underline{s} \in \mathbb{R}^m_{\geq 0}$,

$$
\begin{aligned}
\widetilde{\mathcal{Z}}(\underline{s}) &:= \sum_{i=1}^m \widetilde{Z}^{(i)}(s_i), \\
\overset{\approx}{\mathcal{Z}}(\underline{s}) &:= \sum_{i=1}^m \overset{\approx}{Z}{}^{(i)}(s_i).
\end{aligned}
$$

We will consider separately the initial value problems with vector fields

$$x + \widetilde{\mathcal{Z}} \quad \text{and} \quad \overset{\approx}{\mathcal{Z}} .$$

The next result shows that it is possible to find a unique solution for the initial value problem

$$\begin{cases} \dot{\tau}((t_0, \tau_0, x); t) = (x + \widetilde{\mathcal{Z}})(\tau((t_0, \tau_0, x); t)) , \\ \tau((t_0, \tau_0, x); t_0) = \tau_0 . \end{cases}$$

Later, we will show how to construct a solution of the general problem.

Proposition 3.1. *There exists a unique solution of*

$$\begin{cases} \dot{\tau}((t_0, \tau_0, x); t) = (x + \widetilde{\mathcal{Z}})(\tau((t_0, \tau_0, x); t)), \\ \tau((t_0, \tau_0, x); t_0) = \tau_0 , \end{cases} \tag{22}$$

with $\tau_0 \in \mathbb{R}_{\geq 0}^m$ and $t \geq 0$.

Proof. Observe that (22) is a decoupled system of m equations of type

$$\begin{cases} \dot{\tau}_i((t_0, \tau_0, x); t) = (x_i + \widetilde{Z}_i^{(i)})(\tau_i((t_0, \tau_0, x); t)), & i = 1, \ldots, m , \\ \tau_i((t_0, \tau_0, x); t_0) = \pi_{\{i\}} \tau_0 . \end{cases} \tag{23}$$

where each $\widetilde{Z}_i^{(i)}$ is a Lévy process with no negative jumps. The existence of a unique solution of (23) follows from [10], Section 6.1. ∎

For the proof of the general result, we will need to approximate $\overset{\approx}{\mathcal{Z}}$ with piecewise constant functions. Fix $M \in \mathbb{N}$ and consider the partition

$$\mathcal{T}_M := \left\{ \frac{k}{2^M}, \quad k \geq 0 \right\} .$$

Define the following approximations on the partition $\mathcal{T}_M$:

$$\uparrow \overset{\approx}{Z}^{(i, M)}(t) := \sum_{k=0}^{\infty} \overset{\approx}{Z}_{k/2^M}^{(i)} \mathbb{1}_{[\frac{k}{2^M}, \frac{k+1}{2^M})}(t) ,$$

$$\downarrow \overset{\approx}{Z}^{(i, M)}(t) := \sum_{k=0}^{\infty} \overset{\approx}{Z}_{(k+1)/2^M}^{(i)} \mathbb{1}_{[\frac{k}{2^M}, \frac{k+1}{2^M})}(t) .$$

Introduce, for $\underline{s} \in \mathbb{R}_{\geq 0}^m$, the processes $\uparrow \overset{\approx}{\mathcal{Z}}^{(M)}(\underline{s})$ and $\downarrow \overset{\approx}{\mathcal{Z}}^{(M)}(\underline{s})$ obtained by taking the sums of $\uparrow \overset{\approx}{Z}_{s_i}^{(i, M)}$ and $\downarrow \overset{\approx}{Z}_{s_i}^{(i, M)}$ respectively.

Notation 3.1. Let

$$\Sigma := \bigcup_{i=1}^{m} \{s \geq 0 \mid \Delta \tilde{Z}^{(i)}(s) > 0\}$$

and augment the partition $\mathcal{T}$ with Σ_M. Denote the family obtained in this way by $\mathcal{T}_M^{\Sigma}$.

We will first construct a solution for the equation (20) when $\tilde{\mathcal{Z}}$ is replaced by $\uparrow \tilde{\mathcal{Z}}^{(M)}$.

Hereafter, given $x, y \in \mathbb{R}^m$, we write $x \leq y$ if $x_i \leq y_i$, for all $i = 1, \ldots, m$.

3.2.2. *The algorithm*

Let $\tilde{\mathcal{Z}}$ and $\uparrow \tilde{\mathcal{Z}}^{(M)}$ be defined as above.

Input: Start by defining the random variables

$$\overleftarrow{\sigma}(\omega) := (0, \ldots, 0), \tag{24}$$

$$\overrightarrow{\sigma}(\omega) := (\sigma_1^{(1,M)}(\omega), \ldots, \sigma_1^{(m,M)}(\omega)), \tag{25}$$

where each $\sigma_1^{(i,M)}(\omega)$ is the first jump in the path $t \mapsto \uparrow \tilde{Z}^{(i,M)}(t)(\omega)$.

Step 1: Let $\underline{\tau}((t_0, \tau_0, x); t)$ be the solution of the system (22) starting from

$$t_0 = 0, \quad \tau_0 = (0, \ldots, 0) \quad \text{and} \quad x \in \mathbb{R}_{\geq 0}^m.$$

Consider the solution of (22) for all times t such that

$$\underline{\tau}((t_0, \tau_0, x); t) < \overrightarrow{\sigma}. \tag{†}$$

Let t^* be the first time such that (†) does not hold anymore. Stop the solution $\underline{\tau}((t_0, \tau_0, x); \cdot)$ at time t^*. Observe that the condition (†) is violated if there exists an index $i^* \in \{1, \ldots, m\}$ such that

$$\tau_{i^*}((t_0, \tau_0, x); t^*) = \sigma_1^{(i^*,M)}.$$

Notice here that there might be more than one i^*, where the above equality is valid, however, for the sake of convenience, we assume that there exists only one index for the moment. We will deal with the general case in the proof of Theorem 3.1.

Step 2: Update

$$\overleftarrow{\sigma} := (0, \ldots, \sigma_1^{(i^*, M)}, \ldots, 0), \tag{26}$$

$$\overrightarrow{\sigma} := (\sigma_1^{(1,M)}, \ldots, \sigma_2^{(i^*, M)}, \ldots, \sigma_1^{(m,M)}), \tag{27}$$

$$x := x + \Delta^{\uparrow} \widetilde{Z}^{(M)}(\overleftarrow{\sigma}), \tag{28}$$

where $\sigma_2^{(i^*, M)}(\omega)$ is the second jump in the path $t \mapsto {\uparrow}\widetilde{Z}^{(i^*, M)}(t)(\omega)$.

Step 3: Let $\underline{\tau}((t_1, \tau_1, x_1); t)$ be the solution of the system (22) starting from the *updated* values

$$t_1 = t^*, \quad \tau_1 = \underline{\tau}((t_0, \tau_0, x_0); t^*) \quad \text{and} \quad x_1 = x \in \mathbb{R}_{\geq 0}^m.$$

As before, we let $\underline{\tau}((t_1, \tau_1, x_1); \cdot)$ evolve until

$$\underline{\tau}((t_1, \tau_1, x_1); t^*) < \overrightarrow{\sigma} \tag{29}$$

holds. As soon as this condition does not hold anymore, we stop again the solution.

End: Do iteratively **Step 2** and **Step 3**.

The above algorithm describes the guiding principle for the proof of the next result:

Theorem 3.1. *There exists a solution of*

$$\begin{cases} \underline{\dot{\tau}}^{(M)}((0,0,x);t) = (x + \widetilde{Z} + {\uparrow}\widetilde{Z}^{(M)})(\underline{\tau}^{(M)}((0,0,x);t)), \\ \underline{\tau}^{(M)}((0,0,x);0) = 0. \end{cases} \tag{30}$$

Proof. We already did all the main steps for the proof of this result. Let $\mathcal{T}_M$ and Σ be the sets defined in Notation 3.1. Recall that $\mathcal{T}_M^\Sigma$ is a countable family. Enumerate the elements in $\mathcal{T}_M^\Sigma$ such that $\sigma_k^{(i)}$ denotes the k-th jump of ${\uparrow}\widetilde{Z}^{(i, M)}$. Fix $x \in D$ and set

$$(t_0, \tau_0, x) := (0, 0, x)$$

and

$$\overleftarrow{\sigma} := (0, \ldots, 0),$$

$$\overrightarrow{\sigma} := (\sigma_1^{(1,M)}, \ldots, \sigma_1^{(i,M)}, \ldots, \sigma_1^{(m,M)}),$$

where $\sigma_k^{(i,M)}$ denotes the k-th jump in the path $t \mapsto {\uparrow}\widetilde{Z}^{(i, M)}(t)$ for all $i = 1, \ldots, m$. By definition ${\uparrow}\widetilde{Z}^{(M)}(\underline{s}) = 0$ for all $\underline{s} < \overrightarrow{\sigma}$. Proposition 3.1

gives the existence of the solution of (22) with this set of input parameters. Denote it by $\underline{\tau}((t_0, \tau_0, x); t)$. As soon as the solution $\underline{\tau}((t_0, \tau_0, x); t)$ reaches a jump time for $^{\uparrow}\widetilde{Z}^{(M)}$, the vector field in the equation (30) changes. Precisely, denote by

$$t_1 := \sup\{t > 0 \mid \underline{\tau}((t_0, \tau_0, x); t) < \overrightarrow{\sigma}\}.$$

Again there might be one or more indices i^*, where the condition fails. Collect them in a set $I^* \subseteq \{1, \dots, m\}$. Update the values

$$\begin{aligned}
\pi_{I^*} \overleftarrow{\sigma} &:= \pi_{I^*} \overrightarrow{\sigma}, \\
\pi_{I^*} \overrightarrow{\sigma} &:= \pi_{I^*} \overrightarrow{\sigma}_{++},
\end{aligned} \tag{31}$$

where $\overrightarrow{\sigma}_{++}$ contains the next jumps of $^{\uparrow}\widetilde{Z}^{(i, M)}$ for all $i \in I^*$ after $\overrightarrow{\sigma}_i$. Then define

$$\begin{aligned}
\tau_1 &:= \underline{\tau}((t_0, \tau_0, x); t_1), \\
x_1 &:= x + \Delta^{\uparrow}\widetilde{Z}^{(M)}(\overleftarrow{\sigma}).
\end{aligned}$$

Now, consider again the solution of (22), but this time with parameters (t_1, τ_1, x_1). Denote it by $\underline{\tau}((t_1, \tau_1, x_1); t)$ and observe that it is well defined until all the coordinates of $\tau((t_1, \tau_1, x_1); t)$ stay below the next jump times of $^{\uparrow}\widetilde{Z}^{(M)}$. We obtain the solution of (22) by pasting a finite amount of solutions obtained in the time subintervals defined by $\mathcal{T}_M^{\Sigma}$. Define iteratively, for all $n \geq 1$,

$$t_{n+1} := \sup\{t > t_n \mid \underline{\tau}((t_n, \tau_n, x_n); t_n) < \overrightarrow{\sigma}\}, \tag{32}$$

$$\tau_{n+1} := \underline{\tau}((t_n, \tau_n, x_n); t_{n+1}), \tag{33}$$

$$x_{n+1} := x_n + \Delta^{\uparrow}\widetilde{Z}^{(M)}(\overleftarrow{\sigma}), \tag{34}$$

where, at each step, $\overleftarrow{\sigma}$ and $\overrightarrow{\sigma}$ are updated using the prescription in (31). Continuity follows by construction. ∎

Now that we have found a solution for the approximated problems, we would like to show convergence to the solution of (20).

The following results focus on monotonicity and convergence of (30).

Lemma 3.2. *Let $i = 1, \dots, m$ and $M \in \mathbb{N}$ be fixed. Then, for all $t \geq 0$ it holds*

$$^{\uparrow}\widetilde{Z}^{(i, M)}(t) \leq \widetilde{Z}^{(i)}(t) \leq {}^{\downarrow}\widetilde{Z}^{(i, M)}(t) \text{ almost surely.}$$

Moreover, for each $\omega \in \Omega$, *the sequences* $\{^{\uparrow}\widetilde{Z}^{(i, M)}(\omega)\}_{M \in \mathbb{N}}$ *and* $\{^{\downarrow}\widetilde{Z}^{(i, M)}(\omega)\}_{M \in \mathbb{N}}$ *are monotone in the sense that, for all* $t \geq 0$,

$$^{\uparrow}\widetilde{Z}^{(i, M + 1)}(t)(\omega) \geq {}^{\uparrow}\widetilde{Z}^{(i, M)}(t)(\omega)$$

and

$$^{\downarrow}\widetilde{Z}^{(i, M + 1)}(t)(\omega) \leq {}^{\downarrow}\widetilde{Z}^{(i, M)}(t)(\omega).$$

Proof. By Lemma 3.1 it holds

$$\widetilde{Z}^{(i)}(t) \geq \widetilde{Z}^{(i)}_{k/2^M} = {}^{\uparrow}\widetilde{Z}^{(i, M)}(t), \quad \text{a.s. for all } t \in \left[\frac{k}{2^M}, \frac{k+1}{2^M}\right).$$

For the same reason,

$$\widetilde{Z}^{(i)}(t) \leq \widetilde{Z}^{(i)}_{(k+1)/2^M} = {}^{\downarrow}\widetilde{Z}^{(i, M)}(t), \quad \text{a.s. for all } t \in \left[\frac{k}{2^M}, \frac{k+1}{2^M}\right).$$

Now, since for every $M \in \mathbb{N}$ the partition $\mathcal{T}_{M+1}$ is obtained by halving all the subintervals in the partition $\mathcal{T}_M$, it clearly holds

$$^{\uparrow}\widetilde{Z}^{(i, M + 1)}(t)(\omega) = \begin{cases} ^{\uparrow}\widetilde{Z}^{(i, M)}(t)(\omega), & \text{for all } t \in \left[\frac{2k}{2^{M+1}}, \frac{2k+1}{2^{M+1}}\right), \\[2mm] \widetilde{Z}^{(i)}_{(2k+1)/2^{M+1}}(\omega), & \text{for all } t \in \left[\frac{2k+1}{2^{M+1}}, \frac{2(k+1)}{2^{M+1}}\right). \end{cases}$$

Using again the increasing property of the paths of $\widetilde{Z}^{(i)}$ we conclude that

$$^{\uparrow}\widetilde{Z}^{(i, M)}(t) \geq \widetilde{Z}^{(i)}(t), \quad \text{a.s.}$$

because

$$\widetilde{Z}^{(i)}_{(2k+1)/2^{M+1}} \geq \widetilde{Z}^{(i)}_{2k/2^{M+1}} = \widetilde{Z}^{(i)}_{k/2^M}.$$

The case with $^{\downarrow}\widetilde{Z}^{(i, M)}$ goes analogously. ∎

Proposition 3.2. *Let $M \in \mathbb{N}$ be fixed and denote by $\underline{\tau}^{(M)}((0, 0, x); t)$ the solution of (30) constructed in Theorem 3.1. Then, for all $t \geq 0$ and $x \in \mathbb{R}^m_{\geq 0}$ it holds*

$$\underline{\tau}^{(M)}((0, 0, x); t) \leq \underline{\tau}^{(M+1)}((0, 0, x); t), \ \text{almost surely}.$$

Proof. This follows by construction using the monotonicity proved in Lemma 3.2. Indeed, denote by $\mathcal{T}^{\Sigma}_M := \{\sigma_k^{(M)}\}_{k \in \mathbb{N}}$ and $\mathcal{T}^{\Sigma}_{M+1} := \{\sigma_k^{(M+1)}\}_{k \in \mathbb{N}}$ the set of jump times for $^{\uparrow}\widetilde{Z}^{(M)}$ and $^{\uparrow}\widetilde{Z}^{(M + 1)}$ respectively. By construction $\mathcal{T}^{\Sigma}_M \subset \mathcal{T}^{\Sigma}_{M+1}$ in the sense that, for each $\sigma_k^{(M)} \in \mathcal{T}^{\Sigma}_M$ there exists

$h \in \mathbb{N}$ such that $\sigma_k^{(M)} = \sigma_h^{(M+1)} \in \mathcal{T}_{M+1}^{\Sigma}$. Denote by $\{\sigma_{k_h}^{(M+1)}\}_{h \in \mathbb{N}}$ the jump times of $\uparrow \tilde{Z}^{(M+1)}$ occurring on the subinterval $[\sigma_k^{(M)}, \sigma_{k+1}^{(M)}]$. By construction, there is only one jump inside this interval. Write $\{\sigma_{k_h}^{(M+1)}\}_{h=1,\dots,3}$ with $\sigma_{k_1}^{(M+1)} = \sigma_k^{(M)}$ and $\sigma_{k_3}^{(M+1)} = \sigma_{k+1}^{(M)}$. Then $\underline{\tau}^{(M+1)}$ is obtained by pasting a finite number of solutions of initial value problems with piecewise linear vector field. For each $h = 1, 2, 3$, $\uparrow \tilde{Z}^{(M+1)}(\sigma_{k_h}^{(M+1)}) \geq$ $\uparrow \tilde{Z}^{(M)}(\sigma_k^{(M)})$. Therefore, on each subinterval $[\sigma_k^{(M)}, \sigma_{k+1}^{(M)}]$, the solution $\underline{\tau}^{(M+1)}((t_k, \tau_k, x_k); t)$ is constructed by pasting a finite number of solutions of type $\underline{\tau}((t_{k,h}, \tau_{k,h}, x_{k,h}); t)$ where $x_{k,h}$ is increasing sequence in h. Hence we conclude that, for all $k \in \mathbb{N}$ and for $t \in [\sigma_k^{(M)}, \sigma_{k+1}^{(M)}]$ it holds

$$\underline{\tau}^{(M+1)}((t_k, \tau_k, x_k); t) \geq \underline{\tau}^{(M)}((t_k, \tau_k, x_k); \sigma_k^{(M)}).$$

■

The last monotonicity argument follows directly from the definition of the ODEs:

Lemma 3.3. *Let M, t_0, τ_0 be fixed and $x \leq y$. Consider the systems*

$$\begin{cases} \dot{\underline{\tau}}^{(M)}((t_0, \tau_0, x); t) = (x + \tilde{Z} + \uparrow \tilde{Z}^{(M)})(\underline{\tau}^{(M)}((t_0, \tau_0, x); t)), \\ \underline{\tau}^{(M)}((t_0, \tau_0, x); t_0) = \tau_0. \end{cases}$$

$$\begin{cases} \dot{\underline{\tau}}^{(M)}((t_0, \tau_0, y); t) = (y + \tilde{Z} + \uparrow \tilde{Z}^{(M)})(\underline{\tau}^{(M)}((t_0, \tau_0, y); t)), \\ \underline{\tau}^{(M)}((t_0, \tau_0, y); t_0) = \tau_0. \end{cases}$$

Then, for all $t \geq t_0$ it holds

$$\underline{\tau}^{(M)}((t_0, \tau_0, x); t) \leq \underline{\tau}^{(M)}((t_0, \tau_0, y); t), \text{ almost surely}.$$

Finally, due to monotonicity, we know that the sequence $\underline{\tau}^{(M)}$ admits a limit. With the next result we show that the limit is actually finite and, by monotone convergence, it coincides with a solution of (20), which are by law unique.

Proposition 3.3. *For all $t \geq 0$ and $x \in \mathbb{R}_{\geq 0}^m$ the sequence $\underline{\tau}^{(M)}((0, 0, x); t)$ converges*

$$\lim_{M \to \infty} \underline{\tau}^{(M)}((0, 0, x); t) = \underline{\tau}^{(*)}((0, 0, x); t)$$

and the limit can be identified with a solution of (20) almost surely, whose law, however, is unique.

Proof. Let $\underline{\tau}^{(*)}((0,0,x);\cdot)$ be the limit of the sequence $\{\underline{\tau}^{(M)}((0,0,x);\cdot)\}_{M\geq 0}$. Since the sequence is a monotone sequence and the limit is continuous, the convergence is actually uniform by Dini's theorem. Observe that the same holds for the limit of the sequence of solutions of the system (30) when $\uparrow\widetilde{\mathcal{Z}}^{(M)}$ is replaced by $\downarrow\widetilde{\mathcal{Z}}^{(M)}$. Applying the dominated convergence theorem it follows that $\underline{\tau}^{(*)}((0,0,x);t)$ coincides with a solution of (20). ∎

Remark 3.2. We do believe that solutions of Equation (20) are actually unique but we do not need it here and we therefore do not prove this result. It will follow by methods similar to [11], where weak uniqueness leads to pathwise uniqueness. Notice, however, that our time change setting is different from the classical setting.

4. Pathwise construction of affine processes with time–change

In this section we apply the previous results for the pathwise construction of affine processes in $\mathbb{R}^m_{\geq 0}$. Note that this class is also known in the literature under the name of *multitype continuous-state branching process with immigration*. In particular we are going to show that the process constructed in (17) is adapted with respect to the filtration of the underlying Lévy processes. Then, we will see how to generalize the result for affine processes in $\mathbb{R}^m_{\geq 0} \times \mathbb{R}^n$ with $n > 1$.

We start introducing the notion of multivariate filtration and multivariate stopping time taken from [10].

For all $\underline{s} = (s_1, \ldots, s_{m^2}) \in \mathbb{R}^{m^2}_{\geq 0}$, define the σ-algebra

$$\mathcal{G}_{\underline{s}} := \sigma\left(\{Z^{(h)}(t_h),\, t_h \leq s_h,\, \text{for } h = 1, \ldots, m^2\}\right), \tag{35}$$

where, with an abuse of notation, we denote with $Z^{(h)}$ the h-th coordinate of the process obtained by indexing Z as follows:

$$Z := (Z_1^{(1)}, \ldots, Z_m^{(1)}, \ldots, Z_1^{(m)}, \ldots, Z_m^{(m)}).$$

Then, we complete the σ-algebra by

$$\mathcal{G}_{\underline{s}} = \bigcap_{n\in\mathbb{N}} \mathcal{G}_{\underline{s}^{(n)}} \vee \sigma(\mathcal{N}), \tag{36}$$

where $\mathcal{N}$ is the collection of sets in $\mathcal{G}$ with P-probability zero and $\underline{s}^{(n)}$ is the sequence defined by $s_k^{(n)} = s_k + 1/n$.

Definition 4.1. A random variable $\underline{\tau} = (\tau_1, \ldots, \tau_{m^2}) \in \mathbb{R}^{m^2}_{\geq 0}$ is a $(\mathcal{G}_{\underline{s}})$-stopping time if

$$\{\underline{\tau} \leq \underline{s}\} := \{\tau_1 \leq s_1, \ldots, \tau_{m^2} \leq s_{m^2}\} \in \mathcal{G}_{\underline{s}}, \text{ for all } \underline{s} \in \mathbb{R}^{m^2}_{\geq 0}.$$

If $\underline{\tau}$ is a stopping time,

$$\mathcal{G}_{\underline{\tau}} := \{B \in \mathcal{G} \mid B \cap \{\underline{\tau} \leq \underline{s}\} \in \mathcal{G}_{\underline{s}} \text{ for all } \underline{s} \in \mathbb{R}^{m^2}_{\geq 0}\}.$$

Now that we have introduced the necessary notation, we are ready to prove the following result.

Theorem 4.1. *Let τ be a solution of* (20).

(1) The time–change equation

$$X(t) = x + \sum_{i=1}^{m} Z^{(i)}(\theta_i(t)), \quad \text{with } \theta_i(t) = \int_0^t X_i(r)dr, \qquad (37)$$

admits a solution.
(ii) Define

$$\underline{\theta}^x(t) := (\underbrace{\theta_1(t), \ldots, \theta_1(t)}_{m \text{ times}}, \ldots, \underbrace{\theta_m(t), \ldots, \theta_m(t)}_{m \text{ times}}) \in \mathbb{R}^{m^2}.$$

The random variable $\underline{\theta}^x(t)$ is a $\mathcal{G}_{\underline{s}}$ stopping time for all $t \geq 0$. Hence the time–change filtration

$$\mathcal{G}_{\underline{\theta}^x(t)} := \{A \mid A \cap \{\underline{\theta}^x(t) \leq \underline{s}\} \in \mathcal{G}_{\underline{s}}, \text{ for all } \underline{s} \in \mathbb{R}^{m^2}_{\geq 0}\},$$

is well defined.
(iii) Let R be the function defined as in (9). *The solution of* (37) *is an affine process with functional characteristics $(0, R)$ with respect to the time–changed filtration $(\mathcal{G}_{\underline{\theta}^x(t)})_{t \geq 0}$. In particular the solution of* (37) *is unique in law.*

Proof. Let $Y \in \mathbb{R}^{m^2}$ be the process obtained by casting the solutions of (13) as

$$Y := (Y_1^{(1)}, \ldots, Y_m^{(1)}, \ldots, Y_1^{(m)}, \ldots, Y_m^{(m)}).$$

Then

$$X = x + \sum_{k=1}^{m} Y^{(k)}$$

is a solution of time-change equation (37). Indeed, if $Z_j^{(k)}$ denotes the j-th coordinate of the k-th Lévy process,

$$Z_j^{(k)} \left(\int_0^t f_j^{(k)}(Y(s))ds \right) = Z_j^{(k)} \left(\int_0^t x_j + \sum_{k=1}^m Y_j^{(k)}(s)ds \right) = Z_j^{(k)} \left(\int_0^t X_k(s)ds \right)$$

and

$$X_j(t) = x_j + \sum_{k=1}^m Y_j^{(k)}(t)$$

$$= x_j + \sum_{k=1}^m Z_j^{(k)} \left(\int_0^t X_k(s)ds \right).$$

Now we move on the measurability of the time–change process. Observe

$$\underline{\tau} := (\underbrace{\tau_1, \ldots, \tau_1}_{m \text{ times}}, \ldots, \underbrace{\tau_m, \ldots, \tau_m}_{m \text{ times}}) \in \mathbb{R}^{m^2}.$$

where

$$\tau_k(t) = \int_0^t f_k(Y(s))ds$$

is a $\mathcal{G}_s$ stopping time for all $t \geq 0$. This follows from [10], Theorem VI.2.2.. From the affine relationship between X and Y we conclude that $\underline{\theta}(t)$ is a $\mathcal{G}_s$ stopping time and therefore the time–changed filtration is well defined. Now, we need to check that X is a homogeneous Markov process with respect to $(\mathcal{G}_{\underline{\theta}^x(t)})_{t \geq 0}$. Applying [12], Proposition I.6 at each component $Z^{(k)}$, $k = 1, \ldots, d$ we get that $(\underline{Z}(\underline{\theta}^x(t+h)) - \underline{Z}(\underline{\theta}^x(t)))_{h \geq 0}$ has the same law as $\underline{Z}(\underline{\theta}^x(h))_{h \geq 0}$ and it is independent of $\mathcal{G}_{\underline{\theta}^x(t)}$. Therefore

$$X_{t+h}^x = X^x(t) + N\big(\underline{Z}(\underline{\theta}^x(t+h)) - \underline{Z}(\underline{\theta}^x(t))\big)$$
$$=: \mathcal{S}(t)(\underline{Z}(\underline{\theta}^x(t+h)) - \underline{Z}(\underline{\theta}^x(t)), X^x(t)),$$

with

$$\mathcal{S}(t) : (\mathbb{R}^{m^2}, \prod_{i=1}^m (\mathcal{G}_{\underline{\theta}^x(t)})) \times (\mathbb{R}^m, \mathcal{G}_{\underline{\theta}^x(t)}) \to (\mathbb{R}^m, \mathcal{G}_{\underline{\theta}^x(t)})$$

$$(Z, X) \to X + \sum_{i=1}^m Z^{(i)}.$$

Therefore, we conclude that the conditional law of X_{t+h}^x, given $\mathcal{G}_{\underline{\theta}^x(t)}$, is $X^x(t)$ measurable. Markov property translates into

$$X_{t+h}^x = \mathcal{S}_0(\underline{Z}(\underline{\theta}_h^y), y)|_{y=X^x(t)}.$$

Additionally the time–change process is absolutely continuous with

$$\frac{d}{dt}\theta_i^{(k)}(t) = X_k(t^-), \quad \text{for all } k, i = 1, \ldots, m.$$

The characteristics of the time–changed semimartingale can be computed using the formulas in [13], Theorem 8.4. Then we conclude that the process $(\mathcal{S}_0(\underline{Z}(\underline{\theta}^x(t))), x))_{t \geq 0}$ has characteristics $(\beta(X_-), \alpha(X_-), M(X_-))$, where

$$\beta(x) = x_1\beta_1 + \ldots + x_m\beta_m,$$
$$\alpha(x) = x_1\alpha_1 + \ldots + x_m\alpha_m,$$
$$M(x, B) = x_1 M_1(B) + \ldots + x_m M_m(B), \quad B \in \mathcal{B}(D).$$

∎

The result can be extended very easily for processes in $\mathbb{R}_{\geq 0}^m \times \mathbb{R}^n$ under the assumption that the d Lévy processes additionally satisfy

(A1) for all $k = 1, \ldots, m$ $Z_j^{(k)}(t)$ is a deterministic process for all $j = m+1, \ldots, d$,

(A2) for all $k = m+1, \ldots, d$ $Z_j^{(k)}$ is constantly equal to zero for all $j = 1, \ldots, d$.

Indeed, if $\tau(t) = (\tau_1(t), \ldots, \tau_m(t))$ denotes as before the solution of (16) restricted to $\pi_I Z^{(k)}$ for all $k = 1, \ldots, m$, then

$$\begin{cases} \dot{\tau}_k(t) = f_k(\underline{Z}(\underline{\tau}(t))), t \geq 0, \\ \tau_k(0) = 0, \end{cases} \tag{38}$$

admits a solution for all $k = 1, \ldots, d$. To show this, it suffices to check that for each $k = 1, \ldots, d$, it holds

$$\tau_k(t) = \int_0^t \left(x_k + \sum_{i=1}^d Y_k^{(i)}(s) \right) ds$$

$$= \int_0^t \left(x_k + \sum_{i=1}^d Z_k^{(i)}(\tau_i(s)) \right) ds.$$

In particular, if we have a solution for the system

$$\tau_k(t) = \int_0^t \left(x_k + \sum_{i=1}^m Z_k^{(i)}(\tau_i(s)) \right) ds \quad \text{for all } k = 1, \ldots, m,$$

then, for all $t \geq 0$ and $j = m+1, \ldots, d$, we can compute

$$\tau_j(t) = \int_0^t \left(x_j + \sum_{i=1}^m Z_j^{(i)}(\tau_i(s)) \right) ds.$$

Observe that the right hand side of the last equation does not depend anymore on the left hand side.

Comment. Before to show how to deal with the most general case, we clarify the main steps by means of an easy two dimensional example with $n = m = 1$.

Example 4.1. Suppose that $m = n = 1$. If we have a solution for the time change equation

$$Y_i^{(k)}(t) := Z_i^{(k)}(\tau_k) = Z_i^{(k)} \left(\int_0^t f_k(Y(s))ds \right), \qquad \text{for } k, i = 1, 2 \text{ and } t \geq 0.$$

Inserting the definitions of the $Y_i^{(k)}$, it is clear that X satisfies

$$\begin{pmatrix} X_1 \\ X_2 \end{pmatrix} = \begin{pmatrix} x_1 \\ x_2 \end{pmatrix} + \begin{pmatrix} Z_1^{(1)}(\int_0^\cdot X_1(s)ds) + Z_1^{(2)}(\int_0^\cdot X_2(s)ds) \\ Z_2^{(1)}(\int_0^\cdot X_1(s)ds) + Z_2^{(2)}(\int_0^\cdot X_2(s)ds) \end{pmatrix}.$$

In vector notation, we can write

$$X = x + \sum_{i=1}^{2} Z^{(i)} \left(\int_0^\cdot X_i(s)ds \right)$$

which is indeed the formulation in Theorem 2.2.

However, the previous argument shows that the existence of a solution τ can be generalized in a straightforward way in $\mathbb{R}^d$ only under the additional condition (A1) and (A2). Observe that (A1) is not really a restriction because it follows by the conditions on the admissible parameters. The next proposition shows that, up to a pathwise transformation, also (A2) is not a real restriction. Moreover we show that, up to an enlargement of the state space, any affine process with non zero F can be viewed as an affine process with no state-independent component up to an enlargement of the state space.

Proposition 4.1. *Let X be a conservative affine process taking values on $\mathbb{R}_{\geq 0}^m \times \mathbb{R}^n$. On a possibly enlarged probability space, there exists a process X^∞ such that*

(1) X^∞ is an affine process taking values in $\mathbb{R}_{\geq 0}^{m+1} \times \mathbb{R}^n$ satisfying the following property: there exists a function $\psi^\infty : \mathbb{C}_{\leq 0}^{m+1} \times i\mathbb{R}^n \to \mathbb{C}^{d+1}$ such that for all $(t, x^\infty) \in \mathbb{R}_{\geq 0} \times (\mathbb{R}_{\geq 0}^{m+1} \times \mathbb{R}^n)$ it holds

$$\mathbb{E}^{x^\infty} \left[e^{\langle u, X^\infty \rangle} \right] = e^{\langle x^\infty, \psi^\infty(t,u) \rangle}$$

for $u \in \mathbb{C}_{\leq 0}^{m+1} \times i\mathbb{R}^n$,

(2) for all $u = (u_1, u_2) \in \mathbb{C}_{\leq 0}^{m+1} \times i\mathbb{R}^n$ it holds

$$\pi_{\{m+2,\dots,d+1\}} \psi^{\infty}(t, u_1, u_2) = u_2,$$

for all $t \geq 0$,

(3) the set of admissible parameters for X^{∞} satisfies

- *$(b, a, c, m) = (0, 0, 0, 0)$,*
- *for all $i, j \in J$ it holds $\pi_j(\beta_i) = 0$,*
- *for all $i \in I$ it holds*

$$\int \left(|\pi_I \xi| \wedge |\pi_I \xi|^2 \right) M_i(d\xi), \quad \text{for all} \quad i \in I,$$

- *for all $k = 1, \dots, m+1$, the matrix α_k has the form*

$$
\alpha_k =
\left(
\begin{array}{ccc|c}
0 & & & \\
\vdots & & & \\
0 & & & \\
0 \dots 0 \ (\alpha_k)_{kk} \ 0 \dots 0 & 0 \dots 0 & & \\
0 & & & \\
\vdots & & & \\
0 & & & \\
\hline
0 & & & \\
\vdots & & & \alpha_k^J \\
0 & & & \\
\end{array}
\right),
$$

with $(\alpha_k)_{kk} \geq 0$ and $\alpha_k^J \in S_n^+$.

(4) for all $(t, x) \in \mathbb{R}_{\geq 0} \times D$ and $u \in \mathcal{U}$, define $x^{\infty} = (1, x)$ and $v = (0, u)$. It holds

$$\mathbb{E}^x \left[e^{\langle u, X(t) \rangle} \right] = \mathbb{E}^{x^{\infty}} \left[e^{\langle v, X^{\infty}(t) \rangle} \right].$$

Proof. Given two indices $i, j = 1, \dots, d+1$ with $i < j$ denote by

$$[i : j] := \{i, i+1, \dots, j-1, j\}.$$

We start using [14], Proposition 1.23. Fix $x_0 \in \mathbb{R}_{\geq 0}$ and define

$$x^{\infty} := (x_0, x) \in \mathbb{R}_{\geq 0}^{m+1} \times \mathbb{R}^n, \tag{39}$$

$$\mathcal{U}^{\infty} := \mathbb{C}_{\leq 0}^{m+1} \times i\mathbb{R}^n, \tag{40}$$

$$\psi^{\infty}(t, u_0, u_1, \dots, u_d) := \begin{pmatrix} \varphi(t, u_1, \dots, u_d) + u_0 \\ \psi(t, u_1, \dots, u_d) \end{pmatrix}. \tag{41}$$

Due to regularity in t of $\varphi(t, u)$ and $\psi(t, u)$, we conclude that $\psi^\infty(t, \cdot)$ is a regular semiflow. Hence, from [8], Proposition 7.4, we conclude that there exists an affine process X^∞ with state space $\mathbb{R}_{\geq 0}^{m+1} \times \mathbb{R}^n$ satisfying

$$\mathbb{E}^{x^\infty}\left[e^{\langle u, X^\infty(t)\rangle}\right] = e^{\langle x^\infty, \psi^\infty(t,u)\rangle}, \quad u \in \mathcal{U}^\infty.$$

Now we can apply the method of moving frames (see [15], Theorem 5.1) to the affine process X^∞. Let $(0, \beta, 0, \alpha, 0, 0, 0, M)$ be its set of admissible parameters. Denote by $\mathcal{B}$ the $d \times d$ matrix obtained by placing each β_i, $i = 1, \ldots, d$ as a column

$$\mathcal{B} = \left(\begin{array}{c|c} \mathcal{B}_I & 0 \\ \hline \mathcal{B}_{IJ} & \mathcal{B}_J \end{array}\right). \tag{42}$$

Define the matrix

$$T = \left(\begin{array}{c|c} I & 0 \\ \hline 0 & \mathcal{B}_J^\top \end{array}\right) \in \mathbb{R}^{d \times d}$$

and the map

$$\mathcal{T} : X^\infty \mapsto X^\infty - T^\top \int_0^\cdot X^\infty(s) ds.$$

The process $\mathcal{T} X^\infty$ is an affine process with Fourier–Laplace transform given by

$$\mathbb{E}^{x^\infty}\left[e^{\langle u, \mathcal{T} X^\infty(t)\rangle}\right] = e^{\left\langle \pi_{[1:m+1]} x^\infty, \pi_{[1:m+1]} \psi^\infty(t,u)\right\rangle + \left\langle \pi_{[m+2:d+1]} x^\infty, \pi_{[m+2:d+1]} u\right\rangle}.$$

In particular, the first three conditions are satisfied. Now we move on the structure of the matrices α_k, $k = 1, \ldots, m+1$. Due to the restrictions on the admissible parameters, α_1 is already in the specified form with $(\alpha_1)_{11} = 0$. The matrices α_k, $k = 1, \ldots, m+1$ can be transformed simultaneously into block diagonal form by means of a linear map. See [16]. Finally, if $v = (0, u)$ with $u \in \mathcal{U}$

$$\mathbb{E}^{(1,x)}\left[e^{\langle v, X^\infty(t)\rangle}\right] = e^{\varphi(t,u) + \langle x, \psi(t,u)\rangle} = \mathbb{E}^x\left[e^{\langle u, X(t)\rangle}\right],$$

within

$$\psi^\infty(t, (0, u)) := \left(\begin{array}{c} \varphi(t, u) \\ \psi(t, u) \end{array}\right). \tag{43}$$

■

To summarize, only the equation determining $\pi_I X$ is a real time–change equation. As soon as we provide a strong solution for the system of time–change equations describing the positive components, we automatically find a solution for the components taking values in $\mathbb{R}^n$.

We illustrate the previous proposition with an example

Example 4.2. Let us start by writing (11) componentwise. Denote by $Z_j^{(k)}$ the j-th coordinate of the k-Lévy process. Then (11) reads

$$X_1(t) = x_1 + Z_1^{(0)}(t) + \sum_{k=1}^{d} Z_1^{(k)} \left(\int_0^t X_k(s)ds \right), \quad t \geq 0$$

$$\vdots \tag{44}$$

$$X_d(t) = x_d + Z_d^{(0)}(t) + \sum_{k=1}^{d} Z_d^{(k)} \left(\int_0^t X_k(s)ds \right), \quad t \geq 0.$$

Due to the drift conditions, we conclude that, for $k = m+1, \ldots, d$, $Z^{(k)}$ is a Lévy process with triplet $(\beta_k, 0, 0)$ with $\pi_I \beta_k$ identically zero. Therefore we can write

$$X_1(t) = x_1 + Z_1^{(0)}(t) + \sum_{k=1}^{m} Z_1^{(k)} \left(\int_0^t X_k(s)ds \right), \quad t \geq 0$$

$$\vdots$$

$$X_d(t) = x_d + Z_d^{(0)}(t) + \sum_{k=1}^{m} Z_d^{(k)} \left(\int_0^t X_k(s)ds \right)$$

$$+ \sum_{k=m+1}^{d} \pi_d \beta_k \left(\int_0^t X_k(s)ds \right), \quad t \geq 0.$$

We first transform the process into another affine process with functional characteristic $F = 0$. Just for simplicity assume that $n = m = 1$. Augment the process $X = (X_1, X_2)$ by considering

$$\overline{X} = (\overline{X}_0, \overline{X}_1, \overline{X}_2) := (1, X_1, X_2).$$

Moreover define, for $k = 0, 1, 2$,

$$(\overline{Z}_k^{(0)}, \overline{Z}_k^{(1)}, \overline{Z}_k^{(2)}) := (0, Z_k^{(1)}, Z_k^{(2)}).$$

Then we can write

$$
\begin{pmatrix} \overline{X}_0(t) \\ \overline{X}_1(t) \\ \overline{X}_2(t) \end{pmatrix} = \begin{pmatrix} 1 \\ x_1 \\ x_2 \end{pmatrix} + \overline{Z}^{(0)} \left(\int_0^t \overline{X}_0(s)ds \right) + \overline{Z}^{(1)} \left(\int_0^t \overline{X}_1(s)ds \right)
$$
$$
+ \overline{Z}^{(2)} \left(\int_0^t \overline{X}_2(s)ds \right), \ t \geq 0 .
$$

Observe that the process $\overline{X}$ takes values in $\mathbb{R}^2_{\geq 0} \times \mathbb{R}$. Hence, up to a change of the state space, we are led to consider solutions of

$$
X_1(t) = x_1 + \sum_{k=1}^m Z_1^{(k)} \left(\int_0^t X_k(s)ds \right), \quad t \geq 0
$$

$$
\vdots
$$

$$
X_d(t) = x_d + \sum_{k=1}^m Z_d^{(k)} \left(\int_0^t X_k(s)ds \right) + \sum_{k=m+1}^d \pi_d \beta_k \left(\int_0^t X_k(s)ds \right), \quad t \geq 0.
$$

The second pathspace transformation additionally simplifies the system and allows us to work only with affine processes with admissible parameters satisfying the additional property $\pi_k \beta_j = 0$ for all $j, k \in J$. This means that the Lévy processes $Z^{(k)}$ with $k = m+1, \ldots, d$ are not only deterministic but actually identically equal to zero (as required by the assumption (A2)). This transformation has been introduced in [15] and it is based on the method of the moving frames. Here we focus on the case $n = m = 1$. Let $X = (X_1, X_2)$ be an affine process in $\mathbb{R}_{\geq 0} \times \mathbb{R}$. Consider the process $Y = (Y_1, Y_2)$ with $Y_0 = x$ and

$$
Y_1(t) := X_1(t) - \int_0^t X_1(s)ds, \quad t \geq 0
$$

$$
Y_2(t) := X_2(t) - (\beta_2)_2 \int_0^t X_2(s)ds, \quad t \geq 0 .
$$

From [15], Theorem 5.1 guarantees that Y is again an affine process in $\mathbb{R}_{\geq 0} \times \mathbb{R}$ with admissible parameter $\beta_2^Y = (0,0)$. Moreover this transformation can be inverted. Hence, when $n = m = 1$, up to an invertible pathspace transformation, we can restrict ourselves to the solution of a system of type

$$
X_1(t) = x_1 + Z_1^{(1)} \left(\int_0^t X_1(s)ds \right), \quad t \geq 0 ,
$$

$$
X_2(t) = x_2 + Z_2^{(1)} \left(\int_0^t X_1(s)ds \right), \quad t \geq 0 ,
$$

or more generally

$$X_1(t) = x_1 + \sum_{k=1}^{m} Z_1^{(k)} \left(\int_0^t X_k(s) ds \right), \quad t \geq 0$$

$$\vdots$$

$$X_d(t) = x_d + \sum_{k=1}^{m} Z_d^{(k)} \left(\int_0^t X_k(s) ds \right), \quad t \geq 0.$$

Bibliography

1. J. Kallsen, A didactic note on affine stochastic volatility models, in *From Stochastic Calculus to Mathematical Finance*, (Bachelier Colloquium on Stochastic Calculus and Probability, 2006) p. 343.
2. S. L. Heston, A closed-form solution for options with stochastic volatility with applications to bond and currency options, *The Review of Financial Studies* **6**(2), 327–343 (1993).
3. D. S. Bates, Jumps and stochastic volatility: exchange rate processes implicit in deutsche mark options, *Review of Financial Studies* **9**(1), 69–107 (1996).
4. O. E. Barndorff-Nielsen and N. Shephard, Modelling by Lévy processes for financial econometrics, in *Lévy processes*, (Birkhäuser Boston, Boston, MA, 2001) pp. 283–318.
5. C. Cuchiero and J. Teichmann, Path properties and regularity of affine processes on general state spaces, in *Séminaire de Probabilités XLV*, Lecture Notes in Math. Vol. 2078 (Springer, Cham, 2013) pp. 201–244.
6. M. E. Caballero, J. L. Pérez Garmendia and G. Uribe Bravo, A Lamperti-type representation of continuous-state branching processes with immigration, *The Annals of Probability* **41**, 1585–1627 (May 2013).
7. M. E. Caballero, J. L. Pérez Garmendia and G. Uribe Bravo, Affine processes on $\mathbb{R}_+^m \times \mathbb{R}^n$ and multiparameter time changes, *Ann. Inst. H. Poincaré Probab. Statist.* **53**, 1280–1304 (08 2017).
8. D. Duffie, D. Filipović and W. Schachermayer, Affine processes and applications in finance, *The Annals of Applied Probability* **13**, 984–1053 (2003).
9. M. Keller-Ressel, W. Schachermayer and J. Teichmann, Regularity of affine processes on general state spaces, *Electron. J. Probab.* **18**(43), 1–17 (2013).

10. S. N. Ethier and T. G. Kurtz, *Markov processes* Wiley Series in Probability and Mathematical Statistics: Probability and Mathematical Statistics, Wiley Series in Probability and Mathematical Statistics: Probability and Mathematical Statistics (John Wiley & Sons, Inc., New York, 1986).

11. A. S. Chernyĭ, On strong and weak uniqueness for stochastic differential equations, *Teor. Veroyatnost. i Primenen.* **46**, 483–497 (2001).

12. J. Bertoin, *Lévy Processes* (Cambridge University Press, 1998).

13. O. E. Barndorff-Nielsen and A. Shiryaev, *Change of Time and Change of Measure* (World Scientific, 2010).

14. N. Gabrielli, Affine processes from the perspective of path space valued lévy processes, PhD thesis, ETH Zürich2014.

15. M. Keller-Ressel, W. Schachermayer and J. Teichmann, Affine processes are regular, *Probab. Theory Related Fields* **151**, 591–611 (2011).

16. D. Filipovic and E. Mayerhofer, Affine diffusion processes: Theory and applications, *Advanced Financial Modelling* **8**, 1–40 (2009).

Part II

Innovations in Insurance and Asset Management

Chapter 9

Fixed-Income Returns from Hedge Funds with Negative Fee Structures: Valuation and Risk Analysis

Mohammad Shakourifar*

Sigma Analysis & Management, Toronto, Ontario, Canada
mohammad@sigmanalysis.com

Ranjan Bhaduri[†] and Ben Djerroud[‡]

Sigma Analysis & Management, Toronto, Ontario, Canada
[†]ranjan@sigmanalysis.com
[‡]ben_d@sigmanalysis.com

Fei Meng[§] and David Saunders[¶]

Department of Statistics and Actuarial Science, University of Waterloo, Waterloo, Canada
[§]f7meng@uwaterloo.ca
[¶]dsaunders@uwaterloo.ca

Luis Seco

Department of Mathematics, University of Toronto, Toronto, Canada
seco@math.utoronto.ca

The traditional fixed-income asset class has generated very low returns in recent years. Furthermore, due to long-term market trends it is arguably perceived by investors to be riskier and less diversifying than it has ever been. This has led to the emergence of new products that are designed to appeal to institutional investors in their quest for finding complementary return streams, particularly for liability driven investment (LDI). These bond-like products are often augmented with equity-like positions in investors' portfolios in an attempt to mitigate risk and generate attractive returns. In this paper, we analyze fee structures that have emerged in the hedge fund industry. In particular, we study structures with 'negative fees,' which give hedge fund investments risk-return profiles that more closely resemble traditional fixed-income investments. We analyze the value and risk-return profiles of these investments, and study the incentives that the fee structures create for fund managers. In this paper we discuss how the employment of judicious fee structures in combination with suitable trading strategies can assist in accommodating the appetite of a wide range of investors. We will present a spectrum of fee structures where investors can pinpoint a region of interest which fulfills their desired payoff profile.

---

1. Introduction

According to FitchRatings, the total of sovereign debt with negative yields increased to $11.7 trillion as of June 27, 2016, up $1.3 trillion from the total at the end of May.[a] Major institutional investors have approximately 30% to 50% of their assets allocated to fixed income, which makes them increasingly vulnerable to the interest rate environment (OECD[12]). The low-rate environment has also impacted the manner in which hedge fund managers are compensated. Investors accept paying the traditional fees to hedge fund managers only if the underlying trading strategy generates superior returns (or alpha). However, the lukewarm performance of hedge funds in recent years has pressured the fees as investors need to maintain an acceptable share of gross returns to meet their investment thresholds. The low-rate environment has significantly trimmed the short rebates that managers used to receive on their short book resulting in lower performance of trading strategies in general. This has further undermined the acceptability of traditional 2&20 fee structures (see Bloomberg[2]) and has encouraged investors to seek innovative fee methodologies.[b]

Investors' demand for yield, combined with the difficult market environment and the challenges faced by many hedge fund managers in raising assets, has led institutional investors and fund managers to embrace new fee structures featuring an element of downside protection. In these fee structures, commonly referred to as 'first-loss' or 'shared-loss' structures, the fund manager insures a portion of the investor's losses.

There are many variations on the basic framework of the first-loss fee structure, all of which share the following principle: the fund manager provides downside protection by taking the first tranche of losses, and in return the manager receives a higher percentage of upside participation (higher than the standard performance fee in traditional fee structures). For example, a manager may absorb losses up to 10% and in return may be entitled to a 50% monthly performance fee as opposed to a 20% annual performance fee. Investors gain exposure to the hedge fund investment, with the manager taking the first tranche of losses. He and Kou[9] analyze the first-loss fee structure, examining the incentives that it creates for hedge fund managers, as well as its impact on the utility of both investors and managers. They conclude that for some parameter values, the first-loss fee structure can increase the utility of both the investor and the manager, and result in a less risky investment portfolio. However, at the levels of the performance

---

[a]https://www.fitchratings.com/site/pr/1008156.
[b]The traditional 2&20 fee structure consists of a flat fee of 2% of assets under management together with a performance fee of 20% of net profits.

fee commonly charged in the industry, they find a significant reduction in investor utility.[c] Djerroud *et al.*[3] analyzed the first-loss fee structure using an option-pricing perspective, providing a value of the guarantee offered by the manager to the investor, and compared its value to the performance fee offered by the investor to the manager, providing a way of assessing 'fairness,' which can be used as a benchmark for negotiation of the terms of the fee structure between investor and manager.

In this paper we extend the concept of First Loss by considering a guarantee not just against losses but providing a minimum return guarantee from the manager to the investor. In this regard, the investment starts to look to the investor like a bond with a coupon payment that contains two parts: a fixed one, coming from the return guarantee offered by the hedge fund, and a variable one, arising from the performance of the hedge fund investment net of performance fees. Figure 1 illustrates a spectrum of fee structures from the traditional to the first-loss family of structures and beyond. In the traditional fee structure, also known as '2&20', the investor return varies with the performance of the hedge fund strategy; the investor can experience periods of losses as seen in the leftmost bar in the figure. A simple first-loss structure involves a higher share of the strategy performance allocated to the manager in return for downside protection for the investor. The investor will be less likely to experience periods of losses under this structure; however, the investor return could be zero. A first variant of the first-loss fee structure is the one in which the investor requires a minimum return coupled with a smaller share of the strategy performance in exchange for a higher performance fee paid to the manager. The rightmost bar illustrates a first-loss structure in which the investor 'swaps' the performance of the strategy on its capital for a promised fixed 'coupon'. We refer to these two last structures as a 'negative fee structure'. From left to right, the upside to the investor is gradually reduced in exchange for downside protection, provided by the fund manager. In addition, the investor is more certain to receive a higher minimum return or a larger 'coupon'. It should be noted that the performance fees on the horizontal axis are for illustration purposes only, and the size of the fixed coupon is dependent on the underlying strategy.

The remainder of the paper is structured as follows. The second section discusses hedge fund fee structures. The third section analyzes negative fee structures from an option pricing perspective under a regime-switching model using

---

[c]It should be noted that investor capital brings further benefits to a hedge fund, beyond simply the fees accrued, such as the reputational benefit of having more assets under management.

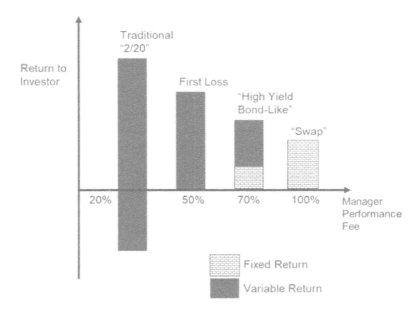

Fig. 1.   Schematic representation of hedge fund fee structures from traditional to first-loss fee structures.

risk-neutral valuation. The fourth section analyzes the risks of the investor's returns under a negative fee structure, now using the real-world measure. The fifth section concludes.

2. Hedge fund fee structures: From traditional fee structures to negative fees

2.1. *Traditional fee structures*

Traditionally, a hedge fund manager charges two types of fees to the fund investors:

- A fixed management fee, usually ranging from 1% to 2% of net asset values.

- A performance fee, most commonly equal to 20% of net profits obtained by the fund.

In this paper we assume a single investor and a single share issued by the fund. The extension to the case of multiple investors and multiple shares is straightforward. Although fees are paid according to a determined schedule (usually monthly or quarterly for management fees and annually for performance fees) we will assume a single payment at the end of a fixed term T.

The initial fund supplied by the investor is denoted by X_0. The hedge fund manager then invests the fund assets to create the future gross values X_t, for $t > 0$. The gross fund value X_t is split between the investor's share I_t (the net asset value) and the manager's fee M_t:

$$X_t = I_t + M_t.$$

At time 0, $I_0 = X_0$ and $M_0 = 0$.

There are countless variations on the basic framework, including hurdles, clawbacks, etc. (for more details on first-loss arrangements see Banzaca[1]). We will ignore these and assume the commonly used version of a management fee equal to $m \cdot X_0$ (m represents a fixed percentage of the initial investment by the investor), and a performance fee of $\alpha \cdot (X_T - (1+m)X_0))_+$, so that the performance fee is payable only when the investor's return is positive, and is zero when it is negative. Hence, the manager's payoff due to fees is:

$$M_T = m \cdot X_0 + \alpha \cdot (X_T - (1+m)X_0)_+$$

In other words, while the management fee is a fixed future liability to the investor, the performance fee is a contingent claim on the part of the manager. As a consequence, we will be pricing the management fee simply as a fixed guaranteed fee with a predetermined future cash value, and we will be valuing the performance fee as the value of a certain call option. In our setting, we will assume a regime-switching process for the invested assets X_t, which allows us to value the performance fee using known results. It is worth mentioning that hedge fund managers can speculate on volatility, credit risks, etc. and in contrast to traditional money managers, they can go long and short. The diversity in investment styles and the different levels of gross and net exposure that they can employ could result in leptokurtic returns, for example through frequent large negative returns in the left tail of the return distribution. Generalization of the current framework to other models of hedge fund returns, for example using stochastic volatility by employing generalized autoregressive conditional heteroskedasticity (GARCH) models, could be a subject for future research.

From a business perspective, it is important to note that the investor has a say in the fees paid to the fund manager: sometimes, as in the case of managed account investments, through a direct negotiation of the fees, at other times, such as in a normal fund structure, through the right not to invest in the fund in the first place. However, when it comes to the choice of the portfolio, the manager has full discretion, within the limits existing in the offering memorandum, without seeking investors' permission or input. This consideration will play a role when we try to extrapolate the results of this article to real investment situations.

2.2. *From first-loss to negative first-loss fee structure*

While the first-loss fee structure protects investors from downside moves in the market, if the manager does not generate returns the investor does not make any profits. A negative fee structure results from modifying the first-loss structure to provide a fixed level of promised return to investors, while maintaining some level of downside protection. The cost of this bond-like return for investors is the increase of the performance fee it pays the manager; we refer to this framework as the 'High-yield bond like' framework. In the limit, the investor has a guaranteed return and pays 100% of the performance beyond the guarantee to the manager. As such, the return profile provided to the investor resembles that of an investor in an asset-backed security, with the underlying portfolio being the assets of the hedge fund; we refer to this framework as the 'swap' framework. In the swap framework, at the end of each period, all returns generated by the strategy are allocated to the investor up to the 'return hurdle' which is negotiated with the hedge fund manager. The remaining returns above the return hurdle are fully allocated to the manager as a performance fee. If the fund return is less than the return hurdle, the manager's deposit is used to make up the difference. In subsequent periods, profits are first used to replenish the manager's deposit, before either the investor's return or the performance fee is paid.

A close look at the negative fee structure reveals that the positions of the investor and the hedge fund manager can be formulated as portfolios of options. The first-loss fee structure was analyzed from an option-pricing perspective using the Black–Scholes model in Djerroud *et al.* [3]. In the next section, we extend that analysis to the negative fee structure under a regime-switching model. Given the bond-like payoff of the negative fee structure, this setting is very similar to the classical Merton model for credit risk (see Merton [11]), with the difference coming from the additional downside protection provided to investors by the hedge fund manager.

Denoting the return threshold by H, the payoff functions of the investor and the manager at the terminal time T are respectively:

$$I_T = \begin{cases} X_0(1+H) & \text{when } (X_T - HX_0) \geq (1-c)X_0 \\ X_T + cX_0 & \text{when } (X_T - HX_0) < (1-c)X_0 \end{cases}$$

$$M_T = \begin{cases} X_T - X_0(1+H) & \text{when } (X_T - HX_0) \geq (1-c)X_0 \\ -cX_0 & \text{when } (X_T - HX_0) < (1-c)X_0 \end{cases}$$

Writing these payoff functions more compactly, we obtain:

$$I_T = X_0(1+H) - ((1-c)X_0 - X_T + HX_0) +$$
$$M_T = X_T - X_0(1+H) + ((1-c)X_0 - X_T + HX_0) + . \tag{1}$$

From the above formulas, we see that the investor (manager) has a short (long) position in a put option on the fund assets, with strike price $(1-c)X_0 + HX_0$. Risk-neutral valuation can be applied to derive the price of the positions.[d]

In particular, the value of the investor's position is:

$$V_I(0) = \exp(-rT)X_0(1+H) - P(X_0, T, (1-c)X_0 + HX_0, r)$$

where $P(X, T, K, r)$ is the price of a put option on a non-dividend paying asset with current value of the underlying X, time to expiration T, strike price K, and where the risk-free interest rate is r. The above framework can be easily extended to the case in which the investor receives a portion of the excess return above the return threshold H.

3. Pricing the payoffs

We assume.a regime-switching model, in which the coefficients of a diffusion process for the value of the hedge funds assets themselves follow continuous-time Markov chains. Regime-switching models have found many applications in finance since the seminal work of Hamilton.[7] They are able to reproduce many features of real-world return distributions, including skewness, volatility clustering, and fat tails. For applications of regime-switching models to insurance products with investment guarantees, similar in sprit to the hedge-fund guarantees considered in this paper, see Hardy,[8] For many other financial applications, see the papers in the volumes Mamon and Elliott,[10] and Zeng and Wu.[13]

---

[d]It should be noted that, similarly to Merton,[11] some of the assumptions used to justify arbitrage-free pricing methods do not hold in practice in the context in which we are applying the model here. In particular, it is typically not possible for the investor to trade in (or even directly observe) the hedge fund assets X_t.

We assume the regime is governed by a finite state continuous-time Markov chain $\varepsilon(t)$ with state space $\mathbb{S} = \{1,2\}$, where state 1 represents the 'normal' regime and state 2 represents the 'stress' regime. The generator of $\varepsilon(t)$ is the matrix:

$$Q = \begin{bmatrix} -\lambda_1 & \lambda_1 \\ \lambda_2 & -\lambda_2 \end{bmatrix},$$

where λ_1 and λ_2 are the transition rates of leaving states 1 and 2 respectively. The value of the hedge fund assets X_t follows a geometric Brownian motion, except that the coefficients of X_t change with the regime:

$$dX_t = \mu_{\varepsilon(t)} X_t dt + \sigma_{\varepsilon(t)} X_t dZ_t$$

where Z_t is a standard Brownian motion, independent of $\varepsilon(t)$, and $\mu_{\varepsilon(t)}$ and $\sigma_{\varepsilon(t)}$ are constants in each state. For simplicity, when $\varepsilon(t) = 1,2$, we use μ_1, μ_2 and σ_1, σ_2 to denote the growth rates and volatilities in each regime. Finally, the risk-free asset B satisfies $B_t = e^{rt}$. The value of the investor's position can be determined using an expectation under a risk-neutral measure (see Elliott *et al.*[4]) to be:

$$V_I^i = \mathbb{E}_{\mathbb{Q}}[I(T)|\varepsilon(0) = i]. \tag{2}$$

Then, we have

$$V_I^i = \exp-rT(1+H) - P_i(X_0, T, (1-c)X_0 + HX_0, r) \tag{3}$$

where $P_i(X,T,K,r) = \mathbb{E}_{\mathbb{Q}}[e^{-rT}(K-S_T)_+|\varepsilon(0) = i], i = 1,2$ is the European put option price under the Markov-modulated geometric Brownian motion model. Moreover, from Guo[6] and Fuh *et al.*,[5] we obtain:

$$P_i(X,T,K,r) = \mathbb{E}_{\mathbb{Q}}[e^{-rT}(K-S_T)_+|\varepsilon(0) = i]$$

$$= e^{-rT} \int_0^{K-1} \int_0^T \frac{y}{K-y} \phi(\ln(K-y), m(t), v(t)) f_i(t,T) dt dy \tag{4}$$

where:

$$m(t) = \ln(X) + (rT - \frac{1}{2}v(t)),$$

$$v(t) = (\sigma_1^2 - \sigma_2^2)t + \sigma_1^2 T,$$

$$f_1(t,T) = e^{-\lambda_1 T} \delta_0(T-t) + e^{-\lambda_2(T-t)-\lambda_1 t}[\lambda_1 I_0(2(\lambda_1\lambda_2 t(T-t))^{1/2})$$

$$+ (\frac{\lambda_1\lambda_2 t}{T-t})^{1/2} I_1(2(\lambda_1\lambda_2 t(T-t))^{1/2})],$$

$$f_2(t,T) = e^{-\lambda_2 T} \delta_0(t) + e^{-\lambda_2(T-t)-\lambda_1 t}[\lambda_2 I_0(2(\lambda_1\lambda_2 t(T-t))^{1/2})$$

$$+ (\frac{\lambda_1\lambda_2(T-t)}{t})^{1/2} I_1(2(\lambda_1\lambda_2 t(T-t))^{1/2})].$$

where $\phi(x, m(t), v(t)$ is the normal density function with mean $m(t)$ and variance $v(t)$, I_0 and I_1 are the modified Bessel functions,

$$I_a(z) = (\frac{z}{2})^a \sum_{k=0}^{\infty} \frac{(a/2)^{2k}}{k!\Gamma(k+a+1)}. \tag{5}$$

and δ_0 is a delta function with a mass at 0.

Figures 2, 3 and 4 illustrate the sensitivity of the value of the investor's payoff to the model parameters. Figure 2 is generated assuming that the market is initially in the normal state ($\varepsilon(0) = 1$). Figure 3 repeats the analysis assuming that the market is initially in the stressed state ($\varepsilon(0) = 2$). Finally, Figure 4 assumes that $\varepsilon(0)$ is random, generated according to the stationary distribution of the Markov chain $\varepsilon(t)$, i.e., $\varepsilon(0) = 1$ with probability $\pi_1 = \lambda_2/(\lambda_1 + \lambda_2)$, and $\varepsilon(0) = 2$ with

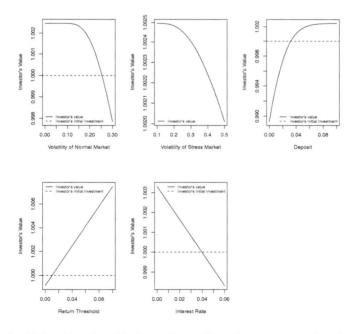

Fig. 2. Sensitivity of the value of the investor's payoff to various parameters, given that the market is initially in the normal state ($\varepsilon(0) = 1$). Benchmark parameter values are $T = \frac{1}{12}$ (the investment horizon is one month), $c = 10\%$ (the manager deposit), $r = 1\%$ (annual risk-free interest rate), $\sigma_1 = 10\%$ (the annual volatility in normal market), $\sigma_2 = 20\%$ (the annual volatility in a stressed market), $\lambda_1 = 1$ (the transition rate in a normal market), $\lambda_2 = 12$ (the transition rate in a stressed market), $X_0 = 1$ (the initial investment), and $H = 4\%$ (the annual return threshold).

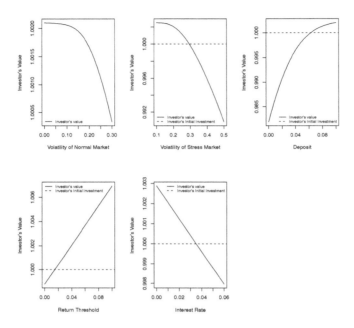

Fig. 3.   Sensitivity of the value of the investor's payoff to various parameters, given that the market is initially in the stressed state($\varepsilon(0) = 2$). Benchmark parameter values are $T = \frac{1}{12}$ (the investment horizon is one month), $c = 10\%$ (the manager deposit), $r = 1\%$ (annual risk-free interest rate), $\sigma_1 = 10\%$ (the annual volatility in a normal market), $\sigma_2 = 20\%$ (the annual volatility in a stressed market), $\lambda_1 = 1$ (the transition rate in a normal market), $\lambda_2 = 12$ (the transition rate in a stressed market), $X_0 = 1$ (the initial investment), and $H = 4\%$ (the annual return threshold).

probability $\pi_2 = 1 - \pi_1$. The parameters are set to $T = \frac{1}{12}$ (the investment horizon is one month), $c = 10\%$ (the manager deposit), $r = 1\%$ (annual risk-free interest rate), $X_0 = \$1$ (the initial investment), and $H = 4\%$ (the annual return threshold). The volatility and transition rate in a normal market are $\sigma_1 = 10\%$ and $\lambda_1 = 1$, while the corresponding parameters in a stressed market are $\sigma_2 = 20\%$ and $\lambda_2 = 12$.

The same basic patterns emerge when looking at the three sets of figures. The volatility sub-figures show that the value of the investor's position is generally a decreasing function of the volatility parameters of the underlying fund. As the volatility becomes very large, the value of the investor's position starts to decline steeply as the hedge fund's put option (in which the investor has a short position) becomes more valuable. The deposit sub-figures (varying c) illustrate that, as expected, the value of the investor's position is an increasing function of the deposit

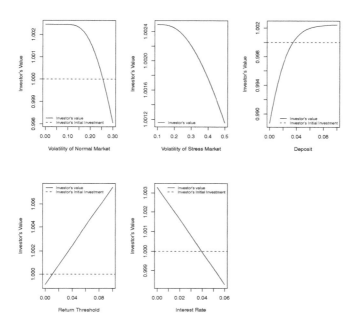

Fig. 4. Sensitivity of the value of the investor's payoff to various parameters, given that $\varepsilon(0)$ is chosen randomly from its stationary distribution. Benchmark parameter values are $T = \frac{1}{12}$ (the investment horizon is one month), $c = 10\%$ (the manager deposit), $r = 1\%$ (annual risk-free interest rate), $\sigma_1 = 10\%$ (the annual volatility in a normal market), $\sigma_2 = 20\%$ (the annual volatility in a stressed market), $\lambda_1 = 1$ (the transition rate in a normal market), $\lambda_2 = 12$ (the transition rate in a stressed market), $X_0 = 1$ (the initial investment), and $H = 4\%$ (the annual return threshold).

level. The return threshold sub-figures show the intuitive monotonic relationship between the value of the investor's position and the return threshold. The value of the investor's position is also a decreasing function of the risk-free rate r, in accord with the bond-like nature of the investor's payoff.

The value of the investor's payoff is lower in a stressed market than in a normal market. The stressed market starts with a higher volatility ($\sigma_2 > \sigma_1$), thus increasing the value of the put option in which the investor has a short position. It is further important to note that given the short time horizon ($T = 1/12$), there is a significant probability that the market will remain in the high volatility, stressed regime over the entire life of the contract. For longer-lived contracts, the discrepancy between the investor's values given that the market is in either the stressed or normal state will be less pronounced. Finally, we note that the figures for when the initial market state is random with distribution equal to the stationary distribution of $\varepsilon(t)$ are close to those for which the market is started in the normal state. This is due to the fact that with our benchmark parameters, the stationary distribution places a high probability of the market being in a normal state ($\pi_1 = 12/13 \approx 92.3\%$), as is common in financial applications of regime-switching models (see the references cited above).

For each figure, one can look for the point where the curve crosses the value 1.0 (if it exists). This allows us to identify the parameter values for which the contract (in terms of risk-neutral valuation in the regime-switching model) favors either the investor or the manager. Parameter values for which the curve is above 1.0 show that the contract favors the investor, while for parameter values where the curve is below 1.0 the contract favors the manager. The point at which the curve crosses 1.0 is the break-even, or indifference, point.

4. Risk analysis of the investor's position as a bond

As noted above, the position of the investor is analogous to a bond, with a promised return of H (received if the hedge fund assets perform sufficiently well). In the event of default, there is a random amount of recovery (again determined by the level of the hedge fund assets). In this section, we examine the properties of the investor's payoff from the perspective of this analogy with a fixed income investment. In particular, we compute default probabilities and expected recovery rates.

In this section, we consider the manager's and investor's expected payoff under real world measure. In order to obtain numerical results, one can discretize the Markov-modulated geometric Brownian motion process as follows:

$$X_{t+\Delta t} = X_t + \mu_{\tilde{\varepsilon}(t)} X_t \Delta t + \sigma_{\tilde{\varepsilon}_t} X_t \sqrt{\Delta t} \cdot \eta_t$$

$$R_t := \frac{X_{t+\Delta t}}{X_t} - 1 = \mu_{\tilde{\varepsilon}(t)} \Delta t + \sigma_{\tilde{\varepsilon}(t)} \sqrt{\Delta t} \cdot \eta_t$$

where the η_t are i.i.d. standard normal random variables, and $\tilde{\varepsilon}(t)$ is a discretized version of the continuous time Markov chain $\varepsilon(t)$, with transition matrix:

$$P = \begin{bmatrix} 1-p & p \\ q & 1-q \end{bmatrix}.$$

where p is the probability of transitioning from state 1 to state 2, and q is the probability of transitioning from state 2 to state 1. The stationary distribution for this Markov chain is $\pi_0 = q(p+q)^{-1}$, $\pi_1 = p(p+q)^{-1}$.

We simulated 5000 scenarios of the returns of the hedge fund using the above model with an annual time horizon and daily time steps. Recall that the payoffs to the hedge fund manager ($\tilde{M}$) and investor ($\tilde{I}$) for the traditional fee structure are:

$$\tilde{M}(T) = \begin{cases} \alpha(X_T - X_0), & X_T \geq X_0, \\ 0, & X_T < X_0. \end{cases}$$

$$\tilde{I}(T) = \begin{cases} X_0 + (1 - \alpha)(X_T - X_0), & X_T \geq X_0, \\ X_T, & X_T < X_0. \end{cases}$$

and the payoffs for the negative loss structure are:

$$M(T) = \begin{cases} X_T - X_0(1 + H), & X_T \geq (1 - c + H)X_0, \\ -cX_0, & X_T < (1 - c + H)X_0. \end{cases}$$

$$I(T) = \begin{cases} X_0(1 + H), & X_T \geq (1 - c + H)X_0, \\ X_T + cX_0, & X_T < (1 - c + H)X_0. \end{cases}$$

Table 1 presents simulated expected returns and standard deviations (with standard errors of the estimates in parentheses) for both the traditional fee structure and the negative fee structure. The volatility in normal markets is set to $\sigma_1 = 0.1$, while in stressed markets it is $\sigma_2 = 0.2$. We consider two different possible growth rates for each state, $\mu_1 = 0.1, 0.15$ and $\mu_2 = -0.05, 0.0$. The probability p is set to 0.01, while q is set to 0.05, indicating a high level of persistence in both states, and a stationary distribution of $(\frac{5}{6}, \frac{1}{6})^T$. In this section, we assume that the initial state of the Markov chain is 1 (normal market). We see that for investors,

Table 1. Expected payoffs (and standard deviations in parentheses) for the traditional fee structure and negative fee structure. $X_0 = 1, T = 1, \alpha = 20\%, p = 0.01, q = 0.05, \sigma_1 = 0.1, \sigma_2 = 0.2, N_{sim} = 5000, H = 0.04,$ and $c = 0.1$.

(μ_0, μ_1)	$\mathbb{E}_{\mathbb{P}}[\tilde{M}(T)]$	$\mathbb{E}_{\mathbb{P}}[\tilde{I}(T)]$	$\mathbb{E}_{\mathbb{P}}[M(T)]$	$\mathbb{E}_{\mathbb{P}}[I(T)]$
$\mu_0 = 0.1, \mu_1 = -0.05$	0.0209 (0.0003)	1.0641 (0.0016)	0.0526 (0.0017)	1.0323 (0.0003)
$\mu_0 = 0.15, \mu_1 = -0.05$	0.0296 (0.0004)	1.1077 (0.0017)	0.097 (0.0019)	1.036 (0.0003)
$\mu_0 = 0.1, \mu_1 = 0$	0.0218 (0.0003)	1.069 (0.0016)	0.063 (0.0017)	1.034 (0.0003)
$\mu_0 = 0.15, \mu_1 = 0$	0.0308 (0.0003)	1.1142 (0.0016)	0.1081 (0.0019)	1.0369 (0.0002)
	S.D. of $\tilde{M}(T)$	S.D. of $\tilde{I}(T)$	S.D. of $M(T)$	S.D. of $I(T)$
$\mu_0 = 0.1, \mu_1 = -0.05$	0.0215 (0.0003)	0.1121 (0.0013)	0.1202 (0.0013)	0.0269 (0.0009)
$\mu_0 = 0.15, \mu_1 = -0.05$	0.0251 (0.0003)	0.1167 (0.0012)	0.1345 (0.0014)	0.0178 (0.0008)
$\mu_0 = 0.1, \mu_1 = 0$	0.0218 (0.0002)	0.1118 (0.0011)	0.1216 (0.0012)	0.0244 (0.0009)
$\mu_0 = 0.15, \mu_1 = 0$	0.0247 (0.0003)	0.1131 (0.0012)	0.1312 (0.0013)	0.0169 (0.0009)

expected payoffs are slightly higher for the traditional fee structure, but standard deviations are also significantly higher in this case. This is consistent with the analogy that the negative fee structure more closely resembles a fixed income investment, while the traditional fee structure gives a more 'equity-like' payoff. In contrast, the manager's expected payoff and standard deviation are higher under the negative fee structure, and lower under the traditional fee structure. As is to be anticipated, expected payoffs are larger when the growth parameters are larger; the standard deviations of payoffs do not change significantly when the μ_i's are varied.

Tables 2 and 3 repeat the analysis with $p = 0.1, q = 0.05$, and $p = 0.01, q = 0.1$ respectively. Comparing to the figures in Table 1, Table 2 was generated assuming a significantly higher (by a factor of 10) probability of transitioning from the normal state to the stressed state, and Table 3 was generated assuming a significantly higher (by a factor of 2) probability of transitioning from the stressed state to the normal state. The stationary distribution for the simulation in Table 2 is $(\frac{1}{3}, \frac{2}{3})^T$ (so that the 'stressed' state is more prevalent), while the stationary distribution for the simulation in Table 3 is $(\frac{10}{11}, \frac{1}{11})^T$. The expected returns and standard deviations of the different payoff structures appear to be relatively insensitive to the choices of the parameters p, q.

Given the similarity of the investor's payoff to the payoff of a fixed income investment, it is interesting to examine the probability of default (i.e. the probability that the investor's return will be lower than the promised hurdle rate H), and the

Table 2.   Expected payoffs (and standard deviations in parentheses) for the traditional fee structure and negative fee structure. $X_0 = 1, T = 1, \alpha = 20\%, p = 0.1, q = 0.05, \sigma_1 = 0.1, \sigma_2 = 0.2, N_{sim} = 5000, H = 0.04$, and $c = 0.1$.

(μ_0, μ_1)	$\mathbb{E}_{\mathbb{P}}[\tilde{M}(T)]$	$\mathbb{E}_{\mathbb{P}}[\tilde{I}(T)]$	$\mathbb{E}_{\mathbb{P}}[M(T)]$	$\mathbb{E}_{\mathbb{P}}[I(T)]$
$\mu_0 = 0.1, \mu_1 = -0.05$	0.0163(0.0004)	1.0057(0.0022)	0.0164(0.0020)	1.0056(0.0009)
$\mu_0 = 0.15, \mu_1 = -0.05$	0.0181(0.0004)	1.0201(0.0022)	0.0277(0.0021)	1.0104 (0.0009)
$\mu_0 = 0.1, \mu_1 = 0$	0.0197(0.0004)	1.0294(0.0023)	0.0374(0.0021)	1.0117(0.0008)
$\mu_0 = 0.15, \mu_1 = 0$	0.0223(0.0004)	1.0452(0.0023)	0.0520(0.0023)	1.0155(0.0008)
	S.D. of $\tilde{M}(T)$	S.D. of $\tilde{I}(T)$	S.D. of $M(T)$	S.D. of $I(T)$
$\mu_0 = 0.1, \mu_1 = -0.05$	0.0248 (0.0004)	0.1576 (0.0017)	0.1426 (0.0021)	0.0633 (0.0011)
$\mu_0 = 0.15, \mu_1 = -0.05$	0.0258 (0.0004)	0.1575 (0.0017)	0.1467 (0.0020)	0.0602 (0.0012)
$\mu_0 = 0.1, \mu_1 = 0$	0.0266 (0.0004)	0.1597 (0.0016)	0.1507 (0.0020)	0.0581(0.0011)
$\mu_0 = 0.15, \mu_1 = 0$	0.0289 (0.0004)	0.1643 (0.0017)	0.1615 (0.0021)	0.0549 (0.0012)

Table 3. Expected payoffs (and standard deviations in parentheses) for the traditional fee structure and negative fee structure. $X_0 = 1, T = 1, \alpha = 20\%, p = 0.01, q = 0.1, \sigma_1 = 0.1, \sigma_2 = 0.2, N_{sim} = 5000, H = 0.04$, and $c = 0.1$.

(μ_0, μ_1)	$\mathbb{E}_\mathbb{P}[\tilde{M}(T)]$	$\mathbb{E}_\mathbb{P}[\tilde{I}(T)]$	$\mathbb{E}_\mathbb{P}[M(T)]$	$\mathbb{E}_\mathbb{P}[I(T)]$
$\mu_0 = 0.1, \mu_1 = -0.05$	0.0227(0.0003)	1.0771(0.0015)	0.0645 (0.0017)	1.0354(0.0003)
$\mu_0 = 0.15, \mu_1 = -0.05$	0.0308(0.0003)	1.1169(0.0015)	0.1095 (0.0018)	1.0382(0.0002)
$\mu_0 = 0.1, \mu_1 = 0$	0.0225(0.0003)	1.0768(0.0015)	0.0637 (0.0017)	1.0356(0.0003)
$\mu_0 = 0.15, \mu_1 = 0$	0.0324(0.0003)	1.1235(0.0015)	0.1179 (0.0018)	1.0381(0.0002)
	S.D. of $\tilde{M}(T)$	S.D. of $\tilde{I}(T)$	S.D. of $M(T)$	S.D. of $I(T)$
$\mu_0 = 0.1, \mu_1 = -0.05$	0.0214 (0.0002)	0.1049 (0.0011)	0.1178 (0.0012)	0.0187 (0.0008)
$\mu_0 = 0.1, \mu_1 = -0.05$	0.0235 (0.0002)	0.1048 (0.0011)	0.1245 (0.0013)	0.0107 (0.0007)
$\mu_0 = 0.1, \mu_1 = 0$	0.0212 (0.0002)	0.1042 (0.0011)	0.1172 (0.0012)	0.0192 (0.0009)
$\mu_0 = 0.15, \mu_1 = 0$	0.0244 (0.0003)	0.1084 (0.0012)	0.1288 (0.0014)	0.0117 (0.0008)

Table 4. Probabilities of default under different parameter assumptions for the regime-switching model. $X_0 = 1, T = 1, \alpha = 20\%, \sigma_1 = 0.1, \sigma_2 = 0.2, N_{sim} = 5000, H = 0.04$, and $c = 0.1$.

(μ_0, μ_1)	Probability of Default		
	$p = 0.01, q = 0.05$	$p = 0.1, q = 0.05$	$p = 0.01, q = 0.1$
$\mu_0 = 0.1, \mu_1 = -0.05$	0.1338 (0.0048)	0.3544 (0.0067)	0.0962 (0.0042)
$\mu_0 = 0.15, \mu_1 = -0.05$	0.0736 (0.0037)	0.3116 (0.0065)	0.0414 (0.0028)
$\mu_0 = 0.1, \mu_1 = 0$	0.1248 (0.0047)	0.2968 (0.0065)	0.0914 (0.0041)
$\mu_0 = 0.15, \mu_1 = 0$	0.0586 (0.0033)	0.2604 (0.0062)	0.0430 (0.0029)

recovery rate (i.e. the fraction of the promised amount $X_0(1 + H)$ that is expected to be recovered conditional upon default having occurred). Simulation results under the regime-switching model for these quantities are provided in Tables 4 and 5 (with standard errors of the estimates in parentheses). Probabilities of default are quite high, ranging from 18% under the best parameter combination to nearly 30% under the worst parameter set. However, these high probabilities of default are mitigated by very high expected recovery rates, in the range of 95-96%.

4.1. *Impact of the manager's deposit c*

A key parameter for first-loss and negative loss fee structures is the manager's deposit c, as it determines the amount of downside protection provided to the

Table 5.   Expected recovery rates under different parameter assumptions for the regime-switching model. $X_0 = 1, T = 1, \alpha = 20\%, \sigma_1 = 0.1, \sigma_2 = 0.2, N_{sim} = 5000, H = 0.04$, and $c = 0.1$.

	Recovery Rate		
(μ_0, μ_1)	$p = 0.01, q = 0.05$	$p = 0.1, q = 0.05$	$p = 0.01, q = 0.1$
$\mu_0 = 0.1, \mu_1 = -0.05$	0.9825 (0.0507)	0.9429 (0.0722)	0.9922 (0.0399)
$\mu_0 = 0.15, \mu_1 = -0.05$	0.9888 (0.0432)	0.9452 (0.0737)	0.9975 (0.0328)
$\mu_0 = 0.1, \mu_1 = 0$	0.9844 (0.0455)	0.9447 (0.0707)	0.9919 (0.0439)
$\mu_0 = 0.15, \mu_1 = 0$	0.9866 (0.0469)	0.9460 (0.0713)	0.9964 (0.0374)

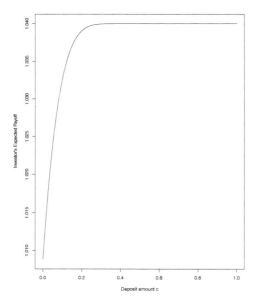

Fig. 5.   Investor's expected payoff as a function of the manager's deposit c. $X_0 = 1, T = 1, \alpha = 20\%, p = 0.01, q = 0.05, \sigma_1 = 0.1, \sigma_2 = 0.2, N_{sim} = 5000, H = 0.04$.

investor by the fund manager (see Djerroud *et al.* [3]). In this section, we investigate the impact of this parameter on the payoffs for the fund investor and manager. Figures 5 and 6 present the expected payoffs of the investor and manager respectively, as the parameter c varies, under the benchmark parameter set used to generate Table 1. We see that for large levels of downside protection, the investor's return quickly approaches the promised value H. For lower levels of insurance,

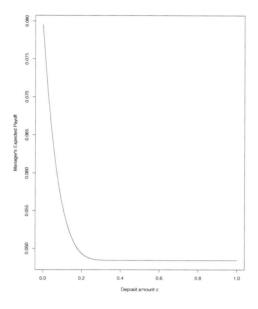

Fig. 6.   Manager's expected payoff as a function of the manager's deposit c. $X_0 = 1, T = 1, \alpha = 20\%, p = 0.01, q = 0.05, \mu_1 = 0.1, \mu_2 = -0.05, \sigma_1 = 0.1, \sigma_2 = 0.2, N_{sim} = 5000, H = 0.04$.

the investor's expected return becomes negative. The manager's expected payoff follows the opposite pattern. Expected payoffs are high for low levels of c, but decrease rapidly as c increases. Similarly, as illustrated in Figures 7 and 8, the volatility of the investor's payoff decreases quickly as the level of downside protection c increases, and the volatility of the manager's payoff increases accordingly. The investor's Sharpe Ratio as a function of c is given in Figure 9 (the risk-free interest rate is set at $r = 1\%$). For very high levels of protection c, the Sharpe ratio grows very quickly (as $H > r$ and a very large level of downside protection virtually guarantees that the investor will receive the return H).

As with many collateralized products, the default and credit risk are intimately related to the market risk and loss quantile of the reference portfolio. In the preceding analysis, we have measured risk using the standard deviations of payoffs and returns. While this is appropriate for normal distributions, the payoffs of the hedge fund manager and investor are non-normal, especially in the context of the regime-switching framework. As a consequence, it is important to consider the tail

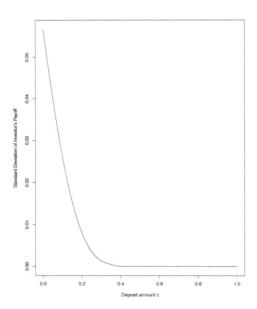

Fig. 7.   Standard deviation of the investor's payoff as a function of the manager's deposit c. $X_0 = 1, T = 1, \alpha = 20\%, p = 0.01, q = 0.05, \mu_1 = 0.1, \mu_2 = -0.05, \sigma_1 = 0.1, \sigma_2 = 0.2, N_{sim} = 5000, H = 0.04$.

risks faced by the investor. We will do this by considering the investor's expected shortfall (also known as conditional Value-at-Risk, or conditional tail expectation), the expectation of losses given that the losses are below a given confidence level of their distribution.

Let

$$L^I = -(I(T) - X_0),$$

so that we have 'positive' loss. Define

$$ES_\beta(L^I) = \mathbb{E}[L^I | L^I \geq VaR_\beta(L^I)]$$

Note that we have a probability mass at the point $-HX_0$. The estimator for expected shortfall is:

$$\widehat{ES}_\beta(L^I) = w \frac{\sum_{i=1}^N \mathbb{I}_{\{L_i^I > \widehat{VaR}_\beta(L^I)\}} L_i^I}{\sum_{i=1}^N \mathbb{I}_{\{L_i^I > \widehat{VaR}_\beta(L^I)\}}} + (1-w)\widehat{VaR}_\beta(L^I)$$

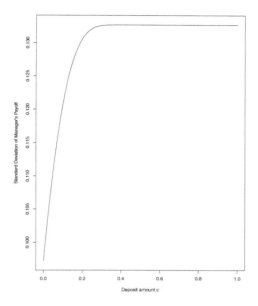

Fig. 8.   Standard deviation of the manager's payoff as a function of the manager's deposit c. $X_0 = 1, T = 1, \alpha = 20\%, p = 0.01, q = 0.05, \mu_1 = 0.1, \mu_2 = -0.05, \sigma_1 = 0.1, \sigma_2 = 0.2, N_{sim} = 5000, H = 0.04$.

where

$$w = \frac{\sum_{i=1}^{N} \mathbb{I}_{\{L_i^I > \widehat{VaR}_\beta(L^I)\}}}{N \cdot (1 - \beta)}$$

We increase the number of scenarios in the simulation to 1,000,000 in order to have more scenarios in the tail and a more accurate estimate of expected shortfall. Figure 10 shows the investor's expected shortfall as a function of the manager's deposit c for $\beta = 0.95, 0.99$. As expected, lower levels of the manager's deposit are associated with higher levels of risk. In particular, for manager deposits near our benchmark level of $c = 10\%$, expected shortfall can exceed 20% of the initial investment, indicating significant losses for investors under extreme scenarios. Because of the large number of scenarios used, the confidence intervals for the estimates are quite small (the lengths of the confidence intervals are around 1.5% of the estimated values).

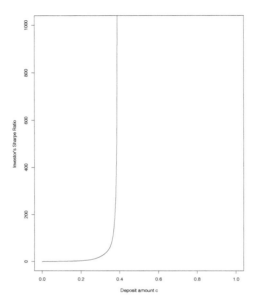

Fig. 9.   Sharpe Ratio of the investor's payoff as a function of the manager's deposit c. $X_0 = 1, T = 1, \alpha = 20\%, p = 0.01, q = 0.05, \mu_1 = 0.1, \mu_2 = -0.05, \sigma_1 = 0.1, \sigma_2 = 0.2, N_{sim} = 5000, H = 0.04$.

5. Conclusion

Recently, market pressures have led to the introduction of innovative hedge fund fee structures, in which the fund manager receives higher performance fees in return for providing downside protection to fund investors. These arrangements are referred to by the general name of first-loss fee structures. An extreme version is the negative fee structure, in which the manager receives all profits above a pre-defined hurdle rate, and for which the investor's position resembles that of an investment in an asset-backed security, with the underlying assets being the hedge fund's portfolio. In this paper we analyzed the negative fee structure in a regime-switching model, both by pricing it using risk-neutral valuation, and performing a risk analysis under the real-world measure (including examining the probability of default and expected recovery rate).

There are a number of important questions that could be considered for future research. The fee structure could be analyzed under other mathematical models, including those that allow more general stochastic behavior of volatility. The incentives of both the manager, in terms of the structuring of the hedge fund port-

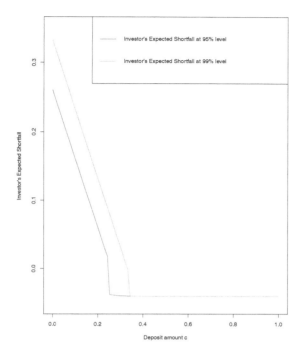

Fig. 10. Expected shortfall of the investor's losses as a function of the manager's deposit c.
$X_0 = 1, T = 1, \alpha = 20\%, p = 0.01, q = 0.05, \mu_1 = 0.1, \mu_2 = -0.05, \sigma_1 = 0.1, \sigma_2 = 0.2, N_{sim} = 1,000,000, H = 0.04$.

folio, and the investor, in terms of the decision to withdraw from the fund, could both be studied, either in isolation (as a stochastic control problem and an optimal stopping problem respectively), or together (in a stochastic game of control and stopping). Finally, the limitations of the assumptions underlying risk-neutral valuation (particularly the ability to observe the value of, and dynamically trade in, the underlying assets of the hedge fund) could be investigated, perhaps through models that more realistically represent the bargaining process between principal (investor) and agent (manager) that we have discussed this paper.

References

1. J. Banzaca, First loss capital arrangements for hedge fund managers: Structures, risks and the market for key terms, *The Hedge Fund Law Report*, **5**(37) (2012).

2. Bloomberg, Pension funds say hedge funds fees too high, (2017). URL `https://www.bloomberg.com/news/articles/2017-06-07/new-york-illinois-pension-funds-say-hedge-funds-fees-too-high`.

3. B. Djerroud, D. Saunders, L. Seco, and M. Shakourifar, Pricing shared-loss hedge fund fee structures. In K. Glau, Z. Grbac, M. Scherer, and R. Zagst, editors, *Innovations in Derivatives Markets: Fixed Income Modeling, Valuation Adjustments, Risk Management, and Regulation*, 369. Springer, (2016).

4. Robert J. Elliott, Leunglung Chan, and Tak Kuen Siu, Option pricing and esscher transform under regime switching, *Annals of Finance*, 1(4):423–432 (Oct2005). ISSN 1614-2454. doi: 10.1007/s10436-005-0013-z. URL `https://doi.org/10.1007/s10436-005-0013-z`.

5. Cheng-Der Fuh, Kwok Wah Remus Ho, Inchi Hu, and Ren-Her Wang, Option pricing with markov switching, *Journal of Data Science*, 3:483–509 (2012).

6. X. Guo, Information and option pricings, *Quantitative Finance*, 1(1):38–44 (2001). doi: 10.1080/713665550. URL `https://doi.org/10.1080/713665550`.

7. J.D. Hamilton, A new approach to the economic analysis of nonstationary time series and the business cycle, *Econometrica*, **57**(2) (1989).

8. M.R. Hardy, *Investment Guarantees: Modeling and Risk Management for Equity-Linked Life Insurance*. John Wiley & Sons, Hoboken, New Jersey (2003).

9. X.D. He and S. Kou, Profit sharing in hedge funds, *Mathematical Finance*, **28**(1):50–81 (2018).

10. R.S. Mamon and R.J. Elliottt, editors, *Hidden Markov Models in Finance*. Springer, New York (2007).

11. R.C. Merton, On the pricing of corporate debt: The risk structure of interest rates, *The Journal of Finance*, **29**:449–470 (1974).

12. OECD, Pension markets in focus. Technical report, OECD (2016).

13. Y. Zeng and S. Wu, editors, *State-Space Models: Applications in Economics and Finance*. Springer, New York (2013).

Chapter 10

Static Versus Adapted Optimal Execution Strategies in Two Benchmark Trading Models

Damiano Brigo* and Clément Piat

Dept. of Mathematics, Imperial College London,
London, United Kingdom
* damiano.brigo@imperial.ac.uk
www.imperial.ac.uk

We consider the optimal solutions to the trade execution problem in the two different classes of i) fully adapted or adaptive and ii) deterministic or static strategies, comparing them. We do this in two different benchmark models. The first model is a discrete time framework with an information flow process, dealing with both permanent and temporary impact, minimizing the expected cost of the trade. The second model is a continuous time framework where the objective function is the sum of the expected cost and a value at risk (or expected shortfall) type risk criterion. Optimal adapted solutions are known in both frameworks from the original works of Bertsimas and Lo (1998) and Gatheral and Schied (2011). In this paper we derive the optimal static strategies for both benchmark models and we study quantitatively the improvement in optimality when moving from static strategies to fully adapted ones. We conclude that, in the benchmark models we study, the difference is not relevant, except for extreme unrealistic cases for the model or impact parameters.

Keywords: optimal trade execution, optimal scheduling, algorithmic trading, calculus of variations, risk measures, value at risk, market impact, permanent impact, temporary impact, static solutions, adapted solutions, dynamic programming.

1. Introduction

A basic stylized fact of trade execution is that when a trader buys or sells a large amount of stock in a restricted amount of time, the market naturally tends to move in the opposite direction. If one assumes an unaffected price dynamics for the traded asset, trading activity will impact this price and lead to an affected price. Supply and demand based analysis says that if a trader begins to buy large amounts, other traders will notice and the affected price will tend to increase. Similarly, if one begins to sell large amounts, the affected price will tend to decrease. This is particularly important when the market is highly illiquid, since in that case no trade goes unnoticed. The goal of optimal execution, or more properly optimal scheduling, is to find how to execute the order in a way such that the expected profit or cost is the best possible, taking into account the impact of the trade on the affected price.

As far as we are concerned in this paper, there are two main categories of trading strategies: deterministic, also called static in the execution literature jargon, and adapted, or adaptive. We will use static/deterministic and adapted/adaptive interchangeably. Deterministic strategies are set before the execution, so that they are independent of the actual path taken by the price. They only rely on information known initially. Adapted strategies are not known before the execution. The amount executed at each time depends on all information known up to this time. Clearly market operators, in reality, will monitor market prices and trade based on their evolution, so that the adapted strategy is the more natural one. However, in some models it is much harder to find an optimal trading strategy in the class of adapted strategies than in the class of static ones.

In 1998, Bertsimas and Lo [6] have defined the best execution as the strategy that minimizes the expected cost of trading over a fixed period of time. They derive the optimal strategy by using dynamic programming, which means that they go backwards in time. The optimal solution is therefore sought in the class of adapted strategies, as is natural from backward induction, but is found to be deterministic anyway. However, once an information process is added, influencing the affected price, the optimal solutions are adapted and no longer static. This approach minimizes the expected trade cost only, without including any risk in the criterion to be optimized. In particular, the criterion does not take into account the variance of the cost function.

Two years later, Almgren and Chriss [2] consider the minimization of an objective function that is the sum of the expected execution cost and of a cost-variance risk criterion. Unlike the previous model, this setting includes in the criterion the possibility to penalize large variability in the trading cost. To solve the resulting mean-variance optimization, Almgren and Chriss assume the solution to be deterministic from the start. This allows them to obtain a closed-form solution. This solution, however, is only the best solution in the class of static strategies, and not in the broader and more natural class of adapted ones.

Gatheral and Schied [13] later solve a similar problem, the main difference being that they assume a more realistic model for the unaffected price. Gatheral and Schied derive an adapted solution by using an alternative risk criterion, the time-averaged value-at-risk function. They obtain closed-form expressions for the strategy and the optimal cost. The solution is not static. However, this does not seem to lead to a solution that is very different, qualitatively, from the static one. Indeed, Brigo and Di Graziano (2014), adding a displaced diffusion dynamics, find that in many situations only the rough statistics of the signal matter in the class of simple regular diffusion models [7]. In this paper we will compare the static and fully adapted solutions in detail.

Since the solutions obtained in the setting of Almgren and Chriss [2] are deterministic, they may be sub-optimal in the set of fully adapted solutions under a cost-variance risk criterion, so several papers have attempted to find adapted solutions by changing the framework slightly. This allows one to take the new price information into account during the execution, and to have more precise models. For example, in 2012 Almgren [5] assumes that the volatility and liquidity are random. He numerically obtains adapted results under these assumptions. Almgren and Lorenz [4] obtain adapted solutions by using an appropriate dynamic programming technique.

Similarly, in this paper we will focus on what one gains from adopting a more general adapted strategy over a simple deterministic strategy in the classic discrete time setting of Bertsimas and Lo [6] with information flow and in the continuous time setting of Gatheral and Schied with time-averaged value-at-risk criterion [13].

The paper is structured as follows. In Section 2 we will introduce the discrete time model by Bertsimas and Lo, looking at the case of permanent market impact on the unaffected price, and including the solution for the case where the price is also affected by an information flow process. We will derive and study the optimal static and fully adapted solutions and compare them, quantifying in a few numerical examples how much one gains from going fully adapted.

In Section 3 we will introduce the continuous time model as in Gatheral and Schied, allowing for both temporary and permanent impact and for a risk criterion based on value at risk. We will report the optimal fully adapted solution as derived in [13] and we will derive the optimal static solution using a calculus of variation technique, similar for example to the calculations in [11]. We will compare the two solutions and optimal criteria in a few numerical examples, to see again how much one gains from going fully adapted.

Section 4 concludes the paper, summarizing its findings, and points to possible future research directions.

2. Discrete time trading with information flow

2.1. *Model formulation with cost based criterion*

Let X_t be the number of units left to execute at time t, such that $X_0 = X$ is the initial amount and $X_T = 0$ at the final time T. In this section we consider a buy order, so that the purpose of the strategy is to buy an amount X of asset by time T, minimizing the expected cost of the trade. The amount to be executed during the time interval $[t, t+1)$ is $\Delta V_t := X_t - X_{t+1}$. We expect ΔV_t to be non-negative, since we would like to implement a pure buy program. However we do not impose a constraint of positivity on ΔV, so that the optimal solution, in principle, might consider a mixed buy/sell optimal strategy. We denote $\mathbb{E}_t()$ the conditional expectation given the information $\mathcal{F}_t$ at time t. We assume that X_t is adapted to the filtration, i.e. X_t is $\mathcal{F}_t$ measurable. Here $\mathcal{F}_t$ models the market information that is accessible at time t.

Since the problem is in discrete time, it is only updated every period so we will assume that the price does not change between two update times.

With that in mind, we assume that the unaffected mid-price process $\widetilde{S}$ is given by

$$\widetilde{S}_t = \widetilde{S}_{t-1} + \gamma Y_t + \sigma \widetilde{S}_0 \Delta W_{t-1}, \tag{1}$$

$$Y_t = \rho Y_{t-1} + \sigma_Y \Delta Z_{t-1}, \tag{2}$$

where the information coefficient γ, and the volatilities σ and σ_Y are positive constants, W and Z are independent standard Brownian motions and the parameter ρ is in $(-1, 1)$. We define $\Delta W_t = W_{t+1} - W_t$, $\Delta Z_t = Z_{t+1} - Z_t$.

$\widetilde{S}$ would be the price if there were no impact from our executions. It follows an arithmetic Brownian motion (ABM) to which an information component Y has been added. The information process Y is an AR(1) process. It could be for example the return of the S&P500 index, or some information specific to the security being traded. γ represents the relevance of that information, that is how much it impacts the price.

Remark 2.1. The ABM is adopted here for tractability. Even though the prices can theoretically become negative, one can keep the probability of negative asset values under control by computing it and monitoring it.

There are two dynamics that we will consider for the real price S, depending on whether the market impact is assumed to be permanent or temporary. We will explain what those terms mean when defining the price dynamics below. We assume that the market impact is linear in both settings, which means that the market reacts proportionally to the amount executed.

In the case of permanent market impact the mid-price dynamics are changed by each execution. This means that when we compute the trade cost, the unaffected price $\widetilde{S}$ is replaced, during the execution, by the impacted or affected price S:

$$S_t = S_{t-1} + \theta \Delta V_{t-1} + \gamma Y_t + \sigma S_0 \Delta W_{t-1}, \quad S_0 = \widetilde{S}_0, \qquad (3)$$

where the permanent impact parameter θ is a positive constant.

In the case of temporary market impact each execution only changes the price for the current time period. The mid-price $\widetilde{S}$ is still given by (1), and the effective price S is derived from $\widetilde{S}$ each period. S has the following dynamics:

$$S_t = \widetilde{S}_t + \eta \Delta V_{t-1}, \quad S_0 = \widetilde{S}_0, \qquad (4)$$

where the temporary impact parameter η is a positive constant.

Remark 2.2. Since one case assumes that the impact lasts for the whole trade, and the other assumes that the impact is instantaneous and affects only an order at the time it is done, both are limit cases of a more general impact pattern that is more progressive, see for example Obizhaeva and Wang [18].

We will keep the two more stylized impact cases and analyze them separately. The problem in both cases is to minimize the expected cost of execution. Since we are considering a buy order, X_t is the number of units left to buy. Hence the optimal expected execution cost at time 0 is

$$C^*(X_0, S_0) := \min_{\{\Delta V\}} C(X_0, S_0, \{\Delta V\}) = \min_{\{\Delta V\}} \mathbb{E}_0 \left[\sum_{t=0}^{T-1} S_{t+1} \Delta V_t \right], \qquad (5)$$

subject to $X_0 = X$, $X_T = 0$.

Remark 2.3. As we mentioned earlier, we do not enforce any constraint on the sign of ΔV, which means that we are allowed to sell in our buy order.

We now present some calculations deriving the optimal solution of problem (5) in the cases of permanent impact.[1] Our calculations in the general setting follow essentially Bertsimas and Lo [6] but with a slightly different notation, as done initially in Bonart, Brigo and Di Graziano [9] and Kulak [16]. We further derive the optimal solution in the static class, using a more straightforward method.

2.2. *Permanent market impact: Optimal adapted solution*

In this section, we solve problem (5) reproducing the solution of Bertsimas and Lo [6], assuming that the market impact is permanent, which means that the affected price follows (3). In the adapted setting, the problem is solved recursively. At any time t, we consider the problem as if t was the initial time, and the execution was optimal from time $t + 1$. We only have to make a decision for the period t, ignoring the past and having already solved the future.

For any t, the execution cost from time t onward is the sum of the cost at time t and the cost from time $t+1$ onward. Taking the minimum of the expectation, this can be written as the Bellman equation:

$$C_t^*(X_t, S_t) = \min_{\Delta V} \mathbb{E}_t \left[S_{t+1}\Delta V_t + C_{t+1}^*(X_{t+1}, S_{t+1}) \right]. \tag{6}$$

Since the execution should be finished by time T ($X_T = 0$), all the remaining shares must be executed during the last period :

$$\Delta V_{T-1}^* = X_{T-1}.$$

Substituting this value into the Bellman equation (6) taken at $t = T - 1$ gives us the optimal expected cost at time $T - 1$:

$$\begin{aligned}
C_{T-1}^*(X_{T-1}, S_{T-1}) &= \min_{\Delta V} \mathbb{E}_{T-1}[S_T \Delta V_{T-1}] \\
&= \mathbb{E}_{T-1}[S_T X_{T-1}] \\
&= \mathbb{E}_{T-1}[(S_{T-1} + \theta X_{T-1} + \gamma Y_T + \sigma S_0 \Delta W_{T-1}) X_{T-1}] \\
&= S_{T-1} X_{T-1} + \theta X_{T-1}^2 + \rho \gamma X_{T-1} Y_{T-1},
\end{aligned}$$

where we used the fact that Y_{T-1}, X_{T-1} and S_{T-1} are known at time $T-1$, as well as the null expectation of standard Brownian motion increments.

---

[1]The case of temporary impact is similar and can be found in the online version of this paper [8].

We now move one step backward to obtain the optimal strategy at time $T - 2$, plugging the expression above in (6) taken at $t = T - 2$ and noting that $X_{T-1} = X_{T-2} - \Delta V_{T-2}$.

$$
\begin{aligned}
C^*_{T-2}(X_{T-2}, S_{T-2}) &= \min_{\Delta V} \mathbb{E}_{T-2}[S_{T-1}\Delta V_{T-2} + C^*_{T-1}(X_{T-1}, S_{T-1})] \\
&= \min_{\Delta V}[S_{T-2}X_{T-2} + \gamma\rho Y_{T-2}X_{T-2}(1 + \rho) \\
&\quad - (\gamma\rho^2 Y_{T-2} + \theta X_{T-2})\Delta V_{T-2} + \theta X^2_{T-2} + \theta\Delta V^2_{T-2}].
\end{aligned}
$$

In order to find the minimum of this expression, we set to zero its derivative with respect to ΔV_{T-2}:

$$
\frac{\partial C_{T-2}(X_{T-2}, S_{T-2})}{\partial \Delta V_{T-2}} = -\theta X_{T-2} - \gamma\rho^2 Y_{T-2} + 2\theta\Delta V_{T-2} = 0.
$$

The solution of this equation is the optimal amount to execute at time $T - 2$:

$$
\Delta V^*_{T-2} = \frac{X_{T-2}}{2} + \frac{\gamma\rho^2 Y_{T-2}}{2\theta}.
$$

The optimal expected cost at time $T - 2$ is

$$
\begin{aligned}
C^*_{T-2}(X_{T-2}, S_{T-2}) &= S_{T-2}X_{T-2} + \frac{3\theta}{4}X^2_{T-2} + \gamma\rho(1 + \frac{\rho}{2})X_{T-2}Y_{T-2} \\
&\quad - \frac{\gamma^2\rho^4}{4\theta}Y^2_{T-2}.
\end{aligned}
$$

More generally, we can see a pattern emerging from the two previous optimal strategies and expected costs results, which can be proven formally by induction.

Theorem 2.1 (Optimal execution strategy). *For any $i \geq 1$ the optimal execution strategy at time $T - i$, subject to $X_0 = X$, is*

$$
X^*_t = \frac{T - t}{T}X - \sum_{k=0}^{t-1}\frac{T - t}{T - k - 1}a_{T-k}Y_k
$$

$$
\text{with } a_i = \frac{\gamma\rho^2}{i\theta(1 - \rho)^2}(\rho^i - i\rho + i - 1) \quad \text{for } i \geq 1.
$$

Theorem 2.2 (Optimal expected cost). *For any $i \geq 1$, the minimum expected cost at time $T - i$ is*

$$C_{ad}^*(X_{T-i}, S_{T-i}) = S_{T-i}X_{T-i} + \frac{i+1}{2i}\theta X_{T-i}^2 + \frac{(i+1)\theta a_{i+1}}{i\rho}X_{T-i}Y_{T-i}$$

$$- b_i Y_{T-i}^2 - (\sum_{k=2}^{i-1} b_k)\sigma_Y^2$$

with $b_i = \dfrac{\gamma^2 \rho^4}{2\theta(1-\rho)^3}\left(\dfrac{1-\rho^{2i}}{1+\rho} - \dfrac{(1-\rho^i)^2}{i(1-\rho)}\right)$ *for* $i \geq 2$.

Corollary 2.1. *In particular, the optimal expected cost at time 0 is*

$$C_{ad}^*(X_0, S_0) = S_0 X + \frac{T+1}{2T}\theta X^2 + \frac{(T+1)\theta a_{T+1}}{T\rho}XY_0 - b_T Y_0^2 - (\sum_{k=2}^{T-1} b_k)\sigma_Y^2.$$

$$(7)$$

Remark 2.4. Although this strategy is adapted, it does not take into account the price, but only the information process. This makes sense because if there was no information, the optimal strategy would be deterministic as shown by Bertsimas and Lo [6].

2.3. *Permanent market impact: Optimal deterministic solution*

We will now constrain the solutions of (5) to be deterministic, so that the strategy is known at time 0 and can be executed with no further calculations, independently of the path taken by the price.

Theorem 2.3 (Optimal deterministic execution strategy). *When we restrict the solutions to the subset of deterministic strategies, the optimal strategy is*

$$X_t^* = \frac{T-t}{T}X + \frac{\gamma Y_0 \rho^2}{\theta(1-\rho)^2}\left[\rho^t - 1 + (1-\rho^T)\frac{t}{T}\right].$$

$$(8)$$

Proof. To solve (5), we will simply assume that every X_t is known at time 0 and compute the expected cost at time 0:

$$C(X_0, S_0, \{\Delta V\})$$

$$= \mathbb{E}_0\left[\sum_{t=0}^{T-1} S_{t+1}\Delta V_t\right]$$

$$= \sum_{t=0}^{T-1} \Delta V_t \mathbb{E}_0[S_{t+1}] \quad \text{since } \Delta V_t = X_t - X_{t+1} \text{ is deterministic}$$

$$= \sum_{t=0}^{T-1} \Delta V_t \left(\mathbb{E}_0[S_t] + \theta \Delta V_t + \gamma \mathbb{E}_0[Y_{t+1}]\right)$$

$$= \sum_{t=0}^{T-1} \Delta V_t \left(S_0 + \theta \sum_{i=0}^{t} \Delta V_i + \gamma Y_0 \sum_{i=1}^{t+1} \rho^i\right) \quad \text{by induction}$$

$$= S_0 X_0 + \sum_{t=0}^{T-1} (X_t - X_{t+1}) \left(\theta \sum_{i=0}^{t} (X_i - X_{i+1}) + \gamma Y_0 \rho \frac{1 - \rho^{t+1}}{1 - \rho}\right)$$

$$= S_0 X_0 + \theta \sum_{t=0}^{T-1} (X_t - X_{t+1})(X_0 - X_{t+1})$$

$$+ \gamma Y_0 \rho \sum_{t=0}^{T-1} \frac{1 - \rho^{t+1}}{1 - \rho} (X_t - X_{t+1}).$$

Problem (5) can be rewritten as

$$C^*(X_0, S_0) = \min_x C(x).$$

To find the minimum, we set to zero the partial derivatives of the expected cost with respect to $X_1, ..., X_{T-1}$. For $t = 1, ..., T-1$ it gives us

$$\frac{\partial C}{\partial X_t} = \theta(X_0 - X_{t+1}) - \theta(X_0 - X_t) - \theta(X_{t-1} - X_t)$$

$$+ \gamma \rho Y_0 \left(\frac{1 - \rho^{t+1}}{1 - \rho} - \frac{1 - \rho^t}{1 - \rho}\right) = 0.$$

We obtain the difference equation

$$X_{t+1} - 2X_t + X_{t-1} = \frac{\gamma Y_0}{\theta} \rho^{t+1}, \tag{9}$$

with boundary conditions $X_0 = X$ and $X_T = 0$.

The solution of (9) is of the form $A + Bt + C\rho^t$ for some constants A, B and C. Plugging this expression back in the equation yields

$$A + B(t+1) + C\rho^{t+1} - 2(A + Bt + C\rho^t) + A + B(t-1) + C\rho^{t-1}$$
$$= \frac{\gamma Y_0}{\theta} \rho^{t+1}$$

$$C\rho^t(\rho - 2 + \rho^{-1}) = \frac{\gamma Y_0}{\theta}\rho^{t+1}$$

$$C = \frac{\gamma Y_0 \rho^2}{\theta(1 - \rho)^2}.$$

From the boundary conditions we have

$$X_0 = A + C = X, \quad A = X - \frac{\gamma Y_0 \rho^2}{\theta(1 - \rho)^2},$$

and

$$X_T = A + BT + C\rho^T = 0, \quad B = -\frac{X}{T} + \frac{\gamma Y_0 \rho^2(1 - \rho^T)}{\theta(1 - \rho)^2 T}.$$

Combining those, we obtain the closed-form formula of the optimal deterministic strategy. $\qquad\square$

Remark 2.5. If $Y_0 = 0$ (no initial information), $\rho = 0$ (information is just noise) or $\gamma = 0$ (information is irrelevant), the strategy consists in splitting the execution in orders of equal amounts over the period T. This is a particular case of the strategy more generally known as VWAP (volume-weighted average price), and is the strategy obtained when there is no information.

Theorem 2.4 (*Expected cost associated with the deterministic strategy*). *The expected cost at time 0 associated with the optimal deterministic strategy is*

$$C_{det}^*(X_0, S_0) = S_0 X + \frac{T+1}{2T}\theta X^2 + \frac{\gamma Y_0 \rho X}{T(1-\rho)}\left(T - \rho\frac{1 - \rho^T}{1 - \rho}\right) - b_T Y_0^2 \tag{10}$$

Proof. For lighter calculations, we set

$$C = \frac{\gamma Y_0 \rho^2}{\theta(1 - \rho)^2}.$$

The optimal expected cost at time 0 is

$$C^*(X_0, S_0) = S_0 X_0 + \theta\sum_{t=0}^{T-1}(X_t^* - X_{t+1}^*)(X_0 - X_{t+1}^*)$$

$$+ \gamma Y_0 \rho \sum_{t=0}^{T-1}\frac{1 - \rho^{t+1}}{1 - \rho}(X_t^* - X_{t+1}^*). \tag{11}$$

We compute the two sums in (11) separately for clarity:
$$C^*(X_0, S_0) = S_0 X_0 + \theta S_1 + \gamma Y_0 \rho S_2.$$

The second sum is

$$S_2 = \sum_{t=0}^{T-1} \frac{1-\rho^{t+1}}{1-\rho} \left(\frac{X}{T} + C \left(\rho^t(1-\rho) + \frac{\rho^T - 1}{T} \right) \right)$$

$$= \frac{X}{T(1-\rho)} \left(T - \rho \frac{1-\rho^T}{1-\rho} \right)$$

$$+ \frac{C}{1-\rho} \left(\frac{1-\rho^T}{1-\rho}(1-\rho) + \rho^T - 1 - \rho \frac{1-\rho^{2T}}{1-\rho^2}(1-\rho) + \rho \frac{(1-\rho^T)^2}{T(1-\rho)} \right)$$

$$= \frac{X}{T(1-\rho)} \left(T - \rho \frac{1-\rho^T}{1-\rho} \right) - \frac{C\rho(1-\rho^{2T})}{1-\rho^2} + \frac{C\rho(1-\rho^T)^2}{T(1-\rho)^2}.$$

The first sum is

$$S_1 = \sum_{t=0}^{T-1} \left(\frac{X}{T} + C \left(\rho^t(1-\rho) + \frac{\rho^T - 1}{T} \right) \right)$$

$$\times \left(\frac{t+1}{T}X - C(\rho^{t+1} - 1 + (1-\rho^T)\frac{t+1}{T}) \right)$$

$$= \sum_{t=0}^{T-1} \frac{t+1}{T^2}X^2 + \sum_{t=0}^{T-1} \frac{CX}{T} \left(1 - \rho^{t+1} + (\rho^T - 1)\frac{t+1}{T} \right)$$

$$+ \sum_{t=0}^{T-1} \frac{t+1}{T}CX \left(\rho^t(1-\rho) + \frac{\rho^T - 1}{T} \right)$$

$$+ \sum_{t=0}^{T-1} C^2 \left(\rho^t(1-\rho) + \frac{\rho^T - 1}{T} \right) \left(1 - \rho^{t+1} + (\rho^T - 1)\frac{t+1}{T} \right)$$

$$= \frac{T(T+1)}{2T^2}X^2 + \sum_{t=0}^{T-1} \frac{CX}{T} \left(-(t+2)\rho^{t+1} + (t+1)\rho^t + 2(t+1)\frac{\rho^T - 1}{T} + 1 \right)$$

$$+ C^2 \sum_{t=0}^{T-1} \left(\rho^t(1-\rho-\rho^{t+1}+\rho^{t+2}) + ((t+1)\rho^t - (t+2)\rho^{t+1} + 1)\frac{\rho^T - 1}{T} \right)$$

$$+ C^2 \sum_{t=0}^{T-1} (t+1)\frac{(\rho^T - 1)^2}{T^2}$$

$$S_1 = \frac{CX}{T} \left(\frac{-(T-1)\rho^{T+2} + T\rho^{T+1} - \rho^2}{(1-\rho)^2} - 2\frac{\rho - \rho^{T+1}}{1-\rho} \right.$$

$$+ \frac{T\rho^{T+1} - (T+1)\rho^T + 1}{(1-\rho)^2} \Bigg)$$

$$+ \frac{CX}{T}\left((T+1)\rho^T - 1\right) + C^2 \sum_{t=0}^{T-1}\left(\rho^{2t+1}(\rho-1) + \frac{(1-\rho)(\rho^T-1)}{T}t\rho^t\right)$$

$$+ C^2 \sum_{t=0}^{T-1}\left(1 - \rho + \frac{\rho^T - 1}{T}(-2\rho+1)\right)\rho^t + \frac{(\rho^T-1)^2}{T^2}(t+1)$$

$$+ \frac{\rho^T - 1}{T} + \frac{T+1}{2T}X^2$$

$$= \frac{CX}{T}\frac{(-T-1)\rho^{T+2} + 2(T+1)\rho^{T+1} + \rho^2 - (T+1)\rho^T + 1 - 2\rho}{(1-\rho)^2}$$

$$+ \frac{CX}{T}\frac{((T+1)\rho^T - 1)(1 + \rho^2 - 2\rho)}{(1-\rho)^2}$$

$$+ C^2\left(\frac{\rho^{2T}-1}{1+\rho}\rho + \frac{\rho^T-1}{T}\rho\frac{(T-1)\rho^T - T\rho^{T-1} + 1}{1-\rho}\right)$$

$$+ C^2\left(\frac{T - T\rho + (1-2\rho)(\rho^T-1)}{T}\frac{1-\rho^T}{1-\rho} + \frac{T+1}{2T}(\rho^T-1)^2 + \rho^T - 1\right)$$

$$+ \frac{T+1}{2T}X^2$$

$$= \frac{C^2}{T(1-\rho^2)}\left(\left(\frac{1-T}{2}\rho^2 + T\rho + \frac{-T-1}{2}\right)\rho^{2T} - \rho^{T+2} + \rho^T + \frac{T+1}{2}\rho^2\right)$$

$$+ \frac{C^2}{T(1-\rho^2)}\left(-T\rho + \frac{T-1}{2}\right) + \frac{T+1}{2T}X^2$$

$$= \frac{C^2(1-\rho)(1-\rho^{2T})}{2(1+\rho)} - \frac{C^2(1-\rho^T)^2}{2T} + \frac{T+1}{2T}X^2.$$

Substituting those results in (11), we obtain

$$C^*(X_0, S_0)$$

$$= S_0 X + \theta\left(\frac{C^2(1-\rho)(1-\rho^{2T})}{2(1+\rho)} - \frac{C^2(1-\rho^T)^2}{2T} + \frac{T+1}{2T}X^2\right)$$

$$+ \gamma Y_0 \rho\left(\frac{X}{T(1-\rho)}\left(T - \rho\frac{1-\rho^T}{1-\rho}\right) - \frac{C\rho(1-\rho^{2T})}{1-\rho^2} + \frac{C\rho(1-\rho^T)^2}{T(1-\rho)^2}\right)$$

$$= S_0 X + \frac{\gamma^2 Y_0^2 \rho^4 (1-\rho^{2T})}{2(1+\rho)\theta(1-\rho)^3} - \frac{\gamma^2 Y_0^2 \rho^4 (1-\rho^T)^2}{2T\theta(1-\rho)^4} + \frac{T+1}{2T}\theta X^2$$

$$+ \frac{\gamma Y_0 \rho X}{T(1-\rho)}\left(T - \rho\frac{1-\rho^T}{1-\rho}\right) - \frac{\gamma^2 Y_0^2 \rho^4 (1-\rho^{2T})}{(1-\rho^2)\theta(1-\rho)^2} + \frac{\gamma^2 Y_0^2 \rho^4 (1-\rho^T)^2}{T(1-\rho)^4\theta}.$$

$$\square$$

2.4. *Permanent market impact: Adapted vs deterministic solution*

We will now quantify the difference between the two strategies obtained above. First, we define the difference.

Definition 2.1 (Absolute difference). *The absolute difference between the deterministic and the adapted optimal expected cost at time 0 is*

$$\epsilon_{abs} := C_{det}^*(X_0, S_0) - C_{ad}^*(X_0, S_0).$$

Proposition 2.1 (Value of the absolute difference). *The value of the absolute difference is*

$$\epsilon_{abs} = \left(\sum_{k=2}^{T-1} b_k \right) \sigma_Y^2. \tag{12}$$

Proof. For a detailed proof, please refer to the full paper [8]. $\square$

Corollary 2.2. *The two strategies have the same expected cost when the information process is not random ($\sigma_Y = 0$).*

Corollary 2.3. *As expected, the adapted strategy is always better than the deterministic one.*

Definition 2.2 (Relative difference). *The relative difference between the deterministic and the adapted optimal expected cost at time 0 is*

$$\epsilon_{rel} := \frac{\epsilon_{abs}}{C_{det}^*(X_0, S_0)}.$$

We now quantify the difference between the deterministic and the adapted strategies through a few numerical examples. The amount of shares to execute X is set at 10^6, big enough to have an impact on the market. The initial price of the stock is $S_0 = \$100$, making it intuitive to take the percentage volatility. The number of periods is $T = 14$ so that there is around one execution every 30 minutes over a trading day for example. The market impact $\theta = 10^{-5}$ is chosen to increase the expected price by a total of 10% over the execution, as done in Bertsimas and Lo [6]:

$$X(S_0 + \theta X) = 1.1 S_0 X.$$

The percentage standard deviation of the price over a time period $\sigma = 0.51\%$ is chosen such that the annual volatility is around 30%, or equivalently the daily volatility is around 1.89%:

$$\sigma \sqrt{14} = 1.89\%.$$

The information process is positively auto-correlated $\rho = 0.5$. Its importance $\gamma = 1$ is chosen arbitrarily. Its volatility $\sigma_Y = 0.44$ is chosen such that the standard deviation of the information component is of the same order as that of the stock price:

$$\sqrt{\mathbb{E}[(\gamma Y_t)^2]} \simeq \frac{\gamma \sigma_Y}{\sqrt{1 - \rho^2}} = 0.51 \quad \text{for t large enough.}$$

By default we assume that there is no initial information $Y_0 = 0$.

The values described above are summarized in Table 1.

Table 1.   Benchmark parameter values

X	10^6
S_0	100
T	14
θ	10^{-5}
σ	0.51%
ρ	0.5
γ	1
σ_Y	0.44
Y_0	0

Remark 2.6. In order to obtain an order of magnitude for the expected cost, note that the best we can do is the cost of an instantaneous execution, which is the cost without market impact, and this would be

$$S_0 X = 10^8.$$

To get an idea of the influence of the initial information on both strategies, we give a few examples of unaffected and affected price paths obtained with different values of Y_0, and their associated strategies in Figures 1, 2 and 3.

The upper plot in Figure 1 represents the evolution of the price throughout the execution. As we can see, the affected price S would be higher than the unaffected price $\tilde{S}$ with both strategies since the market is reacting against a buy order. The lower plot in Figure 1 represents the amount of shares X_t left to be executed throughout the execution. The red curve is the optimal fully adapted strategy. The blue curve is the optimal static or deterministic strategy. Since $Y_0 = 0$, the deterministic strategy is simply a straight line going from the initial value X at time 0 to the final value 0 at time T: the execution is done evenly over the time horizon and this is the well known VWAP strategy. The adapted strategy is roughly the same,

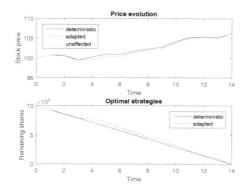

Fig. 1.   One path of a simulated strategy with benchmark parameters $(Y_0 = 0)$

but it is less smooth since the strategy changes according to the path taken by the price during the execution.

With the benchmark parameters, we find that $C^*_{det}(X_0, S_0) = 1.053 \times 10^8$, $C^*_{ad}(X_0, S_0) = 1.0534 \times 10^8$ and $\epsilon_{rel} = 1.97 \times 10^{-4}$. In particular, the costs obtained with the path shown in Figure 1 are $C_{det}(X_0, S_0) = 1.0256 \times 10^8$ and $C_{ad}(X_0, S_0) = 1.0257 \times 10^8$ so the deterministic strategy would have been better than the adapted one in retrospect.

Remark 2.7. The first step is always the same for both strategies since it relies purely on information known at time 0.

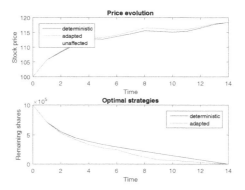

Fig. 2.   One path of a simulated strategy with positive initial information $(Y_0 = 5)$

Since the information process is cumulative and positively auto-correlated, a positive initial information suggests that the information term will be increasing throughout the trade. To minimize the impact of the information, the trade is shifted towards the beginning of the time horizon: we increase the rate at which we buy in a first part. We say that the strategies are "aggressive in the money".

With $Y_0 = 5$, we find that the optimal costs for the static and adapted cases are, respectively, $C^*_{det}(X_0, S_0) = 1.0967 \times 10^8$, $C^*_{ad}(X_0, S_0) = 1.0965 \times 10^8$ and $\epsilon_{rel} = 1.89 \times 10^{-4}$. In particular, the costs obtained in the single path shown in Figure 2 are $C_{det}(X_0, S_0) = 1.1086 \times 10^8$ and $C_{ad}(X_0, S_0) = 1.1082 \times 10^8$.

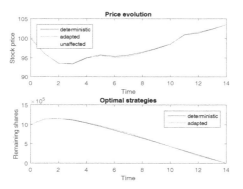

Fig. 3.   One path of a simulated strategy with negative information $Y_0 = -5$.

On the other hand, a negative initial information suggests that the information term will be more and more negative throughout the term, so its impact on the price will be to reduce it more and more. Hence we want to begin buying as late as we can, even selling shares in a first part to maximize the benefits from the price decrease. Indeed, with $Y_0 = -5$, we find that $C^*_{det}(X_0, S_0) = 1.0039 \times 10^8$, $C^*_{ad}(X_0, S_0) = 1.0037 \times 10^8$ and $\epsilon_{rel} = 2.06 \times 10^{-4}$. In particular, the costs obtained in the single path shown in Figure 3 are $C_{det}(X_0, S_0) = 9.8777 \times 10^7$ and $C_{ad}(X_0, S_0) = 9.8758 \times 10^7$. Note that since we begin by selling shares, the effective price goes below the unaffected price at first.

Remark 2.8. In some situations it might be natural to impose a constraint on the sign of ΔV, since one may not wish to sell during a buy order.

Now that we have in mind the path taken by the price and by the strategies for a few examples, we will study the influence of each parameter separately, analyzing in a few numerical examples the impact of the parameters and inputs

$$X, T, \theta, \rho, \gamma, \sigma_Y .$$

In each numerical example, the parameters will be those of Table 1 except for the one whose influence we study. This allows us to study one parameter at a time.

Remark 2.9. Since σ does not appear in the formulas in either case, it has no influence on the optimal expected cost.

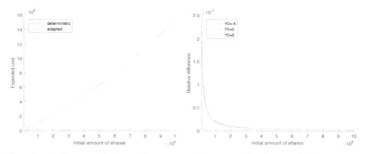

Fig. 4.   Influence of X on the expected costs and relative difference

We begin by studying the influence of X. Figure 4 shows the evolution of the expected costs and the relative difference when X varies from 10^5 to 10^7. The absolute difference does not depend on the amount of shares to execute X, while the expected cost grows with X, so the relative error decreases when X increases. This can be explained by the fact that the market impact parameter θ has been calibrated for a certain X, and its total permanent influence becomes considerable when X is very large. For example, when $X = 10^7$ the permanent impact doubles the price over the execution: the affected price at time T is roughly twice the unaffected price. This is not really representative of the impact of X since θ should be a function of X: the impact we have on the market should not grow linearly with the amount executed, as opposed to our assumption.

We now consider the influence of T. The relative difference between the two strategies increases linearly with the time horizon for T large enough. This stems from the fact that the deterministic strategy is set at time 0, and does not benefit from the information that arrives after, while the adapted strategy will do the best of what is given. Given a full trading week to execute the order, the adapted strategy is almost 0.2% better than the deterministic one.

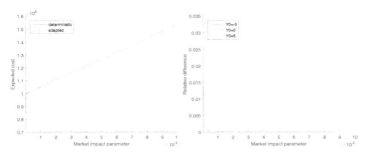

Fig. 5.   Influence of θ on the expected costs and relative difference

We now turn to the influence of θ. As said in the study of the influence of X, when θ increases, the impact we have on the market increases. More and more of the expected cost is unavoidable so it becomes more and more difficult to reduce the expected cost. Hence the relative difference decreases as θ increases. Figure 5 shows the evolution of the expected costs and the relative difference when θ varies from 10^{-8} to 10^{-4}. For a total increase of 1% of the price over the execution ($\theta = 10^{-6}$), the relative difference is 0.21%.

Remark 2.10. It would be interesting to study the joint influence of X and θ, as they depend strongly on each other financially. For example, θ could be taken as a function of X (one could start with a linear function).

We have an interesting pattern on the optimal expected cost when $\theta \downarrow 0$.

Proposition 2.2. *As long as $\sigma_Y \neq 0$, the optimal expected cost tends to $-\infty$ when θ tends to 0. When there is initial information $(Y_0 \neq 0)$, the expected cost associated with the best deterministic strategy tends to $-\infty$ when θ tends to 0.*

To understand the intuition behind this, we will look at a few examples of strategies used for a small value of θ, and initial information. As we can see in Figure 6, the strategies are extremely aggressive when the market impact parameter is small, since we accelerate the execution when the price goes against us. There are strategies related to idealized round trips: due to the cumulative effect of information on the trading price, we quickly buy way more than needed, and sell back later, with a higher information-increased price, until we reach our goal. Without market impact, it seems there is no foreseeable punishment for massively leveraging the information benefit. Note that it is impossible to do this in reality since there is a finite number of shares and this would be prohibited as market manipulation.

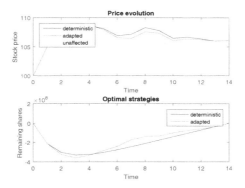

Fig. 6.   One path of a simulated strategy with positive initial information ($Y_0 = 5$) and small market impact ($\theta = 10^{-8}$)

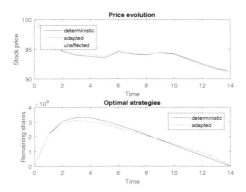

Fig. 7.   One path of a simulated strategy with negative initial information ($Y_0 = -5$) and small market impact ($\theta = 10^{-8}$)

As we can see in Figure 7, when there is negative initial information the strategies are the opposite of the case of positive initial information, since now information will tend to decrease the price cumulatively in time. We sell a lot of shares initially, since we know that the price will go down later due to information, when we will be able to buy back at a much reduced price.

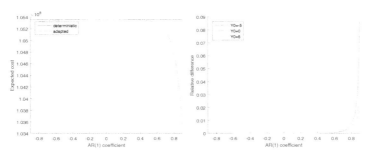

Fig. 8.   Influence of ρ on the expected costs and relative difference

We consider now the influence of ρ. Figure 8 shows the evolution of the expected costs and the relative difference when ρ varies from -0.9 to 0.9. Although there is some noticeable difference in the expected costs for large negative auto-correlations ($\rho < -0.8$), the relative difference is particularly relevant when the information process is strongly positively auto-correlated ($\rho > 0.8$). It then explodes, up to 8.7% when $Y_0 = -5$ and $\rho = 0.9$, but such a huge value does not seem realistic for ρ.

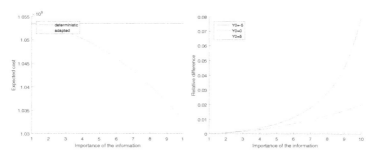

Fig. 9.   Influence of γ on the expected costs and relative difference

As concerns the influence of γ, we have the following results. The relative difference grows with γ, which is intuitive since the more relevant the information is, the more important it is to update our strategy when we receive new information. This seems especially true when the initial information is negative. Figure 9 shows the evolution of the expected costs and the relative difference when γ varies from 1 to 10.

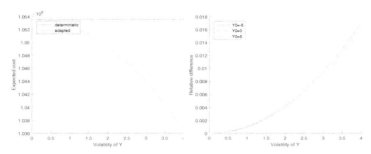

Fig. 10. Influence of σ_Y on the expected costs and relative difference

We finally study the influence of σ_Y. Figure 10 shows the evolution of the expected costs and the relative difference when σ_Y varies from 0 to 4. The volatility of the information process has no influence on the deterministic expected cost, while the adapted expected cost decreases with σ_Y. Hence the relative difference increases with σ_Y.

The solutions derived and their analysis are similar when assuming a temporary market impact. Please refer to the full paper [8].

This concludes our analysis of the discrete time case. We now move to the continuous time case.

3. Continuous time trading with risk function

3.1. *Model formulation with cost and risk based criterion*

In this section we will recall the framework used by Gatheral and Schied [13], with slightly modified notations. Let x_t be the stochastic process for the number of units left to be executed at time t, such that $x_0 = X$ and $x_T = 0$. In the static case x will be a deterministic function of time. We assume $t \mapsto x_t$ to have absolutely continuous paths and to be adapted. The unaffected price $\widetilde{S}$, namely the unaffected price one would observe in the market without our trades, is assumed to follow a geometric Brownian motion (GBM). Hence the unaffected and impacted/affected asset mid-prices are respectively given by

$$d\widetilde{S}_t = \sigma \widetilde{S}_t dW_t, \quad \widetilde{S}_0 = S_0, \tag{13}$$

$$S_t = \widetilde{S}_t + \eta \dot{x}_t + \gamma(x_t - x_0), \tag{14}$$

where the volatility σ, the temporary impact parameter η and the permanent impact parameter γ are positive constants and W is a standard Brownian motion.

The term $\eta \dot{x}_t$ is the temporary impact. As in the discrete time case, it only affects the current execution. The term $\gamma(x_t - x_0)$ is the permanent impact. As in the discrete time case, it has a permanent effect on the price. Indeed, the effect is proportional to the total amount of shares executed up to the current time.

Remark 3.1. Since the unaffected price is a GBM, it can not become negative. This is an improvement compared to the ABM of Bertsimas and Lo. However, we have seen in the examples given by Brigo and Di Graziano [7], where a displaced diffusion is also considered, that this may not make a big difference in practice.

In this setting we will consider a sell order, which means that x_t is the amount of shares left to be sold at time t. At time t, we instantly sell a quantity $-\dot{x}_t dt$ at price S_t. Hence the total execution cost associated with the strategy x_t is

$$C(x) := \int_0^T S_t \dot{x}_t dt = \int_0^T \left[\widetilde{S}_t + \eta \, \dot{x}_t + \gamma(x_t - x_0) \right] \dot{x}_t dt$$

$$= -X S_0 - \int_0^T x_t d\widetilde{S}_t + \eta \int_0^T \dot{x}_t^2 dt + \frac{\gamma}{2} X^2.$$

The problem is to minimize an objective function that consists in both the expected cost and a risk criterion.

The risk term chosen by Gatheral and Schied is

$$\mathbb{E}_0 \left[\widetilde{\lambda} \int_0^T x_t \widehat{S}_t dt \right],$$

where $\widehat{S}_t = \widetilde{S}_t + \gamma x_t$ and the risk aversion parameter $\widetilde{\lambda}$ is a positive constant. We choose to use $\widehat{S}$ instead of $\widetilde{S}$ because we want to take into account the effect of the permanent impact on the mid-price. Gatheral and Schied also consider the simpler case where $\widetilde{S}_t$ enters the risk criterion, instead of $\widehat{S}_t$, see also [7] for the displaced diffusion case.

Remark 3.2. This risk measure can be seen as a Value at Risk (VaR) or an expected shortfall, as shown below.

Proof. Let S_t be a GBM

$$dS_t = \sigma S_t dW_t, \quad S_0.$$

Let $\nu_{\alpha,t,h}$ be the VaR measure computed at time t, for the position, for a given confidence level α over a time horizon h.

$$\mathbb{P}\{x(t)(S_t - S_{t+h}) \leq \nu_{\alpha,t,h} | \mathcal{F}_t\} = \alpha.$$

If at t we have $x(t)$ shares with price S_t, the time t VaR measure for a risk horizon h under DD dynamics at confidence level α would be

$$\begin{aligned}
\nu_t[x(t)(S_t - S_{t+h})] &= x(t)\nu_t[(S_t - S_{t+h})] \\
&= x(t)\nu_t[S_t(1 - \exp(-\sigma^2 h/2 + \sigma(W_{t+h} - W_t)))] \\
&= x(t)S_t q_\alpha[1 - \exp(-\sigma^2 h/2 + \sigma\sqrt{h}\epsilon)] \\
&= x(t)S_t[1 - \exp(-\sigma^2 h/2 + \sigma\sqrt{h}q_{1-\alpha}(\epsilon))] \\
&=: \tilde{\lambda}_\alpha x(t)S_t,
\end{aligned}$$

where ϵ is a standard normal, where we have used the homogeneity of VaR, and where $q_\alpha(X)$ is the α quantile of the distribution of X. This is the VaR measure for the instantaneous position at time t. If we average VaR over the life of the strategy we obtain the risk criterion

$$R^{\mathrm{VaR}_\alpha}(x) := \tilde{\lambda} \int_0^T x(t)(S_t - K)dt.$$

The expected shortfall risk criteria is the same with different λ. □

The objective function to minimize is then

$$\mathbb{E}_0[C(x)] + \tilde{\lambda}\mathbb{E}_0\left[\int_0^T x_t \hat{S}_t dt\right] = -S_0 X + \frac{\gamma}{2}X^2 +$$
$$\mathbb{E}_0\left[\eta \int_0^T \dot{x}_t^2 dt - \int_0^T x_t d\tilde{S}_t + \tilde{\lambda}\int_0^T x_t \hat{S}_t dt\right]. \tag{15}$$

We can simplify the problem easily by taking out the constants. Setting $\lambda = \tilde{\lambda}/\eta$, we now consider the problem

$$\min_x \mathbb{E}_0\left[\int_0^T (\dot{x}_t^2 + \lambda x_t \hat{S}_t)dt\right]. \tag{16}$$

3.2. *Optimal adapted solution under temporary and permanent impact*

We will briefly recall the general (adapted) solutions of problem (16) since they have already been obtained by Gatheral and Schied [13], Theorem 3.2, page 9. Let $\kappa := \sqrt{\lambda\gamma}$.

Theorem 3.1 (Optimal execution strategy). *The unique optimal strategy is*

$$x_t^* = \sinh(\kappa(T-t))\left(\frac{X}{\sinh(\kappa T)} - \frac{\lambda}{2\kappa}\int_0^t \frac{\widetilde{S}_s}{1+\cosh(\kappa(T-s))}ds\right). \quad (17)$$

Theorem 3.2 (Value of the minimization problem). *The value of the minimization problem is*

$$\mathbb{E}_0\left[\int_0^T ((\dot{x}_t^*)^2 + \lambda x_t^* \hat{S}_t^*)dt\right] = \kappa X^2 \coth(\kappa T) + \frac{\lambda X S_0}{\kappa}\tanh\left(\frac{\kappa T}{2}\right)$$
$$-\frac{\lambda^2 S_0^2 e^{\sigma^2 T}}{4\kappa^2}\int_0^T \tanh^2\left(\frac{\kappa t}{2}\right)e^{-\sigma^2 t}dt. \quad (18)$$

3.3. *Optimal static solution under temporary and permanent impact*

We will now solve problem (16) restricted to the set of deterministic strategies.

Theorem 3.3 (Optimal deterministic execution strategy). *The optimal deterministic strategy is*

$$x_t^* = \frac{\sinh(\kappa(T-t))}{\sinh(\kappa T)}X + \frac{\sinh(\kappa(T-t)) + \sinh(\kappa t) - \sinh(\kappa T)}{\sinh(\kappa T)}\frac{S_0}{2\gamma}. \quad (19)$$

Proof. To solve problem (16), we will assume that the strategy x is fully known at time 0. The function we want to minimize is

$$\mathbb{E}_0\left[\int_0^T (\dot{x}_t^2 + \lambda x_t \hat{S}_t)dt\right] = \int_0^T (\dot{x}_t^2 + \lambda x_t \mathbb{E}_0[\hat{S}_t])dt \quad \text{since } x_t \text{ is deterministic}$$
$$= \int_0^T (\dot{x}_t^2 + \lambda x_t (S_0 + \gamma x_t))dt.$$

To find the optimal strategy x^* that minimizes this function, we consider the standard perturbations of the processes x and $\dot{x}$ (see for example [11]):

$$x_t^\epsilon = x(t) + \epsilon h_t,$$
$$\dot{x}_t^\epsilon = \dot{x}_t + \epsilon \dot{h}_t,$$

where the perturbation process h is an arbitrary function satisfying $h_0 = h_T = 0$ and ϵ is a constant. Substituting the perturbed path into the previous formula we obtain

$$H(\epsilon) = \int_0^T (\dot{x}_t + \epsilon \dot{h}_t)^2 + \lambda(x_t + \epsilon h_t)(S_0 + \gamma(x_t + \epsilon h_t))\, dt.$$

The first derivative of H with respect to ϵ is

$$H'(\epsilon) = \int_0^T 2\dot{h}_t(\dot{x}_t + \epsilon \dot{h}_t) + \lambda(x_t + \epsilon h_t)(\gamma h_t) + \lambda h_t (S_0 + \gamma(x_t + \epsilon h_t))\, dt.$$

Evaluating the previous expression at $\epsilon = 0$ gives

$$H'(0) = \int_0^T 2\dot{h}_t \dot{x}_t + \lambda x_t \gamma h_t + \lambda h_t (S_0 + \gamma x_t)\, dt$$

$$= 2\left(h_T \dot{x}_T - h_0 \dot{x}_0\right) - \int_0^T 2h_t \ddot{x}_t dt + \int_0^T \lambda h_t (2\gamma x_t + S_0)\, dt$$

$$= \int_0^T h_t \left(-2\ddot{x}_t + 2\lambda\gamma x_t + \lambda S_0\right) dt.$$

The optimal path is obtained by setting $H'(0) = 0$. Since h is an arbitrary function, the following differential equation must be satisfied for all $t \in [0, T]$:

$$\ddot{x}_t - \kappa^2 x_t = \frac{\lambda S_0}{2}, \tag{20}$$

where we set $\kappa := \sqrt{\lambda\gamma}$ as in the adapted case.

Since λ is positive (the rational trader is risk-averse) and γ is positive (the market reacts against our execution), the roots of the characteristic equation are real. Hence the solution of this differential equation is of the form $A\cosh(\kappa t) + B\sinh(\kappa t) + C$ for some constants A, B and C. Substitute in (20):

$$\kappa^2 A \cosh(\kappa t) + \kappa^2 B \sinh(\kappa t)$$
$$-\kappa^2 \left(A\cosh(\kappa t) + B\sinh(\kappa t) + C\right) = \frac{\lambda S_0}{2}, \quad C = -\frac{S_0}{2\gamma}.$$

From the boundary conditions we have:

$$x_0 = A + C = X, \; A = X + \frac{S_0}{2\gamma}$$

and

$$x_T = A \cosh(\kappa T) + B \sinh(\kappa T) + C = 0,$$
$$B = \frac{-X \cosh(\kappa T)}{\sinh(\kappa T)} + \frac{S_0}{2\gamma} \frac{(1 - \cosh(\kappa T))}{\sinh(\kappa T)}.$$

The solution of (20) is

$$x_t^* = (X - C)\cosh(\kappa t) - \frac{(X - C)\cosh(\kappa T) + C}{\sinh(\kappa T)} \sinh(\kappa t) + C$$
$$= (X - C)\left(\frac{\cosh(\kappa t)\sinh(\kappa T) - \cosh(\kappa T)\sinh(\kappa t)}{\sinh(\kappa T)}\right)$$
$$+ C\left(1 - \frac{\sinh(\kappa t)}{\sinh(\kappa T)}\right).$$

$\square$

Remark 3.3. When $\lambda \downarrow 0$ (no risk in criterion), the deterministic strategy tends to a VWAP.

Theorem 3.4. (*Value of the minimization problem with the deterministic strategy*). *The value of the minimization problem in the deterministic framework is*

$$\mathbb{E}_0\left[\int_0^T ((\dot{x}_t^*)^2 + \lambda x_t^* \hat{S}_t^*) dt\right] = \kappa X^2 \coth(\kappa T) + \frac{\kappa S_0}{\gamma}\left(X + \frac{S_0}{2\gamma}\right)\tanh\left(\frac{\kappa T}{2}\right)$$
$$- \frac{\lambda T S_0^2}{4\gamma}.$$

$$(21)$$

Proof. The value of the minimization problem obtained when following the deterministic strategy of equation 19 is

$$\mathbb{E}_0\left[\int_0^T ((\dot{x}_t^*)^2 + \lambda x_t^* \hat{S}_t^*)dt\right]$$

$$= \int_0^T \left(\frac{-\kappa\cosh(\kappa(T-t))}{\sinh(\kappa T)}X + \frac{\kappa\cosh(\kappa t) - \kappa\cosh(\kappa(T-t))}{\sinh(\kappa T)}\frac{S_0}{2\gamma}\right)^2 dt$$

$$+\lambda S_0\int_0^T\left(\frac{\sinh(\kappa(T-t))}{\sinh(\kappa T)}X + \frac{\sinh(\kappa(T-t)) + \sinh(\kappa t) - \sinh(\kappa T)}{\sinh(\kappa T)}\frac{S_0}{2\gamma}\right)dt$$

$$+\kappa^2\int_0^T\left(\frac{\sinh(\kappa(T-t))}{\sinh(\kappa T)}X + \frac{\sinh(\kappa(T-t)) + \sinh(\kappa t) - \sinh(\kappa T)}{\sinh(\kappa T)}\frac{S_0}{2\gamma}\right)^2 dt$$

$$= \kappa^2\int_0^T\left(\frac{\cosh^2(\kappa(T-t))}{\sinh^2(\kappa T)}X^2\right)dt$$

$$+\kappa^2\int_0^T\left(\frac{\cosh^2(\kappa t) + \cosh^2(\kappa(T-t)) - 2\cosh(\kappa t)\cosh(\kappa(T-t))}{\sinh^2(\kappa T)}\frac{S_0^2}{4\gamma^2}\right)dt$$

$$+2\kappa^2\int_0^T\left(\frac{\cosh^2(\kappa(T-t)) - \cosh(\kappa(T-t))\cosh(\kappa t)}{\sinh^2(\kappa T)}\frac{S_0 X}{2\gamma}\right)dt$$

$$+\kappa^2\int_0^T\left(\frac{\sinh(\kappa(T-t))}{\sinh(\kappa T)}\frac{S_0 X}{\gamma} + \frac{\sinh(\kappa(T-t)) + \sinh(\kappa t) - \sinh(\kappa T)}{\sinh(\kappa T)}\frac{S_0^2}{2\gamma^2}\right)dt$$

$$+\kappa^2\int_0^T\left(\frac{\sinh^2(\kappa(T-t))}{\sinh^2(\kappa T)}X^2 + \frac{(\sinh(\kappa(T-t)) + \sinh(\kappa t) - \sinh(\kappa T))^2}{\sinh^2(\kappa T)}\frac{S_0^2}{4\gamma^2}\right)dt$$

$$+\kappa^2\int_0^T\left(2\frac{\sinh(\kappa(T-t))}{\sinh(\kappa T)}\frac{\sinh(\kappa(T-t)) + \sinh(\kappa t) - \sinh(\kappa T)}{\sinh(\kappa T)}\frac{S_0 X}{2\gamma}\right)dt$$

$$= \kappa^2 X^2\int_0^T\frac{\cosh(2\kappa(T-t))}{\sinh^2(\kappa T)}dt$$

$$+\kappa^2\frac{S_0^2}{4\gamma^2}\int_0^T\left(\frac{\cosh(2\kappa t) + \cosh(2\kappa(T-t)) - 2\cosh(\kappa(T-2t))}{\sinh^2(\kappa T)} - 1\right)dt$$

$$+\kappa^2\frac{S_0 X}{\gamma}\int_0^T\frac{\cosh(2\kappa(T-t)) - \cosh(\kappa(T-2t))}{\sinh^2(\kappa T)}dt$$

$$= \kappa^2 X^2\frac{\sinh(2\kappa T)}{2\kappa\sinh^2(\kappa T)} + \kappa^2\frac{S_0^2}{4\gamma^2}\frac{2\sinh(2\kappa T) - 4\sinh(\kappa T)}{2\kappa\sinh^2(\kappa T)} - \kappa^2\frac{S_0^2 T}{4\gamma^2}$$

$$+\kappa^2\frac{S_0 X}{\gamma}\frac{\sinh(2\kappa T) - 2\sinh(\kappa T)}{2\kappa\sinh^2(\kappa T)}$$

$$= \kappa X^2\frac{\cosh(\kappa T)}{\sinh(\kappa T)} + \kappa\frac{S_0^2}{4\gamma^2}\frac{2\cosh(\kappa T) - 2}{\sinh(\kappa T)} - \kappa^2\frac{S_0^2 T}{4\gamma^2} + \kappa\frac{S_0 X}{2\gamma}\frac{2\cosh(\kappa T) - 2}{\sinh(\kappa T)}.$$

$\square$

3.4. *Comparison of optimal static and adapted solutions*

We will now numerically attempt to quantify the differences in the minimum objective function obtained by the deterministic and by the adapted strategies.

Since we operated a linear transformation from (15) to (16), we will multiply the value of the minimization problems (18) and (21) by η and add back the term $-S_0 X + \frac{\gamma}{2} X^2$ to obtain the value of the objective functions along the optimal solution. We will denote them respectively J^*_{ad} for the fully adapted case and J^*_{det} for the deterministic/static case.

Corollary 3.1 (Minimum of the objective function). *The minimum value of the objective function is*

$$J^*_{ad}(X_0, S_0) = -S_0 X + \frac{\gamma}{2} X^2 + \eta \left(\kappa X^2 \coth(\kappa T) + \frac{\lambda X S_0}{\kappa} \tanh\left(\frac{\kappa T}{2}\right) \right.$$
$$\left. - \frac{\lambda^2 S_0^2 e^{\sigma^2 T}}{4\kappa^2} \int_0^T \tanh^2\left(\frac{\kappa t}{2}\right) e^{-\sigma^2 t} dt \right),$$

and the value of the objective function obtained when using the optimal deterministic strategy is

$$J^*_{det}(X_0, S_0) = -S_0 X + \frac{\gamma}{2} X^2 +$$
$$\eta \left(\kappa X^2 \coth(\kappa T) + \frac{\kappa S_0}{\gamma} \left(X + \frac{S_0}{2\gamma} \right) \tanh\left(\frac{\kappa T}{2}\right) - \frac{\lambda T S_0^2}{4\gamma} \right).$$

Similarly to the cases with no risk criterion, we define the absolute and relative differences.

Definition 3.1 (Absolute difference).

$$\epsilon_{abs} := J^*_{det}(X_0, S_0) - J^*_{ad}(X_0, S_0)$$
$$= \eta \left(\frac{\kappa S_0^2}{2\gamma^2} \tanh\left(\frac{\kappa T}{2}\right) - \frac{\lambda T S_0^2}{4\gamma} + \frac{\lambda^2 S_0^2 e^{\sigma^2 T}}{4\kappa^2} \int_0^T \tanh^2\left(\frac{\kappa t}{2}\right) e^{-\sigma^2 t} dt \right).$$

Proposition 3.1. *Both strategies have the same expected cost when there is no randomness. Hence deciding the strategy entirely before the execution is equivalent to assuming that there is no randomness in the price movements, as in the discrete setting studied in the previous section.*

Proof. For a detailed proof, please refer to the full paper [8].   □

Proposition 3.2 (Sign of the absolute difference). *As expected, the adapted strategy is always better than the deterministic one, in that it results* *in expected risk-adjusted costs that are smaller or equal to the deterministic ones.*

Proof. For a detailed proof, please refer to the full paper [8]. □

Definition 3.2 (Relative difference).

$$\epsilon_{rel} := \frac{\epsilon_{abs}}{|J_{det}^*(X_0, S_0)|}.$$

For the numerical applications we will consider a single stock with current price $S_0 = 100$, making the use of percentage volatility intuitive. We want to sell $X = 10^6$ shares in $T = 1$ day. The stock has a percentage daily volatility $\sigma = 1.89\%$, as in the discrete-time cases. $\gamma = 2 \times 10^{-6}$ is chosen such that the permanent impact is around 10%, assuming there is no risk aversion. The temporary market impact parameter $\eta = 2 \times 10^{-6}$ is chosen such that the impact of an instantaneous execution is 2\$ per share. The risk aversion factor $\widetilde{\lambda} = 0.05$ is taken so that the risk term in the objective function is of the same order as the market impacts.

The values described above are summarized in Table 2.

Table 2.   Benchmark parameter values

X	10^6
S_0	100
T	1
σ	1.89%
γ	2×10^{-6}
η	2×10^{-6}
$\widetilde{\lambda}$	0.05

Remark 3.4. Since this is a sell order, the expected costs should be negative (assuming the trader has no incentive to sell at a loss).

To get an idea of the influence of the risk aversion factor on the strategies, we give a few examples of paths obtained with different values of $\widetilde{\lambda}$ in Figures 11, 12 and 13. With the benchmark parameters, we find that $J_{det}^* = -9.4736 \times 10^7$, $J_{ad}^* = -9.4736 \times 10^7$ and $\epsilon_{rel} = 2.45 \times 10^{-7}$.

With $\widetilde{\lambda} = 10^{-10}$, we find that $J_{det}^* = -9.7000 \times 10^7$, $J_{ad}^* = -9.7000 \times 10^7$ and $\epsilon_{rel} = 0$. Both strategies are straight lines, which means that they practically follow a VWAP. This is consistent with the fact that with very small λ we are close to not having risk in the criterion, leading to the VWAP solution. With $\widetilde{\lambda} = 10$, we find that $J_{det}^* = -5.0391 \times 10^9$, $J_{ad}^* = -5.0385 \times 10^9$ and $\epsilon_{rel} = 1.14 \times 10^{-4}$.

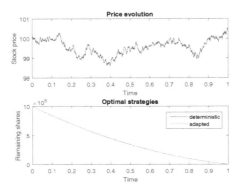

Fig. 11.   One path of a simulated strategy with benchmark parameters ($\widetilde{\lambda} = 0.05$)

Fig. 12.   One path of a simulated strategy with small risk aversion ($\widetilde{\lambda} = 10^{-10}$)

With $\widetilde{\lambda} = 10^3$, we find that $J_{det}^* = -1.1678 \times 10^{12}$, $J_{ad}^* = -1.1680 \times 10^{12}$ and $\epsilon_{rel} = 1.68 \times 10^{-4}$.

The last plots are interesting because they illustrate the fact that when the risk aversion factor is big, as in Figures 13 and 14, we tend to execute everything very fast, even exceeding the amounts we are supposed to execute. At the end of the period we buy back what we need to get back to our objective. The larger the risk factor, the steeper the execution. When λ is very small, the strategies tend to a VWAP. A reasonable value for $\widetilde{\lambda}$ would be something in-between, as in the slightly curved line of Figure 11. Note however that the risk aversion factor is completely arbitrary, and depends only on the trader so any value of $\widetilde{\lambda}$ is possible.

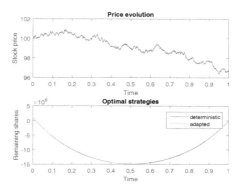

Fig. 13.   One path of a simulated strategy with large risk aversion $(\widetilde{\lambda} = 10)$

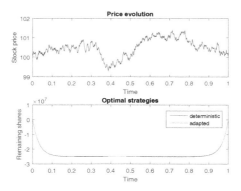

Fig. 14.   One path of a simulated strategy with huge risk aversion $(\widetilde{\lambda} = 10^3)$

To get a more precise idea of the difference between the fully adapted and static optimal strategies, we study the influence of each parameter on the minimized objective functions and their relative difference. In each numerical example, the parameters will be those of Table 2 except for the one whose influence we study. We will consider parameters and inputs

$$X, T, \sigma, \gamma, \eta, \widetilde{\lambda}.$$

Here we only consider the influence of σ and $\widetilde{\lambda}$, as the relative error is smaller for all other parameters, and the plots are similar to those obtained in the setting of Bertsimas and Lo. For a study of every parameter, please refer to the full paper [8].

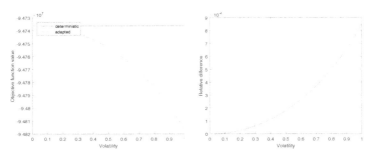

Fig. 15.   Influence of σ on the expected costs and relative difference

As regards the influence of σ, Figure 15 shows the evolution of the expected costs and the relative difference when σ varies from 0 to 100%. When σ increases, the importance of using up to speed price information during the strategy increases, since there is more uncertainty on what the new information will be. The adapted strategy takes incoming price information into account, unlike the deterministic one. Hence the relative difference increases as σ increases. However, even when $\sigma = 1$, which is equivalent to a gigantic annual volatility of 1588%, the relative difference between the two strategies is not even 0.1%. This seems to suggest that with this particular model the optimality does not change much when reducing the strategy class from adapted to deterministic.

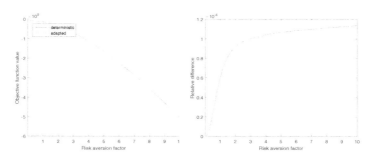

Fig. 16.   Influence of $\widetilde{\lambda}$ on the expected costs and relative difference

Finally, we look at the influence of the risk aversion parameter $\widetilde{\lambda}$. Figure 16 shows the evolution of the expected costs and the relative difference when $\widetilde{\lambda}$ varies from 10^{-5} to 10. The relative difference increases logarithmically with the risk aversion factor. When $\widetilde{\lambda} = 10$, which is big as we have seen in Figure 13, the relative difference is 1.1×10^{-4}.

4. Conclusions and further research

We derived the optimal solutions to the trade execution problem in the two different classes of fully adapted trading strategies and deterministic ones, trying to assess how much optimality was lost when moving from the larger adapted class to the narrow static class. We did this in two different frameworks. The first was the discrete time framework of Bertsimas and Lo with an information flow process, dealing with both cases of permanent and temporary impact. The second framework was the continuous time framework of Gatheral and Schied, where the objective function is the sum of the expected cost and a value at risk (or expected shortfall) risk criterion. Optimal adapted solutions were known in both frameworks from the original works of these authors, [6] and [13]. We derived the optimal static solutions for both approaches. We used those to study quantitatively the advantage gained by adapting our strategy instead of setting it entirely at time 0. Our conclusion is that in our numerical examples there seems to be no sensible difference, except for extreme cases that do not seem realistic. This seems to point in the following direction. As long as we use simple models such as the benchmark models proposed here under reasonable parameters, it does not seem to make much difference to search the solution in the larger adapted class, compared with the narrow static / deterministic class. This indirectly points in the direction where in the similar framework of Almgren and Chriss [2] one may be fine starting from a static solution, which happens to be more tractable, as is indeed done in that paper. While at the moment we can claim a negligible difference only for the numerical examples and the benchmark models we presented, we should investigate the claim more generally in further work.

In terms of further research, we might consider more recent models incorporating jumps, as in [1], or considering daily cycles as in [3]. It may happen that in those cases the difference between the optimal fully adapted solution and the static one is more sizable.

References

1. A. Alfonsi and P. Blanc, Dynamic optimal execution in a mixed-market-impact Hawkes price model. (2014), Available at https://hal-enpc.archives-ouvertes.fr/hal-00971369v2
2. Almgren, R., and Chriss, N., Optimal execution of portfolio transactions. *J. Risk* **3**:5–39.
3. Almgren, R., and Lorenz, J. (2006). Bayesian adaptive trading with a daily cycle. *The Journal of Trading* 1(4):38–46.

4. Almgren, R., and Lorenz, J. (2011). Mean-Variance Optimal Adaptive Execution. *Applied Mathematical Finance* **18**(5):395–422.
5. Almgren, R. (2012). Optimal trading with stochastic liquidity and volatility. SIAM Journal on Financial Mathematics, 3:163-181.
6. Bertsimas, D., and Lo, A.W. (1998). Optimal control of execution costs. Journal of Financial Markets 1:1–50.
7. Brigo, D. and Di Graziano, G. (2014). Optimal trade execution under displaced diffusions dynamics across different risk criteria. Journal of Financial Engineering, 1(2):1–17.
8. Brigo, D., and Piat, C. (2016). Static vs adapted optimal execution strategies in two benchmark trading models. Available at https://arxiv.org/pdf/1609.05523.pdf
9. Bonart, J., Brigo, D., and Di Graziano, G. (2014). Optimal execution strategies across models. Draft research paper, Imperial College London, unpublished.
10. Busseti, E., and Boyd, S. (2015). Volume Weighted Average Price Optimal Execution. Available at https://arxiv.org/pdf/1509.08503.pdf.
11. Di Graziano, G. (2014). Lecture Notes on Algorithmic Trading and Machine Learning, MSc in Mathematics and Finance, Dept. of Mathematics, Imperial College London.
12. Forsyth, P., Kennedy, J.S., Tse, S.T., Windcliff, H. (2011). Optimal Trade Execution: A Mean-Quadratic-Variation Approach. Available at https://cs.uwaterloo.ca/~paforsyt/quad_trade.pdf
13. Gatheral, J., and Schied, A. (2011). Optimal Trade Execution under Geometric Brownian Motion in the Almgren and Chriss Framework. International Journal of Theoretical and Applied Finance, 14(3): 353–368.
14. Ieda, M. (2015). A dynamic optimal execution strategy under stochastic price recovery. Available at https://arxiv.org/abs/1502.04521v1
15. Kato, T. (2014). An Optimal Execution Problem with a Geometric OrnsteinUhlenbeck Price Process. Available at http://arxiv.org/abs/1107.1787v4.
16. Kulak, J.B. (2015). Optimal Execution Problem: Influence of Information and Active Trading Strategies. MSc dissertation for the degree in Mathematics and Finance under the supervision of D. Brigo, Imperial College London.
17. Lorenz, J. (2008). Optimal Trading Algorithms: Portfolio Transactions, Multiperiod Portfolio Selection, and Competitive Online Search. Ph.D. thesis for the degree of Doctor of Sciences under the supervision of A. Steger, ETH Zürich.

18. Obizhaeva, A. and Wang, J. (2006). Optimal trading strategy and supply/demand dynamics, Journal of Financial Markets 16(1):1–32.
19. Shen, J. and Yu, Y. (2014). Styled Algorithmic Trading and the MV-MVP Style. Available at http://ssrn.com/abstract=2507002.

Chapter 11

Liability Driven Investments with a Link to Behavioral Finance

Ludwig Brummer, Markus Wahl and Rudi Zagst*

*Chair of Mathematical Finance, Technical University of Munich,
Parkring 11, 85748 Garching, Germany*
*zagst@tum.de

Liability driven investment (LDI) strategies that take stochastic liabilities into account have become increasingly important for insurance companies and pension funds due to market developments such as low interest rates, high volatility and changes in regulatory requirements. We consider stochastic liabilities in a portfolio optimization framework and include aspects from behavioral finance, in particular cumulative prospect theory (CPT). We study LDI strategies with extended preference structures and probability distortion and derive analytical solutions for a CPT portfolio optimization problem in an LDI context. Within a case study, we compare the optimal investment strategies to existing LDI approaches within traditional frameworks such as the partial surplus optimization presented in [1] and the funding ratio optimization in an expected utility framework as introduced in [2].

Keywords: asset liability management, liability driven investments, cumulative prospect theory.

1. Introduction

In the literature on intertemporal portfolio choice, the optimization of the utility of terminal wealth and consumption as firstly presented in [3] is a widely accepted standard. However, according to regulatory standards, insurance companies and pension funds, e.g., have to consider the level of wealth relative to the value of the liabilities. Consequently, liabilities were included in several different ways into portfolio optimization frameworks in discrete and continuous time. In [1], the authors provide an extension of the mean-variance approach for a one-period setting. The authors of [4] extend the mean-variance framework by considering the downside risk inherent in the liabilities in form of an exchange option and [5] provide a continuous-time version of the surplus management approach from [1]. In a continuous-time model, [6], [7] and [8] consider generalizations of CPPI strategies with a stochastic floor that can be interpreted as stochastic liabilities. In [2], the author argues that what matters is the relative wealth of the asset portfolio with respect to the value of the liabilities and optimizes the terminal wealth of the funding ratio. He develops optimal strategies for a model in which both, the assets and the liabilities, are modeled as geometric Brownian motions. With the recent international accounting standards IFRS (especially IAS 19) for pension funds and the European regulatory requirements Solvency II for insurance companies, the importance of investment strategies that are adapted to stochastic liabilities, has increased. However, this short overview illustrates that no widely accepted scientific standard exists how liabilities should be included in the portfolio optimization.

For the market model from [2], we generalize previous results by embedding funding ratio optimization in a cumulative prospect theory (CPT) framework. The CPT framework provides two further enrichments. Firstly, a probability distortion is included. Within the CPT framework, distortions are used to create subjective probabilities of events. However, distortions can also be used to model heavy-tailed portfolio returns. Secondly, the utility function is extended and assumes risk-seeking behavior in case of underfunding. This extension also contributes to the literature that especially considers underfunded plans, e.g. [9] deal with underfunded plans in a discrete setting.

The article is structured as follows: In Section 2, we introduce the model for assets and liabilities. Optimal investment strategies for the funding ratio are described in Section 3 for an expected utility framework. In Section 4, we consider the optimization of the funding ratio within cumulative prospect theory. This approach is compared to the approach from Section 3 and an application of the approach described in [1] in Section 5. A conclusion is provided in Section 6.

2. A model for assets and liabilities

We introduce a market model on a filtered probability space $(\Omega, \mathcal{A}, \mathbb{P}, \mathcal{F})$ with $\mathcal{F} = \{\mathcal{F}_t; t \geq 0\}$ being the filtration generated by the n-dimensional standard Brownian motion $\tilde{W} := (W^1, \cdots, W^n)'$, satisfying the usual conditions. Following [2], we use $W := (W^1, \cdots, W^{n-1})'$ to model the assets and $W^\epsilon := W^n$ to model the part of the liability risk that cannot be hedged. That means we have $n - 1$ risky assets with price processes $P = (P^1, ... P^{n-1})'$ and one risk-free asset with price process P^0. The assets are assumed to follow a geometric Brownian motion with

$$dP_t^i = P_t^i \left(\mu_i dt + \sigma_i dW_t \right), \; i \in \{1, 2, ..., n-1\},$$

$P_0^i = 1$, $i \in \{1, 2, ..., n-1\}$ and $dP_t^0 = P_t^0 r dt$, $P_0^0 = 1$. The volatility matrix σ with rows σ_i, $i \in \{1, ..., n-1\}$ is assumed to be positive definite. With $\mathbf{1} = (1, 1, ...1)' \in \mathbb{R}^{n-1}$, the market price of risk is then given by

$$\theta := \sigma^{-1}(\mu - r\mathbf{1}).$$

We consider $\mathcal{F}_t$-progressively-measurable, self-financing investment strategies $(\varphi_t^0, \varphi_t)_{t \in [0,T]}$ with $\varphi_t = (\varphi_t^1, ..., \varphi_t^{n-1})'$, φ_t^i being the fraction of wealth invested in asset i at time t satisfying

$$\int_0^T (A_t^\varphi)^2 \|\varphi_t\|^2 dt < \infty \ \mathbb{P} - a.s.,$$

and A_t^φ denoting the wealth process associated with $(\varphi_t^0, \varphi_t)_{t \in [0,T]}$. Its dynamics are given by

$$dA_t^\varphi = A_t^\varphi \left[(r + \varphi_t'(\mu - r\mathbf{1})) dt + \varphi_t' \sigma dW_t \right].$$

The initial wealth A_0 is assumed to be non-negative. By $\Lambda(t, v)$, we denote the set of all admissible investment strategies on $[t, T]$ with $A_t^\varphi = v$ and such that $\mathbb{E}[U(A_T^\varphi)|\mathcal{F}_t]$ is well-defined. Furthermore, let $\Lambda := \Lambda(0, v)$. The performance seeking portfolio (growth optimal portfolio) is known from portfolio optimization without liabilities and logarithmic utility and is defined as

$$\varphi^{PS} := (\sigma\sigma')^{-1}(\mu - r\mathbf{1}). \tag{1}$$

As in [10] and [2], we model the liability process L^ϵ as a geometric Brownian motion following the dynamics

$$dL_t^\epsilon = L_t^\epsilon \left(\mu_L dt + \sigma_L dW_t + \sigma_\epsilon dW_t^\epsilon \right), \ L_0 = 1,$$

with drift μ_L, hedgeable risks related to W and non-hedgeable risks related to W^ϵ, independent of W. In the context of an insurance company or pension fund, the non-hedgeable risks could be, e.g., actuarial risks like longevity risk or underwriting risk. If we have $\sigma_\epsilon = 0$, all the liability risks emerge from W and the liabilities can be hedged. The liability hedging portfolio as introduced in [2] is then given by

$$\varphi^{LH} := (\sigma')^{-1}\sigma_L'. \tag{2}$$

In Section 3, we assume $\sigma_\epsilon \geq 0$ to show that in the expected utility framework, the optimal strategy is independent of the non-hedgeable risks. This observation provides the reasoning for the assumption $\sigma_\epsilon = 0$ which we need in Section 4. Instead of considering the absolute wealth A_t^φ, we consider the funding ratio defined as the relative wealth with respect to the value of the liabilities

$$X_t^\varphi := \frac{A_t^\varphi}{L_t^\epsilon}, \ t \in [0, T]$$

for a corresponding portfolio process φ. By an application of Ito's formula, we get the mean return and volatility of the funding ratio

$$\mu_X^\varphi(t) = r + \varphi_t'(\mu - r\mathbf{1}) - \mu_L + \sigma_L \sigma_L' + \sigma_\epsilon^2 - \sigma_L \sigma' \varphi_t,$$

$$\sigma_X^\varphi(t) = \left((\varphi_t'\sigma - \sigma_L)(\varphi_t'\sigma - \sigma_L)' + \sigma_\epsilon^2 \right)^{\frac{1}{2}}.$$

We define a one-dimensional Brownian Motion $\bar{W}_t$, such that

$$\sigma_X^\varphi(t)\bar{W}_t = (\varphi_t'\sigma - \sigma_L) W_t - \sigma_\epsilon W_t^\epsilon.$$

The funding ratio thus follows the SDE

$$dX_t^\varphi = X_t^\varphi \left[\mu_X^\varphi(t)dt + \sigma_X^\varphi(t)d\bar{W}_t \right], \quad t \in [0, T]$$

or equivalently

$$dX_t^\varphi = X_t^\varphi \left[\mu_X^\varphi(t)dt + (\varphi_t'\sigma - \sigma_L) dW_t - \sigma_\epsilon dW_t^\epsilon \right] \quad t \in [0, T].$$

It is visible in this representation that the liability hedging portfolio φ^{LH} is the portfolio that hedges the liabilities best in the sense that the volatility of the funding ratio is minimized. Let $\sigma_\epsilon = 0$ for the rest of the section and $L = L^0$ denote the corresponding liability process. Then, there exists a unique risk-neutral measure $\mathbb{Q}$ equivalent to $\mathbb{P}$, defined by the Radon-Nikodym derivative (see e.g. [11], Chapter 5)

$$\frac{d\mathbb{Q}}{d\mathbb{P}}|\mathcal{F}_t = \exp(-\frac{1}{2}\theta'\theta t - \theta'W_t)$$

and $\frac{A_t^\varphi}{P_t^0}$ is a $\mathbb{Q}$-martingale. The Pricing Kernel is then given by

$$\tilde{Z}_t := (P_t^0)^{-1}\frac{d\mathbb{Q}}{d\mathbb{P}}|\mathcal{F}_t = \exp\left(-rt - \theta'W_t - \frac{1}{2}\theta'\theta t \right).$$

We change the numéraire from the risk-free asset to the liability process L. To do this, let $\mathbb{Q}^L$ be the risk-neutral measure under the numéraire L. Then, $X_t^\varphi = \frac{A_t^\varphi}{L_t}$ is a $\mathbb{Q}^L$-martingale and the new pricing kernel is given by

$$Z_t^L := \frac{d\mathbb{Q}}{d\mathbb{P}}\frac{d\mathbb{Q}^L}{d\mathbb{Q}}|\mathcal{F}_t = \frac{L_t}{L_0 P_t^0}\frac{d\mathbb{Q}}{d\mathbb{P}}|\mathcal{F}_t = \exp\left(-\frac{1}{2}\|\sigma_L - \theta'\|^2 t + (\sigma_L - \theta')W_t \right).$$

$$(3)$$

Since we only work with this pricing kernel, we set $Z_t := Z_t^L$ and $Z := Z_T^L$. The distribution function of Z is given by

$$F_Z(z) = \mathcal{N}\left(\frac{\ln z + \frac{1}{2}\|\sigma_L' - \theta\|^2 T}{\|\sigma_L' - \theta\|\sqrt{T}}\right) \tag{4}$$

and its quantile function by

$$F_Z^{\leftarrow}(p) = \exp\left(-\frac{1}{2}\|\sigma_L - \theta'\|^2 T + \|\sigma_L - \theta'\|\sqrt{T}\mathcal{N}^{\leftarrow}(p)\right),$$

with $\mathcal{N}$ and $\mathcal{N}^{\leftarrow}$ denoting the distribution function and the quantile of the standard normal distribution.

3. Expected utility framework

3.1. *The optimization problem*

In this section, we go back to the case of possible non-hedgeable risks, so we assume $\sigma_\epsilon \geq 0$ and find an investment strategy φ that solves the optimization problem

$$\sup_{\varphi \in \Lambda} \mathbb{E}\left[U\left(X_T^\varphi\right)\right]$$

for a strictly increasing, strictly concave and twice continuously differentiable utility function satisfying

$$\lim_{x \downarrow 0} U'(x) = \infty, \quad \lim_{x \to \infty} U'(x) = 0,$$

where we will mainly use the power utility function of the form

$$U(x) = \frac{x^\gamma}{\gamma}, \quad \gamma \in (-\infty, 0) \cup (0, 1).$$

The value function is defined as

$$\Phi(t, v) := \sup_{\varphi \in \Lambda(t,v)} \mathbb{E}[U(X_T^\varphi)|F_t]. \tag{5}$$

The following result, which can be found in [2], states an optimal investment strategy for the introduced funding ratio optimization problem.

Theorem 3.1 (Three-Fund Separation, Expected Utility Theory).
The optimal investment strategy φ^* is given by

$$\varphi^*(t, X_t^\varphi) = \left(1 - \lambda^{EU}(t, X_t^\varphi)\right)\varphi^{LH} + \lambda^{EU}(t, X_t^\varphi)\varphi^{PS}$$

with $\lambda^{EU}(t, X_t^\varphi)$ being the inverse of the Arrow-Pratt measure of relative risk aversion (relative risk tolerance) of $\Phi(t, X_t^\varphi)$

$$\lambda^{EU}(t, X_t^\varphi) := -\frac{\frac{\partial}{\partial X_t^\varphi}\Phi(t, X_t^\varphi)}{X_t^\varphi \frac{\partial^2}{\partial^2 X_t^\varphi}\Phi(t, X_t^\varphi)},$$

the liability hedging portfolio as in (2) and the performance seeking portfolio from (1). The remaining fraction of wealth $1 - \varphi^*(t, X_t^\varphi)'\mathbf{1}$ is invested in the risk-free asset.

Proof. The Hamilton-Jacobi-Bellman (HJB) equation associated with (5) can be written as:

$$\frac{\partial}{\partial t}\Phi(t, v) + \sup_{\varphi \in \Lambda(t, v)}\left[\mu_X^\varphi(t)v\frac{\partial}{\partial v}\Phi(t, v) + \frac{1}{2}(\sigma_X^\varphi(t))^2 v^2 \frac{\partial^2}{\partial^2 v}\Phi(t, v)\right] = 0,$$

with terminal condition $\Phi(T, v) = U(v)$, $v \in (0, \infty)$. If there exists a solution to the HJB equation, the optimal strategy can be obtained by calculating the supremum in the HJB equation. For general $\Phi(t, v)$, we obtain the optimal strategy by maximizing the help function

$$M(c) := \mu_X^c(t) \cdot v \cdot \frac{\partial}{\partial v}\Phi(t, v) + \frac{1}{2} \cdot (\sigma_X^c(t))^2 \cdot v^2 \cdot \frac{\partial^2}{\partial^2 v}\Phi(t, v).$$

The first order condition reads

$$((\mu - r\mathbf{1}) - \sigma\sigma_L')\,v\frac{\partial}{\partial v}\Phi(t, v) + (\sigma\sigma'c - \sigma\sigma_L')v^2\frac{\partial^2}{\partial v^2}\Phi(t, v) = 0$$

and holds for

$$c^* = (1 - \lambda^{EU}(t, v))(\sigma')^{-1}\sigma_L + \lambda^{EU}(t, v)(\sigma')^{-1}\theta$$

and thus, the optimal investment strategy is given by

$$\varphi^*(t, X_t^\varphi) = \left(1 - \lambda^{EU}(t, X_t^\varphi)\right)\varphi^{LH} + \lambda^{EU}(t, X_t^\varphi)\varphi^{PS}.$$

$\square$

As in [2], we get a three-fund separation theorem, with the funds being the performance seeking portfolio, liability hedging portfolio and risk-free asset.

Corollary 3.1 (Three-Fund Separation, Power Utility). *For the power utility, we get*

$$\lambda^{EU}(t, X_t^{\varphi}) = \frac{1}{1 - \gamma}.$$

Proof. The statement directly follows with Theorem 3.1 and Appendix A. □

We see that the optimal strategy does not depend on the non-hedgeable risks associated with σ_{ϵ} for the power utility. To cover these risks, an additional capital buffer has to be used. Therefore, we assume in the following that a certain part of the wealth is used for this purpose and we only deal with the hedgeable risks here, i.e. $\sigma_{\epsilon} = 0$ in the following section.

4. Extension to cumulative prospect theory

4.1. *The optimization problem*

The funding ratio optimization can be extended further to Cumulative Prospect Theory (CPT) using the quantile optimization approach by [12]. As it requires a complete market, we set $\sigma_{\epsilon} = 0$ in this section.

Cumulative Prospect Theory is an extension of traditional Expected Utility Theory introduced in [13] and [14]. Its key innovations are a separate treatment of gains and losses with respect to utility and the introduction of a probability distortion function.

Experiments presented in [13] show that people are risk averse with respect to gains and risk friendly when confronted with losses where gains and losses are separated by a reference point. Hence, in case of losses, a convex utility function is used which implies a risk-seeking behavior of the investor. For a pension plan, this could be the case when it is underfunded and aims to eliminate the deficit. In this currently serious situation, the company might be willing to take more risk than in a situation in which the plan is overfunded and the company does not want to put the good funding status at risk.

The probability distortion has two possible interpretations. The first interpretation is the one normally seen for probability distortion functions in a CPT framework. Here, the probability distortion functions are used to model the observation that people overestimate small probabilities and underestimate bigger probabilities. Thus probability distortion functions model an investor-specific, irrational bias. Alternatively, the probability distortion function can also be seen as a property of the asset portfolio rather than the investor. By distorting the probabilities, heavy tails in the distribution of asset returns that are not modeled in a Black-Scholes market can be included and the distortion parameters can thus be fitted using market data. Technical conditions preclude the use of the classical probability distortion functions in this context from [14] and [15]. The authors of [12] introduce their own probability distortion function, however, this distortion function has a large amount of parameters. To simplify the fitting of the parameters and their interpretation, we present an extension of the distortion function introduced in [16] that still allows us to use the quantile optimization approach introduced in [12]. It is reverse-S shaped and has only two parameters. We begin by introducing the optimization approach following [12].

Wealth is considered relative to a *reference point B*, which we assume to be constant in our application. A *CPT utility function* $U : \mathbb{R} \to \mathbb{R}$ is defined by

$$U(x) := U_+((x - B)^+)\mathbf{1}_{x \geq B}(x) - U_-((x - B)^-)\mathbf{1}_{x < B}(x)$$

where

$$(x)^+ = \max\{x, 0\}, (x)^- = -\min\{x, 0\}.$$

and $U_+, U_- : \mathbb{R}_0^+ \to \mathbb{R}_0^+$ are utility functions as in the previously presented expected utility framework with $U_+(0) = U_-(0) = 0$ and $\forall x \in \mathbb{R}^+ :$ $U_-'(x) > U_+'(x)$. The *probability distortion functions* w_+, w_- are required to be twice differentiable, strictly increasing and satisfy:

$$w_\pm : [0, 1] \to [0, 1], \quad w_\pm(0) = 0, \quad w_\pm(1) = 1, \quad w_\pm' > 0.$$

We set $X := X_T^\varphi$. The reference point will be set in such a way that it marks the point where the pension plan is considered to be adequately funded. A natural reference point when optimizing the funding ratio is where the plan is fully funded, i.e. for $B = 1$. We optimize the funding ratio by performing a change of numéraire from the risk-free asset P_T^0 to L_T. Thus we will use the pricing kernel from (3).

To be able to apply the approach from [12], we need to assume that the following *monotonicity condition* holds:

$$\frac{F_Z^\leftarrow(y)}{w_+'(y)} \text{ is non-decreasing for } y \in (0, 1]. \tag{M}$$

In Section 4.2, we introduce and work with a distortion that fulfills (**M**). This is shown explicitly in Lemma 4.1. Using the defined CPT-utility functions and the probability distortion functions, the two value functions for gains and losses are given by

$$\mathbb{V}_+(\bar{X}) := \mathbb{E}\left[U_+(\bar{X})w'_+(1 - F_{\bar{X}}(\bar{X}))\right] = \int_0^\infty w_+(\mathbb{P}(U_+(\bar{X}) > x))dx$$

$$\text{and } \mathbb{V}_-(\bar{X}) := \mathbb{E}\left[U_-(\bar{X})w'_-(1 - F_{\bar{X}}(\bar{X}))\right] = \int_0^\infty w_-(\mathbb{P}(U_-(\bar{X}) > y))dx,$$

where $\bar{X} := X - B$ and $F_{\bar{X}}$ denotes the distribution function of $\bar{X}$. Fitting them together, we define the value function $\mathbb{V}$ as

$$\mathbb{V}(\bar{X}) := \mathbb{V}_+((\bar{X})^+) - \mathbb{V}_-((\bar{X})^-).$$

The optimization problem is then given by:

$$\sup_{\bar{X}} \mathbb{V}(\bar{X})$$

$$s.t. \ \mathbb{E}[Z\bar{X}] = \frac{A_0}{L_0} - B \tag{OP}$$

$$\bar{X} \text{ is } \mathcal{F}_T\text{-measurable and lower-bounded.}$$

To find an optimal solution for (**OP**), we separate (**OP**) into a Gains Problem and a Loss Problem depending on parameters c and v_+ and then find an optimal combination of those parameters in the so-called Gluing Problem. The optimal solution found by this approach is then equivalent to the optimal solution of the Original Problem, as stated in Theorem 4.1. The details of this optimization approach can be found in Appendix B.

Using this setup, the authors of [12] show a way to solve the optimization problem explicitly in the case of power utility functions. We adapt their results to an optimization of the funding ratio. In this section, we work with power utility functions defined as

$$U_+(x) = x^\gamma, \quad U_-(x) = \beta x^\gamma, \quad \gamma \in (0,1), \quad \beta > 1.$$

We define

$$G(c) := \mathbb{E}\left[Z^{\frac{\gamma}{\gamma-1}}w'_+(F_Z(Z))^{\frac{1}{1-\gamma}}\mathbf{1}_{Z\leq c}\right],$$

$$\text{and } k(c) := \frac{\beta w_-(1 - F_Z(c))}{G(c)^{1-\gamma}\mathbb{E}[Z\mathbf{1}_{Z>c}]^\gamma}.$$

The following result, adapted from [12], provides explicit solutions depending on the initial funding $\frac{A_0}{L_0}$ of the investor. We assume that the following condition holds:

$$\inf_{c>0} k(c) \geq 1. \tag{K}$$

Theorem 4.1 (Optimal Payoffs, CPT). *Let (M) and (K) be satisfied. If we start at least funded, i.e. $\frac{A_0}{L_0} \geq B$, then the following holds:*

- *The optimal solution $\bar{X}^*$ to (OP) is given by*

$$\bar{X}^* = (\bar{X}^*)^+ = \frac{\frac{A_0}{L_0} - B}{G(\infty)} \left(\frac{Z}{w'_+(F_Z(Z))} \right)^{\frac{1}{\gamma - 1}}$$

and $X^* = \bar{X}^* + B$.

If we start underfunded, i.e. $\frac{A_0}{L_0} < B$, then the following holds:

- *If $\inf_{c>0} k(c) = 1$, the supremum value of (OP) is 0 but not attainable.*
- *If $\inf_{c>0} k(c) > 1$, the Problem (OP) admits an optimal solution if and only if the problem*

$$\inf_{0 \leq c < \infty} \left(\frac{\beta w_-(1 - F_Z(c))}{\mathbb{E}[Z1_{Z>c}]^\gamma} \right)^{\frac{1}{1-\gamma}} - G(c) \tag{C}$$

admits an optimal solution c^*.

  - *If $c^* = 0$ is the only solution to (C), then*

$$\bar{X}^* = \frac{A_0}{L_0} - B$$

and $X^* = \bar{X}^* + B = \frac{A_0}{L_0}$.
  - *If $c^* > 0$, the optimal solution to (OP) is given by*

$$\bar{X}^* = (\bar{X}^*)^+ - (\bar{X}^*)^-$$

$$= \frac{v_+^*}{G(c^*)} \left(\frac{Z}{w'_+(F_Z(Z))} \right)^{\frac{1}{\gamma - 1}} 1_{Z \leq c^*} - \frac{v_+^* - \frac{A_0}{L_0} + B}{\mathbb{E}[Z1_{Z>c^*}]} 1_{Z>c^*}$$

with

$$v_+^* = \frac{B - \frac{A_0}{L_0}}{k(c^*)^{1/(1-\gamma)} - 1}$$

and $X^* = \bar{X}^* + B$.

Proof. The proof works along [12] with the wealth being replaced by the funding ratio and the change of numéraire as described in Section 2. □

To further specify the optimal solutions and the well-posedness of the optimization problem, probability distortion functions are introduced in the following sections. Using the completeness of the market, we will also derive replicating strategies for the optimal pay-offs.

4.2. *Probability distortion function*

While[1]

$$\bar{w}(p) := \int_0^{F_Z^{\leftarrow}(p)} r f_Z(r)dr = \mathbb{E}\left[Z\mathbf{1}_{Z \leq F_Z^{\leftarrow}(p)}\right] = \mathcal{N}\left(\mathcal{N}^{\leftarrow}(p) - \|\sigma_L - \theta'\|\sqrt{T}\right)$$

with f_Z being the density function of Z, is by definition a probability distortion function, it is not reverse-S-shaped but rather convex. The proof can be found in Appendix C in Lemma C.1.

In order to get reverse S-shaped distortion functions, we introduce an alteration and define the probability distortion function we will work with as

$$w(p) := \mathcal{N}^{\alpha}\left(\mathcal{N}^{\leftarrow}(p) - \delta\|\sigma_L - \theta'\|\sqrt{T}\right),$$

where $\alpha \in (0, 1]$ and $\delta \in (0, 1]$ are parameters that can be chosen to adjust the distortion behavior of w and $\mathcal{N}^{\alpha}(\cdot) := (\mathcal{N}(\cdot))^{\alpha}$. We define furthermore

$$Z_{\delta} := \exp\left(-\frac{1}{2}\delta^2\|\sigma_L - \theta'\|^2 T + \delta(\sigma_L - \theta')W_T\right),$$

which has the cumulative distribution function

$$F_{Z_{\delta}}(z) = \mathcal{N}\left(\frac{\ln z + \frac{1}{2}\delta^2\|\sigma_L - \theta'\|^2 T}{\delta\|\sigma_L - \theta'\|\sqrt{T}}\right)$$

and denote its corresponding density by $f_{Z_{\delta}}$. The quantile function is given by

$$F_{Z_{\delta}}^{\leftarrow}(p) = \exp\left(-\frac{1}{2}\delta^2\|\sigma_L - \theta'\|^2 T + \delta\|\sigma_L - \theta'\|\sqrt{T}\mathcal{N}^{\leftarrow}(p)\right)$$

---

[1]For $\nu \in \mathbb{R}$, $c_1, c_2 \in \mathbb{R}^+$ and $Y \sim \mathcal{LN}(\mu, \sigma^2)$, it holds

$$\mathbb{E}[Y^{\nu}\mathbf{1}_{Y \in (c_1, c_2)}] = \exp\left(\nu\mu + \frac{1}{2}\nu^2\sigma^2\right)\left(\mathcal{N}\left(\frac{\ln c_2 - \mu - \nu\sigma^2}{\sigma}\right) - \mathcal{N}\left(\frac{\ln c_1 - \mu - \nu\sigma^2}{\sigma}\right)\right).$$

and we define

$$\bar{w}_\delta(p) := \int_0^{F_{Z_\delta}^{\leftarrow}(p)} r f_{Z_\delta}(r) dr$$

$$= \mathbb{E}\left[Z_\delta \mathbf{1}_{Z_\delta \leq F_{Z_\delta}^{\leftarrow}(p)} \right] = \mathcal{N}\left(\mathcal{N}^{\leftarrow}(p) - \delta \|\sigma_L - \theta'\|\sqrt{T} \right).$$

Thus, we have

$$w(p) = (\bar{w}_\delta(p))^\alpha.$$

Lemma 4.1. *For* $\delta \in (0,1]$ *and* $\alpha \in (0,1]$, *the distortion function* w *satisfies* (**M**) *and the first derivative is given by*

$$w'(p) = \alpha \mathcal{N}^{\alpha-1}\left(\mathcal{N}^{\leftarrow}(p) - \delta \|\sigma_L - \theta'\|\sqrt{T} \right) F_Z^{\leftarrow}(p)$$

$$\cdot \exp\left(\frac{1}{2}(1 - \delta^2)\|\sigma_L - \theta'\|^2 T + (\delta - 1)\|\sigma_L - \theta'\|\sqrt{T}\mathcal{N}^{\leftarrow}(p) \right).$$

Furthermore, w *is reverse S-shaped for* $\alpha \in (0,1)$.

Proof. See Appendix C. □

Figure 1 shows the probability distortion function for varying parameters. From the definition of $\mathbb{V}_+$ and $\mathbb{V}_-$, we have for a random variable Y with distribution function F_Y and density function f_Y

$$\mathbb{E}\left[U_+(Y)w'_+(1 - F_Y(y)) \right] = \int_{-\infty}^{\infty} U_+(y)w'_+(1 - F_Y(y))f_Y(y)dy.$$

This can be interpreted as an expectation of $U_+(Y)$ under a distorted probability measure with the distorted density function of Y given by

$$f_Y^w(y) := w'_+(1 - F_Y(y))f_Y(y)$$

and the corresponding distribution function given by

$$F_Y^w(y) := \int_{-\infty}^{y} f_Y^w(s)ds = 1 - w_+(1 - F_Y(y)).$$

Figure 2 shows a plot of f_Y^w, with Y being standard normally distributed for illustrative purposes. The influence of different parameter values can be seen clearly: for a fixed α, different values for δ result in a simple shift. When interpreting Y as the return of a portfolio or considering the funding ratio $\bar{X}$, an increase in δ leads to a heavier lower tail of the distribution and can be interpreted as an increase of the downside risk. In case $\alpha = 1$, this corresponds to an increase in downside risk only. A decrease in the parameter α then yields to an increase in the upper tail of the distribution. By combining both effects, the probability for events from both tails is increased by the distortion. This is illustrated with the parameter set $\alpha = 0.5$, $\delta = 1$.

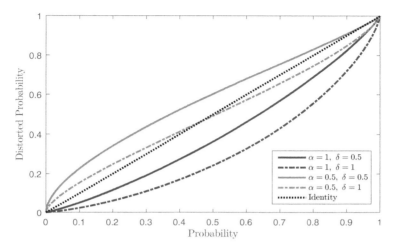

Figure 1. The probability distortion function w. Individual parameters are varied as indicated in the legend.

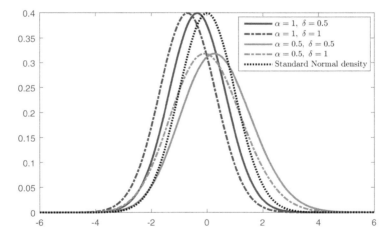

Figure 2. The density of a standard normal random variable that was distorted by the probability distortion function. Individual parameters are varied as indicated in the legend.

Optimal Behavior in the Well-Funded Case

We now assume $\delta_\pm \in (0,1]$, $\alpha_\pm \in (0,1]$ as well as (**K**). Note that (**M**) always holds due to Lemma 4.1 and that the distortion on the losses is especially needed to ensure that the problem is well-posed. Then we derive the optimal strategy in the well-funded case when using w from above.

Theorem 4.2 (Three-Fund Separation, CPT, $\frac{A_0}{L_0} \geq B$). *Let (**K**) be satisfied and $\frac{A_0}{L_0} \geq B$. The optimal terminal funding ratio is then given by*

$$X^* - B = \bar{X}^* = \frac{\frac{A_0}{L_0} - B}{G(\infty)} \left(\frac{Z^{1-\delta_+} \exp\left(\frac{1}{2}(\delta_+^2 - \delta_+)\|\sigma_L - \theta'\|^2 T\right)}{\alpha_+ \mathcal{N}^{\alpha_+ - 1}\left(\frac{\ln Z + (\frac{1}{2} - \delta_+)\|\sigma_L - \theta'\|^2 T}{\|\sigma_L - \theta'\|\sqrt{T}}\right)} \right)^{\frac{1}{\gamma - 1}}$$

and the optimal investment strategy is given by

$$\varphi^*(t) = \lambda^{CPT}((\bar{X}^*)^+(t, Z_t), B)\varphi^{PS} + \left(1 - \lambda^{CPT}((\bar{X}^*)^+(t, Z_t), B)\right)\varphi^{LH},$$

with

$$\lambda^{CPT}((\bar{X}^*)^+(t, Z_t), B) = \frac{-Z_t \frac{\partial}{\partial z}(\bar{X}^*)^+(t, Z_t)}{(\bar{X}^*)^+(t, Z_t) + B},$$

where the funding ratio at time t corresponding to $(\bar{X}^*)^+$ is denoted by

$$(\bar{X}^*)^+(t, Z_t) := \mathbb{E}_{\mathbb{Q}^L}\left[(\bar{X}^*)^+ | \mathcal{F}_t\right]$$

and $\frac{\partial}{\partial z}(\bar{X}^*)^+(t, Z_t)$ is the derivative of $(\bar{X}^*)^+(t, Z_t)$ with respect to the second component.

Proof. Using Lemma 4.1, we have

$$w'_+(F_Z(Z))$$

$$= \alpha_+ \mathcal{N}^{\alpha_+ - 1}\left(\frac{\ln Z + \frac{1}{2}\|\sigma_L - \theta'\|^2 T}{\|\sigma_L - \theta'\|\sqrt{T}} - \delta_+\|\sigma_L - \theta'\|\sqrt{T}\right) \cdot$$

$$\exp\left(-\frac{1}{2}\delta_+^2\|\sigma_L - \theta'\|^2 T + \delta_+\|\sigma_L - \theta'\|\sqrt{T}\frac{\ln Z + \frac{1}{2}\|\sigma_L - \theta'\|^2 T}{\|\sigma_L - \theta'\|\sqrt{T}}\right)$$

$$= \alpha_+ \mathcal{N}^{\alpha_+ - 1}\left(\frac{\ln Z + (\frac{1}{2} - \delta_+)\|\sigma_L - \theta'\|^2 T}{\|\sigma_L - \theta'\|\sqrt{T}}\right) \cdot$$

$$\exp\left(\delta_+ \ln Z - \frac{1}{2}(\delta_+^2 - \delta_+)\|\sigma_L - \theta'\|^2 T\right)$$

$$= \alpha_+ \mathcal{N}^{\alpha_+ - 1}\left(\frac{\ln Z + (\frac{1}{2} - \delta_+)\|\sigma_L - \theta'\|^2 T}{\|\sigma_L - \theta'\|\sqrt{T}}\right) \cdot$$

$$Z^{\delta_+} \exp\left(-\frac{1}{2}(\delta_+^2 - \delta_+)\|\sigma_L - \theta'\|^2 T\right).$$

Hence, using Theorem 4.1 for the well-funded case, $X^* = (\bar{X}^*)^+ + B$, with

$$
(\bar{X}^*)^+ = \frac{\frac{A_0}{L_0} - B}{G(\infty)} \left(\frac{Z}{w'_+(F_Z(Z))} \right)^{\frac{1}{\gamma-1}}
$$

$$
= \frac{\frac{A_0}{L_0} - B}{G(\infty)} \left(\frac{Z^{1-\delta_+} \exp\left(\frac{1}{2}(\delta_+^2 - \delta_+)\|\sigma_L - \theta'\|^2 T\right)}{\alpha_+ \mathcal{N}^{\alpha_+ - 1} \left(\frac{\ln Z + (\frac{1}{2} - \delta_+)\|\sigma_L - \theta'\|^2 T}{\|\sigma_L - \theta'\|\sqrt{T}} \right)} \right)^{\frac{1}{\gamma-1}}.
$$

We use Appendix D with $(\bar{X}^*)^-(t, Z_t) = 0$ to receive the optimal investment strategy for $X^*(t, Z_t) = (\bar{X}^*)^+(t, Z_t) + B$:

$$
\varphi^*(t) = \frac{1}{X^*(t, Z_t)} \left(Z_t \frac{\partial}{\partial z}(\bar{X}^*)^+(t, Z_t)(\varphi^{LH} - \varphi^{PS}) + \left((\bar{X}^*)^+(t, Z_t) + B \right) \varphi^{LH} \right)
$$

$$
= \frac{-Z_t \frac{\partial}{\partial z}(\bar{X}^*)^+(t, Z_t)}{(\bar{X}^*)^+(t, Z_t) + B} \varphi^{PS} + \left(1 - \frac{-Z_t \frac{\partial}{\partial z}(\bar{X}^*)^+(t, Z_t)}{(\bar{X}^*)^+(t, Z_t) + B} \right) \varphi^{LH}.
$$

$\square$

Due to this optimal payoff with $(\bar{X}^*)^- = 0$, the funding ratio never falls below B. We have again a three-fund separation. In order to get a more explicit result for λ^{CPT}, we consider the case $\alpha_+ = 1$ in the following corollary.

Corollary 4.1 (Three-Fund Separation, CPT, $\frac{A_0}{L_0} \geq B$, $\alpha_+ = 1$).
Let (K) be satisfied, $\frac{A_0}{L_0} \geq B$ and $\alpha_+ = 1$. The optimal terminal funding ratio is then given by

$$
X^* - B = \bar{X}^* = (\bar{X}^*)^+
$$

$$
= \left(\frac{A_0}{L_0} - B \right) \exp \left(\frac{1}{2} \frac{(1 - \delta_+)(\delta_+ - \gamma)}{(1 - \gamma)^2} \|\sigma_L - \theta'\|^2 T \right) Z^{\frac{1-\delta_+}{\gamma-1}}
$$

and the optimal investment strategy is given by

$$
\varphi^*(t) = \lambda^{CPT}(X_t^\varphi, B)\varphi^{PS} + (1 - \lambda^{CPT}(X_t^\varphi, B))\varphi^{LH},
$$

with

$$
\lambda^{CPT}(X_t^\varphi, B) = \frac{X_t^\varphi - B}{X_t^\varphi} \cdot \frac{1 - \delta_+}{1 - \gamma}.
$$

Proof. For $\alpha_+ = 1$, we have with the proof of Theorem 4.2

$$
w'_+(F_Z(Z)) = Z^{\delta_+} \exp \left(-\frac{1}{2}(\delta_+^2 - \delta_+)\|\sigma_L - \theta'\|^2 T \right).
$$

Thus, we have with Footnote 1 and with $\nu = \frac{\delta_+ - \gamma}{1-\gamma}, c_2 = c$, and $c_1 = 0$

$$
\begin{aligned}
G(c) &= \mathbb{E}\left[Z^{\frac{\gamma}{\gamma-1}} w'_+ (F_Z(Z))^{\frac{1}{1-\gamma}} \mathbf{1}_{Z \le c} \right] \\
&= \exp\left(-\frac{1}{2} \frac{\delta_+^2 - \delta_+}{1-\gamma} \|\sigma_L - \theta'\|^2 T \right) \mathbb{E}\left[Z^{\frac{\delta_+ - \gamma}{1-\gamma}} \mathbf{1}_{Z \le c} \right] \\
&= \exp\left(\frac{1}{2}\left(\left(\frac{\delta_+ - \gamma}{1-\gamma}\right)^2 - \frac{\delta_+ - \gamma}{1-\gamma} - \frac{\delta_+^2 - \delta_+}{1-\gamma} \right) \|\sigma_L - \theta'\|^2 T \right) \cdot \\
&\quad \mathcal{N}\left(\frac{\ln c + (\frac{1}{2} - \frac{\delta_+ - \gamma}{1-\gamma})\|\sigma_L - \theta'\|^2 T}{\|\sigma_L - \theta'\|\sqrt{T}} \right) \\
&= \exp\left(\frac{1}{2} \frac{(\delta_+ - 1)^2 \gamma}{(1-\gamma)^2} \|\sigma_L - \theta'\|^2 T \right) \mathcal{N}\left(\frac{\ln c + (\frac{1}{2} - \frac{\delta_+ - \gamma}{1-\gamma})\|\sigma_L - \theta'\|^2 T}{\|\sigma_L - \theta'\|\sqrt{T}} \right).
\end{aligned}
$$

Hence, in the well-funded case, the optimal funding ratio is with Theorem 4.2

$$
\begin{aligned}
(\bar{X}^*)^+ &= \frac{\frac{A_0}{L_0} - B}{G(\infty)} \left(Z^{1-\delta_+} \exp\left(\frac{1}{2}(\delta_+^2 - \delta_+)\|\sigma_L - \theta'\|^2 T \right) \right)^{\frac{1}{\gamma-1}} \\
&= \left(\frac{A_0}{L_0} - B \right) \exp\left(-\frac{1}{2}\frac{(\delta_+ - 1)^2 \gamma}{(1-\gamma)^2} \|\sigma_L - \theta'\|^2 T \right) \cdot \\
&\quad Z^{\frac{1-\delta_+}{\gamma-1}} \exp\left(\frac{1}{2}\frac{\delta_+^2 - \delta_+}{\gamma-1} \|\sigma_L - \theta'\|^2 T \right) \\
&= \left(\frac{A_0}{L_0} - B \right) \exp\left(\frac{1}{2}\frac{(1-\delta_+)(\delta_+ - \gamma)}{(1-\gamma)^2} \|\sigma_L - \theta'\|^2 T \right) Z^{\frac{1-\delta_+}{\gamma-1}}.
\end{aligned}
$$

We first compute the value of $(\bar{X}^*)^+$ at time t, denoted by $(\bar{X}^*)^+(t, Z_t)$ using Footnote 1 with $\nu = \frac{1-\delta_+}{\gamma-1}, c_2 = \infty$, and $c_1 = 0$:

$$
\begin{aligned}
(\bar{X}^*)^+(t, Z_t) &= \left(\frac{A_0}{L_0} - B \right) \exp\left(\frac{1}{2}\frac{(1-\delta_+)(\delta_+ - \gamma)}{(1-\gamma)^2} \|\sigma_L - \theta'\|^2 T \right) Z_t^{\frac{1-\delta_+}{\gamma-1}} \cdot \\
&\quad \exp\left(\frac{1}{2}\left(\frac{1-\delta_+}{\gamma-1} + 1 \right) \frac{1-\delta_+}{\gamma-1} \|\sigma_L - \theta'\|^2 (T-t) \right) \\
&= \left(\frac{A_0}{L_0} - B \right) Z_t^{\frac{1-\delta_+}{\gamma-1}} \exp\left(-\frac{1}{2}\left(\frac{1-\delta_+}{\gamma-1} + 1 \right) \frac{1-\delta_+}{\gamma-1} \|\sigma_L - \theta'\|^2 t \right).
\end{aligned}
$$

We know from Appendix D that the corresponding replicating strategy can be written as

$$
\varphi_+(t) = \varphi^{LH} + \frac{1-\delta_+}{1-\gamma}(\varphi^{PS} - \varphi^{LH})
$$

and since $(\bar{X}^*)^-(t, Z_t) = 0$, the optimal investment strategy for $X^*(t, Z_t) = (\bar{X}^*)^+(t, Z_t) + B$ is given by

$$
\begin{aligned}
\varphi^*(t) &= \frac{1}{(\bar{X}^*)^+(t, Z_t) + B} \left((\bar{X}^*)^+(t, Z_t)\varphi_+(t) + B\varphi^{LH} \right) \\
&= \varphi^{LH} + \frac{(\bar{X}^*)^+(t, Z_t)}{(\bar{X}^*)^+(t, Z_t) + B} \cdot \frac{1 - \delta_+}{1 - \gamma}(\varphi^{PS} - \varphi^{LH}) \\
&= \varphi^{LH} + \frac{X^*(t, Z_t) - B}{X^*(t, Z_t)} \cdot \frac{1 - \delta_+}{1 - \gamma}(\varphi^{PS} - \varphi^{LH}).
\end{aligned}
$$

$\square$

The optimal strategy results again in the known separation into performance seeking and liability hedging portfolio with the remaining amount being invested in the risk-free asset. Note that the relative risk aversion of the power utility function, $1 - \gamma$, is positive.

Therefore, we identify $\frac{1-\delta_+}{1-\gamma}$ as investor-specific pre-factor that can be seen as a measure for the risk-appetite of the investor. An increasing δ_+ shifts the density to the left and therefore tempers the influence of the risk-preference of the investor in the strategy, as it makes $\frac{1-\delta_+}{1-\gamma}$ smaller and thus the strategy more cautious in general. In particular, the performance seeking part of the optimal investment strategy corresponds to a CPPI-strategy with multiplier $m := \frac{1-\delta_+}{1-\gamma}$ and this ensures that the funding ratio never falls below B.

Optimal Behavior in the Underfunded Case

We turn to the underfunded case. If $c^* = 0$ is the only solution to the optimization problem (**C**), then Theorem 4.1 states that the optimal funding ratio is

$$
X^* = \frac{A_0}{L_0}.
$$

Therefore, the optimal strategy is to hedge the liabilities perfectly with

$$
\varphi^{LH} = (\sigma')^{-1}\sigma'_L
$$

to keep the funding ratio constant and thus to preserve the current level of funding and not risk an even lower funding for potential profit. Remember that $Z \le c^* \Leftrightarrow X^* \ge B$. So if $c^* = 0$, then

$$
\mathbb{P}(X^* \ge B) = \mathbb{P}(Z \le 0) = 0.
$$

This means that there is zero probability that we will achieve funded or well-funded status and thus no reason to risk anything and try. Therefore, we only consider the case $c^* > 0$ in the following results.

Proposition 4.1 (Optimal Payoff, CPT, $\frac{A_0}{L_0} <$ B). *Let* $\inf_{c>0} k(c) > 1$
be satisfied and $\frac{A_0}{L_0} < 0$. *If* (**C**) *admits an optimal solution* $c^* > 0$, *the
optimal terminal funding ratio is given by*

$$X^* - B = \bar{X}^* = (\bar{X}^*)^+ - (\bar{X}^*)^-,$$

with

$$(\bar{X}^*)^+ = \frac{v_+^*}{G(c^*)} \left(\frac{Z^{1-\delta_+} \exp\left(\frac{1}{2}(\delta_+^2 - \delta_+)\|\sigma_L - \theta'\|^2 T\right)}{\alpha_+ \mathcal{N}^{\alpha_+ - 1} \left(\frac{\ln Z + (\frac{1}{2} - \delta_+)\|\sigma_L - \theta'\|^2 T}{\|\sigma_L - \theta'\|\sqrt{T}} \right)} \right)^{\frac{1}{\gamma - 1}} \mathbb{1}_{Z \le c^*}$$

$$(\bar{X}^*)^- = \frac{v_+^* - \frac{A_0}{L_0} + B}{1 - \mathcal{N}\left(\frac{\ln c^* - \frac{1}{2}\|\sigma_L - \theta'\|^2 T}{\|\sigma_L - \theta'\|\sqrt{T}} \right)} \mathbb{1}_{Z > c^*}$$

and

$$v_+^* = \frac{B - \frac{A_0}{L_0}}{k(c^*)^{1/(1-\gamma)} - 1}.$$

Proof. Proceeding as in the proof of Theorem 4.2, we find with Theorem
4.1

$$(\bar{X}^*)^+ = \frac{v_+^*}{G(c^*)} \left(\frac{Z}{w_+'(F_Z(Z))} \right)^{\frac{1}{\gamma - 1}} \mathbb{1}_{Z \le c^*}$$

$$= \frac{v_+^*}{G(c^*)} \left(\frac{Z^{1-\delta_+} \exp\left(\frac{1}{2}(\delta_+^2 - \delta_+)\|\sigma_L - \theta'\|^2 T\right)}{\alpha_+ \mathcal{N}^{\alpha_+ - 1} \left(\frac{\ln Z + (\frac{1}{2} - \delta_+)\|\sigma_L - \theta'\|^2 T}{\|\sigma_L - \theta'\|\sqrt{T}} \right)} \right)^{\frac{1}{\gamma - 1}} \mathbb{1}_{Z \le c^*}.$$

The second pay-off is given by

$$(\bar{X}^*)^- = \frac{v_+^* - \frac{A_0}{L_0} + B}{\mathbb{E}[Z \mathbb{1}_{Z > c^*}]} \mathbb{1}_{Z > c^*} = \frac{v_+^* - \frac{A_0}{L_0} + B}{1 - \mathcal{N}\left(\frac{\ln c^* - \frac{1}{2}\|\sigma_L - \theta'\|^2 T}{\|\sigma_L - \theta'\|\sqrt{T}} \right)} \mathbb{1}_{Z > c^*}.$$

$\square$

In contrast to the well-funded case, in which the CPPI-part for the
performance seeking portfolio implies that there is no risk of falling below
the reference point B, the optimal strategy in the underfunded case corresponds to a leveraged strategy and thus includes more risk. The reason for
this difference is that in the well-funded case, the risk-seeking area of the
convex utility function below the reference point is never reached, whereas

this area has substantial influence in the case of initial underfunding. The investor tries to achieve a terminal wealth above B by taking additional risk. In case the market evolves in an advantageous way, in particular if $Z \leq c^*$, then the investor receives the payoff $(\bar{X}^*)^+ + B$. In the other case, i.e. $Z > c^*$, the investor suffers a constant loss with terminal wealth $B - (\bar{X}^*)^-$ due to the additional risk. For $\alpha_+ = 1$, the following result states the optimal investment strategy in closed form.

Theorem 4.3 (***Three-Fund Separation, CPT,*** $\frac{\mathbf{A_0}}{\mathbf{L_0}} < \mathbf{B}$, $\alpha_+ = 1$). *Let* $\inf_{c>0} k(c) > 1$ *be satisfied,* $\frac{A_0}{L_0} < 0$ *and* $\alpha_+ = 1$. *If* (**C**) *admits an optimal solution* $c^* > 0$, *the optimal funding ratio is given by*

$$X^* - B = \bar{X}^* = (\bar{X}^*)^+ - (\bar{X}^*)^-,$$

with

$$(\bar{X}^*)^+ = \frac{v_+^*}{\mathcal{N}\left(\frac{\ln c^* + (\frac{1}{2} - \frac{\delta_+ - \gamma}{1-\gamma})\|\sigma_L - \theta'\|^2 T}{\|\sigma_L - \theta'\|\sqrt{T}}\right)} \cdot$$
$$\exp\left(\frac{1}{2}\frac{(1-\delta_+)(\delta_+ - \gamma)}{(1-\gamma)^2}\|\sigma_L - \theta'\|^2 T\right) Z^{\frac{1-\delta_+}{\gamma-1}} 1_{Z \leq c^*},$$

$$(\bar{X}^*)^- = \frac{v_+^* - \frac{A_0}{L_0} + 1}{1 - \mathcal{N}\left(\frac{\ln c^* - \frac{1}{2}\|\sigma_L - \theta'\|^2 T}{\|\sigma_L - \theta'\|\sqrt{T}}\right)} 1_{Z > c^*}$$

and

$$v_+^* = \frac{B - \frac{A_0}{L_0}}{k(c^*)^{1/(1-\gamma)} - 1}.$$

The optimal investment strategy is given by

$$\varphi^*(t) = \lambda^{CPT} \cdot \varphi^{PS} + (1 - \lambda^{CPT}) \cdot \varphi^{LH},$$

with

$$\lambda^{CPT} = \frac{1}{X_t^{\varphi}} \cdot \left(X_+^{\varphi}(t) \cdot \lambda_+ - X_-^{\varphi}(t) \cdot \lambda_- \right)$$

$$\lambda_+ = \left(\frac{1-\delta_+}{1-\gamma} + \frac{1}{\|\sigma_L - \theta'\|\sqrt{T-t}} \cdot \frac{\mathcal{N}'\left(d\left(\frac{c^*}{Z_t}, T-t, \frac{1-\delta_+}{\gamma-1} \right) \right)}{\mathcal{N}\left(d\left(\frac{c^*}{Z_t}, T-t, \frac{1-\delta_+}{\gamma-1} \right) \right)} \right),$$

$$\lambda_- = \frac{\mathcal{N}'\left(d\left(\frac{c^*}{Z_t}, T-t, 0 \right) \right)}{1 - \mathcal{N}\left(d\left(\frac{c^*}{Z_t}, T-t, 0 \right) \right)} \cdot \frac{1}{\|\sigma_L' - \theta\|\sqrt{T-t}},$$

$$X_+^{\varphi}(t) = \frac{v_+^* Z_t^{\frac{1-\delta_+}{\gamma-1}} \cdot \mathcal{N}\left(d\left(\frac{c^*}{Z_t}, T-t, \frac{1-\delta_+}{\gamma-1} \right) \right)}{\mathcal{N}\left(\frac{\ln c^* + (-\frac{1}{2} \cdot \frac{1-\delta_+}{\gamma-1}) \|\sigma_L - \theta'\|^2 T}{\|\sigma_L - \theta'\|\sqrt{T}} \right)}$$

$$\cdot \exp\left(-\frac{1}{2} \left(\frac{1-\delta_+}{\gamma-1} + 1 \right) \cdot \frac{1-\delta_+}{\gamma-1} \|\sigma_L - \theta'\|^2 t \right) \cdot$$

$$X_-^{\varphi}(t) = \frac{v_+^* - \frac{A_0}{L_0} + B}{1 - \mathcal{N}\left(\frac{\ln c^* - \frac{1}{2}\|\sigma_L - \theta'\|^2 T}{\|\sigma_L - \theta'\|\sqrt{T}} \right)} \cdot \left(1 - \mathcal{N}\left(d\left(\frac{c^*}{Z_t}, T-t, 0 \right) \right) \right)$$

and $d(c, s, v) := \frac{\ln(c) - (v + \frac{1}{2})\|\sigma_L - \theta'\|^2 s}{\|\sigma_L - \theta'\|\sqrt{s}}.$

Proof. From the proof of Corollary 4.1, we know that

$$G(c^*) = \exp\left(\frac{1}{2} \frac{(\delta_+ - 1)^2 \gamma}{(1-\gamma)^2} \|\sigma_L - \theta'\|^2 T \right)$$

$$\cdot \mathcal{N}\left(\frac{\ln c^* + (\frac{1}{2} - \frac{\delta_+ - \gamma}{1-\gamma}) \|\sigma_L - \theta'\|^2 T}{\|\sigma_L - \theta'\|\sqrt{T}} \right).$$

Applying Proposition 4.1 yields

$$(\bar{X}^*)^+ = \frac{v_+^*}{G(c^*)} \left(Z^{1-\delta_+} \exp\left(\frac{1}{2}(\delta_+^2 - \delta_+) \|\sigma_L - \theta'\|^2 T \right) \right)^{\frac{1}{\gamma-1}} \mathbf{1}_{Z \le c^*}$$

$$= \frac{v_+^*}{\mathcal{N}\left(\frac{\ln c^* + (\frac{1}{2} - \frac{\delta_+ - \gamma}{1-\gamma}) \|\sigma_L - \theta'\|^2 T}{\|\sigma_L - \theta'\|\sqrt{T}} \right)} \cdot$$

$$\exp\left(\frac{1}{2} \frac{(1-\delta_+)(\delta_+ - \gamma)}{(1-\gamma)^2} \|\sigma_L - \theta'\|^2 T \right) Z^{\frac{1-\delta_+}{\gamma-1}} \mathbf{1}_{Z \le c^*}.$$

We can apply Appendix D to derive

$$(\bar{X}^*)^+(t, Z_t) = \frac{v_+^* Z_t^{\frac{1-\delta_+}{\gamma-1}}}{\mathcal{N}\left(\frac{\ln c^* + (\frac{1}{2} - \frac{\delta_+ - \gamma}{1-\gamma})\|\sigma_L - \theta'\|^2 T}{\|\sigma_L - \theta'\|\sqrt{T}}\right)} \mathcal{N}\left(d\left(\frac{c^*}{Z_t}, T - t, \frac{1-\delta_+}{\gamma-1}\right)\right).$$

$$\exp\left(-\frac{1}{2}\left(\frac{1-\delta_+}{\gamma-1} + 1\right)\frac{1-\delta_+}{\gamma-1}\|\sigma_L - \theta'\|^2 t\right)$$

and the replicating strategy is

$$\varphi_+(t) = \varphi^{LH} + \left(\frac{1-\delta_+}{1-\gamma} + \frac{1}{\|\sigma_L - \theta'\|\sqrt{T-t}} \frac{\mathcal{N}'\left(d\left(\frac{c^*}{Z_t}, T - t, \frac{1-\delta_+}{\gamma-1}\right)\right)}{\mathcal{N}\left(d\left(\frac{c^*}{Z_t}, T - t, \frac{1-\delta_+}{\gamma-1}\right)\right)}\right)$$
$$\cdot (\varphi^{PS} - \varphi^{LH}).$$

The second pay-off is given by Proposition 4.1 and with Appendix D, $c_2 = \infty, c_1 = c^*$ and $\nu = 0$, we have

$$(\bar{X}^*)^-(t, Z_t) = \frac{v_+^* - \frac{A_0}{L_0} + B}{1 - \mathcal{N}\left(\frac{\ln c^* - \frac{1}{2}\|\sigma_L - \theta'\|^2 T}{\|\sigma_L - \theta'\|\sqrt{T}}\right)}\left(1 - \mathcal{N}\left(d\left(\frac{c^*}{Z_t}, T - t, 0\right)\right)\right).$$

Moreover, the replicating strategy φ_- of $(\bar{X}^*)^-$ is

$$\varphi_- = \varphi^{LH} - \frac{\mathcal{N}'\left(d\left(\frac{c^*}{Z_t}, T - t, 0\right)\right)}{1 - \mathcal{N}\left(d\left(\frac{c^*}{Z_t}, T - t, 0\right)\right)} \frac{1}{\|\sigma_L' - \theta\|\sqrt{T-t}}(\varphi^{PS} - \varphi^{LH}).$$

This allows us to compute the replicating strategy of the optimal funding ratio as

$$\varphi^*(t) = \frac{1}{X^*(t, Z_t)}\left((\bar{X}^*)^+(t, Z_t)\varphi_+(t) - (\bar{X}^*)^-(t, Z_t)\varphi_-(t) + B\varphi^{LH}\right)$$

and to represent it as in the statement of the theorem by rearranging the terms and with $X^*(t, Z_t) = (\bar{X}^*)^+(t, Z_t) - (\bar{X}^*)^-(t, Z_t) + B$. $\qquad\square$

5. Comparison

5.1. *Partial surplus optimization*

After the derivation of the optimal strategies, we now show that the CPT approach is a generalization of the funding ratio optimization as well as a continuous-time analogue of the partial surplus optimization. This also establishes the link between partial surplus optimization in discrete time and funding ratio optimization in continuous time.[2] The partial surplus in [1] is defined as $A_T^\varphi - kL_T$, $k \in [0, 1]$ and the surplus return introduced as

$$S_T^\varphi := \frac{A_T^\varphi - kL_T}{A_0} = r_{A^\varphi}(T) - k\frac{L_0}{A_0}r_L(T),$$

with $r_{A^\varphi}(T)$ being the performance of the assets and $r_L(T)$ being the performance of the liabilities from $t = 0$ until $t = T$.

The authors of [1] apply a mean-variance utility to the partial surplus

$$\max_\varphi \mathbb{E}[U(S_T^\varphi)] = \max_\varphi [\mathbb{E}[S_T^\varphi] - \gamma_{MV} Var(S_T^\varphi)] ,$$

with risk aversion parameter $\gamma_{MV} > 0$. They show that this problem can also be written as

$$\max_\varphi \left[\mathbb{E}\left[r_A^\varphi(T)\right] - \gamma_{MV} Var\left[r_A^\varphi(T)\right] + \frac{2\gamma_{MV} kL_0}{A_0} Cov\left[r_A^\varphi(T), r_L(T)\right] \right]. \tag{MV}$$

We consider the logarithmic returns

$$r_{A^\varphi}(T) := \ln\left(\frac{A_T^\varphi}{A_0}\right) \quad \text{and} \quad r_L(T) := \ln\left(\frac{L_T}{L_0}\right).$$

For the market model from the previous sections, we calculate an optimal static investment strategy without allowance for intertemporal portfolio choice.

Theorem 5.1 (*Three-Fund Separation, Mean-Variance Utility*). *The optimal investment strategy for* (MV) *is given by*

$$\varphi_{Sharpe}^* = \lambda^S \varphi^{PS} + (1 - \lambda^S)\frac{kL_0}{A_0}\varphi^{LH},$$

with $\lambda^S = \frac{1}{2\gamma_{MV}+1}$. *The remaining wealth* $1 - 1'\varphi_{Sharpe}^*$ *is invested in the risk-free asset.*

Proof. Setting the gradient of the expected utility equal to zero with respect to φ yields the optimal solution. It is a maximum as the Hessian with respect to φ is negative definite due to $\gamma_{MV} > 0$.

□

---

[2]In contrast to this funding ratio optimization, the intertemporal surplus management approach by [5] cannot be interpreted as a generalization of the funding ratio optimization.

5.2. *Connection between CPT optimization, funding ratio optimization and partial surplus optimization*

After having obtained three-fund separations for the funding ratio optimization in an expected utility framework and in a CPT framework as well as for the partial surplus optimization, we compare the results from Corollary 3.1, Corollary 4.1 and Theorem 5.1. While the optimal investment strategy depends on the initial funding ratio for the static mean-variance approach, the optimal investment strategy for the CPT approach with $\frac{A_0}{L_0} \geq B$ depends dynamically on X_t^φ and the solution for the expected utility approach with power utility is independent of the funding ratio at any time. In Figure 3 and Figure 4, the wealth allocated in the performance seeking portfolio and the liability hedging portfolio at $t = 0$ is illustrated. Unless otherwise stated, the parameters chosen are $\gamma_{MV} = 5$, $k = 0.9$ and $\frac{A_0}{L_0} = 1.1$ for the mean-variance utility approach, $\gamma = -10$ for the expected utility approach with power utility and $B = 0.5$, $\delta_+ = 0.5$ as well as also $\frac{A_0}{L_0} = 1.1$ for the CPT approach. Since we want to consider downside risk only, we set $\alpha = 1$

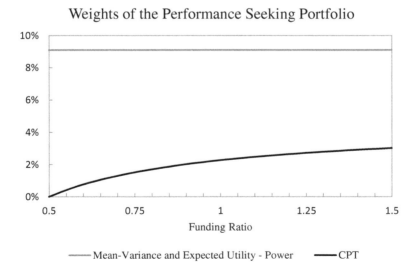

Figure 3.   Weights of the performance seeking portfolio in the different settings.

in the CPT example. If we set $B = 0$, the CPT approach for $\frac{A_0}{L_0} \geq B$ corresponds to a pure CPT funding ratio optimization. The optimal strategy differs from the expected utility approach only by the factor $1 - \delta_+$ caused by the probability distortion. Figures 5 and 6 show that the allocations in the performance seeking portfolio and liability hedging portfolio for the CPT approach converge to the optimal investment strategy in the expected utility approach with power utility when $B \to 0$ and $\delta_+ \to 0$. Thus, the CPT approach is a generalization of the presented expected utility theory approach. On the other hand, CPT is also a generalization of the partial surplus optimization. In the CPT context we optimize the utility of $\bar{X} = X_T^\varphi - B = \frac{A_T^\varphi}{L_T} - B$ and we have

$$\frac{A_T^\varphi}{L_T} - B \geq 0 \quad \Leftrightarrow \quad A_T^\varphi \geq BL_T \quad \Leftrightarrow \quad A_T^\varphi - BL_T \geq 0.$$

Hence, the reference point B, indicating to which extent the liabilities are considered, corresponds to k in the partial surplus optimization.

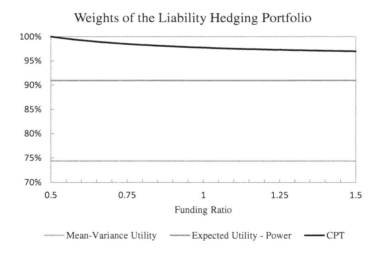

Figure 4.   Weights of the liability hedging portfolio in the different settings.

Weights of the Performance Seeking Portfolio

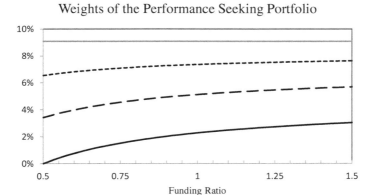

Figure 5. Weights of the performance seeking portfolio in the different settings.

Weights of the Liability Hedging Portfolio

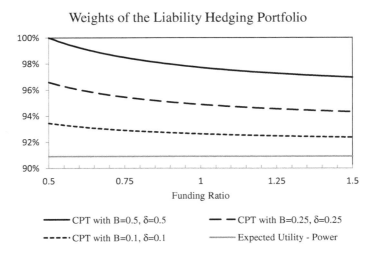

Figure 6. Weights of the liability hedging portfolio in the different settings.

6. Conclusion

Using the market model from [2] for the assets and liabilities, we derive optimal investment strategies in a CPT funding ratio optimization framework with S-shaped utility function and a distortion which has only few parameters but still the desired properties. The optimal investment strategies with initial funding level above and below the reference point differ, but can be represented as a three-fund theorem in each of the two cases. We compare the results from the CPT optimization to the results from [2] obtained for the funding ratio optimization in an expected utility framework and to an application of the partial surplus approach in [1] to our market model. We conclude that the CPT approach can be considered as a generalization of both, the partial surplus approach and the funding ratio optimization.

Acknowledgment

Markus Wahl and Rudi Zagst gratefully acknowledge the support of Allianz Global Investors for this research.

Appendix A. Solution of the HJB equation

We use the well-known separation approach

$$\Phi(t, X_t^\varphi) = U(X_t^\varphi)\Delta(t), \qquad (A.1)$$

where $\Delta : [0, T] \to \mathbb{R}_+$. The function Φ is strictly concave in X_t^φ as U is strictly concave and thus we can find a unique maximizer φ^*. As the relative risk aversion of U is constant $1 - \gamma$, the relative risk tolerance is

$$\lambda^{EUP}(X_t^\varphi, t) = \frac{1}{1 - \gamma}.$$

The resulting maximizer is

$$\varphi^* = \left(1 - \frac{1}{1 - \gamma}\right)\varphi^{LH} + \frac{1}{1 - \gamma}\varphi^{PS},$$

the investment in the risk-free asset is $\varphi_0^* = 1 - \mathbf{1}'\varphi^*$. Using the optimal strategy in $\mu_X^\varphi(t)$ and $\sigma_X^\varphi(t)$ results in

$$\mu_X^{\varphi^*}(t) = r + \varphi_t^{*\prime}(\mu - r\mathbf{1}) - \mu_L + \sigma_L\sigma_L' + \sigma_\epsilon^2 - \sigma_L\sigma'\varphi_t^*$$

$$= r - \mu_L + \frac{1}{1 - \gamma}\sigma_L\sigma_L' + \sigma_\epsilon^2 + \frac{1}{1 - \gamma}\theta'\theta + \left(1 - \frac{2}{1 - \gamma}\right)\sigma_L\theta.$$

and

$$\sigma_X^{\varphi^*}(t)^2 = \left(\varphi_t^{*\prime}\sigma - \sigma_L\right)\left(\varphi_t^{*\prime}\sigma - \sigma_L\right)' + \sigma_\epsilon^2$$

$$= \frac{1}{(1-\gamma)^2}\sigma_L\sigma_L' + 2\frac{1}{1-\gamma}(1 - \frac{1}{1-\gamma})\sigma_L\theta + \frac{1}{(1-\gamma)^2}\theta'\theta + \sigma_\epsilon^2.$$

The assumption on the form of the solution (A.1) and the above results reduces the HJB equation to the ODE

$$0 = \Delta'(t) + \left[\mu_X(\varphi^*, t)\gamma + \frac{1}{2}(\sigma_X(\varphi^*, t))^2\gamma(1-\gamma)\right]\Delta(t).$$

Due to the terminal condition $\Delta(T) = 1$, it has the solution[3]

$$\Delta(t) = \exp\left(\left[\mu_X(\varphi^*, t)\gamma + \frac{1}{2}(\sigma_X(\varphi^*, t))^2\gamma(1-\gamma)\right](T-t)\right).$$

Appendix B. Quantile optimization approach

The optimization approach works by separating the Original Problem (**OP**) into further optimization problems, one for the gains and one for the losses, and a third one that glues them back together. To give an intuition, note that for any feasible solution $\bar{X}$ we have $\bar{X} = (\bar{X})^+ - (\bar{X})^-$ and $(\bar{X})^+$ only influences $\mathbb{V}_+$. In addition, it has a price $\mathbb{E}[Z(\bar{X})^+] =: v_+$ and it only has positive value on an implicitly defined set $A := \{\bar{X} \geq 0\}$. We will call the problem of optimizing $(\bar{X})^+$ the *Gains Problem* (**GP**)

$$\sup_{\bar{X}} \quad \mathbb{V}_+((\bar{X})^+)$$

$$s.t. \ \mathbb{E}[Z(\bar{X})^+] = v_+, \tag{GP}$$

$$\bar{X} \text{ is } \mathcal{F}_T\text{-measurable and lower-bounded.}$$

The other part of the solution $(\bar{X})^-$ only influences $\mathbb{V}_-$, exists on the complement $A^c = \{\bar{X} < 0\}$ and has a price $\mathbb{E}[Z(\bar{X})^-] := v_+ - \left(\frac{A_0}{L_0} - B\right)$.

---

[3]It should be noted that this is a heuristic derivation. For mathematical rigorosity, a verification theorem would have to be shown, which is beyond the scope of this paper. However, for $\gamma \in (0, 1)$, a verification theorem which is directly applicable can be found in [17], Theorem 3.5.2.

The corresponding *Loss Problem* (**LP**) is given by

$$\inf_{\bar{X}} \quad \mathbb{V}_-((\bar{X})^-)$$

$$s.t. \ \mathbb{E}[Z(\bar{X})^-] = v_+ - \left(\frac{A_0}{L_0} - B\right) \tag{LP}$$

$$\bar{X} \text{ is } \mathcal{F}_T\text{-measurable and upper-bounded.}$$

The link between (**GP**) and (**LP**) is the so-called *Gluing Problem*. For this, note that any solutions of both (**GP**) and (**LP**) depend on two common parameters: A and v_+. If any solution depends on those parameters, then so do the optimal solutions. Knowing that the optimal values of the gains problem $\Phi_+(v_+, A)$ and loss problem $\Phi_-(v_+, A)$ depend on v_+ and A, the Gluing Problem boils down to finding an optimal pair (v_+^*, A^*) that maximizes $\Phi_+(v_+, A) - \Phi_-(v_+, A)$. To simplify the Gluing Problem even further, it turns out that an optimal set A^* always has the form $A^* = \{Z \leq c^*\}$, $c \geq 0$ (see [12], Theorem 5.1). Hence, it is enough to look at solutions of the form $\Phi_\pm(v_+, \{Z \leq c\}) =: \Phi_\pm(v_+, c)$. For an indication on why this is true, remember that $F_Z(Z)$ and consequently $1 - F_Z(Z)$ are uniformly distributed on the unit interval and that $A = \{\bar{X} \geq 0\}$. Then we define

$$c := F_Z^\leftarrow(\mathbb{P}(A)) = F_Z^\leftarrow(\mathbb{P}(\bar{X} \geq 0)) = F_Z^\leftarrow(\mathbb{P}(X \geq B))$$

and see that[4]

$$Z \leq c \Leftrightarrow F_Z(Z) \leq \mathbb{P}(\bar{X} \geq 0) \Leftrightarrow 1 - F_Z(Z) \geq \mathbb{P}(\bar{X} < 0) = F_{\bar{X}}(0)$$

$$\Leftrightarrow \bar{X} \overset{d}{=} F_{\bar{X}}^\leftarrow(1 - F_Z(Z)) \geq 0.$$

This means that

$$\mathbb{P}(\bar{X} \geq 0) = \mathbb{P}(Z \leq c)$$

for all relevant $\bar{X}$. The Gluing Problem (**GLUE**) is defined as

$$\sup_{(v_+, c)} \quad \Phi_+(v_+, c) - \Phi_-(v_+, c)$$

$$s.t. \ 0 \leq c \leq \infty. \tag{GLUE}$$

After solving (**GLUE**), we know the optimal parameters c^* and v_+^*. It was shown that $Z \leq c \Leftrightarrow \bar{X} \geq 0$ in all relevant cases, and thus we have for the

---

[4] $\overset{d}{=}$ indicates equivalence in distribution. Also note that $\bar{X}$ is continuous.

optimal solutions of the adjusted problems

$$(\bar{X}^*)^+ = \bar{X}^* \mathbf{1}_{\bar{X}^* \geq 0} = \bar{X}^* \mathbf{1}_{Z \leq c^*}$$

and analogously

$$(\bar{X}^*)^- = -\bar{X}^* \mathbf{1}_{\bar{X}^* < 0} = -\bar{X}^* \mathbf{1}_{Z > c^*}.$$

This means that we can also change the optimization problems (**GP**) and (**LP**) to the equivalent problems

$$\sup_{\bar{X}} \quad \mathbb{V}_+(\bar{X} \mathbf{1}_{Z \leq c})$$

$$s.t. \ \mathbb{E}[Z \bar{X} \mathbf{1}_{Z \leq c}] = v_+, \quad \text{(GP')}$$

$$\bar{X} \mathbf{1}_{Z \leq c} \geq 0$$

and

$$\inf_{\bar{X}} \quad \mathbb{V}_-(-\bar{X} \mathbf{1}_{Z > c})$$

$$s.t. \ \mathbb{E}[-Z \bar{X} \mathbf{1}_{Z > c}] = v_+ - \left(\frac{A_0}{L_0} - B\right) \quad \text{(LP')}$$

$$-\bar{X} \mathbf{1}_{Z > c} \geq 0.$$

Problems (**GP'**) and (**LP'**) can then be solved as described in [12].

Appendix C. Probability distortion

Lemma C.1. *The function* $\bar{w}_\delta : [0, 1] \to [0, 1]$ *with*

$$\bar{w}_\delta(p) = \mathcal{N}\left(\mathcal{N}^{\leftarrow}(p) - \delta\|\sigma_L - \theta'\|\sqrt{T}\right), \ \delta > 0,$$

is convex.

Proof. We know with

$$\bar{w}_\delta(p) = \int_0^{F_{Z_\delta}^{\leftarrow}(p)} r f_{Z_\delta}(r) dr = \int_0^p F_{Z_\delta}^{\leftarrow}(q) dq$$

that

$$\bar{w}_\delta'(p) = F_{Z_\delta}^{\leftarrow}(p) = \exp\left(-\frac{1}{2}\delta^2\|\sigma_L - \theta'\|^2 T + \delta\|\sigma_L - \theta'\|\sqrt{T}\mathcal{N}^{\leftarrow}(p)\right).$$

Thus we have

$$\bar{w}_\delta''(p) = \bar{w}_\delta'(p)\frac{\delta\|\sigma_L - \theta'\|\sqrt{T}}{\mathcal{N}'(\mathcal{N}^{\leftarrow}(p))} \geq 0.$$

The derivative of $w(p) = (\bar{w}_\delta(p))^\alpha$ is given by:

$$
\begin{aligned}
w'(p) =& \alpha(\bar{w}_\delta(p))^{\alpha-1} F_{Z_\delta}^{\leftarrow}(p) \\
=& \alpha \mathcal{N}^{\alpha-1} \left(\mathcal{N}^{\leftarrow}(p) - \delta\|\sigma_L - \theta'\|\sqrt{T} \right) \cdot \\
& \exp\left(-\frac{1}{2}\delta^2\|\sigma_L - \theta'\|^2 T + \delta\|\sigma_L - \theta'\|\sqrt{T}\mathcal{N}^{\leftarrow}(p) \right) \\
=& \alpha \mathcal{N}^{\alpha-1} \left(\mathcal{N}^{\leftarrow}(p) - \delta\|\sigma_L - \theta'\|\sqrt{T} \right) \\
& \exp\left(-\frac{1}{2}\|\sigma_L - \theta'\|^2 T + \|\sigma_L - \theta'\|\sqrt{T}\mathcal{N}^{\leftarrow}(p) \right) \cdot \\
& \exp\left(\frac{1}{2}(1-\delta^2)\|\sigma_L - \theta'\|^2 T + (\delta-1)\|\sigma_L - \theta'\|\sqrt{T}\mathcal{N}^{\leftarrow}(p) \right) \\
=& \alpha \mathcal{N}^{\alpha-1} \left(\mathcal{N}^{\leftarrow}(p) - \delta\|\sigma_L - \theta'\|\sqrt{T} \right) F_Z^{\leftarrow}(p) \cdot \\
& \exp\left(\frac{1}{2}(1-\delta^2)\|\sigma_L - \theta'\|^2 T + (\delta-1)\|\sigma_L - \theta'\|\sqrt{T}\mathcal{N}^{\leftarrow}(p) \right).
\end{aligned}
$$

$\square$

Lemma C.2. *For $\delta \in (0,1]$, $\alpha \in (0,1]$, the probability distortion function w satisfies the monotonicity condition* (**M**)*. Moreover, it is reverse-S shaped if in addition $\alpha \in (0,1)$.*

Proof. To show that (**M**) holds, we have to examine

$$
\frac{F_Z^{\leftarrow}(p)}{w'(p)}.
$$

With

$$
c := F_Z^{\leftarrow}(p), \quad I(c) := \left.\frac{w'(p)}{F_Z^{\leftarrow}(p)}\right|_{p=F_Z(c)} = \frac{w'(F_Z(c))}{c}, \quad H(c) := w(F_Z(c)),
$$

we get

$$
I(c) = \frac{H'(c)}{cF_Z'(c)}
$$

and subsequently

$$
\begin{aligned}
I'(c) =& \frac{H''(c)cF_Z'(c) - H'(c)cF_Z''(c) - H_Z'(c)F_Z'(c)}{(cF_Z'(c))^2} \leq 0 \\
\Leftrightarrow j(c) :=& \frac{cH''(c)}{H'(c)} - \frac{cF_Z''(c)}{F_Z'(c)} = c\left(\frac{H''(c)}{H'(c)} - \frac{F_Z''(c)}{F_Z'(c)} \right) \leq 1.
\end{aligned}
$$

Note that $c > 0$ since Z is log-normally distributed. The following statements are equivalent since F_Z is monotonically increasing:

$$\frac{F_Z^{\leftarrow}(p)}{w'(p)} \text{ is increasing} \quad \Leftrightarrow \quad I(c) \text{ is decreasing} \quad \Leftrightarrow \quad j(c) \leq 1.$$

We have

$$H(c) = w(F_z(c)) = \mathcal{N}^{\alpha}\left(\frac{\ln c + (\frac{1}{2} - \delta)\|\sigma_L - \theta'\|^2 T}{\|\sigma_L - \theta'\|\sqrt{T}}\right).$$

Therefore,

$$H'(c) = \alpha \mathcal{N}^{\alpha-1}\left(\frac{\ln c + (\frac{1}{2} - \delta)\|\sigma_L - \theta'\|^2 T}{\|\sigma_L - \theta'\|\sqrt{T}}\right)$$
$$\mathcal{N}'\left(\frac{\ln c + (\frac{1}{2} - \delta)\|\sigma_L - \theta'\|^2 T}{\|\sigma_L - \theta'\|\sqrt{T}}\right)\frac{1}{c\|\sigma_L - \theta'\|\sqrt{T}} > 0$$

and

$$H''(c) = H'(c)(\alpha - 1)\frac{\mathcal{N}'\left(\frac{\ln c + (\frac{1}{2} - \delta)\|\sigma_L - \theta'\|^2 T}{\|\sigma_L - \theta'\|\sqrt{T}}\right)}{\mathcal{N}\left(\frac{\ln c + (\frac{1}{2} - \delta)\|\sigma_L - \theta'\|^2 T}{\|\sigma_L - \theta'\|\sqrt{T}}\right)}\frac{1}{c\|\sigma_L - \theta'\|\sqrt{T}}$$
$$- H'(c)\left(\frac{\ln c + (\frac{1}{2} - \delta)\|\sigma_L - \theta'\|^2 T}{\|\sigma_L - \theta'\|\sqrt{T}}\right)\frac{1}{c\|\sigma_L - \theta'\|\sqrt{T}} - H'(c)\frac{1}{c}.$$

Thus,

$$\frac{cH''(c)}{H'(c)} = (\alpha - 1)\frac{\mathcal{N}'\left(\frac{\ln c + (\frac{1}{2} - \delta)\|\sigma_L - \theta'\|^2 T}{\|\sigma_L - \theta'\|\sqrt{T}}\right)}{\mathcal{N}\left(\frac{\ln c + (\frac{1}{2} - \delta)\|\sigma_L - \theta'\|^2 T}{\|\sigma_L - \theta'\|\sqrt{T}}\right)}\frac{1}{\|\sigma_L - \theta'\|\sqrt{T}}$$
$$- \left(\frac{\ln c + (\frac{1}{2} - \delta)\|\sigma_L - \theta'\|^2 T}{\|\sigma_L - \theta'\|\sqrt{T}}\right)\frac{1}{\|\sigma_L - \theta'\|\sqrt{T}} - 1.$$

For the distribution of the kernel (see (4)), it holds

$$F_Z'(c) = \mathcal{N}'\left(\frac{\ln c + \frac{1}{2}\|\sigma_L - \theta'\|^2 T}{\|\sigma_L - \theta'\|\sqrt{T}}\right)\frac{1}{c\|\sigma_L - \theta'\|\sqrt{T}}$$

and

$$F_Z''(c) = \mathcal{N}'\left(\frac{\ln c + \frac{1}{2}\|\sigma_L - \theta'\|^2 T}{\|\sigma_L - \theta'\|\sqrt{T}}\right).$$
$$\frac{1}{c\|\sigma_L - \theta'\|\sqrt{T}}\left(-\frac{\ln c + \frac{1}{2}\|\sigma_L - \theta'\|^2 T}{c\|\sigma_L - \theta'\|^2 T} - \frac{1}{c}\right).$$

Thus the second fraction in j is

$$\frac{cF_Z''(c)}{F_Z'(c)} = -\frac{\ln c + \frac{1}{2}\|\sigma_L - \theta'\|^2 T}{\|\sigma_L - \theta'\|^2 T} - 1.$$

Then the function j corresponding to w is

$$j(c) = \frac{\alpha - 1}{\|\sigma_L - \theta'\|\sqrt{T}} \frac{\mathcal{N}'\left(\frac{\ln c + (\frac{1}{2} - \delta)\|\sigma_L - \theta'\|^2 T}{\|\sigma_L - \theta'\|\sqrt{T}}\right)}{\mathcal{N}\left(\frac{\ln c + (\frac{1}{2} - \delta)\|\sigma_L - \theta'\|^2 T}{\|\sigma_L - \theta'\|\sqrt{T}}\right)} + \delta$$

$$= \frac{\alpha - 1}{\|\sigma_L - \theta'\|\sqrt{T}} \frac{\mathcal{N}'\left(d(c, T, \delta - 1)\right)}{\mathcal{N}\left(d(c, T, \delta - 1)\right)} + \delta,$$

with $d(c, T, \delta - 1) := \frac{\ln c + (\frac{1}{2} - \delta)\|\sigma_L - \theta'\|^2 T}{\|\sigma_L - \theta'\|\sqrt{T}}$. Its first term is not positive because $\alpha \in (0, 1]$ and it goes to zero for $c \to \infty$. Thus we can confirm that $j(c) \leq 1 \Leftrightarrow \delta \leq 1$. This means that w satisfies the monotonicity condition (**M**) if and only if $\delta \leq 1$.

Furthermore, we have

$$H'(c) = w'(F_Z(c))F_Z'(c)$$

and

$$H''(c) = w''(F_Z(c))F_Z'(c)^2 + w'(F_Z(c))F_Z''(c)$$
$$= w''(F_Z(c))F_Z'(c)^2 + \frac{H'(c)}{F_Z'(c)}F_Z''(c),$$

as well as

$$w(p) = H(F_Z^{\leftarrow}(p)) = H(c),$$

and

$$w''(F_Z(c)) = \frac{1}{F_Z'(c)^2}\left[H''(c) - \frac{H'(c)}{F_Z'(c)}F_Z''(c)\right].$$

Finally,

$$w''(F_Z(c))$$
$$< 0 \Leftrightarrow H''(c) - \frac{H'(c)}{F_Z'(c)}F_Z''(c) < 0 \Leftrightarrow c\left(\frac{H''(c)}{H'(c)} - \frac{F_Z''(c)}{F_Z'(c)}\right) = j(c) < 0.$$

Hence, w is reverse-S shaped if and only if j is first negative and then positive. For this, we assume that $\alpha \in (0, 1)$ and we note that

$$j(c) = (\alpha - 1)c\frac{\partial}{\partial c}\left(\ln\left(\mathcal{N}\left(d(c, T, \delta - 1)\right)\right)\right) + \delta$$

$$= \delta + \frac{\alpha - 1}{\|\sigma_L - \theta'\|\sqrt{T}}\frac{\partial}{\partial d}\left(\ln\left(\mathcal{N}\left(d\right)\right)\right)|_{d = d(c, T, \delta - 1)}$$

and hence with

$$j(c) = j(d(c)), \ d(c) := d(c, T, \delta - 1)$$

we have

$$j'(c) = \frac{\partial}{\partial d} j(d)|_{d=d(c)} \cdot \frac{\partial}{\partial c} d(c)$$

$$= \frac{\alpha - 1}{\|\sigma_L - \theta'\| \sqrt{T}} \frac{\partial^2}{\partial d^2} \left(\ln \left(\mathcal{N} \left(d \right) \right) \right)|_{d=d(c)} \cdot \frac{\partial}{\partial c} d(c, T, \delta - 1).$$

The factor $\frac{\alpha-1}{\|\sigma_L-\theta'\|\sqrt{T}}$ is negative because $\alpha \in (0,1)$. Furthermore, $\frac{\partial}{\partial c} d(c, T, \delta-1)$ is positive. Thus it remains to be shown that $\frac{\partial^2}{\partial d^2} \left(\ln \left(\mathcal{N} \left(d \right) \right) \right)$ is negative. The normal cumulative distribution function is a log-concave function (see e.g. [18]) which means in this case that $\ln \left(\mathcal{N}(d) \right)$ is concave. It follows that its second derivative is negative and j is monotonically increasing. Additionally we know

$$\lim_{c \to \infty} j(c) = \delta$$

and

$$\lim_{c \to 0} j(c) = \lim_{d \to -\infty} \frac{\alpha - 1}{\|\sigma_L - \theta'\| \sqrt{T}} \frac{\mathcal{N}' \left(d \right)}{\mathcal{N} \left(d \right)} + \delta$$

$$= \lim_{d \to -\infty} \frac{1 - \alpha}{\|\sigma_L - \theta'\| \sqrt{T}} d + \delta = -\infty.$$

For the second limit, we use the l'Hôpital rule and the fact that

$$\mathcal{N}'' \left(d \right) = -d \mathcal{N}' \left(d \right).$$

Hence, j changes sign from negative to positive, i.e. w is reverse-S shaped, if $\delta > 0$. $\qquad \square$

Appendix D. Replicating strategies for selected pay-offs

We want to calculate replicating strategies for general funding ratios $X^{\pm}(t, Z_t)$ first. Using Itô's Lemma and the fact that $X^{\pm}(t, Z_t)$ is a $\mathbb{Q}^L$-martingale, we know that under the measure $\mathbb{Q}^L$, the SDE has the form

$$dX^{\pm}(t, Z_t) = Z_t \frac{\partial}{\partial z} X^{\pm}(t, Z_t)(\sigma_L - \theta') dW_t^{\mathbb{Q}^L}.$$

For the replication, we use the fact that under $\mathbb{Q}^L$ a funding ratio has the form

$$dX^{\pm}(t, Z_t) = X^{\pm}(t, Z_t)(\varphi' \sigma - \sigma_L) dW_t^{\mathbb{Q}^L}. \tag{D.1}$$

Thus we have to find a strategy φ that ensures that both SDEs are the same, i.e.

$$X^{\pm}(t, Z_t)(\varphi(t)'\sigma - \sigma_L) = Z_t \frac{\partial}{\partial z} X^{\pm}(t, Z_t)(\sigma_L - \theta').$$

If we solve this for φ, we find

$$\varphi(t) = \frac{Z_t}{X^{\pm}(t, Z_t)} \frac{\partial}{\partial z} X^{\pm}(t, Z_t)(\sigma')^{-1}(\sigma_L' - \theta) + (\sigma')^{-1}\sigma_L'$$

$$= \frac{Z_t}{X^{\pm}(t, Z_t)} \frac{\partial}{\partial z} X^{\pm}(t, Z_t)(\varphi^{LH} - \varphi^{PS}) + \varphi^{LH}. \qquad (D.2)$$

This allows us to calculate the replicating portfolios of $(\bar{X}^*)^+$ and $(\bar{X}^*)^-$ resulting from CPT optimization. The corresponding strategies will be denoted by φ_+ and φ_- respectively. To discern the replicating portfolio φ^* of X^*, we need some further calculations as the hedging portfolio of the optimal solution is not the sum of the hedging portfolios of the partial optimal solutions. It rather holds

$$dX^*(t, Z_t) = d(\bar{X}^*(t, Z_t) + B) = d((\bar{X}^*)^+(t, Z_t)) - d((\bar{X}^*)^-(t, Z_t)),$$

since $dB = 0$. Using (D.1), this is the same as

$$X^*(t, Z_t)(\varphi'(t)\sigma - \sigma_L)dW_t^{\mathbb{Q}^L} = ((\bar{X}^*)^+(t, Z_t)(\varphi_+'(t)\sigma - \sigma_L)$$
$$- (\bar{X}^*)^-(t, Z_t)(\varphi_-'(t)\sigma - \sigma_L)) dW_t^{\mathbb{Q}^L}$$

or equivalently

$$X^*(t, Z_t)\varphi'(t)\sigma dW_t^{\mathbb{Q}^L}$$
$$= \left[(\bar{X}^*)^+(t, Z_t)\varphi_+'(t)\sigma - (\bar{X}^*)^-(t, Z_t)\varphi_-'(t)\sigma \right.$$
$$\left. + (X^*(t, Z_t) - ((\bar{X}^*)^+(t, Z_t) - (\bar{X}^*)^-(t, Z_t)))\sigma_L \right] dW_t^{\mathbb{Q}^L}.$$

Note that for all $t \in [0, T]$, it holds

$$X^*(t, Z_t) - ((\bar{X}^*)^+(t, Z_t) - (\bar{X}^*)^-(t, Z_t)) = B.$$

Then the replicating portfolio for X^* is given by

$$\varphi^*(t) = \frac{1}{X^*(t, Z_t)} \left((\bar{X}^*)^+(t, Z_t)\varphi_+(t) - (\bar{X}^*)^-(t, Z_t)\varphi_-(t) + B\varphi^{LH} \right).$$

We use (D.2) for φ_+ and φ_- to state

$$\varphi^*(t) = \frac{Z_t}{X^*(t, Z_t)} \left(\frac{\partial}{\partial z}(\bar{X}^*)^+(t, Z_t) - \frac{\partial}{\partial z}(\bar{X}^*)^-(t, Z_t) \right)(\varphi^{LH} - \varphi^{PS}) + \varphi^{LH}.$$

In the well-funded case we have $(\bar{X}^*)^- = 0$. Thus the above formula simplifies to

$$\varphi^*(t) = \frac{Z_t \frac{\partial}{\partial z}(\bar{X}^*)^+(t, Z_t)}{X^*(t, Z_t)}(\varphi^{LH} - \varphi^{PS}) + \varphi^{LH}.$$

If the funding ratio is of the form

$$X(T, Z_T) = Z_T^\nu \mathbf{1}_{Z_T \in (c_1, c_2)},$$

with $\nu \in \mathbb{R}$, $c_1 \geq 0, c_2 > 0$, we can derive the funding ratio at time t and the replicating strategy explicitly. We have $Z_T = Z_t Z_{T-t}$. The funding ratio can also be interpreted as the wealth process, discounted with the liability process L. Thus, the funding ratio is a $\mathbb{Q}^L$-martingale and we have

$$\begin{aligned} X(t, Z_t) &= \mathbb{E}_{\mathbb{Q}^L}\left[Z_T^\nu \mathbf{1}_{Z_T \in (c_1, c_2)} \big| \mathcal{F}_t\right] = \mathbb{E}_{\mathbb{Q}^L}\left[Z_{T-t}^\nu Z_t^\nu \mathbf{1}_{Z_t Z_{T-t} \in (c_1, c_2)} \big| \mathcal{F}_t\right] \\ &= Z_t^\nu \mathbb{E}\left[Z_{T-t}^{\nu+1} \mathbf{1}_{Z_{T-t} \in \left(\frac{c_1}{Z_t}, \frac{c_2}{Z_t}\right)} \Big| \mathcal{F}_t\right]. \end{aligned}$$

Here we can use the results from Footnote 1 and get

$X(t, Z_t)$

$$\begin{aligned} &= Z_t^\nu \exp\left(-\frac{1}{2}(\nu+1)\|\sigma_L' - \theta\|^2(T-t) + \frac{1}{2}(\nu+1)^2\|\sigma_L' - \theta\|^2(T-t)\right) \cdot \\ &\quad \left(\mathcal{N}\left(\frac{\ln\left(\frac{c_2}{Z_t}\right) + \frac{1}{2}\|\sigma_L' - \theta\|^2(T-t) - (\nu+1)\|\sigma_L' - \theta\|^2(T-t)}{\|\sigma_L' - \theta\|\sqrt{T-t}}\right)\right. \\ &\quad \left. - \mathcal{N}\left(\frac{\ln\left(\frac{c_1}{Z_t}\right) + \frac{1}{2}\|\sigma_L' - \theta\|^2(T-t) - (\nu+1)\|\sigma_L' - \theta\|^2(T-t)}{\|\sigma_L' - \theta\|\sqrt{T-t}}\right)\right) \\ &= Z_t^\nu \exp\left(\frac{1}{2}(\nu+1)\nu\|\sigma_L' - \theta\|^2(T-t)\right) \\ &\quad \left(\mathcal{N}\left(\frac{\ln\left(\frac{c_2}{Z_t}\right) - (\nu+\frac{1}{2})\|\sigma_L' - \theta\|^2(T-t)}{\|\sigma_L' - \theta\|\sqrt{T-t}}\right)\right. \\ &\quad \left. - \mathcal{N}\left(\frac{\ln\left(\frac{c_1}{Z_t}\right) - (\nu+\frac{1}{2})\|\sigma_L' - \theta\|^2(T-t)}{\|\sigma_L' - \theta\|\sqrt{T-t}}\right)\right) \\ &= Z_t^\nu \exp\left(\frac{1}{2}(\nu+1)\nu\|\sigma_L' - \theta\|^2(T-t)\right) \cdot \\ &\quad \left(\mathcal{N}\left(d\left(\frac{c_2}{Z_t}, T-t, \nu\right)\right) - \mathcal{N}\left(d\left(\frac{c_1}{Z_t}, T-t, \nu\right)\right)\right), \end{aligned}$$

with $d(c, s, \nu)$ as in Appendix C. Thus all that is left to do is calculating the derivative of the fair price and putting our results together. The derivative is

$$
\frac{\partial}{\partial z} X(t, z) = \exp\left(\frac{1}{2}(\nu + 1)\nu \|\sigma'_L - \theta\|^2 (T - t)\right) \cdot
$$
$$
\left(\nu z^{\nu-1}\left(\mathcal{N}\left(d\left(\frac{c_2}{z}, T - t, \nu\right)\right) - \mathcal{N}\left(d\left(\frac{c_1}{z}, T - t, \nu\right)\right)\right)\right)
$$
$$
- \left(\mathcal{N}'\left(d\left(\frac{c_2}{z}, T - t, \nu\right)\right) - \mathcal{N}'\left(d\left(\frac{c_1}{z}, T - t, \nu\right)\right)\right) \frac{z^{\nu-1}}{\|\sigma'_L - \theta\|\sqrt{T - t}}\right)
$$
$$
= \frac{\nu}{z} X(t, z) - \exp\left(\frac{1}{2}(\nu + 1)\nu \|\sigma'_L - \theta\|^2 (T - t)\right) \cdot
$$
$$
\left(\mathcal{N}'\left(d\left(\frac{c_2}{z}, T - t, \nu\right)\right) - \mathcal{N}'\left(d\left(\frac{c_1}{z}, T - t, \nu\right)\right)\right) \frac{z^{\nu-1}}{\|\sigma'_L - \theta\|\sqrt{T - t}}.
$$

Inserting this and the formula for $X(t, Z_t)$ in (D.2), we see that

$$
\varphi(t) = \varphi^{LH} + \left(\nu - \frac{\exp\left(\frac{1}{2}(\nu + 1)\nu \|\sigma_L - \theta'\|^2 (T - t)\right)}{X(t, Z_t)\|\sigma_L - \theta'\|\sqrt{T - t}} \cdot\right.
$$
$$
\left.\left(\mathcal{N}'\left(d\left(\frac{c_2}{Z_t}, T - t, \nu\right)\right) - \mathcal{N}'\left(d\left(\frac{c_1}{Z_t}, T - t, \nu\right)\right)\right) Z_t^\nu\right) (\varphi^{LH} - \varphi^{PS})
$$
$$
= \varphi^{LH}
$$
$$
+ \left(\nu - \frac{1}{\|\sigma_L - \theta'\|\sqrt{T - t}} \frac{\mathcal{N}'\left(d\left(\frac{c_2}{Z_t}, T - t, \nu\right)\right) - \mathcal{N}'\left(d\left(\frac{c_1}{Z_t}, T - t, \nu\right)\right)}{\mathcal{N}\left(d\left(\frac{c_2}{Z_t}, T - t, \nu\right)\right) - \mathcal{N}\left(d\left(\frac{c_1}{Z_t}, T - t, \nu\right)\right)}\right) \cdot
$$
$$
(\varphi^{LH} - \varphi^{PS})
$$
$$
= \varphi^{LH}
$$
$$
+ \left(-\nu + \frac{1}{\|\sigma_L - \theta'\|\sqrt{T - t}} \frac{\mathcal{N}'\left(d\left(\frac{c_2}{Z_t}, T - t, \nu\right)\right) - \mathcal{N}'\left(d\left(\frac{c_1}{Z_t}, T - t, \nu\right)\right)}{\mathcal{N}\left(d\left(\frac{c_2}{Z_t}, T - t, \nu\right)\right) - \mathcal{N}\left(d\left(\frac{c_1}{Z_t}, T - t, \nu\right)\right)}\right) \cdot
$$
$$
(\varphi^{PS} - \varphi^{LH}).
$$

Bibliography

1. W. Sharpe and L. Tint, Liabilities — a new approach, *Journal of Portfolio Management* **16**(2), 5–10 (Winter 1990).

2. L. Martellini, Managing pension assets: From surplus optimization to liability-driven investment, *EDHEC-Risk Institute Position Papers* (March 2006).

3. R. Merton, Lifetime portfolio selection under uncertainty: The continuous time case, *The Review of Economics and Statistics* **51**, 247–257 (1969).

4. A. Ang, B. Chen and S. Sundaresan, Liability driven investment with downside risk, *Journal of Portfolio Management* **40**, 71–87 (Fall 2013).

5. M. Rudolf and W. T. Ziemba, Intertemporal surplus management, *Journal of Economic Dynamics and Control* **28**, 975–990 (2004).

6. N. Amenc, P. Malaise and L. Martellini, Revisiting core-satellite investing - a dynamic model of relative risk management, *The Journal of Portfolio Management* **31**, 64–75 (2004).

7. J. Kraus, P. Betrand and R. Zagst, Theory of performance participation strategies, *Working paper* (2010).

8. H. Bahaji, Equity portfolio insurance against a benchmark: Setting, replication and optimality, *Economic Modelling* **40**, 382–391 (2014).

9. J. H. van Binsbergen and M. W. Brandt, Optimal asset allocation in asset liability management, *NBER Working Paper No.* **12970** (2007).

10. R. Josa-Fombellida and J. P. Rincón-Zapatero, Optimal risk management in defined benefit stochastic pension funds, *Insurance: Mathematics and Economics* **34**, 489–503 (2004).

11. S. E. Shreve, *Stochastic Calculus for Finance II Continuous-Time Models*, 8th corr. edn. (Springer, Berlin, Heidelberg, 2008).

12. H. Jin and X. Y. Zhou, Behavioral portfolio selection in continuous time, *Mathematical Finance* **18**, 385–426 (2008).

13. D. Kahneman and A. Tversky, Prospect theory: An analysis of decision under risk, *Econometrica: Journal of the Econometric Society* **47**, 263–292 (1979).

14. A. Tversky and D. Kahneman, Advances in prospect theory: Cumulative representation of uncertainty, *Journal of Risk and uncertainty* **5**(4), 297–323 (1992).

15. D. Prelec, The probability weighting function, *Econometrica* **66**, 497–528 (1998).

16. S. S. Wang, A class of distortion operators for pricing financial and insurance risks, *The Journal of Risk and Insurance* **67**(1), 15–36 (2000).

17. H. Pham, *Continuous-time Stochastic Control and Optimization with Financial Applications* (Springer, Berlin, Heidelberg, 2009).

18. M. Bagnoli and T. Bergstrom, Log-concave probability and its applications, *Economic theory* **26**, 445–469 (2005).

Chapter 12

Option Pricing and Hedging for Discrete Time Autoregressive Hidden Markov Model

Massimo Caccia[*] and Bruno Rémillard[†]

Department of Decision Sciences, HEC Montréal,
Montréal (Québec), Canada H3T 2A7
[*] massimo.caccia@hec.ca
[†] bruno.remillard@hec.ca

In this paper we solve the discrete time mean-variance hedging problem when asset returns follow a multivariate autoregressive hidden Markov model. Time dependent volatility and serial dependence are well established properties of financial time series and our model covers both. To illustrate the relevance of our recommended approach, we first compare the proposed model with the well-known hidden Markov model via likelihood ratio tests and a novel goodness-of-fit test on the S&P 500 daily returns. In addition, we present out-of-sample hedging results on S&P 500 vanilla options as well as a trading strategy based on the difference between theoretical and market prices. This strategy is compared to simpler models including the classical Black-Scholes delta-hedging approach.

Keywords: option pricing, dynamic hedging, regime-switching, goodness-of-fit, auto-regressive hidden Markov models.

1. Introduction

The quest for the perfect option pricing model is an important topic in the mathematical finance literature. [1] provided the following observation: if a claim is priced by arbitrage in a world with one asset and one bond, then its value can be found by first adapting the model so that the asset earns the risk-free rate, and then computing the expected value of the claim. The idea of finding a self-financing optimal investment strategy that replicates the terminal payoff of the claim is now known as dynamic hedging.

One can model the underlying asset's returns with the geometric Brownian motion and retrieve a tractable and intuitive way of pricing and replicating options. This is precisely what [2] proposed; it is now called the B&S model. Unfortunately, financial markets are far too complex for a model as simple as this one and this hedging protocol can lead to large hedging errors, as it will be shown later in this paper. The main drawback of this framework is the constant volatility assumption. Indeed, according to [3], [4], volatility seems to vary over time, mainly for macroeconomic reasons. Furthermore, the B&S model assumes serial independence for the returns, which is also an hypothesis that is violated in general.

Optimal hedging was introduced later, and it consists in minimizing the quadratic error of replication. Solutions were derived in continuous time in [5] and later in discrete time in [6]. This methodology can be applied to the B&S model, and more interestingly, to stochastic volatility models.

Hidden Markov models, popularized in [7], [8] were proven to be extremely useful for modeling economic and financial time series. They are robust to time-varying volatility, serial correlation and higher-order moments, which are all well-established stylized facts of asset returns. The premise for these models is that identifiable events can quickly change the characteristics of an asset's returns. This should be taken into account when pricing a derivative. These events could be on a long horizon — fundamental changes in monetary, fiscal or income policies — or on a shorter horizon — news related to the underlying stock or changes in the target band for the federal funds rate. However, the classical implementation of an HMM can't account for multiple horizons.

Elliot's work on energy finance and interest rate modeling, where mean-reversion is a widely accepted feature, addresses this problem. [9] introduced a way to parameterize a regime-switching mean-reverting model with jumps. They found the calibration of the model to be difficult because of the small amounts of jumps exhibited in the time series. [10] later introduced a similar model with no jumps, and where the volatility is subject to mean-reverting regime-switches. The basis was that volatility, being driven by macroeconomic forces, was not to be modeled by price movements. Hence the need to model it by a hidden Markov chain. Finally, [11] investigated the valuation of European and American options under another model where the volatility is subject to regime-switches, but this time the Markov chain was assumed to be observable. This suggests that it would be interesting to develop some methods to determine the optimal number of states for the hidden Markov chain. This is precisely one of the contributions of our paper.

In light of all the above, we decided to generalize the work of [12]: we combine the regime-switching model with an autoregressive parameter to account for trends and mean-reversions without having to change regime. Autoregressive hidden Markov models (ARHMM) have been applied to financial engineering and have shown promising results, see, e.g. [13]. Still, this model has never been used in conjunction with optimal hedging. We derive the solution of the hedging strategy and obtain derivatives prices under this class of models. It is also noteworthy to add that we will use semi-exact techniques to compute expectations necessary for the optimal hedging, instead of Monte Carlo techniques, which will greatly speed up computations. For parameterization, we will implement the EM algorithm of [14] to the ARHMM. This method is widely used in unsupervised machine learning in order to find hidden structures, in our case, the regimes. In order to choose the optimal number of regimes and to assess the suitability of the model, we propose a new goodness-of-fit test based on [15] and [16]. It uses the Rosenblatt transform and parametric bootstrap. Compared to Elliot's work, our model can exhibit mean-reversion but is not restricted to it. It could thus be adequate for the modeling of a wide variety of assets.

In his famous study [17], Fama presented strong and voluminous evidence in favor of the random walk hypothesis. He although suggested that other tests — statistical or profit generating strategies — could either confirm or contradict his findings. In this paper, we will explore both avenues. We will statistically show that the ARHMM is an adequate model for financial modeling using the goodness-of-fit test as well as likelihood ratio tests, and we will show that it is possible to generate money by buying/selling options and replicating them until maturity. To support our approach, we will compare the trading strategy's returns with different methodologies: Black-Scholes delta-hedging and optimal hedging when assets follow a geometric random walk. We will also compare the hedging results with the delta-hedging using the market's implicit volatility.

First, we present likelihood ratio test results confirming the ARHMM is a better fit than the classical HMM on S&P daily returns, in particular, because our model has the capacity for mean-reversion. Secondly, empirical pricing and hedging results suggest that our methodology is superior to its counterparts by achieving the best mean-squared error in six out of eight cases, as well as being the most profitable strategy.

The rest of the paper is organized as follows. Section 2 describes the model and implements the EM algorithm for parameter estimation. In addition, we will introduce the goodness-of-fit test and study its suitability in the financial markets. Then, in Section 3, we will state the optimal dynamic discrete time hedging model when assets follow a ARHMM. The results of the implementation of the dynamic hedging strategies will be presented in Section 4. Section 5 concludes.

2. Regime-switching autoregressive models

The proposed models are quite intuitive. The regime process τ is a homogeneous Markov chain on $\{1, \ldots, l\}$, with transition matrix Q. At period $t - 1$, if $\tau_{t-1} = i$, and the return Y_{t-1} has value y_{t-1}, then at time t, $\tau_t = j$ with probability Q_{ij}, and the return Y_t has conditional distribution $f_j(y_t; y_{t-1})$; here lower case letters $y_1, \ldots, y_n$ are used to denote a realization of $Y_1, \ldots, Y_n$. From this construction it follows that (Y_t, τ_t) is a Markov process. For example, for $j \in \{1, \ldots, l\}$, one could take a Gaussian AR(1) model, meaning that given $Y_{t-1} = y_{t-1}$ and $\tau_t = j$, $Y_t = \mu_j + \Phi_j(y_{t-1} - \mu_j) + \varepsilon_t$, with $\varepsilon_t \sim N(0, A_j)$; the conditional density of Y_t at $y_t \in \mathbb{R}^d$ is

$$f_j(y_t|y_{t-1}) = \frac{e^{-\frac{1}{2}\{y_t - \mu_j - \Phi_j(y_{t-1} - \mu_j)\}^\top A_j^{-1}\{y_t - \mu_j - \Phi_j(y_{t-1} - \mu_j)\}}}{(2\pi)^{d/2}|A_j|^{1/2}}, \qquad (1)$$

where $\mu_j \in \mathbb{R}^d$, Φ_j is a $d \times d$ matrix such that $\Phi_j^n \to 0$ as $n \to \infty$,[1] and A_j is a $d \times d$ non-degenerate covariance matrix. The matrices $\Phi_1, \ldots, \Phi_l$ are mean-reversion parameters. Let $\mathcal{B}_d$ be the set of $d \times d$ matrices B such that $B^n \to 0$ as $n \to \infty$ and let S_d^+ be the set of symmetric positive definite $d \times d$ matrices. Note that $\mathcal{B}_d$ is the set of $d \times d$ matrices with spectral radius smaller than 1, meaning that the eigenvalues are all in the unit complex ball of radius 1; in particular, $I - B$ is invertible for any $B \in \mathcal{B}_d$. Note that the so-called Hidden Markov Model is obtained by setting $\Phi_1 = \cdots = \Phi_l = 0$.

2.1. *Regime prediction*

Since the regimes are not observable, we have to find a way to predict them. This will be of utmost importance for pricing and hedging derivatives.

In many applications, one has to predict an colored a non-observable signal by using observations $Y_1, \ldots, Y_t$ linked in a certain way to the signal. This is known as a filtering problem; see, e.g., [18]. In our case, we need to find at time t the conditional probability $\eta_t(i) = P(\tau_t = i | Y_1 = y_1, \ldots, Y_t = y_t)$. It is remarkable that for the present model, one can compute exactly this conditional distribution, given a starting distribution η_0. For more details, see the extension of the Baum-Welch algorithm in Appendix A.

---

[1] This condition ensures that for any $j \in \{1, \ldots, l\}$, the matrix $B_j = \sum_{k=0}^{\infty} \Phi_j^k A_j \left(\Phi_j^k\right)^\top$ is well defined and satisfies $B_j = \Phi_j B_j \Phi_j^\top + A_j$.

2.1.1. *Filtering algorithm*

Choose an a priori probability distribution η_0 for the regimes. Equivalently, one can choose a positive vector q_0 and set $\eta_0(i) = q_0(i)/Z_0$, where $Z_0 = \sum_{j=1}^{l} q_0(j)$. The choice of q_0 or η_0 is not critical since its impact on predictions decays in time and have virtually no impact on terminal regime probabilities for any reasonable time series length. For simplicity, we assume a uniform distribution, i.e. $q_0 \equiv 1/l$.

For $t \in \{1, \ldots, n\}$, define $q_t(i) = E\left[\mathbf{1}(\tau_t = i) \prod_{k=1}^{t} f_{\tau_k}(y_k|y_{k-1})\right]$, $i \in \{1, \ldots, l\}$, and $Z_t = \sum_{j=1}^{l} q_t(j)$. Note that the first observation of the sequence is burn-in in order to compute $f_{\tau_1}(y_1|y_0)$. Hence, Z_t is the joint density $f_{1:t}(y_1, \ldots, y_t)$ of $Y_1, \ldots, Y_t$ because

$$f_{1:t}(y_1, \ldots, y_t) = E\left[\prod_{k=1}^{t} f_{\tau_k}(y_k|y_{k-1})\right] = \sum_{j=1}^{l} q_t(j) = Z_t.$$

Then if $q_0 = \eta_0$, for any $i \in \{1, \ldots, l\}$, and any $t \geq 1$, we have

$$q_t(i) = E\left[\mathbf{1}(\tau_t = i) \prod_{k=1}^{t} f_{\tau_k}(y_k|y_{k-1})\right]$$

$$= f_i(y_t|y_{t-1}) \sum_{j=1}^{l} E\left[\mathbf{1}(\tau_t = i)\mathbf{1}(\tau_{t-1} = j) \prod_{k=1}^{t-1} f_{\tau_k}(y_k|y_{k-1})\right]$$

$$= f_i(y_t|y_{t-1}) \sum_{j=1}^{l} Q_{ji} E\left[\mathbf{1}(\tau_{t-1} = j) \prod_{k=1}^{t-1} f_{\tau_k}(y_k|y_{k-1})\right]$$

$$= f_i(y_t|y_{t-1}) \sum_{j=1}^{l} Q_{ji} q_{t-1}(j), \tag{2}$$

and

$$\eta_t(i) = P(\tau_t = i|Y_1, \ldots, Y_t) = \frac{q_t(i)}{Z_t}. \tag{3}$$

Having computed the conditional distribution η_t, one can estimate τ_t by

$$\tau_t = \arg\max_i \eta_t(i), \tag{4}$$

i.e. as the most probable regime. In view of applications, it is preferable to rewrite (3) only in terms of η, i.e.,

$$\eta_t(i) = \frac{f_i(y_t|y_{t-1})}{Z_{t|t-1}} \sum_{j=1}^{l} \eta_{t-1}(j) Q_{ji},$$

where $Z_{t|t-1} = \frac{Z_t}{Z_{t-1}} = \sum_{j=1}^{l} \sum_{i=1}^{l} f_i(y_t|y_{t-1})\eta_{t-1}(j)Q_{ji}$. As a result, $Z_{t|t-1}$ is the conditional density of Y_t at y_t, given $Y_1 = y_1, \ldots, Y_{t-1} = y_{t-1}$.

2.1.2. *Conditional distribution*

From the results of the previous section, the joint density $f_{1:t}$ of $Y_1, \ldots, Y_t$ is Z_t. Also, for any $t \geq 2$, the conditional density $f_{t|t-1} = Z_{t|t-1}$ of Y_t given $Y_1, \ldots, Y_{t-1}$, can be expressed as a mixture, viz.

$$f_{t|t-1}(y_t|y_1, \ldots, y_{t-1}) = \sum_{i=1}^{l} f_i(y_t|y_{t-1}) \sum_{j=1}^{l} \eta_{t-1}(j)Q_{ji}$$

$$= \sum_{i=1}^{l} f_i(y_t|y_{t-1})W_{t-1}(i)$$

where $W_{t-1}(i) = \sum_{j=1}^{l} \eta_{t-1}(j)Q_{ji}$, $i \in \{1, \ldots, l\}$. Note that for all $t > 1$, $W_{t-1}(i) = P(\tau_t = i|Y_{t-1} = y_{t-1}, \ldots, Y_1 = y_1)$. As a result, it follows that

$$P(\tau_{t+k} = i|Y_t = y_t, \ldots, Y_1 = y_1) = \sum_{j=1}^{l} (Q^k)_{ji}\eta_t(j), \quad i \in \{1, \ldots, l\}.$$

Next, the conditional law of $Y_{t+1}, \ldots, Y_{t+m}$ given $Y_1, \ldots, Y_t$ has density

$$f_{t+m|t}(y_{t+1}, \ldots, y_{t+m}|y_1, \ldots, y_t) = \sum_{i_0=1}^{l} \sum_{i_1=1}^{l} \cdots \sum_{i_m=1}^{l} \eta_t(i_0)$$

$$\times \prod_{k=1}^{m} Q_{i_{k-1}i_k} f_{i_k}(y_{t+k}|y_{t+k-1}).$$

2.1.3. *Stationary distribution in the Gaussian case*

Suppose that the model specified by (1) holds, ergo the innovations are Gaussian. If Y_n converges in law to a stationary distribution for any given starting point y_0, then this distribution must be Gaussian, with mean μ and covariance matrix A. Suppose the Markov chain is ergodic with stationary distribution ν. Then with probability ν_i, $i \in \{1, \ldots, l\}$, $Y_1 = (I - \Phi_i)\mu_i + \Phi_i Y_0 + \epsilon_i$, where $\epsilon_i \sim N(0, A_i)$ is independent of $Y_0 \sim N(\mu, A)$. It then follows that

$$\mu = \left\{\sum_{i=1}^{l} \nu_i(I - \Phi_i)\right\}^{-1} \left\{\sum_{i=1}^{l} \nu_i\{(I - \Phi_i)\mu_i\}\right\}.$$

Similarly, A must satisfies $A = T(A)$, where

$$T(A) = B + \sum_{i=1}^{l} \nu_i \Phi_i A \Phi_i^\top, \tag{5}$$

with $B = -\mu\mu^\top + \sum_{i=1}^{l} \nu_i \left[(I - \Phi_i)\mu_i + \Phi_i\mu\}\{(I - \Phi_i)\mu_i + \Phi_i\mu\}^\top + A_i\right]$. From the conditions on $\Phi_1, \ldots, \Phi_l$, there is a norm $\|\cdot\|$ on the space of matrices such that $\|\Phi_i\| < 1$ for every $i \in \{1, \ldots, l\}$.[2] The operator T is then a contraction since for any two matrices A_0, A_1, $\|T(A_1) - T(A_0)\| \leq \|A_1 - A_0\| \sum_{i=1}^{l} \nu_i \|\Phi_i\|^2 \leq c\|A_1 - A_0\|$, with $c = \max_{1 \leq i \leq l} \|\Phi_i\|^2 < 1$. Also, since $T(A)$ is a covariance matrix whenever A is one, and B is positive definite, it follows that there is a unique fixed point A of T, meaning that $A = T(A)$, and this unique fixed point A is a positive definite covariance matrix. If fact, A is the limit of any sequence $A_n = T(A_{n-1})$, with A_0 a non-negative definite covariance matrix. For example, one could take even take $A_0 = 0$. This provides a way to approximate the limiting covariance A by setting $A \approx A_n$ for n large enough.

2.2. *Estimation of parameters*

The EM algorithm of [14] is an efficient estimation procedure for incomplete datasets. This is the case here since τ is unobservable. The algorithm proceeds iteratively to converge to the maximum likelihood estimation of parameters. Its implementation for ARHMM is detailed in Appendix A.1. It seems that starting the parameter's estimation of the ARHMM with the HMM parameters' estimate (obtained by setting $\Phi_1 = \cdots = \Phi_d = 0$) is slightly more stable. The optimal number of regimes must be known a priori, an issue we will discuss next.

2.3. *Goodness-of-fit test and selection of the number of regimes*

To select the optimal number of regimes, one must test the adequacy of fitted models with different number of regimes. This is generally done by using a test based on likelihoods. However, according to [19], goodness-of-fit tests based on likelihoods are not recommended for regime-switching models. We opt for a simpler approach based on a parametric bootstrapping. It was shown to work on a large number of dynamic models, including hidden

---

[2]Recall that all norms are equivalent.

Table 1.   P-values (in percentage) for the nonparametric change point test using the Kolmogorov-Smirnov statistic with N=10000 bootstrap samples.

Period	P-value
2000's recovery	39.8
2008-2009 Financial Crisis	0.4
2010's recovery	9.7

Markov models. The test is built on the work of [20] and its implementation is given in Appendix B.

2.3.1. *Selecting the number of regimes*

The goodness-of-fit test described in Appendix B produces P-values from Cramér-von Mises type statistics, for a given number of regimes ℓ. As suggested in [21], it makes sense to choose the optimal number of regimes $\ell^\star$ as the smallest ℓ for which the P-value is larger than 5%. An illustration of this methodology is given in Section 2.4.

2.4. *Application to S&P 500 daily returns*

To assess the relevance of our model on real data, we estimated the parameters on the close-to-close log-returns of the daily price series of the S&P 500 Total Return. To find stationary estimation windows, we used a nonparametric changepoint test for a univariate series using a Kolmogorov-Smirnov type statistic, as in [18]. We focused on recent data, i.e. from early 2000 to the beginning of 2017. We found two stationary estimation windows: from 05/01/2004 to 02/01/2008 and from 05/01/2010 to 20/01/2017. We refer to the former as the 2000's recovery and 2010's recovery for the latter. Results of the tests are presented in Table 1. We also studied the interesting period in between, the 2008-2009 Financial Crisis, even though the null hypothesis of stationarity has a P-value of 0.4%.

Next, we performed the goodness-of-fit test (GoF for short) described in Appendix B for the ARHMM (AR(1)) as well as for the HMM (AR(0)), as a mean of comparison. The results are presented in Tables 2, 4 and 6. According to the selection method described in Section 2.3.1, we selected a three-regime model for the 2000's recovery, since 3 is the smallest number of regimes for which the P-value is larger than 5%. This is also true for the HMM model. Likewise, we chose a three-regime model for the 2008-2009 Financial Crisis, and a four-regime model for the 2010's recovery. Note that in the case of the 2010's Bull markets, a four regime model for the HMM was not enough to get a *P*-value > 5%. Furthermore, to measure the significance of ARHMM over HMM, we performed a likelihood ratio test. This is possible because the HMM is a special case of the ARHMM corresponding to $\Phi_1 = \cdots = \Phi_l = 0$. The corresponding statistic is computed as follows:

$$D = -2\log\left(\frac{L(\hat{\theta}_0|x)}{L(\hat{\theta}_1|x)}\right) = -2\log\left(\frac{f_{1:n}(y_1, \ldots, y_n|\hat{\theta}_0)}{f_{1:n}(y_1, \ldots, y_n|\hat{\theta}_1)}\right)$$

where $\hat{\theta}_0$ are the model's parameters estimated under the null hypothesis, i.e. $\Phi_1 = \cdots = \Phi_\ell = 0$, so the returns follow a Gaussian hidden Markov model, and $\hat{\theta}_1$ are the model's parameters estimated under the alternative, i.e. returns follow an autoregressive hidden Markov model. Under the null hypothesis, the limiting distribution of this statistic is a chi-square distribution with ℓ degrees of freedom, which is the number of extra parameters in the alternative model. Hence, under the null hypothesis, $D \sim \chi^2(\ell)$. The log-likelihoods of both models, the statistical test D and the χ^2 critical value at a significance level of 5% are also presented in Tables 2, 4 and 6. We clearly reject the null hypothesis for all models, proving we should favor ARHMM over HMM for each dataset.

The estimated parameters for the three periods are presented in Tables 3, 5, and 7, where the mean and standard deviation of each AR(1) and AR(0) Gaussian regime density f_i are respectively denoted by μ_i and σ_i, and are presented as annualized percentages values. The tables further contain the stationary regime probabilities ν, together with the estimated transition matrix Q. Regimes are ordered by increasing volatility σ_i, and incidentally by decreasing mean μ_i.

Table 2. P-values (in percentage) for the proposed goodness-of-fit test using N=10000 bootstrap samples on the S&P 500 daily returns for the 2000's recovery, along with the log-likelihood of the models and the P-values (in percentage) of the likelihood ratio test statistic D.

	Number of regimes		
	1	2	3
GoF *P*-value (ARHMM)	0	0	26.51
GoF *P*-value (HMM)	0	0	25.12
Log-likelihood (ARHMM)	3479	3542	3559
Log-likelihood (HMM)	3475	3539	3552
P-value (D)	0.43	3.63	0.18

In the case of the 2000's recovery, regime 1 is associated to Bull markets, which are characterized by strong positive premium and low risk ($\mu_1 =$

Table 3.   Parameters estimation for the three-regime models on the S&P 500 Total Return daily returns for the 2000's recovery.

Parameter	AR(0) Regime			AR(1) Regime		
	1	2	3	1	2	3
μ	31.41	13.88	−17.23	34.89	6.99	−21.60
σ	2.18	10.09	18.02	3.34	11.03	18.95
Φ	0	0	0	−0.14	0.03	−0.19
ν	0.11	0.65	0.24	0.19	0.63	0.18
	0	0.92	0.08	0	0.96	0.04
Q	0.17	0.83	0	0.32	0.68	0
	0	0.03	0.97	0	0.04	0.96

Note: μ and σ are presented as annualized percentage.

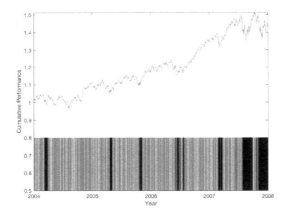

Fig. 1.   Most probable regimes for the three-regime AR(1) model fitted on the S&P 500 Total Return index from 05/01/2004 to 02/01/2008 together with the cumulative performance of the index. Darker areas represent higher volatility states.

35.89 and $\sigma_i = 3.34$). It seems that this state is intermittent in the sense that the Markov chain does not stay or has a very small probability of staying in regime 1 since $Q_{11} \approx 0$. However, this state is not due to outliers since the percentage of time the Markov chain is in this state is 11% for the HMM and 19% for the ARHMM. Regime 2 is an intermediate state. Lastly, regime 3 is associated with bear markets or corrections, as highlighted by the negative premium of −21.60 and the volatility of 18.95. The regimes are less distinct in the HMM case. Also, the likelihood ratio test statistic $D = 15.04$ informs us that ARHMM is a much better fit for the data.

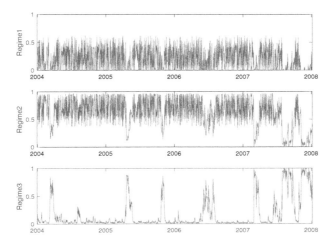

Fig. 2.   Probability of the regimes, i.e. η_t, for the three-regime AR(1) model fitted on the S&P 500 Total Return index from 05/01/2004 to 02/01/2008.

Indeed, we observe strong mean-reversion in regime 1 and 3 ($\Phi_1 = -0.14$ and $\Phi_3 = -0.19$). Figure 1 displays the filtered most probable regimes (as defined in Section 2.1) for the whole time series. The regimes are depicted by different shades of grey, ranging from dark for the high volatility regime to white for the low volatility regime. The probabilities η_t of each regime are displayed in Figure 2. Interestingly enough, the crisis in the subprime mortgage market is adequately captured by the high risk regime.

Table 4.   P-values (in percentage) for the proposed good-ness-of-fit test using N=10000 bootstrap samples on the S&P 500 daily returns for the 2008-2009 Financial Crisis, along with the log-likelihood of the models and the P-values (in percentage) of the likelihood ratio test statistic D.

	Number of regimes		
	1	2	3
GoF *P*-value (ARHMM)	0	0	59.59
GoF *P*-value (HMM)	0	0	72
Log-likelihood (ARHMM)	1,209	1,323	1,334
Log-likelihood (HMM)	1,214	1,318	1.329
P-value (D)	0.19	0.95	2.59

The second period studied is quite interesting. For the 2008-2009 Finan-cial Crisis, regimes are extremely polarized, with expected returns ranging

Table 5. Parameters estimation for the three-regime models on the S&P 500 Total Return daily returns for the 2008-2009 Financial Crisis.

Parameter	AR(0) Regime			AR(1) Regime		
	1	2	3	1	2	3
μ	74.97	−5.28	−66.87	72.22	−0.42	−64.73
σ	5.52	23.17	57.80	5.12	22.56	55.68
Φ	0	0	0	−0.03	−0.16	−0.15
ν	0.15	0.58	0.27	0.14	0.58	0.28
	0	0.97	0.03	0	0.98	0.02
Q	0.25	0.75	0	0.23	0.77	0
	0	0.01	0.99	0	0.01	0.99

Note: μ and σ are presented as annualized percentage.

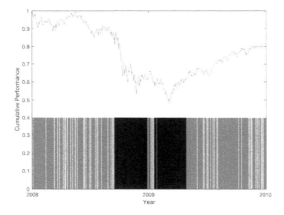

Fig. 3. Most probable regimes for the three-regime AR(1) model fitted on the S&P 500 Total Return index from 03/01/2008 to 04/01/2010, together with the cumulative performance of the index. Darker areas represent higher volatility states.

from 72.22 to −64.73. The bear market regime, i.e. regime 3, is exceptionally persistent and volatile, as highlighted by $Q_{3,3} = 0.99$ and $\sigma_3 = 55.68$. Once more, we find two regimes exhibiting mean-reversion, i.e. $\Phi_2 = -0.16$ and $\Phi_3 = -0.15$. Figures 3 and 4 are analogous to Figures 1 and 2 respectively. We can see that the Markov chain switched to the high risk regime right after the collapse of Lehman Brothers. Remarkably, it stayed in that regime throughout almost all the Banking Crisis, even though we observe numerous small upwards trends, meaning many thought we hit the bottom.

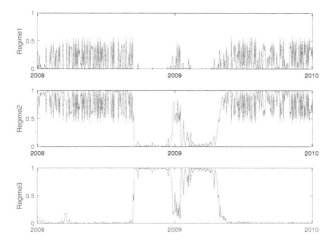

Fig. 4. Probability of the regimes, i.e. η_t, for the three-regime AR(1) model fitted on the S&P 500 Total Return index from 03/01/2008 to 04/01/2010.

Table 6. P-values (in percentage) for the proposed goodness-of-fit test using N=10000 bootstrap samples on the S&P 500 daily returns for the 2010's recovery, along with the log-likelihood of the models and the P-values (in percentage) of the likelihood ratio test statistic D.

	Number of regimes			
	1	2	3	4
GoF P-value (ARHMM)	0	0	0	1.56
GoF P-value (HMM)	0	0	0	5.83
Log-likelihood (ARHMM)	5,696	5,936	5,985	6,012
Log-likelihood (HMM)	5,694	5,931	5,981	6,006
P-value (D)	4.19	1.52	4.46	3.02

Table 7. Parameters estimation for the four-regime models on the S&P 500 Total Return daily returns for the 2010's recovery.

Parameter	AR(0) Regime				AR(1) Regime			
	1	2	3	4	1	2	3	4
μ	29.41	303.07	−68.77	−28.25	32.04	365.83	−68.82	−27.50
σ	6.70	8.13	13.50	29.05	6.73	7.56	13.39	28.50
Φ	0	0	0	0	−0.04	0.14	−0.09	−0.08
ν	0.44	0.09	0.33	0.14	0.45	0.09	0.32	0.14
Q	0.91	0	0.09	0	0.90	0	0.10	0
	0.47	0.07	0.45	0	0.53	0.06	0.41	0
	0	0.23	0.76	0.01	0	0.23	0.76	0.01
	0	0.03	0	0.97	0	0.03	0	0.97

Note: μ and σ are presented as annualized percentage.

For the last period, we chose a model with four regimes. As noted previously, the four-regime HMM did not pass the goodness-of-fit test. We still present the estimated parameters in Table 7 as a mean of comparison.

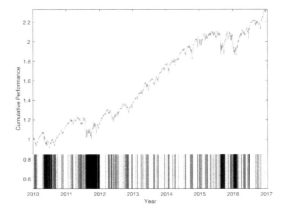

Fig. 5.   Most probable regimes for the four-regime AR(1) model fitted on the S&P 500 Total Return index from 05/01/2010 to 20/01/2017, together with the cumulative performance of the index. Darker areas represent higher volatility states.

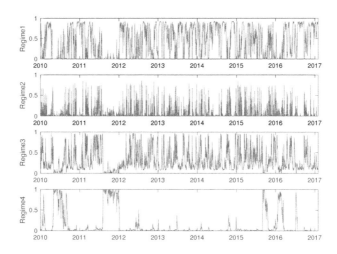

Fig. 6.   Probability of the regimes, i.e. η_t, for the four-regime AR(1) model fitted on the S&P 500 Total Return index from 05/01/2010 to 20/01/2017.

The calibration for this period is less intuitive than the previous ones. The inverse correlation between risk and expected premium is not as strong. Also, both models have a non-persistent regime with huge expected returns, (i.e. regime 2). Nevertheless, we still find modest mean-reversion for two regimes (i.e. regimes 3 and 4), and the high-risk regime is highly persistent, as highlighted by $Q_{4,4} = 0.97$, as it was in the two previous cases. The most probable regimes are displayed in Figure 5, while the probabilities of each regime are presented in Figure 6. Interestingly enough, the crisis in the subprime mortgage market is adequately captured by the high risk regime. The final part of 2011 was marked by fear of the European sovereign debt crisis spreading to Italy and Spain. Once again, the ARHMM isolated the stock markets fall quite accurately. We also estimated the ARHMM on the returns from 01/04/1999 to 01/20/2017. This long period is far from stationary, but it is still interesting to see how the model performs through recessions and recoveries. We chose a four-regime model, as indicated by the goodness-of-fit tests. We can see on Figure 7 that the 2000's bubble burst and the recent financial meltdown (2008-2009) are both correctly captured by the high risk regimes.

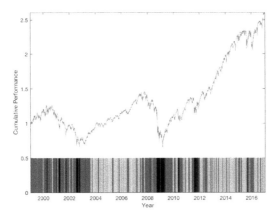

Fig. 7. Most probable regimes for the four-regime AR(1) model fitted on the S&P 500 Total Return index from 01/04/1999 to 01/20/2017, together with the cumulative performance of the index. Darker areas represent higher volatility states.

3. Optimal discrete time hedging

In what follows, we use the notations and results from [22]. Denote the price process by S, i.e., S_t is the value of d underlying assets at period t and let $\mathbb{F} = \{\mathcal{F}_t, \quad t = 0, \ldots, n\}$ a filtration under which S is adapted. Further assume that S is square integrable. Set $\Delta_t = \beta_t S_t - \beta_{t-1} S_{t-1}$, where the discounting factors $\beta_t = e^{-r_t}$ are deterministic for $t = 1, \ldots, n$. We are interested in the optimal initial investment amount V_0 and the optimal predictable investment strategy $\vec{\varphi} = (\varphi_t)_{t=1}^n$ that minimize the expected quadratic hedging error for a given payoff C at time n (e.g a call option). Formally, the problem is stated as

$$\inf_{\{V_0, \vec{\varphi}\}} E[\{G(V_0, \vec{\varphi})\}^2], \tag{6}$$

where $G = G(V_0, \vec{\varphi}) = \beta_n(C - V_n)$ and V_t is the current value of the replicating portfolio at time t. In other words, $\beta_t V_t = V_0 + \sum_{j=1}^t \varphi_j^\top \Delta_j$, for $t = 0, \ldots, n$. To solve (6), set $P_{n+1} = 1$, and define, for $t = n, \ldots, 1$,

$$\gamma_{t+1} = E(P_{t+1}|\mathcal{F}_t),$$
$$\mathfrak{a}_t = E(\Delta_t \Delta_t^\top P_{t+1}|\mathcal{F}_{t-1}) = E(\Delta_t \Delta_t^\top \gamma_{t+1}|\mathcal{F}_{t-1}),$$
$$\mathfrak{b}_t = E(\Delta_t P_{t+1}|\mathcal{F}_{t-1}) = E(\Delta_t \gamma_{t+1}|\mathcal{F}_{t-1}),$$
$$\rho_t = \mathfrak{a}_t^{-1} \mathfrak{b}_t,$$
$$P_t = \prod_{j=t}^n (1 - \rho_j^\top \Delta_j),$$

We now state Theorem 1 of [22], which is a multivariate extension of [6].

Theorem 3.1. *Suppose that $E(P_t|\mathcal{F}_{t-1}) \neq 0$ P-a.s., for 1,...,n. This condition is always respected for regime-switching models. Then, the solution $(V_0, \vec{\varphi})$ of the minimization problem* (6) *is $V_0 = E(\beta_n C P_1)/E(P_1)$, and*

$$\varphi_t = \alpha_t - \check{V}_{t-1} \rho_t, \quad t \in \{1, \ldots, n\}. \tag{7}$$

where

$$\alpha_t = \mathfrak{a}_t^{-1} E(\beta_n C \Delta_t P_{t+1}|\mathcal{F}_{t-1}). \tag{8}$$

and $\check{S}$ and $\check{V}$ are the present values of S and V.

Remark 3.1. V_0 is chosen such that the expected hedging error, G, is zero. [22] also showed that $C_t(S_t, \tau_t)$ given by

$$\beta_t C_t = \frac{E(\beta_n C P_{t+1}|\mathcal{F}_t)}{E(P_{t+1}|\mathcal{F}_t)} \tag{9}$$

is the optimal investment at period t so that the value of the portfolio at period n is as close as possible to C in terms of mean square error G, in particular, $V_0 = C_0$. C_t can be interpreted as the option price at period t. By increasing the number of hedging periods, C_t should tend to a price under a risk-neutral measure; see, e.g., [23]. For example, when there is only one regime, the density is Gaussian and Φ_1 fixed at 0, C_t tends to the usual Black-Scholes price. The optimal hedging implementation for ARHMM is described in [24]. It follows that

$$\check{C}_{t-1} = \beta_{t-1}C_{t-1}\gamma_t = E\{(1 - \rho_t^\top \Delta_t)\check{C}_t|\mathcal{F}_{t-1}), \tag{10}$$
$$\alpha_t = \mathfrak{a}_t^{-1}E(\check{C}_t\Delta_t|\mathcal{F}_{t-1}). \tag{11}$$

To derive the optimal hedging algorithm, we also need the following result, valid for a general ARHMM. First, write $S_t = D(S_{t-1})e^{Y_t}$, where e^{Y_t} is the vector with components $e^{(Y_t)_j}$, and $D(s)$ is the diagonal matrix with diagonal elements $(s)_j$, $j \in \{1, \ldots, d\}$. The proof of the following theorem is given in [24].

Theorem 3.2. *For any $t \in \{1, \ldots, n\}$, set*

$$\mathfrak{a}_t = D(\check{S}_{t-1})a_t(Y_{t-1}, \tau_{t-1})D(\check{S}_{t-1}),$$
$$\mathfrak{b}_t = D(\check{S}_{t-1})b_t(Y_{t-1}, \tau_{t-1}),$$
$$\rho_t = D^{-1}(\check{S}_{t-1})h_t(Y_{t-1}, \tau_{t-1}),$$
$$\gamma_t = g_t(Y_{t-1}, \tau_{t-1}),$$

with $h_t = a_t^{-1}b_t$, where a_t, b_t, and g_t are deterministic functions given by

$$a_t(y, i) = E\left\{\zeta_t\zeta_t^\top g_{t+1}(Y_t, \tau_t)|Y_{t-1} = y, \tau_{t-1} = i\right\}, \tag{12}$$
$$b_t(y, i) = E\left\{\zeta_t g_{t+1}(Y_t, \tau_t)|Y_{t-1} = y, \tau_{t-1} = i\right\}, \tag{13}$$
$$g_t(y, i) = E\left\{g_{t+1}(Y_t, \tau_t)|Y_{t-1} = y, \tau_{t-1} = i\right\} \tag{14}$$
$$-b_t^\top(Y_{t-1}, \tau_{t-1})h_t(Y_{t-1}, \tau_{t-1}),$$

with $\zeta_t = e^{Y_t - r_t} - \mathbf{1}$, and $g_{n+1} \equiv 1$.
If in addition $\beta_n C = \Psi_n(\check{S}_n)$, then $\check{C}_t = \Psi_t(\check{S}_t, Y_t, \tau_t)$, where

$$\Psi_{t-1}(s, y, i)$$
$$= E\left[\Psi_t\left\{D(s)e^{Y_t - r_t}, Y_t, \tau_t\right\}\left\{1 - h_t(y, i)^\top\zeta_t\right\}|Y_{t-1} = y, \tau_{t-1} = i\right], \tag{15}$$

and

$$\alpha_t = D^{-1}(\check{S}_{t-1})a_t^{-1}(Y_{t-1}, \tau_{t-1})\mathbf{A}_t(\check{S}_{t-1}, Y_{t-1}, \tau_{t-1}), \tag{16}$$

where

$$\mathbf{A}_t(s, y, i) = E\left[\Psi_t\left\{D(s)e^{Y_t - r_t}, Y_t, \tau_t\right\}\zeta_t|Y_{t-1} = y, \tau_{t-1} = i\right]. \tag{17}$$

For example, for a call option with strike K, $\Psi_n(s) = \max(0, s - \beta_n K)$.

3.1. *Implementation issues*

There are two main problems related to the implementation of the hedging strategy: a_t, b_t, g_t, Ψ_t and A_t defined in expressions (12)-(17) must be approximated and regimes must be predicted. We approximate a_t, b_t g_t for values y on a finite grid and then use linear interpolation. In a similar manner, we approximate Ψ_t and A_t for values s and y on a (product) grid and then use interpolation. This way, the recursion formulas given by (15)-(17) can be solved. This approach was proposed in [12], where stratified Monte Carlo sampling was also used. Because the simulations are computationally expensive and introduce variability, we propose a novel technique to approximate these integrals using semi-exact calculations, inspired by [18] Chapter 3. The details for the semi-exact calculations are presented in [24].

We also tested the Monte Carlo sampling procedure as a mean of comparison. Interestingly, we found that by simply rescaling the Monte Carlo samples to the desired mean and volatility, we achieved results as accurate as the semi-exact calculations, as pointed out in Section 3.3.

As for defining the points on the grids, previous literature suggest choosing 10^3 equidistant points marginally covering at least 3 standard deviations under the respective highest volatility regimes. Importantly, we found that strategically choosing the points with respect to the percentiles of simulated processes significantly reduces the number of points needed while keeping the accuracy at a reasonable level.

Next, we need to predict τ_1 based on R_1, R_0, τ_0 and so on. The predicted regime $\hat{\tau}$ is the one having the largest probability given the information on prices up to time t, i.e. the *most probable regime* given by (4). Note that this methodology introduces a bias. We also studied the less biased approach of weighting the regimes proportionally to η_t, but since the results were comparable and did not lead to any significant improvement, they are omitted from the analysis. For more details on regime predictions, see Section 2.1. Then, according to (7) and (16), the optimal hedging weights φ_t for period $[t-1, t)$, for $k = n, \ldots, 1$, are approximated by

$$\hat{\varphi}_t = \alpha_t(\check{S}_{t-1}, Y_{t-1}, \hat{\tau}_{t-1}) - D^{-1}(\check{S}_{t-1})\check{V}_{t-1}h_t(Y_{t-1}, \hat{\tau}_{t-1}). \tag{18}$$

V_0 is approximated by $C_0(S_0, \hat{\tau}_0, 0)$ while the remaining monies, $V_0 - \hat{\varphi}_1^\mathsf{T} S_0$, are invested in the riskless asset. Next, as S_1 is observed, one first computes the actual portfolio value V_1, then predicts the current regime τ_1 and finally approximates the optimal weights φ_2. This process is iterated until expiration of the option.

3.1.1. *Using regime predictions*

Here, we obtain option prices and strategies that depend on the unobservable regimes τ, since (S_t, τ_t) is a Markov chain. However, [25] proposed a very interesting approach: they showed that (S_t, η_t) is Markov, so one can obtain prices and hedging strategies depending on (S_t, η_t) instead. This makes sense financially. However, this new Markov chain lives in a $l + d - 1$-dimensional space, because the values of η_t belong to the simplex $\mathcal{S}_l = \{(x_1, \ldots, x_l); \quad x_i \geq 0, x_1 + \cdots + x_l = 1\}$. [25] considered only 2 regimes and one asset, so the real dimension is 2. When $l > 3$, this becomes numerically intractable.

3.2. *Optimal hedging vs delta-hedging*

In optimal hedging, the strategy φ takes into account the hedging error at each time period, as exemplified by equation (7), since it depends explicitly on the previous value of the portfolio. For delta-hedging, this is not the case since it is assumed that the hedging error is 0 at each period, so there is no correction term depending on the value of the portfolio.

3.3. *Simulated hedging errors*

To assess the proposed strategy's accuracy, we simulated 10000 trajectories under ARHMM and we hedged identical options under different hedging strategies. To be realistic, the parameters were taken from Table 3. The hedging methodologies are the classical Black-Scholes delta-hedging (B&S) and optimal hedging under ARHMM (OH-ARHMM), HMM (OH-HMM) and Gaussian (OH-B&S) returns (i.e., considering only 1 regime). We also compared semi-exact approximation to Monte-Carlo. The option in question is a call with S_0 and K equal to 100, risk-free rate $r = 0.01$, 3 month maturity (63 days) with daily hedging. Hedging error statistics are given in Table 8, while the estimated densities are displayed in Figure 8. OH-ARHMM achieves a 33% reduction in RMSE compared to B&S and OH-B&S and a 26% to OH-HMM. The latter is quite impressive, as it highlights how big of an impact the autoregressive dynamic has.

4. Out-of-sample vanilla pricing and hedging

4.1. *Methodology*

To exhibit the behavior of the hedging protocols, we buy and sell vanilla options on the S&P 500 depending on how the market prices compare with

Table 8.   Statistics for the hedging errors in an autoregressive hidden Markov model, using 10000 simulated portfolios.

	B&S	OH-B&S	HMM	HMM MC	ARHMM	ARHMM MC
Average	−0.105	−0.084	0.004	**0.003**	0.025	0.030
Median	−0.236	−0.202	−0.085	−0.086	**−0.019**	**−0.019**
Volatility	0.611	0.626	0.559	0.559	**0.411**	0.412
Skewness	1.715	1.948	1.639	**1.629**	4.644	4.738
Kurtosis	7.737	9.558	9.464	9.356	**71.834**	78.219
Minimum	**−1.658**	**−1.658**	−4.649	−4.633	−2.477	−2.413
VaR (1%)	−1.110	−1.118	−1.087	−1.086	−0.749	**−0.741**
VaR (99%)	2.069	2.227	1.987	1.982	**1.526**	1.531
Maximum	**4.886**	6.725	6.538	6.520	12.958	14.266
RMSE	0.620	0.632	0.559	0.559	**0.411**	0.413

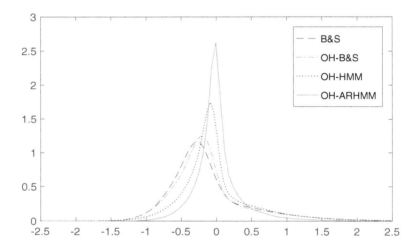

Fig. 8.   Estimated densities for the hedging errors in an autoregressive hidden Markov model, using 50000 portfolios. Only the semi-exact densities are shown, as they were indiscernible from the Monte Carlo ones.

our theoretical prices. Then, we hedge the positions until expiration. We then assess the impact of model specification on the delta-hedging strategy by examining the statistical properties of the hedging error and of the strategy's returns. All hedging portfolios are re-balanced on a daily basis, as is often assumed in the volatility timing literature; see e.g., [26]. The market price of an option is defined as the last (i.e. as 4:15 PM EST) midpoint between the bid and the ask. The price of the underlying is its listed close value. For simplicity, we neglect issues related to time-varying discount rates by assuming constant continually compounded daily rates. Risk-free rates, r, are linearly interpolated for a given maturity, n, from the zero-coupon U.S. yield curve.

Remark 4.1. For the implementation, we chose to present only the results using the most probable regime for the computation of the hedging strategy. These results are a little bit better than those obtained by weighting the hedging strategy according to $\eta_t(1), \ldots, \eta_t(l)$ at period t.

4.1.1. *The underlying asset*

We make the reasonable assumption that the spot S&P 500 is investable and tradable at a minimal cost. The forward rate is retrieved for the maturities of interest directly from the option data at hand, as proposed by [27]. From put-call parity, the option implied forward value at n, F_n, is

$$F_n = (\tilde{C}(\tilde{K}, n) - \tilde{P}(\tilde{K}, n))e^{r_n n} + \tilde{K},$$

where $C(\tilde{K}, T)$ and $P(\tilde{K}, T)$ are respectively the call and put *market* values expiring at T with strike K and $\tilde{K}$ is the at-the-money strike value minimizing $|C(\tilde{K}, T) - P(\tilde{K}, T)|$ for all strikes offered by the exchange. We use at-the-money options because they are the most liquid and are thus less likely to provide *cash-and-carry* type arbitrage opportunities. We then compute the daily forward rate as $f_n = \frac{1}{n}\log(F_n/S_0)$ and the associated daily discounting factor $\beta = e^{-f_n}$, which reflects the current risk-free return on capital net of the implied continuous dividend yield.

4.1.2. *Option dataset*

Exchange-traded options on the S&P 500 are European, heavily traded and have a high number of strikes and maturities. To assess the accuracy of our model, we will analyze two periods with very different characteristics: the 2008 Financial Crisis, and a chunk of the recent recovery. Dates range from 09/24/2007 to 09/20/2009 and from 09/23/2013 to 07/08/2015, respectively. This will help us discern the impact on hedging and pricing when a dramatic regime change occurs, in the former, and when it does not, in the latter. In order to minimize the effect of varying maturities, we built the dataset of options having a maturity of about 1 year, more precisely from 231 to 273 trading days till expiration. Also, because *in-the-money* and *out-of-the-money* are less liquid, we only included options where moneyness (strike value divided by the underlying value) is between 0.9 and 1.1. So we were left with a total of 180 options for the first period, and 478 options for the second period. Note that at a given date, more than one option can meet these criteria.

4.1.3. *Backtesting*

We applied the AR(1) regime-switching optimal hedging methodology with 3 regimes (ARHMM). We chose 3 regimes because it is the number of regimes that seemed the best given the time windows studied, which we will describe in the next paragraph. We compared it to the case with 1 regime and Φ fixed at 0, corresponding to the optimal hedging under the B&S model (OH-B&S).

For each option in the dataset, we estimated the ARHMM parameters on the S&P 500 log-returns with a 500 and 2000 day trailing window. We chose to backtest the methods using 2 estimation windows in order to have a more in-depth understanding of model specifications on pricing and hedging. The 2000 day trailing window always included the previous financial meltdown, i.e., dot-com bubble for our first analysis, and the 2008 financial crisis for the second one. The 500 day trailing window didn't. Similarly, we applied this methodology to all the hedging protocols included in the analysis, which will be introduced below.

From [28], for a given *moneyness*, the value of an option is homogeneous of degree one with respect to the underlying value. Thus, for each inception date, we normalize the option prices, the strike values and the underlying path at an initial S&P 500 value of 100. Results can thus be aggregated through time and interpreted as a percentage of S&P 500. Note that for each inception date, the hedging protocols are applied out-of-sample until maturity. To ensure comparability, OH-B&S assumes the stationary distribution of the ARHMM when the autoregressive parameter $\Phi = 0$. The OH-B&S optimal hedging exposure is derived from an algorithm similar to the one presented in Section 3. Optimal hedging under unconditional distributions is presented in [18]. Both strategies minimize the expected quadratic hedging error under their respective null hypothesis, namely that the returns follow an autoregressive regime-switching model (ARHMM), and a Gaussian model (OH-B&S).

OH-B&S methodology is not to be confused with the classical Black-Scholes delta hedging protocol. Indeed, the terminology only reflects the fact that we hedge and price under the Black-Scholes framework hypothesis, namely that assets follow geometric Brownian motions. Even though the OH-B&S prices converge to the usual Black-Scholes prices as the number of hedging periods tends to infinity, the discrete time hedging strategies will not necessarily be the same. For this reason, the classical Black-Scholes delta-hedging methodology (B&S) is also considered. Similarly to OH-B&S, the B&S volatility is calibrated to the stationary volatility of ARHMM.

We added a final benchmark to our analysis, one that reflects how well the market would hedge the same options, namely the delta-hedging methodology where the volatility is calibrated to the implied volatility at each hedging period (B&S-M). It informs us how well the models compare to market's intuition. The effect of using implied volatility was discussed in [29]. However, his theoretical analysis cannot be performed here.

To recap, we buy and sell options depending on their market value compared to the theoretical prices, and hedge the positions until maturity. We analyze the P&L of the different methodologies, as well as the hedging errors. Two periods are studied: the 2008 Financial Crisis and a chunk of the following recovery spanning from mid-2013 to mid-2015.

4.2. *Empirical results*

We define the hedging error as the present value of the liability $\beta_n C$ minus the present value of terminal portfolio $\beta_n V_n$. The options' maturity being set to one year, the annualized root-mean-squared hedging error can be computed by $\sqrt{\hat{E}(\beta_n V_n - \beta_n C)^2}$. This realized risk is the empirical counterpart of the quantity we minimized and as such, is the most relevant metric for comparing the different models. Keep in mind that there is a lot of overlap in our dataset, so the hedging error values are not independent, nor identically distributed since the moneyness or other parameters are not constant. Despite these inconveniences, the hedging errors are still useful to compare the models.

Concerning the trading strategy, if the market is overvalued with respect to the model, we sell the option and hedge our position. Thus, the present value of the return is $(C_0 - V_0) - (\beta_n C_n - \beta_n V_n)$. If the market is undervalued, we buy the option and hedge our position. The return will be the negative of the former.

4.2.1. *2008–2009 Financial Crisis*

In this section, we will focus on options with inception dates from September 24th 2007 to September 20th 2009. This period is really interesting. In the first part, the market experienced a huge increase in volatility and decrease in returns. In the second part, it is the opposite.

We will first turn our attention to the 500 trailing window case. Table 9 and Figure 9 present the hedging error's statistics and density approximation, while the results of the trading strategy, i.e., the cumulative value of a portfolio that traded the 90 options, are displayed in Figure 10. The horizontal axis is the cumulative number of options traded in chronological order. In this case, ARHMM is by far the superior methodology. It achieved the best hedging error considering all the metrics for both calls and puts. Furthermore, it is the best trading strategy for both type of options, even though the hedging errors are almost entirely negative in the calls case. Note that the "Bias" statistic refers to the difference between the market price and the theoretical price. Therefore, it is always 0 for the BS-M, since the implied volatility is used.

Note that according to Figure 4, around 2009, the asset spends a lot of time in regime 3, which is characterized by a very large volatility and a very large negative mean; see, e.g., Table 5. When volatility increases and returns turn negative, the puts' value increase and need to be hedged accordingly. B&S and B&S-M failed to do so, resulting in huge hedging errors and large negative P&L values. This explains the difference between put and calls in Table 9.

Table 9.   Hedging error statistics for the 90 calls and the 90 puts traded in the 2008-2009 Financial Crisis with 500 days trailing estimation window.

	Calls				Puts			
	B&S-M	B&S	OH-B&S	ARHMM	B&S-M	B&S	OH-B&S	ARHMM
RMSE	3.87	5.27	4.53	**0.61**	39.95	42.52	4.53	**0.98**
Bias	0	−4.52	−4.37	−5.35	0	−1.05	−0.91	−1.87
VaR 1%	−7.64	−12.02	−12.47	**−3.17**	−28.39	−33.24	−12.47	**−3.18**
Median	2.9	3.82	2.68	**−1.65e-04**	30.78	29.77	2.68	**0.01**
VaR 99%	9.16	8.61	7.57	**−1.97e-09**	72.9	77.22	7.57	**4.75**

Similar results are presented in Table 10 and Figures 11 and 12, although the trailing estimation window, previously set to 500 days, is now 2000 days. This estimation window includes another financial crisis, the Dot-com Bubble. The same conclusions as in the previous experience can be drawn.

Table 10.   Hedging error statistics for the 90 calls and the 90 puts traded in the 2008-2009 Financial Crisis with 2000 days trailing estimation window.

	Calls				Puts			
	B&S-M	B&S	OH-B&S	ARHMM	B&S-M	B&S	OH-B&S	ARHMM
RMSE	3.87	4.26	3.15	**0.33**	39.95	40.87	3.15	**1.25**
Bias	0	−4.86	−4.69	−4.91	0	−1.4	−1.23	−1.44
VaR 1%	−7.64	−4.76	−4.27	**−1.43**	−28.39	−28.68	−4.27	**−1.4**
Median	2.9	3.26	1.93	**0.01**	30.78	27.74	1.93	**0.35**
VaR 99%	9.16	8.93	7.62	**0.33**	72.9	74.76	7.62	**4.83**

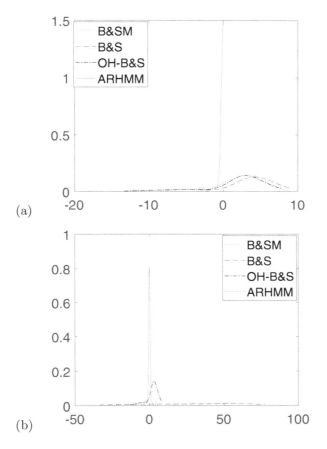

Fig. 9. Hedging error density approximation for the 90 calls (a) and 90 puts (b) traded in the 2008-2009 Financial Crisis with 500 days trailing estimation window.

4.2.2. *2013–2015 Bull markets*

Our second and last analysis focuses on a part of the recent recovery spanning from September 23th 2013 to August 7th 2015. This period is quite the opposite of a financial crash, with the exception of periods spent in regime 3, which has a very large negative mean and a large volatility. This also affects negatively the performance of hedging error statistics of the B&S methods for the puts. Again, we start with the small estimation window. The results are presented in Table 11 and Figures 13 and 14. Considering the hedging errors, OH-B&S and ARHMM achieved the best and pretty

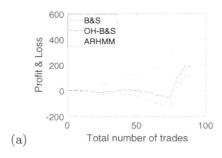
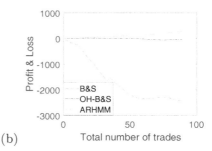

(a)

(b)

Fig. 10.   Profit & Loss of trading strategy for the 90 calls (a) and 90 puts (b) traded in the 2008-2009 Financial Crisis with 500 days trailing estimation window.

similar statistics for both put and calls. Similarly to the previous experience in Section 4.2.1, B&S and B&S-M replicated poorly the put options.

Table 11.   Hedging error statistics for the 239 calls and the 239 puts traded in the 2013-2015 Bull markets with 500 days trailing estimation window.

	Calls				Puts			
	B&S-M	B&S	OH-B&S	ARHMM	B&S-M	B&S	OH-B&S	ARHMM
RMSE	1.09	1.64	**0.84**	0.99	18.12	11.6	**0.84**	0.99
Bias	0	0.12	0.22	0.59	0	−4.08	−3.98	−3.62
VaR 1%	−2.63	−2.53	**−1.45**	−2.47	−41.63	−26.59	**−1.45**	−2.46
Median	−0.2	0.14	−0.02	**−0.01**	−12.12	−8.6	−0.02	**−0.01**
VaR 99%	**1.39**	4.42	3.7	3.54	9.42	6.78	3.7	**3.53**

Finally, the results for the longer estimation window case are presented in Table 12 and Figures 15 and 16. This is probably the worst environment for the ARHMM, as the estimation window includes a financial crisis (i.e. 2008-2009 Financial Crisis) and the out-of-sample returns are slow and steady. Because our trading strategy takes into account the actual hedging error according to (7), the simpler models should perform better. In spite of that, ARHMM managed to outperform B&S and B&-M for the put options. The fact that pricing bias for the calls are strongly positive is noteworthy. In theory, the pricing bias should be negative, to account for the risk premium. In this case, it seems that the market was pretty confident about returns and volatility staying low. In insight, it was right.

Lastly, we aggregated the P&L over all the experiences for B&S, OH-B&S and ARHMM in Table 13. For a fair comparison, we normalized the number of traded options in each cases to 100. Remember that the option prices, strike prices and underlying paths are also normalized at an initial S&P 500 value of 100. Impressively, ARHMM accomplished a 106% increase in P&L compared to the second best, OH-B&S, for the 2-year

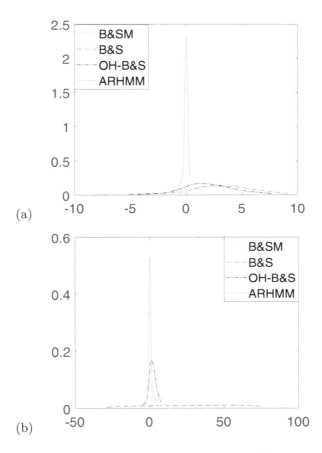

Fig. 11. Hedging error density approximation for the 90 calls (a) and 90 puts (b) traded in the 2008-2009 Financial Crisis with 2000 days trailing estimation window.

Table 12. Hedging error statistics for the 239 calls and the 239 puts traded in the 2013-2015 Bull markets with 2000 days trailing estimation window.

	Calls				Puts			
	B&S-M	B&S	OH-B&S	ARHMM	B&S-M	B&S	OH-B&S	ARHMM
RMSE	**1.09**	5.32	4.84	8.57	18.12	14.75	**4.84**	8.6
Bias	0	4.71	4.54	4.18	0	0.52	0.34	−0.01
VaR 1%	−2.63	−10	−8.93	−31.27	−41.63	−27.66	−8.93	−31.39
Median	−0.2	−4.67	−4.09	−2.82	−12.12	−12.5	−4.09	−2.81
VaR 99%	1.39	−1.79	−1.76	−0.04	9.42	1.41	−1.76	−0.04

trailing window, and is only 9% behind the first for the 8-year case, which is again OH-B&S.

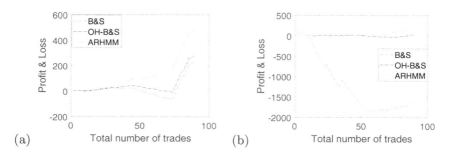

(a)   (b)

Fig. 12. Profit & Loss of trading strategy for the 90 calls (a) and 90 puts (b) traded in the 2008-2009 Financial Crisis with 2000 days trailing estimation window.

Table 13. Total normalized P&L

Trailing window (years)	B&S	OH-B&S	ARHMM
2	−1286.78	685.32	**1409.54**
8	−1761.77	**594.56**	546.38

Overall, by achieving the best Root Mean Square Error (RMSE) two times out of four for both the 2-year and 8-year window, and by being the most profitable strategy three times out of four for the 2-year window and two times out of four for the 8-year window, the ARHMM is the superior hedging protocol. However, practitioners should keep in mind that if the ARHMM is estimated on a window including a financial crisis, they should expect higher hedging errors than the simpler models if returns stay slow and steady. From our results, we strongly suggest using a 2-year trailing window as it consistently achieved an RMSE lower than 1, i.e., the ARHMM can accurately hedge options in a financial crisis.

5. Conclusion

In this paper, we proposed an autoregressive hidden Markov model to fit financial data, and we showed how to implement an optimal hedging strategy when the underlying asset returns follow an autoregressive regime-switching random walk. First, we presented estimation and filtering procedures for the ARHMM. In order to determine the optimal number of regimes, we proposed a novel goodness-of-fit test for univariate and multivariate ARHMM based on the work of [30], [20] and [12].

To illustrate the proposed strategy, we modeled three daily return series of the S&P 500. Using likelihood test, we show that the ARHMM

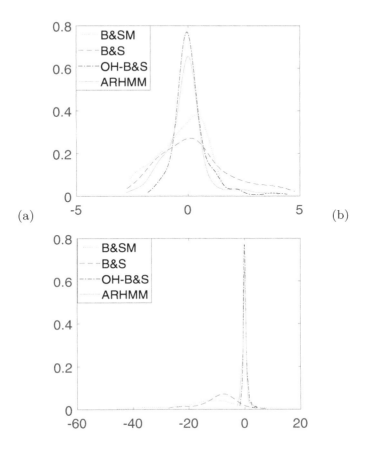

(a)   (b)

Fig. 13.   Hedging error density approximation for the 239 calls (a) and 239 puts (b) traded in the 2013-2015 Bull markets with 500 days trailing estimation window.

is a much better fit than the classical HMM, particularly because it has the capacity to model mean-reversion. Moreover, we presented the implementation of the discrete-time optimal hedging algorithm minimizing the mean-squared hedging error. Because it performs pricing, we implemented a trading strategy consisting of selling overpriced and buying underpriced options and hedging the position till maturity. Out of eight cases and compared to three other hedging protocols, our strategy achieves the best root-mean-squared hedging error four times and is the most profitable strategy five times. Furthermore, it realized the best total P&L. Because of its

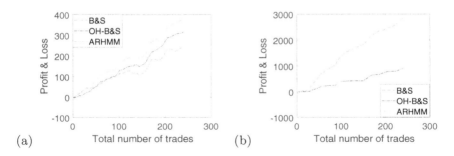

Fig. 14.   Profit & Loss of trading strategy for the 239 calls (a) and 239 puts (b) traded in the 2013-2015 Bull markets with 500 days trailing estimation window.

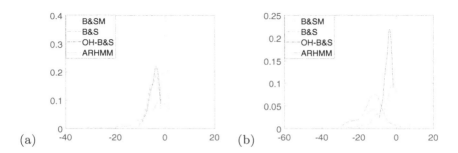

Fig. 15.   Hedging error density approximation for the 239 calls (a) and 239 puts (b) traded in the 2013-2015 Bull markets with 2000 days trailing estimation window.

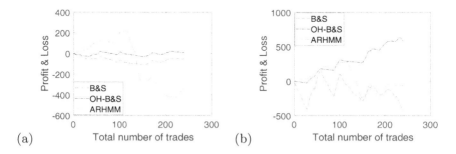

Fig. 16.   Profit & Loss of trading strategy for the 239 calls (a) and 239 puts (b) traded in the 2013-2015 Bull markets with 2000 days trailing estimation window.

ability to model regime switches as well as mean-reversion, it would be interesting to see this model applied to multivariate time series. The hedging algorithm can also be applied to multivariate or American options.

Appendix A. Extension of Baum-Welch algorithm

For $i \in \{1, \ldots, l\}$ and $t \in \{1, \ldots, n\}$, define

$$\lambda_t(i) = P(\tau_t = i | Y_1, \ldots, Y_n).$$

Also, for $i, j \in \{1, \ldots, l\}$ and $t \in \{1, \ldots, n-1\}$, define

$$\Lambda_t(i, j) = P(\tau_t = i, \tau_{t+1} = j | Y_1, \ldots, Y_n),$$

and let $\bar{\eta}_t(i)$ be the conditional density of $(Y_{t+1}, \ldots, Y_n)$, given Y_t and $\tau_t = i$. Further set $\bar{\eta}_n \equiv 1$. Note that $\lambda_n(i) = \eta_n(i)$, and $\Lambda_n(i, j) = \lambda_n(i)Q_{ij}$, for any $i, j \in \{1, \ldots, l\}$. The proof of the following proposition is given in [24].

Proposition A.1. *For all $i, j \in \{1, \ldots, l\}$, and any $t \in \{0, \ldots, n-1\}$,*

$$\eta_{t+1}(i) = \frac{f_i(Y_{t+1}|Y_t) \sum_{\beta=1}^{l} \eta_t(\beta) Q_{\beta i}}{\sum_{\alpha=1}^{l} \sum_{\beta=1}^{l} f_\alpha(Y_{t+1}|Y_t) \eta_t(\beta) Q_{\beta\alpha}}, \, , \tag{A.1}$$

$$\bar{\eta}_t(i) = \sum_{\beta=1}^{l} Q_{i\beta} \bar{\eta}_{t+1}(\beta) f_\beta(Y_{t+1}|Y_t), \tag{A.2}$$

$$\lambda_t(i) = \frac{\eta_t(i)\bar{\eta}_t(i)}{\sum_{\alpha=1}^{l} \eta_t(\alpha)\bar{\eta}_t(\alpha)}, \tag{A.3}$$

$$\Lambda_t(i, j) = \frac{\eta_t(i)Q_{ij}\bar{\eta}_{t+1}(j)f_j(Y_{t+1}|Y_t)}{\sum_{\alpha=1}^{l} \eta_t(\alpha)\bar{\eta}_t(\alpha)}. \tag{A.4}$$

In particular, $\sum_{\beta=1}^{l} \Lambda_t(i, \beta) = \lambda_t(i)$, for all $t \in \{0, \ldots, n\}$.

Appendix A.1. *Estimation of regime-switching models*

To describe the EM algorithm for the estimation, suppose that at step $k \geq 0$, one has the parameters Q, μ_i, Φ_i, A_i, $i \in \{1, \ldots, l\}$. Let $w_t(i) = \lambda_t(i) / \sum_{k=1}^{n} \lambda_k(i)$, and set $\bar{y}_i = \sum_{t=1}^{n} w_t(i)y_t$ and $\underline{y}_i = \sum_{t=1}^{n} w_t(i)y_{t-1}$, $i \in \{1, \ldots, l\}$, where λ_t and Λ_t are given in Proposition A.1. Then, at step $k+1$, for $i, j \in \{1, \ldots, l\}$, one has

$$Q_{ij}^{(k+1)} = \frac{\sum_{t=1}^{n} \Lambda_{t-1}(i, j)}{\sum_{\beta=1}^{l} \sum_{t=1}^{n} \Lambda_{t-1}(i, \beta)} = \frac{\sum_{t=1}^{n} \Lambda_{t-1}(i, j)}{\sum_{t=1}^{n} \lambda_{t-1}(i)}, \tag{A.5}$$

$$\mu_i^{(k+1)} = \left(I - \Phi_i^{(k+1)}\right)^{-1} \left(\bar{y}_i - \Phi_i^{(k+1)} \underline{y}_i\right), \tag{A.6}$$

$$\Phi_i^{(k+1)} = \left\{ \sum_{t=1}^{n} w_t(i) \left(y_{t-1} - \underline{y}_i \right) \left(y_{t-1} - \underline{y}_i \right)^{\top} \right\}^{-1} \tag{A.7}$$

$$\times \left\{ \sum_{t=1}^{n} w_t(i) \left(y_t - \bar{y}_i \right) \left(y_{t-1} - \underline{y}_i \right)^{\top} \right\},$$

$$A_i^{(k+1)} = \sum_{t=1}^{n} w_t(i) e_{ti} e_{ti}^{\top}, \tag{A.8}$$

where $e_{ti} = y_t - \bar{y}_i - \Phi_i^{(k+1)} \left(y_{t-1} - \underline{y}_i \right)$, $t \in \{1, \ldots, n\}$.

For a proof of these formulas, see [24].

Appendix B. Goodness-of-fit test for ARHMM

Here, we state the main formulas needed to implement the goodness-of-fit test, which can be performed to assess the suitability of a Gaussian AR(1) regime-switching models as well as to select the optimal number of regimes, l^*. The proposed test, based on the work of [31], [20] and [32], uses the Rosenblatt's transform. For conciseness, we detail the implementation for two dimensional Gaussian AR(1) regime-switching models, but the approach can be easily generalized.

Appendix B.1. *Rosenblatt's transform*

Let $i \in \{1, \ldots, l\}$ be fixed, and let R_i be a random vector with density f_i. For any $q \in \{1, \ldots, d\}$, denote by $f_{i,1:q}$ the density of $\left(R_i^{(1)}, \ldots, R_i^{(q)} \right)$, and by $f_{i,q}$ the density of $R_i^{(q)}$ given $\left(R_i^{(1)}, \ldots, R_i^{(q-1)} \right)$. Further denote by $F_{i,q}$ the distribution function associated with density $f_{i,q}$. By convention, $f_{i,1}$ denotes the *unconditional* density of $R_i^{(1)}$. Then, the Rosenblatt's transform $x \mapsto T_i(x) = \left(F_{i,1}(x^{(1)}), F_{i,2}(x^{(1)}, x^{(2)}), \ldots, F_{i,d}(x^{(1)}, \ldots, x^{(d)}) \right)^{\top}$ is such that $T_i(R_i)$ is uniformly distributed in $[0, 1]^d$. For example, if f_i is the density of a bivariate Gaussian distribution with mean μ_i and covariance

$$\Sigma_i = \begin{pmatrix} v_i^{(1)} & \rho_i \sqrt{v_i^{(1)} v_i^{(2)}} \\ \rho_i \sqrt{v_i^{(1)} v_i^{(2)}} & v_i^{(2)} \end{pmatrix},$$

$f_{i,2}$ is the density of a Gaussian distribution with mean $\mu_i^{(2)} + \beta_i \left(y_i^{(1)} - \mu_i^{(1)} \right)$ and variance $v_i^{(2)} (1 - \rho_i^2)$, with $\beta_i = \rho_i \sqrt{v_i^{(2)} / v_i^{(1)}}$. These results can easily be extended to the Gaussian AR(1) distribution.

However, for regime-switching random walks models, past returns must also be included in the conditioning information set. For any $x^{(1)}, \ldots, x^{(d)} \in \mathbb{R}$, the ($d$-dimensional) Rosenblatt's transform Ψ_t corresponding to the density (5) conditional on $x_1, \ldots, x_{t-1} \in \mathbb{R}^d$ is given by

$$\Psi_t^{(1)}(x_t^{(1)}) = \Psi_t^{(1)}\left(x_1, \ldots, x_{t-1}, x_t^{(1)}\right) = \sum_{i=1}^{l} W_{t-1}(i) F_{i,1}(x_t^{(1)})$$

and

$$\Psi_t^{(q)}\left(x_1^{(1)}, \ldots, x_t^{(q)}\right) = \Psi_t^{(q)}\left(x_1, \ldots, x_{t-1}, x_t^{(1)}, \ldots, x_t^{(q)}\right)$$
$$= \frac{\sum i = 1^l W_{t-1}(i) f_{i,1:q-1}\left(x_t^{(1)}, \ldots, x_t^{(q-1)}\right) F_{i,q}(x_t^{(q)})}{\sum_{i=1}^{l} W_{t-1}(i) f_{i,1:q-1}\left(x_t^{(1)}, \ldots, x_t^{(q-1)}\right)},$$

for $q \in \{2, \ldots, d\}$. Suppose $R_1, \ldots, R_n$ is a sample of size n of d-dimensional vectors drawn from a joint (continuous) distribution P. Also, let $\mathcal{P}$ be the parametric family of Gaussian AR(1) regime-switching models with l regimes. Formally, the hypothesis to be tested is

$$\mathcal{H}_0 : P \in \mathcal{P} = \{P_\theta; \theta \in \Theta\} \quad vs \quad \mathcal{H}_1 : P \notin \mathcal{P}.$$

Under $\mathcal{H}_0$, it follows that

$$U_1 = \Psi_1(R_1, \theta), U_2 = \Psi_2(R_1, R_2, \theta), \ldots, U_n = \Psi(R_1, \ldots, R_n, \theta)$$

are independent and uniformly distributed over $[0, 1]^d$, where $\Psi_1(\cdot, \theta)$, ..., $\Psi_n(\cdot, \theta)$ are the Rosenblatt's transforms conditional on the set of parameters $\theta \in \Theta$. Since θ is unknown, it must be estimated by some θ_n. Then, the *pseudo-observations*, $\left(\hat{U}_1 = \Psi_1(R_1, \theta_n), \ldots, \hat{U}_n = \Psi_n(R_1, \ldots, R_n, \theta_n)\right)$ are *approximately* uniformly distributed over $[0, 1]^d$ and *approximately* independent. We propose a test statistic based on these pseudo observations.

Appendix B.2. *Test statistic*

The test statistic is based on the empirical process $D_n(u) = \frac{1}{n} \sum_{t=1}^{n} \prod_{q=1}^{d} \mathbb{I}(\hat{U}_t^{(q)} \leq u^{(q)})$, $u \equiv (u^{(1)}, \ldots, u^{(d)}) \in [0, 1]^d$.

To test $\mathcal{H}_0$ against $\mathcal{H}_1$ we propose a Cramér-von Mises type statistic:

$$S_n \equiv B_n(\hat{U}_1, \ldots, \hat{U}_n) = n \int_{[0,1]^d} \left\{ D_n(u) - \prod_{q=1}^{d} u^{(q)} \right\}^2 du$$

$$= \frac{1}{n} \sum_{t=1}^{n} \sum_{k=1}^{n} \prod_{q=1}^{d} \left\{ 1 - \max \hat{U}_t^{(q)}, \hat{U}_k^{(q)} \right\} - \frac{1}{2^{d-1}} \sum_{t=1}^{n} \prod_{q=1}^{d} (1 - \hat{U}^{(q)2}) + \frac{n}{3^d}.$$

Since $\hat{U}_i$ is almost uniformly distributed under $\mathcal{H}_0$, large values of S_n should lead to rejection of $\mathcal{H}_0$. Unfortunately, the limiting distribution of the test statistic depends on the unknown parameter θ. This is why we use the parametric bootstrap to compute P-values. Its validity has been shown for a wide range of assumptions in [20]. These results were recently extended to dynamic models in [16], including regime-switching random walks.

Appendix B.3. *Parametric bootstrap algorithm*

(1) For a given number of regimes, estimate parameters with θ_n computed from the EM algorithm applied to $(R_1, \ldots, R_n)$.
(2) Compute the test statistic $S_n = B_n(\hat{U}, \ldots, \hat{U}_n)$, from the estimated pseudo observations, $\hat{U}_i = \Psi_i(R_1, \ldots, R_i, \theta_n)$, for $i \in \{1, \ldots, n\}$.
(3) For some large integer N (say 1000), repeat the following steps for every $k \in 1, \ldots, N$:

   (a) Generate a random sample $\{R_1^k, \ldots, R_n^k, \theta_n^k\}$ from distribution P_{θ_n}
   (b) Compute θ_n^k by applying the EM algorithm to the simulated sample, $R_1^k, \ldots, R_n^k$.
   (c) Let $\hat{U}_i^k = \Psi_i(R_1^k, \ldots, R_i^k, \theta_n^k)$ for $i \in 1, \ldots, n$, and finally compute $S_n^k = B_n\left(\hat{U}_1^k, \ldots, \hat{U}_n^k\right)$.

Then, the approximated P-value for the test based on the Cramér von Mises statistic S_n is given by $\frac{1}{N} \sum_{k=1}^{N} \mathbb{I}\left(S_n^k > S_n\right)$.

References

[1] J. Cox and S. Ross, The valuation of options for alternative stochastic processes, *Journal of Financial Economics* **3**, 145–166 (1976).
[2] F. Black and M. Scholes, The pricing of options and corporate liabilities, *Journal of Political Economy* **81**, 637–654 (1973).
[3] G. W. Schwert, Why does stock market volatility change over time?, *Journal of Finance* **44**, 1115–1153 (1989).

[4] J. D. Hamilton and G. Lin, Stock market volatility and business cycle, *Journal of Applied Econometrics*, 573–593 (1996).

[5] M. Schweizer, Mean-variance hedging for general claims, *Ann. Appl. Probab.* **2**, 171–179 (1992).

[6] M. Schweizer, Variance-optimal hedging in discrete time, *Math. Oper. Res.* **20**, 1–32 (1995).

[7] J. D. Hamilton, A new approach to the economic analysis of non-stationary time series and the business cycle, *Eonometrica*, 357–384 (1989).

[8] J. D. Hamilton, Analysis of time series subject to changes in regime, *J. Econometrics* **45**, 39–70 (1990).

[9] P. Wu and R. J. Elliott, Parameter estimation for a regime-switching mean-reverting model with jumps, *Int. J. Theor. Appl. Finance* **8**, 791–806 (2005).

[10] R. J. Elliott, H. Miao and Z. Wu, An asset pricing model with mean reversion and regime switching stochastic volatility, in *The Oxford handbook of nonlinear filtering*, (Oxford Univ. Press, Oxford, 2011) pp. 960–989.

[11] R. J. Elliott, L. Chan and T. K. Siu, Option valuation under a regime-switching constant elasticity of variance process, *Appl. Math. Comput.* **219**, 4434–4443 (2013).

[12] B. Rémillard, A. Hocquard, H. Lamarre and N. A. Papageorgiou, Option pricing and hedging for discrete time regime-switching model, *Modern Economy* **8**, 1005–1032 (September 2017).

[13] S. Shi and A. S. Weigend, Taking time seriously: hidden Markov experts applied to financial engineering, *Computational Intelligence for Financial Engineering (CIFEr)*, 244 (1997).

[14] A. P. Dempster, N. M. Laird and D. B. Rubin, Maximum likelihood from incomplete data via the EM algorithm, *J. Roy. Statist. Soc. Ser. B* **39**, 1–38 (1977).

[15] C. Genest, J.-F. Quessy and B. Rémillard, Goodness-of-fit procedures for copula models based on the integral probability transformation, *Scand. J. Statist.* **33**, 337–366 (2006).

[16] B. Rémillard, *Validity of the Parametric Bootstrap for Goodness-of-Fit Testing in Dynamic Models*, tech. rep., SSRN Working Paper Series No. 1966476 (2011).

[17] E. F. Fama, The behavior of stock-market prices, *Journal of Business* **38**, 34–105 (1965).

[18] B. Rémillard, *Statistical Methods for Financial Engineering* Chapman and Hall/CRC Financial Mathematics Series, Chapman and Hall/CRC Financial Mathematics Series (Taylor & Francis, 2013).

[19] O. Cappé, E. Moulines and T. Rydén, *Inference in Hidden Markov Models* Springer Series in Statistics, Springer Series in Statistics (Springer, New York, 2005).

[20] C. Genest and B. Rémillard, Validity of the parametric bootstrap for goodness-of-fit testing in semiparametric models, *Ann. Inst. H. Poincaré Sect. B* **44**, 1096–1127 (2008).

[21] N. Papageorgiou, B. Rémillard and A. Hocquard, Replicating the properties of hedge fund returns, *Journal of Alternative Investments* **11**, 8–38 (2008).

[22] B. Rémillard and S. Rubenthaler, Optimal hedging in discrete time, *Quantitative Finance* **13**, 819–825 (2013).

[23] B. Rémillard and S. Rubenthaler, *Option pricing and hedging for regime-switching geometric Brownian motion models*, working paper series, SSRN Working Paper Series No. 2599064 (2016).

[24] M. Caccia and B. Rémillard, *Option pricing and hedging for discrete time autoregressive hidden Markov model*, Tech. Rep. G-2017-60, GERAD (2017).

[25] P. François, G. Gauthier and F. Godin, Optimal hedging when the underlying asset follows a regime-switching Markov process, *European Journal of Operational Research* **237**, 312–322 (2014).

[26] J. Fleming, C. Kirby and B. Ostdiek, The economic value of volatility timing, *The Journal of Finance* **56**, 329–352 (2001).

[27] A. Buraschi and J. Jackwerth, The price of a smile: hedging and spanning in option markets, *The Review of Financial Studies* **14**, 495–527 (2001).

[28] R. C. Merton, Theory of rational option pricing, *The Bell Journal of Economics and Management Science* **4**, 141–183 (1973).

[29] P. Carr, *FAQ's in option pricing theory*, tech. rep., NYU (2002).

[30] J. Bai, Testing parametric conditional distributions of dynamic models, *The Review of Economics and Statistics* **85**, 531–549 (2003).

[31] F. X. Diebold, T. A. Gunther and A. S. Tay, Evaluating density forecasts with applications to financial risk management, *International Economic Review* **39**, 863–883 (1998).

[32] B. Rémillard, Tests of independence, in *International Encyclopedia of Statistical Science*, ed. M. Lovric (Springer Berlin Heidelberg, 2011) pp. 1598–1601.

Chapter 13

Interest Rate Swap Valuation in the Chinese Market

Wei Cui

RMB Market Department, China Foreign Exchange Trade System &
National Interbank Funding Center, Shanghai 201203, China
cuiwei@chinamoney.com.cn

Min Dai*, Steven Kou†, and Yaquan Zhang‡

Department of Mathematics and Risk Management Institute,
National University of Singapore, 119613 Singapore
* matdm@nus.edu.sg
† matsteve@nus.edu.sg
‡ rmizhya@nus.edu.sg

Chengxi Zhang§ and Xianhao Zhu¶

Risk Management Institute,
National University of Singapore, 119613 Singapore
§ rmizcxi@nus.edu.sg
¶ rmizx@nus.edu.sg

Following the 2008 financial crisis, the dual curve discounting method became widely used in valuing interest rate swaps denominated in major currencies, which implies the market consensus of accepting Overnight Indexed Swap rates as new proxies of risk-free rates. However, in the Chinese market, the outdated single curve discounting method is still widely used, because there is no consensus on the choice of the risk-free rate proxy. We apply the dual curve discounting method to the Chinese interest rate swap market and recommend using the 7-day fixing repo rate, a benchmark interest rate of the Chinese repo market, as the risk-free rate. Empirically, using the single curve discounting method may significantly undervalue a swap contract to the fixed rate receiver.

Keywords: multi-curve models, short rate models, pricing of interest rate swaps, the Chinese market, risk-free rate, repo rate.

1. Introduction

In financial markets, interest rate swaps have long been used as a tool of investment and risk management. The most common type is the "plain vanilla" interest rate swap. In this swap, one party periodically pays a cash flow determined by a fixed swap rate and receives a cash flow determined by a reference floating interest rate. This is the only type of interest rate swap traded in the Chinese market, and the focus of this paper.

Pricing an interest rate swap has different meanings in different contexts. In the market, only new contracts are frequently traded. These contracts are quoted by the fixed swap rates such that the contracts are worth zero at initiation. Therefore, to price a new interest rate swap means to determine the swap rate. The other case is to price an existing swap contract with a known swap rate. In this case, to price it usually means to calculate its net present value, which is important for accounting, risk management or early termination of the contract. In this paper, the swap valuation equations are given to serve the second case. However, one can easily modify them to get the swap rates of new contracts by rearranging the terms.

The benefit of having an appropriate swap valuation equation is not limited to calculating swap prices correctly. Typically, interest rates, such as Libor or Shibor, are only quoted with short maturities of up to 1 year, whereas their swaps can have much longer maturities. Therefore, market participants rely on the swap rates to derive interest rate term structures in long tenors. This technique is known as bootstrapping, which is the inverse of the swap valuation equation. Therefore, an appropriate valuation equation is crucial for the market to derive term structures properly.

Internationally, before the 2008 financial crisis, to price interest rate swaps, the industry practice was to regard Xibor rate[1] as a risk-free rate, and to project and discount the Xibor swap cash flows using the rate itself. Since only the Xibor curve is involved in this procedure, this valuation method is referred to as single curve discounting.

However, Xibor rate is not truly risk-free. It is an unsecured lending rate among financial institutions. For example, Collin-Dufresne and Solnik [1] argued that Libor has the same credit risk as AA rated financial institutions. Before the 2008 financial crisis, the risk embedded in Xibor was not significant in practice and the spreads between Xibor and the Overnight Indexed Swap (OIS)[2] curves were small. After the 2008 financial crisis, as shown in Fig. 1, these spreads became increasingly significant. Hull and

---

[1]Xibor rate refers to the group of interbank offered rates. For the U.S. dollar (USD), this rate is the London Interbank Offered Rate, or Libor. For the Euro (EUR), it refers to the Euro Interbank Offered Rate, or Euribor. For onshore Chinese Yuan (CNY), it refers to the Shanghai Interbank Offered Rate, or Shibor.

[2]OIS swaps refer to the swaps in which an overnight rate is chosen as the floating rate. In USD-dominated OIS, the federal funds rate is the choice. In EUR-dominated OIS, Euro Overnight Index Average, or Eonia, is the choice.

White [2] pointed out that the spreads reflect the credit concerns of banks about each other. This phenomenon makes the practice of discounting cash flows with Xibor curves questionable.

To account for the risks embedded in Xibor, practitioners have switched to a new valuation method known as dual curve discounting. Under this framework, in the valuation of Xibor swaps, another choice of risk-free rate curve is used in discounting the cash flows. Since the choice of the risk-free rate curve is usually the OIS rate for major currencies, this method is also known as OIS discounting, which has been documented by Grbac and Runggaldier [3] and many others.

The over-the-counter trading of interest rate swaps in the onshore Chinese market started in 2006. During the past decade, the Chinese swap market has made considerable progress. In 2016, there were more than 87 thousand swap transactions with a notional value of 9.9 trillion CNY. The popular benchmark floating rates are the 7-day interbank fixing repo rate (7D Repo rate), which accounts for 86% of market share, and the 3-month Shibor (3M Shibor), which accounts for 11% of market share.

Figure 1 shows the spread between the 3M Shibor and the 7D Repo rate in the Chinese market. This spread is more significant than the spread between the risky and risk-free rates observed in the U.S. market. This spread needs to be taken into account to properly price swap contracts.

Despite the rapid growth of market size, the valuation methodology used in the Chinese market lags behind. Market participants still price the swaps on risky floating rates with the single curve method. The following are some examples of using the single curve method in the Chinese market.

(1) China Foreign Exchange Trading System (CFETS) is a government institution organizing and supervising the Chinese interest rate swap market. It reports the forward rates of a few benchmark floating rates on its website[3] on a daily basis. These forward rates are obtained by stripping the market swap rates using the single curve method.

(2) Other than reporting the forward rates, CFETS also provides the bilateral early termination service of swap contracts. In this service, CFETS calculates the values of the contracts to be terminated using the single curve method.

(3) Bloomberg L.P. provides an interest rate swap valuation service through its terminals. It offers the dual curve stripping of a range of major

---

[3]http://www.chinamoney.com.cn.

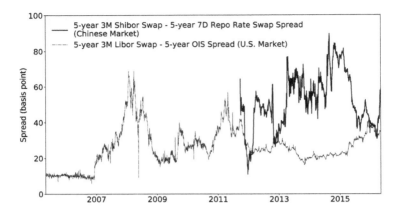

Fig. 1.   The dotted line shows the spread between the five-year swap rates of the 3M Libor and the five-year OIS rate in the U.S. market. The solid line shows the spread between the five-year swap rates of the 3M Shibor and the 7D Repo rate in the Chinese market. The historical swap rate data in the Chinese market started in mid 2012.

currencies including USD and EUR, but not CNY. In the Bloomberg valuation of CNY denominated swaps, the forward rates are stripped using the single curve method.

The contribution of this paper is two-fold. Firstly, we compare a few interest rates in the Chinese market. We suggest using the 7D Repo rate as the risk-free rate for the valuation of swaps. Secondly, we test the dual curve discounting method in the Chinese market. Our results show the current single curve discounting method may significantly undervalue a swap contract to the fixed rate receiver.

The rest of the paper is organized as follows. Section 2 revisits the modeling framework and valuation equations of interest rate swaps, and mathematically analyses how the change of valuation method affects the valuation results. Section 3 discusses the choice of risk-free rate proxy in the Chinese swap market. In Sec. 4, using data from the Chinese market, we price a Shibor swap contract using both the single and the dual curve discounting method and analyse the valuation difference. Lastly, we conclude in Sec. 5.

2. Pricing model

2.1. *Dual curve discounting*

For the completeness of later analysis, we first introduce the notations and review the pricing formulas of interest rate swaps. There is abundant literature discussing post-crisis interest rate models. Some examples are Ametrano and Bianchetti [4], Filipovic and Trolle [5] and Grbac and Runggaldier [3]. Despite their results being very similar, their terminologies and middle steps have subtle differences. In this paper, we generally follow the logic of Grbac and Runggaldier [3], for its similarity to the pre-crisis single curve settings.

The dual curve modeling framework starts from the prices of risk-free zero coupon bonds, denoted by $D_{\rm rf}(t, T)$.[4] The risk-free zero coupon bond curve at time t refers to the function $T \to D_{\rm rf}(t, T)$. Corresponding to the zero coupon bonds, we define the continuously-compounded risk-free instantaneous forward rates as $f_{\rm rf}(t, T) := -\partial_T \log D_{\rm rf}(t, T)$, and define the continuously-compounded risk-free short rate as $r_{\rm rf}(t) = f_{\rm rf}(t, t)$.

Let $\mathbb{Q}$ denote a risk-neutral measure, under which the numeraire is the money market account $B_{\rm rf}(0, t) = \exp\left(\int_0^t r_{\rm rf}(u)du\right)$. Under this measure, a direct result of the fundamental theorem of asset pricing is that the risk-free bond price is $D_{\rm rf}(t, T) = E^{\mathbb{Q}}\left[\exp\left\{-\int_t^T r_{\rm rf}(u)du\right\}|\mathcal{F}_t\right]$. We further define the forward measure $\mathbb{Q}^T$ using $D_{\rm rf}(t, T)$ as the numeraire.

In the market, there are (at least) two simple interest rates. Denote by $R_{\rm rf}(t_i, t_j)$ the risk-free rate and $R_{\rm risky}(t_i, t_j)$ the risky rate.[5] Both rates are fixed and take effect at t_i, and mature at t_j. Then $R_{\rm rf}(t_i, t_j)$ is the simple interest rate over time $[t_i, t_j]$ of an investment of buying a risk-free bond with maturity t_j at t_i, mathematically,

$$R_{\rm rf}(t_i, t_j) = \left(\frac{1}{D_{\rm rf}(t_i, t_j)} - 1\right)\frac{1}{t_j - t_i}.$$

Sometimes, we simply use $R_{\rm rf}$ and $R_{\rm risky}$ to refer to the interest rates when the tenors are not important.

---

[4]In Grbac and Runggaldier [3], this term is referred to as OIS bonds, because OIS rates are commonly used as the proxy of risk-free rate. In the Chinese market, there is no consensus on the proxy choice yet. Therefore, in the modeling framework, we do not link it to a specific interest rate in the market, though our analysis shows that the 7D Repo rate seems to be the best available choice in the current Chinese market. In some contexts, the zero coupon bond prices are also referred to as discount factors.

[5]In swap markets denominated in major currencies, $R_{\rm risky}$ is usually taken to be Xibor.

We denote the discretely compounded forward rates of R_{rf} and R_{risky} at time $t < t_i$ by $F_{\mathrm{rf}}(t; t_i, t_j)$ and $F_{\mathrm{risky}}(t; t_i, t_j)$ respectively. In the rest of this paper, they are referred to as *forward rates*. Following Grbac and Runggaldier [3], they are defined as follows:

$$
\begin{aligned}
F_{\mathrm{rf}}(t; t_i, t_j) &:= E^{\mathbb{Q}^{t_j}}[R_{\mathrm{rf}}(t_i, t_j)|\mathcal{F}_t], \\
F_{\mathrm{risky}}(t; t_i, t_j) &:= E^{\mathbb{Q}^{t_j}}[R_{\mathrm{risky}}(t_i, t_j)|\mathcal{F}_t].
\end{aligned}
$$

We denote a payment schedule by $t_{0 \leq i \leq n}$ with $t_i = t_{i-1} + \Delta$, where t_0 is the start date and Δ is a time interval of fixed length.[6] The dual curve interest rate swap valuation equations can be found in Grbac and Runggaldier [3].[7] More precisely, we refer to an interest rate swap with floating rate R_{rf} or R_{risky} as a R_{rf} swap or a R_{risky} swap respectively. At time $t \leq t_1$, the prices of a R_{rf} swap and a R_{risky} swap to the fixed rate receiver are as follows:

$$
V_{\mathrm{rf}}(t) = N \sum_{i=0}^{n-1} D_{\mathrm{rf}}(t, t_{i+1}) \Delta[s_{\mathrm{rf}} - F_{\mathrm{rf}}(t; t_i, t_{i+1})],
$$

$$
V_{\mathrm{risky}}(t) = N \sum_{i=0}^{n-1} D_{\mathrm{rf}}(t, t_{i+1}) \Delta[s_{\mathrm{risky}} - F_{\mathrm{risky}}(t; t_i, t_{i+1})]. \tag{1}
$$

where N is the notional amount, and s_{rf} and s_{risky} are the respective swap rates.

To use Eq. (1) to value a R_{risky} swap, one needs to calibrate the discount factors D_{rf} by the interest rate curve of R_{rf}, and calibrate the forward rates by the interest rate curve of R_{risky}. Since two curves are involved in this approach, it is named *dual curve*.

However, it is rare for simply compounded interest rates with long tenors to be directly quoted in the market. For example, the longest maturities

---

[6]Some papers introduce two separate payment schedules, with one for fixed rate payments and one for floating rate payments. However, in the Chinese market, the payment dates of the two legs of swaps usually coincide.

[7]Following Grbac and Runggaldier [3], in swap valuation, we assume the contracts are free of counterparty credit risk. This assumption is valid because of the fact that almost all swap contracts in the Chinese market were collateralized. In 2016, among the 9.9 trillion swap transactions, 9.8 trillion is fully collateralized, and the risk exposure is marked to market on a daily basis. Johannes and Sundaresan [6] theoretically proved that collateralized swaps are free of counterparty risk. Although in their proof, they refer to the floating rate of the swap as Libor, the proof can be generally applied to collateralized swaps with any floating rates.

for both Libor and Shibor are 1 year. To obtain the whole interest rate curves, the market practice is to use a method known as bootstrapping, which is essentially the inverse of the swap valuation equations. The input of this method is a series of market swap rates. Standardized swap contracts with long tenors are traded frequently in the market. The output of the method is a curve of discount factors or forward rates, which can be then used to value non-standard or existing swap contracts. The reader is referred to Ametrano and Bianchetti [4] for detailed implementations. Note that, apart from swap rates, the bootstrapping procedures in Ametrano and Bianchetti [4] also use futures contracts as inputs. Since futures on Shibor are not available in the Chinese market, we use only swap rates in the implementation.

In the above derivation, we purposely ignore the subtle differences resulting from day count conventions for the clarity of the notations. However, in implementation, we should take them into account to produce the correct numerical results. For more details on day count conventions, see Henrard [7].

2.2. *Single curve discounting*

As mentioned in the introduction, in the current Chinese market, the single curve discounting method still prevails in pricing swaps. In order to analyse the numerical difference of the two methods, we briefly introduce the single curve approach.

The difference between the single and the dual curve discounting methods lies in the valuation of R_{risky} swaps. Under the single curve modeling framework, R_{risky} is also regarded as risk-free, despite its riskiness. The valuation equation is given by:

$$V_{\text{risky}}(t) = N \sum_{i=0}^{n-1} D_{\text{risky}}(t, t_{i+1})\Delta[s_{\text{risky}} - F_{\text{risky}}(t; t_i, t_{i+1})], \qquad (2)$$

where $D_{\text{risky}}(t, t_{i+1})$ is the discount factor calculated under the wrong assumption that R_{risky} is risk-free. See Brigo and Mercurio [8] for the derivation of the single curve valuation equation.

Using both R_{rf} and R_{risky} as proxies for the risk-free rate is acceptable in practice if the two interest rate curves are close. However, as shown by Fig. 1, in the Chinese market, there is a dramatic spread between the 7D Repo rate and the 3M Shibor. Therefore, the single curve approach is clearly problematic.

Lastly, similar to the dual curve case, to implement Eq. (2), one needs to first perform bootstrapping with swap rates of R_{risky} swaps as inputs. One can still refer to Ametrano and Bianchetti [4] for how bootstrapping is performed under the single curve approach. Note that the bootstrapping method relies on the swap valuation equation. Therefore, with the same swap rates as inputs, changing the valuation equation leads to different discount factors, forward rates and valuation results.

2.3. *Valuation difference*

In this part, we analyse the valuation difference resulting from switching from the single to the dual curve method in valuing a R_{risky} swap. We attempt to empirically identify the drivers of this valuation difference.

Suppose initially we enter into a R_{risky} swap contract from the fixed rate receiver side. We denote the fixed rate of this contract by $s_{\text{risky}}^{\text{fix}}$ and its value by V_{risky}. After some time, we enter into a new contract with the same reference floating rate as the fixed rate payer. The new contract is designed to have identical maturity, payment dates and notional value as the previous one. As a result, the future cash flows generated from the floating legs of the two contracts will offset each other. Assume this new contract is entered into at time t, with swap rate $s_{\text{risky}}^{\text{par}}$, which is chosen so that the value of this contract is zero at time t. Note that the swap rate of this new contract is exactly the par rate of the old contract at t. Assume further that both $s_{\text{risky}}^{\text{fix}}$ and $s_{\text{risky}}^{\text{par}}$ are taken from a liquid market so that the values are independent of our choice of valuation method.

Consider the value of the portfolio consisting of the two swaps. Note the second contact has zero value at t. Therefore, the value of the portfolio is the same as the value of the old swap. Again, the cash flows generated by the floating legs of these two swaps are canceled. The values of the R_{risky} swap under the dual and the single curve discounting approach are respectively given by:

$$V_{\text{risky}}^{\text{dual}}(t) \quad = V_{\text{risky}}^{\text{dual}}(t) + 0 = N \sum_{i=0}^{n-1} (s_{\text{risky}}^{\text{fix}} - s_{\text{risky}}^{\text{par}}) D_{\text{rf}}(t, t_{i+1}) \Delta,$$
$$V_{\text{risky}}^{\text{single}}(t) = V_{\text{risky}}^{\text{single}}(t) + 0 = N \sum_{i=0}^{n-1} (s_{\text{risky}}^{\text{fix}} - s_{\text{risky}}^{\text{par}}) D_{\text{risky}}(t, t_{i+1}) \Delta,$$

where $V_{\text{risky}}^{\text{dual}}(t)$ and $V_{\text{risky}}^{\text{single}}(t)$ stand for the valuation derived from the dual curve and single curve methods. Taking the difference of the two, then the change in valuation resulting from switching valuation method is given precisely by

$$V_{\text{risky}}^{\text{dual}}(t) - V_{\text{risky}}^{\text{single}}(t) = N \sum_{i=0}^{n-1} (D_{\text{rf}}(t, t_{i+1}) - D_{\text{risky}}(t, t_{i+1}))(s_{\text{risky}}^{\text{fix}} - s_{\text{risky}}^{\text{par}})\Delta.$$

Benefiting from this equation, we do not need to deal with untraceable forward rates in our later analysis. It is now clear that the valuation difference has two drivers, namely the difference of the discount factors used in the two methods, and the difference between the stipulated swap rate and its par rate at the time of valuation.

The difference caused by the discount factors is determined by the spread between the risky floating rate and the risk-free rate on the valuation date. Typically, this difference is positive. This is pretty intuitive. D_{risky} is obtained from the risky interest rate with an implicit but wrong assumption that the rate is risk-free. The market asks for a premium for taking the risk and the corresponding discount factors are smaller.

We analyse the difference $(s_{\text{risky}}^{\text{fix}} - s_{\text{risky}}^{\text{par}})$ from two aspects. Firstly, the term structure of the swap rates in the market is usually upward sloping, i.e. a swap rate with a long maturity is larger than a rate with short maturity. Note that the par rate is effectively the swap rate of a new swap with short maturity. If the interest rate market remains stable, the stipulated fixed rate will be larger than the par rate at the time of valuation. This is especially the case for contracts signed long before the valuation time. Secondly, the difference will be affected by market fluctuations. Note that the par rate is determined by the market condition at the time of valuation. In particular, if the market rates continuously rise after the swap contract was signed, the effect of the first aspect will be offset and the valuation difference will not be material. In contrast, if the market rates move downwards, the difference between the swap rate and par rate will be correspondingly enlarged. In most cases, $(s_{\text{risky}}^{\text{fix}} - s_{\text{risky}}^{\text{par}})$ is positive and it is not unusual to observe a difference as large as a hundred basis points.

In summary, in most cases, using the single curve method tends to undervalue interest rate swap contracts on the fixed rate receiver side. In particular, the valuation bias is most significant for contracts that still have a long time to maturity, and when the market rates have moved continuously downwards after inception of the contracts. This argument is demonstrated using market data in later sections. However, we have to stress that the above analysis is empirical. The actual difference depends heavily on market conditions.

3. Candidates for the risk-free rate in the Chinese swap market

In valuation theory, the risk-free rate is an important building block. In financial markets, however, there is hardly a perfect proxy of the risk-free rate. All practitioners can do is to compare the available candidates in the market and choose the one with the least disadvantage. For example, to justify the effectiveness of the OIS rate in the U.S. market, Hull and White [2] compared it against Libor, treasury and repo rate. Here, we will have the same discussion to compare the 7D Repo rate with Chinese government bond yields and other interest rates in the Chinese market. Some arguments are borrowed from the U.S. market.

Chinese Government Bond Yields: Chinese government bonds are frequently traded in the onshore Chinese market. These bonds are backed by the Chinese government and are the safest investment in China. The most recognized government bond yield curve is published by China Central Depository & Clearing (CCDC), which is a government institution. The yield curve is calculated daily using market prices and has tenors up to 50 years. The yield curve data set is available on the CCDC website.[8] We denote the yield at time t with maturity $t + \delta$ by $Y(t, t + \delta)$. If the government yields are the proxy of the risk-free rate, then the corresponding zero coupon bond prices are given by

$$D_{\text{bond}}(t, t + \delta) = \frac{1}{(1 + Y(t, t + \delta))^\delta}, \qquad (3)$$

Government bond yields in China have similar drawbacks as U.S. treasury rates. Firstly, the coupon payments of government bonds are non-taxable. This tax benefit makes government bond yields artificially low. Secondly, government bonds are often used as collaterals in repurchase transactions. This extra demand also brings down the yield. Note that these are also the reasons for not using U.S. treasury rates as risk-free rate in the U.S. market; see Hull [9]. If government bond yields are used as a risk-free rate proxy, the resulting discount factors will be artificially large. For this reason, government bond yields may not be a good proxy for the risk-free rate.

7D Repo Rate: In 2016, the total notional value of repo transactions in the Chinese repo market was 831 trillion CNY, which is around 6 times of total bond transactions. Among all the maturities, the overnight repo

---

[8]http://www.chinabond.com.cn.

contracts are the most liquid, followed by 7-day contracts. As a benchmark rate in the repo market, the interbank fixing repo rates are calculated and published by CFETS each trading day. Since repo transactions are always collateralized, the repo rate appears to be a good indicator of the risk-free rate.

Of course, the 7D Repo rate is still not a perfect choice. Firstly, Hull and White [2] observed that repo rates in the U.S. market have great cross-sectional variation: repos secured by U.S. treasuries have lower rates than repos secured by other debts. Although there has been no report of this observation in the Chinese market so far, we should not totally ignore this problem. Another potential problem is liquidity. 7-day repo transactions are not as liquid as overnight transactions, which may be a better proxy of the risk-free rate. However, in the current market, there is no interest rate swap on the overnight repo rate and there is no way to determine a full term structure.

Other Candidates: As an overnight interest rate, Overnight Shibor appears to be a good proxy of the risk-free rate at first glance. There are also Overnight Shibor swaps traded in the Chinese market. However, the trading volume of Overnight Shibor swaps is very limited: they constitute less than 3% of market share. Therefore, the resulting swap curves are not supported by sufficient market information. Moreover, the longest maturity of swaps on Overnight Shibor is only 3 years. There is no way to determine the term structure at long tenors for this interest rate.

Another potential choice is the fixing depository-institutions repo rate. This is a new benchmark rate of the repo market published by CFETS. As the name suggests, this rate is calculated based on the repo transactions among only the depository institutions. However, at the time of writing, the historical data of this rate is still not sufficient to support any conclusive analysis. We leave this new interest rate for future study.

To numerically compare government bond yields and the 7D Repo rate, Table 1 gives the average discount factors assuming the corresponding market rate is risk-free. More precisely, it reports the average discount factors in the time interval $[t, t + \delta]$ with t being the trading days from January 1, 2016 to December 31, 2016. δ is chosen to be 1 year, 3 years, 5 years, 7 years and 10 years. The discount factors corresponding to the government bond yields are calculated using Eq. (3) with yield curves published by CCDC. The 7D Repo rate discount factors are calculated using the bootstrapping method mentioned in Sec. 2.1.

From Table 1, we can see that the discount factors corresponding to government bond yields are universally larger than those of the 7D Repo rate, which is consistent with previous analysis.

Table 1.   The average discount factors in 2016 corresponding to Chinese government bond yields and 7D Repo rate respectively.

δ	Average Discount Factors	
	Government Bond Yield	7D Repo Rate
1 Year	0.978	0.975
3 Years	0.928	0.924
5 Years	0.876	0.867
7 Years	0.819	0.813
10 Years	0.752	0.736

4. Numerical test

In the Chinese market, the current market practice is to price 3M Shibor swaps using the single curve valuation Eq. (2). To demonstrate the possible magnitude of the valuation bias resulting from this practice, we give valuation to a 3M Shibor interest rate swap contract. The contract is chosen based on the criterion summarized in Sec. 2.3 so that the valuation difference between the dual and the single curve discounting method is significant.

On December 26, 2013, the 5-year 3M Shibor swap rate published by CFETS was 5.6827%. This swap rate was calculated based on quotes from major market participants and was a good representation of the market condition at the time. After this day, the interest rates in the Chinese market moved continuously downwards. At the beginning of 2016, the 5-year 3M Shibor swap rate dropped to around 3%.

Suppose a 5-year 3M Shibor contract with notional value of 1 million CNY is signed on December 26, 2013 with a swap rate of 5.6827%. Table 2 and Fig. 2 present the valuation results from 2014 to 2016. The contract is priced using both the current single curve practice and the dual curve valuation method. In the dual curve discounting, we choose the 7D Repo rate and the government bond yield as the risk-free rate respectively. Since the 7D Repo rate is recommended, the results corresponding to this rate are used as the benchmark. All the valuation is performed from the fixed rate receiver side.

DV01, or dollar value of one basis point, is obtained from the dual curve discounting method using the 7D Repo rate as the risk-free rate. In practice, DV01 is calculated by shifting the input swap rate curve[9] up and down by x basis points. We denote the resulting valuation by V_{up} and V_{down} respectively, then

$$\text{DV01} = \frac{V_{\text{up}} - V_{\text{down}}}{2x}.$$

The choice of x is empirical. CFETS takes $x = 5$ (see Lai [10]) and Bloomberg L.P. takes $x = 10$ (see Wu [11]). We follow the choice of CFETS.

To measure the significance of the valuation difference, we also report the value *DV01 Difference*. The unit of this value is basis point. A DV01 difference of x basis points has the following interpretation: if the valuation discounted by the 7D Repo rate is correct, then using the corresponding method leads to a valuation bias equivalent to shifting the input 3M Shibor swap rate curve by x basis points.

There are a few interesting points about the valuation results. First of all, the current Chinese market practice is to price 3M Shibor swaps using the single curve discounting method. Both Bloomberg and CFETS will give valuations close to the numbers shown in the columns under *Single Curve*[10] of Table 2. Compared with the dual curve method with the 7D Repo rate, the current single curve method may undervalue the 1 million swap contract by up to 1.4 thousand CNY. In terms of DV01, the difference reached 4.37 basis points, which means the difference is equivalent to shifting the floating rate curve by 4.37 basis points. In the 749 trading days from 2014 to 2016, the average valuation difference and DV01 difference are respectively 701.47 CNY and 2.24 basis points. In comparison, from 2014 to 2016, the median of daily absolute change of 5-year swap rate of the 3M Shibor was only 1.48 basis points. These results suggest that using the current single curve method in the market may significantly undervalue swap contracts for fixed rate receivers and bring great model risks to the market.

Secondly, as shown in Fig. 2, between the dual curve method with the 7D Repo rate and the single curve method, the valuation differences firstly enlarged, then reached the maximum after the contract had been signed for one and a half years, and dropped afterwards. This pattern is in line with our previous analysis in Sec. 2.3. In the first one and a half years, the market interest rates moved continuously downwards. As a result, $(s_{\text{risky}}^{\text{fix}} - s_{\text{risky}}^{\text{par}})$

---

[9]The swap rate curve is used in the bootstrapping method; see the last part of Sec. 2.1.
[10]The actual valuation given by Bloomberg or CFETS might be slightly different from these results for reasons such as interpolation.

Table 2.   Valuation of the 3M Shibor swap contract using two methods, namely the single curve discounting method, and the dual curve discounting method with 7D Repo rate. The contract is priced at the end of each quarter from 2014 to 2016. The units of valuation, DV01 and valuation difference are CNY. To measure the significance of the difference, the valuation differences are also divided by DV01. Between these two methods, the valuation difference achieves the maximum on April 28, 2015 (labeled with *).

| Valuation Date | Dual Curve: 7D Repo Rate | | Single Curve | | |
	Valuation (CNY) (1)	DV01 (CNY) (2)	Valuation (CNY) (3)	Valuation Difference (CNY) (4) = (1) − (3)	DV01 Difference (basis points) (5) = (4) / (2)
Mar 31, 2014	18755.07	401.6	18391.44	363.62	0.91
Jun 30, 2014	40525.02	385.99	39773.68	751.34	1.95
Sep 30, 2014	62715.31	369.24	61702.59	1012.72	2.74
Dec 31, 2014	54587.37	347.74	53654.2	933.17	2.68
Mar 31, 2015	44129.94	324.21	43379.73	750.2	2.31
Apr 28, 2015*	67460.15	331.49	66010.05	1450.1*	4.37
Jun 30, 2015	71114.23	308.99	69865.16	1249.07	4.04
Sep 30, 2015	69280.04	286.03	68258.7	1021.34	3.57
Dec 31, 2015	73364.5	263.83	72490.22	874.28	3.31
Mar 31, 2016	74964.68	240.67	74409.61	555.07	2.31
Jun 30, 2016	64186.53	216.59	63718.15	468.38	2.16
Sep 30, 2016	59563.74	192.9	59300.7	263.04	1.36
Dec 30, 2016	33366.13	167.89	33209.17	156.96	0.93

enlarged and dominated the change of the valuation difference. Starting from the second half year of 2015, the market gradually became stable and so is $(s_{\text{risky}}^{\text{fix}} - s_{\text{risky}}^{\text{par}})$. In this period, $(D_{\text{rf}} - D_{\text{risky}})$ dominated the change. As the remaining life of the swap contract reduced, $(D_{\text{rf}} - D_{\text{risky}})$ became smaller, which led to the decrease of the valuation difference.

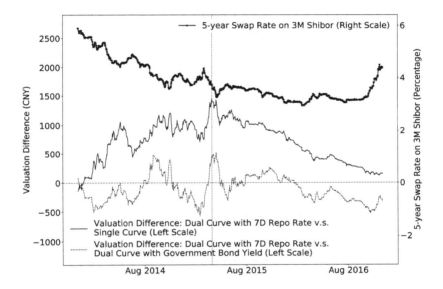

Fig. 2.   *The left scale*: The valuation difference between the dual curve method with the 7D Repo rate and the single curve method, and the valuation difference between the dual curve method with the 7D Repo rate and the dual curve method with government bond yields. *The right scale*: Five-year swap rate of 3M Shibor swaps. These swap rates represent the market movements. The vertical line is April 28, 2015, on which the valuation difference between the dual curve method with the 7D Repo rate and the single curve method achieved the maximum.

The final observation is that, as shown in figure Fig. 2, between the dual curve method with the 7D Repo rate and the dual curve method with government bond yield, the valuation differences are negative on most trading days, which suggests using government bond yields as a risk-free rate proxy overvalues the swap contracts for fixed rate receivers. This is consistent with the results in Table 1, as higher discount factors lead to higher valuation results. In the 749 trading days, the largest valuation bias in magnitude was 569.83 CNY, which is equivalent to a DV01 difference of 2.70 basis points.

5. Conclusion

In this paper, we first theoretically analysed the difference between the valuation results of the single and the dual discounting methods. The conclusion was then verified using data from the Chinese interest rate swap market. We have shown that the single curve method tends to undervalue swap contracts from the fixed rate receiver side. The bias is most significant for old contracts that still have a long time to maturity and when the market rates have moved continuously downwards. Our numerical test showed that the size of the valuation bias can be as large as 3 times that of typical daily movements in the Chinese swap market. Another important discussion in the paper is the choice of the risk-free rate proxy for the Chinese swap market. After comparing with the Chinese government bond yields and other interest rates, we found that the 7D Repo rate appeared to be the most appropriate choice to be used in dual curve discounting. We hope these results bring some attention and insight to interest rate swap valuation issues in the Chinese market.

This research can be extended in many ways. First of all, to choose a proxy of the risk-free rate, we compared three different interest rates in the market. In this comparison, we are aware that our supporting arguments are empirical. A more systematic justification is required. Secondly, interest rate swaps are not the only financial assets that need to be valued in the dual curve framework. This method is also applicable to many other assets such as cross currency swaps and swaptions. It will be interesting to look at how the change of valuation method will affect the valuation of these assets in the Chinese market.

References

1. P. CollinDufresne and B. Solnik, On the term structure of default premia in the swap and libor markets, *J. Financ.* **56**, 1095–1115 (2001).
2. J. Hull and A. White, Libor vs. OIS: The derivatives discounting dilemma, *Journal Of Investment Management* **11**(3), 14–27 (2012).
3. Z. Grbac and W. J. Runggaldier, *Interest rate modeling: post-crisis challenges and approaches* (Springer, 2015).

4. F. M. Ametrano and M. Bianchetti, Everything you always wanted to know about multiple interest rate curve bootstrapping but were afraid to ask (2013).

5. D. Filipovi and A. B. Trolle, The term structure of interbank risk, *J. Financ. Econ.* **109**(3), 707–733 (2013).

6. M. Johannes and S. Sundaresan, The impact of collateralization on swap rates, *J. Financ.* **62**, 383–410 (2007).

7. M. Henrard, Interest rate instruments and market conventions guide, *OpenGamma Quantitative Research* (2012).

8. D. Brigo and F. Mercurio, *Interest Rate Models-Theory and Practice: With Smile, Inflation and Credit* (Springer Science & Business Media, 2007).

9. J. Hull, *Options, Futures and Other Derivatives*, 3rd Edn. (Pearson, 2015).

10. Y. Lai, *Introduction to the interest rate swap intraday fixing curves, closing curves and valuation methodology*, tech. rep., China Foreign Exchange Trading System (2012).

11. Z. Wu, *DV01 Calculation Method*, tech. rep., Bloomberg Professional (2011), Available at: subscription service.

Chapter 14

On Consistency of the Omega Ratio with Stochastic Dominance Rules

Bernhard Klar

Department of Mathematics,
Karlsruhe Institute of Technology (KIT), Germany
bernhard.klar@kit.edu

Alfred Müller

Department of Mathematics,
University of Siegen, Germany
mueller@mathematik.uni-siegen.de

Omega ratios have been introduced in [1] as a performance measure to compare the performance of different investment opportunities. It does not have some of the drawbacks of the famous Sharpe ratio. In particular, it is consistent with first order stochastic dominance. Omega ratios also have an interesting relation to expectiles, which found increasing interest recently as risk measures. There is some confusion in the literature about consistency with respect to second order stochastic dominance. In this paper, we clarify this and extend it to a consistency result with respect to stochastic dominance of order $1 + \gamma$ recently introduced in [2] and generalizing the classical concepts of stochastic dominance of first and second order. Several examples illustrate the usefulness of this result. Finally, some consistency results for even more general stochastic dominance rules are shown, including the concept of ϵ-almost stochastic dominance introduced in [3].

Keywords: omega ratio, stochastic dominance, expectiles, integrated distribution function.

1. Introduction

There is an ongoing debate on how to compare the performance of different investment opportunities. Very often one tries to use a performance measure that can be interpreted as a return-risk ratio. The most famous example is the *Sharpe ratio*, introduced in [4] to compare the performance of funds. It works well under the assumption that returns are normally distributed, but it has well known serious drawbacks if one dispenses from that unrealistic assumption. One of the problems with the Sharpe ratio is that it is not consistent with first order stochastic dominance (abbreviated as FSD from now on). This implies that an investor maximizing the Sharpe ratio may have a preference for an investment A over an investment B even though its returns are smaller for sure. This is clearly irrational behavior.

As an alternative, [1] introduced the *Omega ratio*, a concept that has been received with great interest. One of its advantages over the Sharpe ratio is its consistency with FSD. There is a bit of confusion in the literature whether or not it is also consistent with second order stochastic dominance (SSD). Wrong claims that this holds for all benchmarks can be found e.g. in [5] and [6]. An accurate statement showing that this depends on the used benchmark was recently published in [7]. There is also some recent interest in portfolio optimization problems using the Omega ratio. [8] introduce a linear programming algorithm to find an optimal portfolio maximizing the Omega ratio. [9] and [10] also discuss portfolio optimization problems using Omega ratio as a performance measure. In [9] it is shown that for some benchmarks this is an ill-posed problem in their setting, as the optimal Omega ratio may be infinite.

The increasing interest in the Omega ratio is also related to the fact that Omega ratios are strongly related to *expectiles*, which recently found a lot of attention as risk measures after it was shown that they are the only risk measures having the property of being coherent and elicitable at the same time, see e.g. [11] and [12].

This inspired us to reconsider the problem of consistency of the Omega ratio with stochastic dominance rules. In this contribution, we clarify the consistency properties with FSD and SSD and show that indeed these results can be unified and generalized by using the concept of fractional stochastic dominance of order $1 + \gamma$ recently introduced in [2]. In Example 2.10 of that paper, it was already observed that comparing a distribution with a degenerate one with respect to stochastic dominance of order $1 + \gamma$ holds for all γ larger than the Omega ratio. Therefore it is not surprising that we can show a much more interesting result about consistency of Omega ratios with respect to this kind of stochastic dominance in Theorem 2.3 below.

The rest of the paper is organized as follows. In Section 2, we first introduce the main concepts used in this paper including the definition of Omega ratio and expectiles and the formal definitions of stochastic dominance rules. We then show our main result in Theorem 2.3 and illustrate its usefulness by several examples. In Section 3, these results are extended to more general combined convex and concave stochastic dominance rules, which generalize the well known concept of ϵ-almost stochastic dominance introduced in [3].

2. Omega ratios and stochastic dominance

Let X be a real valued random variable with a finite mean EX, describing the return of an asset. We denote by $F_X(t) = P(X \leq t)$ its distribution function, and by

$$\phi_X(t) = \int_{-\infty}^{t} F_X(z) \, dz = E(X - t)_-$$

the integrated distribution function of X, where here and in the following we use the abbreviations $x_+ := \max\{x, 0\}$ and $x_- := \max\{-x, 0\}$ for the positive and negative part of x. Note that $x = x_+ - x_-$.

It should be emphasized that

$$\bar{\delta}_X = \phi_X(EX) = E|X - EX|/2$$

is the absolute semideviation (from the mean). Its use as a risk measure is examined in [13].

[1] introduced the *Omega ratio* with benchmark t as

$$\Omega_X(t) = \frac{E(X - t)_+}{E(X - t)_-}. \tag{1}$$

The following properties are immediate. The function Ω_X is strictly positive, continuous and strictly decreasing from infinity to zero on its domain and $\Omega_X(EX) = 1$.

From

$$EX - t = E(X - t)_+ - E(X - t)_- \tag{2}$$

we can derive the following representation using the integrated distribution function:

$$\Omega_X(t) = \frac{EX - t + E(X - t)_-}{E(X - t)_-} = 1 + \frac{EX - t}{\phi_X(t)}. \tag{3}$$

Therefore we can also derive the integrated distribution function from the Omega ratio via

$$\phi_X(t) = \frac{EX - t}{\Omega_X(t) - 1}, \quad t \neq EX, \tag{4}$$

which can be continuously extended in $t = EX$. This shows that the Omega ratio determines the distribution. Taking the right derivative in (4) and taking into account that $EX = \Omega_X^{-1}(1)$ we get the following explicit expression for the distribution function in terms of the Omega ratios:

$$F_X(t) = \frac{1 - \Omega_X(t) + \Omega_X'^+(t) \cdot (t - \Omega_X^{-1}(1))}{(1 - \Omega_X(t))^2}, \quad t \neq \Omega_X^{-1}(1).$$

It is basically equivalent to a corresponding formula already mentioned in [14] as Theorem 1 (iv), where a very similar formula is stated for continuously differentiable distribution functions in the context of expectiles.

Recall that the expectiles $e_X(\alpha)$ of a random variable $X \in L^2$ have been defined by [14] as the minimizers of an asymmetric quadratic loss:

$$e_X(\alpha) = \arg \min_{t \in \mathbb{R}} \left\{ E\ell_\alpha(X - t) \right\}, \tag{5}$$

where

$$\ell_\alpha(x) = \begin{cases} \alpha x^2 & \text{if } x \geq 0, \\ (1 - \alpha)x^2 & \text{if } x < 0, \end{cases}$$

and $\alpha \in (0, 1)$. For $X \in L^1$, Equation (5) has to be modified (see [14]) to

$$e_X(\alpha) = \arg \min_{t \in \mathbb{R}} \left\{ E \left[\ell_\alpha(X - t) - \ell_\alpha(X) \right] \right\}. \tag{6}$$

The minimizer in (5) or (6) is always unique and is identified by the first order condition

$$\alpha E \left(X - e_X(\alpha) \right)_+ = (1 - \alpha)E \left(X - e_X(\alpha) \right)_- . \tag{7}$$

From this equation, the one-to-one relation between expectiles and Omega ratios given below immediately follows, see [15]. It holds

$$e_X(\alpha) = \Omega_X^{-1} \left(\frac{1 - \alpha}{\alpha} \right), \quad \Omega_X(t) = \frac{1 - e_X^{-1}(t)}{e_X^{-1}(t)}. \tag{8}$$

Next we recall the basic definitions of stochastic dominance. The well known concepts of first order stochastic dominance (FSD) and second order stochastic dominance (SSD) are defined as follows. We say that $X \leq_{FSD} Y$ if $Eu(X) \leq Eu(Y)$ for all increasing utility functions u, i.e. if all rational utility maximizers prefer Y to X. This holds if and only if $F_X(t) \geq F_Y(t)$ for all t. We say that $X \leq_{SSD} Y$ if $Eu(X) \leq Eu(Y)$ for all increasing and concave utility functions u, i.e. if all rational and risk averse utility maximizers prefer Y to X. This holds if and only if $\phi_X(t) \geq \phi_Y(t)$ for all t. In the mathematical literature, FSD is also known under the name *(usual) stochastic order* denoted by $X \leq_{st} Y$, and SSD is known as *increasing concave order* denoted by $X \leq_{icv} Y$, see e.g. [16] or [17]. In this paper, we stick to the notation FSD and SSD as usually used in the literature on finance and economics.

The following consistency result holds for the Omega ratio. We will give a simple proof of a more general result below in Theorem 2.3.

Theorem 2.1. *a) If $X \leq_{FSD} Y$ then $\Omega_X(t) \leq \Omega_Y(t)$ for all t.*
b) If $X \leq_{SSD} Y$ then $\Omega_X(t) \leq \Omega_Y(t)$ for all $t \leq EY$.

For $t > EY$ the Omega ratio is not consistent with SSD. Indeed, if $EX = EY$ and $X \leq_{SSD} Y$, then it follows immediately from (3) that $\Omega_X(t) \geq \Omega_Y(t)$ with strict inequality if $\phi_X(t) > \phi_Y(t)$.

[2] introduce a concept of generalized stochastic dominance with a real valued parameter $1+\gamma$ interpolating between FSD ($\gamma = 0$) and SSD ($\gamma = 1$). We repeat here the definitions and the main result.

Definition 2.1. For $0 \leq \gamma \leq 1$ let $\mathcal{U}_\gamma$ be the class of continuously differentiable functions u such that

$$0 \leq \gamma u'(y) \leq u'(x) \quad \text{for all } x \leq y. \tag{9}$$

Definition 2.2. For $0 \leq \gamma \leq 1$ we say that Y dominates X by $(1+\gamma)$-SD, denoted $X \leq_{(1+\gamma)-SD} Y$, if $Eu(X) \leq Eu(Y)$ for all functions $u \in \mathcal{U}_\gamma$.

Note that $u \in \mathcal{U}_0$ if and only if u is non-decreasing, and $u \in \mathcal{U}_1$ if and only if u is increasing and concave. Thus, $\gamma = 0$ corresponds to FSD and $\gamma = 1$ corresponds to SSD, with $0 < \gamma < 1$ corresponding to preference relations falling between FSD and SSD. The parameter γ provides a bound on how much marginal utility $u'(x)$ can decrease as x decreases, and its reciprocal $1/\gamma$ gives a bound on how much marginal utility can increase as x increases.

In Theorem 2.4 of [2], the following equivalence is shown, which yields a method to check this kind of stochastic dominance.

Theorem 2.2. *The following conditions are equivalent:*
a) $X \leq_{(1+\gamma)-SD} Y$,
b) $\int_{-\infty}^{t} (F_Y(z) - F_X(z))_+ \, dz \leq \gamma \int_{-\infty}^{t} (F_X(z) - F_Y(z))_+ \, dz$ for all $t \in \mathbb{R}$.

From this characterization we can deduce a condition for the comparison of a random variable X with a constant random variable c, see Example 2.10 in [2].

Corollary 2.1. *If $\Omega_X(c) \leq \gamma$, then we have $X \leq_{(1+\gamma)-SD} c$ for the constant random variable c.*

We can now show the following result generalizing Theorem 2.1.

Theorem 2.3. *If $X \leq_{(1+\gamma)-SD} Y$ and $\Omega_Y(t) \geq \gamma$ then $\Omega_X(t) \leq \Omega_Y(t)$.*

Proof. Assume $\Omega_Y(t) = \delta \geq \gamma$. Then $Y \leq_{(1+\delta)-SD} t$ follows from Corollary 2.1. Since $\delta \geq \gamma$, we have $\mathcal{U}_\delta \subseteq \mathcal{U}_\gamma$, and thus

$$X \leq_{(1+\delta)-SD} Y \leq_{(1+\delta)-SD} t.$$

By transitivity, $X \leq_{(1+\delta)-SD} t$, which implies $\Omega_X(t) \leq \delta$, i.e. $\Omega_X(t) \leq \Omega_Y(t)$. $\square$

Notice that Theorem 2.1 is just a special case of Theorem 2.3. Part a) of Theorem 2.1 follows by choosing $\gamma = 0$ and part b) by choosing $\gamma = 1$.

We will now give some illustrative examples showing the usefulness of this result. We start with a comparison of a normal and an exponential distribution, where we can compute the Omega ratios as well as the conditions for $(1+\gamma)$-dominance explicitly.

Example 2.1. Consider a normally distributed random variable X with mean μ and standard deviation σ, denoted from now on as $X \sim N\left(\mu, \sigma^2\right)$, and an exponential random variable Y with mean $1/\lambda$, denoted as $Y \sim Exp(\lambda)$. The integrated distribution functions are given by

$$\phi_X(t) = (t - \mu)\Phi_{\mu,\sigma^2}(t) + \varphi_{\mu,\sigma^2}(t), \quad t \in \mathbb{R},$$
$$\phi_Y(t) = t - (1 - \exp(-\lambda t))/\lambda, \quad t > 0,$$

where Φ_{μ,σ^2} and φ_{μ,σ^2} denote the cumulative distribution function (cdf) and density of X, respectively. Using (3), the pertaining Omega ratios can be derived explicitly.

To be more specific, take $X \sim N\left(3/4, (3/2)^2\right)$ and $Y \sim Exp(1)$. The cdfs F and G of X and Y have two crossing points $x_1 = 0.633$ and $x_2 = 3.692$ with $F(x) \geq G(x)$ for $x \leq x_1$ and $x \geq x_2$ and $F(x) \leq G(x)$ for $x_1 \leq x \leq x_2$. Setting $x_0 = -\infty$ and $x_3 = \infty$, the areas

$$A_i = \int_{x_{i-1}}^{x_i} (F(x) - G(x)) \, dx, \quad i = 1, 2, 3,$$

are given by $A_1 = 0.378$, $A_2 = -0.138$, $A_3 = 0.0108$. By Corollary B.1 in [2], we have $X \leq_{(1+\gamma)-SD} Y$ if and only if

$$\gamma \geq \max\left\{\frac{-A_2}{A_1}, \frac{-A_2}{A_1 + A_3}\right\} = \frac{-A_2}{A_1} = 0.367 = \gamma_{\min}.$$

Now, $\Omega_Y(t) \geq \gamma_{\min}$ if $t \leq t_0 = 1.418$. Therefore, Theorem 2.3 yields $\Omega_X(t) \leq \Omega_Y(t)$ for $t \leq t_0$. Figure 1 shows the distribution functions and

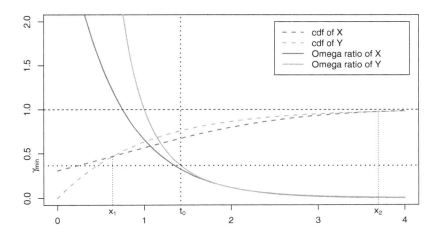

Fig. 1.   Cdfs and Omega ratios of $X \sim N\left(3/4, (3/2)^2\right)$ and $Y \sim Exp(1)$.

Omega ratios of X and Y. We will reconsider this example later in Examples 3.1 and 3.2 where we derive further related inequalities.

The example shows that $\Omega_X(t) \leq \Omega_Y(t)$ for $t \leq t^*$ does not necessarily imply $X \leq_{(1+\gamma^*)-SD} Y$, where $\gamma^* = \Omega_Y(t^*)$. The situation is different for the case of distributions from the same location-scale family that we consider in the following. To this end, assume

$$F(x) = H\left(\frac{x - \mu_1}{\sigma_1}\right) \quad \text{and} \quad G(x) = H\left(\frac{x - \mu_2}{\sigma_2}\right), \tag{10}$$

where H is the continuous cdf of a random variable with mean zero and standard deviation one. Then F and G have means μ_1 and μ_2 and standard deviations σ_1 and σ_2. Let $X \sim F$ and $Y \sim G$. A necessary and sufficient condition for $X \leq_{SSD} Y$ is $\mu_1 \leq \mu_2$ and $\sigma_1 \geq \sigma_2$. The cdfs are single-crossing at

$$x_1 = \frac{\mu_2 \sigma_1 - \mu_1 \sigma_2}{\sigma_1 - \sigma_2}. \tag{11}$$

If F single-crosses G from above, Corollary 2.5 in [2] shows that $X \leq_{(1+\gamma)-SD} Y$ if and only if $\gamma A \geq B$, where

$$A = \int_{-\infty}^{x_1} (F(x) - G(x))\ \mathrm{d}x \quad \text{and} \quad B = \int_{x_1}^{\infty} (G(x) - F(x))\ \mathrm{d}x. \tag{12}$$

We get the following result.

Theorem 2.4. *Let X and Y be from the same location-scale family as given in (10) with $\mu_1 \leq \mu_2$ and $\sigma_1 \geq \sigma_2$. Define $\gamma^* = \Omega_X(x_1)$, where x_1 is the single crossing point of the cdfs of X and Y given in (11). Then, $X \leq_{(1+\gamma^*)-SD} Y$. Furthermore, $\Omega_X(t) \leq \Omega_Y(t)$ if and only if $t \leq x_1$.*

Proof. First, we get

$$\Omega_X(x_1) = \frac{E(X - x_1)_+}{E(X - x_1)_-} = \frac{\int_{x_1}^{\infty} \left(1 - H\left((x - \mu_1)/\sigma_1\right)\right) \, dx}{\int_{-\infty}^{x_1} H\left((x - \mu_1)/\sigma_1\right) \, dx}$$

$$= \frac{\sigma_1 \int_{\frac{x_1-\mu_1}{\sigma_1}}^{\infty} \left(1 - H(z)\right) \, dz}{\sigma_1 \int_{-\infty}^{\frac{x_1-\mu_1}{\sigma_1}} H(z) \, dz} =: \frac{\sigma_1 \tilde{B}}{\sigma_1 \tilde{A}}.$$

Similarly,

$$\Omega_Y(x_1) = \frac{\sigma_2 \int_{\frac{x_1-\mu_2}{\sigma_2}}^{\infty} \left(1 - H(z)\right) \, dz}{\sigma_2 \int_{-\infty}^{\frac{x_1-\mu_2}{\sigma_2}} H(z) \, dz} = \frac{\sigma_2 \tilde{B}}{\sigma_2 \tilde{A}},$$

since

$$\frac{x_1 - \mu_1}{\sigma_1} = \frac{x_1 - \mu_2}{\sigma_2} = \frac{\mu_2 - \mu_1}{\sigma_1 - \sigma_2}.$$

Putting $\gamma^* = \Omega_X(x_1) = \Omega_Y(x_1)$, we get for the areas A and B defined in (12)

$$\frac{B}{A} = \frac{E(X - x_1)_+ - E(Y - x_1)_+}{E(X - x_1)_- - E(Y - x_1)_-} = \frac{(\sigma_1 - \sigma_2)\tilde{B}}{(\sigma_1 - \sigma_2)\tilde{A}} = \gamma^*.$$

Hence, $X \leq_{(1+\gamma^*)-SD} Y$ by the remark preceding the theorem.

Now, assume $t \leq x_1$. Then, $t_1 = (t - \mu_1)/\sigma_1 \geq t_2 = (t - \mu_2)/\sigma_2$ since $F(t) = H(t_1) \geq H(t_2) = G(t)$. Then, the same considerations as above yield $\Omega_X(t) \leq \Omega_Y(t)$. The case $t \geq x_1$ follows by analogous reasoning. □

Theorem 2.4 yields simple explicit expressions for the important case of normally distributed random variables that is considered in the following example.

Example 2.2. As an illustration of Theorem 2.4, Figure 2 shows the cdfs and Omega ratios of $X \sim N(1, 1)$ and $Y \sim N\left(3/2, (1/4)^2\right)$. Here, $x_1 = 5/3$, and $\Omega_X(5/3) = 0.185$. Hence, according to Theorem 2.4, $X \leq_{(1+\gamma)-SD} Y$ with $\gamma = 0.185$. Further, $\Omega_X(t) \leq \Omega_Y(t)$ on $(-\infty, x_1]$, and $\Omega_X(t) \geq \Omega_Y(t)$ on $[x_1, \infty)$.

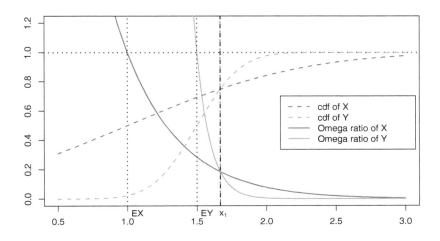

Fig. 2.   Cdfs and Omega ratios of $X \sim N(1,1)$ and $Y \sim N\left(3/2, (1/4)^2\right)$.

We next consider an example where using the Sharpe ratio leads to irrational behavior, as it is not consistent with FSD. This example is quite realistic as it is simply obtained by comparing a normally distributed return with a truncated one, which is obtained by selling a call option at a price of zero. We also investigate in this case how the preference of selling such a call option for a fixed price depends on the benchmark that we use for the Omega ratio. The example shows that the chosen benchmark represents the risk aversion of the decision maker in a similar way as does the parameter γ in the generalized stochastic dominance rule.

Example 2.3. Consider an investment with an excess return over the risk free rate X with $X \sim N(\mu, \sigma)$ with $\mu = 2$ and $\sigma = 1$. Assume that we have the opportunity to sell a call option with strike price $K = 3$ for a price $C \geq 0$. If we give the call option away for free $(C = 0)$ we get as remaining return Y a normal random variable right-censored at 3. No rational decision maker would do this, as $Y \leq_{FSD} X$. If we consider the Sharpe ratio, however, then it turns out that we should prefer Y to X: expected value and variance of Y are given by (see, e.g. [18], p. 763)

$$EY = \Phi(\alpha)(\mu + \sigma\lambda) + (1 - \Phi(\alpha))\,K,$$
$$V(Y) = \sigma^2\Phi(\alpha)\left(\left(1 - \left(\lambda^2 - \lambda\alpha\right)\right) + (\alpha - \lambda)^2\left(1 - \Phi(\alpha)\right)\right)$$

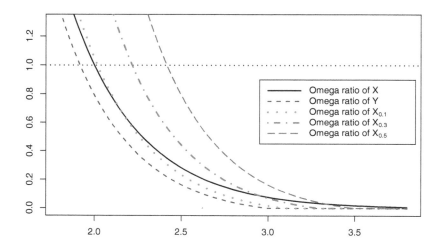

Fig. 3.   Omega ratios of X, Y, and X_C for $C = 0.1, 0.3, 0.51$.

where

$$\alpha = \frac{K - \mu}{\sigma}, \quad \lambda = -\frac{\varphi(\alpha)}{\Phi(\alpha)}.$$

This yields $EY = 1.917, \sigma_Y = 0.867$, and $EY/\sigma_Y = 2.212$, whereas $EX/\sigma_X = 2$.

If we sell the call option for a price $C > 0$ then we get a return $X_C = Y + C$. The distribution function of X_C is given by

$$F_{X_C}(t) = F_X(t - C), \ t < K + C, \quad \text{and} \quad F_{X_C}(t) = 1, \ t \geq K + C,$$

where $F_X(t) = \Phi((t - \mu)/\sigma)$. Hence,

$$\phi_{X_C}(t) = \int_{-\infty}^{t} F_{X_C}(x) \mathrm{d}x = \begin{cases} \phi_X(t - C), & t < K + C, \\ \phi_X(K) + t - (K + C), & t \geq K + C. \end{cases}$$

Figure 3 shows the Omega ratios of X, Y, and X_C for $C = 0.1, 0.3, 0.5$.
We further obtain

$$\Omega_{X_C}(1) \geq \Omega_X(1) \text{ if and only if } C \geq 0.029,$$
$$\Omega_{X_C}(2) \geq \Omega_X(2) \text{ if and only if } C \geq 0.083,$$
$$\Omega_{X_C}(3) \geq \Omega_X(3) \text{ if and only if } C \geq 0.32,$$
$$\Omega_{X_C}(4) \geq \Omega_X(4) \text{ if and only if } C \geq 1.03.$$

Note that $EX_C = EY + C$. Hence, $EX_{0.029} = 1.95, EX_{0.083} = 2, EX_{0.32} = 2.23$, and $EX_{1.03} = 2.94$. Thus we see that for a small benchmark we may accept an investment with a smaller mean than EX, and thus the decision is not too different from what we get when using the Sharpe ratio, as has been empirically observed by [19]. But in contrast to the Sharpe ratio our decisions are always consistent with FSD. We are never willing to give away an option for free. If we use a benchmark above the expected return of the investment, however, then even SSD dominance is not sufficient to choose X_C. Then we need a stronger dominance than SSD, meaning that our decisions are not consistent with SSD anymore.

We could also define a new stochastic dominance rule by requiring all Omega ratios for all benchmarks to be larger, or equivalently all expectiles to be larger. This concept is studied in detail in [15], where it is called *expectile ordering*. There it is shown that this is a strictly weaker condition than FSD and is not equivalent to any of the many known stochastic orders.

3. Omega ratios and combined concave and convex stochastic dominance

In [2], the combined concave and convex stochastic dominance of order $(1 + \gamma_{cv}, 1 + \gamma_{cx})$ is introduced, which generalizes the concept of $(1 + \gamma)$-dominance and is defined as follows.

Definition 3.1. a) For $0 \leq \gamma_{cv}, \gamma_{cx} \leq 1$ let $\mathcal{U}_{\gamma_{cv}, \gamma_{cx}}$ be the class of continuously differentiable functions u such that

$$0 \leq \gamma_{cv} u'(y) \leq u'(x) \leq \frac{1}{\gamma_{cx}} u'(y) \quad \text{for all } x \leq y.$$

If $\gamma_{cx} = 0$ this shall mean that the last inequality can be omitted.
b) For $0 \leq \gamma_{cv}, \gamma_{cx} \leq 1$ we say that Y dominates X by $(1 + \gamma_{cv}, 1 + \gamma_{cx})$-SD, denoted

$$X \leq_{(1+\gamma_{cv}, 1+\gamma_{cx})-SD} Y,$$

if $Eu(X) \leq Eu(Y)$ for all functions $u \in \mathcal{U}_{\gamma_{cv}, \gamma_{cx}}$.

Note that $X \leq_{(1+\gamma_{cv}, 1+\gamma_{cx})-SD} Y$ implies $X \leq_{(1+\tilde{\gamma}_{cv}, 1+\tilde{\gamma}_{cx})-SD} Y$, where $\gamma_{cv} \leq \tilde{\gamma}_{cv} \leq 1, \gamma_{cx} \leq \tilde{\gamma}_{cx} \leq 1$. The case $\gamma_{cv} = \gamma, \gamma_{cx} = 0$ is concave $(1 + \gamma)$-SD from Definition 2.2 and therefore we get a generalization of that concept. In the following, we consider two other interesting special cases:

- The case $\gamma_{cv} = 0, \gamma_{cx} = \gamma$ is convex $(1 + \gamma)$-SD, corresponding to preference relations falling between FSD and convex (risk-seeking) SSD (for the latter, see, e.g. [20], sec 3.11).
- The case $\gamma_{cv} = \gamma_{cx} = \gamma = \varepsilon/(1-\varepsilon)$ is ε-almost first degree stochastic dominance (ε-AFSD, [3]) with $\varepsilon = \gamma/(1+\gamma)$.

Theorem 4.3 in [2] provides an integral condition for $(1+\gamma_{cv}, 1+\gamma_{cx})$-SD. In particular, for $\gamma_{cv} = 0$, $X \leq_{(1,1+\gamma_{cx})-SD} Y$ if and only if

$$\int_t^\infty (F_Y(z) - F_X(z))_+ \, \mathrm{d}z \leq \gamma_{cx} \int_t^\infty (F_X(z) - F_Y(z))_+ \, \mathrm{d}z \ \forall t \in \mathbb{R}, \ (13)$$

and for $\gamma_{cv} = \gamma_{cx} = \gamma$, $X \leq_{(1+\gamma,1+\gamma)-SD} Y$ if and only if

$$\int_{-\infty}^\infty (F_Y(z) - F_X(z))_+ \, \mathrm{d}z \leq \gamma \int_{-\infty}^\infty (F_X(z) - F_Y(z))_+ \, \mathrm{d}z. \qquad (14)$$

For convex $(1 + \gamma)$-SD, we have the following result.

Theorem 3.1. *If $X \leq_{(1,1+\gamma_{cx})-SD} Y$ and $\Omega_X(t) \leq 1/\gamma_{cx}$ then $\Omega_X(t) \leq \Omega_Y(t)$.*

Proof. First, note that $X \geq_{(1,1+\gamma_{cx})-SD} c$ if and only if $\Omega_X(c) \geq 1/\gamma_{cx}$ (see [2]). Now, assume $\Omega_X(t) = 1/\delta_{cx} \leq 1/\gamma_{cx}$. Then, $X \geq_{(1,1+\delta_{cx})-SD} t$. Since $\delta_{cx} \geq \gamma_{cx}$, we obtain

$$Y \geq_{(1,1+\delta_{cx})-SD} X \geq_{(1,1+\delta_{cx})-SD} t.$$

By transitivity, $Y \geq_{(1,1+\delta_{cx})-SD} t$, which in turn implies $\Omega_Y(t) \geq 1/\delta_{cx}$, i.e. $\Omega_Y(t) \geq \Omega_X(t)$. $\qquad \square$

If the cdf F of X single-crosses the cdf G of Y from above, condition (13) entails that X dominates Y via convex $(1 + \gamma_{cx})$-SD if and only if $B/A \geq 1/\gamma_{cx}$, where A and B are defined in (12). For this, it is necessary that $B - A = EX - EY \geq 0$. For location-scale families, we get the following result, which can be proven similar as Theorem 2.4.

Theorem 3.2. *Let X and Y be from the same location-scale family as given in (10) with $\mu_1 \geq \mu_2$ and $\sigma_1 \geq \sigma_2$. Define $\gamma^* = 1/\Omega_X(x_1)$, where x_1 is the single crossing point of the cdfs of X and Y given in (11). Then, $X \geq_{(1,1+\gamma^*)-SD} Y$. Furthermore, $\Omega_X(t) \geq \Omega_Y(t)$ if and only if $t \geq x_1$.*

The subsequent example considers distribution functions having two crossing points.

Example 3.1. In Example 2.1, the cdfs F and G of X and Y have two crossing points x_1 and x_2 with $F(x) \geq G(x)$ for $x \leq x_1$ and $x \geq x_2$ and

$F(x) \leq G(x)$ for $x_1 \leq x \leq x_2$. Writing again

$$A_i = \int_{x_{i-1}}^{x_i} (F(x) - G(x)) \, dx, \quad i = 1, 2, 3,$$

it is easy to see that $X \leq_{(1, 1+\gamma_{cx})-SD} Y$ if and only if

$$\gamma \geq \max \left\{ \frac{-A_2}{A_3}, \frac{-A_2}{A_1 + A_3} \right\} = \frac{-A_2}{A_3} = \gamma_{cx}^{\min}.$$

In Example 2.1, we get $\gamma_{cx}^{\min} = 12.82$. Now, $\Omega_X(t) \leq 1/\gamma_{cx}^{\min} = 0.078$ if $t \geq t_1 = 2.99$. Therefore, Theorem 3.1 yields $\Omega_X(t) \leq \Omega_Y(t)$ for $t \geq t_1$.

Finally, we consider almost first degree stochastic dominance. If F single-crosses G from above, Equation (14) shows that $X \leq_{(1+\gamma, 1+\gamma)-SD} Y$ if and only if $\gamma A \geq B$, which is the same condition as for concave $(1+\gamma)$-SD. In particular, $X \leq_{(1+\gamma, 1+\gamma)-SD} c$ if $\Omega_X(c) \leq \gamma$. Using the same arguments as in the proof of Theorem 2.3 provides the following strengthening of Theorem 2.3.

Theorem 3.3. *If $X \leq_{(1+\gamma, 1+\gamma)-SD} Y$ and $\Omega_Y(t) \geq \gamma$ then $\Omega_X(t) \leq \Omega_Y(t)$.*

Example 3.2. Again, we consider the situation of Example 2.1 with two crossing points. With a view to Equation (14), $X \leq_{(1+\gamma, 1+\gamma)-SD} Y$ if and only if

$$\gamma \geq \frac{-A_2}{A_1 + A_3} = \tilde{\gamma}_{\min}.$$

For the distributions used in Example 2.1, $\tilde{\gamma}_{\min} = 0.356$, and $\Omega_Y(t) \geq \tilde{\gamma}_{\min}$ if $t \leq \tilde{t}_0 = 1.431$. Therefore, Theorem 3.3 yields $\Omega_X(t) \leq \Omega_Y(t)$ for $t \leq \tilde{t}_0$. Thus we get a slightly better result in comparison to Example 2.1 as we use a weaker stochastic dominance rule here.

References

1. C. Keating and W. F. Shadwick, A universal performance measure, *J. Perform. Measurement* **6**(3), 59–84 (2002).
2. A. Müller, M. Scarsini, I. Tsetlin and R. L. Winkler, Between first and second-order stochastic dominance, *Management Science* **63**(9), 2933–2947 (2017).
3. M. Leshno and H. Levy, Preferred by "all" and preferred by "most" decision makers: Almost stochastic dominance, *Management Science* **48**(8), 1074–1085 (2002).
4. W. F. Sharpe, Mutual fund performance, *The Journal of Business* **39**, 119–138 (1966).

5. J.-L. Prigent, *Portfolio Optimization and Performance Analysis* (CRC Press, 2007).
6. W. M. Fong, Stochastic dominance and the omega ratio, *Finance Research Letters* **17**, 7–9 (2016).
7. S. Balder and N. Schweizer, Risk aversion vs. the omega ratio: Consistency results, *Finance Research Letters* **21**, 78–84 (2017).
8. H. Mausser, D. Saunders and L. Seco, Optimizing omega, *Risk*, 88–92 (2006).
9. C. Bernard, S. Vanduffel and J. Ye, Optimal strategies under omega ratio, Working paper (2018). Available at SSRN: https://ssrn.com/abstract=2947057 or http://dx.doi.org/10.2139/ssrn.2947057.
10. M. R. Metel, T. A. Pirvu and J. Wong, Risk management under omega measure, *Risks* **5**(2), 27 (2017). Available at https://doi.org/10.3390/risks5020027.
11. F. Bellini, B. Klar, A. Müller and E. R. Gianin, Generalized quantiles as risk measures, *Insurance: Mathematics and Economics* **54**, 41–48 (2014).
12. J. F. Ziegel, Coherence and elicitability, *Mathematical Finance* **26**, 901–918 (2016).
13. W. Ogryczak and A. Ruszczyński, From stochastic dominance to mean-risk models: Semideviations as risk measures, *European Journal of Operational Research* **116**, 33–50 (1999).
14. W. K. Newey and J. L. Powell, Asymmetric least squares estimation and testing, *Econometrica* **55**, 819–847 (1987).
15. F. Bellini, B. Klar and A. Müller, Expectiles, omega ratios and stochastic ordering, *Methodology and Computing in Applied Probability* , p. in print (2017).
16. A. Müller and D. Stoyan, Comparison methods for stochastic models and risks, *Wiley: New York* (2002).
17. M. Shaked and G. Shanthikumar, *Stochastic orders* (Springer, 2007).
18. W. H. Greene, *Econometric Analysis*, 5 edn. (Prentice Hall, 2003).
19. M. Eling and F. Schuhmacher, Does the choice of performance measure influence the evaluation of hedge funds?, *Journal of Banking & Finance* **31**, 2632–2647 (2007).
20. H. Levy, *Stochastic dominance: Investment decision making under uncertainty* (Springer, 2016).

Chapter 15

Chance-Risk Classification of Pension Products: Scientific Concepts and Challenges

Ralf Korn

Dept. Mathematics, Univ. Kaiserslautern,
Kaiserslautern, 67663, Germany
and
Dept. Financial Mathematics, Fraunhofer ITWM,
Kaiserslautern, 67663, Germany
korn@mathematik.uni-kl.de

Andreas Wagner

Dept. Mathematics Group, Fraunhofer ITWM,
Kaiserslautern, 67663, Germany
andreas.wagner@itwm.fraunhofer.de

We survey the underlying scientific concepts and aspects of the implementation of the classification of state-subsidized private German pension products into five different chance-risk classes. The topics range from the choice and calibration of the capital market model via simulation issues of various pension products to specific research topics such as the behavior of chance-risk curves or new valuation algorithms for cliquet-type options.

Keywords: chance-risk classification, pension products, Monte Carlo simulation.

1. Introduction

The introduction of bonus schemes (such as the *Riester Rente*) or schemes that lead to tax advantages (such as the *Basis Rente*) in Germany had the clear intention to give the public an incentive to enter into private pension contracts as a necessary add-on to their state pension. As understanding general pension products and judging their risk and return potential usually requires deep actuarial knowledge, the German Ministry of Finance introduced a new standardized information document (*Produktinformationsblatt*)[1] for those products to help the customer in comparing the

---

[1]Similar to the KID in the European PRIIPS regulation.

products and finding a suitable choice. Besides some product and concept descriptions, the leaflet has to contain two key figures

- a so-called *chance-risk class* ranging from 1 to 5 expressing the character of the chances and risks associated with the product,
- the *reduction in yield* expressing that part of the potential yield of the product that is lost due to costs charged by the issuing company (such as administration costs, costs of sales and management, or costs of capital or of investment).

It is required that the chance-risk classification has to be based on stochastic simulations of the evolution of the contract value of a product up to the end of the accumulation period. A chance-risk class of 1 is characterized by a low risk and a low return potential of the product, i.e. the customer should have a precise idea about the available money at the end of the accumulation period. In addition, the contract value has to increase over time, and there is a money-back-guarantee at the end of the accumulation period. A product having been assigned the chance-risk class 5 shows a high return potential, but also admits a high risk. Its capital at the end of the accumulation period is not required to stay above a positive bound. The classes 2, 3, 4 fill the space between 1 and 5 in increasing order of return potential and riskiness. Of those, only chance-risk class 2 in addition contains a money-back-guarantee. More details will be found in the sections below.

We will in the following only consider aspects of the chance-risk classification and do not comment on the concept and the computation of the reduction in yield.[2]

As the chance-risk classification has to be done by an independent organization, the Fraunhofer Institute for Industrial Mathematics ITWM in Kaiserslautern was chosen as the result of a public competition. A separate legal entity was formed, the *Produktinformationsstelle Altersvorsorge gGmbH* which is responsible for the classification of the products. However, all mathematical concepts underlying the whole classification process have been developed by the Financial Mathematics Department of Fraunhofer ITWM. These include suggestions for

- the form of the capital market model underlying the simulation of the contract values at the end of the accumulation period,

---

[2]To learn more about the concept and the actual computation of the reduction in yield see www.produktinformationsstelle.de/effektivkosten.html.

- the choice of the risk measure and the chance measure that form the basis for the chance-risk-classification of the pension products,
- the determination of the five different chance-risk classes,
- the simulation algorithms to obtain the contract value at the end of the accumulation period for the different pension products,
- the algorithms for calculating the reduction in yield for the different pension product types,

where the Ministry of Finance of Germany had the final say about accepting these suggestions.

We will in the following present the main conceptual ideas behind this project in general and will in particular concentrate on issues of financial mathematics and simulation. Let us also state in this introductory section that all the classifications have to be done for four different times until the end of the accumulation phase T of the product in years with

$$T \in \{12, 20, 30, 40\}. \tag{1}$$

This does not only result in an enormous simulation effort for just one product, but also leads to the possibility that one product can have four different chance-risk classes for the four different maturities. However, given that the product parameters (in particular with regard to its assigned costs) do not change dramatically with the maturities, the scenario of having different classifications for different maturities is not very likely. The extreme case of four different classes is extremely unlikely.

Of course, it would be desirable to be able to classify products of exactly that form that is tailored to the customer's personal needs. However, the resulting variety of products and of needed simulation and classification work cannot be delivered, at least not without exploding classification costs. As a compromise, the classification is only done for a prototypical customer who is assumed to pay a monthly contribution (before costs) of 100 Euros (where state bonuses are assumed to be included when they are granted) until the last month of the accumulation products, i.e. we assume $12 \cdot T$ payments. Further, we perform 10000 simulations of the wealth at the end of the accumulation period with a monthly time discretization as the basis for determining the chance and the risk measure.

We will in the following present

- the main types of private pension products offered in Germany,
- the concepts underlying the classification,

- the capital market model underlying the simulation together with some product specific issues,
- some scientific challenges that are a consequence of experiences made in the first years of the classification.

2. Typical private pension products offered in Germany

The variety of offered private pension products greatly influences the classification effort, both from a conceptional point of view and from the purely technical issue of coding the algorithms. We therefore give a short and incomplete survey of the main types of private pension products offered at the German market that are eligible for state bonuses or tax advantages.

In former times, the market for private pension products in Germany was dominated by traditional life insurance contracts with surplus participation offering a high degree of safety and by unit-linked fund investments offering a high return potential, but leaving the investment risk with the policy holder. During recent years and particularly motivated by the current low interest rate phase, the diversity of state subsidized private pension products has enormously increased. Besides the above mentioned two standard types, there is nowadays a wide range of hybrid products that combine fund investment with guarantee components, new forms of the participating life insurance, savings plans, or index participations, just to name the main families. Most of these products also have variants containing a money-back guarantee, i.e. their contract value $V(T)$ at the end of the accumulation period exceeds the sum of contributions paid in by the customer and potential bonuses assigned by the state. This property is a strict requirement for the products to fall in the range of the so-called *Riester-Rente*, the main German bonus scheme for private pension products. All German employees and their spouse are eligible for subsidy under the *Riester-Rente* scheme.

To give the reader a survey on the main characteristics of all those product classes, we will roughly describe them below. While in the actual simulation we are working on the basis of monthly premium payments by the policy holder, it will here be beneficial for simplicity of the presentation that we assume annual contributions by the policy holder only in this work.

In the following, $B(t)$ denotes the annual premium that the policy holder contributes at the beginning of year t until the end of the accumulation period which can — again for simplicity — be identified with the beginning of the retirement phase of the policy holder. We make the usual convention that the contract starts at $t = 0$ with the first contribution. We also introduce $V(t)$ to be the policy value at time t, $N(t)$ the net savings premium after deduction of initial costs $C(t)$ from the contribution $B(t)$, i.e.

$$N(t) = B(t) - C(t) .$$

Further costs that are annually deducted from the contract value are denoted by $C_a(t)$. Note that the costs can also vary in their functional form over time. A typical feature causing this is the so-called *Zillmerung* which assigns the main parts of the compensation for the agent selling the product to the first five years of the contract.

Traditional life insurance with surplus participation. We start with the classical pension product where each initial contribution $B(t)$ is decomposed into costs $C(t)$ and the net savings $N(t)$. The complete contract value is then invested in the actuarial reserve fund (ARF) of the insurer which is a special fund made up of various asset classes. At the end of the year, the contract value is assigned a surplus participation $i(t)$ based on the performance of the ARF (and of saved costs, mortality gains and further reserves gained from earlier periods and/or the (assigned) differences between market and book value of the assets in the ARF). This surplus participation has to exceed the promised guarantee rate at the start of the contract $i_G(0)$ which currently is $0,9\%$ in Germany, i.e. $i(t) \geq i_G(0)$. The contract value thus evolves according to

$$V(t) = (V(t-1) - C_a(t))(1 + i(t)) + N(t), \qquad (2)$$

where bonuses $R(t)$ from the state may also be granted. As they depend on both the actual contribution $B(t)$ and the personal situation of the policy holder (married, children, income, ...), we omit them here for simplicity (although this can be quite a rough simplification, it is in line with the requirements for the simulation given by the German Ministry of Finance).

There also exist variants where the guarantee rate $i_G(0)$ is reduced, sometimes even to zero. This variant is often called *neo classic* or *capital efficient classic*. Further, there are variants where a part of the surplus is invested into a fund.

However, the main challenge in the current interest rate environment — independent of the product type — is the money-back guarantee

$$V(T) \geq \sum_{t=0}^{T-1} B(t). \qquad (3)$$

Index participations. Index participations allow the policy holder to benefit from a positive evolution of a stock index although all the (net savings) contributions of the policy holder are invested into the ARF. However, that part of the annual surplus that is not needed to ensure the money-back guarantee can be used to buy an option on the annual performance of an index. To obtain a significant chance for additional return, typically an option with a high leverage is used. An example which is popular is a so-called *locally capped and globally floored cliquet-option* with a payoff at time $t + 1$ of

$$Z(t+1; C) = \tilde{V}(t) \left(\sum_{i=1}^{12} \min \left(C, \frac{S\left(t + \frac{i}{12}\right) - S\left(t + \frac{i-1}{12}\right)}{S\left(t + \frac{i-1}{12}\right)} \right) \right)^{+}. \quad (4)$$

Here, C is called the *index cap* and is determined by the money available for buying the option. $\tilde{V}(t)$ denotes the contract value at time t after all costs are deduced, $S(t)$ the value of the index at time t. At time $t + 1$ the payment $Z(t + 1)$ is added to the contract value. Variants using other option types exist at the market.

The particular feature of option type payoffs as in Equation (4) is that on the one hand they provide the possibility of high returns on the contract value by leveraging the contract value (there have been annual returns realized in practice of about 20%) while on the other hand the downside risk is limited by the option price paid. Compare this to either a full (!) investment of the contract value in the fund underlying the index which can lead to a higher return but does not provide any guarantee, or to the investment of the surplus in the index which can only generate a high return on the surplus and not (!) on the whole contract value. Of course, an option payment of zero does also appear quite often.

Unit-linked life insurance. Here, the net savings contribution of the policy holder is invested into a fund. The evolution of the contract value is given by

$$V(t) = (V(t-1) - C_a(t))(1 + r_F(t)) + N(t) \quad (5)$$

with

$$1 + r_F(t) = \frac{F(t) - F(t-1)}{F(t-1)} \quad (6)$$

where $F(t)$ denotes the value of the fund at time t. Typically, the investment risk stays with the customer. To highlight this feature, we have used a notation of the fund return that differs from $i(t)$ which has been the return in the traditional life insurance product with surplus participation.

There are also special variants of unit-linked products including guarantees. They are then summarized under the name *hybrid products*.

Hybrid products. The term hybrid product is assigned to those products where money is allocated to both a guarantee component and to a pure investment component. Hybrid products mainly differ in the way how the given guarantee (such as the money-back-guarantee or the guarantee of a fixed percentage of all contributions) is generated. Typically, a life insurer uses the ARF as the guarantee component. A fund provider instead has to rely on the capital market and either uses a bond strategy, put options, or a sophisticated portfolio strategy such as a *CPPI-strategy* (see e.g. [2], [6]). Hybrid products are also distinguished according to the nature of their investment strategy. There are so-called *static hybrids* where the allocation of the net savings contribution to the guarantee and to the investment part of the product stays constant over time. In *dynamic hybrids* this strategy is state and time dependent. According to the funds used there exist two- and three-fund hybrids. In the two-fund setting there typically exist a strict guarantee part such as the ARF and a second fund that has a lower guarantee (a usual ingredient is a fund that guarantees 80% of its initial value and which is typically hold for one month or one year). The three-fund version in addition contains the possibility to invest in a fund that does not promise any kind of guarantee.

Savings plans. A savings plan is typically offered by banks. Here, the full contributions of the customer are added to the contract account. At the end of the year a fixed, a variable, or a combined interest rate $i(t)$ is assigned to the contract value. This is often a market rate such as the rate for 10 year bonds minus a predefined deduction. Thus, costs are introduced in an indirect way. The evolution of the contract is thus given by

$$V(t) = V(t-1)(1 + i(t)) + N(t).$$ (7)

Due to a possible non-negativity condition or to a bonus scheme, the determination of the interest rate $i(t)$ can also contain non-linearities.

More products. There are many more different products which we do not describe here as they do not constitute a significant part of the German pension market. Of course, they still have to be simulated and classified. As they often also have features such as e.g. a so-called *intelligent volatility control*, a complicated fund investment strategy, separate treatment of state bonuses and of contributions made by the policy holder, they often cause a large effort with respect to the actual implementation of the simulation procedure.

3. Aspects of chance-risk classification concepts

There are well-known relations between chance and risk as e.g. expressed in a mean-variance or a mean-standard-deviation diagram for the return of an asset. The use of those diagrams is a natural basis for setting up chance-risk classes (CRC). However, we first have to decide about the form of the measures that stand for chance/return and for risk.

As the prototypical customer pays the fixed contribution of 100 Euro every months, the use of the (continuous) yield Y that is determined from the mean of the 10000 simulated contract values at the end of the accumulation period is the choice for the chance measure. We thus have to solve

$$100 \, (1 + Y/12) \, \frac{(1 + Y/12)^{12T} - 1}{Y/12} = \frac{1}{10000} \sum_{i=1}^{10000} V^{(i)}(12T) \qquad (8)$$

where $V^{(i)}(12T)$ denotes the final contract value in the i th simulation run. Note that we take the yield corresponding to the average of the simulated realizations of the accumulated final contract value and not (!) the average yield. The reason for this is that we are thus in line with the definition of the yield of a zero bond and with the expected value of a stock.

As a surprisingly high return constitutes no risk at all for a pensioner, we solely concentrate of the downside risk. A number which is based on the philosophy of the expected short fall measure is obtained using the 2000 worst simulated final contract wealth and then calculate the corresponding yield as in Equation (8) where of course, we have to divide by 2000 only. We will call this solution X.

Having decided on the chance and on the risk measures, our next task is to determine the five different chance-risk classes. For this we define reference portfolios which mirror the intended behavior of the class. For example, the reference portfolio attached to CRC 1 solely consists of AAA-bonds which mature at the end of the accumulation period T. The portfolio attached to CRC 5 invests in our prototypical fund with a volatility of 20%. The reference pairs of the chance measure and risk measure points are then put into a diagram that displays the chance measure on the y-axis and the (negative (!) of the) risk measure on the x-axis. This way of display ensures that moving to the top (in terms of a higher chance) and moving to the left (in terms of a lower risk) is desirable. Different product types and their chance-risk pairs are plotted in Figure 1.

Chance-risk classification for different pension product types

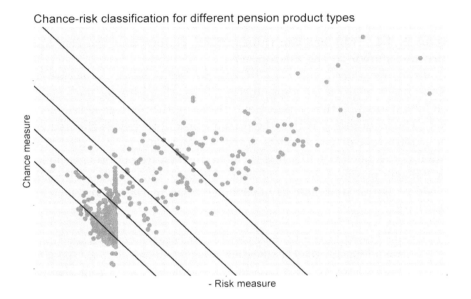

Fig. 1. Chance and risk pairs for classified products (12T = 30).

To separate the different CRC we draw lines with a slope of −1 lying in the middle between the points that represent the reference portfolios. The justification for the slope of −1 of the separating lines lies in the relation between the reference portfolios and the actually offered products. For the reference portfolios, the chance and the risk measure are calculated based on the simulated wealth at the end of the accumulation period without considering any costs. Due to the similar, mainly linear form of both the chance and the risk measure, the actual costs reduce them both in a similar, typically parallel way for real-life pension products. Of course, this parallelism is slightly disturbed when the money-back guarantee gets binding.

There is a clear criticism for this way of constructing the areas for the chance-risk classification. Leaving aside the influence of the money-back guarantee, it seems that a product can stay in the same chance-risk class when the costs are arbitrarily increased. However, increasing costs will lead to an increase in the reduction in yield, the second quantity besides the chance-risk class that is shown to the customer. And of course, a high reduction in yield will make a product unattractive to the customer. So, the reduction in yield helps to force the product provider to offer products with as few costs as possible.

Remark 3.1. Why are the values of the chance and the risk measure not shown to the customer?

As already mentioned, only the CRC of a product is shown to the customer as the result of the simulation process. Thus, the customer does not get the full information that is generated. However, there are good reasons for that. The main reason is that the primary task of the whole simulation of the performance of the products in the accumulation phase is the classification in the different CRC. It is therefore the relative performance among the different products that is sufficient. Although the real-life performance should be mirrored as close as possible, an exact image cannot be created due to e.g.

- differences in the time discretization between real-life and model simulation (in the classification process, all calculations and simulations have to based on a monthly scale why in real-life there are many advanced products that use weekly or daily reallocation of the portfolios),
- only approximate knowledge of the reallocation algorithm (as the exact form of the allocation algorithm and in particular strategic decision plans of the product providers are often proprietary knowledge, we receive only simplified forms of both),
- the worst-case principle (i.e. using upper bounds) that has to be applied with regard to variable costs and that does not allow to consider the possibility of kick backs.

All these reasons might lead to an under performance of the products in the simulation in absolute terms. In relative terms between the different products, however, this is mainly not the case.

On the other hand, the way of calculation of the prices of options that are ingredients of various products (such as e.g. index participations) assumes a liquid market. In real-life, those prices can be significantly higher due to the fact that full liquidity and market efficiency for such option types is not given. This might lead to significantly higher market prices than model prices. Thus, those products might perform worse in the real markets than in the simulations.

It has therefore been decided that the CRC and the reduction in yield are the only informations passed on to the customer that are generated on the basis of the stochastic market model.

4. Capital market model and simulation of important product ingredients

The choice of the capital market model is crucial for both the simulation effort and also for the realism of the classification. As for the majority of existing pension contracts bonds are the most important investment asset and as the duration of the contract is long, we decided to choose a two-factor Hull-White model stated in the so-called $G2 - ++$ formulation (see [3]). The model has the advantage of being a well-tested and applied model. Also, as a two factor model, it avoids the problem of perfect correlation between short- and long-term interest rates. Further, as it admits a normally distributed short-rate behavior, it has the potential to model negative interest rates. And finally, it allows for a perfect initial calibration to the bond market.

The model is given by the equations

$$dx\left(t\right) = -ax\left(t\right)dt + \sigma dW_1\left(t\right), \tag{9}$$
$$dy\left(t\right) = -bx\left(t\right)dt + \eta\left(\rho dW_1\left(t\right) + \sqrt{1-\rho^2}dW_2\left(t\right)\right), \tag{10}$$
$$r^*\left(t\right) = x\left(t\right) + y\left(t\right) + \zeta\left(t\right) \tag{11}$$

describing the dynamics of the short rate $r(t)^*$ under a risk-neutral measure Q. $W_i(t)$ are independent one-dimensional Brownian motions. The function

$$\zeta\left(t\right) = f^M\left(0,t\right) + \frac{\sigma^2}{2a^2}\left(1 - e^{-at}\right)^2 +$$
$$\frac{\eta^2}{2b^2}\left(1 - e^{-bt}\right)^2 + \rho\frac{\sigma\eta}{ab}\left(1 - e^{-at}\right)\left(1 - e^{-bt}\right) \tag{12}$$

contains the model parameters that are calibrated to market prices of swaptions, while the initial market forward rate curve $f^M(0,t)$ is obtained from the Nelson-Siegel-Svensson curve of the Deutsche Bundesbank.

As for the classification purposes we have to simulate all relevant processes under a real-world measure P, we have to add a risk premium to obtain the final short rate process

$$r(t) := r^*(t) + \lambda_r(t).$$ (13)

To determine it, we use the annual predictions by the OECD on the expected future development of the interest rate market. We here do not go into further technical details.

On the stock side, we use a generalized Black-Scholes model given by

$$S(t) = s_0 \exp\left(\int_0^t r(s)\,ds + \left(\lambda_S - 0.5\,\sigma_S^2\right)t + \sigma_S W(t)\right)$$ (14)

for modeling the dynamics of a reference stock index. Here, the one-dimensional Brownian motion $W(t)$ can also be correlated to $W_i(t)$.

Based on an analysis of the EuroStoxx 50, we have chosen the parameters $\lambda = 0.04$ and $\sigma = 0.2$ to give $S(t)$ comparable dynamics. If a product is based on another index or stock, then we assume that it has the dynamics as our basic index $S(t)$, but with individual σ and a risk premium of λ determined by

$$\lambda = \lambda_S \frac{\sigma}{\sigma_S}.$$ (15)

Remark 4.1. *Why not using a more general stock price model?*

Of course, one can think about introducing jumps or even Lévy-type models for the evolution of the stock index. However, the choice of the market model had to be a compromise between generality, stability of calibration and the market standards. Note that for some products, we need option prices, continuous-time approximations for discrete formulas and other features where more complicated models do not offer stable or unique solutions (think about e.g. option prices in incomplete markets!). Due to the long running contracts and the dominance of bond investments in life insurance, our preference was to consider (at least) a two-factor model for the short rate and not to introduce a more complicated stock price model.

Having specified the basic processes for our capital market, we now have to come up with the simulation of some important components that are crucial for many products. The most prominent of those components is the ARF of an insurance company and — as a consequence of its annual performance — the surplus declaration mechanism.

How to simulate the surplus declaration in a participating life insurance contract? Our modeling approach is based on the following ideas: We assume an insurer to buy bonds of duration d at par every year. Thus, the main risk is the re-investment risk when those bonds mature. Otherwise, we know their annual coupons precisely in advance. Let, therefore be $k_d(t-i)$ be the coupon rate of a d-year bond bought at time $t-i$. It will pay out those coupons at years $t-i+1, ..., t-i+d$. Assuming a stationary state of the insurance company in the sense that the number of bonds hold are constant over the years, we arrive at a mean annual bond return of

$$R_{B,d}(t) = \frac{1}{d} \sum_{i=1}^{d} k_d(t-i).$$

Further, we assume a constant proportion investment strategy over time, i.e. the insurer always rebalances the holdings at time t such that the fraction invested in stocks (or a comparable fund) equals $\psi \in [0,1]$.

To model the smoothing algorithm for the surplus rates over time applied by a life insurance company, we assume that the geometric average over the returns of the last three years (including the current one) is the basis for the surplus declaration. It is given by

$$R(t) = \sqrt[3]{\prod_{i=0}^{2} \left(\psi \frac{F(t-i)}{F(t-i-1)} + (1-\psi)(R_{B,d}(t-i)+1) \right)} - 1.$$

Based on this, we assign the following surplus rate to the actuarial reserve fund

$$g(t+1) = i_G(0) + (0.9 * (R(t) - K) - i_G(0))^+,$$

where $i_G(0)$ is the guarantee rate which has been valid when entering the contract. Note that the second term on the right hand side contains the minimal part (by law 90%) of the returns $R(t)$ after capital costs K that the insurer has to assign to the surplus rate, in case that this part is positive.

Our algorithm is a suggestion to capture the freedom of the insurer to decide about direct assignments of gains to the individual contracts or to a collective bonus account without (!) directly introducing this feature. Introducing all kinds of accounts and legal aspects goes beyond the scope of this paper. However, for a detailed treatment of the use of bonus accounts, reserve accounts and liabilities, we refer to [5].

How to generate guarantee mechanisms? Given the above relation for the surplus rate, we can at least assume a return of $i_G(0)$ each year. It is thus the classical tool for a life insurer to generate guarantees, simply by contract agreement, not so much by the use of the capital market. Therefore, the actuarial reserve fund is also used by insurers in hybrid products. However, depending on the construction of the hybrid product, the hybrid product will attain the full surplus or only a part of the surplus that the holder of a classical product with participation receives.

If however the actuarial reserve fund can not be used (for e.g. contractual reasons) or if the provider of a pension product simply does not have an actuarial reserve fund (think of a bank or an investment company) then CPPI-type strategies using bonds or option based strategies are popular alternatives.

How are de-risking strategies implemented? Reducing the investment risk with approaching end of the accumulation phase is a typical strategy to avoid big losses when there is not a long time remaining to correct them. While there are small differences in the ways this is implemented in various products offered at the market, the main form consists of a linear reduction of stock-type parts down to zero close to the end of the accumulation phase.

5. Scientific challenges and outlook

Of course, the whole project of chance-risk classification of publicly available pension products is not a playground for scientific experiments. On one hand, well established models and methods should be used while on the other hand, it needs a very efficient implementation of the simulation process of a wide range of diverse products. Thus, there is always room for improvement, in particular as also new products will enter the scene.

The simulation of some products needs a particularly high computational effort. Given that we have to simulate 10000 paths of the evolution of the contract value over 40 years, efficiency can be greatly improved if regularly appearing tasks can be accelerated.

Improved Monte Carlo algorithms for pricing options in an index participation. A prototypical example of both high computational effort per simulation path and of accelerating regularly appearing tasks is the calculation of the implied monthly cap on the index return in index participation products. Here, we refer the reader to Korn, Temocin and Wenzel

[8] where a completely new control variate approach for pricing cliquet-style options is developed. It rests on the use of a control variate that has been derived using the central limit theorem. More precisely, by identifying the twelve capped monthly returns

$$R^c(i) = \min \left\{ \frac{S(t+i/12) - S(t+(i-1)/12)}{S(t+(i-1)/12)}, c \right\}, \; i = 1, 2, ..., 12,$$

in the cliquet option payment as independent and identically distributed random variables in the Black-Scholes setting, we use the approximation

$$\left(\sum_{i=1}^{12} R_i \right)^+ \approx X^+$$

with $X \sim N(12E(R_i), 12Var(R_i))$. This is motivated by the central limit theorem (although 12 might appear to be quite small for the use of an asymptotic result). While the approximate option price $E(exp(-r)X^+)$ (under the risk-neutral measure) can be obtained as an explicit analytical formula and is surprisingly close to the exact option price, it is not close enough to replace the option price fully as an approximation. However, using this approximate price as a control variate delivers a great variance reduction in the Monte Carlo simulation.

The resulting control variate method can numerically outperform the standard semi-closed formula solution as given by Bernard and Li [1]. Even more, it can be extended to more general model frameworks such as the Heston model and also to other types of options used in index participations such as the asymmetric participation option (see again [8]). The latter is not dealt with by Bernard and Li [1].

The projection of general assets to the two basic asset classes. Many investment positions hold by life insurance companies are no pure bond or stock products. Examples are defaultable bonds, investment in buildings, wind parks, just to name a few. They typically contain aspects of a bond-type and also of a stock-type investment. Also, derivatives such as stock options have a mixed character. The projection of such assets in a suitable way to the two basic asset classes is an important issue for the realistic simulation (and performance) of the actuarial reserve fund. A corresponding decomposition algorithm that assigns an investment prod-uct must be simple and also convincing from a conceptual point of view. Therefore, the simulation model for official classifications has recently been extended to allow for a more complex structure of the ARF.

Effects in the evolution of the yield curve. The so-called yield curve for zero bonds with maturity x is defined as the equivalent constant interest rate $y(x)$ that one receives when buying a zero bond now for the price of $P(0, x)$ and holding it until maturity x. The most popular forms of the function $y(x)$ are a *normal yield-curve* if it is increasing and concave, an **inverse yield curve** if it is decreasing and convex, and a *humped yield curve* if it contains exactly one interior maximum. Of course, further forms of yield curves are possible, and some also have names.

Simple short rate models such as the one-factor Vasicek model have a tendency to produce a higher fraction of inverse term structures with ongoing time. The reason for this is based on the following two facts (see e.g. [4]):

- For large values of x in the Vasicek model we have that $y(x)$ converges to a fixed value $\bar{y}$.
- The stationary distribution of the short rate $r(t)$ has a median that is bigger than $\bar{y}$.

Thus, due to the fact that the current value of the short rate determines the form of the yield curve, we will asymptotically observe more than 50% of inverse or humped yield curves in the Vasicek model. This follows from the fact that for initial short rate values above y the yield curve in the Vasicek model can only be inverse or humped (see again Chapter 8 in [4]).

The two-factor Hull-White variant that we are using has a similar behavior, but the relations are more subtle and in particular also depend very much on the initial yield curve that we obtain from calibrating the model to the yield curve of the Deutsche Bundesbank. Obtaining a simple relation between the starting yield curve and the distribution of future forms of the yield curve at some fixed time point is therefore an obvious research challenge.

The form of chance-risk curves. An effect that is at first sight surprising is the dependence of the form of the chance-risk curve on its ingredients. Knowing the typical form of a classical mean-standard deviation diagram, we would also expect a typical form for the chance-risk curve as in Figure 2. We have plotted the chance measure on the y-axis and have plotted the risk measure on the x-axis, but in inverted order. This is done to have a high risk on the right hand side of the figure (as in the usual risk-return plots). One can however show that in a simple Black-Scholes setting for a high risk premium of stock investment, for long time to maturity T or for

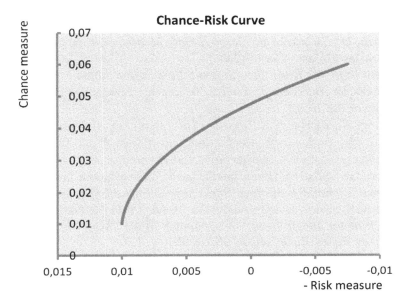

Fig. 2. A form of a chance-risk-curve similar to a mean-standard-deviation curve.

a low volatility σ there can occur different forms. Thus, to obtain explicit descriptions of the form of the chance-risk curve in dependence of the input parameters and ingredients (such as the initial yield curve) is another desirable goal.

More challenges. Due to the low interest rate environment, we expect pension products to use even more complicated investment and guarantee strategies in the future. Products that use a daily asset reallocation strategy already exist. Other products contain a volatility control that uses the volatility estimation on the basis of daily asset prices. Of course, for every such product, it is a challenge to find approximation algorithms that are based on our monthly discretization. Further challenges will appear with every new generation of products.

References

1. Bernard, C., Li, W.V.: *Pricing and hedging of cliquet options and locally-capped contracts.* SIAM J. Fin. Math. 4, 353–371 (2013).

2. Black, F., Jones, R.: *Simplifying portfolio insurance*, Journal of Portfolio Management 14, 48–51 (1987).
3. Brigo, D., Mercurio, F.: *Interest Rate Models: Theory and Practice.* Springer Finance, Berlin (2001).
4. Desmettre, S., Korn, R.: *Moderne Finanzmathematik – Theorie und praktische Anwendung, Band 2.* To appear: Springer Spektrum, Heidelberg (2018).
5. Kling, A., Richter, A., Russ, J.: *The Interaction of Guarantees, Surplus Distribution, and Asset Allocation in With Profit Life Insurance Policies*, Insurance: Mathematics and Economics 40, 164–178 (2007).
6. Korn, R.: *Moderne Finanzmathematik – Theorie und praktische Anwendung, Band 1.* Springer Spektrum, Heidelberg (2014).
7. Korn, R., Korn, E., Kroisandt, G.: *Monte Carlo Methods and Models in Finance and Insurance.* Chapman & Hall/CRC Financial Mathematics Series, Boca Raton, USA (2010).
8. Korn, R., Temocin, B., Wenzel, J.: *Applications of the Central Limit Theorem for Pricing Cliquet-Style Options.* European Actuarial Journal, doi=10.1007/s13385-017-0158-y (2017).

Chapter 16

Forward versus Spot Price Modeling

Jan-Frederik Mai

XAIA Investment,
Sonnenstraße 19, 80331 München, Germany
jan-frederik.mai@xaia.com

It is possible to base an equity derivatives pricing model on a stochastic driving process for the share price (spot), or for the equity forward. While the former is the classical approach pioneered by Black and Scholes [9], the latter approach separates the modeling of exogenous random price fluctuations from the cost-of-carry modeling of the stock, probably the first and most prominent example of this technique being the paper by Black [8]. While the Black–Scholes spot price approach and Black's forward approach are equivalent, the present note demonstrates that the introduction of local volatility and/ or level-dependent default intensity into the stochastic driving process destroys this equivalence, if applied carelessly. The advantages and disadvantages of both approaches are discussed.

Keywords: equity forward, derivative pricing, dividend modeling, credit-equity modeling, CEV model, JDCEV model.

1. Introduction

Today's equity derivative pricing algorithms are based on stochastic modeling of the underlying equity. The pioneering paper by Black and Scholes [9] paved the road for dozens of different models with varying complexity, which all have in common that the underlying share price process is modeled exogenously by some more or less complex stochastic process. The price of a derivative is then given as the expected value of the derivative's payoff function with respect to a so-called risk-neutral probability measure. Due to arbitrage constraints the drift of the share price process under the risk-neutral pricing measure is determined, in the sense that the stochastic process which describes the discounted wealth from holding a portfolio that is long one share becomes a (local) martingale.[1] The incorporation

---

[1]This is roughly the statement of the so-called 1st fundamental theorem of asset pricing, cf. [13], [14] for detailed background.

of a deterministic interest rate, a continuous rate accounting for proceeds from holding the stock (e.g. due to dividends and/ or the possibility for stock lending via repos[2]), or even discrete cash dividends into the stock price model in general is a non-trivial, or at least inconvenient, task that must be executed in accordance with these arbitrage constraints. Not much later than the invention of the pioneering Black–Scholes model in 1973, in 1976 Black [8] already proposed a trick to circumvent this difficult task by modeling the equity forward[3] process exogenously (instead of the share price). While the spot price S_t of an equity is the price at which one share can be bought or sold at time t, the equity forward $F(t,T)$ is defined as the market's expectation at time t about the value of the spot at some fixed future time $T \geq t$. The difference between the share price (spot) and its forward is the cost-of-carry between t and T, which consists precisely of the components mentioned before: interest rates, repo rates, and dividends. Consequently, the task of modeling the forward process $\{F(t,T)\}_{t\in[0,T]}$ exogeneously is a task that is free from these considerations,[4] and after having modeled the forward process exogeneously as an arbitrary (local) martingale, one may include interest rate, repo, and dividend considerations in a separate step.

For the sake of a clear presentation, throughout the present paper we assume that there is a deterministic, risk-free short rate $r(.)$ used for discounting cash flows, and a deterministic, continuous yield $\delta(.)$ accounting for proceeds from stock possession, so that at time t the relation between the share price S_t and the equity forward $F(t,T)$ with maturity $T > t$ is given by

$$S_t = e^{-\int_t^T \left(r(s)-\delta(s)\right)\,\mathrm{d}s}\, F(t,T), \quad 0 \leq t \leq T. \tag{1}$$

In particular, for the sake of simplicity the model abstracts from the fact that in reality dividends are paid at discrete time points, but we discuss the possibility for the inclusion of discrete cash dividends in Section 5. Furthermore, the inclusion of stochastic interest rates is no problem on a generic level, but only disturbs from the main message we like to convey, which is the sole reason why we assume interest rates to be deterministic

---

[2]By "repo" we mean a repurchasement agreement.

[3]Black [8] considers a commodity as underlying and distinguishes "spot" and "futures price", which in our equity setting and today's terminology corresponds to "spot" and "equity forward".

[4]Except for the starting value $F(0,T)$, which depends on the current spot price S_0 as well as the market's expected cost-of-carry between $[0,T]$, see Formula (1) for $t = 0$.

throughout. Equation (1) shows that one of the two stochastic quantities S_t and $F(t, T)$ is obtained from the other by multiplying it with a deterministic process under our assumptions. When it comes to stochastic modeling, the only constraint from arbitrage pricing theory is that the process $\{F(t, T)\}_{t \in [0,T]}$ is a (local) martingale. For instance, if $\{F(t, T)\}_{t \in [0,T]}$ is modeled as a driftless diffusion, this implies that $\{S_t\}_{t \in [0,T]}$ is a diffusion with drift $r(.) - \delta(.)$. Consequently, one would guess that it makes no difference whether one models the spot process $\{S_t\}_{t \in [0,T]}$ exogenously and derives the forward process $\{F(t, T)\}_{t \in [0,T]}$ from it, or vice versa. Indeed, the classical Black–Scholes spot model defines $\{S_t\}_{t \in [0,T]}$ as a geometric Brownian motion, which is equivalent to the Black forward model that defines the forward process $\{F(t, T)\}_{t \in [0,T]}$ as a geometric Brownian motion, with the same volatility but different drift. However, the present article points out that this equivalence hinges upon the assumption of constant volatility. When the driving geometric Brownian motion is replaced by some more general diffusion process with state-dependent local volatility, the parameters $r(.)$ and $\delta(.)$ must be incorporated in a deliberate way into the local volatility term in order for both approaches to be equivalent, see the following example.

Example 1.1 (Drift effect on local volatility). *Assume that the forward process* $\{F(t, T)\}_{t \in [0,T]}$ *follows a local volatility model of the form*

$$dF(t, T) = F(t, T)\, \sigma_F\big(F(t, T), t\big)\, dW_t, \tag{2}$$

where $\{W_t\}$ *denotes a standard Brownian motion. According to (1), Itô calculus implies that* $\{S_t\}_{t \in [0,T]}$ *follows the diffusion*

$$dS_t = S_t\left([r(t) - \delta(t)]\, dt + \sigma_S\big(S_t, t\big)\, dW_t\right), \tag{3}$$

where the spot price local volatility σ_S *is related to the forward local volatility* σ_F *via*

$$\sigma_S(S_t, t) := \sigma_F\left(S_t\, e^{\int_t^T r(s) - \delta(s)\, ds}, t\right) = \sigma_F\big(F(t, T), t\big). \tag{4}$$

Consequently, apart from the differing drift terms in (2) and (3), that result from no arbitrage considerations, also the forward local volatility functions σ_F *and* σ_S *must differ by the discount factor term in the middle expression in (4) in order for (2) and (3) to become equivalent. If, instead of (3), we model the share price dynamics as*

$$dS_t = S_t\left([r(t) - \delta(t)]\, dt + \sigma_F\big(S_t, t\big)\, dW_t\right), \tag{5}$$

i.e. if we use the same driving process as in the forward model only with different drift, we end up with a spot price model that in general is not equivalent to the forward model (2), even though it is also a share price model that is consistent with arbitrage pricing theory.

In Example 1.1 we purposely distinguish the spot local volatility $\sigma_S(.,.)$ and the forward local volatility $\sigma_F(.,.)$, because they are different in general. In practical modeling, in a first (purely stochastic, non-economic) step, one typically decides for some diffusion model with drift $\mu(.)$ and a parametric family of local volatility functions $\sigma(.,.)$, still without economic meaning. The economic interpretation is attached to the model in a second step, when one decides whether the diffusion represents the share price (in which case one sets $\mu = r - \delta$) or the forward (in which case one sets $\mu(t) \equiv 0$). However, it is unusual to incorporate the parameters $r(.)$ and $\delta(.)$ into the local volatility model $\sigma(.,.)$. The present article's purpose is to point out that the decision between "spot modeling" and "forward modeling" can have economic effects that one should keep in mind. Concretely, we investigate the difference between the two different spot price dynamics (3) and (5) of Example 1.1. Furthermore, in order to be even more general, additional to the local volatility part we also include a state-dependent default intensity into the model. For the state-dependence of the latter default intensity there are similar constraints for the equivalence of spot and forward model as in the case of the local volatility.

The remainder of the article is organized as follows. Section 2 introduces both the spot model and the forward model based on a general defaultable Markov diffusion as stochastic driving process. Section 3 provides an elaborate example for how different both modeling approaches can be, when a so-called CEV driving diffusion is chosen. However, the example is still rather theoretic with the sole purpose of clearly pointing out that the two approaches are not the same. More practically oriented, Section 4 calibrates the two different modeling approaches based on a so-called JDCEV driving process to the same observed market data and discusses the resulting differences. With a solid understanding of the differences between forward and spot modeling at hand, Section 5 discusses the basis for decision-making between the two approaches. In particular, since the possibility to include discrete cash dividends into the pricing model is one of the main advantages of the forward modeling approach, the respective technique of [3] to accomplish this task is reviewed and slightly enhanced as well in this section. Finally, Section 6 concludes, and a technical appendix explains two important computations in the context of defaultable Markov diffusions for the readers' convenience.

2. Spot and forward model

As driving equity process for either share price (spot) or forward, we consider a defaultable Markov diffusion model,[5] which is based on a stochastic process $\{Z_t^{(\mu)}\}$. The latter is given by

$$dZ_t^{(\mu)} = Z_t^{(\mu)} \left(\left[\mu(t) + \lambda(Z_t^{(\mu)}) \right] dt + \sigma(Z_t^{(\mu)}) \, dW_t \right),$$

with starting value denoted by $z_0 := Z_0^{(\mu)} > 0$, where $\mu : [0, \infty) \to \mathbb{R}$ is some deterministic drift function, and $\lambda, \sigma : \mathbb{R} \to (0, \infty)$ are smooth enough for the defining stochastic differential equation (SDE) to have a non-explosive weak solution under the constraint that the state zero, if attainable at all, is an absorbing boundary.[6] For an exponential random variable ϵ with unit mean, that is independent of the Brownian motion $\{W_t\}$, we further define the random variable

$$\tau^{(\mu)} := \inf \left\{ t > 0 : \int_0^t \lambda(Z_s^{(\mu)}) \, ds > \epsilon \text{ or } Z_t^{(\mu)} = 0 \right\}.$$

In the sequel, we use the stochastic process $\{Z_t^{(\mu)} 1_{\{\tau^{(\mu)} > t\}}\}$ as a basis for modeling either the share price process ($\mu = r - \delta$) or the equity forward process ($\mu \equiv 0$), and then study the difference between both approaches. In particular, we are only interested in the diffusion process $Z_t^{(\mu)}$ until time $\tau^{(\mu)}$, when we pin it to zero. Since the model is used for pricing applications, it is defined directly under a risk-neutral probability measure. It is well-known that the stochastic process

$$e^{-\int_0^t \mu(s) \, ds} Z_t^{(\mu)} 1_{\{\tau^{(\mu)} > t\}}, \quad t \geq 0,$$

is a local martingale[7] with respect to the filtration $\{\mathcal{F}_t\}$ that is generated jointly by the Brownian motion $\{W_t\}$ and the default indicator process $\{1_{\{\tau^{(\mu)} > t\}}\}$. This filtration is used as market filtration. The random variable $\tau^{(\mu)}$ is interpreted as the occurrence of a bankruptcy event, at which the share price and the equity forward drop to zero and remain there. The stochastic process $\{\lambda(Z_t^{(\mu)})\}$ is called *default intensity*, and intuitively

---

[5] Such models are treated, e.g., in [1],[2],[4]–[7],[10]–[12].
[6] Concrete examples satisfying these demands are given in Sections 3 and 4 below.
[7] For the reader's convenience, the Appendix provides a proof.

represents the instantaneous bankruptcy probability according to the first
order approximation formula

$$\mathbb{P}\big(\tau^{(\mu)} \le t + \Delta \,|\, \tau^{(\mu)} > t\big) \approx \lambda\big(Z_t^{(\mu)}\big)\,\Delta.$$

In light of this formula, the function $\lambda(.)$ allows to model a reciprocal relationship between the value of $Z_t^{(\mu)}$ and the bankruptcy likelihood. Moreover, the function $\sigma(.)$ allows to model a local volatility component. For
the sake of generality, we do not further specify the functions $\lambda(.)$ and $\sigma(.)$
here, but provide parametric examples later. Depending on the choice of
these model functions, the random variable $\tau^{(\mu)}$ may also be infinity, as
Example 2.1 below shows.

2.1. *Spot model*

The drift function $\mu(.)$ is interpreted as the difference between a risk-free
discounting rate $r(.)$ and a continuous yield $\delta(.) \ge 0$ accounting for proceeds
from stock possession, i.e. $\mu := r - \delta$. Based on the model $\big(\{Z_t^{(r-\delta)}\}, \tau^{(r-\delta)}\big)$,
the defaultable Markov diffusion model for the evolution of the share price
$\{S_t\}_{t \ge 0}$ is the stochastic process defined as

$$S_t := Z_t^{(r-\delta)}\, 1_{\{\tau^{(r-\delta)} > t\}}, \quad t \in [0, T], \tag{6}$$

where T is a finite model horizon, and $z_0 := Z_0^{(r-\delta)} = S_0$. The model is in
accordance with arbitrage pricing theory in the sense that the process

$$e^{-\int_0^t r(s)\,\mathrm{d}s}\, e^{\int_0^t \delta(s)\,\mathrm{d}s}\, S_t, \quad t \in [0, T],$$

which equals precisely the discounted wealth process from a portfolio that
is long the stock, is a (non-negative) local martingale with respect to the
market filtration $\{\mathcal{F}_t\}$. In particular, for $\delta \equiv 0$ the discounted share price
process is a local martingale and for $\delta(.) > 0$ it is a supermartingale. Within
this share price model the equity forward process for $0 \le t \le T$ is given by

$$F(t, T) = \mathbb{E}\big[S_T \,|\, \mathcal{F}_t\big] = e^{\int_t^T \big(r(s) - \delta(s)\big)\,\mathrm{d}s}\, Z_t^{(r-\delta)}\, 1_{\{\tau^{(r-\delta)} > t\}},$$

so that, in particular,

$$F(0, T) = e^{\int_0^T \big(r(s) - \delta(s)\big)\,\mathrm{d}s}\, S_0. \tag{7}$$

Example 2.1 (Geometric Brownian motion). *If $\lambda(z) \equiv \lambda \ge 0$ and
$\sigma(z) \equiv \sigma > 0$ are both constant, then $\tau^{(r-\delta)} = \epsilon/\lambda$ has an exponential*

distribution with mean $1/\lambda$, *which is independent of* $\{W_t\}$. *The unique strong solution of the driving process SDE is given by*

$$Z_t^{(\mu)} = S_0 \, e^{\int_0^t \left(r(s)-\delta(s)\right)ds + \left(\lambda-\frac{\sigma^2}{2}\right)t + \sigma \, W_t}, \quad t \geq 0,$$

so that $\log(Z_t^{(\mu)}/S_0)$ *has a normal distribution with mean* $\int_0^t \left(r(s) - \delta(s)\right)ds + \left(\lambda - \frac{\sigma^2}{2}\right)t$ *and variance* $\sigma^2 t$. *The share price process is given by*

$$S_t = S_0 \, e^{\int_0^t \left(r(s)-\delta(s)\right) ds + \left(\lambda-\frac{\sigma^2}{2}\right)t + \sigma \, W_t} \, 1_{\{\epsilon > \lambda \, t\}}.$$

Finally, we'd like to remark that in the special case $\lambda = 0$ *bankruptcy cannot happen, i.e.* $\tau^{(r-\delta)} = \infty$, *and the model boils down to the famous Black–Scholes share price model, cf. [9].*

2.2. *Forward model*

Instead of modeling the share price process exogenously and deriving the equity forward process, one may instead choose to model the equity forward process $\{F(t,T)\}_{t\in[0,T]}$ exogenously and derive the share price process $\{S_t\}_{t\in[0,T]}$ from it via the relation (1). The main motivation for this modeling approach is the separation of interest rate/ repo/ dividend modeling and stochastic modeling (captured in the model for $F(t,T)$), which are multiplicatively separated in (1). There is no need to consider $r(.)$ and $\delta(.)$ when modeling $F(t,T)$, because it is already incorporated adequately into the share price process according to Formula (1), one only needs to make sure that $\{F(t,T)\}_{t\in[0,T]}$ is a (local) martingale. The only thing which depends on $r(.)$ and $\delta(.)$ is the starting value $F(0,T)$ of the forward process. Consequently, basing the stochastic modeling of the equity forward process on the model $\left(\{Z_t^{(\mu)}\}, \tau^{(\mu)}\right)$, it is natural to set $\mu \equiv 0$ and define

$$F(t,T) := Z_t^{(0)} \, 1_{\{\tau^{(0)} > t\}}, \quad t \in [0,T], \tag{8}$$

where $z_0 := Z_0^{(0)} = \exp\left(\int_0^T \left(r(s) - \delta(s)\right) ds\right) S_0$ in accordance with (7). This model for $F(t,T)$ depends on $r(.)$ and $\delta(.)$ only through its starting value z_0. Summarizing, the resulting share price process in this approach is given by

$$S_t := e^{-\int_t^T \left(r(s)-\delta(s)\right) ds} \, Z_t^{(0)} \, 1_{\{\tau^{(0)} > t\}}, \quad t \in [0,T].$$

Example 2.2 (Geometric Brownian motion, contd.). *Like in Example 2.1, assume that* $\lambda(z) \equiv \lambda \geq 0$ *and* $\sigma(z) \equiv \sigma > 0$ *are both constant.*

Then we have

$$Z_t^{(0)} = S_0 \, e^{\int_0^T \left(r(s) - \delta(s) \right) \, ds} \, e^{\left(\lambda - \frac{\sigma^2}{2} \right) t + \sigma W_t}, \quad 0 \le t \le T,$$

and $\tau^{(0)} = \epsilon/\lambda = \tau^{(r-\delta)}$ is an exponential random variable with mean $1/\lambda$, independent of $\{W_t\}$. Consequently,

$$S_t = e^{-\int_t^T \left(r(s) - \delta(s) \right) \, ds} \, Z_t^{(0)} \, 1_{\{\tau^{(0)} > t\}}$$

$$= S_0 \, e^{\int_0^t \left(r(s) - \delta(s) \right) \, ds + \left(\lambda - \frac{\sigma^2}{2} \right) t + \sigma W_t} \, 1_{\{\epsilon > \lambda t\}},$$

which coincides exactly with the share price model in Example 2.1. Hence, for constant $\lambda(.)$ and $\sigma(.)$ the share price model approach and the forward model approach are equivalent. Finally, we'd like to remark that in the special case $\lambda = 0$ bankruptcy cannot happen, i.e. $\tau^{(0)} = \infty$, and the model for $F(t, T)$ boils down to the famous Black–model for the forward process, cf. [8]. In particular, the Black–forward model and the Black–Scholes share price model are equivalent.

2.2.1. *Wealth process model*

Modeling the forward process by (8) implies that the starting value of the driving process $z_0 = F(0, T)$ depends on the model horizon T. This is a drawback compared with the spot model approach (6), where the starting value of the driving process is simply the current share price $z_0 = S_0$, independent of T. In particular, when derivatives with different maturities have to be priced, the forward modeling approach has the disadvantage that different forward processes, with different time horizons and starting values, are required.

A third modeling approach, which shares with the forward model approach that the driving process is a (local) martingale, and which shares with the spot model approach the independence of the driving process' starting value of T, is to model the discounted wealth process $\{V_t\}_{t \in [0,T]}$ that arises from holding a portfolio which is long one share and continuously rehypothecates all proceeds from stock possession into more shares, given by

$$V_t := e^{-\int_0^t \left(r(s) - \delta(s) \right) \, ds} S_t = e^{-\int_0^T \left(r(s) - \delta(s) \right) \, ds} F(t, T).$$

Like in the forward model approach, since $\{V_t\}$ is a (local) martingale, a natural definition based on the model $\left(\{Z_t^{(\mu)}\}, \tau^{(\mu)} \right)$ is to set $\mu \equiv 0$ and

$$V_t := Z_t^{(0)} \, 1_{\{\tau^{(0)} > t\}}, \quad t \in [0, T],$$

where $z_0 := Z_0^{(0)} = S_0$. Consequently, the share price in this setup is derived from the discounted wealth process via

$$S_t = e^{\int_0^t r(s) - \delta(s) \, ds} V_t, \quad t \in [0, T].$$

Remark 2.1 (Wealth modeling $\equiv$ forward modeling). *As the wealth process $\{V_t\}$ equals the forward process $\{F(t, T)\}$ up to a multiplicative constant which is independent of time t, the wealth process approach and the forward model approach are equivalent under the condition that the functions $\lambda(z)$ and $\sigma(z)$ depend on their argument z only through the fraction z/z_0, i.e. default intensity and local volatility are independent of the starting value z_0 of the driving process. This is often satisfied in applications, and in particular in all examples within the present article. Consequently, we do not further distinguish between wealth process approach and forward model approach in the remainder of this article.*

3. First example: CEV model

As demonstrated in Example 2.2, the spot model approach is equivalent to the forward model approach if the functions $\lambda(.)$ and $\sigma(.)$ are constant. However, if they are not constant, both approaches imply different models, which is illustrated in Figure 1 below.

Figure 1 depicts two simulated paths of $\{S_t\}_{t \in [0,20]}$, one simulated according to the spot model approach, the other according to the forward modeling approach. Both simulations are accomplished via an Euler scheme based on exactly the same path of the underlying Brownian motion. It is assumed that $\lambda \equiv 0$, but the local volatility component is modeled with a constant elasticity of variance (CEV) term $\sigma(z) = 0.6 \sqrt{z_0/z}$, cf. Delbaen and Shirakawa [15], who prove the existence of a non-explosive weak solution of the defining SDE, which also follows from the more general results in [10]. It is obvious from Figure 1 that the two modeling approaches are not equivalent. Most outstanding is the observation that the two paths have a different bankruptcy time. This difference can also be observed analytically as follows. For $\mu \geq 0$, the probability $\mathbb{P}(S_T = 0)$ is computed explicitly by Delbaen and Shirakawa [15]. In case of the spot modeling approach, it is given by

$$\mathbb{P}(S_T = 0) = \mathbb{P}\big(\tau^{(\mu)} \leq T\big) = \exp\left(-\frac{\mu}{0.18 \left(1 - e^{-\mu T}\right)}\right).$$

In particular, as the model horizon T tends to infinity, this probability tends to the value $\exp(-\mu/0.18)$, which is smaller than one for $\mu > 0$. This

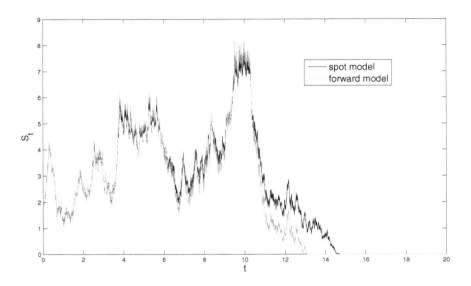

Fig. 1.   Share price process $\{S_t\}_{t \in [0,20]}$, once simulated from the spot model, and once from the forward model. The parameters are chosen as $\mu(t) = r(t) - \delta(t) \equiv 0.025$, $S_0 = 2$, with $\lambda(z) \equiv 0$, and $\sigma(z) = 0.6\sqrt{z_0/z}$.

means that there is a positive probability that bankruptcy never occurs. In contrast, in case of the forward modeling approach, this probability is independent of μ and given by

$$\mathbb{P}(S_T = 0) = \mathbb{P}\big(F(T,T) = 0\big) = \mathbb{P}\big(\tau^{(0)} \leq T\big) = \exp\Big(\frac{-1}{0.18\,T}\Big),$$

which tends to one as the model horizon T tends to infinity. It is intuitive that the difference between spot and forward approach increases with increasing T, since the economic difference between spot and forward increases as well. Figure 2 depicts the probabilities $T \mapsto \mathbb{P}(S_T = 0)$ in dependence on T for the two different models.

4. Second example: JDCEV model

The CEV example of the previous section is rather academic in the following sense: comparing spot modeling approach and forward modeling approach with exactly the same parameters for their driving process is comparing

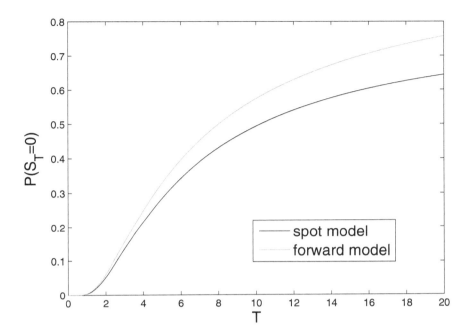

Fig. 2.   The function $T \mapsto \mathbb{P}(S_T = 0)$ for the spot model and the forward model, with the same parameters as in Figure 1.

apples to oranges. In practice, either model is calibrated to one set of observed price data, so that the resulting spot model parameters and forward model parameters are typically different. In such a case, an investigation of the difference between both calibrated models is more delicate and interesting. In the sequel, we are going to carry out such a comparison for a particular model.

One of the most popular models for the joint pricing of credit- and equity-related derivatives is the so-called jump-to-default extended constant elasticity of variance (JDCEV) model of Carr and Linetsky [10], see also [1]. It extends the previously mentioned CEV model by a state-dependent default intensity term. More specifically, we consider the following parametric specification of the JDCEV model in the sequel:

$$\lambda(z) := \lambda_0 \left(\frac{z}{z_0} \right)^{2\beta}, \quad \sigma(z) := \sigma_0 \left(\frac{z}{z_0} \right)^{\beta},$$

with parameters $\lambda_0, \sigma_0 > 0$, and $\beta < 0$. The existence of a non-explosive weak solution for the defining SDE is shown in [10], who also explain that the stopping time $\tau^{(\mu)}$ happens almost surely by the integrated default intensity exceeding ϵ, and not via diffusion of $\{Z_t^{(\mu)}\}$ through zero. Notice in particular that in our parameterization $\lambda(z)$ and $\sigma(z)$ depend on their argument z only via the fraction z/z_0, so that the forward and wealth process modeling approaches are equivalent according to Remark 2.1. Furthermore, the power 2β in the default intensity is twice the power β of the local volatility, which is a deliberate choice making the model analytically tractable. In particular, with an arbitrary[8] function $h : (0, \infty) \to \mathbb{R}$, it is shown in [10], Lemma 5.4, that

$$\mathbb{E}\left[h(Z_T^{(\mu)}) 1_{\{\tau^{(\mu)} > T\}}\right] = z_0 \, \mathbb{E}\left[\frac{h\left(e^{\int_0^T \mu(s)\,\mathrm{d}s} \left(|\beta| \sqrt{c\,X}\right)^{\frac{1}{|\beta|}}\right)}{\left(|\beta| \sqrt{c\,X}\right)^{\frac{1}{|\beta|}}}\right], \qquad (9)$$

where the auxiliary random variable X has a non-central χ^2-distribution with non-centrality parameter $z_0^{2|\beta|}/(c\,\beta^2)$ and $2\lambda_0/(|\beta| \sigma_0^2) + 1/|\beta| + 2$ degrees of freedom, and

$$c = c(T, \sigma_0, z_0, \beta, \mu) = \frac{\sigma_0^2}{z_0^{2\beta}} \int_0^T e^{-2|\beta| \int_0^u \mu(s)\,\mathrm{d}s} \, \mathrm{d}u.$$

In particular, the default probability is computed from the last formula with $h \equiv 1$ as

$$\mathbb{P}\left(\tau^{(\mu)} \leq T\right) = 1 - z_0 \, \mathbb{E}\left[\left(|\beta| \sqrt{c\,X}\right)^{-\frac{1}{|\beta|}}\right].$$

This default probability depends critically on the drift function $\mu(.)$, hence on $r(.) - \delta(.)$, which directly carries over to the probability

$$\mathbb{P}(S_T = 0) = \mathbb{P}\left(\tau^{(\mu)} \leq T\right)$$

within the spot model approach. In contrast, for the forward model approach this default probability is independent of $\mu(.)$ (and hence independent of both $r(.)$ and $\delta(.)$), since it is given by

$$\mathbb{P}(S_T = 0) = \mathbb{P}\left(\tau^{(0)} \leq T\right).$$

Consequently, interest rate and repo/ dividend parameters have a direct effect on default probabilities only within the spot price model.

We consider a credit default swap (CDS) par spread curve with maturities ranging from one year to ten years, referring to a company XY. We also consider European out-of-the-money (OTM) call and put options

---

[8]"Arbitrary" in the sense of a practitioner, of course, measurability issues swept under the carpet.

with maturity $T \approx 1.425$ years on the stock of company XY. The current stock price is $S_0 = 53.48$ and the forward $F(0, T) \approx 50.74$, implying a constant yield $\delta \approx 3.32\%$, where at the same time the discount rate $r(.)$ has been bootstrapped in a piecewise constant manner from observed prices of interest rate swaps with a 3-month tenor. This example is inspired by a real-world case.

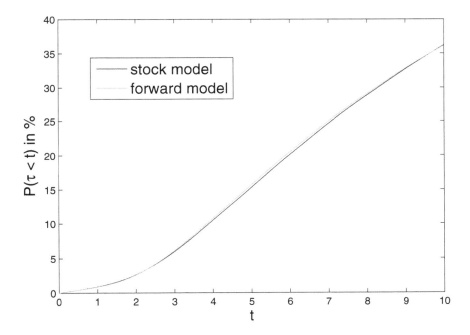

Fig. 3.   Default probabilities for the next ten years in spot and forward model, both models being calibrated to the same CDS curve.

The JDCEV model parameters are fitted to the observed CDS quotes, which results in a perfect and unambiguous[9] model fit in both cases. More precisely, the fitted parameters in spot (S) and forward (F) model[10] are

---

[9]The observed CDS data already determines the model parameters uniquely.

[10]We actually use the wealth process modeling approach because we deal with different maturities, but according to Remark 2.1 the wealth process modeling approach is equivalent to the forward modeling approach.

given by

$$\beta_S = -0.8,\ \sigma_S = 0.30,\ \lambda_S = 0.0077091,$$
$$\beta_F = -0.6,\ \sigma_F = 0.39,\ \lambda_F = 0.0077091.$$

Notice in particular that $\lambda_S = \lambda_F$, because this parameter can directly be read off from the short end of the observed CDS par spread curve. Both models calibrate perfectly to the observed CDS prices, which is illustrated by Figure 3 that depicts induced default probabilities for the next ten years. Notice that the CDS prices depend only on these probabilities, assuming a constant recovery rate, as usual. It is observed that both models imply almost perfectly the same default probabilities, hence CDS prices. Now what about the option data?

The distribution function of S_T has a jump at zero (corresponding to the default probability $\mathbb{P}(S_T = 0) > 0$) and is continuously differentiable on $(0, \infty)$. The top plot in Figure 4 shows the density function $f_S(.; T) := \frac{\partial}{\partial x} \mathbb{P}(S_T \leq x)$ for $x > 0$, which is derived from Formula (9) in the Appendix. Whereas the expected value of S_T, which is the forward $F(0, T)$, is identical in both models, it is observed that the stock price has higher variance in the forward model. Consequently, the option prices in the forward model are higher than in the spot model, which is depicted in the bottom plot of Figure 4. The observed market prices of the options in the current example are perfectly in line with the option prices of the spot model, and are overestimated by the forward model.

Finally, Figure 5 visualizes the sensitivities of CDS prices on changes in the stock price with both considered JDCEV models. It is observed that the CDS spreads are more sensitive with regards to changes in the stock price within the stock price model, which is due to the fact that $|\beta_S| > |\beta_F|$.

Concluding, the two different models (spot and forward) differ significantly in the present use case. They differ with respect to the computation of price sensitivities, and they also differ in their projections of equity derivative prices from observed CDS prices, which is the most prominent application of such credit-equity models.

5. Implications for modeling

As demonstrated in the previous paragraph, when volatility and/ or default intensity in an equity model are allowed to depend on the current equity level, it makes a difference whether we decide to model the share price process (like in the Black–Scholes model), or instead we opt for modeling

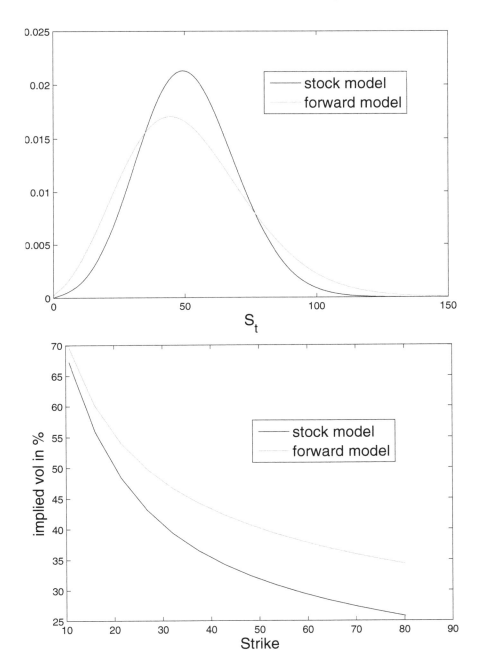

Fig. 4.   Top: The risk-neutral density function $f_S(.;T)$ of S_T for $T \approx 1.425$ in spot and forward model.   Bottom: Implied volatilities for European OTM calls and OTM puts with maturity $T \approx 1.425$ in spot and forward model.

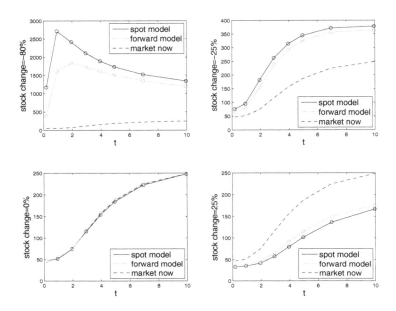

Fig. 5.   Effect of stock price change on the shape of a CDS par spread curve (computed with recovery rate 40% and running coupon 500 bps). Northwest: Stock price drops 80%. Northeast: Stock price drops 25%. Southwest: Stock price unchanged, current CDS par spread curve. Southeast: Stock price rises 25%.

the forward equity process (like in the Black–model). Moreover, Example 2.2 shows that this difference is not present in the classical Black–Scholes model with constant volatility (and zero default intensity), so it is an issue emerging only in advanced equity models, for instance with local volatility and/ or the possibility for a bankruptcy event sending the share price to zero. Since both spot and forward approach imply arbitrage-consistent pricing models, the decision between either one of them must be based on one's opinion regarding the economic interpretation. Within the cosmos of defaultable Markov diffusion models considered in the present paper, the important question that needs to be answered is: "Do we want the dividend/ repo/ interest rate parameters to have influence on the default probabilities and local volatility of the equity process?" If the answer is "yes", one prefers the spot model approach, if it is "no", one prefers the forward model approach. If one does not care, it is also possible to work with both models and prefer the one that fits observed price data better. For example, in the real-world case of the previous paragraph the market stock option data (which is not depicted in Figure 4) is explained better within the spot model. But the author wishes to mention that he could instead have easily presented another use case with the forward model being closer to the market data as well.

One of the most important advantages of the forward model over the spot model is the possibility to include discrete cash dividends in a simple manner, as described by Bernhart and Mai [3]. In this case, neglecting proceeds from stock lending[11] and focusing on proceeds from dividends only, a continuous dividend yield $\delta(.)$ is not required, since dividends are modeled by discrete cash payments. If we want to include discrete cash dividends (which is straightforward in the forward model), but also want to make sure that interest rate and dividends have an influence on default probabilities (which requires the spot model), what can we do? We can use a hybrid model, using aspects of both discrete cash dividend modeling and continuous dividend modeling as follows. The discrete cash dividend model of [3] specifies a dividend payment at time t_k as a function $D_{t_k} = f\big(F(t_k, T)\big)$ of the forward at t_k. The forward process $\{F(t, T)\}_{t \in [0,T]}$ is the driving process of the model, for instance being given by default intensity $\lambda(.)$ and local volatility $\sigma(.)$ according to the defaultable Markov diffusion considered in Section 4 of the present paper. The stock price is finally given by

$$ S_t = F(t, T)\, e^{-\int_t^T r(s)\,\mathrm{d}s} + \sum_{t < t_k \leq T} e^{-\int_t^{t_k} r(s)\,\mathrm{d}s}\, \mathbb{E}[D_{t_k} \,|\, \mathcal{F}_t], \qquad (10) $$

where the sum is taken over all dividend payment dates between t and T. Using Equation (1) with $t = 0$ and different forward maturities, the observable quantities S_0 and $\{F(0, \tilde{T})\}_{\tilde{T} \in [0,T]}$ may be used to extract a continuous dividend yield parameter $\delta(.)$, for instance in a piecewise-constant manner with jumps at a discrete set of observed forward maturities $\tilde{T}$. This parameter $\delta(.)$ may now be incorporated into the model (10) at one or both of the following two places:

---

[11]Only for the sake of a simplified notation. It is easily possible to keep a part of δ as continuous yield from stock lending and only transform the remaining dividend part into discrete payments.

(i) In order to make D_{t_k} dependent on both $r(.)$ and $\delta(.)$, we may change its definition to

$$D_{t_k} := f\left(e^{-\int_{t_k}^{T} r(s)-\delta(s)\, \mathrm{d}s}\, F(t_k,T)\right).$$

(ii) In order to make interest rate and dividends affect default probabilities and local volatility we change the default intensity and local volatility of the driving forward process from $\lambda(.)$ and $\sigma(.)$ to

$$\lambda_F\big(F(t,T),t\big) := \lambda\left(e^{-\int_{t}^{T} r(s)-\delta(s)\, \mathrm{d}s}\, F(t,T)\right),$$

$$\sigma_F\big(F(t,T),t\big) := \sigma\left(e^{-\int_{t}^{T} r(s)-\delta(s)\, \mathrm{d}s}\, F(t,T)\right).$$

In particular, we introduce a dependence on the time t.

The inspiration for both adjustments (i) and (ii) above relies on the relation

$$S_t \approx e^{-\int_{t}^{T} r(s)-\delta(s)\, \mathrm{d}s}\, F(t,T), \quad 0 \le t \le T, \tag{11}$$

which is no longer an equality in the presence of discrete cash dividends, but now only an approximation of the discrete relationship (10). The discrete payments cause jumps in the stock price process on the left-hand side of (11), whereas the right-hand side of (11) only represents a continuous proxy for the stock price (10), with the aforementioned definitions (i) and (ii) being in place. Altering the model of [3] in this way, it features jumps (of possibly random, state-dependent size) in the stock price process on dividend dates t_k, but there is also an effect of dividends and interest rates on default probability and local volatility, which is modeled continuously and non-random. In this sense, it is a hybrid model. The tractability of the model, which relies heavily on the fact that the forward modeling approach is chosen, is still huge, as can be seen from Equation (10): based on a stochastic differential equation for the driving forward process, standard finite difference techniques may be applied in a straightforward manner to compute the value of equity derivatives on the share price. The interested reader is referred to [3] for details.

6. Conclusion

We investigated the potential differences between basing an equity derivatives pricing model on either the share price or the equity forward. It has been demonstrated that it can be a crucial economic difference whether default intensity and local volatility of the driving process is modeled dependent on the spot-level or the forward-level. Since both approaches imply arbitrage-consistent pricing models, the choice between them depends on the user's preference and economic interpretation.

Appendix A. Martingale property of driving process

We write $Z_t := \exp(-\int_0^t \mu(s)\,\mathrm{d}s)\,Z_t^{(\mu)}$ and $\tau = \tau^{(\mu)}$, i.e. in particular we omit the superscript (μ) for notational simplicity. We furthermore introduce the notation $Y_t := Z_t\,1_{\{\tau>t\}}$, $t \geq 0$, and aim to prove that $\{Y_t\}$ is a local martingale with respect to the market filtration that is generated by the Brownian motion and the observable default indicator. Fix $T \geq t \geq 0$. We compute the dynamics of the process $\left\{ Z_u \exp\left(-\int_t^u \lambda(Z_s)\,\mathrm{d}s \right) \right\}_{u \geq t}$ and observe

$$\mathrm{d}\!\left(Z_u\, e^{-\int_t^u \lambda(Z_s)\,\mathrm{d}s} \right) = e^{-\int_t^u \lambda(Z_s)\,\mathrm{d}s}\,\mathrm{d}Z_u - \lambda(Z_u)\,Z_u\, e^{-\int_t^u \lambda(Z_s)\,\mathrm{d}s}\,\mathrm{d}u$$

$$= e^{-\int_t^u \lambda(Z_s)\,\mathrm{d}s}\,Z_u\,\sigma(Z_u)\,\mathrm{d}W_u.$$

Consequently, the latter process is driftless, showing that itself is a local martingale with respect to the natural filtration $\{\mathcal{F}_t^{(W)}\}_{t \geq 0}$ of the Brownian motion W. Hence, there exists an increasing sequence of $\{\mathcal{F}_t^{(W)}\}$-stopping times $(T_n)_{n \in \mathbb{N}}$, such that $\lim_{n \to \infty} T_n = \infty$ and the stopped processes are martingales. Since $\mathcal{F}_t^{(W)} \subset \mathcal{F}_t$, $(T_n)_{n \in \mathbb{N}}$ is also a sequence of $\{\mathcal{F}_t\}$-stopping times. We denote by $Y^{[T_n]} := \{Y_{T_n \wedge t}\}_{t \geq 0}$ the process Y stopped at T_n, and show that $Y^{[T_n]}$ is a martingale for each n.

$$\mathbb{E}\big[Y_T^{[T_n]} \,\big|\, \mathcal{F}_{t \wedge T_n}\big] = \mathbb{E}[Z_{T \wedge T_n}\,1_{\{\tau > T \wedge T_n\}} \,|\, \mathcal{F}_{t \wedge T_n}]$$

$$= 1_{\{\tau > t \wedge T_n\}}\,\mathbb{E}[Z_{T \wedge T_n}\,1_{\{\tau > T \wedge T_n\}} \,|\, \mathcal{F}_{t \wedge T_n}]$$

$$= 1_{\{\tau > t \wedge T_n\}}\,\mathbb{E}[Z_{T \wedge T_n}\,\mathbb{E}[1_{\{\tau > T \wedge T_n\}} \,|\, \mathcal{F}_{t \wedge T_n} \vee \mathcal{F}_T^{(W)}] \,|\, \mathcal{F}_{t \wedge T_n}]$$

$$= 1_{\{\tau > t \wedge T_n\}}\,\mathbb{E}[Z_{T \wedge T_n}\,\mathbb{E}[1_{\{\int_0^{T \wedge T_n} \lambda(Z_s)\,\mathrm{d}s < \epsilon\}} \,|\, \mathcal{F}_{t \wedge T_n} \vee \mathcal{F}_T^{(W)}] \,|\, \mathcal{F}_{t \wedge T_n}]$$

$$\overset{(*)}{=} 1_{\{\tau > t \wedge T_n\}}\,\mathbb{E}[Z_{T \wedge T_n}\,\mathbb{E}[e^{-\int_{t \wedge T_n}^{T \wedge T_n} \lambda(Z_s)\,\mathrm{d}s} \,|\, \mathcal{F}_{t \wedge T_n} \vee \mathcal{F}_T^{(W)}] \,|\, \mathcal{F}_{t \wedge T_n}]$$

$$= 1_{\{\tau > t \wedge T_n\}}\,\mathbb{E}[Z_{T \wedge T_n}\, e^{-\int_{t \wedge T_n}^{T \wedge T_n} \lambda(Z_s)\,\mathrm{d}s} \,|\, \mathcal{F}_{t \wedge T_n}] \overset{(**)}{=} 1_{\{\tau > t \wedge T_n\}}\,Z_{t \wedge T_n} = Y_t^{[T_n]},$$

where Equality $(*)$ follows from the lack-of-memory property of the exponential distribution

$$\mathbb{P}(\epsilon > b \,|\, \epsilon > a) = \mathbb{P}(\epsilon > b - a), \quad b \geq a \geq 0,$$

and $(**)$ follows from the fact that $\left\{ Z_u \exp\left(-\int_t^u \lambda(Z_s)\,\mathrm{d}s \right) \right\}_{u \geq t}$ is a local martingale.

Appendix B. Density of S_T in JDCEV model

We briefly demonstrate how to derive the probability law of S_T from Formula (9). First of all, we consider the following bijection on $(0, \infty)$:

$$g(x) = \left(|\beta|\sqrt{cx}\right)^{\frac{1}{|\beta|}}, \quad g^{-1}(s) = s^{2|\beta|}\frac{1}{c\beta^2}, \quad g'(x) = \frac{1}{2}\sqrt{\frac{c}{x}}\left(|\beta|\sqrt{cx}\right)^{\frac{1}{|\beta|}-1}.$$

Formula (9) states that

$$\mathbb{E}\left[h(Z_T^{(\mu)})1_{\{\tau^{(\mu)}>T\}}\right] = z_0\,\mathbb{E}\left[\frac{h\left(e^{\int_0^T \mu(s)\,ds}\,g(X)\right)}{g(X)}\right],$$

where the random variable X has density f_X of a certain non-central χ^2-distribution. Consequently, we observe with the change of variables $u = e^{\int_0^T \mu(s)\,ds}\,g(x)$ that

$$\mathbb{E}\left[h(Z_T^{(\mu)})1_{\{\tau^{(\mu)}>T\}}\right] = z_0\int_0^\infty \frac{h\left(e^{\int_0^T \mu(s)\,ds}\,g(x)\right)}{g(x)}f_X(x)\,dx$$

$$= z_0\int_0^\infty \frac{h(u)\,f_X\left(g^{-1}\left(u\,e^{-\int_0^T \mu(s)\,ds}\right)\right)}{u\,g'\left(g^{-1}\left(u\,e^{-\int_0^T \mu(s)\,ds}\right)\right)}\,du$$

$$= \int_0^\infty h(u)\underbrace{\frac{2\,z_0\,f_X\left(\frac{\left(u\,e^{-\int_0^T \mu(s)\,ds}\right)^{2|\beta|}}{c\beta^2}\right)}{u\,c\,|\beta|\left(u\,e^{-\int_0^T \mu(s)\,ds}\right)^{1-2|\beta|}}}_{=:f_Z(u;T,\mu)}\,du.$$

In the spot model we have $S_t = Z_t^{(\mu)}1_{\{\tau^{(\mu)}>0\}}$, hence

$$\mathbb{E}\left[h(S_T)\right] = \mathbb{E}\left[h(S_T)1_{\{S_T>0\}}\right] + h(0)\,\mathbb{P}(S_T = 0)$$

$$= \mathbb{E}\left[h(Z_T^{(\mu)})1_{\{\tau^{(\mu)}>T\}}\right] + h(0)\,\mathbb{P}(\tau^{(\mu)} \leq T)$$

$$= \int_0^\infty h(u)\,f_Z(u;T,\mu)\,du + h(0)\left(1 - \int_0^\infty f_Z(u;T,\mu)\,du\right),$$

which shows that $f_Z(.;T,\mu)/\int_0^\infty f_Z(u;T,\mu)\,du$ equals the density of S_T conditioned on the event $\{S_T > 0\}$. The complementary event $\{S_T = 0\}$ has probability $1 - \int_0^\infty f_Z(u;T,\mu)\,du$. In other words, $f_S(x;T) := \frac{\partial}{\partial x}\mathbb{P}(S_T \leq x) = f_Z(x;T,\mu)$ for $x > 0$.

In the wealth process model, which is equivalent to the forward model by Remark 2.1, we have $S_t = e^{\int_0^t r(s)-\delta(s)\,ds}\,Z_t^{(0)}1_{\{\tau^{(0)}>t\}}$, hence the same computation as above shows

$$\mathbb{E}\Big[h(S_T)\Big] = \mathbb{E}\Big[h(S_T)\,1_{\{S_T>0\}}\Big] + h(0)\,\mathbb{P}(S_T = 0)$$

$$= \mathbb{E}\Big[h\Big(e^{\int_0^T r(s)-\delta(s)\,\mathrm{d}s}\,Z_T^{(0)}\Big)\,1_{\{\tau^{(0)}>T\}}\Big] + h(0)\,\mathbb{P}(\tau^{(0)} \le T)$$

$$= \int_0^\infty h\Big(e^{\int_0^T r(s)-\delta(s)\,\mathrm{d}s}\,u\Big)\,f_Z(u;T,0)\,\mathrm{d}u + h(0)\Big(1 - \int_0^\infty f_Z(u;T,0)\,\mathrm{d}u\Big).$$

Substituting $x = e^{\int_0^T r(s)-\delta(s)\,\mathrm{d}s}\,u$, this implies for $x > 0$ that

$$f_S(x;T) = \frac{\partial}{\partial x}\mathbb{P}(S_T \le x) = e^{-\int_0^T r(s)-\delta(s)\,\mathrm{d}s}\,f_Z(e^{-\int_0^T r(s)-\delta(s)\,\mathrm{d}s}\,x;T,0).$$

References

1. L. Andersen and D. Buffum, Calibration and implementation of convertible bond models, *Journal of Computational Finance* **7:2**, 1–34 (2004).
2. E. Ayache, P. Forsyth and K. Vetzal, The valuation of convertible bonds with credit risk, *Journal of Derivatives* **11**, 9–29 (2003).
3. G. Bernhart and J.-F. Mai, Consistent modeling of discrete cash dividends, *Journal of Derivatives* **22**, 9–19 (2015).
4. T.R. Bielecki, S. Crépey, M. Jeanblanc and M. Rutkowski, Arbitrage pricing of defaultable game options with applications to convertible bonds, *Quantitative Finance* **8:8**, 795–810 (2008).
5. T.R. Bielecki, S. Crépey, M. Jeanblanc and M. Rutkowski, Defaultable options in a Markovian intensity model of credit risk, *Mathematical Finance* **18:4**, 493–518 (2008).
6. T.R. Bielecki, S. Crépey, M. Jeanblanc and M. Rutkowski, Valuation and hedging of defaultable game options in a hazard process model, *Journal of Applied Mathematics and Stochastic Analysis*, Article ID 695798 (2009).
7. T.R. Bielecki, S. Crépey, M. Jeanblanc and M. Rutkowski, Convertible bonds in a defaultable diffusion model, in *Stochastic Analysis with Financial Applications*, eds. A. Kohatsu-Higa, N. Privault and S.J. Sheu (2011) pp. 255–298.
8. F. Black, The pricing of commodity contracts, *Journal of Financial Economics* **3**, 167–179 (1976).
9. F. Black and M.S. Scholes, The pricing of options and corporate liabilities, *Journal of Political Economy* **81**, 637–654 (1973).

10. P. Carr and V. Linetsky, A jump to default extended CEV model: an application of Bessel processes, *Finance and Stochastics* **10:3**, 303–330 (2006).
11. P. Carr and D. Madan, Local volatility enhanced by a jump to default, *SIAM Journal on Financial Mathematics* **1:1**, 2–15 (2010).
12. P. Carr and L. Wu, Stock options and credit default swaps: a joint framework for valuation and estimation, *Journal of Financial Econometrics* **8:4**, 409–449 (2010).
13. F. Delbaen and W. Schachermayer, A general version of the fundamental theorem of asset pricing, *Mathematische Annalen* **300:1**, 463–520 (1994).
14. F. Delbaen and W. Schachermayer, The fundamental theorem of asset pricing for unbounded stochastic processes, *Mathematische Annalen* **312**, 215–250 (1998).
15. F. Delbaen and H. Shirakawa, A note on option pricing for the constant elasticity of variance model, *Asia-Pacific Financial Markets* **9:2**, 85–99 (2002).
16. V. Linetsky, Pricing equity derivatives subject to bankruptcy, *Mathematical Finance* **16:2**, 255–282 (2006).

Chapter 17

Replication Methods for Financial Indexes

Bruno Rémillard*, Bouchra Nasri† and Malek Ben-Abdellatif‡

*Department of Decision Sciences, HEC Montréal,
Montréal (Québec), Canada H3T 2A7*
* *bruno.remillard@hec.ca*
† *bouchra.nasri@hec.ca*
‡ *malek.ben-abdellatif@hec.ca*

In this paper, we first present a review of statistical tools that can be used in asset management either to track financial indexes or to create synthetic ones. More precisely, we look at two important replication methods: the strong replication, where a portfolio of very liquid assets is created and the goal is to track an actual index with the portfolio, and weak replication, where a portfolio of very liquid assets is created and used to either replicate the statistical properties of an existing index, or to replicate the statistical properties of a custom asset. In addition, for weak replication, the target is not an index but a payoff, and the replication amounts to hedge the portfolio so it is as close as possible to the payoff at the end of each month. For strong replication, the main tools are predictive tools, so filtering techniques and regression play an important role. For weak replication, which is the main topic of this paper, in order to determine the target payoff, the investor has to find or choose the distribution function of the target index or custom index, as well as its dependence with other assets, and use a hedging technique. Therefore, the main tools for weak replication are modeling (estimation and goodness-of-fit) and optimal hedging. For example, an investor could wish to obtain Gaussian returns that are independent of some ETFs replicating the Nasdaq and S&P 500 indexes. In order to determine the dependence of the target and a given number of indexes, we introduce a new class of easily constructed models of conditional distributions called B-vines. We also propose to use a flexible model to fit the distribution of the assets composing the portfolio and then hedge the portfolio in an optimal way. Examples are given to illustrate all the important steps required for the implementation of this new asset management methodology.

Keywords: ETF, hedge funds, replication, smart beta, copulas, B-vines, HMM, hedging.

1. Introduction

Historically, hedge funds have been an important class of alternative investment assets for diversifying portfolios. The early sales pitch was that hedge funds offer superior returns, due to use of leverage, derivatives, short sales and other non-traditional investment strategies. The new sales pitch is that there are diversification benefits due to low correlation with traditional assets classes. However, investors are still often rebutted in investing in hedge funds, mainly because of high management and performance fees, lack of liquidity and significant lock-up periods, and lack of transparency.

Mainly based on the work on [1], [2] and [3], major investors like financial institutions looked for more efficient and affordable methods to generate the same kind of returns. This was mainly done by strong replication, i.e., by constructing portfolios of very liquid assets tracking a hedge fund index. Nowadays, smart beta methods, a new brand name for replication techniques, offer even more flexibility to small investors as well, through ETFs. For example, Horizons HFF (hhf.to) is an ETF targeting the Morningstar Broad Hedge Fund Index SM, while State Street SPDR ETF (spy) tracks S&P 500 index.

In addition to strong replication, weak replication, based of the payoff distribution model of [4], was proposed by [5] and extended by [6]. This innovative approach consists in constructing a dynamic strategy to track a payoff, in order to reproduce the statistical properties of hedge fund returns together with their dependence with a selected investor portfolio. It can also be used to construct synthetic indexes with tailor-made properties, which is an advantage over strong replication since the latter can only replicate an existing index.

In Section 2, we review the main statistical techniques to replicate indexes, including a new "Smart Beta" approach that can be used to diversify investors portfolios. In order to implement the proposed methodology, a new family of conditional distributions called B-vines are introduced in Section 3. The essential steps of modeling and hedging are discussed in Section 4. Examples of applications are then given in Section 5.

2. Replication methods

There are basically two replication approaches: strong replication, where the target is the index (naive or imitative method, and factor-based method), and weak replication, where the target is a payoff determined by the distribution of an existing index or a custom index, also called synthetic index. In both cases, the idea is to construct a portfolio of liquid assets with end of the month values as close as possible to the target.

Strong replication is divided in two sub-groups. On one hand, there is the "naive replication", where the investor try to imitate the hedge fund manager investment strategy or the index composition. This is kind of easy for indexes when their composition is known, but it is far from obvious when the strategy or composition is unknown. For example, for a Merger Arbitrage Fund index, the idea is to long (potential) sellers and short (potential) buyers.

On the other hand, the factorial approach attempts to reproduce hedge fund returns or indexes by investing in a portfolio of assets that provide similar end of month returns. The implementation of the factorial approach is described in Section 2.1, while the multi-asset extension of the weak replication is discussed in Section 2.2.

Alternative beta funds based on the factorial approach have been launched by several institutions including Goldman Sachs, JP Morgan, Deutsche Bank, and Innocap, to name a few. According to [7], the short version Verso of Innocap, based on filtering methods, performed best in the turbulent period 2008–2009. Note also that [8] showed that factor-based replicators produce independent returns over time, which might be interesting from an investor's perspective. Furthermore, an investor can easily track the performance of a given replicator. However, in a recent study, [9] found very high correlations between factor-based replicators and indexes like S&P 500. This undesirable dependence show that these replicators cannot really be used for diversification purposes, contrary to synthetic indexes that can be built with weak replication techniques. An illustration of this powerful technique is given in Section 5.4.

Before presenting the mathematical framework defining strong and weak replication, we summarize in Table 1 the main differences between the two approaches.

Table 1. Main differences between strong replication and weak replication.

Method	Target	Tracking	Synthetic index	Controlled dependence
Strong	Index	Yes	No	No
Weak	Payoff	Possible	Possible	Possible

Note: Tracking is possible for weak replication if the value of the payoff is posted at the end of the month. In this case, the analog of the tracking error is the RMSE (root mean square error) of the hedging error. This important value appears in our examples of implementation in Section 5. For synthetic indexes, it is possible to control the dependence.

2.1. *Factorial approach for strong replication*

To implement the factorial approach, one needs the returns[1] $R_t^\star$ of the target fund $S^\star$ and one needs to select appropriate liquid assets (factors) $\mathbf{S} = \left(S^{(1)}, \ldots, S^{(p)} \right)$ composing the replication portfolio. The returns of $\mathbf{S}$ are denoted by $\mathbf{R}_t = \left(R_t^{(1)}, \ldots, R_t^{(p)} \right)$, and the associated weights are denoted by $\boldsymbol{\beta}_t = (\beta_{t,1}, \ldots, \beta_{t,p})$. The model is written in the linear form

$$R_t^\star = \boldsymbol{\beta}_t^\top \mathbf{R}_t + \varepsilon_t, \tag{1}$$

where the ε_t's are non-observable tracking error terms.

The unknown weights $\boldsymbol{\beta}_t$ are then evaluated from a predictive method using relation (1), e.g., by using a rolling-window regression over the last 24 months, or by using filtering methods. Note that for filtering, one must also define the (Markovian) dynamics of the weights $\boldsymbol{\beta}_t$; see, e.g., [10].

To measure the performance of a replicating method, one uses the tracking error (TE), defined in the in-sample case by

$$\mathrm{TE}_{in} = \left\{ \frac{1}{n} \sum_{t=1}^{n} \left(R_t^\star - \hat{\boldsymbol{\beta}}_t^\top \mathbf{R}_t \right)^2 \right\}^{1/2},$$

while for the out-of-sample, it is defined by

$$\mathrm{TE}_{out} = \left\{ \frac{1}{n} \sum_{t=1}^{n} \left(R_t^\star - \hat{\boldsymbol{\beta}}_{t-1}^\top \mathbf{R}_t \right)^2 \right\}^{1/2},$$

where $\hat{\boldsymbol{\beta}}_t$ is the vector of predicted weights using returns $(R_t^\star, \mathbf{R}_t)$, $(R_{t-1}^\star, \mathbf{R}_{t-1})$,…… The out-of-sample tracking error is a more realistic measure of performance, since the error $R_t^\star - \hat{\boldsymbol{\beta}}_{t-1}^\top \mathbf{R}_t$ is the one monitored by investors. As seen in the example below, filtering usually yields better results than regression in terms of tracking error.

Example 2.1. This example is taken from [11], Chapter 10. The target is HFRI Fund Weighted Composite Index, and the factors are S&P500 Index TR, Russel 2000 Index TR, Russell 1000 Index TR, Eurostoxx Index, Topix, US 10-year Index, 1-month LIBOR.[2] Here, two methods were used to compute the dynamic weights $\boldsymbol{\beta}$: a regression with a 24-month window, and a Kalman filter, where the dynamics of the $\boldsymbol{\beta}$'s is a random walk, meaning that $\boldsymbol{\beta}_t = \boldsymbol{\beta}_{t-1} + \boldsymbol{\eta}_t$, where the innovations $\boldsymbol{\eta}_t$ are assumed to be independent and identically distributed.

---

[1]Typically monthly returns, especially in the case of hedge fund indexes.
[2]Data, from April 1997 to October 2008, were provided by Innocap.

Table 2. In-sample and out-of-sample statistics.

Portfolio	TE	Corr	Mean	Std	Skew	Excess kurt
			In-sample statistics			
Target	—	1.00	8.12	7.72	−0.59	2.45
Regression	10.58	0.93	8.79	8.32	−0.69	2.22
Kalman	8.54	0.95	9.68	7.75	−0.59	2.53
			Out-of-sample statistics			
Target	—	1.00	8.12	7.72	−0.59	2.45
Regression	19.27	0.83	9.30	9.86	−0.11	3.34
Kalman	14.71	0.86	9.97	8.20	−0.40	2.63

Note: Values are expressed in annual percentage. The excess kurtosis of the Gaussian distribution is 0.

This is a very basic and unrealistic model, but it can be improved, e.g., by adding dependence in the increments or adding constraints on the portfolio compositions. In this case, the Kalman filter assumptions are no longer met, and one should use for example a particle filter; see, e.g., [11], Chapter 9. However, even with a simple model and the Kalman filter, the results are surprisingly good, better than the rolling-window regression. In-sample and out-of-sample statistics for our example are displayed in Table 2.

In general, the β_t are much less variable in the Kalman filter case, leading to less expensive transactions, in addition to being a better tracking method. See, e.g., [11], Chapter 10.

Before ending this section, it is worth noting that one could also use machine learning methods for tracking purposes. It would be interesting to compare the performance of machine learning vs filtering. This will be done in a forthcoming work.

2.2. *Weak replication*

Weak replication is an alternative replication method proposed by [5] and later extended by [6] based on the payoff distribution model of [4]. The aim was to replicate hedge fund returns or hedge fund indexes not by identifying the return generating betas as in the factor-based approach, but by building a trading strategy that can be used to generate the (statistical) distribution of the hedge fund returns or indexes. The implementation proposed in [6] is subject to several shortcomings and inconsistencies. Improvements of the Kat-Palaro method were proposed in [12] for a start.

In view of applications to asset management, and mainly for diversification purposes, it is desirable to generalize the Kat-Palaro approach (limited to only one reference asset). To this end, it was suggested in [13] to consider a multivariate asset **S** of $p = d + 1$ components, where $S^{(1)}, \ldots, S^{(d)}$

represent the value of reference portfolios of the investor, and the so-called reserve asset $S^{(d+1)}$.[3] As before, $S^\star$ is the index one seeks to replicate. The aim is not to reproduce the monthly values of $S^\star$, which might not even exists, but rather reproduce its statistical properties.

The steps required to implement the proposed weak replication method are given next.

2.2.1. *Implementation steps*

(1) Determine the joint distribution of the (daily) returns $\mathbf{R}_k$ of $\mathbf{S}_k$.

We suggest to use a Gaussian Hidden Markov Model (HMM). This model is described in Section 4.1. However any dynamic model is permitted, as long as it fits the data.

(2) Find a compatible distribution for the monthly returns $\mathbf{R}_{0,T}$. In particular, find the marginal distributions $F_1, \ldots, F_d$ of $\mathbf{R}_{0,T}^{(ref)} = \left(R_{0,T}^{(1)}, \ldots, R_{0,T}^{(d)} \right)$, find the copula of $\mathbf{R}_{0,T}^{(ref)}$, and find the conditional distribution $\mathcal{F}(\cdot, \mathbf{x})$ of $R_{0,T}^{(res)}$ given $\mathbf{R}_{0,T}^{(ref)} = \left(R_{0,T}^{(1)}, \ldots, R_{0,T}^{(d)} \right) = \mathbf{x}$.

This can be done by simulation from daily returns, as suggested in Section 4.2. Again, we suggest to use a Gaussian HMM. We strongly advise against using real monthly returns to complete this step since in general the sample size for estimation purposes is not long enough, and in addition, there is a lack of compatibility between the distribution of the daily and monthly returns, thus creating a bias.

(3) Find or choose the distribution function $F_\star$ of the return $R_{0,T}^\star$ of the target index $S^\star$.

If the asset $S^\star$ does not exists, i.e., we are creating a synthetic index, then the investor must choose $F_\star$. Interesting choices of distributions are the Gaussian, truncated Gaussian, and the Johnson SU distribution. Even if the index $S^\star$ exists, one can try to fit these three distributions.

---

[3]E.g., equal weighted portfolio of highly liquid futures contracts.

(4) Find or choose the conditional distribution function $\mathcal{H}(\cdot, \mathbf{x})$ of $R_{0,T}^{\star}$ given $\mathbf{R}_{0,T}^{(ref)} = \mathbf{x}$, which can be expressed as

$$\mathcal{H}(y, \mathbf{x}) = \mathcal{C}\{F_{\star}(y), \mathbf{F}(\mathbf{x})\},$$

where $\mathbf{F}(\mathbf{x}) = (F_1(x_1), \dots, F_d(x_d))$, and $\mathcal{C}(\cdot, \mathbf{v})$ is the conditional distribution of $U = F_{\star}(R_{0,T}^{\star})$ given $\mathbf{V} = \mathbf{F}\left(\mathbf{R}_{0,T}^{(ref)}\right) = \mathbf{v}$.

If the index $S^{\star}$ does not exists, then the investor must choose $\mathcal{C}$. In any case, we recommend to choose or try to fit a B-vine model, as defined in Section 3. The importance of the choice of $\mathcal{C}$ is discussed in Section 2.2.3.

(5) Compute the return function g given by

$$g(\mathbf{x}, y) = \mathcal{Q}\left\{\mathcal{F}(y, \mathbf{x}), \mathbf{x}\right\}, \tag{2}$$

where $\mathcal{Q}(\cdot, \mathbf{x})$ is the conditional quantile function, defined as the inverse of $\mathcal{H}(\cdot, \mathbf{x})$. For more details on copula-based conditional quantiles, see the recent articles [16], [14]. The function g can also be expressed as

$$g(\mathbf{x}, y) = F_{\star}^{-1}\left[\mathcal{C}^{-1}\left\{\mathcal{F}(y, \mathbf{x}), \mathbf{F}(\mathbf{x}))\right\}\right]. \tag{3}$$

The reason for defining g this way is that the joint distribution of $\left(R_{0,T}^{\star}, \mathbf{R}_{0,T}^{(ref)}\right)$ is the same as the joint distribution of $\left(g(\mathbf{R}_{0,T}), \mathbf{R}_{0,T}^{(ref)}\right)$. This means that $g(\mathbf{R}_{0,T})$ has distribution function $F_{\star}$, and that the conditional distribution of $g(\mathbf{R}_{0,T})$ given $\mathbf{R}_{0,T}^{(ref)} = \mathbf{x}$ is $\mathcal{H}(\cdot, \mathbf{x})$. In particular the statistical properties of $R_{0,T}^{\star}$ are the same as the statistical properties of $g(\mathbf{R}_{0,T})$.

(6) Compute the payoff function G defined by

$$G\left(\mathbf{S}_T\right) = 100 \exp\left\{g\left(\mathbf{R}_{0,T}\right)\right\}.$$

The interpretation of the payoff function is the following: if one starts by investing 100\$, and one can replicate exactly this payoff with a hedging portfolio, then one would get the return $g(\mathbf{R}_{0,T})$. In particular the distribution function of the portfolio return is $F_{\star}$, and it is obtained without investing in $S^{\star}$.

(7) Construct a dynamic portfolio $\{\mathcal{V}_k(\mathcal{V}_0, \varphi)\}_{k=0}^{n}$ of the assets $\mathbf{S}$, traded daily, in order to generate the payoff $G\left(\mathbf{S}_T\right)$ at the end of the month.

More precisely, letting $\beta_k = e^{-rkT/n}$ be the discounting factors, the discounted value of the portfolio at the end of the month is

$$\beta_n \mathcal{V}_n = \mathcal{V}_0 + \sum_{k=1}^{n} \boldsymbol{\varphi}_k^\top \left(\beta_k \mathbf{S}_k - \beta_{k-1} \mathbf{S}_{k-1} \right),$$

where $\varphi_k^{(j)}$ is number of shares of asset $S^{(j)}$ invested during $((k-1)T/n, kT/n]$, and $\boldsymbol{\varphi}_k$ may depend only on $\mathbf{S}_0, \ldots, \mathbf{S}_{k-1}$. Initially, the portfolio initial value is $\mathcal{V}_0$.

This hedging problem is typical in financial engineering, where $\mathcal{V}_0$ can be interpreted as the value of an option on $\mathbf{S}$ having payoff G at maturity T, and one wants to replicate the payoff. Usually, we are more interested in the price of the option, while here the emphasis is on the hedging portfolio, which is the object of the investment.

For hedging, we suggest to use the discrete time hedging method defined in Section 4.3. This strategy, adapted for a continuous time model, is optimal with respect to minimizing the square hedging error.

2.2.2. *K-P measure*

If the goal is attained, i.e., $\mathcal{V}_n = G\left(\mathbf{S}_T\right)$, the return of the portfolio is

$$\log(\mathcal{V}_n/\mathcal{V}_0) = \log(100/\mathcal{V}_0) + g\left(\mathbf{R}_{0,T}\right),$$

which has the same distribution as $\alpha + S^\star$, where $\alpha = \log(\mathcal{V}_0/100)$ can be used to estimate manager's alpha or the feasibility of the replication. In the context of replicating hedge funds, it is suggested in [6] that the initial amount $\mathcal{V}_0$ to be invested in the portfolio be viewed as a measure of performance of the hedge fund manager. Here we prefer to use α which we call the K-P measure. It can be interpreted as follows:

- If $\alpha = 0$, i.e., $\mathcal{V}_0 = 100$, the strategy generates the same returns as $S^\star$ (in distribution);
- If $\alpha < 0$, i.e., $\mathcal{V}_0 < 100$, it is worth replicating, generating superior returns (in distribution), while if $\alpha > 0$, i.e., $\mathcal{V}_0 > 100$, it may be not worth replicating.

Note that centered moments like standard deviation, skewness, kurtosis, are not affected by the value of the K-P measure α. However, the expected value of the portfolio is $\alpha + E(S^\star)$.

Example 2.2. A simple example in risk management is an investor interested in creating a portfolio $S^\star$ with a specific distribution function $F_\star$, which would be independent of several reference indexes, so that the return of the hedging portfolio will not be affected by extreme behavior of the reference indexes. In this case, g is given by

$$g(\mathbf{x}, y) = F_\star^{-1} \{\mathcal{F}(y, \mathbf{x})\}. \tag{4}$$

An example of implementation of this model is given in Section 5.4.

Remark 2.1. It makes sense that $\alpha > 0$, especially if the target distribution of $S^\star$ is not realistic. For example, one could wish to generate Gaussian returns with annual mean of 30% and a volatility of 1% that is independent of $S^{(1)}$, but the real distribution would be Gaussian with mean $.3 - 12\alpha$. In fact, if the joint distribution of the monthly returns is Gaussian, with annual means μ_1, μ_2, μ_3, annual volatilities $\sigma_1, \sigma_2, \sigma_3$ and correlations ρ_{12}, ρ_{13}, then, according to Equation (2),

$$
g(x, y) = \frac{1}{12} \left\{ \mu_3 - r + \sigma_3 \left(\frac{x - \mu_1}{\sigma_1} \right) \left(\rho_{13} - \rho_{12} \sqrt{\frac{1 - \rho_{13}^2}{1 - \rho_{12}^2}} \right) \right.
$$
$$
\left. + \sigma_3 \left(\frac{y - \mu_2}{\sigma_2} \right) \sqrt{\frac{1 - \rho_{13}^2}{1 - \rho_{12}^2}} \right\},
$$

so using the Black-Scholes setting with associated risk neutral measure $\mathbb{Q}$,

$$
\mathcal{V}_0 = 100 e^{-r/12} E^{\mathbb{Q}} \left\{ e^{g\left(R_{0,1/12}^{(1)}, R_{0,1/12}^{(2)}\right)} \right\} = 100 e^\alpha,
$$

with

$$
\alpha = \frac{\mu_3}{12} - \frac{r}{12} - \frac{1}{12} \left\{ \mu_1 \frac{\sigma_3}{\sigma_1} + \mu_2 \frac{\sigma_3}{\sigma_2} \sqrt{\frac{1 - \rho_{13}^2}{1 - \rho_{12}^2}} - \frac{\sigma_3^2}{2} \right\}
$$
$$
+ \frac{1}{12} \left\{ \frac{\sigma_3}{\sigma_1} \left(r - \frac{\sigma_1^2}{2} \right) \left(\rho_{13} - \rho_{12} \sqrt{\frac{1 - \rho_{13}^2}{1 - \rho_{12}^2}} \right) \right.
$$
$$
\left. + \frac{\sigma_3}{\sigma_2} \left(r - \frac{\sigma_2^2}{2} \right) \sqrt{\frac{1 - \rho_{13}^2}{1 - \rho_{12}^2}} \right\}.
$$

As a result, the genuine mean of the target is independent of μ_3! For example, if $r = 1\%$, $\mu_1 = 8\%$, $\mu_2 = 6\%$, $\sigma_1 = 10\%$, $\sigma_2 = 8\%$, $\sigma_3 = 1\%$, $\rho_{12} = 0.25$ and $\rho_{13} = 0$, then $\alpha = \frac{\mu_3}{12} - \frac{.02499}{12}$, and we would get a Gaussian distribution with an annual mean of 2.499% and an annual volatility of 1% that is independent of $S^{(1)}$. It is interesting to look at the real annual mean of the portfolio (assuming perfect hedging) as a function of ρ_{13}. This is illustrated in Figure 1. Note that the maximum value 2.501% is attained for $\rho_{13} = -0.072$.

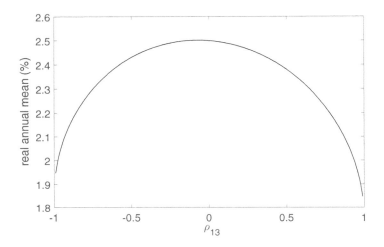

Fig. 1. Real annual mean in percent of the Gaussian distribution of the monthly return $R^\star$ as a function of the correlation ρ_{13} with monthly return $R^{(1)}$.

2.2.3. *Choice of $\mathcal{C}$*

First, note that $\mathcal{C}$ is a function of the copula C of $(U, \mathbf{V})$ viz.

$$\mathcal{C}(u, \mathbf{v}) = \frac{\partial_{v_1} \cdots \partial_{v_d} C(u, v_1, \ldots, v_d)}{c_{\mathbf{V}}(1, v_1, \ldots, v_d)}, \quad (u, \mathbf{v}) \in (0, 1)^{1+d}, \qquad (5)$$

where $c_{\mathbf{V}}$ is the density of the copula $C_{\mathbf{V}}(\cdot) = C(1, \cdot)$. When $d = 1$, we can take $\mathcal{C}(u, v) = \partial_v C(u, v)$ for any copula C. However, if $d \geq 2$, then the copula of $\mathbf{V}$ matters. One cannot just take any $d+1$-dimensional copula C. To solve this intricate problem, we propose to use a construction similar to the one used for vine copulas. This new construction is described in Section 3, after we discuss why the choice of $\mathcal{C}$ matters.

To this end, let $\tilde{\mathcal{C}}$ be an arbitrary conditional distribution function of U given a d-dimensional random vector $\tilde{\mathbf{V}}$ associated with the copula $\tilde{C}$ of $(U, \tilde{\mathbf{V}})$, and define

$$\tilde{g}(\mathbf{x}, y) = F_\star^{-1} \left[\tilde{\mathcal{C}}^{-1} \left\{ \mathcal{F}(y, \mathbf{x}), \mathbf{F}(\mathbf{x}) \right\} \right].$$

Setting $\mathcal{Z} = \mathcal{F}\left(R_{0,T}^{(res)}, \mathbf{R}_{0,T}^{(ref)}\right)$, one gets

$$P\left[\tilde{g}(\mathbf{R}_{0,T}) \le y, \mathbf{R}_{0,T}^{(ref)} \le \mathbf{x}\right] = P\left[\mathcal{Z} \le \tilde{C}\left\{F_\star(y), \mathbf{F}\left(\mathbf{R}_{0,T}^{(ref)}\right)\right\}, \mathbf{R}_{0,T}^{(ref)} \le \mathbf{x}\right]$$

$$= E\left[\tilde{C}\left\{F_\star(y), \mathbf{V}\right\} \mathbb{I}\left(\mathbf{V} \le \mathbf{F}(\mathbf{x})\right)\right]$$

$$= \int_{(0, \mathbf{F}(\mathbf{x})]} \tilde{C}\left\{F_\star(y), \mathbf{v}\right\} c_{\mathbf{V}}(\mathbf{v}) d\mathbf{v},$$

since $\mathcal{Z}$ is uniformly distributed and is independent of $\mathbf{R}_{0,T}^{(ref)}$, according to [15]. So, in general, $\tilde{F}_\star(y) = E\left[\tilde{C}\left\{F_\star(y), \mathbf{V}\right\}\right]$ is not the target distribution function $F_\star$. However, $\tilde{F}_\star = F_\star$ if $\tilde{C}(1, \mathbf{v}) = C_{\mathbf{V}}(\mathbf{v})$. This shows that one then must be careful with the choice of $\mathcal{C}$ in order to have compatibility.

3. B-vines models

The aim of this section is to find a flexible way to construct a conditional distribution of a random variable Y given a d-dimensional random vector $\mathbf{X}$. Using the representation of conditional distributions in terms of copulas, this problem amounts to constructing the conditional distribution $\mathcal{C}$ of a uniform random variable U given a random vector $\mathbf{V}$ (with uniform margins) that is coherent with the distribution function $C_{\mathbf{V}}$ of $\mathbf{V}$. Unfortunately, the usual vines models for multivariate copulas cannot be used here, because of this compatibility constraint. For more details on unconstrained vine models applied to conditional distributions, see, e.g., [16].

As noted before, when $d = 1$, the compatibility condition is not a constraint at all since $C_V(v) = v$, $v \in [0,1]$, and the solution is simply to take $\mathcal{C}(u, v) = \partial_v C(u, v)$, for a copula C that is smooth enough.

Next, in the case $d = 2$, if D_1 and D_2 are bivariate copulas, with conditional distributions $\mathcal{D}_j(u, t) = \partial_t D_j(u, t)$, $j \in \{1, 2\}$, and $C_{\mathbf{V}}$ is the copula of $\mathbf{V} = (V_1, V_2)$, then

$$\mathcal{C}(u, \mathbf{v}) = \mathcal{D}_2\left\{\mathcal{D}_1(u, v_1), \partial_{v_1} C_{\mathbf{V}}(v_1, v_2)\right\}, \quad \mathbf{v} = (v_1, v_2) \in (0, 1)^2, \quad (6)$$

defines a conditional distribution for U given $\mathbf{V} = v$, compatible with the law of $\mathbf{V}$. This construction is a particular case of a D-vine copula, as defined in [17], [18].

Guided by formula (6), let D_j, $j \in \{1, \ldots, d\}$ be bivariate copulas and let $\mathcal{D}_j(u, t) = \partial_t D_j(u, t)$ be the associated conditional distributions. For $j \in \{1, \ldots, d\}$, further let $\mathcal{R}_{j-1}(v_1, \ldots, v_j)$ be the conditional distribution of V_j given $V_1 = v_1, \ldots, V_{j-1} = v_{j-1}$, with $\mathcal{R}_0(v_1) = v_1$, and for $(u, \mathbf{v}) \in (0,1)^{d+1}$, set $\mathcal{C}_0(u) = u$, and

$$\mathcal{C}_j(u, v_1, \ldots, v_j) = \mathcal{D}_j \{ \mathcal{C}_{j-1}(u, v_1, \ldots, v_{j-1}), \mathcal{R}_{j-1}(v_1, \ldots, v_j) \}. \quad (7)$$

Note that $E\{ \mathcal{C}_j(u, v_1, \ldots, v_{j-1}, V_j) | V_1 = v_1, \ldots, V_{j-1} = v_{j-1} \}$ is given by

$$\int_0^1 \mathcal{C}_j \{ u, v_1, \ldots, \mathcal{R}_{j-1}(v_1, \ldots, v_j) \} d\mathcal{R}_{j-1}(v_1, \ldots, v_j)$$

$$= \int_0^1 \mathcal{D}_j \{ \mathcal{C}_{j-1}(u, v_1, \ldots, v_{j-1}), t \} dt$$

$$= \mathcal{D}_j \{ \mathcal{C}_{j-1}(u, v_1, \ldots, v_{j-1}), 1 \}$$

$$= \mathcal{C}_{j-1}(u, v_1, \ldots, v_{j-1}).$$

It follows that $\mathcal{C}_j$ is the conditional distribution of U given $V_1, \ldots, V_j$. The conditional quantile of U given $V_1, \ldots, V_j$ is also easy to compute, satisfying a recurrence relation similar to (7). In fact, if the conditional quantile of $\mathcal{C}_j$ is denoted by Γ_j, then for any $j \in \{1, \ldots, d\}$, and for any $u, v_1, \ldots v_d \in (0,1)$,

$$\Gamma_j(u, v_1, \ldots, v_j) = \Gamma_{j-1} \left[\mathcal{D}_j^{-1} \{ u, \mathcal{R}_{j-1}(v_1, \ldots, v_j) \}, v_1, \ldots, v_{j-1} \right]. \quad (8)$$

In general, this construction does not lead to a proper vine copula since all copulas involved are not bivariate copulas, the copula of $\mathbf{V}$ being given. In fact, it is more general than the pair-copula construction method used in vines models. Nevertheless, this type of model will be called B-vines and its construction is illustrated below, where the underlined variables (in red) mean that their distributions $\mathcal{R}_0, \ldots, \mathcal{R}_{d-1}$ are known,[4] and the conditional copulas $\mathcal{D}_1, \ldots, \mathcal{D}_d$ have to be chosen, in order to determine

---

[4]$\mathcal{R}_0, \ldots, \mathcal{R}_{d-1}$ are called the Rosenblatt's transforms and are particularly important in simulating copulas or for testing goodness-of-fit. See, e.g., [11].

$\mathcal{C}_1, \ldots, \mathcal{C}_d$.

$$
\text{Level 1:} \quad \overset{\mathcal{C}_0}{U} \quad | \quad \overset{\overset{\mathcal{D}_1}{}}{\overset{\mathcal{R}_0}{V_1}} \quad \Longrightarrow \mathcal{C}_1
$$

$$
\text{Level 2:} \quad \overset{\mathcal{C}_1}{U|V_1} \quad | \quad \overset{\overset{\mathcal{D}_2}{}}{\overset{\mathcal{R}_1}{V_2|V_1}} \quad \Longrightarrow \mathcal{C}_2
$$

$$
\vdots \quad \cdots \qquad\qquad\qquad \ddots
$$

$$
\text{Level } j: \quad \overset{\mathcal{C}_{j-1}}{U|V_1, \ldots, V_{j-1}} \quad | \quad \overset{\overset{\mathcal{D}_j}{}}{\overset{\mathcal{R}_{j-1}}{V_j|V_1, \ldots, V_{j-1}}} \quad \Longrightarrow \mathcal{C}_j
$$

$$
\vdots \quad \cdots \qquad\qquad\qquad\qquad \ddots
$$

$$
\text{Level } d: \quad \overset{\mathcal{C}_{d-1}}{U|V_1, \ldots, V_{d-1}} \quad | \quad \overset{\overset{\mathcal{D}_d}{}}{\overset{\mathcal{R}_{d-1}}{V_j|V_1, \ldots, V_{d-1}, V_d}} \quad \Longrightarrow \mathcal{C}_d
$$

Note that B-vines can be particularly useful in conditional mean regression (OLS, GAM, GLM, etc,) and conditional quantile settings, where the distribution of the covariates is often given; see, e.g., [14]. It can also be used in our replication context when the target $S^\star$ exists; in this case, we could look at B-vines constructed from popular bivariate families like Clayton, Gumbel, Frank, Gaussian and Student, and find the ones that fit best the data, in the same spirit as the choice of vines for copula models in the R packages *CDVine* or *VineCopula*. In a future work we will propose goodness-of-fit tests for these models.

4. Modeling and hedging

In what follows, building on [12], we propose a model to fit the data and deal with numerical problems arising from using a larger number of assets for hedging.

To implement successfully the proposed replication approach, one needs to model the distribution of the returns $\mathbf{R}_t$ and $\mathbf{R}_{0,T}$ for steps (1) and (2) described in Section 2.2.1. Once this is done, we will have as a by-product the conditional distribution $\mathcal{F}$ and the Rosenblatt's transforms $\mathcal{R}_0, \ldots, \mathcal{R}_{d-1}$ used for computing the conditional distribution $\mathcal{C}$, as in Section 3. For replicating an existing asset $S^\star$, one further needs the joint distribution of $\left(R_{0,T}^\star, \mathbf{R}_{0,T}^{(ref)}\right)$. To do this, we propose to use Gaussian Hidden Markov Models (HMM) as defined in [19]. This model is described next in Section

4.1. Next, one needs to find a distribution of the monthly returns compatible with the distribution of the daily returns. A solution to this problem is proposed in Section 4.2. Finally, a replication method is suggested in Section 4.3.

4.1. *Gaussian HMM*

Regime-switching models are quite intuitive. First, the regimes $\{1, \ldots, l\}$ are not observable and are modeled by a finite Markov chain with transition matrix $\mathbf{Q}$. At period t, given that the previous regime τ_{t-1} has value i, the regime $\tau_t = j$ is chosen with probability Q_{ij}, and given $\tau_t = j$, the log-returns $\mathbf{R}_t$ have a Gaussian distribution with mean $\boldsymbol{\mu}_j$ and covariance matrix $\mathbf{B}_j$.

The law of most financial time series can be modeled adequately by a Gaussian HMM, provided the number of regimes is large enough. Indeed, the serial dependence in regimes propagates to returns and captures the observed autocorrelation in financial time series. Also, the conditional distribution is time-varying, leading to conditional volatility, as well as conditional asymmetry and kurtosis. Finally, the Black-Scholes framework is a particular case of this model when the number of regimes is 1. Parameters are quite easy to estimate and there is also an easy way to choose the number of regimes, depending on the results of goodness-of-fit tests; see, e.g., [19] for more details.

In the next section, we introduce the continuous time limit of a Gaussian HMM, the main reason being that for this limiting process, one can show that there exists an equivalent martingale measure that is optimal in the sense of [20] and that can be used for pricing and hedging; see, e.g., [21].

4.1.1. *Continuous time limiting process*

Under weak conditions, the continuous time limit of a Gaussian HMM is a regime-switching geometric Brownian motion (RSGBM). Using the same notations as in [21], let $\mathcal{T}$ be a continuous time Markov chain on $\{1, \ldots, l\}$, with infinitesimal generator $\boldsymbol{\Lambda}$. In particular, $P(\mathcal{T}_t = j | \mathcal{T}_0 = i) = P_{ij}(t)$, where the transition matrix $\mathbf{P}$ can be written as $\mathbf{P}(t) = e^{t\boldsymbol{\Lambda}}$, $t \geq 0$. Then, the (continuous) price process $\mathbf{X}$ modeled as a RSGBM satisfies the stochastic differential equation

$$d\mathbf{X}_t = D(\mathbf{X}_t)\boldsymbol{v}(\mathcal{T}_t)dt + D(\mathbf{X}_t)\sigma(\mathcal{T}_{t-})d\mathbf{W}_t, \tag{9}$$

where $D(\mathbf{s})$ is the diagonal matrix with diagonal elements $(s_j)_{j=1}^d$ and $\mathbf{W}$ is a d-dimensional Brownian motion, independent of $\mathcal{T}$. Note that the time scale is in years, and we assume that $a(j) = \sigma(j)\sigma(j)^\top$ is invertible for any $j \in \{1, \dots, l\}$.

4.1.2. *Relationship between discrete time and continuous time parameters*

The relationship between the continuous-time parameters $(\boldsymbol{v}, \mathbf{a}, \boldsymbol{\Lambda})$ of the limiting RSGBM and the parameters of the Gaussian HMM is the following: if the parameters $\boldsymbol{\mu}_h, \mathbf{B}_h, \mathbf{Q}_h$ of the discrete time model are obtained from data sampled $1/h$ times a year, then $\boldsymbol{v}(j) \approx \left[\boldsymbol{\mu}_h(j) + \frac{1}{2}\mathrm{diag}\{\mathbf{B}_h(j)\}\right]/h$, where $\mathrm{diag}(\mathbf{B})$ is the vector of the diagonal elements of a matrix $\mathbf{B}$, $\mathbf{a}(j) \approx \mathbf{B}_h(j)/h$, and $\Lambda \approx (\mathbf{Q}_h - I)/h$. For example, for daily data, one usually takes $h = 1/252$.

Note that if we define $\mathbf{X}_{h,t} = \mathbf{S}_{\lfloor t/h \rfloor}$ and $\mathcal{T}_{h,t} = \tau_{\lfloor t/h \rfloor}$, where $\lfloor a \rfloor$ stands for the integer part of $a \in \mathbb{R}$, then the processes $(\mathbf{X}_{h,t}, \mathcal{T}_{h,t})$ converge in law to $(\mathbf{X}, \mathcal{T})$. Note also that the optimal hedging strategy converges as well; see, e.g., [22].

4.2. *Monthly returns compatibility*

Compatibility means that the distribution of the monthly returns $\mathbf{R}_{0,T}$ is the same as the distribution of the sum of typically $n = 21$ consecutive daily returns. Since the hedging will be done under a continuous time RSGBM, there is no compatibility problem. However, since we need the distribution of $\log(\mathbf{X}_T)$ to construct the payoff, and the latter is not known explicitly, we propose to simulate a large number of monthly returns $\log(\mathbf{X}_T)$, say 10000, which is impossible to get in practice, and then fit a Gaussian HMM to these simulated data. The joint distribution of the monthly returns is then approximated by a mixture of (multivariate) Gaussian distributions, and the conditional distribution function $\mathcal{F}$ is also a (univariate) Gaussian mixture. See, e.g., [19] for more details.

4.3. *Discrete time hedging*

Since we fitted a Gaussian HMM to the daily returns, an obvious solution of the hedging problem would be to use the results of [23] for optimal hedging in discrete time; see also [11]. However, implementing this methodology requires interpolating functions on a $(d + 1)$-dimensional grid. Since we are aiming for applications with $d \geq 2$, this approach leads to too much imprecision. For example, a (too) small grid of 100 points for each asset would require computing and storing $10^{2(d+1)}$ points, while a relatively precise grid of 1000 points for each asset requires $10^{3(d+1)}$ points. Even with $d = 2$, this means storing 10^9 points, which is way too much.

This is why we consider a continuous-time approximation, which does not require any interpolation or grid construction and works in any dimension. It is easy to show, see, e.g., [22] that many interesting discrete time models can be approximated by continuous time models. In particular, this is true for the Gaussian HMM whose continuous time limit is the RSGBM. Option pricing and optimal quadratic hedging have been studied recently for this process in [21], and it turns out that the optimal hedging strategy and option price can be deduced from an equivalent martingale measure. Under this equivalent martingale measure, assets still follow a RSGBM, with the additional feature that the distribution of the regimes is now an inhomogeneous continuous time Markov time. Nevertheless, this model is quite easy to simulate and does not require any calibration to option prices.

4.3.1. *Continuous time approximation*

Because we have possibly more than 2 risky assets, and based on the results in [22], [21], we approximate φ_k by $\phi_{\frac{k-1}{n}T}$, where ϕ is the optimal hedging strategy of the RSGBM obtained from [21], Lemma 4.1.

To get nearly optimal hedging strategies in discrete time, we first use Monte Carlo methods by simulating the process $\mathbf{X}$ under the optimal martingale measure, as given by Equation (A.2), to obtain the values $C_{kT/n}(\mathbf{s}, i)$ and $\nabla_{\mathbf{s}} C_{kT/n}(\mathbf{s}, i)$ given by formulas (A.3) and (A.4). Then we simply discretize the continuous time optimal hedging values (A.5)–(A.6) to get, for $k \in \{1, \ldots, n\}$,

$$\varphi_k = \nabla_{\mathbf{s}} C_{(k-1)T/n}(\mathbf{S}_{k-1}, \hat{\tau}_{k-1}) + G_{k-1} D^{-1}(\mathbf{S}_{k-1}) \rho(\hat{\tau}_{k-1})/\beta_{k-1}, \quad (10)$$

$$\tilde{\mathcal{V}}_k = \tilde{\mathcal{V}}_{k-1} + \varphi_k^{\top} \left(\beta_k \mathbf{S}_k - \beta_{k-1} \mathbf{S}_{k-1} \right), \quad (11)$$

$$G_k = \beta_k C_{kT/n}(\mathbf{S}_k, \hat{\tau}_k) - \tilde{\mathcal{V}}_k, \quad (12)$$

where $\tilde{\mathcal{V}}_0 = \mathcal{V}_0 = C_0(\mathbf{S}_0, \hat{\tau}_0)$, $G_0 = 0$, and $\tilde{\mathcal{V}}_k = \beta_k \mathcal{V}_k$ are the discounted portfolio values. In particular, $\varphi_1 = \nabla_{\mathbf{s}} C_0(\mathbf{S}_0, \hat{\tau}_0)$.

Remark 4.1. One could replace $C_{kT/n}(\mathbf{S}_k, \hat{\tau}_k)$ by the weighted average $\sum_{j=1}^{l} C_{kT/n}(\mathbf{S}_k, j) \eta_k(j)$, where $\eta_k(j)$ is the predicted probability of $\tau_k = j$, given the past observations.

We now have the necessary tools to tackle the implementation problem. Two examples of application are presented next.

5. Examples of application

In this section, we provide some empirical evidence regarding the ability of the model to replicate a synthetic index. In the implementation of the replication model, we consider a 3-dimensional problem.

5.1. *Assets*

The first step is to select two reference portfolios $P^{(1)}$ and $P^{(2)}$ and the reserve asset $P^{(3)}$. These 3 portfolios are dynamically traded on a daily basis, so we choose very liquid instruments with low transaction costs. We therefore restrict the components of the portfolios to be Futures contracts. The cash rate is the BBA Libor 1-month rate. Log-returns on futures are calculated from the reinvestment of a rolling strategy in the front contract. The front contract is the nearest to maturity, on the March/June/September/December schedule and is rolled on the first business day of the maturity month at previous close prices. Each future contract is fully collateralized, so that, the total return is the sum of the rolling strategy returns and the cash rate.

The first investor portfolio is related to equities while the second is related to bonds. The reserve asset is a diversified portfolio. The composition of these portfolios is detailed in Table 3. As in [13], we use daily returns from 01/10/1999 to 30/04/2009 (115 months). Table 4 presents some descriptive statistics of the daily returns $R^{(1)}, R^{(2)}, R^{(3)}$.

Table 3. Portfolios' composition.

$P^{(1)}$	60%	S&P/TSE 60 IX future
	40%	S&P500 EMINI future
$P^{(2)}$	100%	CAN 10YR BOND future
$P^{(3)}$	10%	E-mini NASDAQ-100 futures
	20%	Russell 2000 TR
	20%	MSCI Emerging Markets TR
	10%	GOLD 100 OZ future
	10%	WTI CRUDE future
	30%	US 2YR NOTE (CBT)

Table 4. Summary statistics for the 3 portfolios.

Statistics	$R^{(1)}$	$R^{(2)}$	$R^{(3)}$
	Daily returns		
Mean	0.0198	0.0209	0.0363
Volatility	0.1327	0.0592	0.1238
Skewness	−0.6447	−0.3261	−0.4418
Excess kurtosis	8.5478	2.0583	5.1415

Note: Values are reported on an annual basis.

5.2. *Modeling*

As discussed in Section 4.1, we use a Gaussian HMM to model the joint distribution of the returns of the 3 portfolios. The choice of the number of regimes is done as suggested in [19]: we choose the lowest number of regimes m so that the goodness-of-fit test for m regimes has a P-value larger than 5%. This leads to a selection of 6 regimes for the daily returns. The large number of regimes for the daily returns is due to the fact that the sample period contains the last financial crisis. Usually, for non-turbulent periods, 4 regimes are sufficient for fitting daily returns. The estimated parameters are given in Table 5. The associated transition matrix for daily returns of the Gaussian HMM is

$$\mathbf{Q}_{daily} = \begin{pmatrix} 0.9608 & 0.0000 & 0.0181 & 0.0000 & 0.0000 & 0.0211 \\ 0.0160 & 0.1494 & 0.3384 & 0.0000 & 0.4962 & 0.0000 \\ 0.0000 & 0.0579 & 0.6746 & 0.0108 & 0.2567 & 0.0000 \\ 0.0000 & 0.0000 & 0.0000 & 0.9823 & 0.0177 & 0.0000 \\ 0.0176 & 0.0993 & 0.2753 & 0.0175 & 0.5882 & 0.0021 \\ 0.0599 & 0.0000 & 0.0000 & 0.0000 & 0.0071 & 0.9330 \end{pmatrix},$$

and the infinitesimal generator associated with the limiting RSGBM is

$$\mathbf{\Lambda}_{daily} = \begin{pmatrix} -9.8765 & 0.0000 & 4.5658 & 0.0000 & 0.0000 & 5.3107 \\ 4.0402 & -214.3435 & 85.2680 & 0.0000 & 125.0353 & 0.0000 \\ 0.0000 & 14.5863 & -81.9990 & 2.7205 & 64.6922 & 0.0000 \\ 0.0000 & 0.0052 & 0.0004 & -4.4624 & 4.4569 & 0.0000 \\ 4.4414 & 25.0201 & 69.3636 & 4.4157 & -103.7633 & 0.5226 \\ 15.0866 & 0.0000 & 0.0000 & 0.0000 & 1.7858 & -16.8724 \end{pmatrix}.$$

Finally, for the last observation, corresponding to the beginning of the hedging, the estimated probability of occurrence of each regime is

$$\mathbf{\eta}_{daily} = (0.9433, 0.0003, 0.0246, 0.0000, 0.0006, 0.0312).$$

Therefore, we will take for granted that at time $t = 0$, we are in regime 1.

Table 5. Estimated parameters for the Gaussian HMM fitted on daily returns.

Regime	$\boldsymbol{\mu}_j$		$\mathbf{B}_j$		
	−0.0182	0.0250	−0.0026		0.0157
1	0.0409	−0.0026	0.0028		−0.0021
	−0.1706	0.0157	−0.0021		0.0200
	0.1709	0.0131	−0.0000		0.0114
2	−1.6439	−0.0000	0.0040		0.0009
	0.1790	0.0114	0.0009		0.0170
	0.6694	0.0050	0.0002		0.0018
3	0.0619	0.0002	0.0036		−0.0006
	0.9667	0.0018	−0.0006		0.0040
	0.1486	0.0042	−0.0002		0.0028
4	0.0286	−0.0002	0.0018		0.0000
	0.2178	0.0028	0.0000		0.0047
	−0.6934	0.0084	−0.0013		0.0049
5	0.2548	−0.0013	0.0023		−0.0009
	−0.9222	0.0049	−0.0009		0.0067
	−0.4565	0.1169	−0.0115		0.0788
6	0.0749	−0.0115	0.0099		−0.0110
	−0.4082	0.0788	−0.0110		0.0889

Note: Values are expressed on an annual basis.

5.2.1. *Monthly returns*

As suggested in Section 4.2, we simulated 10 000 values of monthly returns under the estimated RSGBM. We fitted a Gaussian HMM and found that 3 regimes were necessary, which is larger than usual, but we have to remember that we are fitting 10 000 values. The estimated parameters are given in Table 6, and the associated transition matrix is

$$\mathbf{Q}_{monthly} = \begin{pmatrix} 0.1209 & 0.6788 & 0.2003 \\ 0.1719 & 0.6184 & 0.2097 \\ 0.1926 & 0.5846 & 0.2229 \end{pmatrix}.$$

Finally, for the last observation, corresponding to the beginning of the hedging, the estimated probability of occurrence of each regime is $\boldsymbol{\eta}_{monthly} = (0.1796, 0.7635, 0.0569)$. In particular, it means that the probability $\boldsymbol{\pi}_{next}$ of being in each regime next month is

$$\boldsymbol{\pi}_{next} = \boldsymbol{\eta}_{monthly} \mathbf{Q}_{monthly} = (0.1639, 0.6273, 0.2088). \tag{13}$$

It then follows that the conditional distribution $\mathcal{F}(\cdot, \mathbf{x})$ is mixture of 3 Gaussian distributions, with mean $\alpha_j + \boldsymbol{\beta}_j^\top \mathbf{x}$ and standard deviation σ_j, $j \in \{1, 2, 3\}$, and weights given by (13), where the values of the parameters

Table 6. Estimated parameters for the Gaussian HMM fitted on 10 000 simulated monthly returns under RSGBM.

Regime	$\boldsymbol{\mu}_j$		$\mathbf{B}_j$	
	0.0728	0.0085	−0.0006	0.0067
1	0.0320	−0.0006	0.0027	−0.0004
	0.1081	0.0067	−0.0004	0.0096
	−0.4201	0.0726	−0.0117	0.0396
2	0.0050	−0.0117	0.0067	−0.0067
	−0.2813	0.0396	−0.0067	0.0421
	−0.4201	0.0726	−0.0117	0.0396
3	0.0050	−0.0117	0.0067	−0.0067
	−0.2813	0.0396	−0.0067	0.0421

Note: The values are expressed on an annual basis.

are given in Table 7. More precisely,

$$
\mathcal{F}(y, \mathbf{x}) = \sum_{j=1}^{3} \pi_{next}(k) \Phi \left(\frac{y - \alpha_j - \boldsymbol{\beta}_j^\top \mathbf{x}}{\sigma_j} \right), \quad (y, \mathbf{x}) \in \mathbb{R}^3, \qquad (14)
$$

where Φ is the distribution function of the standard Gaussian.

Table 7. Parameters of the conditional distribution of $R_{0,T}^{(3)}$ given $\left(R_{0,T}^{(1)}, R_{0,T}^{(2)} \right)$.

Regime	α_j	$\boldsymbol{\beta}_j$	σ_j	π_j
1	0.0037	(0.6343 , −0.3353)	0.0463	0.1639
2	−0.0014	(0.6090 , −0.1828)	0.0296	0.6273
3	−0.0063	(0.6876 , 0.1661)	0.0231	0.2088

5.3. *Target distribution function*

For this example, the target distribution $F_\star$ is a truncated Gaussian distribution at $-a$, with (annual) parameters $\mu_\star$ and $\sigma_\star$, meaning that

$$
F_\star(y) = \begin{cases} 0, & y \leq -a; \\[2ex] \dfrac{\Phi\left(\frac{y - \mu_\star/12}{\sigma_\star/\sqrt{12}} \right) - \Phi\left(\frac{-a - \mu_\star/12}{\sigma_\star/\sqrt{12}} \right)}{\Phi\left(\frac{a + \mu_\star/12}{\sigma_\star/\sqrt{12}} \right)}, & y \geq -a. \end{cases} \qquad (15)
$$

Setting $z = \frac{a + \mu_\star/12}{\sigma_\star/\sqrt{12}}$ and $\kappa = \Phi'(z) \Big/ \Phi(z)$, the mean of this distribution is $\frac{\mu}{12} + \frac{\sigma}{\sqrt{12}} h$, while the standard deviation is $\frac{\sigma_\star}{\sqrt{12}} \sqrt{1 - h^2 - 2hz}$. With $a = 0.02$, $\mu_\star = 0.08$ and $\sigma_\star = 0.05$, one gets an annual mean of 0.0842, and an annual volatility of 0.0477. Note that $F_\star(0) = 1 - \Phi\left(\frac{\mu_\star}{\sqrt{12}\sigma_\star}\right)/\Phi(z) = 0.3$. The density is displayed in Figure 2.

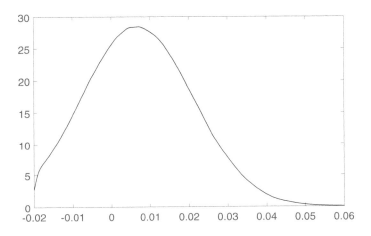

Fig. 2.   Target density for the monthly returns.

In the remaining of the section, we try to replicate the monthly returns of a synthetic hedge fund having distribution $F_\star$ given by (15). We will rebalance the portfolio once a day, so $n = 21$. For simplicity, we take $\mathbf{S}_0 = (1,1,1)$ and $r = 0.01$. We will consider two models: the first one is the independence model, meaning that $\mathcal{C}(u, v_1, v_2) = u$, so that the return function g is given by (4). This model is studied in Section 5.4. We consider another model, called the Clayton model, define using the B-vines representation by $D_1(u,t) = \left[\max\left\{0, u^{-\theta} + t^{-\theta} - 1\right\}\right]^{-1/\theta}$, which is the so-called Clayton copula of parameter $\theta \in (-1,1)$, with Kendall's $\tau = \frac{\theta}{\theta+2}$, and $D_2(u,t) = ut$, the independence copula. For this case, we take $\theta = -2/3$, leading to a Kendall's tau of -0.5. This means that we require a negative dependence with asset $P^{(1)}$.

Finally, for each model, we simulated 1000 replication portfolios.

5.4. *Synthetic index independent of the reference portfolios*

The results of this first experiment are quite interesting, as can be seen from the statistics displayed in Table 8, especially the tracking error given by the

RMSE. Note also that the mean of the hedging error is significantly smaller that 0, meaning that the portfolio is doing better on average than the target payoff, even if the K-P measure $\alpha = 0.0078$ is positive. The target distribution is also quite well replicated. The distribution of the hedging errors is also quite good, as can be seen from the estimated density displayed in Figure 3. Finally, letting $\tau^{(1)}$ and $\tau^{(2)}$ represent the estimated Kendall's tau between the variable and the returns of portfolio $P^{(1)}$ and $P^{(2)}$ respectively, one can see that the returns of the hedged portfolio are independent of the returns of the reference portfolios, as measured by Kendall's tau, meaning that the synthetic asset has the desired properties.

Table 8.   Descriptive statistics for the independence model.

Statistics	HE	$G(\mathbf{S}_{21})$	$\mathcal{V}_{21}$	$g(\mathbf{R}_{21})$	$\log(\mathcal{V}_{21}/\mathcal{V}_0)$	Target
Average	−0.012	100.770	100.782	0.0076	−0.0001	0.0078
Median	−0.012	100.741	100.760	0.0074	−0.0003	0.0073
Volatility	0.035	1.299	1.290	0.013	0.013	0.013
Skewness	0.431	0.201	0.192	0.172	0.162	0.267
Kurtosis	7.939	2.581	2.614	2.559	2.593	2.760
Minimum	−0.145	98.083	98.013	−0.019	−0.028	−0.02
Maximum	0.241	104.987	104.926	0.049	0.040	
RMSE	0.037					
$\tau^{(1)}$				0.023	0.024	0
$\tau^{(2)}$				−0.061	−0.060	0

Note: The hedging error HE is defined by HE $= G(\mathbf{S}_{21}) - \mathcal{V}_{21}$, and $\tau^{(j)}$, $j \in \{1, 2\}$, is the estimated Kendall's tau between the variable and the returns of portfolio $P^{(j)}$. The results are based on 1000 repetitions. Here $\mathcal{V}_0 = 100.645$ and $\alpha = \log \mathcal{V}_0/100 = 0.0064$. The statistics for the target distribution are also displayed for sake of comparison. Note also that $\varphi_1 = (-26.464, 5.630, 42.050)$, showing that we are short of the first asset at the beginning.

5.5. *Synthetic index with Clayton level-1 dependence*

The results of this second experiment are also quite interesting, but for different reasons. As can be seen from the results displayed in Table 9, our goal of replicating the distribution is not achieved. The tracking error given by the RMSE is too large, the average gain of the portfolio is negative and its volatility is too large to be interesting for an investor, even if the K-P measure $\alpha = 0.0064$ is smaller than in the independence model. This might be due to the fact that initially, the weight of the assets in the portfolio are quite large, since $\varphi_1 = (-724.845, 84.394, 648.811)$. Furthermore, the distribution of the hedging errors is not good at all, as can be seen from the estimated density displayed in Figure 4. The conclusion is that the

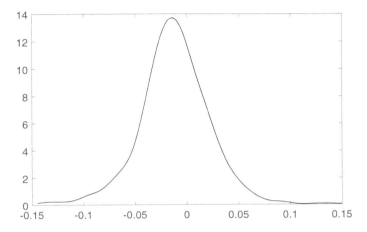

Fig. 3. Estimated density of the hedging error $G(\mathbf{S}_{21}) - V_{21}$ for the independence model based on 1000 replications. Here $\mathcal{V}_0 = 100.7864$ and $\alpha = \log \mathcal{V}_0 / 100 = 0.007833$.

target distribution is not quite well replicated, and one should not invest in this strategy. The only positive point is that the dependence between the returns of the payoff and portfolio seems to match the theoretical one, as measured by Kendall's tau.

Table 9. Descriptive statistics for the Clayton model.

Statistics	HE	$G(\mathbf{S}_{21})$	$\mathcal{V}_{21}$	$g(\mathbf{R}_{21})$	$\log(\mathcal{V}_{21}/\mathcal{V}_0)$	Target
Average	−1.152	100.689	101.842	0.00680	−0.0271	0.0078
Median	3.399	100.608	97.071	0.0061	−0.0362	0.0073
Volatility	27.739	1.235	28.917	0.0122	0.2784	0.0133
Skewness	−0.772	0.268	0.753	0.240	0.077	0.267
Kurtosis	3.697	2.610	3.616	2.586	2.525	2.760
Minimum	−140.008	98.126	48.336	−0.019	−0.733	−0.02
Maximum	50.675	104.836	244.844	0.047	0.889	
RMSE	27.763					
$\tau^{(1)}$				−0.443	−0.461	−0.5
$\tau^{(2)}$				0.093	0.111	

Note: HE $= G(\mathbf{S}_{21}) - \mathcal{V}_{21}$, and $\tau^{(j)}$, $j \in \{1, 2\}$, is the estimated Kendall's tau between the variable and the returns of portfolio $P^{(j)}$. The results are based on 1000 repetitions. Here $\mathcal{V}_0 = 100.645$ and $\alpha = \log \mathcal{V}_0 / 100 = 0.0064$. The statistics for the target distribution are also displayed for sake of comparison.

To conclude this section, we computed the K-P measure for Clayton models as a function of Kendall's τ. This is illustrated in Figure 5 and it is

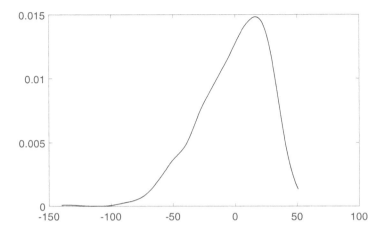

Fig. 4.   Estimated density of the hedging error $G(\mathbf{S}_{21}) - V_{21}$ for the Clayton model with $\tau = -0.5$ based on 1000 replications.

coherent with the fact that the conditional distribution $\mathcal{D}_{1,\tau}$, with $\tau = \frac{\theta}{\theta+2}$, are ordered according to Lehmann's order. It then follows from (3) that the payoff are ordered as well, so the value of the option increases with τ.

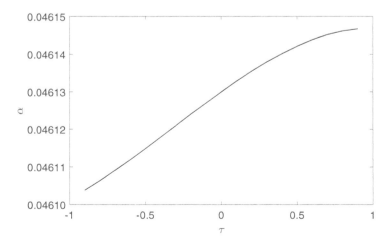

Fig. 5.   Graph of the K-P measure $\alpha = \log(\mathcal{V}_0/100)$ as a function of Kendall's τ for the Clayton model.

5.6. *Discussion*

Before deciding to replicate an asset S^*, we should always perform a Monte Carlo experiment as we did in Sections 5.4–5.5. Using simulations, we can decide in advance if an asset S^* is worth replicating. For example, for our data, it is worth using the independence model, but it is not worth using the Clayton model. Simulations can also be useful in tracking a more realistic P&L since transactions costs can be included in the Monte Carlo experiment.

We notice that in all cases, the initial investment is more than 100, meaning that the K-P measure is positive. This can be attributed to the choice of the reserve asset. Indeed, [12] showed that the choice of the reserve asset can affect the replication results especially the mean return, which depends linearly on the K-P measure. Nevertheless, at least in the case of the independence, we were able to achieve our goal.

It is also worth mentioning that due to (3), if two dependence models C_1 and C_2 are ordered according to Lehmann's order, i.e., for any $\mathbf{v} \in (0,1)^d$, $C_1(u, \mathbf{v}) \leq C_1(u, \mathbf{v})$, for all $u \in [0,1]$, then the K-P measures are also ordered.

6. Conclusion

We looked at two important methods of replication of indexes: strong and weak replication. For strong replication, the aim is to construct a portfolio of liquid assets that is as close as possible to an existing index, so statistical methods related to prediction like regression and filtering play an important role. For weak replication, the aim is to construct a portfolio of liquid assets that is as close as possible to a payoff constructed in such a way that the portfolio returns have predetermined distributional properties, such as the marginal distribution and the conditional distribution relative to some reference assets entering in the construction of the portfolio.

We also introduced a new family of conditional distribution models called B-vines that can be useful in many fields, not just weak replication of indexes.

We showed how to implement weak replication in general framework, and we showed that it is possible to construct efficiently a synthetic asset that is independent of prescribed asset classes, with a predetermined distribution. Using simulations, we can decide in advance if an asset S^* is worth replicating. For example, for our data, it is worth using the independence model, but it is not worth using the Clayton model.

For future work, we plan to investigate the performance of machine learning methods compared to filtering methods for strong replication purposes. We will also propose goodness-of-fit tests for the B-vines models introduced in Section 3.

Acknowledgments

The authors thank the referee and the editors for their useful comments and suggestions. Partial funding in support of this work was provided by the Natural Sciences and Engineering Research Council of Canada, by the Fonds Québécois de Recherche sur la Nature et les Technologies, and by the Groupe d'études et de recherche en analyse des décisions (GERAD).

Appendix A. Optimal hedging in continuous time

For $j \in \{1, \ldots, l\}$, let $\mathbf{m}(j) = (\boldsymbol{v}(j) - r\mathbf{1})$, where $\mathbf{1}$ is the vector with all components equaled to 1, $\boldsymbol{\rho}(j) = \mathbf{a}(j)^{-1}\mathbf{m}(j)$, and set $\ell_j = \boldsymbol{\rho}(j)^{\top}\mathbf{m}(j) = \boldsymbol{\rho}(j)^{\top}\mathbf{a}(j)\boldsymbol{\rho}(j) \geq 0$. Further set $\boldsymbol{\gamma}(t) = e^{(T-t)\{\boldsymbol{\Lambda} - D(\ell)\}}\mathbf{1}$. Next, define

$$(\tilde{\boldsymbol{\Lambda}}_t)_{ij} = \boldsymbol{\Lambda}_{ij}\gamma_j(t)/\gamma_i(t), \quad i \neq j, \qquad (\tilde{\boldsymbol{\Lambda}}_t)_{ii} = -\sum_{j \neq i}(\tilde{\boldsymbol{\Lambda}}_t)_{ij}. \qquad (\text{A.1})$$

Then $\tilde{\boldsymbol{\Lambda}}_t$, $t \in [0,T]$, is the infinitesimal generator of a time inhomogeneous Markov chain.

In [21], it is shown that the optimal hedging problem is related to an equivalent martingale measure $\mathbb{Q}$, in the sense that under the risk neutral measure $\mathbb{Q}$, if the price process $\mathbf{X}$ satisfies

$$d\mathbf{X}_t = rD(\mathbf{X}_t)dt + D(\mathbf{X}_t)\boldsymbol{\sigma}(\mathcal{T}_{t-})d\mathbf{W}_t, \qquad (\text{A.2})$$

and $\mathcal{T}$ is a time inhomogeneous Markov chain with generator $\tilde{\boldsymbol{\Lambda}}_t$, then the value of an option with payoff Φ at maturity T is given by

$$C_t(\mathbf{s}, i) = e^{-r(T-t)}E^{\mathbb{Q}}\left[\Phi(\mathbf{X}_T)|\mathbf{X}_t = \mathbf{s}, \mathcal{T}_t = i\right]. \qquad (\text{A.3})$$

If the payoff is smooth enough so that it is differentiable almost everywhere, then

$$\nabla_{\mathbf{s}}C_t(\mathbf{s}, i) = e^{-r(T-t)}D^{-1}(\mathbf{s})E^{\mathbb{Q}}\left[\Phi'(\mathbf{X}_T)\mathbf{X}_T|\mathbf{X}_t = \mathbf{s}, \mathcal{T}_t = i\right], \quad i \in \{1, \ldots, l\}. \qquad (\text{A.4})$$

Since C_t and $\nabla_{\mathbf{s}}C_t$ are related to expectations, one can use Monte Carlo methods to obtain unbiased estimates of these values.

Next, setting $\boldsymbol{\alpha}_t(s, i) = \nabla_s C_t(s, i) + C_t(s, i)D^{-1}(s)\boldsymbol{\rho}(i)$, and $\mathcal{G}_t = e^{-rt}C_t(\mathbf{X}_t, \mathcal{T}_t) - \mathcal{V}_t$, with $\mathcal{G}_0 = 0$, where $\mathcal{V}_t$ is the discounted value of the (continuous time) hedging portfolio at time t, then the optimal hedging strategy is

$$\phi_t = \boldsymbol{\alpha}_t(X_t, \mathcal{T}_{t-}) - e^{rt}\mathcal{V}_{t-}D^{-1}(\mathbf{X}_t)\rho(\mathcal{T}_{t-}) \qquad (A.5)$$
$$= \nabla_{\mathbf{s}}C_t(\mathbf{X}_t, \mathcal{T}_{t-}) + e^{rt}\mathcal{G}_{t-}D^{-1}(\mathbf{X}_t)\rho(\mathcal{T}_{t-}). \qquad (A.6)$$

References

[1] W. Fung and D. Hsieh, The risk in hedge fund strategies: Theory and evidence from trend followers, *Review of Financial Studies* **14**, 313–341 (2001).

[2] W. Fung and D. Hsieh, Hedge fund benchmarks: A risk-based approach, *Financial Analysts Journal* **60**, 65–80 (2004).

[3] J. Hasanhodzic and A. W. Lo, Can hedge-fund returns be replicated?: The linear case, *Journal of Investment Management* **5**, 5–45 (2007).

[4] P. H. Dybvig, Distributional analysis of portfolio choice, *The Journal of Business* **61**, 369–393 (1988).

[5] G. Amin and H. M. Kat, Hedge fund performance 1990-2000: Do the "money machines" really add value, *Journal of Financial and Quantitative Analysis* **38**, 251–274 (2003).

[6] H. M. Kat and H. P. Palaro, *Who needs hedge funds? A copula-based approach to hedge fund return replication*, tech. rep., Cass Business School, City University (2005).

[7] E. Wallerstein, N. S. Tuchschmid and S. Zaker, How do hedge fund clones manage the real world?, *The Journal of Alternative Investments* **12**, 37–50 (2010).

[8] P. Laroche and B. Rémillard, *On the Serial Dependence of Hedge Fund Indices Returns*, tech. rep., Innocap (2008).

[9] M. Towsey, *Hedge Fund Replication*, tech. rep., Aon Hewitt (2013).

[10] T. Roncalli and J. Teïletche, *An alternative approach to alternative beta*, tech. rep., Société Générale Asset Management (2007).

[11] B. Rémillard, *Statistical Methods for Financial Engineering* Chapman and Hall/CRC Financial Mathematics Series, Chapman and Hall/CRC Financial Mathematics Series (Taylor & Francis, 2013).

[12] N. Papageorgiou, B. Rémillard and A. Hocquard, Replicating the properties of hedge fund returns, *Journal of Alternative Investments* **11**, 8–38 (2008).

[13] M. Ben-Abdellatif, Réplication des fonds de couverture, Master's thesis, HEC Montréal (2010).

[14] B. Rémillard, B. Nasri and T. Bouezmarni, On copula-based conditional quantile estimators, *Statistics & Probability Letters* **128**, 14–20 (2017), September 2017.

[15] M. Rosenblatt, Remarks on a multivariate transformation, *Ann. Math. Stat.* **23**, 470–472 (1952).

[16] D. Kraus and C. Czado, D-vine copula based quantile regression, *Computational Statistics & Data Analysis* **110**, 1–18 (2017).

[17] H. Joe, Families of m-variate distributions with given margins and $m(m-1)/2$ bivariate dependence parameters, in *Distributions with fixed marginals and related topics*, Eds. L. Rüschendorf, B. Schweizer and M. D. Taylor, Lecture Notes–Monograph Series, Vol. 28 (Institute of Mathematical Statistics, Hayward, CA, 1996) pp. 120–141.

[18] K. Aas, C. Czado, A. Frigessi and H. Bakken, Pair-copula constructions of multiple dependence, *Insurance Math. Econom.* **44**, 182–198 (2009).

[19] B. Rémillard, A. Hocquard, H. Lamarre and N. A. Papageorgiou, Option pricing and hedging for discrete time regime-switching model, *Modern Economy* **8**, 1005–1032 (September 2017).

[20] M. Schweizer, Mean-variance hedging for general claims, *Ann. Appl. Probab.* **2**, 171–179 (1992).

[21] B. Rémillard and S. Rubenthaler, *Option pricing and hedging for regime-switching geometric Brownian motion models*, working paper series, SSRN Working Paper Series No. 2599064 (2016).

[22] B. Rémillard and S. Rubenthaler, *Optimal hedging in discrete and continuous time*, Tech. Rep. G-2009-77, Gerad (2009).

[23] B. Rémillard and S. Rubenthaler, Optimal hedging in discrete time, *Quantitative Finance* **13**, 819–825 (2013).